CONTENTS

8 ABOUT CASINO GAMBLING 220

9 WHERE TO STAY 250

10 SIDE TRIPS FROM LAS VEGAS 323

11 PLANNING YOUR TRIP TO LAS VEGAS 345

LIST OF MAPS

ABOUT THE AUTHOR

Rick Garman began visiting Las Vegas as soon as he was not barred from doing so by pesky things like laws. He started writing about the city in 1997 when he and his best friend Mary Herczog were invited to write Frommer's Las Vegas. He went on to create Vegas4Visitors.com, one of the most respected Las Vegas travel resources on the Web and has appeared in various outlets as a self-proclaimed Vegas expert, although most of that expertise has been gained sitting at a slot machine with a glazed look in his eye while mumbling incoherently to himself. When not gambling away his life savings, Rick lives in Los Angeles and works in the travel industry.

A NOTE FROM THE AUTHOR

Mary Herczog wrote this book for more than a decade, starting with the 1998 edition that we co-authored, our first collaboration as professionals but certainly not as best friends. For much of that decade she also battled breast cancer but through it all she never lost her warmth, her humor, and her love for all things travel. Shortly before she died on February 16, 2010 she asked me to take over this book and I am both humbled and honored to do so. Although my name is on the title page, this was and always will be her book. Viva Las Vegas, Mary . . . the city will not be the same without you.

HOW TO CONTACT US

In researching this book, we discovered many wonderful places—hotels, restaurants, shops, and more. We're sure you'll find others. Please tell us about them, so we can share the information with your fellow travelers in upcoming editions. If you were disappointed with a recommendation, we'd love to know that, too. Please write to:

Frommer's Las Vegas 2013
John Wiley & Sons, Inc. • 111 River St. • Hoboken, NJ 07030-5774
frommersfeedback@wiley.com

ADVISORY & DISCLAIMER

Travel information can change quickly and unexpectedly, and we strongly advise you to confirm important details locally before traveling, including information on visas, health and safety, traffic and transport, accommodation, shopping and eating out. We also encourage you to stay alert while traveling and to remain aware of your surroundings. Avoid civil disturbances, and keep a close eye on cameras, purses, wallets and other valuables.

While we have endeavored to ensure that the information contained within this guide is accurate and up-to-date at the time of publication, we make no representations or warranties with respect to the accuracy or completeness of the contents of this work and specifically disclaim all warranties, including without limitation warranties of fitness for a particular purpose. We accept no responsibility or liability for any inaccuracy or errors or omissions, or for any inconvenience, loss, damage, costs or expenses of any nature whatsoever incurred or suffered by anyone as a result of any advice or information contained in this guide.

The inclusion of a company, organization or website in this guide as a service provider and/or potential source of further information does not mean that we endorse them or the information they provide. Be aware that information provided through some websites may be unreliable and can change without notice. Neither the publisher or author shall be liable for any damages arising herefrom.

FROMMER'S STAR RATINGS, ICONS & ABBREVIATIONS

Every hotel, restaurant, and attraction listing in this guide has been ranked for quality, value, service, amenities, and special features using a **star-rating system.** In country, state, and regional guides, we also rate towns and regions to help you narrow down your choices and budget your time accordingly. Hotels and restaurants are rated on a scale of zero (recommended) to three stars (exceptional). Attractions, shopping, nightlife, towns, and regions are rated according to the following scale: zero stars (recommended), one star (highly recommended), two stars (very highly recommended), and three stars (must-see).

In addition to the star-rating system, we also use **seven feature icons** that point you to the great deals, in-the-know advice, and unique experiences that separate travelers from tourists. Throughout the book, look for:

special finds—those places only insiders know about

fun facts—details that make travelers more informed and their trips more fun

kids—best bets for kids and advice for the whole family

special moments—those experiences that memories are made of

overrated—places or experiences not worth your time or money

insider tips—great ways to save time and money

great values—where to get the best deals

The following abbreviations are used for credit cards:

AE	American Express	**DISC**	Discover	**V**	Visa
DC	Diners Club	**MC**	MasterCard		

TRAVEL RESOURCES AT FROMMERS.COM

Frommer's travel resources don't end with this guide. Frommer's website, www.frommers.com, has travel information on more than 4,000 destinations. We update features regularly, giving you access to the most current trip-planning information and the best airfare, lodging, and car-rental bargains. You can also listen to podcasts, connect with other Frommers.com members through our active-reader forums, share your travel photos, read blogs from guidebook editors and fellow travelers, and much more.

THE BEST OF LAS VEGAS

t seems as if Las Vegas was designed to overwhelm the senses at every turn. The glow-in-the-dark skyline of gleaming modern towers and replicas of ancient wonders is a "where do I look first?" wonderland; everything from buffets to gourmet restaurants will keep your taste buds busy; the booming beats on the nightclub dance floors will have your ears ringing; the luxurious spas will make your skin tingle; and you may detect the sweet scent of success, or more likely failure, in the casinos. These sights, sounds, tastes, smells, and touches are the embodiment of excess; a pure expression of the id that makes Las Vegas one of the most irresistible cities in the world.

Things to Do   If you find yourself in Vegas with nothing to do, you really aren't paying attention. Walk out onto the Strip and just look around; there are more things here designed to amuse you than you'll know what to do with. Wonder at the delirious architecture, with appropriated landmarks like the **Eiffel Tower** at **Paris Las Vegas** and the Sphinx at **Luxor;** get your camera ready for the delightful dancing waters of the **Fountains at Bellagio** and the lava-spewing drama of the **Mirage Volcano;** or pull out your wallet and try your luck in one of the dozens of opulent casinos.

Shopping   It's easy to be distracted by the theme-park-worthy malls like **The Forum Shops at Caesars Palace,** full of decadent Roman splendor, and **The Grand Canal Shoppes,** complete with its own Venetian canals and gondoliers. But don't let the bling stop you from discovering real gems like the blast-from-the-past amusements at **The Toy Shack** or the Sin City collectibles at **Retro Vegas.**

PREVIOUS PAGE: **Fountain of the Gods at Caesars Palace.** ABOVE: **The Bellagio fountain show at night.**

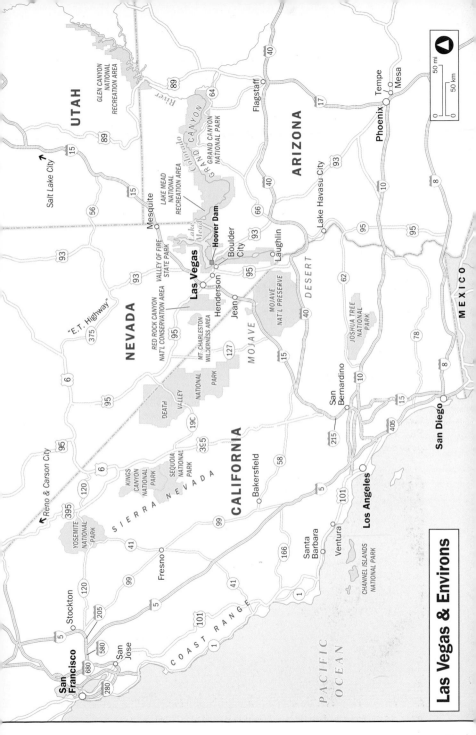

Las Vegas & Environs

3

Restaurants & Dining   Once an outpost of cheap buffets and barely edible prime-rib specials, Las Vegas is now an epicurean destination. You'll do fine at celebrity chef outlets from **Emeril Lagasse** and **Wolfgang Puck,** but dig deeper to find the spectacularly intricate French cuisine at **L'Atelier de Joël Robuchon** or the modern, luxurious interpretation of an all-you-can-eatery at the **Buffet at Wynn Las Vegas.** True foodies get off the Strip to experience eclectic Japanese at **Raku Grill** or the gourmet delights of **Todd's Unique Dining.**

Nightlife & Entertainment   Las Vegas comes alive at night, with a club scene that rivals Ibiza for its intensity and enough dazzling shows to give Broadway a run for its money. **Marquee** at The Cosmopolitan and **XS** at Encore are two of the better party-spot options these days, while almost all of the **Cirque du Soleil** productions are worth their high ticket prices. If you can snag tickets for a headliner like **Garth Brooks** or are willing to take a chance on lesser known shows like *Absinthe,* you're in for a treat.

THE most unforgettable LAS VEGAS EXPERIENCES

o **Strolling on the Strip After Dark:** You haven't really seen Las Vegas until you've seen it at night. This neon wonderland is the world's greatest sound-and-light show. Begin at Luxor and work your way past the incredible hotels and their attractions. You'll probably be exhausted, both physically and mentally, by the time you get to the halfway mark around Caesars Palace, but forge ahead and you could go all the way to the Stratosphere Tower for a bird's-eye view of the city from more than 1,000 feet up. Make plenty of stops en route to see the Mirage Volcano erupt, take a photo of the full moon over the Eiffel Tower, and marvel at the choreographed water-fountain ballet at Bellagio.

Hang out with dolphins at the Mirage's Dolphin Habitat.

- **Casino Hopping on the Strip:** The interior of each lavish hotel-casino is more outrageous and giggle-inducing than the last. Just when you think they can't possibly top themselves, they do. From Venice to Paris, from New York City to the Manhattan-style chic of CityCenter, it is all, completely and uniquely, Las Vegas. See chapter 8 for more information on casinos and check out the "The Best Casino Experiences" later in this section.

- **Sleeping In:** Come on! You're on vacation! Yes, there are lots of things to see and do in Las Vegas, but with tens of thousands of the most luxurious hotel rooms in the world, don't you just want to stay in one of those big fluffy beds and maybe order room service? We know we do. For "Best Las Vegas Hotel Bets," see p. 251.

Glide on a gondola through The Grand Canal Shoppes at The Venetian.

- **Visiting an Only-in-Vegas Museum:** Sadly, the Liberace Museum is gone but there are still several museums that are worthy of their Sin City locales. Go nuclear at the **National Atomic Testing Museum** (p. 74), go naughty at the **Erotic Heritage Museum** (p. 73), or get "made" at the **Mob Museum** (p. 70).

- **Spending a Day (and Night) in Downtown:** Glitter Gulch is undergoing a renaissance with updated and upgraded hotels and casinos like **The Plaza** (p. 298); terrific new dining options such as **Oscar's** (p. 130) from the former mayor of Vegas; fun and funky bars like **Insert Coin(s)** (p. 195); and must-see attractions like the **Fremont Street Experience** (p. 69) and the **Mob Museum** (p. 70).

- **Shopping until You're Dropping:** Take what Napoleon called "the greatest drawing room in Europe," replicate it, add shops, and you've got **The Grand Canal Shoppes** at The Venetian (p. 163)—it's St. Mark's Square, complete with canals and working gondolas. See Chapter 6 for the low-down on the shopping scene and don't miss "The Best Shopping Experiences" on p. 11.

- **Dressing Up for a Show:** You don't have to get gussied up to see one of the mind-boggling Cirque du Soleil productions or one of your favorite headliners, but there's something about putting on your best suit or fanciest dress for an evening at the "thea-tuh" that can't be beat. See Chapter 7 for reviews of the major shows and check out "The Best Las Vegas Entertainment Experiences" on p. 12.

- **Getting Away from It All:** Las Vegas can be overwhelming, so be sure to put some time on your itinerary to find your Zen at such scenic spots as the Valley of Fire State Park or Red Rock Canyon. See chapter 10 for more ideas for side trips from Vegas.

Elephant Rock, Valley of Fire State Park.

THE best FOOD & DRINK EXPERIENCES

o **Feasting Like a Gourmet:** Once an outpost of nearly inedible buffets and food-as-fuel diners, Las Vegas restaurants now regularly find spots on epicurean "best of" lists and award nominations. **Joël Robuchon Restaurant** (p. 100), from the lauded French chef, is shockingly expensive, but most true gourmands agree that it is totally worth it.

o **Bingeing at Buffets:** The indelibly Vegas all-you-can-eat buffet has grown up, transcending the concept of warmed-over food in trays to sit down restaurant–quality meals. Need proof? Check out the fine-dining caliber selections at the **Buffet at Wynn Las Vegas** (p. 150).

o **Dining with the Stars:** While it's true that few celebrity chefs are cooking in the kitchens of their Vegas restaurants, you can always tell your friends that you dined with Emeril Lagasse at **Delmonico** (p. 110) or Bobby Flay at

Gorge yourself on high-class treats at the Wynn Las Vegas Buffet.

Mesa Grill (p. 113). Who knows? They may actually believe you!

o **Hunting for a Meal Deal:** As restaurant quality has gone up, so to have the prices, but bargain hunters can still find some incredible edible deals (T-bone dinner for $9.99!) at places like **Bougainvillea** (p. 137) or the cafe at **Ellis Island** (p. 138).

o **Partying the Night Away:** The club scene in Vegas is one of the hottest in the world with debaucherous party spots in virtually every hotel. **Marquee** (p. 204) and **1 OAK** (p. 201) are among the best at keeping the party going until dawn.

o **Bar Hopping in Downtown:** The revival of Downtown Las Vegas has been led, in part, by the proliferation of casually fun bars in the area. Must visits include **Insert Coin(s)** (p. 195), a video gamers paradise, and **Vanguard Lounge** (p. 196), a craft cocktail haven with surprisingly delicious and inexpensive cocktails.

Marquee at the Cosmopolitan is one of the city's hottest clubs.

o **Mixing It Up with the Mixologists:** If the idea of drinking anything other than top-shelf liquor horrifies you, check out the almost scientifically designed concoctions at **Petrossian** (p. 198), the homemade flavors at **Vanguard Lounge** (p. 196), or the lively cocktails at the second-floor level of **The Chandelier** (p. 197).

THE best FREE & DIRT CHEAP EXPERIENCES

o **Watching the Waters Dance:** The intricately choreographed water ballet that is the **Fountains at Bellagio** (p. 66) would be worth repeated viewings even if they charged to see it. The fact that they don't makes it an almost perfect Vegas experience.

o **Enjoying the Changing of the Seasons:** There are five seasons in the elaborately designed, free to visit, botanical gardens of the **Bellagio Conservatory** (p. 66): Winter (holiday), Chinese New Year, Spring, Summer, and Fall. No matter which is on display during your visit, make sure your digital camera has a full battery charge. You'll want lots of pictures.

o **Seeing a Volcano Erupt:** When the free **Mirage Volcano** (p. 66) first "erupted" in 1989, shooting flames and faux lava into the sky, it literally stopped traffic on the Strip. That it doesn't today only means that it has more competition for your attention, not that it is any less fun.

o **Watching the Sky Light Up:** Many people considered it almost sacrilegious to convert the famed Glitter Gulch in Downtown Vegas into a pedestrian mall with a free light-and-sound show broadcast on a massive LED canopy overhead. Now the **Fremont Street Experience** (p. 69) is considered a must-visit.

o **Playing a Penny Slot:** Yes, in order to win the big bucks—sometimes millions of them—on a modern penny slot you have to bet much more than just one penny. But if you're okay with smaller rewards and losses, you could stretch a dollar into 100 spins.

o **Beating the High Score:** It's free to just look at the restored classic machines at the **Pinball Hall of Fame** (p. 76), and if you want to do more than just look, it'll only cost you a couple of quarters. What other museum lets you play with its works of art?

o **Making Your Own Postcard:** Just down the road from the southern-most edge of the Strip is one of the most photographed and imitated signs in the world. Get a picture of you at the **Welcome to Fabulous Las Vegas Sign** (p. 67) and you'll have a postcard-worthy souvenir.

THE best WAYS TO SEE LAS VEGAS LIKE A LOCAL

o **Gambling on a Budget:** Finding a local at a Strip casino is rare. Why? Because Vegas residents know the limits are lower and the payback is often higher at neighborhood casinos like **Cannery** (p. 246) and **Green Valley Ranch Resort** (p. 248).

o **Eating off the Strip:** Those same locals who don't gamble on the Strip usually don't eat on the Strip either, unless they are trying to impress visitors. Instead they dine at the less expensive but still fantastic local eateries such as **Lola's: A Louisiana Kitchen** (p. 132) or **Todd's Unique Dining** (p. 139).

o **Becoming an Arts Lover:** Leave the tacky Las Vegas snow globes for the souvenir hunting tourists and get yourself some unique Vegas keepsakes at one of the arts collectives instead. **Emergency Arts** (p. 68) and **The Arts Factory** (p. 68) are leading the charge for the burgeoning arts scene in the city.

o **Hunting for Treasure:** It may be surprising to find out that in a city like Las Vegas, where history is often disposed of with carefully

Photographing the popular Welcome to Las Vegas sign won't cost you a cent, but you may have to wait in line.

timed implosions, that antique shopping is a favored pastime of locals and visitors alike. Check out the fun finds at **Retro Vegas** (p. 167) or the flea-market bonanza of **Not Just Antiques Mart** (p. 167).

o **Catching a Broadway Show:** The 2012 opening of the stunning (both visually and aurally) **Smith Center for the Performing Arts** (p. 71) has been a boon to the cultural life of Las Vegas, giving a proper home to everything from the philharmonics and dance troupes to their popular Broadway Series featuring titles like *Mary Poppins* and *Wicked.*

Hip boutiques abound at the Emergency Arts Collective.

o **Walking the Streets:** No, not that way. Instead, check out the fun **First Friday Las Vegas** street fair (p. 72), which brings the local (and tourist) community together with live entertainment, art vendors, and lots of state fair–type food. Did we mention deep-fried cookie dough? We thought that would get your attention.

THE best CASINO EXPERIENCES

o **Saying "Vegas, Baby!" in a Classic Casino:** On the Strip there is no place that honors its history quite like **Caesars Palace** (p. 66), where you can still enjoy the classic Roman decadence that has been wowing gamblers since

The art, music, and food at the monthly First Friday street fair draws locals as well as visitors.

1966. And though they no longer have the World Series of Poker, serious players still head directly to **Binion's** (p. 242) for its *Swingers* vibe and lively table game action.

o **Seeing the Future in a Modern Casino:** When we first saw the contemporary, cutting-edge decor at **Aria Las Vegas** (p. 235) we thought that nothing could top it in terms of modern casino luxury, but then along came the bold, artistic statement of **The Cosmopolitan of Las Vegas** (p. 236) and we realized we just might have a competition on our hands.

o **Gambling in Glitter Gulch:** Downtown Las Vegas casinos often have lower limits and friendlier dealers, two things that can make losing money less egregious. The best of the breed in the area are the **Golden Nugget** (p. 244), all warm hues and laid-back fun; **Main Street Station** (p. 244), a charming turn-of-the-20th-century San Francisco–themed joint; and the newly revamped **Plaza** (p. 244), with a chic, yet comfortable, modern design.

o **Living It Up Like the Locals:** Most neighborhood casinos are low-limit, no-frills joints, but the casinos at **Red Rock Resort** (p. 316), **Green Valley Ranch** (p. 308), and **M Resort** (p. 310) are as stylish as many on the Strip. That they can be that visually appealing and still maintain most of the thrifty attitude that the locals' casinos are known for is almost a miracle.

o **Getting Rewards with a Players' Club:** Covering the casinos at places like Bellagio, Aria Las Vegas, and Mandalay Bay, **M life** is the loyalty program for all MGM Resorts International properties and offers multiple ways to earn points for comps, cash, and one-of-a-kind rewards like backstage tours of shows and exclusive dining opportunities. For more on players' clubs, see p. 232.

Casino at The Cosmopolitan of Las Vegas.

Casino at the M Resort.

o **Playing an Old School Slot:** Those seeking a retro feeling should head to the **Eastside Cannery** (p. 248), where they'll find a selection of "classic" machines that still take and dispense actual coins!

o **Chatting with a Dealer:** The dealers at most casinos on the Strip are all business, but those at **The Cosmopolitan of Las Vegas** (p. 236) are among the friendliest in town. Downtown Las Vegas is where a lot of people go to find a more laid-back, friendly attitude at the gaming tables, and you'll find it in spades (and hearts and clubs and diamonds) at the **Four Queens** (p. 242).

o **Stretching Your Gambling Budget:** You won't find any ostentatious opulence at **The Orleans** (p. 245), but you will find thousands of low-limit slot and video poker machines and dozens of gaming tables that won't cost you an arm and a leg to join. Although farther away from the Strip than most people are willing to travel, the casino at **Santa Fe Station** (p. 247) also offers a great place to gamble for the budget conscious without sacrificing style or comfort.

THE best SHOPPING EXPERIENCES

o **Hanging at the Mall:** The deliriously over-the-top togas-and-sandals theme at Caesars Palace continues into **The Forum Shops** (p. 162), where you can do you window-shopping through a replica of an ancient Roman street scene complete with talking statues!

o **Running Up Your Credit Card Balance:** You'll need to have some pretty high credit card limits to truly enjoy the shops at **The Esplanade at Wynn Las Vegas** (p. 161), which include such pricey options as Cartier, Chanel, and Christian Dior (and those are just the C's).

o **Finding the Best Bargains:** The outlet malls in Las Vegas often don't provide the kind of deep discounts that you will find about 40 miles south of town at the **Fashion Outlets Las Vegas** (p. 161). Yes, it's a bit of a drive (they offer a shuttle service), but it can be worth it for the money you'll save.

o **Laughing at the Wacky Souvenirs:** They call themselves the "world's largest gift shop" and although we're not sure who keeps track of claims like that, we're inclined to believe that the **Bonanza Gift and Souvenir Shop**

TOP 10 THINGS I MISS ABOUT BEING MAYOR BY OSCAR B. GOODMAN

1. My constituents, or as I like to call them, my peeps.

2. My mayoral parking placard.

3. My showgirls.

4. My throne.

5. Playing the mayor of Las Vegas on *CSI*.

6. Everyone takes your call when you are calling as the mayor of Las Vegas.

7. The 12 different bobble heads made in my likeness.

8. My lucky mayor's casino chips with my caricature on them.

9. Welcoming visitors and conventions to fabulous Las Vegas.

10. Visitors to my office bearing gifts of Bombay Sapphire Gin.

Oscar B. Goodman was first elected mayor in 1999 and went on to serve three terms, becoming one of the most popular politicians in the city's history. The former Mafia lawyer (who had a cameo in the movie *Casino* playing himself) was Las Vegas's biggest cheerleader and drove the development of many notable projects, including the Mob Museum (p. 70). His colorful style (he usually showed up at events with showgirls on his arms and had a throne in his office) and say-anything attitude (he often professed his fondness for gin and the "good old days" of Vegas when disputes were settled in the desert with baseball bats) earned him some controversy, but also the respect of constituents who saw him as the perfect ambassador for America's most outrageous city. Goodman's tenure as mayor ended in 2011 due to term limits, but he has kept himself busy with his own restaurant, Oscar's (p. 130), and kept the showgirls on his arm as the de facto "ambassador" for the Las Vegas Convention and Visitors Authority.

(p. 173) could hold that title. If you are looking for anything with Las Vegas emblazoned on it—seriously, almost anything—you'll find it here.

o **Reliving Your Childhood:** Regardless of whether your favorite childhood toy was something standard like a Barbie or Hot Wheels car or something obscure like a Big Trak or GI Joe Aircraft Carrier, **The Toy Shack** (p. 176) will probably have at least one of them in stock—and if they don't, they can probably get it for you.

o **Taking Vegas Home with You:** You could make your own casino at home with the almost endless supply of gaming accoutrement and keepsakes at the **Gamblers General Store** (p. 174). Permission from local authorities or your spouse not included.

THE best LAS VEGAS ENTERTAINMENT EXPERIENCES

o **Being Wowed by a Cirque Show:** The wow-factor winner is a tossup between **Cirque du Soleil's *KÀ*** (p. 181) and *Mystère* (p. 181). The latter is more traditional—if you can call a human circus that mixes dazzling acrobatics with

Cirque du Soleil's *KÀ* is noteworthy for its use of a traditional storyline.

dramatic visuals "traditional"—in that it has only a loose semblance of narrative, whereas *KÀ* actually has a plot. Both are dazzling and, given the extremely high production values, seem worth the extremely high ticket prices.

o **Embracing the Past with a Classic Show:** You know: big, huge stage sets, pointless production numbers, showgirls, nipples on parade, Bob Mackie headdresses. Ah, ***Jubilee!*** (p. 187), this world would be dreary without you. But if you want more than just a musty blast from the past, check out ***Vegas! The Show*** (p. 193), which celebrates multiple eras of classic Sin City entertainment in one spectacular package.

o **Pretending You're Brainier Than You Are with a Smart Show:** This town isn't good enough for either **Blue Man Group** (p. 179) or **Penn & Teller** (p. 190). The former is a wacky yet surprisingly cerebral performance art piece starring guys with their heads painted blue; the latter is a master class in the art and artifice of illusion taught by guys who will both amuse and amaze.

o **Asking "How Did He Do That?" at a Magic Show:** It's almost as much of a comedy show as it is a magic one, but the set done by **Mac King** (p. 189) will leave you astounded with some great close-up tricks and laughing your head off at the same time. Mixing traditional illusions (big sets and big shocks) with a rock-'n'-roll aesthetic, **Criss Angel: *Believe*** (p. 183) will make you rethink everything you thought about magic shows.

The traditional Vegas showgirl is disappearing but still makes waves at *Jubilee!*

o **Going Out on the Edge with an Adult Show:** The "edge" in the case of *Absinthe* (p. 179) is both in the so-close-you-could-get-hurt acrobatic and stunt acts and in the so-funny-you-forget-to-be-offended X-rated comedy.

o **Seeing a Legend:** The stripped-down show put on by country superstar **Garth Brooks** (p. 186), featuring him and his guitar and nothing else, is not only one of the best entertainment experiences in Las Vegas, it is one of the best shows anywhere at any cost. Meanwhile, pop royalty Sir Elton John is back on the Vegas stages with a *The Million Dollar Piano* (p. 185).

THE best OUTDOOR EXPERIENCES

o **Catching Some Rays at the Pool:** There are acres of water park fun at **Mandalay Bay** (p. 257), including a wave pool, lazy river, beach, regular swimming pools, and even its own open-air casino. Meanwhile, the lush landscaping, fountains, and water slides at **The Mirage** (p. 278) will make you feel like you're in a tropical paradise. For more picks for our favorite pools, see p. 279.

o **Sinking the Perfect Putt:** The greens fees are outrageously high but the course at **Wynn Las Vegas** (p. 91) is one of the most lush in town. "Real" golfers head to **TPC Las Vegas** (p. 91) for its challenging holes, gorgeous scenery, and occasional Justin Timberlake sightings.

o **Going for a Drive:** The 13-mile **Red Rock Scenic Drive** (p. 336) provides a way to enjoy the colorful rocks and canyons without leaving the air-conditioned comfort of your car. On the other hand, you could get a good breeze going at about 140 mph in one of the race cars you can drive yourself at the **Las Vegas Motor Speedway** (p. 77).

○ **Getting Away from the Madness:** If you need a respite from the hustle and bustle of Las Vegas, head north to **Mount Charleston** (p. 339) for a relaxed mountain retreat or to work up a sweat while hiking or snowboarding.

○ **Seeing a Man-Made Wonder:** One of the greatest engineering feats in history is the 726-foot-tall **Hoover Dam** (p. 324). You can take tours of the mighty facility and learn how it made Las Vegas (and much of the American Southwest) possible.

○ **Relaxing at a Spa:** Okay, technically it's not an outdoor experience, but you won't care once you experience the **Spa at Encore** (p. 94), a 70,000-square-foot oasis for the mind, body, and spirit, with a gorgeous Moroccan-infused design and full menu of pampering delights. Meanwhile, we only wish our own gym were as handsomely equipped as the one at the **Canyon Ranch SpaClub** (p. 93) in The Venetian, which also has a number of other high-priced treatments on which you can blow your blackjack winnings. For more great spa options, see p. 93.

The Venetian's Canyon Ranch Spa.

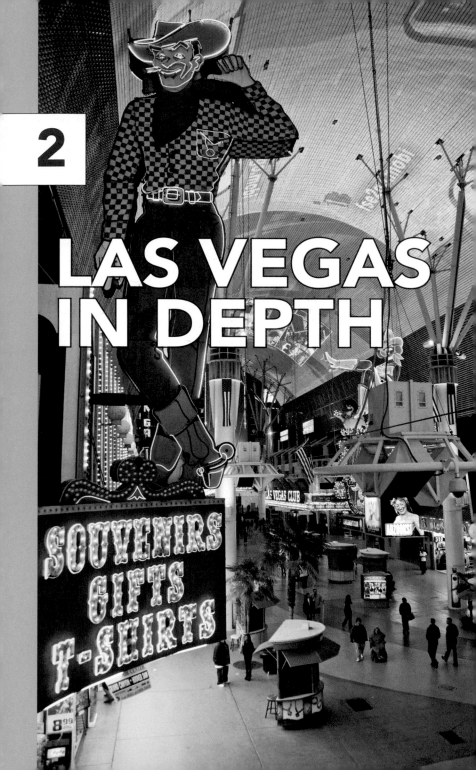

LAS VEGAS IN DEPTH

There has rarely been a time in Vegas's post-Bugsy history when the city wasn't booming, but lately the boom, while not quite a "bust," has certainly been less sonic. Proving that no corner of the globe was immune to the global recession, Las Vegas of late has struggled with the same kind of debt-to-asset imbalances that people everywhere have, only on a scale measured in billions. While new development is still happening, its pace has slowed to a crawl and the entire city seems to be poised for yet another reinvention. It wouldn't be the first time.

LAS VEGAS TODAY

No major city in America has reinvented itself as many times, especially in such a short period, as Las Vegas. Just look at the recent decades. In the '80s, it was a discount afterthought. In the '90s, it was family and theme heaven. The new millennium brought in ultraluxury and sky-high prices on everything from rooms to shampoo in the sundry stores.

For the better part of the new millennium, the watchword was "expensive." The average room rate soared to over $200 a night, significantly higher than the visitors, once lulled by lower double-digit bargains, were used to paying. It was not unusual for the high-end hotels to be charging $400 or even $500 for a standard room.

And why not? The crowds kept coming. Occupancy rates in Vegas were well over 90%, nearly 30% higher than the national average. Flush with big returns on their stock investments, equity in their home, or simply easy-flowing credit, those who could afford it flocked to the city in record numbers, generating record profit for the casinos. Vegas became hip, drawing a younger, more affluent demographic that lined up to pay for the fancy hotel rooms, the exclusive nightclubs, the celebrity-chef restaurants, and the high-limit gaming tables.

The Average Joe, on the other hand, got priced right out of town. For a lot of people—the people whose money helped build those massive hotels and casinos—the idea of a Vegas vacation became cost prohibitive.

Ultramodern CityCenter.

But then came the global economic meltdown, and Vegas has been hit hard. The number of visitors coming to the city dropped dramatically, and those who came spent a lot less money in the casinos. By 2010, the average room rate plunged to the lowest level in nearly a decade and more rooms were going empty, with occupancy rates in the low 80% range—still good when compared to the national average, but scary low for a city that depends upon filling those rooms to keep its economy going.

Many gaming companies fell into bankruptcy, and while their casinos have remained open, their bank accounts have slammed shut. Just like many Americans who ran up too much credit card debt, the gaming companies are operating under obligations that run into the billions, and they are having a hard time paying the bills.

As the national economy improved as we moved into the second decade of the new millennium, so did the Las Vegas economy. Visitation and occupancy rates perked up and people seem to be willing to spend money again.

In the long run, this could wind up being good news for the Average Joe tourist. Room rates have remained lower and most of the new stuff planned for the city—attractions, shows, restaurants, and so on—is aimed squarely at the midmarket crowd. "Expensive" seems to have been replaced by "value" as a watchword. While rates will certainly go up when the economy improves, the hotel companies are skittish about the idea of returning them to their sky-high levels because they are worried that the national mood of extravagant spending has changed.

Welcome back, Joe. Las Vegas has missed you.

Tourists vs. Natives

Las Vegas Boulevard is the epicenter of the tourism industry in the city, drawing tens of millions of people each year to roughly a 4-mile stretch of road. However, most of the people who actually live and work in Las Vegas never go to the Strip unless they are employed by one of the hotels there. But this doesn't mean that they don't gamble, eat at the hotel restaurants, and drink in the casino lounges. Scattered around town are dozens of big and small properties that are known as locals' casinos. The larger of them offer just about everything the Strip hotels do—casinos, multiple restaurants, bars and clubs, movie theaters, bowling alleys, and more—often for a fraction of the cost. Consequently, that's where the smart folks who inhabit the city spend most of their time.

It's also where the smart, budget-conscious visitor can spend a lot of time. You will need a rental car to get to and fro, but, even with that added expenditure, you can save a significant amount of money by choosing to stay somewhere other than the Strip.

Bumper-to-bumper traffic on the Strip.

There's even better news in terms of the friendliness factor. As prices went up on the Strip, so did the snootiness, to the point where it's hard to get even a smile out of check-in agents or blackjack table dealers. Locals' hotels are an entirely different animal altogether, in that you can often find the kind of familial service that can make a huge difference in how much you enjoy your stay. Save money and get a smile? Hard to beat that.

Adapting to Las Vegas

Las Vegas is, for the most part, a very casual city. Although there are a few restaurants that have a restrictive dress code, most of them—and all of the showrooms, casinos, and attractions—are pretty much come as you are. Some people still choose to dress up for their night on the town, resulting in a strange dichotomy where you might see a couple in a suit and evening gown sitting next to a couple in shorts and sandals at a show or in a nice restaurant.

Generally speaking, spiffy casual (slacks or nice jeans, button-up shirts or blouses, a simple skirt or dress) is the best way to go in terms of what to wear, allowing you to be comfortable in just about any situation. Go too far to one extreme or the other and you're bound to feel out of place somewhere.

The only exception to this rule is the nightclubs, which often have very strict policies on what you can and cannot wear. They vary from club to club, but, as a general rule, sandals or flip-flops, shorts, and baseball caps are frowned upon. A nice pair of jeans, a clean T-shirt, and a simple pair of sneakers will get you in the door, while fancier clothes (jackets, cocktail dresses) may get you past the velvet rope a little faster.

Yes, it does get hot in Las Vegas, so you really should factor that in when you're planning your wardrobe for your trip. It's important to note that every enclosed space (casino, showroom, restaurant, nightclub, and so on) is heavily air-conditioned, so it can actually get a bit chilly once you get inside. Think light layers and you should be okay.

Las Vegas is a 24-hour town, so you can find something to eat or drink all the time; but many of the nicer restaurants open only for dinner, with 5 or 6pm to 10 or 11pm the standard operating hours. Nightclubs usually open around 10pm and go until dawn, with the bulk of the crowds not showing up until midnight at the earliest. There are a few afternoon shows, but most are in the evenings and often run two shows a night with start times that range from 7 until 10:30pm. Casinos and most regular bars are open 24 hours a day.

LOOKING BACK: LAS VEGAS HISTORY

The Early 1900s: Las Vegas Takes Shape

For many years after its formal creation in 1905, Las Vegas was a mere whistle-stop town. That all changed in 1928 when Congress authorized the building of nearby Boulder Dam (later renamed Hoover Dam), bringing thousands of workers to the area. Although gambling still happened in the backrooms of saloons after it became illegal in 1909, the lifting of those prohibitions in 1931 is what set the stage for the first of the city's many booms. Fremont Street's gaming emporiums and speakeasies attracted dam workers and, upon the dam's completion, were replaced by hordes of tourists who came to see the engineering marvel (it was called "the Eighth Wonder of the World"). But it wasn't until the early years of World War II that visionary entrepreneurs began to plan for the city's glittering future.

The 1940s: The Strip Is Born

Contrary to popular lore, developer Bugsy Siegel didn't actually stake a claim in the middle of nowhere—his Flamingo opened in 1946 just a few blocks south of already-existing properties.

The true beginnings of what would eventually become the Las Vegas Strip started years earlier. According to lore, Thomas Hull was driving toward Downtown's already booming Fremont Street area when his car broke down just outside of the city limits. As he stood there sweating in the desert heat, he envisioned, or perhaps just wished for, a cool swimming pool in the scrub brush next to the highway. Luckily, Hull was a hotel magnate and he put his money where his mirage was. El Rancho Vegas, ultraluxurious for its time and complete with a sparkling pool facing the highway, opened in 1941 across the street from where the recently closed Sahara now stands. Scores of Hollywood stars were invited to the grand opening, and El Rancho Vegas soon became the hotel of choice for visiting film stars.

Beginning a trend that continues today, each new property tried to outdo existing hotels in luxurious amenities and thematic splendor. Las Vegas was on its way to becoming America's playground.

Las Vegas promoted itself in the 1940s as a town that combined Wild West frontier friendliness with glamour and excitement. As chamber of commerce president Maxwell Kelch put it in a 1947 speech, "Las Vegas has the impact of a Wild West show, the friendliness of a country store, and the sophistication of Monte Carlo." Throughout the decade, the city was Hollywood's celebrity retreat. The Hollywood connection gave the town glamour in the public's mind. So did the mob connection (something Las Vegas has spent decades trying to live

Classic Vegas

down), which became clear when notorious underworld gangster Bugsy Siegel built the fabulous Flamingo, a tropical paradise and "a real class joint."

A steady stream of name entertainers came to Las Vegas. In 1947, Jimmy Durante opened the showroom at the Flamingo. Other headliners of the 1940s included Dean Martin and Jerry Lewis, tap-dancing legend Bill "Bojangles" Robinson, the Mills Brothers, skater Sonja Henie, and Frankie Laine. Future Las Vegas legend Sammy Davis, Jr., debuted at El Rancho Vegas in 1945.

While the Strip was expanding, Downtown kept pace with new hotels such as the El Cortez and casinos like the Golden Nugget. By the end of the decade, Fremont Street was known as "Glitter Gulch," its profusion of neon signs proclaiming round-the-clock gaming and entertainment.

The 1950s: Building Booms & A-Bombs

Las Vegas entered the new decade as a city (no longer a frontier town), with a population of about 50,000. Hotel growth was phenomenal, with legendary names like the Sahara, the Dunes, the Sands, and the Tropicana, all gaining neon-lit fame.

The Desert Inn, which opened in 1950 with headliners Edgar Bergen and Charlie McCarthy, brought country-club elegance (including an 18-hole golf course and tennis courts) to the Strip.

In 1951, the Eldorado Club Downtown became Benny Binion's Horseshoe Club, which would gain fame as the home of the annual World Series of Poker.

In 1955, the Côte d'Azur–themed Riviera became the ninth big hotel to open on the Strip. Breaking the ranch-style mode, it was, at nine stories, the Strip's first high-rise. Liberace, one of the hottest names in show business, was paid the unprecedented sum of $50,000 a week to dazzle audiences in the Riviera's posh Clover Room.

Elvis appeared at the New Frontier in 1956 but wasn't a huge success; his fans were too young to fit the Las Vegas tourist mold.

In 1958, the $10-million, 1,065-room Stardust upped the spectacular stakes by importing the famed *Lido de Paris* spectacle from the French capital. It became one of the longest-running shows ever to play Las Vegas.

Two performers whose names have been linked to Las Vegas ever since—Frank Sinatra and Wayne Newton—made their debuts there. Mae West not only performed in Las Vegas, but also cleverly bought up a half-mile of desolate Strip frontage between the Dunes and the Tropicana.

In the 1950s, the wedding industry helped make Las Vegas one of the nation's most popular venues for "goin' to the chapel." Celebrity weddings of the 1950s that sparked the trend included singer Dick Haymes and Rita Hayworth, Joan Crawford and Pepsi

Tests of the atomic bomb just outside Vegas were a major tourist attraction in the 1950s.

chairman Alfred Steele, Carol Channing and TV exec Charles Lowe, and Paul Newman and Joanne Woodward.

On a grimmer note, the '50s also heralded the atomic age in Nevada, with nuclear testing taking place just 65 miles northwest of Las Vegas. A chilling 1951 photograph shows a mushroom-shaped cloud from an atomic bomb test visible over the Fremont Street horizon. Throughout the decade, about one bomb a month was detonated in the nearby desert (an event, interestingly enough, that often attracted loads of tourists).

The 1960s: The Rat Pack & the King

The very first month of the new decade made entertainment history when the Sands hosted a 3-week "Summit Meeting" in the Copa Room that was presided over by "Chairman of the Board" Frank Sinatra, with Rat Pack cronies Dean Martin; Sammy Davis, Jr.; Peter Lawford; and Joey Bishop (all of whom happened to be in town filming *Ocean's Eleven*). The series of shows helped to form the Rat Pack legend in Vegas and, in many ways vice versa, making the town hip and cool—the ultimate '60s swinging retreat.

It needed the help. After nearly a decade of almost constant building and expansion (no fewer than 10 major resorts opened in the 1950s), a crackdown on the Mafia and its money, which had fueled the city's development, brought construction to a halt. Only two major properties opened during the decade—the Road to Morocco–themed Aladdin in 1963 and the Roman Empire bacchanalia that was Caesars Palace in 1966. Perhaps trying to prove that the mob was gone for good, Las Vegas became a family destination in 1968, when Circus Circus burst onto the scene with the world's largest permanent circus and a "junior casino" featuring dozens of carnival midway games on its mezzanine level.

Elvis officially became part of the Vegas legend with the release of the film *Viva Las Vegas* in 1964, which not only furthered the city's "cool" quotient but gave it an enduring theme song that remains a part of the city's identity more than 50 years later. But it was not until 1969 that the King's place in Sin City history would be cemented with his triumphant return to Las Vegas at the International's showroom with a series of concerts that made him one of the city's all-time legendary performers. His fans had come of age.

The 1970s: The Glamour Fades

The image of Las Vegas that emerged in the 1970s was one that it would take decades to shed itself of: a tacky tourist trap with aging casinos, cheap restaurants, and showrooms filled with performers whose careers were on their last legs. With a few exceptions, investment had slowed to a crawl and Vegas didn't

The Vegas Rat Pack.

Elvis may have left the building, but Vegas has plenty of dedicated impersonators who keep his spirit alive.

seem as exciting anymore, especially when it was forced to compete with the sparkling newness of Atlantic City, where gambling was legalized in 1976.

There were some bright spots. In 1971, the 500-room Union Plaza opened at the head of Fremont Street, on the site of the old Union Pacific Station. It had what was, at the time, the world's largest casino, and its showroom specialized in Broadway productions.

The year 1973 was eventful: Over at the Tropicana, illusionists extraordinaire Siegfried & Roy began turning women into tigers and themselves into legends in the *Folies Bergere*. Meanwhile, just up the street, the original MGM Grand (now Bally's) trumped the Plaza as the largest hotel and casino in the world with Dean Martin as the opening evening's host.

Las Vegas made its way into America's living rooms with two very different television programs. Merv Griffin began taping his daytime talkfest in 1971 at Caesars Palace, taking advantage of a ready supply of local headliner guests. Then in 1978 *Vega$* debuted, instantly emblazoning the image of star Robert Urich cruising down the Strip in his red Thunderbird convertible on the minds of TV viewers everywhere.

As the decade drew to a close, an international arrivals building opened turning McCarran Field into McCarran International Airport, and dollar slot machines caused a sensation in the casinos.

The 1980s: The City Erupts

As the '80s began, Las Vegas was suffering an identity crisis. The departure of the mob and its money combined with a struggling economy and Reagan-era conservatism put a damper on the shining star of the desert. There was little new

THE mob IN LAS VEGAS

The role of the Mafia in the creation of Las Vegas is little more than a footnote these days, but it isn't too bold of a statement to suggest that without organized crime the city would not have developed in the ways that it did and its past would have certainly been less colorful.

Meyer Lansky was a big name in the New York crime syndicate in the 1930s, and it was largely his decision to send Benjamin "Bugsy" Siegel (pictured below) west to expand their empire. Although the Strip had already begun to form with the opening of El Rancho in 1941 and the Frontier in 1942, it was Bugsy's sparkling Flamingo of 1946 that began a Mafia-influenced building boom and era of control that would last for decades. Famous marquees, such as the Desert Inn, the Riviera, and the Stardust, were all built, either in part or in whole, from funding sources that were less than reputable.

During the '60s, negative attention focused on mob influence in Las Vegas. Of the 11 major casino hotels that had opened in the previous decade, 10 were believed to have been financed with mob money. Then, like a knight in shining armor, Howard Hughes rode into town and embarked on a $300-million hotel- and property-buying spree, which included the Desert Inn itself (in 1967). Hughes was as "Bugsy" as Benjamin Siegel any day, but his pristine reputation helped bring respectability to the desert city and lessen its gangland stigma.

During the 1970s and 1980s, the government got involved, embarking on a series of criminal prosecutions across the country to try to break the back of the Mafia. Although not completely successful, it did manage to wrest major control of Las Vegas away from organized crime, aided by new legislation that allowed corporations to own casinos. By the time Steve Wynn built The Mirage in 1989, the Mafia's role was reduced to the point where the most it could control were the city's innumerable strip clubs.

These days strict regulation and billions of dollars of corporate money keep things on the up and up, but the mob's influence can still be felt even at the highest levels of Las Vegas government. Former Mayor Oscar B. Goodman, first elected mayor in 1999, was a lawyer for the Mafia in the 1960s and 1970s, defending such famed gangsters as Meyer Lanksy and Anthony "Tony the Ant" Spilotro. The popular and colorful Goodman cheerfully refers to his Mafia-related past often, joking about his desire to settle conflicts in the desert at night with a baseball bat like "in the good old days."

As if to bring things full circle, Goodman championed **The Mob Museum** (p. 70), a stunning facility that examines the history and influence of the Mafia in America and Las Vegas in particular. It is located in a former courthouse that was the site of the Mafia-related Kefauver hearings of the 1950s.

development and a lot of the "classic" hotels became rundown shadows of their former selves.

A devastating fire in 1980 at the original MGM Grand killed more than 80 people, and just a few months later another at the Las Vegas Hilton killed eight more. In some ways these tragedies helped to further the transformation of the public's view of the entire city. Las Vegas became tacky, desperate, and possibly unsafe.

Even the showrooms, once the magnificent Elvis/Sinatra klieg light that lured people from around the world, had become something of a joke. For entertainers, Vegas was where you played when your career was over, not when you were on top.

So the city started creating its own stars. Siegfried & Roy's show, *Beyond Belief,* ran for 6 years at the Frontier, playing a record-breaking 3,538 performances to sellout audiences every night. It became the most successful attraction in the city's history.

But no number of white tigers could stop the decline the city's image was taking. What Las Vegas really needed was a white knight, and they got one in the form of Golden Nugget owner Steve Wynn.

Wynn gambled big—$630 million big. Financed mostly through the sale of junk bonds, he began construction on a place that would eventually change the course of Las Vegas history.

His gleaming white-and-gold Mirage opened in 1989, fronted by five-story waterfalls, lagoons, and lush tropical foliage—not to mention a 50-foot volcano that dramatically erupted regularly! Wynn gave world-renowned illusionists Siegfried & Roy carte blanche (and more than $30 million) to create the most spellbinding show Las Vegas had ever seen and brought in world-class chefs to banish the idea that all you could eat in the town were all you-can-eat spreads and $4.99 prime rib.

It was an immediate success; from a financial perspective, of course, but more importantly from a perception one. Almost overnight, Las Vegas became cool again and everyone wanted to go there.

The Mirage's lush tropical atrium.

The 1990s: King Arthur Meets King Tut

The 1990s began with a blare of trumpets heralding the rise of a turreted medieval castle, fronted by a moated drawbridge and staffed by jousting knights and fair damsels. Excalibur reflected the '90s marketing trend to promote Las Vegas as a family-vacation destination.

Was that successful? Well, Chevy Chase did take his family on a *Vegas Vacation* in 1997, but the city kept the Sin part of its name alive, at least in popular culture, with Robert Redford making an *Indecent Proposal* (1993); Nicholas Cage hitting rock bottom in *Leaving Las Vegas* (1995); and Elizabeth Berkley strutting her stuff in the widely derided *Showgirls* (1995).

The Excalibur—a monument to the Vegas theme era and the city's failed attempt to seduce families.

Canadian circus/theater group Cirque du Soleil transformed the entertainment scene in Las Vegas with the 1993 debut of *Mystère* at the newly opened Treasure Island. It would be the first of no fewer than seven Cirque shows that would launch over the next 2 decades.

The era of megahotels continued on the Strip, including the *new* MGM Grand hotel, backed by a full theme park (it ended Excalibur's brief reign as the world's largest resort), Luxor Las Vegas, and Steve Wynn's Treasure Island.

In 1993, a unique pink-domed 5-acre indoor amusement park, Grand Slam Canyon (later known as Adventuredome), became part of the Circus Circus hotel. In 1995, the Fremont Street Experience was completed, revitalizing Downtown Las Vegas. Closer to the Strip, rock restaurant magnate Peter Morton opened the Hard Rock Hotel, billed as "the world's first rock-'n'-roll hotel and casino." The year 1996 saw the advent of the French Riviera–themed Monte Carlo and the Stratosphere Las Vegas Hotel & Casino, its 1,149-foot tower the highest building west of the Mississippi. The unbelievable New York–New York arrived in 1997.

But it all paled compared with 1998 to 1999. As Vegas hastily repositioned itself from "family destination" to "luxury resort," several new hotels, once again eclipsing anything that had come before, opened. Bellagio was the latest from Vegas visionary Steve Wynn, an attempt to bring grand European style to the desert, while at the far southern end of the Strip, Mandalay Bay charmed. As if this weren't enough, The Venetian's ambitiously detailed re-creation of everyone's favorite Italian city came along in May 1999, and was followed in short order by the opening of Paris Las Vegas in the fall of 1999.

The 2000s: The Lap of Luxury

The 21st century opened up with a bang as the Aladdin blew itself up and gave itself a from-the-ground-up makeover (which in turn only lasted for a handful of years before Planet Hollywood took it over and changed it entirely), while Steve Wynn blew up the Desert Inn and built a new showstopper named for himself. Along the way, everyone expanded, and then expanded some more, ultimately adding thousands of new rooms. Caesars produced two new towers, plus a multistory addition to its Forum Shops. Bellagio and The Venetian followed suit with their own additional towers. Mandalay Bay upped the ante by making its new tower an entirely separate establishment, THEhotel, which sent the signal that the priorities in this latest incarnation of Vegas had shifted. There is no casino in THEhotel (though guests have adequate access to the one in Mandalay Bay), while rooms are all one-bedroom suites, permanently breaking with the convention that no one comes to Vegas to spend time in their room. Other hotels followed with similar plush digs. The watchword became "luxury," with a secondary emphasis on "adult." Little by little, wacky, eye-catching themes were phased out (as much as one can when one's hotel looks like a castle) and generic sophistication took its place. Gaming is still number one, but the newer hotels are trying to top each other in terms of other recreations—decadent nightclubs, celebrity chef–backed restaurants, fancy spas, and superstar shows.

"More is more" seemed to be the motto, and so The Venetian's annex, The Palazzo, is taller than Encore, the extension of the Wynn. Eclipsing all of it—for the moment, anyway—is the massive CityCenter, perhaps the most ambitious project in the city yet. Composed of a 4,000-room megaresort, two 400-room boutique hotels, condos, shopping, dining, clubs, and more, it covers more than 60 acres and, as such, is a city-within-the-city. Gone are the outrageous themes, replaced by cutting-edge modernism—all sleek lines of glass and metal designed with the future in mind, not only from an architectural standpoint but from an ecological one as well. Sure, building the massive CityCenter probably made the earth shudder a bit, but its advanced green building and sustainable operating systems helped to ensure that the planet didn't just collapse in on itself from the weight of it all.

The excess of Vegas was spotlighted in popular culture as well. *Ocean's Eleven* got a new millennium makeover in 2001 with a cast of superstars like George Clooney, Brad Pitt, and Julia Roberts. Then in 2009, *The Hangover* took it all to a new level with a raunchy morality tale of a Vegas bachelor party gone horribly awry.

Colorful artwork in the lobby of Wynn Las Vegas, the resort that launched the Las Vegas luxe era.

criss angel's **FAVORITE LAS VEGAS TV**

Although most people immediately think of movies when they think of Las Vegas in pop culture, there have been some classic television series and episodes set in Sin City as well. We asked superstar magician Criss Angel (and star of A&E's hit series *Criss Angel Mindfreak*) to pick his favorites:

- *Criss Angel Mindfreak* (2005–current). I'm a little biased, but we've done six seasons, a lot of it in Vegas including an episode where I floated more than 500 feet above Las Vegas Boulevard in the Luxor Light. Taxis literally crashed watching.

- *Vega$* (1977–79). Robert Urich, Tony Curtis, the Desert Inn, and that red Thunderbird cruising the Strip. Does it get any cooler than this?

- *CSI: Crime Scene Investigation* (2000–current). There's a dark side to Vegas behind the neon lights, and this gory (in a good way) show captures it perfectly.

- *Las Vegas* (2003–2008). I'm especially fond of the November 2005 episode "Bold, Beautiful & Blue" where I got accused of stealing a priceless diamond. It wasn't me, I swear.

- *Friends* ("The One in Vegas"; May 1999). Ross and Rachel get drunk and wind up married. In other words, a typical weekend in Vegas.

- *The Simpsons* ("Viva Ned Flanders"; January 1999). Homer takes Ned to Vegas for a lesson on how to live fully, get drunk . . . and wind up married. Sensing a theme here?

- *The Real World Las Vegas* (2002–2003). Okay, there may be nothing "real" about living in a casino, but it did leave behind a suite at the Palms that you can rent and make your own Vegas reality show.

- *Roseanne* ("Vegas, Vegas"; November 1991). Thinking she's dealing with an impersonator, Roseanne heckles the real Wayne Newton during a concert. Anything with Mr. Las Vegas in it is an instant classic.

- *The Stand* (miniseries; 1994). When the world is ending, where would you want to go? Vegas, of course!

- *Blanksy's Beauties* (1977). Does anyone else remember this sitcom with Nancy Walker as a den mother to a bunch of Las Vegas showgirls? Just me? Okay.

Even the city's motto, which became a popular part of the American lexicon, was a winking nod to the seemingly endless ways to satisfy the id: "What happens in Vegas, stays in Vegas."

Once known solely as an outpost of all-you-can-eat buffets and $4.99 prime rib specials, Las Vegas has become one of the top dining destinations in the world. Every celebrity chef worth his or her sea salt has a restaurant here, and the level of culinary quality has risen almost as fast as the prices. Take a look at some of the famous names attached to Vegas restaurants: Emeril Lagasse, Wolfgang Puck, Gordon Ramsay, Bobby Flay, Todd English, Hubert Keller, Bradley Ogden, Joël de Robuchon, Thomas Keller, and Julian Serrano. It's a veritable who's who of the culinary world. Dining in Las Vegas is now one of the top reasons people want to visit the city.

And proving that Las Vegas really is a 24-hour town, the nightlife scene exploded in Vegas. Megaclubs like PURE (p. 205) at Caesars Palace, XS (p. 206) at Encore Las Vegas, and Marquee (p. 204) at The Cosmopolitan pull in droves of the young and beautiful (or people who think they are, or who just want to be around them) who do not seem to be deterred by the eye-popping high prices ($20–$50 cover, $10–$15 drinks), long lines (expect to wait at least an hour), and lack of personal space. It's a see-and-be-seen scene, where you better dress to impress or expect to be relegated to the darker corners (if you get in at all).

Céline Dion made it safe to be a Vegas headliner again as she kicked off a 5-year residency at Caesars Palace in 2003. She would be followed by big-ticket names like Elton John, Bette Midler, Cher, and Garth Brooks, all of whom made Vegas their performing home for at least a little while.

Just before 2010 came to end, the last major resort for the foreseeable future opened in the form of the audaciously designed Cosmopolitan of Las Vegas, complete with a three-story chandelier that doubles as a bar. It was designed as one big art project, with graffiti artist renderings on the walls of the parking garages, support columns in the lobby clad in video screens showing fields or champagne bubbles, and even vending machines that dispense $5 packets of art instead of cigarettes.

Clearly, no one can rest on their laurels in Vegas, for this is not only a town that never sleeps, but also one in which progress never stops moving, even for a heartbeat.

WHEN TO GO

Most of a Las Vegas vacation is usually spent indoors, so you can have a good time here year-round. The most pleasant seasons are spring and fall, especially if you want to experience the great outdoors.

Weekdays are slightly less crowded than weekends. Holidays are always a mob scene and come accompanied by high hotel prices. Hotel prices also skyrocket when big conventions and special events are taking place. The slowest times of year are June, July, and August; the week before Christmas; and the week after New Year's.

If a major convention is to be held during your trip, you might want to change your date. Check the box on p. 33 for convention dates, and contact the **Las Vegas Convention and Visitors Authority** (*(*0*877/847-4858** or 702/892-7575; www.visitlasvegas.com), as convention schedules often change.

Climate & Current Weather Conditions

First of all, Vegas isn't always hot, but when it is, it's *really* hot. One thing you'll hear again and again is that even though Las Vegas gets very hot, the dry desert heat is not unbearable. We know this is true because we spent a couple of days there in 104°F (40°C) weather and lived to say, "It wasn't all that bad, not really." The humidity averages a low 22%, and even on very hot days, there's apt to be a breeze. Having said that, once the temperature gets into triple digits, it is wise to limit the amount of time you spend outdoors and to make sure you are drinking plenty of water even while you are inside enjoying the blessed air-conditioning (which is omnipresent). Dehydration and heatstroke are two of the most common ailments that affect tourists—don't be a victim of one of them. Also, except on the hottest summer days, there's relief at night, when temperatures often drop by as much as 20 degrees.

Las Vegas's Average Temperatures (°F & °C) & Rainfall

	JAN	FEB	MAR	APR	MAY	JUNE	JULY	AUG	SEPT	OCT	NOV	DEC
AVERAGE (°F)	49	54	60	67	78	87	93	91	83	70	57	48
(°C)	9	12	16	19	26	31	34	33	28	21	14	9
HIGH TEMP. (°F)	58	63	70	78	89	99	104	102	94	81	67	57
(°C)	14	17	21	26	32	37	40	39	35	27	19	14
LOW TEMP. (°F)	39	44	49	56	66	75	81	79	71	59	47	39
(°C)	4	7	9	13	19	24	27	26	22	15	8	4
RAINFALL (IN.)	0.6	0.8	0.4	0.2	0.1	0.1	0.4	0.3	0.3	0.3	0.4	0.5

But this is the desert, and it's not hot year-round. It can get quite cold, especially in the winter, when at night it can drop to 30°F (–1°C) and lower. Although rare, it does snow occasionally in Las Vegas. The winter of 2008 to 2009 dropped nearly 3 inches of snow on the Strip. There's nothing quite like the sight of Luxor's Sphinx covered in snow. The breeze can also become a cold, biting wind of up to 40 mph and more. And so there are entire portions of the year when you won't be using that hotel pool at all (even if you want to; most of the hotels close huge chunks of those pool areas for "the season," which can be as long as the period from Labor Day to Memorial Day). If you aren't traveling in the height of summer, bring a jacket. Also, remember sunscreen and a hat—even if it's not all that hot, you can burn very easily and very fast.

Holidays

Banks, government offices, post offices, and many stores, restaurants, and museums are closed on the following legal national holidays: January 1 (New Year's Day), the third Monday in January (Martin Luther King, Jr., Day), the third Monday in February (Presidents' Day), the last Monday in May (Memorial Day), July 4 (Independence Day), the first Monday in September (Labor Day), the second Monday in October (Columbus Day), November 11 (Veterans Day/Armistice Day), the fourth Thursday in November (Thanksgiving Day), and December 25 (Christmas). The Tuesday after the first Monday in November is Election Day, a federal government holiday in presidential-election years (held every 4 years, and next in 2012).

Las Vegas Calendar of Events

You may be surprised that Las Vegas does not offer as many annual events as most other tourist cities. The reason is Las Vegas's very raison d'être: the gaming industry. This town wants its visitors spending their money in the casinos, not at Renaissance fairs and parades.

When in town, check the local paper and contact the **Las Vegas Convention and Visitors Authority** (✆ **877/847-4858** or 702/892-7575; www.visitlasvegas.com) or the **Las Vegas Chamber of Commerce** (✆ **702/735-1616;** www.lvchamber.com) to find out about other events scheduled during your visit.

For an exhaustive list of events beyond those listed here, check http://events.frommers.com, where you'll find a searchable, up-to-the-minute roster of what's happening in cities all over the world.

wild **WEATHER**

Las Vegas rests in the middle of a desert, so how wacky can the weather possibly get? A lot crazier than you think. Although Las Vegas's location results in broiling-hot temperatures in the summer, many people tend to forget that deserts get cold and rainy, while wind is also a potential hazard.

Winter temperatures in Las Vegas have been known to dip below 30°F (–1°C), and when you toss in 40 mph winds, that adds up to a very chilly stroll on the Strip. And snow is not an unheard-of occurrence. Most years see a flurry or two falling on Las Vegas, and since 1949, a total of 12 "storms" have resulted in accumulations of 2 inches or greater, with the largest storm dropping 9 inches onto the Strip in January 1949. In December 2003, parts of Las Vegas got 6 inches of the white stuff, and although it didn't stick around too long on the Strip, the sight of the famous "Welcome to Fabulous Las Vegas" sign in the middle of a driving blizzard was quite a spectacle. And more recently (the winter of 2008–09), Vegas received nearly 3 inches of snow on the Strip itself, with nearly 10 inches accumulating in other areas of town. Locals usually find the snow a charming addition to the city (and the stuff melts completely in a day or two, so they don't have to shovel it—lucky them).

But although snow is a novel quirk that many Vegas residents and visitors welcome, rain isn't always as well received. The soil in Las Vegas is parched most of the year, making it difficult for the land to absorb large amounts of water coming down in a short time. Between June and August, when most of the area's rainfall takes place due to the Southwest's monsoon season, there is a good possibility of flash flooding.

At times, the skies just open up, resulting in flooding that wreaks havoc on Sin City. On July 9, 1999, Mother Nature unleashed more than 3 inches of rain *in just a few hours* on a city that averages about 4 inches of rain a year. The deluge killed two people, swamped hundreds of cars, and destroyed millions of dollars in property. As the Strip turned into a raging river, tourists took refuge in the hotels, but at least one resort—Caesars Palace—had to close its casino and shopping arcade because of flooding. This kind of storm (and rain in general) is rare, but even a light shower can make things treacherous on the roads, the sidewalks, and the slippery marble walkways that front almost every casino in town.

The topography of the Las Vegas region also makes it prone to high, often damaging winds. Situated at the bottom of a bowl ringed by mountains, 15 to 20 mph steady winds are not uncommon and gusts of 70 to 80 mph have been recorded. In 1994, a brief windstorm knocked down the massive sign at the Las Vegas Hilton and in 2010 a storm tore apart the Cloud 9 balloon, billed as the largest tethered helium balloon in the world.

FEBRUARY

The Super Bowl. Granted, the actual game is not held in Las Vegas, but the numbers of people it brings to the city rival those that go to wherever the big game is being held. Sports fans and sports bettors come out in droves to watch the action on the big screens around town and to lay down a wager or two on the outcome. Usually the first weekend in February.

Valentine's Day. This is the marriage (and possibly divorce) capital of the world and the betrothed line up to exchange their vows all across town on Cupid's day. The city's Marriage Bureau stays open 24 hours during the weekend and some chapels literally perform dozens of weddings. February 14.

MARCH

NASCAR. The **Las Vegas Motor Speedway,** 7000 Las Vegas Blvd. N. (© **800/644-4444;** www.lvms.com), has become one of the premier facilities in the country, attracting races and racers of all stripes and colors. The biggest races of the year are the Sam's Town 300 and the Kobalt Tools 400, held in early March.

March Madness. Remember everything we just said about the Super Bowl? Apply it here for the NCAA college basketball championships held over several weekends in March.

JUNE

World Series of Poker. When Harrah's Entertainment bought the legendary Binion's Horseshoe, in Downtown Vegas, out of bankruptcy, it quickly turned around and sold the hotel but kept the hosting rights to this famed event, moving its location and place on the calendar. Now held at the **Rio All-Suite Hotel and Casino,** 3700 W. Flamingo Rd. (© **800/752-9746**), in June and July (with the final table held in Nov for some incomprehensible reason), the event features high-stakes gamblers and showbiz personalities competing for six-figure purses. There are daily events, with entry stakes ranging from $125 to $5,000. To enter the World Championship Event players must pony up $10,000 but could win a fortune (the 2011 top prize was $8.71 million). It costs nothing to crowd around the tables and watch the action, but if you want to avoid the throngs, you can catch a lot of it on TV. For more information, visit www.wsop.com.

OCTOBER

Halloween. Las Vegas gets even scarier than normal on and around Halloween with "spooky" twists to many of the major attractions (Adventuredome becomes

"Fright Dome" with haunted houses and more), debaucherous costume parties at the nightclubs, and a parade and festivities in Downtown Las Vegas.

DECEMBER

National Finals Rodeo. This is the Super Bowl of rodeos, attended by about 200,000 people each year and offering nearly $5 million in prize money. Male rodeo stars compete in calf roping, steer wrestling, bull riding, team roping, saddle bronco riding, and bareback riding. Women compete in barrel racing. An all-around Cowboy of the Year is chosen. In connection with this event, hotels book country stars into their showrooms, and a cowboy shopping spree—the **NFR Cowboy Christmas Gift Show,** a trade show for Western gear—is held at Cashman Field. The NFR runs for 10 days, during the first 2 weeks of December, at the 17,000-seat Thomas & Mack Center of the University of Nevada, Las Vegas (UNLV). Order tickets as far in advance as possible (© **866/388-3267**). For more information, see www.nfrexperience.com.

MAACO Bowl Las Vegas Week. A championship college football event in mid-December pits the winners of the Mountain West Conference against the fourth or fifth selection of the Pac-10 Conference. The action takes place at the 32,000-seat Sam Boyd Stadium. Call © **702/732-3912,** or visit www.lvbowl.com for ticket information.

New Year's Eve. Between 300,000 and 400,000 people descend on Las Vegas to ring in the New Year, making it one of the largest gatherings for the holiday outside of New York's Times Square. Fireworks are the dominant entertainment, with pyrotechnics launched from the roofs of many hotels on the Strip and under the canopy at Fremont Street in Downtown Las Vegas. The Strip is closed to vehicles for the night, and so traffic and parking are a nightmare, as is booking a room, which should be done well in advance (and expect to pay a hefty premium).

MAJOR convention DATES FOR 2013

Listed below are Las Vegas's major annual conventions, with projected attendance figures for 2013; believe us, unless you're coming for one of them, you probably want to avoid the biggies. Because convention schedules frequently change, contact the **Las Vegas Convention and Visitors Authority** (© **877/847-4858** or 702/892-7575; www.visitlasvegas.com) to double-check the latest info before you commit to your travel dates.

Event Attendance	Dates	Expected
Consumer Electronics Show	Jan 8–11	140,000
Adult Entertainment Expo	Jan 8–11	40,000
International Builders Show	Jan 22–25	62,000
International Pizza Expo	Mar 19–21	10,000
Nightclub and Bar Show	Mar 20–21	31,000
Associated Surplus Dealers	Mar 26–29	41,000
Int'l Esthetics, Cosmetics & Spa Conference	May 4–6	32,000
National Hardware Show	May 7–9	35,000
RECon 2013	May 20–22	30,000
Associated Surplus Dealers	Aug 11–14	41,000
Interactive Manufacturing Experience	Sep 9–12	20,000
2013 Pack Expo	Sep 23–25	26,000
Global Gaming Expo	Sep 24–26	17,000
International Baking Industry Expo	Oct 6–9	35,000
ABC Kids Expo	Oct 15–18	14,000
National Business Aviation Association	Oct 22–24	32,000
ISSA/INTERCLEAN North America	Nov 19–21	18,000
SEMA/Automotive Aftermarket Industry Week	Nov 4–7	150,000

RESPONSIBLE TRAVEL

Las Vegas is a city that was built on the concept of mass consumption—overconsumption, really—of just about everything. Water, electricity, food, alcohol—you name it and probably too much of it is used here. The fact that all of this consumption happens in the middle of a desert where such resources are scarce only amplifies the problem.

Drought is a major concern here, with water levels at the major lakes and reservoirs in the area falling to dangerously low levels. You can do your part by limiting the amount of water your vacation consumes in a couple of simple yet

GENERAL RESOURCES FOR responsible TRAVEL

In addition to the resources for Las Vegas listed below see frommers.com/planning for more tips on responsible travel.

o **Responsible Travel** (www.responsible travel.com) is a great source of sustainable travel ideas; the site is run by a spokesperson for ethical tourism in the travel industry. **Sustainable Travel International** (www.sustainable travelinternational.org) promotes ethical tourism practices and manages an extensive directory of sustainable properties and tour operators around the world.

o **Carbonfund** (www.carbonfund.org), **TerraPass** (www.terrapass.org), and

Cool Climate (http://coolclimate. berkeley.edu) provide info on "carbon offsetting," or offsetting the green-house gas emitted by airplanes during flight.

o **Greenhotels** (www.greenhotels.com) recommends green-rated member hotels around the world that fulfill the company's stringent environmental requirements. **Environmentally Friendly Hotels** (www.environmentally friendlyhotels.com) offers more green accommodations ratings.

effective ways. First, although that soaking tub looks tempting, perhaps a short shower will do the trick. Second, reuse your towels whenever possible so they don't have to be run through the laundry every day. Most housekeeping staff will only launder towels left on the floor and will leave those on racks alone.

Many newer hotels (CityCenter and The Palazzo, to name a couple) have been built with sustainable practices that limit the amount of energy you use while visiting. Some have automatic shutdown systems that turn off all the lights when you leave the room and then restore your settings when you return, but if yours doesn't, there is always the light switch. Use it.

For transportation, the greenest (and most scenic) way of getting around is your own two feet. Vegas, especially on the Strip, is very pedestrian-friendly provided you follow the marked crosswalks and signals. But if you need wheels, most major rental-car companies in town have hybrids or electric vehicles in their fleet. We don't recommend trying to use a bicycle around the Strip—it's just too difficult to navigate the crowds and the traffic—but if you really want to, your hotel's concierge can direct you to the nearest local bike-rental company. And if you're staying at Aria Las Vegas, they'll even valet your two-wheeler for you!

3

SUGGESTED
LAS VEGAS
ITINERARIES

When you visit Las Vegas, you certainly won't be lacking in things to do. But the sheer enormity of the city and its laundry list of sights, attractions, restaurants, shows, recreation, and other activities could leave even the most intrepid traveler feeling a little overwhelmed.

The itineraries in this chapter are designed to help narrow the big list down a little while maximizing your time. This way you can spend less energy planning and more simply having fun. Each has a theme, but you can always mix and match to create your perfect Las Vegas getaway.

Instead of a step-by-step tour, the itineraries are broken down by morning, afternoon, and nighttime activities with multiple suggestions for each, again allowing you to customize your vacation in a way that makes sense for you.

CITY LAYOUT

Located in the southernmost precincts of a wide, pancake-flat valley, Las Vegas is the biggest city in the state of Nevada. Treeless mountains form a scenic backdrop to hotels awash in neon glitter. Although bursting with residents and visitors, the city is quite compact, geographically speaking.

There are two main areas of Las Vegas: the **Strip** and **Downtown.** The former is probably the most famous 4-mile stretch of highway in the nation. Officially called Las Vegas Boulevard South, it contains most of the top hotels in town and offers almost all the major showroom entertainment. First-time visitors will, and probably should, spend the bulk of their time on the Strip.

Downtown, meanwhile, is where Vegas started its Glitter Gulch fame, complete with neon ambassadors Vegas Vic and Sassy Sally watching over the action.

For many people, that's all there is to Las Vegas. But there is actually more to the town than that: Although maybe not as glitzy and glamorous as the Strip and Downtown—okay, definitely not—Paradise Road and east Las Vegas are home to quite a bit of casino action; Maryland Parkway boasts mainstream and some alternative-culture shopping; and there are different restaurant options all over the city. Many of the "locals' hotels," most of which are off the regular tourist track, offer cheaper gambling limits plus budget food and entertainment options. Confining yourself to the Strip and Downtown is fine for the first-time visitor, but repeat customers (and you will be) should get out there and explore. Las Vegas Boulevard South (the Strip) is the starting point for addresses; any street that crosses it starts with 1 East and 1 West at its intersection with the Strip (and goes up from there).

All major Las Vegas hotels provide comprehensive tourist information at their reception and/or sightseeing and show desks.

Other good information sources are the **Las Vegas Convention and Visitors Authority,** 3150 Paradise Rd. (© **877/847-4858** or 702/892-7575; www.visitlasvegas.com), open Monday through Friday 8am to 6pm and Saturday and

PREVIOUS PAGE: **Limos are a common sight in fabulously over-the-top Vegas.**

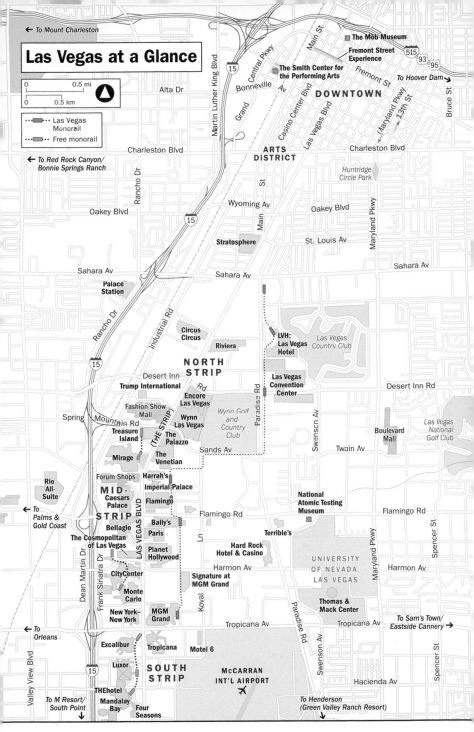

Las Vegas at a Glance

← To Mount Charleston

0   0.5 mi
0   0.5 km

···▭··· Las Vegas Monorail
···▭··· Free monorail

← To Red Rock Canyon/ Bonnie Springs Ranch

To Mount Charleston

Alta Dr

Martin Luther King Blvd

Bonneville Av

Central Pkwy

Grand

Main St

The Mob Museum

Fremont Street Experience

The Smith Center for the Performing Arts

Casino Center Blvd

Las Vegas Blvd

Fremont St

DOWNTOWN

515

93

95

To Hoover Dam →

Maryland Pkwy

13th St

Bruce St

Charleston Blvd

ARTS DISTRICT

Charleston Blvd

Huntridge Circle Park

Rancho Dr

Oakey Blvd

Main St

Wyoming Av

Oakey Blvd

St. Louis Av

Maryland Pkwy

Sahara Av

Stratosphere

Sahara Av

Sahara Av

Palace Station

Sahara Av

Industrial Rd

Circus Circus

Riviera

LVH: Las Vegas Hotel

Las Vegas Country Club

15

Rancho Dr

NORTH STRIP

Desert Inn Rd

Las Vegas Convention Center

Desert Inn Rd

Trump International

Rd

Encore Las Vegas

Wynn Golf and Country Club

Paradise Rd

Swenson Av

Twain Av

Boulevard Mall

Las Vegas National Golf Club

Spring Mountain Rd

Fashion Show Mall

(THE STRIP)

Wynn Las Vegas

Treasure Island

The Palazzo

Mirage

The Venetian

Sands Av

Forum Shops

Harrah's

Imperial Palace

National Atomic Testing Museum

Rio All-Suite

MID-CAESARS PALACE STRIP

Flamingo

Flamingo Rd

Flamingo Rd

← To Palms & Gold Coast

Bellagio

Bally's Paris

Terrible's

LAS VEGAS BLVD

The Cosmopolitan of Las Vegas

Planet Hollywood

Hard Rock Hotel & Casino

Harmon Av

UNIVERSITY OF NEVADA, LAS VEGAS

Maryland Pkwy

Spencer St

Harmon Av

Dean Martin Dr

Frank Sinatra Dr

CityCenter

Monte Carlo

Signature at MGM Grand

Koval Ln

New York–New York

MGM Grand

Thomas & Mack Center

To Sam's Town/ Eastside Cannery →

← To Orleans

Excalibur

Tropicana

Motel 6

Tropicana Av

Paradise Rd

Tropicana Av

Swenson Av

Spencer St

Valley View Blvd

Luxor

SOUTH STRIP

McCARRAN INT'L AIRPORT ✈

15

THEhotel

To M Resort/ South Point ↓

Mandalay Bay

Four Seasons

Hacienda Av

To Henderson (Green Valley Ranch Resort) ↓

37

Help for Troubled Travelers

The **Travelers Aid Society** is a social-service organization geared to helping travelers in difficult straits. Its services include reuniting families separated while traveling, feeding people stranded without cash, and even providing emotional counseling. If you're in trouble, seek them out. In Las Vegas, services are provided by **Help of Southern Nevada,** 1640 E. Flamingo Rd., Ste. 100, near Maryland Parkway (© **702/369-4357;** www.helponv.org). Hours are Monday through Thursday 7am to 5pm.

Sunday 8am to 5pm; the **Las Vegas Chamber of Commerce,** 6671 Las Vegas Blvd. S., Ste. 300 (© **702/735-1616;** www.lvchamber.com), open Monday through Friday 8am to 5pm; and, for information on all of Nevada, including Las Vegas, the **Nevada Commission on Tourism** (© **800/638-2328;** www.travel nevada.com), open 24 hours.

NEIGHBORHOODS IN BRIEF

SOUTH STRIP

For the purposes of organizing this book, we've divided the Strip into three sections. The **South Strip** can be roughly defined as the portion of the Strip south of Harmon Avenue, including the MGM Grand, Mandalay Bay, the Monte Carlo, New York–New York, Luxor, CityCenter, and many more hotels and casinos. First-timers should consider staying here or in the Mid-Strip area simply because this is where the bulk of the stuff you're going to want to see, do, and eat are located.

MID-STRIP

The **Mid-Strip** is a long stretch of the Las Vegas Boulevard South between Harmon Avenue and Spring Mountain Road, which includes such big-name casinos

The North Strip is home to several resorts, the iconic Stratosphere, and the Fashion Show mall.

as Planet Hollywood, The Cosmopolitan of Las Vegas, Bellagio, Caesars, The Mirage, Treasure Island, Bally's, Paris Las Vegas, Flamingo Las Vegas, Harrah's, and more. As mentioned above, this is a great area for newbies and it's also the preferred location for people with mobility issues since fewer steps will get you to more places.

NORTH STRIP

The **North Strip** stretches north from Spring Mountain Road all the way to the Stratosphere and includes Wynn Las Vegas, Encore, the Riviera, and Circus Circus, to name a few. Although there are certainly things to see along this chunk of the Strip, development has mostly stalled so you'll see more things closed or partially constructed in this area than you will open and completed. With the exception of Wynn/Encore, it is the lower-rent part of the Strip, with all of the good and bad that comes along with it.

DOWNTOWN

Also known as **"Glitter Gulch"** (narrower streets make the neon seem brighter), Downtown Las Vegas, which is centered on Fremont Street, between Main and 9th streets, was the first section of the city to develop hotels and casinos. With the exception of the Golden Nugget, which looks like it belongs in Monte Carlo, this area has traditionally been more casual than the Strip. But between the **Fremont Street Experience** (p. 69), the **East Fremont District** (p. 52), and a general resurgence, Downtown offers a more affordable yet still entertaining alternative to the Strip.

The area between the Strip and Downtown is a seedy stretch dotted with tacky wedding chapels, bail-bond operations, pawnshops, and cheap motels. However, the area known as the **18b Arts District** (roughly north and south of Charleston Blvd. to the west of Las Vegas Blvd. S.) is starting to make a name for itself as an artists' colony. Studios, galleries, antique stores, bars, small cafes, and the fun **First Friday Las Vegas** festival (p. 72) can be found in the vicinity. Eventually it may warrant its own neighborhood designation, but for now we are including it in the Downtown category.

"Sassy Sally" is one of several old-style neon signs overlooking Downtown Las Vegas.

JUST OFF THE STRIP

With land directly on the Strip at a premium, it isn't surprising that a veritable cottage industry of casinos, hotels, restaurants, nightclubs, attractions, and services have taken up residence in the areas immediately surrounding the big megaresorts. Within a mile in any given direction you'll find major hotels such as Rio Las Vegas, Orleans, the Las Vegas Hotel (formerly the Las Vegas Hilton), and the Hard Rock, to name a few, as well as important visitor destinations such as the Las Vegas Convention Center. You'll also find many smaller chain/name-brand hotels and motels offering reliable service at rates that are usually cheaper than you'll pay in a big casino-hotel on the Strip.

SOUTH & EAST OF THE STRIP

Once you get a little bit of distance between you and the Strip, you'll start getting into the types of neighborhoods that will look much more familiar to you—except, perhaps, with a lot more desert landscaping. Shopping centers and housing tracts dominate the landscape of the bedroom community of Henderson, while lower-priced motels and chain restaurants take up a lot of space along the Boulder Highway corridor on the far-east side of town. But sprinkled throughout are some fun, low-cost casino-hotels and some out-of-the-way restaurants and attractions worth knowing about.

NORTH & WEST OF THE STRIP

The communities of Summerlin and North Las Vegas are where many of the people who work on the Strip live, shop, eat, and play. Yes, there are some major casino-hotels in the area, including the stunning Red Rock Resort and a few notable restaurants, but for the most part what you'll find here are dependable chain stores and eateries that offer comfort shopping and food at better-than-Strip prices.

ICONIC LAS VEGAS

There are many things with which Las Vegas has become synonymous: gambling and all things excess are probably at the top of the list, but there are also the dancing waters, the dolphins, the buffets, the Cirque du Soleil shows, the steakhouses, the offbeat museums, the wild nightlife, and much more. This itinerary will guide you to the must-see and must-do, all of which are fun for first-timers or repeat offenders. Have your cameras ready!

Mornings

Start your day with a photo opportunity at the **Welcome to Fabulous Las Vegas Sign,** perhaps the city's most iconic symbol of all. Then keep your "say cheese" smile in place as you take a walking or driving tour past the only-in-Vegas, postcard-worthy exteriors of hotels like the pyramid-shaped **Luxor,** the castle-themed **Excalibur,** the Gotham re-creation of **New York–New York,** the modern wonder of **CityCenter,** the Italian villa charm of **Bellagio,** the Gallic splendor of **Paris Las Vegas,** and the Roman decadence of **Caesars Palace.** There are more,

Mon Ami Gabi at Paris Las Vegas.

of course, but you only have so much room on your digital camera's memory card and there is much more to see.

If you started early enough and still have time before lunch, check out one (or both preferably) of the city's more colorful attractions with the glorious botanical gardens at the **Bellagio Conservatory** or the majestic animals at the **Mirage Secret Garden & Dolphin Habitat.** Both are fun to look at, but more importantly offer a bit of a peaceful respite from the madness that is Las Vegas. Trust us, you'll need a break every now and then!

Afternoons

You can go one of two ways for lunch, either with a classic Vegas buffet or a view of the throngs of humanity that crowd the Strip. For the former, check out the **Carnival World Buffet** at Rio Suites or **Le Village Buffet** at Paris Las Vegas. Both offer a seemingly endless array of well-prepared food; while they may not be the cheapest buffets in town, neither are they the most expensive, so you can have your proverbial, or literal, cake and eat it too.

The other way to go would be to have a nosh at a Strip-side cafe so you can do some people-watching while you eat. The best of the bunch are **Mon Ami Gabi,** offering Americanized twists on classic French bistro cuisine, and the **Sugar Factory,** which serves up a laundry list of hearty dishes from burgers to steaks with stops at crêpes and waffles in between. Both are at Paris Las Vegas.

After you have refueled, head to one (or more, if time allows) of the city's offbeat, unique museums. Tops on our list are the **National Museum of Organized Crime and Law Enforcement,** aka the Mob Museum, which takes a look at the Mafia and its influence on the country and Vegas in particular; the **National Atomic Testing Museum,** which explores the history of the nuclear age with a special focus on the nearby Nevada Testing Site; and the **Erotic Heritage Museum,** which examines human sexuality in both thought-provoking and titillating ways.

Close out your afternoon with some shopping, window or otherwise. Las Vegas is one of the top shopping destinations in the world, and even if you can't afford to buy anything, a stroll through the highly themed malls like **The Forum Shops** or **Grand Canal Shoppes** should keep you entertained.

Nights

If you didn't do the buffet at lunch you may want to consider one for dinner, but our preference would be to send you to a steakhouse. Virtually every hotel in town has at least one and they are practically a requirement for nonvegetarian Vegas visitors. The best of the bunch are **Old Homestead Steakhouse** at Caesars Palace, a Vegas version of the famed New York City restaurant that has been in business since 1868; **Strip House** at Planet Hollywood, which has fantastically flavorful cuts of meat and a peek-a-boo bordello theme; and the simply named **The Steakhouse** at Circus Circus, which has an old-school charm, terrific food, and affordable prices.

We hope you didn't eat too much because your night is just getting started. Next it's on to one of the shows by Cirque du Soleil, the French-Canadian circus troupe that reinvented and now rules the Las Vegas entertainment scene. There are many to choose from, but our favorites include the dreamy wonder of *Mystère* at Treasure Island, the martial arts spectacle of *KÀ* at MGM Grand, or the water ballet of **O** at Bellagio.

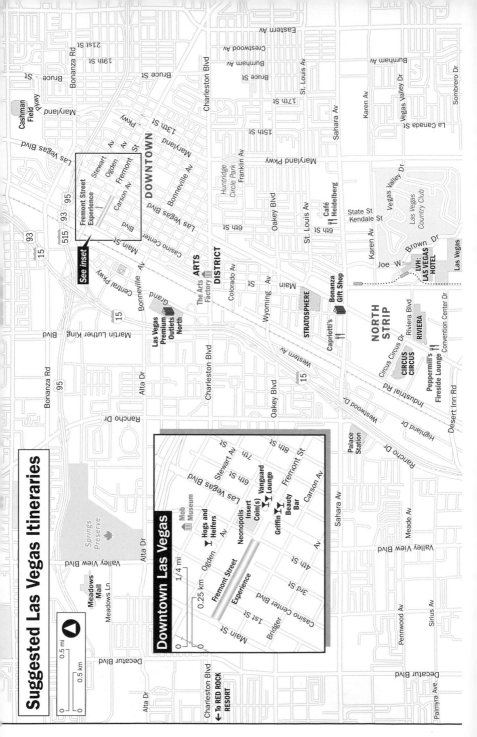

Suggested Las Vegas Itineraries

Downtown Las Vegas

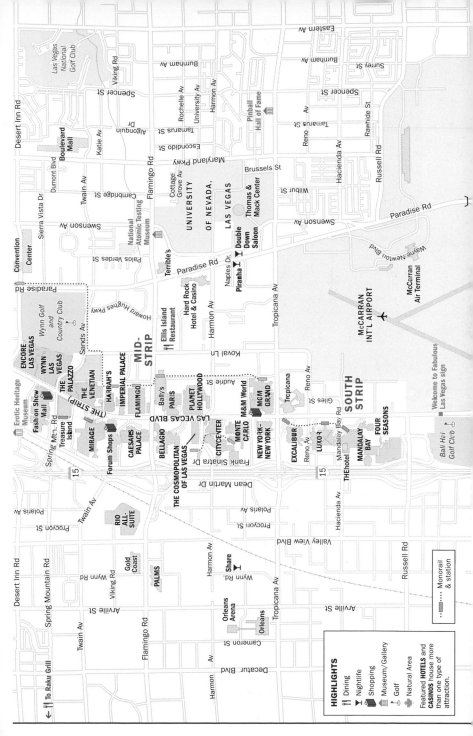

The Red Room at PURE.

From there it's on to the truly iconic Las Vegas experiences, which are all best viewed at night. The dancing waters of the **Bellagio Fountains** are worth visiting no matter how many times you have seen them, the **Mirage Volcano** is still a lava-spewing delight, and the **Fremont Street Experience** in Downtown Las Vegas will immerse you in the neon-lit glory that is Glitter Gulch.

End your day dancing the night away at one of the city's hot nightclubs like **1 OAK** at The Mirage or **PURE** at Caesars Palace, or put some money down in the casino. It certainly doesn't get more iconic Vegas than that.

OVER-THE-TOP LAS VEGAS

Las Vegas was built on the idea that "average" and "normal" were adjectives that should never be used to describe the city. They don't just build hotels here; they build the biggest hotels in the world. And then they throw a roller coaster or a volcano or a $500-per-person golf course or a $400-per-meal restaurant into the mix. Vegas is all about extravagance, so this itinerary will help you find the biggest of the big, the wildest of the wild, and the most outrageous, over-the-top experiences the city has to offer.

Mornings

You're going to have a busy day of excess, so it's important to start out with a hearty breakfast to keep your energy level high. Room service is always an option—there's nothing quite as extravagant as having people bring you food without ever getting out of bed—but if you feel like getting out and about, try the sumptuous **brunch buffets at Wynn Las Vegas or Bellagio.** Both offer an almost mind-boggling amount of food, all of which is a cut above your standard buffet. Handmade omelets and crêpes, freshly baked breads, and heaping mounds of bacon, sausage, and even steak will go well with your unlimited mimosas. At nearly $40 per person (for the weekend champagne brunch), the price will remind you that this is no pedestrian all-you-can-eat experience.

The a.m. hours are the best time to schedule your outdoor activities. Not only are crowds often lighter, as a lot of people sleep in (it is a vacation after all), but temperatures are also more moderate, especially in the summer when an afternoon stroll down the Strip can emulate a trek across the desert. So use this time to catch some rays poolside or, if you are recreationally minded, work up a moderate sweat with a round of golf.

To fit with this over-the-top theme, consider staying at hotels where the experience of sunbathing is taken to a different level, such as **The Four Seasons,** where they provide chilled towels and have people walking around spritzing you with Evian

One of the many tempting offerings at the Wynn Las Vegas Buffet.

water (at your request, of course). Or, if you are a guest of **Wynn Las Vegas** or **Encore,** you can play the links at the **Wynn Las Vegas Golf Club** for a princely sum of $300 per person.

End your morning with a visit to a spa for some pampering and luxuriating. The **Qua Baths & Spa at Caesars Palace** offers virtually every massage, aromatherapy, skin-care treatment, and relaxation technique known to man—some of which will cost you more for 30 minutes than you are paying for your hotel room. Soak in the Jacuzzi or sit in the unique ice room before heading out for the rest of the day.

Afternoons

If you worked off your breakfast with all that massaging and lying around by the pool, you'll need to find a good lunch spot to refuel. Belly up to the **Burger Bar** in Mandalay Place and order the Kobe beef patty topped with black truffles, and voilà! You have spent $45 on a burger. Congratulations!

Then it's off to the shopping malls where the true excess can really begin. **The Forum Shops at Caesars Palace,** the **Grand Canal Shoppes at The Venetian, Crystals at CityCenter,** and the **Miracle Mile at Planet Hollywood** are all filled with high-end retailers that are designed to drain your checking

Qua Bath & Spa's luxurious Roman Baths.

account and max out your credit cards. Pick up a little bauble at **Harry Winston Jewelers** or a pair of those *Sex in the City*–endorsed **Manolo Blahnik** shoes. Or if you're feeling that a $100,000 diamond tiara just isn't "over the top" enough, then head to the **Ferrari-Maserati dealership,** at Wynn Las Vegas, to get something to park in your driveway that will make the neighbors really jealous.

If those are a little out of your price range, consider going the completely opposite direction at the **Bonanza Gift and Souvenir Shop.** Billed as the largest souvenir shop in the world, this is the place where you can find pretty much anything—from tacky to, well, more tacky—emblazoned with the words "Las Vegas" on it. The kitsch factor here is off the charts.

Finally, experience some of the quintessential, only-in-Vegas attractions, such as riding a gondola through a shopping mall at **The Venetian,** or watching the **Fountains of Bellagio** put on a water ballet.

Nights

Start your evening with a meal at **Joël Robuchon,** the multi-Michelin-star-winning darling of the foodie world—and with good reason. It'll only cost you a mere $300 a person (and that's before wine) to find out why. Or if your extravagance knows no bounds, try the FleurBurger at **Fleur by Hubert Keller.** The Wagyu beef, foie gras truffle, and a bottle of 1995 Chateau Petrus costs a measly $5,000.

Next you'll want to see a show, and you should focus on those that can only be seen here. If **Garth Brooks** or **Céline Dion** is in town, you should seize the

VEGAS BY air

Most people are satisfied with the views of Las Vegas from terra firma. Walking or driving up the Strip, especially at night, is a requirement for the first-time Vegas visitor. But, for some, there is no better way to see Sin City in all its neon glamour than from the air. If you are one of these intrepid souls, then a helicopter tour of Las Vegas is what you're looking for.

There are more than a dozen competing companies offering tours of the city and surrounding areas, and most offer the same type of services at very similar prices. We're including a few of the more well-known companies below, but comparison shopping and checking out safety records are highly encouraged.

Maverick Helicopters (☎ **888/261-4414;** www.maverickhelicopter.com) is one of the most well-known tour operators in Las Vegas. Its large fleet of ECO-Star helicopters has one of the best safety records in the business, and a variety of packages are available,

including twilight and night flights over the Strip. If you want to venture farther, Hoover Dam and Grand Canyon packages are available. Rates start at around $115 per person and go up from there, depending on the length and distance of the tour you choose. Most include transportation to and from your hotel.

VegasTours.com (☎ **866/218-6877;** www.vegastours.com) features a similar list of air adventures, including a nighttime flight over Vegas and several to the Grand Canyon, while **Papillon Tours** (☎ **888/635-7272;** www.papillon.com) not only offers helicopter tours, but also airplane and ground excursions as well.

opportunity to catch one of their concerts at Encore or Caesars Palace respectively, because they aren't playing anywhere else. Or check out any of the Cirque du Soleil productions that are Vegas-only experiences, the best of which are **O**, at Bellagio, and **KÀ**, at MGM Grand. Each is set in its own multimillion-dollar theater, with stage sets—a giant pool and an enormous revolving platform, respectively—unlike anything you are likely to have seen before.

Nighttime is the best time for getting the true Strip experience, so how about renting a limousine (maybe one of those superstretch Hummers, if you are feeling really crazy) and instruct the driver to just cruise Las Vegas Boulevard. Hanging out of the sunroof with a cocktail in your hand is discouraged, but people do it anyway.

Most of the Vegas club scene starts late (11pm or midnight), so have your driver take you to one of the hip hot spots, such as **XS**, at Encore, **1 OAK** at The Mirage, or **Marquee** at The Cosmopolitan of Las Vegas. These are see-and-be-seen places, so dress to impress and be on the lookout for a celebrity or three hanging out in the VIP areas. You can drop a grand easily if you want to sit at a table with bottle service.

If it's more of the classic Las Vegas vibe you're looking for, try **Peppermill's**, with its retro-'70s/'80s interior. So cheesy, it's hip again.

Your final destination should be in the spot that makes Vegas tick, the casino. Yes, there are casinos all over the country now, but there's nothing quite like tossing the dice at a craps table at **Caesars Palace** or spinning the reels in the high-limit lounge at **Wynn Las Vegas.**

GUYS' GETAWAY

Not every trip to Vegas with the guys needs to get as crazy as the movie *The Hangover,* but if you're looking for a real man's man experience, no other city does it quite like this one. Whether it's a bachelor blowout weekend or just an excuse to blow off steam without your significant other giving you disapproving glances, this itinerary is designed to explain why they call this place "Sin City."

Mornings

You were probably out late the night before and there may have been alcohol involved, so start your morning with a hearty guy's breakfast at **Hash House a Go Go.** Its huge portions of twisted farm food are chest-poundingly substantial, and there is even a specialty called O'Hare of the Dog—a Budweiser served in a paper bag with a side of bacon.

To get your body in shape for the day ahead, spend the morning taking advantage of the various sports and recreation options available around town. Nearly every hotel has a fitness center and some, such as Bally's and the Flamingo, offer full tennis courts. If you're a fan of the fairway, head over to **Bali Hai golf course,** located conveniently on the Strip, for 18 holes and some wheeling around in their GPS-enabled golf carts. Or, if you need something more extreme, visit the **Adventure Spa,** at Red Rock Resort, where you can arrange everything from rock climbing to horseback riding to river rafting.

If you're serious about your gambling, then late mornings are a great time to hit the casinos as well. The crowds are thinner, so you'll usually be able to find a table or a slot easily, while the blackjack limits are often lower so you can save money for your big day ahead.

Afternoons

Continue your guy's gone wild day with a stop at **Gilley's** for some great down-home grub and even a ride on the mechanical bull if you feel like proving your manliness.

Daytime is playtime in Las Vegas, where the newest trend is to have night-club-worthy experiences during the afternoon at some of the hotel pools. **Bare Pool Club** at The Mirage, **Tao Beach** at The Venetian, and **Encore Beach Club** at Encore Las Vegas are all open to the general public (for a cover charge) and include everything from live DJs to fully stocked bars and certainly a bevy of bikini-wearing partyers.

Next, head back to the casino for a little sports book action. You can place a wager on just about any type of sporting event in existence (cricket, anyone?), and, depending on the season and the day of the week, you might be able to catch a game in action. The **sports books** at The Mirage and Caesars Palace are always good options for their huge screens and high energy, but you may want to consider the M Resort, The Venetian, or The Palazzo, which offer in-running betting. Popular in the U.K., this means that you can not only wager on the outcome of the game but also place bets during the action as well.

And if you need to get your adrenaline flowing, consider one of the serious thrill rides in town, such as the extreme adventures atop the 1,000-foot **Stratosphere Tower,** at the Stratosphere Hotel. You can play a little game and make whichever of your friends who screams the loudest while on **Insanity: The Ride** or **SkyJump** buy the first round of drinks later that night.

Nights

We know. We already sent you to some sports books, but you should go back to the only one that is a real restaurant. The 45,000-square-foot **Lagasse's Stadium** is a sports bar on steroids, with 100 flatscreen TVs and a menu crammed with highlights from Emeril's American and Creole cuisine.

Bali Hai offers 18 lush holes smack in the middle of the desert.

Marquee at The Cosmopolitan.

Now for some nighttime entertainment. If you want class, try the topless showgirl beauties in the (admittedly cheesy) *Jubilee!* at Bally's. If you want crass, go for **Crazy Girls,** at the Riviera, where taste is not on the menu. But if you want it "just right," go for the peek-a-boo fairy tale *Peepshow,* at Planet Hollywood, which usually has a rotating cast of comely C-list celebrities—such as *The Girls Next Door* star Holly Madison—in the partially clad cast.

Time to hit the dance floor. **PURE,** at Caesars Palace, is an obvious place to start, but **Marquee,** at The Cosmopolitan, is where the action really is. The party gets started late in Vegas, so you might want to start at a bar or two, such as **Coyote Ugly,** at New York–New York (just like the movie only you pay more), or **Hogs & Heifers,** in Downtown Las Vegas.

What's that? You haven't had enough gambling? Well, head over to Planet Hollywood's **Passion Pit,** complete with lingerie-clad dealers at the blackjack tables and go-go girls.

And if you want more girly action, there are **strip clubs** aplenty. We have reviewed them in chapter 7. You're a guy; you'll know which one appeals to you most.

GIRLS' GETAWAY

With the plethora of strip clubs and showgirls in this town, you'd think that Vegas is a man's world. Not so! There are plenty of activities and attractions for the ladies, from wild-weekend, bachelorette-style craziness to relaxing, leave-your-cares-at-home-style getaways. Here are just a few suggestions.

Mornings

If you dream of going to Paris, skip the hotel of the same name and go more or less across the street to Caesars Palace and **Payard Patisserie & Bistro** for breakfast. The chef is from the City of Lights, and you'll know it when you taste his croissants. The food is not cheap, but it is high quality, generously portioned, and just plain delightful. (It's also worth an evening stop for the amazing desserts.)

Vegas is retail heaven, and you could spend your whole day going to branches of pretty much every designer name you can think of in the major hotel malls (**Crystals** at CityCenter, **The Forum Shops** at Caesars Palace, **The Grand Canal Shoppes** at Venetian/Palazzo, **Miracle Mile** at Planet Hollywood,

Bellagio, Wynn Las Vegas). In particular, it is worth noting the branch of NYC's fashion apex **Barney's** department store and a **Christian Louboutin** at The Palazzo, **Tiffany & Co.** and **Hermes Paris** at Crystals, and **Agent Provocateur** and **H&M** in The Forum Shops. Bargain shoppers will want to check out the **Las Vegas Premium Outlets North** near Downtown. Truth be told, there are not a lot of bargains there, but it's an outlet, so something will turn up.

Afternoons

You can have a fabulous girly lunch at the pink-and-orange **Serendipity 3,** a branch of the beloved New York establishment. The hot dogs are authentic, but, more to the point, it's got the frozen hot chocolate!

Okay, it's time for some serious pampering. You could just stretch out by the pool (didn't you just buy a new bikini this morning?), but it's hot outside. So make your way to the spas at **Encore, Bellagio,** or **The Venetian** (which is a branch of the Canyon Ranch) for a full menu of massages, facials, weird treatments imported from countries you've never heard of, and lots more—all designed to make you feel as relaxed and limp as an al dente noodle.

Nights

If your girls' getaway weekend is of the rowdy bachelorette variety, have dinner at **Tacos & Tequila,** at Luxor. Not only is the food fun and frivolous, the Margaritas are also among the best in town. If it's a more laid-back experience you need, then get a patio table at **Estiatorio Milos** at The Cosmopolitan and enjoy their amazingly fresh Mediterranean seafood and other Greek specialties.

Hey, speaking of getting rowdy, not to mention all those signs with scantily clad women all over the place, equal time can be attained at such shows as the male-stripper review *Thunder From Down Under,* at Excalibur. Or get your

Serendipity 3's legendary frozen hot chocolate is worth every calorie.

High-end boutiques dominate the offerings at The Shoppes at The Palazzo.

performance art on at the **Blue Man Group**—they are weird and wonderful, and they make the audience go berserk.

The **Petrossian** bar at Bellagio is a calm, sophisticated place to have a tipple to gear up for the rest of your evening. Plus, the bartenders generally are trained mixologists who really know how to prepare a classic drink, not to mention pour a mean glass of champagne. A somewhat more gearing-up-for the clubs atmosphere is across the way at **Hyde Bellagio,** which in addition to having fun cocktails (is that a Belini cart? Why, yes, it is!) also has the best view of the Bellagio Fountains from its lakeside patio.

Finally, strap on that pair of Christian Louboutin's you bought earlier today (lucky you), because it's time to go dancing. If you're single and looking to mingle (or whatever, we don't judge), the scenes at **PURE** at Caesars Palace, **XS** at Encore Las Vegas, and **Marquee** at The Cosmopolitan of Las Vegas are such that people will stand in line for hours (and pay outrageous cover charges) just to get inside. We have to admit they are awfully fun.

Wanna just go dance and not be bothered by the meat-market scene? Consider going to gay clubs, such as **Krave Las Vegas,** at Planet Hollywood, or **Piranha** or **Share,** both just off the Strip. They welcome women, but remember that you aren't going to be the priority here.

UNLIKELY LAS VEGAS

It's really hard to overlook the Strip—after all, a number of people have spent billions and billions of dollars to ensure that you don't—but there are still some surprisingly unusual and captivating sights to see in and around Las Vegas. This itinerary is designed to help you discover them. You will need a car to do this tour.

Mornings

Those pricey buffets at the casinos may offer you truckloads of food, but even the ones at the out-of-the-way hotels are the very definition of "discovered." Instead, go down home for the delightful Southern cooking at M&M Soul Food cafe. Chicken and waffles, biscuits and gravy, or anything with grits is a great way to start the day as far as we're concerned.

Walk off that breakfast by exploring the nearby **18b Arts District,** home to a number of art galleries and studios, bravely taking a stance against prefab, soulless Vegas. You might take special note of **The Arts Factory,** a collection of art spaces. If it's the first Friday of the month, you could come back and stroll here in the evening, as that's when the galleries come into the streets for a food, art, and entertainment festival.

Springs Preserve is a remarkable destination, focused on nature and ecological concerns. The interpretive center examines the history of the region as related to water consumption,

Desert flowers in the gardens at Springs Preserve.

which sounds "dry" but really isn't. Need proof? Try the so-real-you-are-there flash-flood exhibit or the 3-D movie theater that puts you atop the Hoover Dam as it is being built. Outside are trails through the wetlands, animal habitats, and other exhibition halls dealing with the environment and recycling. The place is informative, entertaining, and absolutely vital in this day and age, and you can't believe that something of this quality and social significance is anywhere near Vegas.

Afternoons

We have a soft spot for old school, or should we say in this case, *alte Schule,* and **Hofbrauhaus** is just that sort of place. We're talking schnitzel. We're talking polka music. We're talking German beer. We are not talking $45 hamburgers with Kobe beef and truffles. Get the picture?

From there, we're recommending a duo of only-in–Las Vegas museums. Begin with the **National Atomic Testing Museum.** It's about more than just the 5 minutes when the bomb was awesome (apparently people really thought that—they have photos that you won't believe; check out the one of Miss Atomic Bomb), instead tracing the history of the atomic age and focusing specifically on the aboveground nuclear testing that occurred just outside of Las Vegas. It's a fascinating and sobering experience.

Then you're off to the **Pinball Hall of Fame,** where you can not only appreciate but actually play classic machines and arcade games from the 1960s to the present day.

If you want to skip the latter, consider taking in the afternoon show by **Mac King** at Harrah's Las Vegas, considered one of the best shows in Vegas and a good value for the money. King is an illusionist and comedian of great personal charm, who still practices magic that doesn't require computer technology. You can often get discounted (or even two-for-one) tickets in local magazines or at the players' club desk at Harrah's.

Nights

Now we'll send you far west to a place only foodies tend to know about: **Raku Grill,** a Japanese *robata* (charcoal grill) restaurant that is a hangout for many of the chefs in town when they get off work cooking for other people.

After dinner, why not do something completely "unlikely," like perform on the Las Vegas Strip? There are several hotel lounges that offer karaoke, but the singalong fun at **Gilley's** at Treasure Island is probably the best.

End your night exploring the booming bar scene Downtown's **East Fremont District** with the funky taverns like **Griffin, Beauty Bar, Insert Coin(s), Vanguard Lounge,** and more, all within steps of each other. Each has its own vibe and is mostly populated by locals, so try them on for style and see which one fits.

EATING LAS VEGAS

Las Vegas is a mecca for food lovers, offering you almost endless opportunities to gorge yourself on virtually every type of cuisine, from cheap eats to gourmet meals. This itinerary presumes you are very hungry and want to at least sample as much of it as you can, throwing waistlines, cholesterol counts, and common sense to the wind. You will need a car to do this tour, although you may want to consider walking as much of it as you can to give yourself the illusion that you are getting a little exercise in between binges.

Mornings

There are plenty of ways to overdo it from a food perspective first thing in the morning. You could go big with the insane portions of the deliriously over-the-top selections at **Hash House a Go Go** or get an entire day's worth of calories at an inexpensive buffet like the **Main Street Garden Court** in Downtown Las Vegas, but let's be reasonable, shall we? After all, you don't want to get too full before the day has really even started.

So instead, go for something a little more light but still packed with flavors, like the delightful crêpes at the **Sugar Factory** or the sumptuous quiche at **Bouchon.** Both come in very satisfying portions but will keep you from getting too loaded down.

If you decided to sleep in a bit (and really, who could blame you?), then you could go for a brunch at **Mon Ami Gabi,** which offers their own crêpes and quiches.

Otherwise the rest of your morning should be spent exploring various sweet shops so you can stock up on quick hits of sugar to get you through the rest of the day. **M&M World** allows you to mix and match your own selection of candy, while local favorite **Ethel M Chocolates** serves a finer brand of confections. Or you could simply stay at the aforementioned **Sugar Factory,** which in addition to having a full-service restaurant has a massive candy store with contemporary and blast-from-the-past treats plus their line of signature, celebrity-endorsed lollipops.

Afternoons

For lunch, we're going to start to get a little more serious and substantial. The inspired pub grub at **Todd English P.U.B.** is a terrific way to do it, especially if you go for the "carvery" portion of the menu, which allows you to mix and match meat, bread, cheese, and toppings to create your own sandwiches.

Speaking of sandwiches, we'd be totally remiss if we didn't mention **Capriotti's** here as a perfect place to have lunch. Their divine submarine sandwiches (we're partial to the Bobby, which is like Thanksgiving on a bun) will make you consider getting the epic 20-inch size and calling it a day, but try to restrain yourself with one of the smaller versions.

Burgers would be another way to go and there are lots of options in Vegas, including the fantastic offerings at **munchbar** or **Holstein's Shakes and Buns.** But if we had to pick just one burger favorite it would have to be the barbecue bacon variety at **KGB**: **Kerry Simon Burgers,** which will pretty much destroy your taste for anything ordered through a clown's mouth ever again.

As you are digesting, take a stroll over to Bellagio to visit the **Jean-Philippe Patisserie** and sample the finest chocolate available in Las Vegas, or go to Monte Carlo and check out **The Cupcakery** for their mouth-watering temptations. Regarding the latter, if you can only choose one go for the Oh My Gosh, Ganache, which has chocolate ganache baked *into* the cake!

Food trucks abound at the First Friday street festival.

If you're lucky enough to be visiting on the first Friday of the month, be sure to go to the **First Friday** street festival in the Arts District, where you'll find a parking lot's worth of food trucks and vendors serving everything from pizza to sushi to barbecue and more. Don't miss the state fair–style selections, including the genius deep-fried chocolate-chip cookie dough. Missing this will haunt you, trust us.

Nights

Finally, we're going to go whole hog, or cow as the case may be, by sending you to dinner at one of the city's steakhouses. **The Steakhouse** at Circus Circus is a local favorite, offering full meals at the same prices that others charge for an a la carte selection. **Strip House** at Planet Hollywood puts a modern spin on things with a charming peek-a-boo bordello theme and fantastic cuts of meat. But for our money you can't beat **Old Homestead Steakhouse** at Caesars Palace, a sister of the New York City restaurant that has been in business since 1868. The portions here are huge, which is appropriate since this is the restaurant that claims to have invented the doggie bag.

If a steak seems like too much of a commitment to you, you could try one of the growing number of restaurants that serves small bites instead of full meals. Chief among them would be **L'Atelier** at MGM Grand by master chef Joël Robuchon, where you can get various-size tasting menus or order small plates on your own, each of which will be better than the last. **Fleur** at Mandalay Bay from chef Hubert Keller has a similar concept of gourmet cuisine served in small-bite sizes. Another great choice in this category would be **Raku Grill,** where you can get fantastic skewers of meat, vegetables, seafood, and more done over a Japanese charcoal grill. Just be warned that even though the portions are small, you'll wind up ordering a lot of them and it could end up costing you more than just a standard meal.

But wait, we're not done. This is a 24-hour town, and lots of restaurants are open all night to satisfy those 2am cravings. **Central** at Caesars Palace is a modern interpretation of the 24-hour coffee shop, serving upscale but accessible takes on classic diner food. The real stuff, however, can be found at classic eateries like **Ellis Island Restaurant,** which is a meal-deal hunter's dream.

Of course, you also get some symmetrical closure on your day by going back to the **Sugar Factory,** which is also open 24 hours a day.

If you're hungry and looking for a deal, stop in at Ellis Island Restaurant any time of the day or night; the prices are good and the portions are huge.

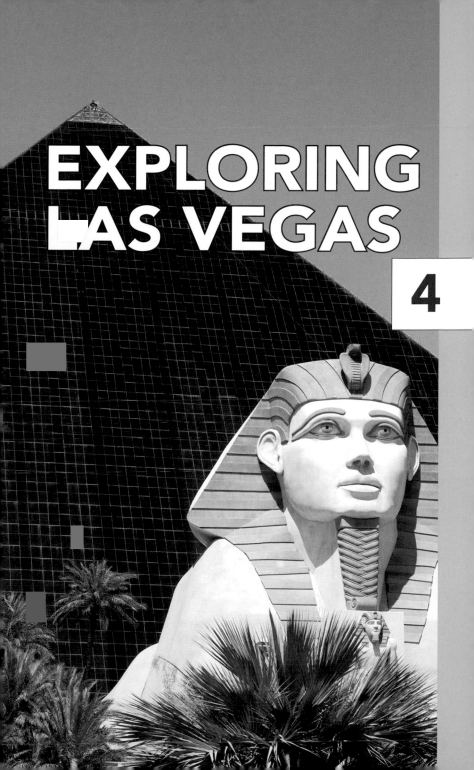

EXPLORING LAS VEGAS

4

Y
ou aren't going to lack for things to do in Las Vegas. More than likely, you've come here for the gambling, which should keep you pretty busy. But you can't sit at a slot machine forever. After all, you're going to have to get up to go to the restroom at some point! When you do, maybe you should look around at some of the other things here that can keep you entertained.

Just walking on the Strip and gazing at the gaudy, garish, absurd wonder of it all can occupy quite a lot of time. This is the number-one activity we recommend in Vegas; at night, it is a mind-boggling sight. And, of course, there are shows and plenty of other nighttime entertainment. Vegas is firmly set in such an "adult" entertainment direction that many attractions, particularly those with kid appeal, have closed, and though new, equally expensive options may come along to take their place, the emphasis right now seems to be on mature fun—drinking, gambling, nightclubbing, and the like.

Don't forget to check out the **free hotel attractions,** such as Bellagio's water-fountain ballet, The Mirage's volcano, and the Show in the Sky at the Rio. Oh, yeah, and the utter piece of hooey that masquerades as the pirate show at Treasure Island. You can probably give that a miss.

There are also plenty of out-of-town sightseeing options, such as **Hoover Dam** (a major tourist destination), **Red Rock Canyon,** and excursions to the **Grand Canyon.** We've listed the best of these in chapter 10.

LAS VEGAS'S TOP SIGHTS & ATTRACTIONS

o **Best Free Attractions:** Even if they charged money to see the dancing waters of the **Bellagio Fountains** (p. 66) or the dazzling light-and-sound show that is the **Fremont Street Experience** (p. 69), they'd be totally worth it. The fact that they are free is like winning a jackpot.

o **Best Museums:** Las Vegas has its own idea of what constitutes culture, and nowhere is that more apparent than at the **Erotic Heritage Museum** (p. 73), a titillating and thought-provoking examination of human sexuality. If you're looking for something even more explosive, try the **National Atomic Testing Museum** (p. 74) for its absorbing examination of the good, the bad, and the ugly aspects of our atomic age. Last but certainly not least, the **National Museum of Organized Crime and Law Enforcement (Mob Museum)** (p. 70) is a fascinating and fun peek into the Mafia underworld and one of the best museums in the country.

o **Best Animal Attraction:** The **Mirage Dolphin Habitat** (p. 63) is a most un-Vegas experience. Watch these gorgeous mammals frolic in their cool blue pool. If you're really lucky, they'll play ball with you.

PREVIOUS PAGE: **A replica of the Sphinx guards entrance to the Luxor.**

The Venetian, lit up at night, is one of the prettiest sights on the Strip.

o **Best Way to Get Back to Nature:** Las Vegas exists because of the natural springs that once fed the valley and provided an oasis in the desert. The **Springs Preserve** (p. 78) examines the history, future, and impact of water in the region alongside relaxing nature trails and preserves.

o **Best Ways to Get Your Heart Pounding:** We get our pulses up by playing the $5 slot machines, but if you want some serious thrills check out the high-altitude craziness of **Stratosphere Thrill Rides** (p. 65), including one that lets you jump off the top of a 100-story building. For those with a taste of adventure but a touch

One of many colorful rock formations at Red Rock Canyon.

more sanity, go zipping down the **Fremont Street Flightlinez** (p. 69) directly under the light-and-sound-show canopy.

o **Best Ways to Keep the Kids Entertained:** Las Vegas is not really a family destination, but there are still things for the wee ones to do, including playing their own games of chance at the **Circus Circus Midway** (p. 289) or riding the roller coasters and other junior thrills inside the blessedly air-conditioned theme park that is **Adventuredome** (p. 64).

o **Best Places to Get Hitched:** If you want a friendly, low-key wedding, walk down the aisle at the oldest chapel in Las Vegas, the **Wee Kirk O' the**

Heather (p. 86). But this is Vegas—why would you want a low-key wedding? Instead, try one of the extravaganzas at the **Viva Las Vegas Wedding Chapel** (p. 85), where you can choose among themes ranging from Elvis to vampires to outer space and more.

SOUTH STRIP

Bodies . . . The Exhibition ★★ EXHIBIT   A stunning and controversial exhibit featuring what can be best described as real live dead bodies (over 200 full and partial specimens). Utilizing a patented freeze-dry operation, full bodies (donated by their former inhabitants, though that's where some controversy comes in), artfully dissected body parts, and stripped cadavers are on display not for sensationalism—though it is pretty sensational in nearly all senses of the word—but for visitors to fully appreciate the wonder and mechanics that go into our transient flesh. When a body is positioned in an athletic pose, you can see how the muscles work, and when a cross section of a lung afflicted with cancer is right in front of you, you may well be glad Vegas has passed stricter smoking laws. It's educational and bizarre and not something you are likely to forget soon. Surprisingly, not grotesque, but not for the ultrasqueamish.

In the Luxor, 3900 Las Vegas Blvd. S. www.bodiestheexhibition.com/lasvegas. ℭ **702/262-4400.** Admission $32 adults, $30 seniors 65 and over, $24 ages 4–12, free 3 and under, $29 Nevada residents. Daily 10am–10pm; last admission 9pm.

CityCenter Fine Art Collection ★ ART MUSEUM   Previous attempts at displaying fine art have met with mixed success in Las Vegas. Of the four major galleries/museums to open over the last couple of decades, only the one at Bellagio remains. But CityCenter has gone a different route, choosing to integrate its fine art collection throughout the resort, turning the entire place into one big gallery of sorts. There's a sculpture from Maya Lin, designer of the Vietnam War Memorial, over the check-in desk; the iconic *Reclining Connected Forms* sculpture by Henry Moore; a massive installation of canoes and rowboats in a valet

Anatomical exhibit at Bodies . . . The Exhibition.

Big Edge by Nancy Rubin, CityCenter Fine Art Collection.

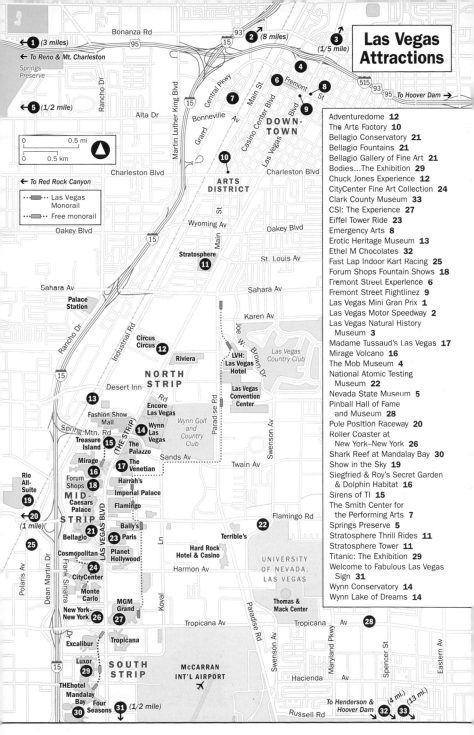

Las Vegas Attractions

Adventuredome **12**
The Arts Factory **10**
Bellagio Conservatory **21**
Bellagio Fountains **21**
Bellagio Gallery of Fine Art **21**
Bodies...The Exhibition **29**
Chuck Jones Experience **12**
CityCenter Fine Art Collection **24**
Clark County Museum **33**
CSI: The Experience **27**
Eiffel Tower Ride **23**
Emergency Arts **8**
Erotic Heritage Museum **13**
Ethel M Chocolates **32**
Fast Lap Indoor Kart Racing **25**
Forum Shops Fountain Shows **18**
Fremont Street Experience **6**
Fremont Street Flightlinez **9**
Las Vegas Mini Gran Prix **1**
Las Vegas Motor Speedway **2**
Las Vegas Natural History
    Museum **3**
Madame Tussaud's Las Vegas **17**
Mirage Volcano **16**
The Mob Museum **4**
National Atomic Testing
    Museum **22**
Nevada State Museum **5**
Pinball Hall of Fame
    and Museum **28**
Pole Position Raceway **20**
Roller Coaster at
    New York–New York **26**
Shark Reef at Mandalay Bay **30**
Show in the Sky **19**
Siegfried & Roy's Secret Garden
    & Dolphin Habitat **16**
Sirens of TI **15**
The Smith Center for
    the Performing Arts **7**
Springs Preserve **5**
Stratosphere Thrill Rides **11**
Stratosphere Tower **11**
Titanic: The Exhibition **29**
Welcome to Fabulous Las Vegas
    Sign **31**
Wynn Conservatory **14**
Wynn Lake of Dreams **14**

area by Nancy Rubins; and a 250-foot-long LED display from street artist Jenny Holzer, to name a few. You can pick up a brochure and map at the concierge desk at Aria Las Vegas that will guide you to the major works or there's even "an app for that"—download it for free to your iPhone and it will guide you to the works and give you in-depth background. Wear comfortable shoes; there is a lot of walking involved.

At CityCenter, 3730 Las Vegas Blvd. S. www.citycenter.com. ℭ **702/590-7111.** Free admission. Most artworks are outdoors or in 24-hour public spaces.

CSI: The Experience ★ ☺ ENTERTAINMENT COMPLEX   Although spinoffs have moved the sleuthing to Miami and New York, the original *CSI* television show takes place in Las Vegas, so how apropos is this major attraction, which allows you to work a crime scene right here on the Strip? Three different crimes have occurred—a car has crashed into a house, a woman has been murdered behind a motel, and a skeleton has been found in the desert—and it's up to you to examine the crime scene, look for clues, take notes, and then run it all through an interactive lab of sorts with help from videos of various stars of the show (we miss you, Gil Grissom!) and real-life CSI technicians. It's silly, gory fun and highly engrossing if you have an analytical mind (all but the most sullen of teenagers will love this).

In MGM Grand, 3799 Las Vegas Blvd. S. http://lasvegas.csiexhibit.com. ℭ **877/660-0660.** Admission $28 for the first crime scene, $26 per experience after that. Daily 10am–10pm (last admission 8:30pm).

Roller Coaster at New York–New York ★ ☺ THRILL RIDE   As if the outside of this hotel weren't busy enough, someone decided to knock it up a few notches by having a roller coaster wind around the whole thing. The whimsically designed cars evoke Manhattan taxi cabs and run at speeds up to 67 mph while going through drops of as much as 144 feet, a full loop, and the "heartline" twist, which simulates a jet-fighter barrel roll. Adrenaline junkies may find it too tame, but the average fun-seeker will do a lot of screaming.

In New York–New York, 3790 Las Vegas Blvd. S. www.newyorknewyork.com. ℭ **702/740-6969.** Single rides $14 adults; all-day pass $25. Must be 54 in. tall to ride. Sun–Thurs 11am–11pm; Fri–Sat 10:30am–midnight. Closed during inclement weather.

Shark Reef at Mandalay Bay ★ ☺ ZOO   Given that watching fish can lower your blood pressure, it's practically a public service for Mandalay Bay to provide this facility in a city where craps tables and other gaming areas can bring your excitement level to dangerous heights. Although we admire the style (it's built to look like a sunken temple), and standing in the all-glass tunnel surrounded by sharks is cool, it's just a giant aquarium, which we like,

A "crime scene" at CSI: The Experience.

Titanic: The Exhibition.

Shark Reef at Mandalay Bay.

but not at these prices. **Note:** It is *waaay* off in a remote part of Mandalay Bay, which might be a hassle for those with limited mobility.

In Mandalay Bay, 3950 Las Vegas Blvd. S. www.sharkreef.com. (C) **702/632-4555.** Admission $18 adults, $12 children 5–12, free for children 4 and under, $15 Nevada residents. Sun–Thurs 10am–8pm; Fri–Sat 10am–10pm. Last admission 1 hr. before closing.

Titanic: The Exhibition ★ EXHIBIT   It's too easy to say "you've seen the movie, now see the exhibit." But that is sort of the case; if you were captivated by the Oscar-winning epic, you will definitely want to take in this exhibit on the unsinkable luxury liner that sank on its maiden voyage. While it's a can't-miss for buffs, it might still be of some interest for those with only marginal feelings about the massive 1912 disaster. It's a strangely somber subject for Vegas. It features displays explaining the ship's ill-fated maiden voyage; relics salvaged from the sunken liner; and even re-creations of sample cabins from first, second, and third class, including atmospheric conditions, giving you a sense of how it felt to travel aboard what was an incredible vessel. There is even a large chunk of real ice standing in for the culprit berg.

In the Luxor, 3900 Las Vegas Blvd. S. www.luxor.com. (C) **702/262-4400.** Admission $32 adults, $30 seniors 65 and over, $24 children 4–12, free for children 3 and under, $29 Nevada residents with ID. Daily 10am–10pm (last admission 9pm).

MID-STRIP

Bellagio Gallery of Fine Art ★ ART MUSEUM   This small but effective gallery is one of the few remaining places on the Strip where you can see fine art, if you are so inclined. Works by brand-name artists (like Warhol, Picasso, and Ansel Adams) give it legitimacy, and shows from more unexpected choices (actor/comedian Steve Martin, for instance) give it cachet. Will there be as interesting a show when you go? Beats us. (When we wrote this, it was a collection of works by Claude Monet.) Then there's that ticket price. Do let us point out that admission to the Louvre—needless to say, quite a bit larger and with, one can safely say, some notable works—is about the same price as this gallery.

In Bellagio, 3600 Las Vegas Blvd. S. www.bellagio.com. ✆ **702/693-7871.** Admission $15 adults, $12 seniors and Nevada residents, $10 teachers and students with ID. Sun–Tues and Thurs 10am–6pm; Wed and Fri–Sat 10am–7pm (last admission half-hour prior to closing).

Eiffel Tower Ride ✋ OBSERVATION TOWER   Whether this is worth the dough depends on how much you like views. The "ride" portion is a glass-enclosed elevator to the top as a guide delivers a few facts—this is a half-size exact replica, down to the paint color of the original. Once you reach the upper-most platform, you are welcome to stand around and look out for as long as you want, which probably isn't 2 hours, the length of the average movie, which costs about what this does. Nice view, though.

In Paris Las Vegas, 3655 Las Vegas Blvd. S. www.parislv.com. ✆ **702/946-7000.** Admission $10 adults 9:30am–7:30pm, $15 7:30pm–close; $7 seniors 65 and over and children 6–12 9:30am–7:30pm, $10 7:30–close; free for children 5 and under. Daily 9:30am–12:30am, weather permitting.

Madame Tussauds Las Vegas ★★ ☺ MUSEUM   Madame Tussauds's waxworks exhibition has been a top London attraction for nearly 2 centuries, so even if you aren't a fan of wax museums this is probably worth a stop—if you can stomach the admission price. Figures here are state of the art, painstakingly constructed to perfectly match the real person. Truth be told, while some are nearly identical to their living counterparts—Brad Pitt gave us a start—others look about as much like the celebrity in question as a department-store mannequin. All the waxworks are free-standing, allowing, and indeed encouraging, guests to get up close and per-sonal. Go ahead, lay your cheek next to Elvis's or Sinatra's and have your photo taken. Or put on a wedding dress and get "married" to "George Clooney" (you know you want to). Or fondle J. Lo's butt (she won't mind). There's also a behind-the-scenes look at the lengthy process involved in creating one of these figures.

In The Venetian, 3355 Las Vegas Blvd. S. www.madametussauds.com/lasvegas. ✆ **702/862-7800.** Admission $26 adults, $19 student/military w/ID, $16 children 7–12, free for children 6 and under. Discounts for booking online. Sun–Thurs 10am–9pm; Fri–Sat 10am–10pm; hours vary seasonally; may close early for private events and holidays.

LEFT: **The gift shop at the Bellagio Gallery of Fine Art.** RIGHT: **The nighttime view from the Eiffel Tower Ride is superb if expensive.**

Siegfried & Roy's Secret Garden & Dolphin Habitat ★★★ ☺ ZOO

Animals belonging to or once featured in the illusion-packed show of this facility's namesakes are on display in the **Secret Garden,** which is basically a zoo glorified by celebrity benefactors. No, the white tiger that (allegedly) tried to eat Roy is probably not going to be on display, but there are other examples of the breed plus more big cats and even an elephant. Zoo purists will be horrified at the smallish spaces the animals occupy, but all the animals are rotated between here and their more lavish digs at the illusionist team's home. What this does allow you to do is get safely close to a tiger, which is quite a thrill—those paws are massive indeed.

The **Dolphin Habitat** is more satisfying than the Secret Garden. It was designed to provide a nurturing environment and to educate the public about marine mammals and their role in the ecosystem. Specialists worldwide were consulted in creating the habitat. The pool is more than eight times larger than government regulations require, and its 2.5 million gallons of human-made seawater are cycled and cleaned every 2 hours. The Mirage displays only dolphins already in captivity—no dolphins are taken from the wild. You can watch the dolphins frolic both above and below ground through viewing windows, in three different pools. The knowledgeable staff members, who surely have the best jobs in Vegas, will answer questions. If they aren't doing it already, ask them to play ball with the dolphins; they toss large beach balls into the pools, and the dolphins hit them out with their noses, leaping out of the water, cackling with dolphin glee. You catch the ball, getting nicely wet, and toss it back to them. If you have never played ball with a dolphin, shove

Get up close with Elvis and other wax celebrities at Madame Tussauds Las Vegas.

A white tiger in the Secret Garden.

that happy child next to you out of the way and go for it. You can stay as long as you like, which might just be hours. True dolphin fanatics can become a trainer for a day, complete with pool time, for $550.

In The Mirage, 3400 Las Vegas Blvd. S. www.mirage.com. ℂ **702/791-7111.** Admission $20 adults, $12 children 4–10, free for children 3 and under. Mon–Fri 11am–5:30pm; Sat–Sun and holidays 10am–5:30pm.

NORTH STRIP

Adventuredome ★ ☺ AMUSEMENT PARK   This is an okay place to spend a hot afternoon, especially since it's one of the few family-friendly attractions in town. Plus, unlike most theme parks, it's indoors! The glass dome that towers overhead lets in natural light so you get the best of both worlds—sunlight and air-conditioning. A double-loop roller coaster careens around the simulated Grand Canyon, and there's the requisite water flume, a laser-tag area, some bouncy/twirly/stomach-churning rides, and a modest number of other, tamer rides for kids of all ages. Video games and a carnival-style arcade are separate from the attractions, though it all still feels pretty hectic. The SpongeBob SquarePants 4-D ride is disappointing, as the technology is about 10 years behind the times and the story is hard to follow, thanks to bad acoustics. We suggest that you not leave kids here alone; they could easily get lost.

2880 Las Vegas Blvd. S. (behind Circus Circus). www.adventuredome.com. ℂ **702/794-3939.** Free admission; $5–$8 per ride; daily pass $27 adults, $17 children 33–47 in. tall. Mon–Thurs 11am–6pm, Fri–Sat 10am–midnight, Sun 10am–9pm; hours vary seasonally.

Chuck Jones Experience ★★ ☺ ENTERTAINMENT COMPLEX   A lot of people don't know the name Chuck Jones, but they certainly know his work: Bugs Bunny, the Road Runner, Wile E. Coyote, *How the Grinch Stole Christmas.* As an animator, screenwriter, and director, Jones had a huge impact on art and popular culture, and his career and life are lovingly celebrated here at this 10,000-square-foot museum, art, and play space. Designed to look like an Acme warehouse from the classic Looney Tunes cartoons, the fun starts out front with

Rollercoaster inside Adventuredome.

Insanity, Stratosphere.

oversized toys and sculptures that make noise and allow for some hands-on amusements. Inside is a theater showing classic Jones cartoon shorts and a substantial art gallery space with his animation and other artwork. The real fun starts when you get to the interactive section that features opportunities to create your own basic animations, sound effects, and voices. A digital archive allows access to all of Jones art and cartoons, which, we should warn you, could be a major time waster. You try walking away after watching *What's Opera, Doc?* A creativity center has drawing tables for kids (and giddy adults) and even offers classes and seminars from animators and artists. **Note:** Kids will be bored by the extensive art gallery section, so weary parents may want to rush forward to the hands-on sections that will provide much more entertainment for the tykes.

In Circus Circus, 2880 Las Vegas Blvd. S. www. chuckjonesexperience.com. ⓒ **702/734-0410.** Admission $20 adults; $15 kids 5–17, seniors 65 and up, military with ID, and students with ID; free for kids 3 and under. Daily 10am–10pm.

Stratosphere Thrill Rides ★★ ☺

THRILL RIDE Atop the 1,149-foot Stratosphere Tower are four marvelous thrill rides that will test your mettle and perhaps how strong your stomach is. The **Big Shot** is a breathtaking free-fall ride that thrusts you 160 feet in the air along a 228-foot spire at the top of the tower, and then plummets back down again. Sitting in an open car, you seem to be dangling in space over Las Vegas. We have one relative, a thrill-ride enthusiast, who said he never felt more scared than when he rode the Big Shot. After surviving, he promptly put his kids on it; they loved it. Amping up

SkyJump, Stratosphere.

free VEGAS

Vegas used to be the land of freebies—or at least, stuff so cheap it seemed free. Those days are an increasingly dim memory, but some hotels still offer free attractions designed to lure you into their casinos, where you might well then drop far more than the cost of a day ticket to Disney World. Here's a handy list of the best of the free bait, er, sights:

Bellagio Conservatory ★★★

(in Bellagio) PARK/GARDEN   A totally preposterous idea, a larger-than-life greenhouse atrium, filled with seasonal living foliage in riotous colors and styles, changed with meticulous regularity. From Easter to Chinese New Year, events are celebrated with carefully designed splashes of flowers, plants, and remarkable decorations—it's an incredible amount of labor for absolutely no immediate financial payoff. No wonder it's one of the most popular sights in Vegas. Open 24 hours.

Bellagio Fountains ★★★ (out-

side Bellagio) ICON   Giant spouts of water shoot up and down and sideways, and dance their little aquatic hearts out to music ranging from show tunes to Chopin. When we tell people about this, they roll their eyes when they think we aren't looking, and then they go see it for themselves . . . and end up staying for several numbers. Shows are daily every half-hour, starting early afternoon, then every 15 minutes 8pm to midnight. Closed when it's windy.

The Forum Shops Fountain Shows ★ (in The Forum Shops at

Caesars) ICON   The first established of the free shows and easily the stupidest. We love it—in theory, at least—as giant "marble" Greco-Roman statues come to creaky animatronic life and deliver a largely unintelligible speech, mostly exhorting the crowds to eat, drink, and get so merry they will think nothing of dropping a bundle at the slots. A second show in another part of the mall adds fire, so that's cool. Not quite so bad it's good, but one day they are going to wise up and make the thing more high-tech, and a little something special will be lost. Daily every hour, starting at 10am.

Mirage Volcano ★★ (outside The

Mirage) ICON   When it first opened with the hotel in 1989, this erupting "volcano" literally stopped traffic on the Strip. The fact that it's not quite as spectacular these days—even after a 2008 makeover amped up the fire, lights, sound, and effects to a much more entertaining level—says more about how jaded we've become than how cool it is. Get up close to feel the heat of the "lava" blasts and the rumble of the sound system. Eruptions are daily on the hour after dark until midnight.

Show in the Sky ★ (in the Rio;

pictured left) ENTERTAINMENT COMPLEX   Like TI's pirates, this formerly wholesome, if a bit weird, show has undergone a revamp to make it more sexy and adult oriented. Giant carnival-style floats scoot about above the audience, manned by sexy, dancing, scantily

clad men and women—and then more of them come out to sing, dance, and pelvic thrust their way through a stage show on the casino floor. Note that the later it gets, the more adult it gets; if you've got kids, take them to one of the early shows and you'll only be slightly embarrassed. Performed hourly from 7pm until midnight Thursday through Sunday.

Sirens of TI ★ (outside Treasure Island; pictured above) ICON   We gave it a star because it has such high production values, but man, it hurt us to do even that. Once a fun, inoffensive stunt show about pirates attacking a British sailing vessel, complete with cannons and sinking ships, it now features lingerie-clad lovelies luring the pirates to their sexy doom. Stuff happens, but no one really cares; either you like the scantily clad chicks, or you are so horrified by the whole spectacle because it's so appallingly bad that plot twists don't matter much. *Parents, be warned:* Cleavage and seaman "jokes" abound. Shows are daily at 5:30, 7, 8:30, 10, and 11:30pm (the latter in summer only), weather permitting.

Welcome to Fabulous Las Vegas Sign ★★★ ICON   Erected in 1959, this colorfully lit neon sign is probably the most iconic and most photographed attraction in Las Vegas. Located in the median of Las Vegas Boulevard about a mile south of Mandalay Bay, visiting was made easier in 2008 with the addition of a small parking lot, which means you no longer need to play chicken with oncoming traffic to get to it. It has no formal address but GPS users should use 5200 Las Vegas Blvd. S. to get in the vicinity. The lot is open 24 hours, but go at night when it's all lit up for the best photo opportunities.

Wynn Conservatory ★ (in Wynn Las Vegas) PARK/GARDEN   Although not as jaw-dropping as its spiritual cousin the Bellagio Conservatory, this indoor atrium of floral displays is still worth a gander, if for no other reason than it's on your way from the front door to the casino. The arrangements change regularly, though they may reflect the striking floral mosaics on the floor below. It's open 24 hours.

Wynn Lake of Dreams ★ (in Wynn Las Vegas) ICON   Masked as it is from the street by a 150-foot-tall "mountain," this light, laser, fog, and special-effect show can only be seen from select areas inside the hotel, mostly in bars requiring you to buy expensive drinks. Should you bother? Maybe. Basically, twice an hour, a lake lights up with pretty colors, cued to tunes ranging from classical to Louis Armstrong for "interludes." At the top of the hour are bigger extravaganzas of weird hologram erotic-psychedelic images projected on the wall waterfall, while shapes and puppets pop out for even more weird action, with some rather adult imagery at times. Shows are every 30 minutes, from 6pm to midnight.

the terror factor is **X-Scream,** a giant teeter-totter–style device that propels you in an open car off the side of the 100-story tower and lets you dangle there weightlessly before returning you to relative safety. Then there's the aptly named **Insanity,** a spinning whirligig of a contraption that straps you into a seat and twirls you around 1,000 feet or so above terra firma. Insanity is right.

Finally, if whirling and twirling and spinning around at the top of the tower is just not good enough for you, there's **SkyJump,** in which you get to leap off the top of the thing. Although we kind of wish we were kidding, we're really not. Jumpers are put into flight suits and harnesses, then taken up to the 108th floor where they get connected to a big cable/winch thing. Then, they jump. It's a "controlled" descent, meaning that you don't just drop the roughly 830 feet to the landing pad, but you are flying down at speeds of up to 40 mph with nothing but a couple of metal wires keeping you in place. There are lots of safety features that they tout and the three other SkyJumps around the world (in New Zealand, China, and South Korea) have sterling safety records. Nevertheless, they may call the other ride Insanity, but we think this one is the truly insane option. *Note:* The rides are shut down in inclement weather and high winds.

Atop Stratosphere Las Vegas, 2000 Las Vegas Blvd. S. www.stratospherehotel.com. ℂ **702/380-7777.** Big Shot $13, X-Scream $12, Insanity $12, SkyJump $110. Tower admission waived with SkyJump. Multiride and all-day packages available. Sun–Thurs 10am–1am; Fri–Sat 10am–2am; hours vary seasonally. Minimum height 48 in. for Big Shot, 52 in. for X-Scream and Insanity. Maximum weight 275 lbs. for SkyJump.

Stratosphere Tower ★ ☺ OBSERVATION TOWER Indoor and outdoor decks provide some pretty remarkable views of Las Vegas, southern Nevada, and perhaps even California on a clear day from this, the tallest observation tower west of the Mississippi (more than 1,100 ft.). It is worth noting, however, that these are views from a macro level with a lot of "they look like ants" type of commentary going on, so if it is an up-close, detailed scenery you are looking for, try the Eiffel Tower at Paris Las Vegas. Obviously, acrophobics should avoid this at all costs.

Atop Stratosphere Las Vegas, 2000 Las Vegas Blvd. S. www.stratospherehotel.com. ℂ **702/380-7777.** Admission $16 adults; $12 seniors, Nevada residents and hotel guests; $10 children 4–12; free for children 3 and under. Sun–Thurs 10am–1am; Fri–Sat 10am–2am; hours vary seasonally.

DOWNTOWN

The Arts Factory ★ 📷 COMMERCIAL ART GALLERY Believe it or not, Las Vegas has a pretty decent art scene (what some would consider soul crushing is what others consider inspirational), and this complex, located in the 18b Arts District, is the place to find proof. It features several galleries, boutiques, and a number of work spaces for local artists plus a bistro and bar.

107 E. Charleston Blvd. www.theartsfactory.com. ℂ **702/383-3133.** Free admission. Hours vary by gallery.

Emergency Arts ★★ 📷 COMMERCIAL ART GALLERY The artists in residence here rescued a derelict downtown building that was once a medical clinic and turned it into a funky, fun, bohemian space dedicated to the creation and conservation of all things art. The first floor has a small cafe (perfect for having a coffee while discussing Sartre, we think), a used record store, and the temporary home of the Burlesque Hall of Fame and Museum. The latter is a small

First Friday event at The Arts Factory.

couple of rooms with what is said to be a tiny fraction of photos and memorabilia honoring the peek-a-boo art form. The rest of the first and all of the second floor of the space are taken up by small boutiques where local artists show and sell their wares. There are paintings, sculpture, jewelry, clothing, and much more, and while the quality obviously varies from artist to artist, it is all totally unique and a much better way to spend your souvenir dollars than on a Las Vegas snow globe.

520 E. Fremont St. www.emergencyartslv.com. ⓒ **702/686-3164.** Free admission. Hours vary by gallery.

Fremont Street Experience ★★★ ICON

The Fremont Street Experience is a 5-block open-air landscaped strip of outdoor snack shops, vendor carts, and colorful kiosks purveying food and merchandise. Overhead is a 90-foot-high steel-mesh "celestial vault" that at night becomes **Viva Vision,** a high-tech video-and sound show (the canopy is equipped with more than 12.5 million lights), enhanced by a concert hall–quality sound system. There are a number of different shows, and there's music between the light performances as well. It's really cool, in that Vegas over-the-top way that we love so much. Go see for yourself; you will be pleased to see how a one-time ghost town of tacky, rapidly aging buildings, in an area with more undesirables than not, is now a bustling, friendly, safe place. It's a place where you can stroll, eat, or even dance to the music under the lights.

> ### 💬 When Downtown Ruled
>
> Fremont Street was the hub of Las Vegas for almost 4 decades, before the first casino hotel, El Rancho, opened on the Strip in 1941.

Fremont St. (btw. Main St. and Las Vegas Blvd.), Downtown. www.vegasexperience.com. Free admission. Shows nightly on the hour.

Fremont Street Flightlinez ★★ THRILL RIDE

If jumping off the top of the Stratosphere Tower with its SkyJump feature is a little too, well, insane for you, then consider zipping down the Fremont Street Experience instead. Instead of starting from 100 stories up, you launch from a platform about 65 feet above the street and then ride the zip line down to a second platform near Binion's at speeds approaching 35 mph. Thrill junkies may scoff, but this is still a heart-pounding ride that even the most acrophobic seem to have an easier time of handling. The staff is very friendly and extremely patient, even with big chickens like us. Pay the extra $5 to ride it at night so you can cruise under the Viva Vision canopy while it is all lit up. That's a Vegas experience you will not forget anytime soon.

425 E. Fremont St. www.fremontstreetflight line.com. (℃) **702/410-7999.** Rides $15 before 6pm, $20 after 6pm. Sun–Thurs noon–midnight; Fri–Sat noon–2am.

Las Vegas Natural History Museum ★ ☺ MUSEUM This humble temple of taxidermy harkens back to elementary-school field trips, around 1965, when stuffed elk and brown bears forever protecting their kill were as close as most of us got to exotic animals. Worn around the edges but very sweet and relaxed, the museum is

Fremont Street Flightlinez lets you soar over Glitter Gulch.

enlivened by a hands-on activity room and two life-size dinosaurs that roar at one another intermittently. A small boy was observed leaping toward his dad upon watching this display, so you might want to warn any sensitive little ones that the big tyrannosaurs aren't going anywhere. Surprisingly, the gift shop here is particularly well stocked with neat items you won't too terribly mind buying for the kids.

900 Las Vegas Blvd. N. (at Washington Ave.). www.lvnhm.org. (℃) **702/384-3466.** Admission $10 adults; $8 seniors, students, and military; $5 children 3–11; free for children 2 and under. Daily 9am–4pm. Closed Thanksgiving and Dec 25.

The Mob Museum ★★★ MUSEUM Vegas has a long history with the Mafia. Most of the classic hotels—the ones that helped define the city like the Flamingo, the Dunes, the Sands, and the Stardust—were built, in part or in

Dinosaur exhibit in the Las Vegas Natural History Museum.

The Mob Museum.

whole, with mob money, and organized crime virtually ran Sin City for decades. When Senator Estes Kefauver headed an early 1950s committee to investigate the mob and its power, hearings were held in cities around the country, including in a courthouse in Las Vegas. That courthouse is now the Mob Museum.

The three-story facility has been lovingly restored and features 17,000 square feet of exhibit space examining the Mafia in America, from its beginnings in New York and Chicago through Prohibition, its expansion to Las Vegas, and its influence on everything from law enforcement to popular culture. Although the topic is deadly serious, the museum itself is dynamic and engaging, using the latest state-of-the-art tricks to bring the stories it is telling to life. A video about the St. Valentine's Massacre is broadcast on the actual wall against which seven mob associates were gunned down in Chicago; touch-screen displays allow visitors to try to identify mug shots; a Tommy gun bucks and makes gunshot noises when you pull the trigger; old slot machines have modern interfaces that explain casino cheats; and so much more. Each exhibit is a highlight of its own, including the actual Kefauver hearing courtroom, which now has video and 3-D displays that evoke the feeling that you are watching the real thing happening in the room in which it did.

Officially known as the National Museum of Organized Crime and Law Enforcement, this endlessly fascinating, brilliantly executed facility deserves to become a Las Vegas icon—the kind of must-see attraction that should be on everyone's list when visiting the city and a reason to come here all by itself.

300 Stewart Ave. www.themobmuseum.org. (✆) **702/229-2734.** Admission $18 adults; $12 children 5–17 and students with ID; $14 seniors, military, law enforcement, and teachers. Sun–Thurs 10am–7pm; Fri–Sat 10am–8pm.

The Smith Center for the Performing Arts ★★★ ☺ PERFORMING
ARTS VENUE   Although Las Vegas has been synonymous with entertainment for decades, filled with showrooms and theaters galore, the one thing the city never had was a true performing arts venue—the kind of place where symphonies and true Broadway shows (not the cut-down versions that happen on the Strip) could spread their wings. The Smith Center changes all that and should firmly establish Sin City as a cultural center to be reckoned with.

The buildings are stunning, designed with a timeless Art Deco style inspired by Hoover Dam—notice the chandeliers, which look like an inverted version of the water intake towers. The whole thing is bright, modern, and dramatic, yet

THE resurgence OF DOWNTOWN LAS VEGAS

For decades, the bulk of the attention, and development dollars, in Las Vegas has been paid to the Strip, while the original part of Sin City, the Downtown area, languished and seemed on the verge of extinction.

Credit, at least in part, online retailer Zappos.com for changing all that. Its plan to move its headquarters and a couple thousand employees into the former city hall building in 2013 has spurred a resurgence in Downtown Las Vegas, with major revamps to old hotels, new restaurants, fun and funky bars, attractions, street festivals, and more all lending a new sense of life to the area.

The bulk of the action happens on the **Fremont Street Experience,** the pedestrian only mall on Fremont Street between Main Street and Las Vegas Boulevard. That's where you'll find most of the casinos, shopping, and restaurants.

The **Fremont East District** takes up several blocks of Fremont Street just east of Las Vegas Boulevard and has several bars, lounges, and clubs all within a few feet of each other, so no matter how much you may be stumbling, you can probably still make it to the next one in your all-night pub crawl.

The **18b Arts District** is a few blocks south of Fremont Street bounded, more or less, by Las Vegas Boulevard to the east, Commerce Street to the west, Hoover Avenue on the north, and Colorado Avenue on the south. Art galleries, antique and collectible stores, and more than a few pawn shops and bail bonds offices (to give it color, we suppose) are scattered about the neighborhood, giving it a refreshingly bohemian feeling as it sits in the shadow of the overprocessed Strip.

The monthly **First Friday Las Vegas** street festival happens in the heart of the 18b Arts District on the blocks surrounding the intersection of Casino Center Drive and Colorado Avenue. Local artists hawk their wares while live bands and DJs keep the crowds moving, play areas (complete with a video game truck) keep the kids entertained, and a sea of food vendors and food trucks keep everyone fat and happy. It's one of the few places where there is a true sense of community in Vegas. It happens, appropriately enough, on the first Friday of every month from 5 until 11pm. For more information visit www.firstfridaylasvegas.com.

Las **Vegas StrEATS** is another street festival occurring on the second Saturday of every month on the Jackie Gaughan Plaza near the El Cortez Hotel in the Fremont East District. This one is a little more urban in feeling, with the vendors focusing on street art and streetwear and the entertainment leaning toward indie rock, but it's the parking lot full of the city's best food trucks that really bring out the crowds. For more information visit www.vegasstreats.com.

comfortable and familiar and built to last. While many Vegas buildings attempt scope and grandeur, they feel impermanent somehow—as if they are just waiting to be imploded so the next big thing can be built. The Smith Center feels like the kind of place that will be here for centuries.

The main space, Reynolds Hall, is a finely tuned, Carnegie Hall–worthy, 2,050 seat concert venue that hosts philharmonics, headliners, and touring versions of Broadway shows like *Wicked.* The 300-seat Cabaret Theater, which features a jazz series and former Strip headliner Clint Holmes, is a classic nightclub-style space with big windows, giving it a sense of airiness missing in most theaters. A third, 200-seat "black box"–style theater holds smaller theater and dance productions. Outside is a beautiful park that can also be used for performances or just as place to sit and enjoy the view.

The complex will also be home to the Discovery Children's Museum by early 2013.

361 Symphony Park Ave. (at Grand Central Pkwy.). www.thesmithcenter.com. *(C)* **702/749-2000.** Prices and times vary by show.

JUST OFF THE STRIP

Erotic Heritage Museum ★★★ 🎁 MUSEUM It sounds like something you'd find next door to a strip club, and in fact it is, but this adjunct of the Institute for Advanced Study of Human Sexuality is not about cheap thrills. Instead, it's a totally engrossing (and sometimes simply gross) museum/art gallery devoted to the exploration of all things sex. Exhibits include artwork, sculpture, video, photographs, artifacts, interactive displays, and more that run the gamut from the ancient rituals of deflowerization to the peek-a-boo naughtiness of Bettie Page to the hard-core adult film industry, with stops at bondage, peep shows, the First Amendment, Tom of Finland, and Larry Flynt along the way. It is at turns sobering (the AIDS panels on display are still moving), silly (a sculpture of a male, uh, "appendage" made of 100,000 pennies), and shocking (the mechanics of sadomasochism) and absolutely geared toward adults with an open mind. If you are one, this is one of the most original, informative, and entertaining museums anywhere in the world. A full erotic library, gift shop, performing arts/arts instruction venue, and even an erotic wedding chapel fill out the massive space.

3275 Industrial Rd. (at Desert Inn Rd.). www.eroticheritagemuseumlasvegas.com. *(C)* **702/369-6442.** Admission $15 adults; $10 students, seniors, locals, and military. Not appropriate for children 17 and under. Sun and Tues–Thurs 11am–4pm; Fri–Sat noon–10pm.

Fast Lap Indoor Kart Racing.

Fast Lap Indoor Kart Racing ★★
☺ ENTERTAINMENT COMPLEX
When NASCAR pro Kurt Busch is in Las Vegas, this is the place he comes to play. Tucked away on a dead-end street in a mostly industrial part of town near the Strip, this is a no-frills go-kart experience, with a short track filling a former warehouse space that still looks like a warehouse. The gasoline-powered karts are equipped with 200cc Honda motors, allowing you to push the little monsters up to 50 mph (if you dare) as you battle in 10-minute-long races (as many laps as you can get) against other drivers. While bumping and other unsportsman-like contact is officially frowned upon, in reality this is a grown-up (mostly testosterone-driven) sport. So put your foot on the gas and see if you can be first to the checkered flag! *Note:* You must be at

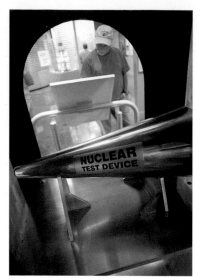

The Atomic Testing Museum.

least 5 feet tall to participate, and children 17 and under must be accompanied by a parent or guardian.

4288 Polaris Ave. www.fastlaplv.com. ✆ **702/736-8113.** $25 per race or $60 for 3 races. Mon–Sat 11am–11pm; Sun 11am–9pm.

National Atomic Testing Museum ★★★ 🎁 MUSEUM   From 1951 until 1992, the Nevada Test Site was this country's primary location for testing nuclear weapons. Aboveground blasts in the early days were visible to the tourists and residents of Las Vegas. This well-executed museum, library, and gallery space (a Smithsonian affiliate) offers visitors a fascinating glance at the test site from ancient days through modern times, with memorabilia, displays, official documents, videos, interactive displays, motion-simulator theaters (such as sitting in a bunker, watching a blast), and emotional testimony from the people who worked there. It respectfully treads that tricky line between honoring the work done at the site and understanding its terrible implications. Not to be missed, even if it's only because of the Albert Einstein action figure in the gift shop. Visitors should plan on spending at least an hour.

755 E. Flamingo Rd. www.nationalatomictestingmuseum.org. ✆ **702/794-5151.** Admission $14 adults; $11 kids 7–17, seniors, military, students with ID, and Nevada residents; free for children 6 and under. Mon–Sat 10am–5pm; Sun noon–5pm. Closed Thanksgiving, Dec 25, and Jan 1.

SOUTH & EAST OF THE STRIP

Clark County Museum ★★☺🎁 MUSEUM   Someday, one of these casino moguls (yeah, we're lookin' at you, Trump) is going to take just some of those megamillions they are pouring into yet another Strip hotel and put it into the museum that this bizarre town, and its ridiculously rich 100-year history, deserves. Until then, this dear little place will have to do its best—and that best is actually pretty good. With everything from dioramas of dinosaurs to a small street filled with original buildings, including the 1932 Boulder City train depot,

Ghost Town at the Clark County Museum.

this is a throwback to ghost towns and other low-tech diversions—sweet, informative, and you can't beat the price. ***Note:*** Hot days will make the outdoor portions less than bearable.

1830 S. Boulder Hwy., Henderson. www.clarkcountynv.gov. ☏ **702/455-7955.** Admission $2 adults, $1 seniors and children 3–15, free for children 2 and under. Daily 9am–4:30pm. Closed Thanksgiving, Dec 25, and Jan 1.

Ethel M Chocolates ★ ☺ FACTORY TOUR   Ethel Mars began making fine chocolates in a little candy kitchen in the early 20th century. Her small enterprise evolved to produce not only dozens of varieties of superb boxed chocolates, but also some of the world's most famous candies: M&Ms, Milky Way, 3 Musketeers, Snickers, and Mars bars. Alas, the tour lasts only about 10 minutes and consists entirely of viewing stations with an audiotape explaining the chocolate-making process. Even more sadly, you get only one small chocolate as a sample—delicious, but hardly satisfying. Of course, there is a fully-stocked gift shop if you want to buy more. ***Note:*** Come before 2:30pm, which is when the workers start to pack up and go home.

What's really worth seeing is outside: a lovely and extensive **4-acre garden** ★ displaying over 300 species of rare and exotic cacti with signs provided for self-guided tours. It's best

Cactus garden at Ethel M Chocolates.

75

appreciated in spring when the cacti are in full bloom, or in December when the entire garden is bedecked with holiday lights.

2 Cactus Garden Dr. (just off Mountain Vista and Sunset Way, in the Green Valley Business Park). www.ethelschocolate.com. ℭ **888/627-0990** or 702/433-2500 for recorded information. Free admission. Daily 8:30am–6pm. Self-guided chocolate factory tours daily 8:30am–4:30pm. Holiday hours may vary. Closed Dec 25.

Pinball Hall of Fame and Museum ★★ 🎁 ☺ MUSEUM

There's plenty of old-school fun to be had at the Pinball Hall of Fame and Museum.

Picture this: You walk into the Louvre in Paris and instead of gazing at the art on the walls from a safe distance, you are able to take it down, examine it from different angles, and even paint some strokes on top of the canvases. Of course, you'd never do that in a museum elsewhere, but this is Las Vegas and that is what you get to do with the pieces of art here at the Pinball Hall of Fame. More than 100 lovingly restored pinball machines from the 1960s through modern times are lined up and waiting for you to play. Try your hand at getting a ball into a dinosaur's mouth in the mid-1990s *Jurassic Park* machine, or giggle at the Elton John costumes on the artwork while you're playing the 1975 *Captain Fantastic* machine. They also have a big section of classic arcade games from Donkey Kong to Super Mario Brothers if you feel like going back to the '80s for a while. Note that many of the machines have QR bar codes on them, so you can use your smart phone to surf for additional info about these masterpieces.

1610 E. Tropicana Ave. www.pinballmuseum.org. ℭ **702/597-2627.** Free admission; game costs vary. Sun–Thurs 11am–11pm; Fri–Sat 11am–midnight.

NORTH & WEST OF THE STRIP

Las Vegas Mini Gran Prix ★★☺ ENTERTAINMENT COMPLEX   Finally, after all our yammering about how Vegas isn't for families and how most of the kid-friendly options are really overpriced tourist traps, we can wholeheartedly recommend an actual family-appropriate entertainment option. Part arcade, part go-kart racetrack, this is exactly what you want to help your kids (and maybe yourselves) work their ya-yas out. The arcade is well stocked, with a better quality of prizes than one often finds, but we suggest not spending too much time in there and instead hustling outside to the slide, the little roller coaster, and best of all, the four go-kart tracks. Each offers a different thrill, from the longest track in Vegas, full of twists and turns as you try to outrace other drivers (be a sport, let the little kids win occasionally), to a high-banked oval built just so you can try to make other drivers take spills onto the grass, to, best of all, a timed course. The last requires a driver's license, so it's for you rather than your kids (but the wee ones will find the fourth course is just for them), and here you can live out your Le Mans or police-chase fantasies as you blast through twisting runs one kart at a time, trying to beat your personal best. The staff is utterly friendly, and the pizzas at the food court are triple the size and half the price of those found in your hotel. The one drawback: It's far away from main Strip action, so you'll need that rental car. *Note:* Kids have to be at least 36 inches tall to ride any of the attractions.

1401 N. Rainbow Rd. (just off U.S. 95 N.). www.lvmgp.com. © **702/259-7000.** Ride tickets $7 each, $6.50 for 5 or more; ride wristbands $20 per hr. Mon–Fri 11am–9pm; Sat–Sun 10am–9pm.

Las Vegas Motor Speedway ★★ RACECOURSE This 176,000-seat facility was the first new superspeedway to be built in the Southwest in over 2 decades. A $200-million state-of-the-art motorsports entertainment complex (with tens of millions more dumped into it since it opened), it includes a 1½-mile superspeedway, a 2½-mile FIA-approved road course, paved and dirt short-track ovals, and a 4,000-foot drag strip. Also on the property are facilities for go-kart, Legends Car, Sand Drag, and Motocross competition. Some major hotels have shuttles to the speedway during big events, so check with your hotel's front desk or concierge.

Several famous names in racing offer driving schools and experiences at the LVMS, including Mario Andretti, Dale Jarrett, and the **Richard Petty Driving Experience** (© **800/237-3889;** www.drivepetty.com), where you can pilot your own NASCAR racer around the track at speeds of more than 140 mph. Talk about a thrill ride!

7000 Las Vegas Blvd. N. (directly across from Nellis Air Force Base). www.lvms.com. © **702/644-4443.** Tickets $10–$75 (higher for major events). Race days vary. Take I-15 north to exit 54.

Nevada State Museum MUSEUM Long delayed due to state budget cuts, this new home to the history of the Silver State has only about 13,000 square feet of exhibit space in which they try to cram several millennia worth of the flora, fauna, people, and events that shaped Nevada. The result is a disappointingly cursory glance at the topics, most of which are presented in a fairly dry manner with very little of the hands-on interactivity that is fashionable in museums these days. But in what other museum would you find a

Las Vegas Mini Gran Prix.

Racing at the Las Vegas Motor Speedway.

mammoth skeleton near a wall of showgirl costumes? That might make it worth visiting in and of itself, but if not consider the fact that it is free with your admission to the endlessly fascinating Springs Preserve next door (see below).

309 S. Valley View Blvd. (at Meadows Lane) http://museums.nevadaculture.org. ℂ **702/486-5205.** Tickets $20 ($9.95 for NV residents), free for children 17 and under. Admission free with paid admission to neighboring Springs Preserve. Fri–Mon 10am–6pm.

Pole Position Raceway ★ ☺ ENTERTAINMENT COMPLEX   Similar in concept to the Fast Lap facility (p. 74), Pole Position is a more polished go-kart racing venue owing to its sleek, modern facility and electric-powered racers. The indoor course is short but satisfying, and the lack of gas-powered engines doesn't mean you sacrifice any of the speed. You may retain your hearing for longer, which is definitely a good thing. It's worth noting that the karts are small and the mandatory helmets are tight, so claustrophobics may want to seek alternative fun. The facility also has a small video and virtual-reality game arcade and a gift shop.

4175 S. Arville Rd. www.polepositionraceway.com. ℂ **702/227-7223.** Adults 56 in. or taller $25, kids 17 and under or 48 in. and taller $22; multirace packages available. Sun–Thurs 11am–11pm; Fri–Sat 11am–midnight.

Springs Preserve ★★★ ☺ NATURAL RESERVE   By now, perhaps you've learned that *Las Vegas* is Spanish for "The Meadows." This facility is set on the 180-acre site of the original springs that fed Las Vegas until it dried in the 1960s (told you that Hoover Dam comes in handy). These days, Las Vegas is an environmental nightmare, along with much of the rest of this planet, and this remarkable recreational attraction is here to educate us about the possibilities to reverse some of the damage.

Set amid nature and hiking trails, plus man-made wetlands, which is an interesting concept, the focal point is a large interpretive center that gives the history of Las Vegas from a land- and water-use perspective. The displays are creative and interactive, including a room with a reproduction flash flood that

Springs Preserve.

coming ATTRACTIONS

This city is always coming up with new ways to entertain its visitors, so it is no surprise that there are several major attractions in development that were not open at press time but should be (or should be close) by the time you pick up this book.

Long in the works is a permanent home for **The Neon Museum.** This collection of classic neon signs and artwork from historic Vegas hotels and businesses has been showing some of its restored pieces on Fremont Street, but the bulk of its inventory has been sitting in a dusty lot for years. A full visitor center (created out of the shell of the old La Concha motel lobby) and a park with restored signs is scheduled to be open by the time you read this. Follow the progress at www.neonmuseum.org.

Splash Canyon is the city's first water park since the much beloved Wet 'n Wild on the Strip closed in 2004. Located on the far west side of town, it may not be as convenient for tourists, but its 20 water slides, 17,000-acre wave pool, 1,000-foot-long lazy river, and other attractions may just make it worth the jaunt. It is expected to open by summer 2013. Visit www.splashlv.com for more information.

The delightful Lied Discovery Children's Museum in Downtown Las Vegas will getting a new home and new name in early 2013. Soon to be known as just the **Discovery Children's Museum,** the new facility will be located on the campus of the Smith Center for the Performing Arts and will feature more than 58,000 square feet (twice the size of the original) of nine exhibition halls geared toward expanding young minds with science, art, and more. Visit www.nowtowow.org for updates.

The biggest attraction for Vegas doesn't have an official name as of this writing, but its code name, **Project Linq,** hints at the scope and purpose. An alley between the Flamingo and the Imperial Palace will be converted to an entertainment destination with shops, bars, restaurants, and more linking the two hotels and nearby Harrah's into one big destination. It will all lead to a 550-foot-tall observation wheel at the back of the properties near the Las Vegas monorail. O'Shea's casino, located between the two hotels, will be torn down and the Imperial Palace will get a major makeover that will most likely include a new name and theme. The project is expected to be finished by the summer of 2013.

uses 5,000 gallons of water and one with a simulation of the experience of working on Hoover Dam. The other buildings are all built according to standards that have the least environmental impact, using modern construction versions of adobe and other green concepts. Each building tackles an aspect of desert living and the environment, including one that instructs kids on the glories of recycling, complete with a compost tunnel to crawl through! Other displays focus on environmentally friendly kitchens and bathrooms, while the gardens demonstrate environmentally friendly gardening, including a section instructing seniors and those with disabilities how to garden despite physical limitations.

The outdoor kids' play area is made from recycled materials and has big fake animals to climb on and real live ones to look at, in case the kiddies have grown tired of learning responsible stuff. Given the care, knowledge, and urgency of the issues addressed, this is an extraordinary facility for any town, but particularly for this one.

Note: Admission includes entrance to the adjacent Nevada State Museum reviewed above.

333 S. Valley View Blvd. www.springspreserve.org. © **702/822-8344.** Admission $19 adults, $17 seniors and students with ID, $11 children 5–17, free for children 4 and under, $9.95 Nevada residents. Free admission to trails and gardens. Daily 10am–6pm.

ESPECIALLY FOR KIDS

To put things simply, Las Vegas makes money—lots and lots of money—by promoting gambling, drinking, and sex. These are all fine pursuits if you happen to be an adult, but if you haven't reached the magical age of 21, you really don't count in this town. In any case, the casinos and even the Strip itself are simply too stimulating, noisy, and smoky for kids.

Nevertheless, you may have a perfectly legitimate reason for bringing your children to Las Vegas (like Grandma was busy, or you were just stopping off on your way from somewhere else), so be on the lookout throughout this chapter for the Kids icon. These are places we think your children either might enjoy or, at the very least, might not detest.

In addition to those picks, note that **Circus Circus** (p. 289) has ongoing circus acts throughout the day, a vast video game–and-pinball arcade, and dozens of carnival games on its mezzanine level; **Excalibur** (p. 263) offers video, carnival, and thrill cinemas; and **The Forum Shops at Caesars Palace** (p. 66) has animated talking statues.

Consider carefully the attractions at Luxor Las Vegas: **Bodies . . . The Exhibition** (p. 58) may be too intense for kids, depending on their age, though others will be happily grossed out and might even learn a thing or two, while only those with interest in the high seas, disasters, the Titanic, or the eponymous movie will want to browse through **Titanic: The Exhibition** (p. 61).

Beyond the city limits (see chapter 10 for details on all of these) is **Bonnie Springs Ranch/Old Nevada,** with trail and stagecoach rides, a petting zoo, old-fashioned melodramas, stunt shootouts, a Nevada-themed wax museum, crafts demonstrations, and more. **Lake Mead** has great recreational facilities for family vacations. Finally, organized tours (p. 89) to the **Grand Canyon** and other interesting sights in southern Nevada and neighboring states can be fun family activities. Check with your hotel sightseeing desk.

Also note that there are several **Kids Quest** facilities around town where you can dump your kids while you're off gambling—we mean, place them under the caring guidance of trained professionals at a well-stocked play and activity centers that have everything from games to learning centers. The closest one to the Strip is at the **Palms,** 4321 W. Flamingo Rd. (© **866/942-7777**), but you can check the website at www.kidsquest.com for other locations that may be more convenient.

GETTING MARRIED

Getting hitched is one of the most popular things to do in Las Vegas. Just ask Britney Spears—as she rather infamously revealed, it's all too easy to get married here. See that total stranger/childhood friend standing next to you? Grab him or her and head down to the **Clark County Marriage License Bureau,** 201 Clark Ave. (© **702/761-0600;** daily, including holidays, 8am–midnight), to get

Clark County Marriage License Bureau.

your license. Find a wedding chapel (not hard, as there are about 50 of them in town; they line the north end of the Strip, and most hotels have them) and tie the knot. Just like that. No blood test, no waiting period—heck, not even an awkward dating period . . . though you may have a potentially very awkward time explaining it afterward to your mother, your manager, and the press.

Even if you have actually known your intended for some time, Las Vegas is a great place to get married. The ease is the primary attraction, but there are a number of other appealing reasons. You can have any kind of wedding you want, from a big, traditional production number to a small, intimate affair; from a spur-of-the-moment "just-the-happy-couple-in-blue-jeans" kind of thing to an "Elvis-in a pink Cadillac-at-a-drive-through-window" kind of thing (see the box "An Elvis Impersonator's Top 10 Reasons to Get Married in Las Vegas," below). The wedding chapels take care of everything; usually they'll even provide a limo to take you to the license bureau and back. Most offer all the accessories, from rings to flowers to a videotaped record of the event.

We personally know several very happy couples who opted for the Vegas route. Motivations differed, with the ease factor heading the list (though the Vegas-ness of the whole thing came in a close second), but one and all reported having great fun. Is there a more romantic way to start off your life together than in gales of laughter?

In any event, the more than 100,000 couples who yearly take advantage of all this can't be wrong. If you want to follow in the footsteps of Elvis and Priscilla (at the first incarnation of the Aladdin Hotel), Michael Jordan, Jon Bon Jovi, Richard Gere and Cindy Crawford, Pamela Anderson and ill-fated husband no. 3, Angelina Jolie and Billy Bob, and, of course, Britney and What's-His-Name, you'll want to peruse the following list of the most notable wedding chapels on or near the Strip.

With regard to decor, there isn't a radical difference between the major places, though some are decidedly spiffier and less sad than others. Attitude certainly makes a difference with several and varies radically, depending on who's working at any given time. Given how important your wedding is—or should be—we encourage you to give yourself time to comparison shop and spurn anyone who doesn't seem eager enough for your business.

You can also call **Las Vegas Weddings** (ℂ **800/322-8697;** www.lasvegas weddings.com), which offers one-stop shopping for wedding services.

> # AN ELVIS IMPERSONATOR'S TOP 10
> # REASONS TO get married IN LAS VEGAS

Jesse Garon has appeared in numerous Las Vegas productions as "Young Elvis." He arrives at any special event in a 1955 pink, neon-lit Cadillac, and does weddings, receptions, birthdays, conventions, grand openings, and so on. For all your Elvis impersonator needs, call © **702/588-8188,** or visit his website at www.vegaselvis.com.

1. It's the only place in the world where Elvis will marry you, at a drive-up window, in a pink Cadillac—24 hours a day.

2. Chances are, you'll never forget your anniversary.

3. Where else can you treat all your guests to a wedding buffet for only 99¢ a head?

4. Four words: One helluva bachelor party.

5. On your wedding night, show your spouse that new "watch me disappear" act you learned from Siegfried & Roy.

6. Show your parents who's boss—have your wedding your way.

7. Wedding bells ring for you everywhere you go. They just sound like slot machines.

8. You can throw dice instead of rice.

9. Easy to lie about age on the marriage certificate—just like Joan Collins did!

10. With all the money you save, it's dice clocks for everyone!

Weddings can be very inexpensive in Vegas: A license is $60 and a basic service not much more. Even a full-blown shebang package—photos, music, flowers, video, cake, and other doodads—will run only about $500 total. We haven't quoted any prices here because the ultimate cost depends entirely on how much you want to spend. Go cheap, and the whole thing will set you back maybe $150, including the license; go elaborate, and the price is still reasonable by today's wedding-price standards. Be sure to remember that there are often hidden charges, such as expected gratuities for the minister (about $25 should do; no real need to tip anyone else), and so forth. If you're penny-pinching, you'll want to keep those in mind.

Be aware that Valentine's Day is a very popular day to get married in Vegas. Some of the chapels perform as many as 80 services on February 14. But remember, you also don't have to plan ahead. Just show up, get your paperwork, close your eyes, and pick a chapel. And above all, have fun. Good luck and best wishes to you both.

Note: When we describe the following chapels and say "flowers," don't think fresh (unless it's part of a description of services provided); the permanent decorations are artificial and of varying levels of quality.

Chapel of the Bells Sporting perhaps the largest and gaudiest wedding chapel sign on the Strip, this is also one of the longest-running chapels, operating since 1957. This combination of classic Vegas "style" and "tradition" is most of what this place has going for it. The chapel is pretty, garnished with swaths of white material and light green accents, seating 25 to 35, but nothing dazzling. It's not particularly distinctive, but Kelly Ripa got married here, so there is that. The chapel prefers advance booking but can do same-day ceremonies.

2233 Las Vegas Blvd. S. (at Sahara Ave.). www.chapelofthebellslasvegas.com. © **800/233-2391** or 702/735-6803. Mon–Thurs 9am–10pm; Fri–Sat 9am–1am. Open as late as needed on holidays.

Chapel of the Flowers ★★
This chapel's claim to fame is that Dennis Rodman and Carmen Electra exchanged their deathless vows here—but don't hold it against the place. A 2010 extreme makeover turned an already lovely facility into a truly stunning one, with gardens, updated decor in all three chapels, full services from photos to flowers, and more. The La Capella Chapel fits 50 and has a rustic Tuscan feel, with wood pews and frosted glass sconces. The Victorian chapel, which holds only 30, has white walls and dark-wood pews and doesn't look very Victorian at all—but as the plainest, it's also the nicest. The smallest is the Magnolia Chapel, done in simple white marble with a free-standing arch. If you want an outdoor vow exchange, you might choose the gazebo by a running stream and waterfall that nearly drowns out Strip noise. There's also a medium-size reception room and live organ music upon request, plus Internet streaming of services is available for those of you who have second thoughts about not inviting the family to your vows. It's a pretty, friendly place (owned by the same family for more than 50 years) that seems to keep an eye on its bustling business. It does not allow rice or confetti throwing.

1717 Las Vegas Blvd. S. (at E. Oakey Blvd.). www.littlechapel.com. © **800/843-2410** or 702/735-4331. Mon–Thurs 7am–8pm; Fri 7am–9pm; Sat 7am–9pm.

Graceland Wedding Chapel ★
Housed in a landmark building that's one of the oldest wedding chapels in Vegas, the Graceland bills itself as "the proverbial mom and pop outfit." No, Elvis never slept here, but one of the owners was friends with Elvis and asked his permission to use the name. This is a tiny New England church building with a small bridge and white picket fence out front. Inside is a 30-seat chapel; the walls are off white, with a large, modern stained-glass window of doves and roses behind the pulpit. The pews are dark-blond wood. It's not the nicest of the chapels, but Jon Bon Jovi and Billy Ray Cyrus got married here (though not to each other). An Elvis package is available, and weddings can be viewed online 45 minutes after the ceremony.

619 Las Vegas Blvd. S. (at E. Bonneville Ave.). www.gracelandchapel.com. © **800/824-5732** or 702/382-0091. Daily 9am–11pm.

Little Church of the West ★★
Built in 1942 on the grounds of the Frontier, this gorgeous traditional chapel has been moved three times in its history and has hosted weddings for everyone from Judy Garland to Angelina Jolie. Elvis even got married here, at least on film—the building played the backdrop for his nuptials to Ann-Margret in *Viva Las Vegas*. There are rich wood walls, ceiling, and pews; stained-glass windows; and a traditional steeple amongst the well-landscaped grounds, making it a really lovely option for those looking to walk down the aisle.

4617 Las Vegas Blvd. S. (at Russell Rd.). www.littlechurchlv.com. © **800/821-2452** or 702/739-7971. Daily 8am–11pm.

Little White Wedding Chapel
This is arguably the most famous of the chapels on the Strip, maybe because there is a big sign saying Michael Jordan and Joan Collins were married here (again, not to each other), maybe because they were the first to do the drive-up window, or maybe because this is where

Britney and that guy who isn't the guy from *Seinfeld* began their 51 hours of wedded bliss (no, we will never, ever get tired of mocking that bit of bad decision making). It is indeed little and white. However, it has a factory-line atmosphere, processing wedding after wedding all day. Move 'em in and move 'em out. No wonder they put in that drive-up window! The staff, dressed in no-nonsense black, is brusque, hasty, and has a bit of an attitude. Although the chapels are fine, if you want something special, there are probably better choices.

1301 Las Vegas Blvd. S. (btw. E. Oakey and Charleston boulevards). www.alittlewhite chapel.com. ✆ **800/545-8111** or 702/382-5943. Daily 8am–midnight.

Mon Bel Ami Wedding Chapel ★

Formerly the Silver Bells chapel, this got a spanking new redo a few years back that is holding up well; a pretty

FROM TOP: **Drive-up window at Little White Wedding Chapel. Mon Bel Ami Wedding Chapel.**

little churchlike building complete with a big gold- and flower-bedecked chapel room (maybe the taller peaked ceiling gives that effect) fitted with surround-sound speakers. The cupid bas-relief is a bit much. The chapel does frilly and fancy wedding receptions, as well as events where white doves are released. Perhaps because of this, the establishment seems to attract fewer walk-ins than prebooked weddings, so you should call in advance, or you might be stuck in the Strip-side gazebo. Along with Elvis, Tom Jones, Marilyn Monroe, and Elvira (!) impersonators are available.

607 Las Vegas Blvd. S. (at E. Bonneville Ave.). www.monbelami.com. ✆ **866/503-4400** or 702/388-4445. Sun–Fri 10am–8pm; Sat 10am–10pm.

A Special Memory Wedding Chapel ★ This is a very nice wedding chapel, particularly compared to the rather tired facades of the classics on the Strip. This is absolutely the place to go if you want a traditional, big-production wedding; you won't feel it the least bit tacky. It's a New England church–style building, complete with steeple. The interior looks like a proper church (well, a plain one—don't think ornate Gothic cathedral), with a peaked roof, pews with padded red seats, modern stained-glass windows of doves and flowers, and lots of dark wood. It's all very clean and new and seats about 87 comfortably. There is a short staircase leading to an actual bride's room; she can make an entrance coming down it or through the double doors at the back. The area outside the chapel is like a minimall of bridal paraphernalia stores. Should all this just be too darned nice and proper for you, they also offer a drive-up window (where they do about 300 weddings a month!). They have a photo studio on-site and will do receptions featuring a small cake, cold cuts, and champagne. There is a gazebo for outside weddings, and they sell T-shirts!

800 S. 4th St. (at Gass Ave.). www.aspecialmemory.com. ✆ **800/962-7798** or 702/384-2211. Sun–Thurs 8am–10pm; Fri–Sat 8am–midnight.

Viva Las Vegas Weddings ★★ Yes, you could come to Las Vegas and have a traditional wedding in a tasteful chapel where you walk down the aisle to a kindly minister. But wouldn't you rather literally ride into the chapel in the back of a pink Cadillac and get married by Elvis? Or wade in through dry ice fog while Dracula performs your ceremony? This is the mecca of the wacky themed Vegas wedding, complete with indoor and outdoor spaces, tux and costume rentals, florists, theme rooms for receptions, and a staff of former stage performers who love to put on a show. *This* is what a Vegas wedding should be like.

1205 Las Vegas Blvd. S. (btw. Charleston and Oakey boulevards). www.vivalasvegasweddings.com. ✆ **800/574-4450** or 702/384-0771. Sun–Thurs 9am–9pm; Fri–Sat 8am–10pm.

A Special Memory Wedding Chapel.

Theme wedding at Viva Las Vegas Weddings.

Wee Kirk O' the Heather ★   This is the oldest wedding chapel in Las Vegas (it's been here since 1940; ah, Vegas, and its mixed-up view of age) and the one at the very end of the Strip, right before Downtown (and thus close to the license bureau). It was originally built as a house in 1925 for a local minister, but marriage bureau officials kept sending couples there to get married and they eventually just gave up and turned it into a chapel. The decor is entirely fresh, and while that means gold-satin-patterned wallpaper in the chapel, we like it a great deal. Just the right balance between kitsch and classic, and that's what you want in a Vegas wedding chapel. Plus, if there were a competition for the friendliest chapel in town, this one would win hands down.

231 Las Vegas Blvd. S. (btw. Bridger and Carson aves.). ℭ **800/843-5266** or 702/382-9830. www.weekirk.com. Daily 10am–8pm.

VOWS **WITH A VIEW**

Almost every major resort has a wedding chapel (or four), and while most of them are nice enough, they are usually pretty bland—which isn't something you should want for any wedding, much less a Sin City one. But a few hotels offer only-in-Vegas experiences that make for great memories (and wedding photos!).

If you want to have the iconic dancing waters as a backdrop, you can get married on a balcony overlooking the Bellagio Fountains at **Bellagio,** 3600 Las Vegas Blvd. S. (www.bellagio.com/weddings; ℭ **702/693-7700**). As you might expect, it ain't cheap, but you can even time your "I do" to the fountains' big climax.

An almost aerial view of the fountains is available across the street from the Eiffel Tower at **Paris Las Vegas,** 3655 Las Vegas Blvd S. (www.parislv.com; ℭ **877/650-5021**). You can get married on the observation deck at the top of the tower replica.

An even higher view is available at the top of the **Stratosphere Las Vegas,** 2000 Las Vegas Blvd. S. (www.chapelintheclouds.com; ℭ **800/789-9436**). Their chapels overlook the entire city from more than 100 stories up, or you can get married on the indoor or outdoor observation decks. They even have packages that will include the thrill rides, so you can take the plunge both metaphorically and literally.

OUTDOOR ACTIVITIES

Biking

Bicycle rentals can be arranged through the concierge at most of the major hotels in town. If you'd prefer to do it on your own, check out **Las Vegas Cyclery** (www.lasvegascyclery.com; ✆ **702/596-2953**), a rental and tour operator offering everything from street to mountain to tandem bikes and the necessary safety equipment and accessories. Guided tours of Red Rock Canyon, Mount Charleston, and more are also offered. Prices for rentals start at around $25 for a half-day and guided tours at around $110.

Boating & Fishing

The bulk of the water-based activities in the area take place at the **Lake Mead National Recreation Area**, located about 20 miles east of Las Vegas. Several harbors offer rentals of power, fishing, and house boats and personal watercraft. They can also help you with fishing licenses and equipment. For more information, see chapter 10, "Side Trips from Las Vegas."

Golf

See "Fore! Great Desert Golf" (p. 89).

Gyms

All of the major hotels (and many of the minor ones) have fully stocked gyms on the premises. The size and quality varies, of course, but the bigger resorts have facilities that would make most commercial fitness centers green with envy. The bad news is that there is usually a fee to use the gym, which can range between $15 and $35 per day (unless it is already included in the resort fee that many hotels are charging these days). Several national chains, including **24 Hour Fitness,** have outlets in Las Vegas, and your membership may allow you to use the local branch.

Hiking

We consider the length you have to walk between hotels on the Strip or from your room to the front door enough of a hike, but if you are looking for something more traditional, the **Red Rock Canyon** and **Mount Charleston** areas have numerous hiking trails. For more information, see chapter 10, "Side Trips from Las Vegas."

Horseback Riding

Looking to indulge your inner cowboy/girl? There are several stables and horseback-tour companies in town, most of which are located near **Red Rock Canyon** and **Mount Charleston.** For more information, see chapter 10, "Side Trips from Las Vegas."

Ice Skating

The **SoBe Ice Arena** at the Fiesta Rancho, 2400 N. Rancho Rd. (www.fiesta rancholasvegas.com; ✆ **702/631-7000**), features an NHL regulation–size rink and offers daily open skating hours, lessons, and equipment rental. Public skating times vary from week to week based upon the schedules of the various hockey leagues that use the facility; usually the rink is open for at least a couple of hours every afternoon and after 8pm on Friday and Saturday nights, when a DJ and nightclub-worthy lighting may help mask the sound and sight of you falling down a lot.

Skiing & Snowboarding

The **Las Vegas Ski and Snowboard Resort,** Highway 156, Mount Charleston (www.skilasvegas.com; © **702/385-2754**), offers 11 trails ranging from beginner to advanced, including a half-pipe and the Darkside Park with tabletop jumps and assorted rails. Lift tickets are $40 to $60 for adults, and $25 to $45 for children 18 and under and seniors 60 and over. The facility offers a full array of equipment and clothing rentals; there's also a small snack bar and sundry shop if you forgot to bring a camera with which to record yourself in full downhill glory (or falling repeatedly if you are like us). It is usually open late November through early April from 9am until 4pm, but that may vary based on conditions.

Swimming

Part of the delight of the Vegas resort complexes is the gorgeous pools—what could be better for beating the summer heat? But there are pools and there are pools, so you'll need to keep several things in mind when searching for the right one for you.

During the winter, it's often too cold or windy to do much lounging, and even if the weather is amenable, the hotels often close part of their pool areas during winter and early spring. The pools also are not heated for the most part, but in fairness, they largely don't need to be.

Most hotel pools are shallow, chest-high at best, only about 3 feet deep in many spots (the hotels want you gambling, not swimming). Diving is impossible—not that a single pool allows it anyway.

And finally, during those hot days, be warned that sitting by pools next to heavily windowed buildings such as The Mirage and Treasure Island allows you to experience the same thing a bug does under a magnifying glass with a sun ray directed on it (see the Vdara "Death Ray" on p. 263). Regardless of time of year, be sure to slather on the sunscreen; there's a reason you see so many unhappy lobster-red people roaming the streets. Many pool areas don't offer much in the way of shade. On the other hand, if your tan line is important to you, head for Caesars, Mandalay Bay, Wynn Las Vegas, or Stratosphere (to name a few), all of which have topless sunbathing areas where you can toast even more flesh than at the other hotels.

At any of the pools, you can rent a cabana (which often includes a TV, special lounge chairs, and even better poolside service), but these should be reserved as far in advance as possible, and, with the exception of the Four Seasons' complimentary shaded lounging area, most cost a hefty fee. If you are staying at a chain hotel, you will most likely find an average pool, but if you want to spend some time at a better one, be aware that most of the casino-hotel pool attendants will ask to see your room key. If they are busy, you might be able to sneak in, or at least blend in with a group ahead of you.

Tennis

Tennis used to be a popular pastime in Vegas, but these days, buffs only have a couple of choices at hotels in town that have courts. **Bally's** (© **702/739-4111**)

organized TOURS

Just about every hotel in town has a tour desk offering a seemingly infinite number of sightseeing opportunities in and around Las Vegas. You're sure to find a tour company that will take you where you want to go.

○ **Gray Line** (ℂ 800/634-6579; www. grayline.com) offers a rather comprehensive roster, including the following:

○ A pair of 5- to 6-hour **city tours** (day or night) with various itineraries, including visits to **Ethel M Chocolates** and the **Fremont Street Experience**

○ Half-day excursions to **Hoover Dam** and **Red Rock Canyon** (see chapter 10 for details)

○ A half-day tour to **Lake Mead** and **Hoover Dam** (see chapter 10 for details)

○ Several full-day **Grand Canyon** excursions (see chapter 10 for details)

Call for details or inquire at your hotel's tour desk, where you'll also find free magazines with coupons for discounts on these tours.

---

has eight night-lit hard courts. Fees start at $20 per hour for guests of Bally's or Paris Las Vegas and $25 per hour for nonguests, with rackets available for rental. Facilities include a pro shop. Hours vary seasonally. Reservations are advised. The **Las Vegas Hotel** (ℂ 702/732-5009) has six outdoor hard courts (four night-lit) and a pro shop. It's open to the public but hours vary seasonally. Rates are $20 per hour for guests and $25 per hour for nonguests. Lessons are available. Reservations are required.

FORE! GREAT DESERT GOLF

In addition to the listings below, there are dozens of local courses, including some very challenging ones that have hosted PGA tournaments. *Note:* Greens fees vary radically depending on time of day and year. Also, call for opening and closing times, because these change frequently. Because of the heat, you will want to take advantage of the cart that in most cases is included in the greens fee.

Angel Park Golf Club ★★   This 36-hole, par-70/71 public course is a local favorite. Arnold Palmer originally designed the Mountain and Palm courses (the Palm Course was redesigned several years later by Bob Cupp). Players call this a great escape from the casinos, claiming that no matter how many times they play it, they never get tired of it. The Palm Course has gently rolling fairways that offer golfers of all abilities a challenging yet forgiving layout. The Mountain Course has rolling natural terrain and gorgeous panoramic views.

   Yardage: Palm Course 6,525 championship, 5,438 resort; Mountain Course 6,722 championship, 5,718 resort.

   Facilities: Pro shop, night-lit driving range, 18-hole putting course, restaurant, cocktail bar, snack bar, and beverage cart.

100 S. Rampart Blvd. (btw. Summerlin Pkwy. and Alta St., 20 min. NW of the Strip). www.angelpark. com. ℂ **888/446-5358** or 702/254-4653. Greens fees $30–$155. Internet specials available.

Angel Park Golf Club.

Arroyo Golf Club ★   Also designed by Arnold Palmer, this 18-hole, par-72 course is one of the more scenic in town owing to its location nestled along Red Rock Canyon. Stunning mountains on one side and Las Vegas in the distance on the other side; what more could you want? Well, you get a challenging (but not insanity inducing) course that will keep all but the most competitive of golfers entertained.

Yardage: 6,883 resort.

Facilities: Pro shop, night-lit driving range, 18-hole putting course, restaurant, cocktail bar, snack bar, and beverage cart.

2250 C Red Springs Dr. (just west of the 215, 25 min. NW of the Strip). www.thearroyogolfclub. com. 🕐 **866/934-4653** or 702/258-3200. Greens fees $89–$149.

Bali Hai Golf Club ★★★   One of the most exclusive golf addresses belongs to this multimillion-dollar course, built in 2000, on the Strip, just south of Mandalay Bay. Done in a wild South Seas theme, the par-72 course has over 7 acres of water features, including an island green, palm trees, and tropical foliage everywhere you look. Not impressed yet? How about the fact that all their golf carts are equipped with GPS? Okay, if that doesn't convince you of the upscale nature of the joint, check out the greens fees. Even at those prices, tee times are often booked 6 months in advance.

Yardage: 7,002 championship.

Facilities: Pro shop, putting green, gourmet restaurant, grill, and lounge.

5150 Las Vegas Blvd. S. www.balihaigolfclub.com. 🕐 **702/479-6786.** Greens fees $125–$395.

Bear's Best Las Vegas ★★★   Golf legend Jack Nicklaus has designed hundreds of courses around the world, but here he has taken 18 of his favorite holes and put them all together in one delightfully challenging package. From courses in Mexico to Montana and back again, the bunkers, water features, and traps have all been faithfully re-created, giving you an opportunity to try the best of "The Bear."

Yardage: 7,194 championship.

Facilities: Pro shop, putting green, restaurant (with Nicklaus memorabilia), and club house.

11111 W. Flamingo Rd. www.clubcorp.com. 🕐 **702/605-0649.** Greens fees $79–$249.

Black Mountain Golf & Country Club ★★ Two new greens have recently been added to this 27-hole, par-72 semiprivate course, which requires reservations 4 days in advance. It's considered a great old course, with lots of wildlife, including roadrunners. However, unpredictable winds may affect your game.

Yardage: 6,550 championship; 6,223 regular; 5,518 ladies.

Facilities: Pro shop, driving range, putting green, restaurant, cocktail lounge, and snack bar.

500 Greenway Rd., Henderson. www.golfblackmountain.com. ✆ **866/596-4833.** Greens fees $40–$95.

Las Vegas National Golf Club ★ This 18-hole, par-71 public course is one of the most historic in town. Built in 1961, it was at various times associated with or run by the Stardust, Sahara, and the Las Vegas Hilton. Yes, the Rat Pack played here, and you can, too. The course itself is classically designed (not the desert layout that most in Vegas have), and although it's not the most challenging in town, it will keep you entertained.

Yardage: 6,815 championship; 6,418 regular; 5,741 ladies.

Facilities: Pro shop, driving range, restaurant, cocktail lounge, and golf school.

1911 Desert Inn Rd. (btw. Maryland Pkwy. and Eastern Ave.). www.lasvegasnational.com. ✆ **866/ 695-1961.** Greens fees $69–$129.

Rio Secco Golf Club ★★ You don't have to be staying at the Rio Suites (or another Caesars Entertainment property) to play this gorgeous 18-hole course, but you get preferred tee times and discounts if you do. Set in the foothills of the mountains overlooking Las Vegas, the views are incredible and the course, designed by Rees Jones, is one of the most in demand in town.

Yardage: 7,313 championship; 6,927 back; 6,356 middle; 5,759 forward.

Facilities: Pro shop, driving range, restaurant, and bar.

2851 Grand Hills Dr., Henderson. www.riosecco.net. ✆ **888/867-3226.** Greens fees $110–$275.

TPC Las Vegas ★★ Justin Timberlake has held his charity golf tournament at this course, so if it's good enough for him, it should be good enough for you, right? Luckily the sexy-back guy has good taste as this scenic course, which follows the arroyos and plateaus of the terrain, is also a favorite of the PGA. That should tell you there are no windmills or clown's mouths here. It's a very challenging course, so bring your A game.

Yardage: 7,081 championship.

Facilities: Pro shop, driving range, restaurant, clubhouse, and golf school.

9851 Canyon Run Dr. www.tpc.com. ✆ **702/256-2500.** Greens fees $79–$249.

Wynn Las Vegas Golf Club ★★ Before Mr. Wynn came along and bulldozed the legendary Desert Inn Golf Club, he rescued a bunch of the landscaping and then reinstalled it here on his elegant 18-hole, par-70 course behind Wynn Las Vegas. The facility is as gorgeous as you would expect it to be, with waterfalls, lush foliage, and stunning greens designed by the acclaimed Thomas Fazio. It ain't cheap, but many golfers say it is totally worth it. Note that it is only open to guests of Wynn or Encore.

Yardage: 7,042 championship.

Facilities: Pro shop, driving range, putting green, and food service.

At Wynn Las Vegas, 3131 Las Vegas Blvd. S. www.wynnlasvegas.com. ✆ **888/320-7122.** Greens fees $300 and up.

4

EXPLORING LAS VEGAS

Fore! Great Desert Golf

striking **OUT**

Las Vegas is one of the favorite cities in the world for bowlers of all levels, with several huge alleys offering everything from regular bowling to rock-'n'-roll style action.

- **Gold Coast Bowling Center,** 4000 W. Flamingo Rd. (at Valley View; *©* **702/367-7111**), has a 70-lane bowling center open daily 24 hours.

- The **Orleans Bowling Center,** 4500 W. Tropicana Ave. (*©* **702/365-7400**), has 70 lanes, a pro shop, lockers, meeting rooms, and more open daily 24 hours.

- **Red Rock Lanes,** 11011 W. Charleston Ave. (*©* **702/797-7467**), is a luxury bowling center with 72 lanes, plasma TVs, and VIP suites where you can pick your own music and get bottle service. It's open Monday through Thursday from 8am until 2am and 24 hours on Fridays and Saturdays.

- **Santa Fe Station Bowling Center,** 4949 N. Rancho Rd. (*©* **702/658-4995**), has a 60-lane alley with the most modern scoring equipment, new furnishings, a fun and funky bar, a small cafe, and much more. Open Sunday through Thursday 7am until midnight, Friday and Saturday 7am until 1am.

- **Sam's Town Bowling Center,** 5111 Boulder Hwy. (*©* **702/456-7777**), offers 56 lanes plus a snack shop, cocktail lounge, video arcade, day-care center, pro shop, and more. It's open daily 24 hours.

- **South Point Bowling Center,** 9777 Las Vegas Blvd. (*©* **702/797-8080**), has a 64-lane facility with a similar divided layout to its sister at Suncoast (see below). It has all the latest gee-whiz scoring and automation, plus the usual facilities, and is open 24 hours.

- **Strike Zone** at Sunset Station, 1301 W. Sunset Rd., in Henderson (*©* **702/547-7467**), has a high-tech 72-lane facility with all the latest automated scoring gizmos, giant video screens, a full bar, a snack shop, a pro shop, a video arcade, and more.

- **Suncoast Bowling Center,** 9090 Alta Dr., in Summerlin (*©* **702/636-7111**), offers 64 lanes divided by a unique center aisle. The high-tech center with touch-screen scoring has become a regular stop on the Pro Bowlers tours. It's open daily 24 hours.

- **Texas Star Lanes,** 2101 Texas Star Lane (*©* **702/631-8128**), offers a 60-lane alley, video arcade, billiards, a snack bar and lounge, and more. It's open daily 24 hours.

Bowling alley in The Orleans.

SPAS

Most of the major resorts in Las Vegas have spa facilities that range from pretty basic (sauna, Jacuzzi, some treatment rooms for massages) to extravagant (is that a rock climbing wall?), but many are only available to guests of the hotels in which they are located. Our favorite in that category is contemporary and dramatic **Bathhouse Spa,** 3950 Las Vegas Blvd. S. (www.mandalaybay.com; ℭ 877/632-9636), which requires you to be a guest of Mandalay Bay or THE-hotel. It's a gorgeous, sun-dappled cave of a space and it would be totally worth it to get a room upstairs just so you can use this.

The spas that follow all have hours during which they are open to the general public. Those hours change seasonally and sometimes even weekly based on hotel guest demand, so call ahead or visit the websites for more details.

Aquae Sulis Spa ★★   The centerpiece here is the "Ritual," a series of dunks and soaks in cold, warm, hydrotherapy, and floating pools, some of which are outside in a gorgeously landscaped grotto. It's totally unique and worth the 20-minute drive from the Strip.

At the JW Marriott, 221 N. Rampart Blvd. (at Summerlin Parkway). www.jwlasvegasresort.com. ℭ **877/869-8777.** Massage and treatments $70–$245.

Canyon Ranch SpaClub ★   The largest spa in Las Vegas has more than 130,000 square feet worth of treatment rooms, workout facilities, and even a rock climbing wall. Although they do a good job of keeping things relatively peaceful, the sheer size of the place and the number of people that visit may inhibit your relaxation efforts. Note that prices are more expensive on the weekends, so go on a weekday if you can.

At The Venetian, 3355 Las Vegas Blvd. S. www.venetian.com. ℭ **877/220-2688.** Massage and treatments $155–$530.

Qua Baths & Spa ★★   Check out the Environment rooms at this lavishly designed spa, which include the Arctic Ice room complete with snow showers and a Roman Baths section that would make Caesar proud. Treatments and massages are not cheap, but the spa faithful say this is one of the best in town.

At Caesars Palace, 3570 Las Vegas Blvd. S. www.caesarspalace.com. ℭ **866/782-0655.** Massage and treatments $140–$250.

Red Rock Resort Adventure Spa ★★★   The facility has the requisite spa accoutrement—a Zen-like space, massages, facials, sauna, and so on—but it's the "Adventure" part of the program that makes it truly unique. Capitalizing on the hotel's location on the edge of the Red Rock Canyon National Conservancy Area, the spa offers horseback riding, river rafting, kayaking, hiking, rock climbing, biking, and more. Go get a great outdoors workout and then come back for a massage to soothe your aches and pains.

At Red Rock Resort, 11011 W. Charleston Ave (at I-215). www.redrocklasvegas.com. ℭ **866/328-9270.** Massage and treatments $85–$225.

Spa at Bellagio ★★   The surroundings are luxe and the staff is so soothingly attentive that you just know it's going to cost you a fortune to get worked on here—but it's totally worth it. Few other spas in town will make you feel so richly pampered.

Canyon Ranch Spa.

At Bellagio, 3600 Las Vegas Blvd. S. www.bellagio.com. ✆ **702/693-7472.** Massage and treatments $85–$310.

Spa at Encore ★★★   By far the most beautifully designed spa in Las Vegas, the Moroccan garden decor is at once breathtaking and calming. Your bill can get shocking really fast, but one walk down the lantern-lit treatment room hallway will make all your cares melt away.

At Encore Las Vegas, 3121 Las Vegas Blvd. S. www.encorelasvegas.com. ✆ **702/770-4772.** Massage and treatments $85–$425.

SIGHTS & ATTRACTIONS BY THEME

AMUSEMENT PARKS
Adventuredome ★ (North Strip, p. 64)

ART MUSEUMS
Bellagio Gallery of Fine Art ★ (Mid-Strip, p. 61)
CityCenter Fine Art Collection ★ (South Strip, p. 58)

COMMERCIAL ART GALLERIES
The Arts Factory ★ (Downtown, p. 68)
Emergency Arts ★★ (Downtown, p. 68)

ENTERTAINMENT COMPLEXES
Chuck Jones Experience ★★ (North Strip, p. 64)
CSI: The Experience ★ (South Strip, p. 60)
Fast Lap Indoor Kart Racing ★★ (Just Off the Strip, p. 74)
Las Vegas Mini Gran Prix ★★ (North & West of the Strip, p. 76)
Pole Position Raceway ★ (North & West of the Strip, p. 78)
Show in the Sky (Just Off the Strip, p. 66)

EXHIBIT

Bodies . . . The Exhibition ★★ (South Strip, p. 58)

Titanic: The Exhibition ★ (South Strip, p. 61)

FACTORY TOURS

Ethel M Chocolates ★ (South & East of the Strip, p. 75)

ICONS

Bellagio Fountains ★★★ (Mid-Strip, p. 66)

The Forum Shops Fountain Shows ★ (Mid-Strip, p. 66)

Fremont Street Experience ★★★ (Downtown, p. 69)

Mirage Volcano ★★ (Mid-Strip, p. 66)

Sirens of TI ★ (Mid-Strip, p. 67)

Welcome to Fabulous Las Vegas Sign ★★★ (Just Off the Strip, p. 67)

Wynn Lake of Dreams ★ (North Strip, p. 67)

MUSEUMS

Clark County Museum ★★ (South & East of the Strip, p. 74)

Erotic Heritage Museum ★★★ (Just Off the Strip, p. 73)

Las Vegas Natural History Museum ★ (Downtown, p. 70)

Madame Tussauds Las Vegas ★★ (Mid-Strip, p. 62)

The Mob Museum ★★★ (Downtown, p. 70)

National Atomic Testing Museum ★★★ (Just Off the Strip, p. 74)

Nevada State Museum (North & West of the Strip, p. 77)

Pinball Hall of Fame and Museum ★★ (South & East of the Strip, p. 76)

NATURAL PRESERVES

Springs Preserve ★★★ (North & West of the Strip, p. 78)

OBSERVATION TOWERS

Eiffel Tower Ride (Mid-Strip, p. 62)

Stratosphere Tower ★ (North Strip, p. 68)

PARKS & GARDENS

Bellagio Conservatory ★★★ (Mid-Strip, p. 66)

Wynn Conservatory ★ (North Strip, p. 67)

PERFORMING ARTS VENUES

The Smith Center for the Performing Arts ★★★ (Downtown, p. 71)

RACECOURSE

Las Vegas Motor Speedway ★★ (North & West of the Strip, p. 77)

THRILL RIDE

Fremont Street Flightlinez ★★ (Downtown, p. 69)

Roller Coaster at New York–New York ★ (South Strip, p. 60)

Stratosphere Thrill Rides ★★ (North Strip, p. 65)

ZOOS

Shark Reef at Mandalay Bay ★ (South Strip, p. 60)

Siegfried & Roy's Secret Garden & Dolphin Habitat ★★★ (Mid-Strip, p. 63)

WHERE TO EAT

5

as Vegas is one of the top dining destinations in the world. As evidence, take a look at some of the names behind the restaurants: Wolfgang Puck, Emeril Lagasse, Joël Robuchon, Thomas Keller, Julian Serrano, Bobby Flay, Gordon Ramsay, Alain Ducasse, Charlie Palmer . . . the list goes on and on. If you don't know who these people are, you don't watch the Food Network enough. Fine dining has never been this fine in Vegas, but the good news for folks with less adventurous palates or less extravagant budgets is that there is plenty to eat here for everyone. All-you-can-eat buffets still abound; cheap eats can still be found if you know where to look; and moderately priced restaurants are making a big comeback. We hope you're hungry!

BEST LAS VEGAS DINING BETS

o **Best Strip Restaurants:** The seafood at **Estiatoria Milos** (p. 112) will make people who don't like fish change their minds while their Greek specialties will make everyone yell "Opa!" We're also big fans of the simple, yet fantastic, pub grub at **Todd English P.U.B.** (p. 109).

o **Best Off-Strip Restaurants: Raku Grill** is a 10- to 20-minute drive from the Strip, but the flavorful Japanese grill specialties here make it totally worth the trip. See p. 143.

o **Best Theme Restaurant:** Generally speaking, we think theme restaurants are overpriced tourist traps, but **Gilley's** has such great down-home cooking that we're willing to overlook the mechanical bull. See p. 120.

o **Best Steakhouses:** Based on the NYC restaurant that has been in business for more than 150 years, **Old Homestead Steakhouse** serves hugely flavorful cuts of meat that are just plain old huge. They did invent the doggy bag, after all. See p. 114.

o **Best Inexpensive Meal: Capriotti's** serves monster, well-stuffed submarine sandwiches with fresh ingredients both traditional (ham and cheese) and offbeat (the Bobby is like Thanksgiving on a bun). Even better, most are under $10. See p. 137.

o **Best Buffets:** It's expensive, but the **Buffet at Wynn Las Vegas** (p. 150) serves high-quality food worthy of tablecloths and candlelight. Bargain hunters, however, won't need to sacrifice quality at the **Main Street Garden Court Buffet** (p. 151).

o **Best Hamburgers: KGB: Kerry's Gourmet Burgers** gives you a choice of creating your own burger or ordering one of theirs. Either way you can't go wrong. See p. 121.

PREVIOUS PAGE: **Gorging on sweet treats at a buffet is an integral Vegas experience.**

LEFT: **Dining room at L'Atelier de Joël Robuchon.**
RIGHT: **Alizé mixes fine cuisine with top-notch views of the Strip.**

- **Best Desserts:** It's not just chocolate at **Max Brenner Chocolate Restaurant**—their dessert menu is 10 pages long—but if you just stop at the chocolate selections we won't blame you. See p. 122.

- **Best Splurge:** Food should not cost as much as it does at **Joël Robuchon at the Mansion** (p. 100) and the slightly less expensive sibling **L'Atelier de Joël Robuchon** (p. 100), but a few bites of the exquisite cuisine will make you understand why it does.

- **Best Views:** You can see the entire city, and big chunks of southern Nevada, from the revolving **Top of the World,** situated more than 800 feet up the Stratosphere Tower. See p. 128.

- **Best Spot for a Romantic Dinner: Alizé,** at the top of the Palms, has a virtually unobstructed view of the Strip and delightfully crafted French cuisine that may make you forget the view entirely. See p. 134.

- **Best Breakfast:** The twisted farm food at **Hash House a Go Go** features things like pancakes the size of pizzas and waffles with bacon baked right in. Forget the warmed-over eggs at the buffets and come here instead. See p. 120.

PRICE CATEGORIES

Very Expensive	Main courses $35 and up
Expensive	Main courses $25–$35
Moderate	Main courses $15–$25
Inexpensive	Main courses under $15

SOUTH STRIP

Very Expensive

Andre's ★★ FRENCH The original and much-beloved Andre's, in Downtown Las Vegas, closed in 2008, but never fear—the branch at Monte Carlo is still going strong. While it may not have the ambience, it certainly has the menu, still overseen by owner/chef Andre Rochat, who brings over 40 years of experience to the table. Much of the waitstaff is also French, and they will happily lavish attention on you and guide you through the menu. The food presentation is exquisite and choices change seasonally; examples might be an appetizer of foie gras served with fig confiture and drizzled with a balsamic reduction, or a main course of an apple-stuffed pork tenderloin with sautéed Brussels sprouts. You get the idea. Desserts are similarly lovely, an exotic array of rich delights. An extensive wine list (more than 1,500 selections) is international in scope and includes many rare vintages; consult the sommelier.

In Monte Carlo, 3770 Las Vegas Blvd. S. www.andrelv.com. ✆ **702/798-7151.** Reservations required. Main courses $36–$68. AE, DC, MC, V. Tues–Sun 5:30–10:30pm.

Aureole ★★★ NEW AMERICAN This branch of a New York City fave (it's pronounced Are-ree-*all*), run by Charlie Palmer, is noted for its glass wine tower. It's four stories of what is probably the finest wine collection in Vegas, made even more sensational thanks to catsuit-clad lovelies who are hoisted on wires to reach bottles requested from the uppermost heights, all navigable via a tablet computer brought to your table. Amid this Vegas-show glitz is one of the better of the fine-dining experiences around. The menu is a three-course prix fixe, though if you are winsome enough, they might send out luxurious extras, such as pâté on brioche topped with shaved truffles, or an espresso cup of cold yellow-pepper soup with crab. Otherwise, expect such marvels as a tender roasted lamb loin and braised shoulder, or a rack of venison accompanied by sweet-potato purée and chestnut crisp. Everything demonstrates the hand of a true chef in the kitchen, someone paying close attention to his work and to his customers. Desserts are playful, including a bittersweet chocolate soufflé with a tangerine creamsicle and candied kumquat.

In Mandalay Bay, 3950 Las Vegas Blvd. S. www.aureolelv.com. ✆ **877/632-1766.** Reservations required. Prix-fixe dinner $75; tasting menu $95. AE, DISC, MC, V. Daily 5:30–10:30pm. Lounge 5:30pm–midnight.

Charlie Palmer Steak ★★ STEAK There are many, many steakhouses in Vegas, as if there were some natural law stating that any hotel without one will suffer from entropy and eventually collapse into a black hole. Most are pedestrian; this one is not. The slabs o' meat are as tender as anything because with the big bucks, which these cost, you do get the best cuts. We prefer the flavorful rib-eye to the other favorite, the charcoal-grilled filet, but that pork tenderloin and the goat cheese–crusted lamb do look (and taste) mighty tempting. Desserts are stylish creations, and the entire place is set in a generic fancy space that can be a bit noisy and crowded, so if romance is on the agenda, ask for one of the two-person tables in the back. Charlie Palmer, by the way, is the chef mind behind Aureole, on the other side of Mandalay Bay; this makes two for two for this celeb chef.

In Four Seasons Hotel, 3960 Las Vegas Blvd. S. www.charliepalmersteaklv.com. © **702/632-5120.** Reservations recommended. Main courses $27–$57. AE, DC, DISC, MC, V. Daily 5–10:30pm.

Joël Robuchon Restaurant ★★★ FRENCH   This is listed under Very Expensive only because there is no category for Unbelievably, Heart-Stoppingly, Stratospherically Expensive. But it's here because legendary chef Joël Robuchon—the first (and youngest) chef to win three consecutive Michelin stars—who closed his restaurants in France (where he was proclaimed "chef of the century") at the height of his fame, has proven that all the hype is justified. This is not food as fuel, food to bolt down greedily (even though you may want to), but to slowly savor. Pay attention as you chew, and notice how many layers of interest are revealed. Great care was taken in choosing and combining ingredients, to create not fuss but both surprise and a sense of rightness. Exquisite, superb—name your superlative, and it's been levied toward this remarkable restaurant.

Chef Robuchon is not personally in the kitchen that often, but he oversees the menu, which changes very frequently and features many key ingredients flown in daily from France. And the service reminds one that Michelin ratings take more than just the food into account, too. None of this comes cheap. Could it possibly be worth it? When restaurant critics claim they would spend their own money to dine here, quite very possibly, yes.

In MGM Grand, 3799 Las Vegas Blvd. S. www.joel-robuchon.net. © **702/891-7925.** Reservations strongly recommended. Jacket recommended. Prix-fixe tasting menus $120–$240; 16-course tasting menu $425. AE, DC, DISC, MC, V. Sun–Thurs 5:30–10pm; Fri–Sat 5:30–10:30pm.

L'Atelier de Joël Robuchon ★★★ FRENCH   Despite the four-star *L.A. Times* and *N.Y. Times* reviews for the main establishment reviewed above, trustworthy foodies tipped this place as actually superior. Then it won the James Beard Foundation Award for best new restaurant in 2007, which only adds to the debate. You won't go wrong either way. Certainly, it's relatively cheaper here, but the casual, almost entirely counter seating (it's like an extremely high-style diner) might dismay those looking for a different sort of atmospheric experience. But food is supposed to be fun, and interacting with the charming staff on the other side only adds to the great good pleasure. Portions are small but exquisitely conceived and constructed. The seasonal tasting menu is probably your best way to go, but consider coming just to treat yourself to a couple of dishes, such as the bacon-and-onion tart with asparagus sprigs; the wee, perfect burgers topped with foie gras; or the signature foie gras–stuffed quail. The artistry only continues with dessert. A marvelous culinary experience.

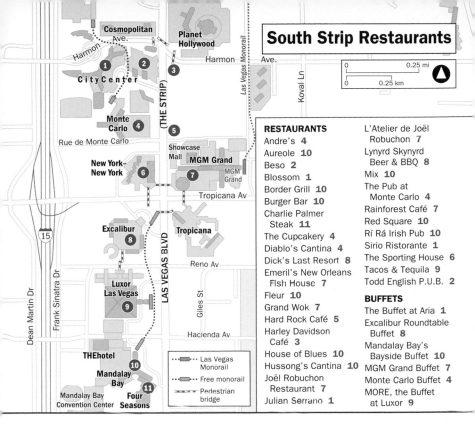

South Strip Restaurants

0 — 0.25 mi
0 — 0.25 km

RESTAURANTS
Andre's **4**
Aureole **10**
Beso **2**
Blossom **1**
Border Grill **10**
Burger Bar **10**
Charlie Palmer
  Steak **11**
The Cupcakery **4**
Diablo's Cantina **4**
Dick's Last Resort **8**
Emeril's New Orleans
  Fish House **7**
Fleur **10**
Grand Wok **7**
Hard Rock Café **5**
Harley Davidson
  Café **3**
House of Blues **10**
Hussong's Cantina **10**
Joël Robuchon
  Restaurant **7**
Julian Serrano **1**

L'Atelier de Joël
  Robuchon **7**
Lynyrd Skynyrd
  Beer & BBQ **8**
Mix **10**
The Pub at
  Monte Carlo **4**
Rainforest Café **7**
Red Square **10**
Rí Rá Irish Pub **10**
Sirio Ristorante **1**
The Sporting House **6**
Tacos & Tequila **9**
Todd English P.U.B. **2**

BUFFETS
The Buffet at Aria **1**
Excalibur Roundtable
  Buffet **8**
Mandalay Bay's
  Bayside Buffet **10**
MGM Grand Buffet **7**
Monte Carlo Buffet **4**
MORE, the Buffet
  at Luxor **9**

In MGM Grand, 3799 Las Vegas Blvd. S. www.joel-robuchon.net. ℂ **702/891-7358.** Reservations strongly recommended. Main courses $38–$70; 8-course discovery menu $168; small plates $20–$39. AE, DC, DISC, MC, V. Sun–Thurs 5:30–10:30pm; Fri–Sat 5–10:30pm.

Mix ★ NEW AMERICAN   The setting for highly revered French chef Alain Ducasse's cuisine certainly makes a statement. The space-age interior, all white and silver with a chandelier of blown-glass balls, is starkly stunning and the view from the top of THEhotel's tower is photograph worthy. The food itself is perhaps not quite as adventurous, but there are some noteworthy items. The menu changes seasonally but look for the charcuterie platter (and especially the Italian rosemary ham) for a starter, the pepper-crusted bison tenderloin for a main course, and Ducasse's signature potato gnocchi, with veal *jus*, as a side. The steaks are underwhelming in a town filled with so many better examples, and the desserts are light, airy, and generally forgettable (although the caramelized pear turnover almost captured our attention). All of it is fine, certainly, even very good in bright spots, but given the remarkable things going on in some other kitchens around town—and given the prices here—you have better options for dinner.

In THEhotel, 3950 Las Vegas Blvd. S. www.mandalaybay.com. ℂ **702/632-9500.** Reservations recommended. Main courses $34–$69. AE, DISC, DC, MC, V. Daily 6–11pm.

Red Square ★★ CONTINENTAL/RUSSIAN   The beheaded and pigeon-droppings-adorned statue of Lenin outside and the Bolshevik trappings inside

SHHHHHH . . . half-price MEALS, ON THE STRIP & OFF

Here's the latest in restaurant discounting: Cut-price meals at some of the city's top eateries are being sold by Tix4Tonight, the same people who peddle theater tickets. Either stop by a booth, call ⓒ **800/269-8499,** or visit www.tix4dinner.com. Request a reservation from their list of partner restaurants (which vary often but can include gourmet to buffet), pay a small fee, and get discounts of up to 50% off. Reservations must be made in person at a Tix4Tonight booth (see locations below).

Booths can be found at the following locations:

- In the Fashion Show mall (across from the Wynn)

- In the Hawaiian Marketplace (near Harmon St.)

- At the Circus Circus main registration desk (North Strip)

- At Slots A Fun (next to Circus Circus)

- In Bill's Casino (at the corner of Flamingo Blvd.)

- In the Showcase Mall (at the base of the giant Coca-Cola bottle)

- In the Four Queens Casino (Downtown, on Fremont St.)

- In the Casino Royale (across from The Mirage)

- At the Town Square shopping center (across from Claim Jumper)

make this one big post-Communist party (sorry, we had to say it). But if you can tear your eyes away from the theme run amok, you might notice that the menu is quite good. Blow your expense account on some caviar (we found we liked nutty osetra better than stronger beluga), properly chilled in ice, served with the correct pearl spoon. Or, more affordably, nosh on Siberian nachos—smoked salmon, citron caviar, and crème fraîche. The chef's special is a Roquefort-crusted tender filet mignon, with some soft caramelized garlic and a fine reduction sauce. Try a silly themed drink, such as the Sputnik, which is raspberry vodka and triple sec; or, better still, take advantage of the vodka menu (one of the largest in town, served at an ice-topped bar). Desserts are not so clever but the warm chocolate cake with a liquid center and strawberry sauce is fit for a czar.

In Mandalay Bay, 3950 Las Vegas Blvd. S. www.mandalaybay.com. ⓒ **702/632-7407.** Reservations recommended. Main courses $27–$39. AE, DC, MC, V. Sun–Thurs 5–10:30pm; Fri–Sat 5–11pm.

Expensive

Border Grill ★★ MEXICAN   This big, cheerful space (like a Romper Room for adults) houses a branch of the much-lauded Los Angeles restaurant, conceived and run by Mary Sue Milliken and Susan Feniger, hosts of the 1990s Food Network show *Two Hot Tamales*. This is truly authentic Mexican home cooking—the Tamales learned their craft south of the border—but with a *nuevo* twist. So don't expect precisely the same dishes you'd encounter in your favorite corner joint, but do expect fresh and fabulous food, sitting as brightly on the plates as the decor on the walls. Stay away from the occasionally bland fish and head right toward rich and cheesy dishes such the citrus chicken quesadilla or turkey tostada. Don't miss the dense but fluffy Mexican chocolate cream pie.

In Mandalay Bay, 3950 Las Vegas Blvd. S. www.bordergrill.com. (℃ **702/632-7403.** Main courses $16–$26 lunch, $19–$36 dinner. AE, DC, DISC, MC, V. Daily 11:30am–10pm.

Emeril's New Orleans Fish House ★ CREOLE/SEAFOOD Celeb chefs don't get any more "celeb" than Emeril Lagasse—if there's a cooking show, he's probably been on it—and that's probably what will lure you to this Vegas version of his justifiably famed New Orleans restaurant. The bad news is it isn't as good as the original; the good news is that if you've never eaten at the original, you will probably be satisfied with your choice. Despite the name, it's the nonfish items we were most impressed with, including a Creole-spiced rib-eye that was as good as any we have eaten at a steakhouse. The Crescent City favorites, including barbecue shrimp and shrimp étouffée with andouille pork sausage, are zesty delights and desserts like Emeril's trademark banana cream pie with chocolate and caramel are worth saving room for. Still, after you've eaten here, maybe you should book your next vacation to New Orleans so you can taste what Emeril can really do.

In MGM Grand, 3799 Las Vegas Blvd. S. www.emerils.com. (℃ **702/891-7374.** Reservations recommended. Main courses $16–$40 lunch, $16–$41 dinner (more for lobster). AE, DC, DISC, MC, V. Daily 11:30am–2:30pm and 5–10pm.

Fleur by Hubert Keller ★★★ CONTINENTAL A reboot of Hubert Keller's divine Fleur de Lys, Fleur focuses on a continental selection of small plates, served in more casual surroundings than its predecessor. Choose a seat on the (indoor) patio, a comfy leather club chair, or a traditional table to enjoy selections like a miniature croque-monsieur, dripping with cheese and loaded with finely smoked ham; or a small slice of tender skirt steak served with a fingerling potato and chimichurri. The construction is divine and the ingredients are noteworthy for their freshness. The good news/bad news of small plates is you get to sample more but you also have more opportunity for some bum notes, of which we had one or two (the pork schnitzel was a little tough), but it's strictly by comparison to the rest of the fabulous flavors. And even though individually the small plates have small prices, you can also run up a hefty bill by ordering multiple options—and that's even if you don't get the $5,000 Wagyu beef hamburger (it comes with a bottle of 1995 Chateau Petrus).

In Mandalay Bay, 3950 Las Vegas Blvd. S. www.hubertkeller.com. (℃ **702/632-9400.** Reservations recommended. Small plates $9–$22; full plates $24–$95. AE, DC, DISC, MC, V. Daily 11am–3pm and 5–11pm.

Julian Serrano ★★ SPANISH Serrano is most famous in Vegas for his Picasso restaurant at Bellagio, a place that paved the way for all of the ultraexclusive, large-check restaurants that came after it. His eponymously named restaurant at Aria Las Vegas is much more accessible, both from a menu and price perspective. Tapas are the main draw here, allowing you to load up on small plates of often exquisite dishes, many with a Spanish flair to them. The chorizo was surprisingly mild but still playfully flavorful, and the lobster with a molecular pineapple gelatin will convert even non–seafood fans. Check out the "new" tapas section with funky combos such as ahi tuna with avocado and mango, and fried potatoes, eggs, and chorizo (breakfast on a stick!). If the small selections aren't doing it for you, go big with one of the signature paellas. The Valenciana has chicken and rabbit in a not-too-spicy Spanish rice, large enough to feed at least two people. The food, service, and ambience are all superb, although it is worth noting that the bill can add up quickly if you go too crazy with tapas sampling.

In Aria Las Vegas, 3730 Las Vegas Blvd. S. www.arialasvegas.com. © **877/230-2742.** Reservations recommended. Main courses $24–$45; tapas $8–$25. AE, DC, DISC, MC, V. Sun–Thurs 11:30am–11pm; Fri–Sat 11:30am–11:30pm.

Sirio Ristorante ★★ ITALIAN   From the same family that brought us Le Cirque and Circo, Sirio serves decidedly upscale Italian fare with a heavy Tuscan influence, meaning simple concepts and ingredients often thrown together in revelatory ways. Start with a build-your-own antipasti platter, and if you don't get the smoked rosemary ham as one of your choices, you only have yourself to blame. Hand-rolled spaghetti in a three-meat ragu is heavenly, as is the pan-roasted tenderloin in garlic and Gorgonzola. Designer pizzas, salads, more pasta, seafood, and traditional favorites with words like *scallopini* and *Alfredo* in their title round out a very complete menu. Oh, and do not ignore the desserts. There are simply too many wonders to choose just one, but if you must, go for the trio of tiramisu (traditional, strawberry, and caramel).

In Aria Las Vegas, 3730 Las Vegas Blvd. S. www.arialasvegas.com. © **877/230-2742.** Reservations recommended. Main courses $17–$49. AE, DC, DISC, MC, V. Daily 5–10:30pm.

Moderate

Blossom ★★ CHINESE   Chef Chi Kwun Choi is not a household name like Emeril or Wolfgang, but his resume reads like a master class in the art of Chinese cuisine. He worked at some of the most prestigious restaurants in Hong Kong and, since coming to Vegas, has cooked at notable eateries like Pearl and Fin. His cuisine incorporates classic Chinese flavors into modern interpretations of the dishes. We know you're hungry, but do not skip the appetizer section with its deliciously doughy pot stickers or the interesting version of egg rolls with finely chopped vegetables instead of the shredded, indefinable goo you find in lesser restaurants. Then you can move on to the extensive main menu for meat (everything from Peking duck to lamb chops, but a big thumbs up for the pan-fried shredded beef tenderloin), hot pot, noodle, rice, and veggie dishes. Or you can forget all that and go directly for the two pages' worth of seafood options, unbelievably fresh considering the fact that the restaurant is in the middle of a desert. Prices may be shocking to people who are used to takeout, but they have to pay for that Zen gorgeous dining room somehow.

In Aria Las Vegas, 3730 Las Vegas Blvd. S. www.arialasvegas.com. © **877/230-2742.** Reservations recommended. Main courses $14–$30. AE, DC, DISC, MC, V. Daily 5:30–10:30pm.

Burger Bar ★ DINER   The burgers-done-your-way experience starts with Ridgefield Farm (most recommended) and Black Angus beef, and all the toppings (the usuals, such as bacon and avocado, but also six kinds of cheese, prosciutto, chopped scallions, and even anchovies and lobster, for Pete's sake), plus a choice of bun. It adds up to a hilarious and, if you have a deft touch, delicious experience—albeit an expensive one considering you are really just having a hamburger. Shakes are creamy, fries aren't bad (we like the skinny ones better than the fat ones), though if you haven't before, try the sweet-potato fries. One of the most clever desserts in town lurks on this menu, a "sweet burger"—a slab of really fine chocolate pâté "burger" on a warm donut "bun," topped with cunningly crafted strawberry "tomato" slices, mint "lettuce," and translucent passionfruit "cheese." Skip the highfalutin' burger options—Kobe beef is too soft to use as burger meat, while foie gras is just wasted in this context. In other words, don't show off, but do have fun.

In Mandalay Place, 3930 Las Vegas Blvd. S. www.burger-bar.com. ℂ **702/632-9364.** Main courses $8–$60 (burgers start at $8.50, depending on kind of meat; toppings start at 45¢ and go way up). AE, DISC, MC, V. Sun–Thurs 11am–11pm; Fri–Sat 11am–1am.

Diablo's Cantina ★★ MEXICAN   Located right on the Strip with some fun people-watching views, Diablo's is a dark pueblo of a space serving up traditional Mexican fare at prices that will remind you that eating in Vegas doesn't need to be a bank-draining occasion. The menu, while not as mind-bogglingly expansive as similar restaurants, certainly covers all the basics, with burritos, tacos, quesadillas, enchiladas, and fajitas, plus some sandwiches, burgers, and salads thrown in for those who need a little less spice in their life. Standouts include the Club Quesadilla, three layers of steak, pulled pork, and guacamole; and the tender steak fajitas, served sizzling—the way God intended them to be.

In Monte Carlo, 3770 Las Vegas Blvd. S. www.montecarlo.com. ℂ **702/730-7979.** Main courses $13–$22. AE, MC, V. Daily 11am–10pm.

Dick's Last Resort ★★ AMERICAN   Boy food for the boisterous. This is not the place to go for a relaxing or dainty meal. The gimmick is customer abuse—yes, you pay for the privilege of having waitstaff hurl napkins and cheerful invective at you. But they mean it with love. Sounds a bit strange, but it works, in a party-hearty way. Speaking of, the food itself is hearty indeed, with house specialties (barbecue ribs, honey-glazed chicken) arriving in buckets. Entrees are substantial, both in quantity and construction—look for chickenfried steak, fried chicken, and meats or pastas covered in cream sauces. The most successful item could well be their burger, a juicy mammoth. Probably best for rowdy teenagers or stag parties, but both attitude and grub might be a relief after all those houses of reverent culinary worship.

In Excalibur, 3850 Las Vegas Blvd. S. www.dickslastresort.com. ℂ **702/597-7991.** Main courses $13–$26. AE, MC, V. Daily 11am–late.

Grand Wok ★★ 🍴 ASIAN   This place is no longer thoroughly Pan-Asian but is still a solid choice for sushi and, more importantly, budget fare in the form of the combo soup full of noodles and different kinds of meat. It's particularly nice and more affordable than the usual hotel restaurant—and the primarily Asian clientele clearly agrees. Note that soup portions are most generous; four people could easily split one order and have a nice and very inexpensive lunch, an unexpected bargain option for the Strip.

In MGM Grand, 3799 Las Vegas Blvd. S. www.mgmgrand.com. ℂ **702/891-7777.** Main courses $13–$42; sushi rolls and pieces $7–$30. AE, DC, DISC, MC, V. Sun–Thurs 11am–10pm; Fri–Sat 11am–1am.

Hussong's Cantina ★ MEXICAN   It is based on the legendary Ensenada bar, in business since 1892, which claims to have been the site where the margarita was invented (a bartender reportedly concocted the mixture in 1941 for

YOU GOTTA HAVE A theme

It shouldn't be too surprising to learn that a town devoted to gimmicks has just about every gimmick restaurant there is. No matter your interest, there is probably a theme restaurant here for you, from sports to pop culture and back again. Fans should have a good time checking out the stuff on the walls, but for the most part the memorabilia is usually more interesting than the food. Here are some of the best of the bunch.

The House of Blues ★ ★, in Mandalay Bay, 3950 Las Vegas Blvd. S. (www.hob.com; ℂ **702/632-7607;** Sun–Thurs 8am–11pm, Fri–Sat 7am–midnight), has a Mississippi Delta blues theme complete with frequent concerts and a gospel brunch. The food is down-home Southern and there is lots of it for pretty decent prices.

Southern staples are also on tap at the **Harley-Davidson Café** ★, 3725 Las Vegas Blvd. S., at Harmon Avenue (www.harley-davidsoncafe.com; ℂ **702/740-4555;** Sun–Thurs 11am–midnight, Fri–Sat 11am–2am), alongside shrines to the easy-rider lifestyle evoked by the motorcycle brand.

And as long as we're on a Southern-fried kick, check out the fine barbecue offerings at **BB King's Blues Club** ★ in The Mirage, 3400 Las Vegas Blvd. S.

(www.bbkingclubs.com; ℂ **702/242-5464;** daily 7am–11pm), served in a roadhouse setting with frequent live blues music as accompaniment. BB even plays there occasionally.

The Hard Rock Cafe ★, 3771 Las Vegas Blvd. S. (www.hardrock.com; ℂ **702/733-7625;** Sun–Thurs 11am–midnight, Fri–Sat 11am–1am), has decent burgers and all of the requisite music memorabilia you have come to expect packed in a massive, 42,000-square-foot, three-level behemoth with a gigantic gift shop, a 1,000-seat concert venue, and more. **Note:** There is a second Hard Rock Cafe at the Hard Rock Hotel, 4475 Paradise Rd., at Harmon Avenue (ℂ **702/733-8400**).

Parrot Heads, as fans of Jimmy Buffet refer to themselves, like to party it up at **Margaritaville** ★, at the Flamingo,

either the daughter of a Mexican ambassador or Rita Hayworth, depending on who you ask—there was alcohol involved so the history is understandably fuzzy). Hussong's boldly proclaims to have "the Best Tacos in Town." Okay. Gauntlet thrown. You can build your own combo platter of three starting with steak, *carnitas*, chicken, lobster, or goat (no, really) and then add from over a dozen different toppings (cheeses, pico de gallo, onions, guacamole, and more) on a soft corn tortilla. We haven't sampled *every* taco in town but we can say without a doubt that these are worthy contenders for the "Best" title. The steak was the winner of the three, all smoky charbroiled goodness, but my-oh-my the *carnitas* (shredded, spiced pork) were pretty darned good, too. Other options include burritos the size of a spare tire with a perfectly flaky crust, enchiladas, quesadillas, and all the other usual Mexican suspects. The margaritas are good, but perhaps floating a bit too much on their "we invented it!" reputation. You can get better just down the hall at Tacos & Tequila (p. 108). The only disappointment was the too-short and too-traditional dessert menu. Fried ice cream? Yawn.

At Mandalay Place, 3930 Las Vegas Blvd. S., no. 121B. www.hussongslasvegas.com. ℂ **702/553-0123.** Main courses $12–$22. AE, DISC, MC, V. Daily 11am–11pm.

3555 Las Vegas Blvd. S. (www.margarita villelasvegas.com; ☎ **702/733-3302;** Sun–Thurs 8am–2am, Fri–Sat 8am–3am), the singer's tropical-themed cafe/bar/ club. The menu runs a range from Mexican to something sort of Caribbean themed to basic American, and it's not all that bad, considering. Partaking in lots of fruity tropical drinks doesn't hurt, either.

If the rodeo is more your style, the Pro Bull Riding organization has its own place at the **PBR Rock Bar & Grill** ★ at Planet Hollywood, 3663 Las Vegas Blvd. S. (www.pbrrockbar.com; ☎ **702/750-1685;** daily 8am–late). It serves up down-home American food in a country-western environment complete with a mechanical bull and tire swings above the tables.

The Sporting House, at New York–New York, 3790 Las Vegas Blvd. S. (www.sportinghouselv.com; ☎ **702/740-6766;** Mon–Thurs 4pm–midnight, Fri–Sat 11:30am–1am; Sun 11:30am–

midnight), took over the space once occupied by the ESPN Zone and pretty much changed nothing. There are lots of TVs, a big bar, a game arcade, and a big menu of American comfort food.

You would think the celebrity shrine and memorabilia factory that is the **Planet Hollywood** restaurant would be in the Planet Hollywood Resort. But you'd be wrong. Instead, it's at Caesars Palace in The Forum Shops, 3500 Las Vegas Blvd. S. (www.planethollywood. com; ☎ **702/791-7827;** Sun–Thurs 9am–11pm, Fri–Sat 9am–midnight).

Lastly, if all of this mass consumption has got you a bit down, try the eco-themed **Rainforest Café** in the MGM Grand, 3799 Las Vegas Blvd. S. (www. rainforestcafe.com; ☎ **702/891-8580;** Sun–Thurs 8am–11pm, Fri–Sat 8am–midnight). Not only do they have a full menu of interesting food items (barbecue to seafood), but the 10,000-gallon aquarium and earth-friendly decor create a festive environment. Great for kids!

The Pub at Monte Carlo ★ PUB FARE   The former Monte Carlo Pub and Brewery still looks almost exactly as it did before the name change. The good news is that's kind of okay because we liked the old place, and we like the new place, too. It's a two-story brew pub with a big bar serving more than 200 beers on tap (including their own in-house labels), lots of TVs showing the latest games, an entertainment area with a stage and dance floor, and a restaurant, of course. It's mainly pub-grub food—lots of sandwiches and some really fantastic burgers (try the build-your-own section where you can create dozens of different combinations), salads, and a few American entrees. There's nothing unexpected, but it's all surprisingly flavorful and well prepared for a very moderate price. Note that frequent live entertainment and DJs can make this a fun but noisy spot at night.

In Monte Carlo, 3770 Las Vegas Blvd. S. www.montecarlo.com. ☎ **702/730-7420.** Main courses $11–$23. AE, DC, DISC, MC, V. Sun–Thurs 11am–11pm; Fri–Sat 11am–3am.

Rí Rá Irish Pub ★★ IRISH   Is it too much of a cliché to say that the one dish you should not pass up at an Irish pub is the potato-cake appetizer? Perhaps, but one bite of the pan-seared, delicately seasoned dish covered in Irish sour cream and drizzled with balsamic oil and you will not care a whit about stereotypes. But don't stop there. Traditional favorites include fish and chips, shepherd's pie, bangers and mash, and corned beef and cabbage, although you could also play it safe with a variety of burgers, sandwiches, and salads, many of which have *Erin go bragh* twists like Irish bacon or Guinness barbecue sauce. Be sure to ask for a tour of the restaurant from your server (many of whom are as authentically Irish as the food) to see the restored pub once run by the owner's aunt, the tile floors from the shipyard office of the company that built the Titanic, and the massive 500-pound statue of St. Patrick found in an Irish farmer's field.

At Mandalay Place, 3930 Las Vegas Blvd. S. www.rira.com. ✆ **702/632-7771.** Main courses $12–$26. AE, DC, DISC, MC, V. Sun–Thurs 10am–3am; Fri–Sat 10am–4am.

Tacos & Tequila ★★ MEXICAN   If you can get past the trendy trappings (bold colors, metal sculptures, a DJ!), the food and the drinks at this Mexican restaurant overlooking the Luxor lobby are about as good as you'll find anywhere in town—provided you like Mexican food, that is. Although there are more than a dozen varieties of tacos (Kobe beef, lobster, beer-battered tilapia, and more) and more than 100 different tequilas, the menu goes beyond their namesake to include tostadas, enchiladas, burritos, quesadillas, seafood, soups, and salads, all done with an organic freshness that sets the dishes apart from the chain restaurants you're

quick BITES

Food courts are a dime a dozen in Vegas, but the one in **New York–New York,** 3790 Las Vegas Blvd. S. (✆ **702/740-6969**), deserves a mention for two reasons. First, it's the nicest setting for this sort of thing on the Strip, sitting in the Greenwich Village section of New York–New York, which means scaled replica tenement buildings, steam rising from the manhole covers, and more than a little (faux, naturally) greenery, a nice change from unrelentingly shrill and plastic mall decor. Second, the selections are the usual, but it's a better-than-average food court, with Chinese food and pizza (as befitting an ode to NYC), and excellent if expensive (for this situation) double-decker burgers, plus **Ben & Jerry's** ice cream.

The **Monte Carlo,** 3770 Las Vegas Blvd. S., between Flamingo Road and Tropicana Avenue (✆ **702/730-7777**), has traditional offerings like **McDonald's** and **Subway,** but the main reason you should know about it is the branch of our beloved **The Cupcakery** (p. 144) located just down the hall. That's a reason to go all by itself. The food court is open daily from 6am to 3am.

The food court at **Flamingo Las Vegas,** 3555 Las Vegas Blvd. S. (✆ **702/733-3111**), has a couple of interesting outlets like **Pan Asian Express** and

Johnny Rockets hamburgers, among others. Hours vary, but it's usually open from 8am until 2am.

And if you head farther down the Strip, to **The Grande Canal Shoppes** at The Venetian, 3355 Las Vegas Blvd. S. (✆ **702/414-4500**), you can find another decent food court, with a **Panda Express,** a good pizza place (despite the confusing name of **LA Italian Kitchen**), and more. Plus, it's right by the canals of this faux Venice, one of our favorite places in Vegas.

We've already alluded to the rock-bottom budget meals and graveyard specials available at casino hotel restaurants, quality not assured and Pepto-Bismol not provided. As prices and deals can change without notice, we don't want to list examples, but finding a full prime-rib dinner for around $5 is not rare (pun definitely intended).

Your best bet is to keep your eyes open as you travel through town, as hotels tend to advertise their specials on their marquees. Or you can go to www.vegas.com and click on **"Dining"** and then **"Dining Bargains,"** though the tips and prices may be somewhat out-of-date. Following are three examples of current options for late-night munchies: **Ellis Island** offers a $9.99 10-ounce steak (plus potato and other sides), and $7.99 gets you a porterhouse steak at **Arizona Charlie's Boulder.** At the Hard Rock Hotel, **Mr. Lucky's 24/7** is a particularly good diner, with particularly good people-watching. And then ask your server about the $7.77 steak, three barbecued shrimp, and sides; it's not on the menu, so you have to know about it.

probably used to. A Sunday-only Mariachi Brunch adds a variety of breakfast items to the offerings, including *huevos con tocino* or *chorizo*, burritos, and huevos rancheros. As good as the food is, you would be doing yourself a disservice if you don't try the margaritas, all made with hand-squeezed lime juice, organic agave nectar, and your choice of tequilas and flavors. We know people who are very picky about their margaritas and have declared these the best they have ever tasted. Prices are high for a Mexican joint but relatively affordable for a Strip restaurant.

In Luxor, 3900 Las Vegas Blvd. S. www.tacosandtequilalv.com. ✆ **702/262-5225.** Reservations suggested for dinner. Main courses $10–$24. AE, MC, V. Daily 11am–11pm.

Todd English P.U.B. ★★★ PUB FARE   English's Olives restaurant (p. 117) up the street at Bellagio is one of our favorites, so we had high hopes for his new pub concept at CityCenter. Hopes met and exceeded. A huge beer and wine list is enticing, as are the sun-dappled interiors with lots of TVs on which to catch your favorite game, but it is the menu that really seals the proverbial deal here. Want a sandwich? Make your own from the Carvery, with your choice of meat (prime beef, roasted chicken, turkey, duck, salmon, and pastrami for starters), bread, and condiments. Be sure to accompany that with the spectacular prime rib chili, slathered in cheese and moderate on the spicy scale. Burgers, salads, bangers and mash, fish and chips, potpies, and a host of other sandwiches round out the menu. Best of all are the moderate prices. Forget the lunch buffets and come here instead.

In Crystals at CityCenter, 3720 Las Vegas Blvd. S. www.toddenglishpub.com. ✆ **702/489-8080.** Reservations recommended. Main courses $13–$24. AE, DC, DISC, MC, V. Sun–Thurs 11am–11pm; Fri–Sat 11am–midnight.

Inexpensive

Lynyrd Skynyrd Beer & BBQ ★ BARBECUE   We freely admit to being barbecue snobs, but the fact that the 'que here didn't live up to our insanely high standards doesn't mean that it isn't darned good and among the best you're going to find on the Las Vegas Strip. Offerings are done old school with a pit card that you take to a serving line for your selections. You can do premade sandwiches, but the better approach is to just get the meat (the ham, sausage, and brisket are all worthy of your attention) and a few slices of classic white bread that go along with it. The classic Southern rock band most famous for their songs "Free Bird" and "Sweet Home Alabama" gives the place its name and theme, done up like a well-lit roadhouse with Skynyrd memorabilia. A big stage helps turn the place into a rocking joint late at night.

In Excalibur, 3850 Las Vegas Blvd. S. www.lynyrdskynyrdlv.com. ✆ **702/597-7818.** Main courses $5–$15. AE, DISC, MC, V. Mon–Fri 11am–midnight; Sat–Sun 9am–midnight.

MID-STRIP

Very Expensive

B&B Ristorante ★★ ITALIAN   Long-time Food Network staple Mario Batali has a couple of Vegas outposts, and this is perhaps the most notable. It looks like an über-Italian trattoria, full of dark wood, quite inviting, and unfortunately very loud. Naturally, the desirable room is in the wine cellar. The menu options are a little too casual for the price, and might be intimidating for those uninitiated in Batali, but there's probably no one in Vegas doing such interesting Italian food. To that end, you might be best served sticking with the *primi* (pasta selections), which are cheaper and arguably more interesting than the *secondi,* though portions are not hearty. Don't miss the beef-cheek ravioli with duck liver, but other notables are the Mint Love Letters with lamb sausage, and the stinging nettle *pappardelle* with wild-boar ragu. Or you could go crazy with the $120 pasta tasting menu. Meanwhile, if you are lucky, Chef himself might be roaming the place in his famous clogs.

In The Venetian, 3355 Las Vegas Blvd. S. www.bandbristorante.com. ✆ **702/266-9977.** Main courses $25–$55. AE, DISC, MC, V. Daily 5–11pm.

Circo ★★ ITALIAN   Yes, this is the less expensive offering from the same family that brings you Le Cirque, but going to one does not excuse you from going to the other. (By the way, "less expensive" is a relative term.) Le Cirque's gourmet French haute cuisine does not prepare you for what to expect from Circo, or, for that matter, vice versa. Ignore the bright primary-color scheme, meant to evoke the circus but instead sadly recalling outdated hotel buffets (albeit with expensive wood grain), in favor of watching the dancing fountains outside. And then order the *mista di campo,* a lovely little salad, both visually and in terms of taste; it's a creative construction of vegetables bound with cucumber and topped with a fab balsamic vinaigrette. Follow that with a perfect tagliatelle with rock shrimp—it comes loaded with various crustacean bits in a light sauce. Note that appetizer portions of pastas are plenty filling and cheaper than full-size servings. Entrees usually include more elaborate dishes, such as breast of Muscovy duck with dried organic fruit in port-wine sauce. Save room for desserts such as *panna cotta* (Italian cream–filled doughnuts) or *tutto cioccolato,* consisting of chocolate mousse, ice cream, and crumb cake.

In Bellagio, 3600 Las Vegas Blvd. S. www.bellagio.com. ✆ **702/693-7223.** Reservations recommended. Main courses $23–$85. AE, DC, DISC, MC, V. Daily 5:30–10:30pm (last seating 10pm).

Delmonico Steakhouse ★★ CREOLE/STEAK   You might well feel that Emeril Lagasse is omnipresent. This incarnation is a steakhouse version of his

Mid-Strip Restaurants

0   0.25 mi
0   0.25 km

- Las Vegas Monorail
- Free monorail
- Pedestrian bridge

Spring Mountain Rd.

Sands Ave.

1 Treasure Island
2 The Palazzo
The Venetian
3
Mirage **4**
Casino Royale
5 Harrah's
Harrah's/ Imperial Palace
6 Forum Shops
7 Imperial Palace
(THE STRIP)
Caesars Palace **8**
Flamingo **9**
Flamingo/ Caesars Palace
Bill's Gamblin' Hall & Saloon
Flamingo Rd.
Bally's
Frank Sinatra Dr.
15
Flamingo Rd.
LAS VEGAS BLVD.
Paris **11**
Bellagio **10**
The Cosmopolitan of Las Vegas **13**
Planet Hollywood **12**
Dean Martin Dr.
Frank Sinatra Dr.
Harmon Ave.
CityCenter
Harmon Ave.

RESTAURANTS
B&B Ristorante **3**
BB King's Blues Club **4**
Bouchon **3**
Cabo Wabo Cantina **12**
Canter's Deli **1**
Carnegie Deli **4**
Central Michel Richard **8**
China Pobano **13**
Circo **10**
Comme Ça **13**
Cypress Street Marketplace **8**
Delmonico Steakhouse **3**
Earl of Sandwich **12**
Estiatorio Milos **13**
FIRST Food and Bar **2**
Flamingo Food Court **9**
Gilley's **1**
Grand Canal Shoppes Food Court **3**
Hash House a Go Go **7**
Holstein's Shakes & Buns **13**
Jean Philippe Patisserie **10**
KGB: Kerry's Gourmet Burgers **5**
Lagasse's Stadium **2**
Le Cirque **10**
Margaritaville **9**
Max Brenner Chocolate Restaurant **8**
Mesa Grill **8**

Michael Mina **10**
Mon Ami Gabi **11**
munchbar **8**
Old Homestead Steakhouse **8**
Olives **10**
The Palm **6**
Payard Patisserie & Bistro **3**
PBR Rock Bar & Grill **12**
Picasso **10**
Pink's **3**
Pinot Brasserie **3**
PJ Clarke's **6**
Planet Hollywood **6**
Public House **2**
Rao's **8**
Sensi **10**
Serendipity 3 **8**
Spago **8**
Strip House **12**
Sugar Factory **11**
Table 10 **2**

BUFFETS
Bellagio Buffet **10**
The Buffet at TI **1**
Flamingo Paradise Garden Buffet **9**
Flavors at Harrah's **5**
Le Village Buffet **11**
Mirage Cravings Buffet **4**
Spice Market Buffet **12**
Wicked Spoon Buffet **13**

hard-core classic Creole restaurant; this ever-so-slight twist is just enough to make it a superior choice over the more disappointing New Orleans locale. You can't go wrong with most appetizers, especially the superbly rich smoked mushrooms with homemade tasso ham over pasta—it's enough for a meal in and of itself. The same advice holds for any of the specials or the gumbo, particularly if it's the hearty, near-homemade country selection. If you want to experiment, definitely do it with the appetizers; you're better off steering clear of complex entrees, no matter how intriguing they sound; the deceptively simple choices are more successful. The bone-in rib-eye steak is rightly recommended (skip the gummy béarnaise sauce in favor of the fabulous homemade Worcestershire or A.O.K. sauce). The tableside-made Caesar was dubbed "transcendental" by one astute diner. Sides are hit or miss—the creamed spinach was too salty, but a sweet-potato purée (a special, but maybe they'll serve you a side if you ask sweetly) is most definitely a winner. Too full for dessert? No, you aren't. Have the Emeril's trademark banana cream pie or the lemon icebox pie, a chunk of curd that blasts tart lemon through your mouth.

In The Venetian, 3355 Las Vegas Blvd. S. www.emerils.com. ✆ **702/414-3737.** Reservations strongly recommended for dinner. Main courses $36–$52. AE, DC, DISC, MC, V. Daily 11:30am–2pm; Sun–Thurs 5–10pm; Fri–Sat 5–10:30pm.

carbon **COPY CUISINE**

There are many restaurants in Las Vegas that you can only find here, but one of the ways that the city has built its reputation for top-notch cuisine is by importing popular dining establishments from other places. By and large, meals at these restaurants are fine-dining experiences, but too often whatever secret sauce made them special in their original locations is lost in the translation. Don't get us wrong—you will most likely have a fine meal at any of the following restaurants, but we think there are others that do what they do better.

Beso, in Crystals at CityCenter, 3720 Las Vegas Blvd. S. (www.besolasvegas.com; **℃ 702/254-2376;** Sun–Thurs 5–10pm; Fri–Sat 5–11pm), is based on the L.A. restaurant of the same name from former *Desperate Housewives* star Eva Longoria and celebrity chef Todd English. It's a Spanish steakhouse heavy on the seafood and cuts of beef, many of which have a spicy kick to them, and a few Latin specialties like their *taqueria* (taco) tasting. The steaks are not quite as adventurous unless you go nuts with the sauces (tequila peppercorn, anyone?), which you probably should.

Le Cirque, in Bellagio, 3600 Las Vegas Blvd. S. (www.bellagio.com; **℃ 702/693-7223;** Tues–Sun 5:30–10pm), has been wowing New York diners for nearly 4 decades with its upscale French cuisine. Too bad the one here in Vegas isn't as wow-worthy. It's not that the food is bad—quite the contrary—but it's not the very best in town, and it is among the most expensive. We think there are better French meals to be had here.

We were a little disappointed in the seafood at **Michael Mina,** in Bellagio, 3600 Las Vegas Blvd. S. (www.michael mina.net; **℃ 702/693-7223;** Thurs–Tues 5:30–10pm), which is puzzling because the San Francisco original gets rave reviews and lots of stars from those other guides.

You can't swing a feathered headdress without hitting a steakhouse in this town, which is why the Las Vegas branch

Estiatorio Milos ★★★ GREEK/SEAFOOD   As the waitstaff gives you a tour of the open fish market–style stands with dozens of fresh catches on ice, note the fact that it doesn't reek like a fish market. That should tell you how fresh the selections are—stunning if for no other reason than many of the options are regional specialties that you won't find too often outside the Mediterranean, such as fangri or skaros. Don't know what those are? That's okay; the server will describe them to you and give you a comparison that will help you understand. Selections are prepared whole, lightly dressed in olive oil and lemon juice, and not placed directly on the grill; instead the fish are sort of suspended above it so as not to lose any of their flavor before being deboned and served. Seafood that tastes like this could convert people who say they don't like seafood. It's all bursting with freshness and is the first time we have ever been able to say "it doesn't taste fishy" with a straight face. Nonseafood eaters have a few choices, including lamb chops and a few choice Black Angus steaks that are dry aged and prepared with as much care as the seafood selections. As good as all the main courses are, we would be remiss if we didn't tell you to begin your meal with the Milos Special, a stack of thinly sliced zucchini and eggplant, gently fried and served with *manaki* cheese and homemade yogurt dip. The quality and attention to detail of the venerable New York eatery **The Palm,** in The Forum Shops at Caesars Palace, 3570 Las Vegas Blvd. S. (www.thepalm.com; ℂ **702/732-7256;** daily 11:30am–11pm), is probably not as noteworthy as the original. Red-meat lovers will probably still be happy with the high-quality cuts of beef, but with so many better choices, why settle for anything less than the best?

At this point in the game, **Spago,** in Caesars Palace, 3570 Las Vegas Blvd. S. (www.wolfgangpuck.com; ℂ **702/369-6300;** dining room daily 5:30–10pm; cafe Sun–Thurs 11:30am–11pm, Fri–Sat 11:30am–midnight), represents both the best and the worst of the celebrity chef phenomenon. If you eat at Wolfgang Puck's Beverly Hills location, you might well have the very best meal of your life, but the expensive California/Asian cuisine here is simply not our first, nor even our second, choice for ways for you to spend your hard-won jackpot money.

Rao's, in Caesars Palace, 3570 Las Vegas Blvd. S. (www.raos.com; ℂ **877/346-4642;** daily 5–midnight), is a meticulous re-creation of the famous 110-year-old East Harlem restaurant, which is notorious in equal measure for "Uncle Vincent's lemon chicken" and the near impossibility of getting a seat; however, because this isn't revelatory Italian cooking, you may justly wonder what all the fuss is about.

Finally, **Gordon Ramsay,** the guy that does all the yelling on TV, will have opened his first Las Vegas restaurant at Paris Las Vegas by the time you read this. Although it hadn't bowed by the time we went to press, it is not expected to be exactly a carbon copy of his other establishments around the world, but it is going to be a steakhouse so we're not exactly bowled over by the originality of the idea. Still, we have high hopes if for no other reason than we like to watch chefs cry. Check out www.parislasvegas.com for information.

here is almost astounding. The honey they drizzle on top of their yogurt? It comes from real Greek bees who feed on only wild thyme flowers. It's classic Greek and will have you longing for a vacation to a seaside cafe in Santorini.

In The Cosmopolitan of Las Vegas, 3708 Las Vegas Blvd. S. www.milos.ca. ℂ **702/698-7930.** Reservations required. Main courses $28–$65. AE, DC, DISC, MC, V. Daily noon–2:30pm and 5:30pm–midnight.

Mesa Grill ★★ SOUTHWESTERN   Food Network darling Bobby Flay has his fans and his detractors, and we aren't going to mediate that argument here, especially since the man isn't cooking in the kitchen any more often than most celebrity chefs in this town. More significantly, regardless of where you fall in the debate, this is a worthy restaurant, if, like so much in Vegas, a bit overpriced. Just about every well-spiced entree is over $30, and sometimes well over. Still, there is so much that is fun here: blue-corn pancakes with barbecue duck, or the chicken quesadilla (made in a special dedicated oven) that comes with garlic crème fraîche. Presentation is over the top—yes, this is playful food, we get it, now stop it—but those who are a bit on the wimpy side when it comes to spices will appreciate how each entree comes with its own cooling element (the aforementioned crème fraîche, for example). Desserts are equally frivolous, though not particularly theme intensive (unless you consider deep-dish banana cream pie "Southwestern"). Those wishing to try it without breaking the bank should either come at lunch or consider splitting appetizers as a light meal.

In Caesars Palace, 3570 Las Vegas Blvd. S. www.mesagrill.com. ✆ **877/346-4642.** Main courses $15–$24 brunch and lunch, $25–$48 dinner. Mon–Fri 11am–2:30pm and 5–11pm; Sat–Sun 10:30am–3pm and 5–11pm.

Old Homestead Steakhouse ★★★ STEAK   The original version of this classic American steakhouse debuted in New York City in 1868 and claims to have invented the doggy bag. This should tell you a lot about how good the food is (you don't stay in business for more than 150 years without doing something right) and how big the portions are. The menu is mostly steakhouse classic, with beef and seafood leading the charge, but there are a few twists thrown in just to keep things interesting. Don't miss the Kobe beef meatball appetizer, which is roughly the size of your head and drowning in a tangy tomato sauce. And if you never listen to anything we say, listen to this: The potato gnocchi, served in an insanely rich truffle-butter-cream sauce, will make the trip worth it all on its own. The steaks themselves are massive (we're talking pounds of meat here), and although you can get sauces and toppings to spice them up, they really don't need it. Whether Old Homestead can make it 150 years in Vegas is yet to be seen, but with food this good, they deserve to.

In Caesars Palace, 3570 Las Vegas Blvd. S. www.theoldhomesteadsteakhouse.com. ✆ **877/346-4642.** Reservations required. Main courses $40–$110. Sun–Thurs 5–10:30pm; Fri–Sat 5–11pm.

Picasso ★★★ FRENCH   A Spanish chef who cooks French cuisine in an Italian-themed hotel in Vegas? Trust us, it works. This is one of the best restaurants in Vegas, and given serious competition for such a title, that says a lot. This is an extraordinary dining experience that includes the thrill of having millions of dollars worth of Picassos gaze down over your shoulders while you eat. Serrano's cooking is a work of art that can proudly stand next to the masterpieces. The menu changes nightly and always offers a choice between a four- or five-course prix-fixe dinner or a tasting menu. The night we ate there, we were bowled over by roasted Maine lobster with a trio of corn—kernels, sauce, and a corn flan—that was like slightly solid sunshine. Hudson Valley foie gras was crusted in truffles and went down most smoothly. A filet of roasted sea bass came with a light saffron sauce and dots of cauliflower purée. And, finally, pray that they're serving the lamb rôti—it was an outstanding piece of lamb, perfectly done, tender, and crusted with truffles. Portions are dainty but so rich that you'll have plenty to eat without groaning and feeling heavy when you leave. Desserts are powerful yet prettily constructed. A molten chocolate cake leaves any other you may have tried in the dust and comes with ice cream made with imported European chocolate. A crisp banana tart with coconut ice cream is a fine nonchocolate (foolish you) choice, while a passion-fruit flan in a citrus-soup sauce is perfect if you don't have much room left. Everything is delivered by attentive staff that makes you feel pampered. Can we go back soon and try it all again?

In Bellagio, 3600 Las Vegas Blvd. S. www.bellagio.com. ✆ **866/259-7111.** Reservations recommended. Prix-fixe 4-course dinner $113; 5-course degustation $123. AE, DC, DISC, MC, V. Wed–Mon 6–9:30pm.

Strip House ★★ STEAK   What turns a pedestrian steakhouse visit, admittedly a dime-a-dozen experience in Vegas, into something truly special? Here it comes down to the two prime ingredients: the atmosphere and the steaks. The place is done in a cheeky bordello theme, with red-flocked walls adorned with black-and-white photos of peek-a-boo strippers from the bygone days when stripping seemed slightly naughty as opposed to today's raunchiness. These Bettie Page–like works of art are endlessly entertaining to look at, not for the titillation but for the kitsch factor. It is worth noting that while most of the photos are safe for young eyes, there are a few in the mix that are decidedly PG-13, so parents with children may want to scan the walls before sitting to make sure there are no uncomfortable questions during the appetizer course. Speaking of which, there are the traditional (shrimp cocktail, clams casino), but head directly for the warm garlic bread served in a bed of Gorgonzola fondue, cholesterol numbers be darned. Follow that up with any of the fine cuts of beef, all done in a black-pepper rub that might be overwhelming to some with the first few bites, but go with it and you'll be rewarded with one of the best and most flavorful steaks on the Strip.

In Planet Hollywood Resort & Casino, 3667 Las Vegas Blvd. S. www.striphouse.com. (*) **702/737-5200.** Reservations recommended. Main courses $29–$54. AE, DC, MC, V. Sun–Thurs 5–11pm; Fri–Sat 5–11:30pm.

Expensive

Bouchon ★★★ BISTRO   Thomas Keller made his name with his Napa Valley restaurant French Laundry, considered by many to be the best restaurant in the United States. Bouchon is a version of his Napa Valley bistro which is not nearly as lauded, so imagine our surprise when we discovered that humble though these dishes sound, in nearly every case they are gold-standard versions of classics. Someone is certainly keeping a close eye on this kitchen, and that someone has learned the lessons well. Ever wondered why people get worked up over raw oysters? The sweet and supremely fresh (kept in water until the moment they are served to you) Snow Creek oysters will enlighten you, as they seem to melt on contact with your tongue. Fifty dollars seems like a lot for pâté, but here a complex multiday preparation produces a buttery whip that is so rich, it's an appropriate—and highly recommended—appetizer for four. Don't miss the bacon-and–poached egg frisée salad, or the cleanly seared salmon over poached leeks, prepared to such perfection it doesn't need the accompanying sauce. Gnocchi is earthy and assertive, a peasant version of an Italian favorite, while beef Bourguignon is exactly as you expect it to be, in the divine perfection sense. This is a superlative Vegas restaurant, and while it may be hard to reconcile the prices with the apparent simplicity of the food, recall that it takes serious skill to make even the most humble of dishes correctly, as your palate will reassure you.

In The Venetian, 3355 Las Vegas Blvd. S. www.bouchonbistro.com. (*) **702/414-6200.** Reservations strongly recommended. Main courses $19–$45 dinner, $12–$34 brunch. AE, DC, DISC, MC, V. Mon–Fri 7am–3pm and 5–10pm; Sat–Sun 8am–2pm (brunch) and 5–10pm. Oyster bar daily 3–10pm.

China Poblano ★ CHINESE/MEXICAN   Mixing Chinese and Mexican cuisines may not seem like the most obvious choice. Chef José Andrés defends the

A SEAT AT THE table

Opportunities to sample cuisines from master chefs in interesting surroundings abound in Las Vegas, but if you want to expand your horizons beyond the four walls of the traditional restaurants, **Project Dinner Table** offers some of the most truly unique dining experiences in town. Some of the city's top culinary geniuses design lavish, multicourse meals that are served at one long, family-dining-style table in interesting locations to raise money for various local charities. Past events have included cuisine from Fluer's Hubert Keller, Central's Michel Richard, and Sensi's Roy Ellmar at once-in-a-lifetime spots like on the baseball diamond at Cashman Field, in the middle of an orchard, in the courtyard of the World Market Center, and in the park at the Town Square shopping center. Dinners are once a month from April to November and the $140 tickets include the meal, drinks, and entertainment with proceeds going to local charities. For more information, visit www.project dinnertable.com.

concept with a history lesson about Spanish galleons sailing the Asian seas and bringing spices and fruit to Mexico. Okay, but it still takes a moment to reconcile a menu that has dim sum and tacos on the same page. They don't actually mix the two cuisines—no sweet and sour burritos, darn it—but instead offer small plates that can be mixed, matched, and shared. The success or failure of the concept totally depends on what you order, and the more you stick to similarly sweet or savory or spicy, the better off you'll be. For instance, the Chinese barbecue pork steamed buns have a sticky sweet flavor that goes well with the pork belly with pineapple, but not so much with the spicy *carnitas*. Sadly, mixing two cuisines that aren't famous for their desserts doesn't help here, so skip the flan and the sticky mango rice and go get a cupcake instead.

In The Cosmopolitan of Las Vegas, 3708 Las Vegas Blvd. S. www.chinapoblano.com. (C) 702/698-7900. Reservations recommended at dinner. Small plates $5–$22. AE, DC, DISC, MC, V. Mon–Thurs 11:30am–11:30pm; Fri–Sun 10am–11:30pm.

Comme Ça ★★ FRENCH

Chef David Myers' resume reads like a culinary dream; he's worked for Charlie Trotter and Daniel Boulud and has been endorsed by *Wine Spectator* and Oprah. This version of his popular Los Angeles restaurant is his first venture in Sin City and he seems determined to give the other French bistros in town a run for their money. The space certainly deserves attention; it's a gorgeously bright room featuring floor-to-ceiling windows overlooking the Strip and a big outdoor dining patio pointed directly at the Eiffel Tower at Paris Las Vegas, just to put you in a Gallic mood. The menu is traditional French but in a safe Julia Child way (coq au vin, *côte de boef*, cassoulet, and so forth), so those usually intimidated by the cuisine can feel at ease. Kick things off with a selection of cheeses or meat from the charcuterie (think of it as a deli platter), and then be sure to ask about the soups and hope they have the sweet tomato and cream available. If not, the cheesy, gooey French onion is a good second choice. The beef Bourguignon is a fine main course choice, with tender braised beef, slow cooked and lightly seasoned; and the Wagyu steaks are worth their elevated cost (although we would've preferred a better side than fries and a bland garlic aioli).

In The Cosmopolitan of Las Vegas, 3708 Las Vegas Blvd. S. www.commecarestaurant.com. *©* **702/698-7910.** Reservations required. Main courses $20–$38. AE, DC, DISC, MC, V. Lunch/ brunch Fri–Sun noon–5pm; dinner Mon–Thurs 5:30–11pm, Fri–Sun 5–11pm.

Olives ★★ ITALIAN/MEDITERRANEAN   If there was an Olives in our neighborhood, we would eat there regularly. A branch of Todd English's original Boston-based restaurant, Olives is a strong choice for a light lunch that need not be as expensive as you might think. Here's how to enjoy a moderately priced meal here: Munch on the focaccia bread, olives, and excellent tapenade they give you at the start, have a lovely salad (maybe of bibb lettuce, Maytag blue cheese, and walnut dressing), and then split a flatbread—think pizza with an ultrathin crust (like a slightly limp cracker), topped with delicious combinations such as the highly recommended Moroccan-spiced lamb, eggplant purée, and feta cheese, or our other favorite, fig, prosciutto, and Gorgonzola. They are rich and wonderful—split one between two people, and you have an affordable and terrific lunch. Or try pasta; we were steered toward the simple but marvelous spaghettini with roasted tomatoes, garlic, and Parmesan, and were happy with it. The constructed, but not too fussy, food gets more complicated and costly at night, adding an array of meats and chickens, plus pastas such as butternut squash with brown butter and sage.

In Bellagio, 3600 Las Vegas Blvd. S. www.bellagio.com. *©* **866/259-7111.** Reservations recommended. Main courses $17–$28 lunch, $24–$51 dinner. AF, DC, DISC, MC, V. Daily 11am–2:45pm and 5–10:30pm.

Pinot Brasserie ★★ BISTRO   A sister to the well-regarded Los Angeles restaurant Patina, this casual bistro reliably delivers French and American favorites that are thoughtfully conceived and generally delicious. It's an excellent choice if you want a special meal that is neither stratospherically expensive nor too complex. And the space is highly attractive, with various props culled from French auctions and flea markets forming the archetypal, clubby bistro feel. We particularly like the small room off the bar to the right—just perfect for a tête-à-tête.

Salads are possibly fresher and more generous than other similar starters in town (thank that California influence), and they can come paired with various toppings for *crostini* (toasted slices of French bread) such as herbed goat cheese. The signature dish, beloved by many, is a roasted chicken accompanied by heaping mounds of garlic fries; but if you wish to get a little more elaborate (and yet rather light), thin slices of smoked salmon with celery rémoulade could be a way to go. Desserts are lovely, and the ice cream is homemade—the chocolate alone should make you wish you'd never eaten at 31 Flavors because it was wasted calories compared to this.

In The Venetian, 3355 Las Vegas Blvd. S. www.patinagroup.com. *©* **702/414-8888.** Reservations recommended for dinner. Main courses $15–$32 lunch, $25–$49 dinner. AE, DISC, MC, V. Sun–Thurs 11:30am–3pm and 5:30–10pm; Fri–Sat 11:30am–3pm and 5:30–10:30pm.

Public House ★ GASTROPUB   The gastropub trend is already threatening to collapse in on itself, with waves of self-consciously hip eateries mixing beer lists that are longer than the walk from your hotel room to the casino and food that attempts to be epicurean fun but usually just ends up being twee and bland. This one, however, is a prime example of what can happen when the booze and the food have the creativity and execution to back up the bluster. At first glance the epic beer list (four pages of really small print) and some of the "with the what now?" menu selections (poutine, pork rinds, duck rillettes) may make you groan, but dig past it for some true rewards. Ask their in-house cicerone (the beer version of a sommelier) to suggest a brew and then try the brilliant pork fillet, juicy and fork-cutting tender, or the roasted free ranch chicken, which could challenge Zankou for "best chicken ever." Lamb pierogies are another interesting option but if you can't handle the offbeat offerings, just go for the pub burger served with bacon marmalade and Gruyère cheese. Or just keep having the cicerone bring you beer—a few of them and the grilled octopus, roasted bone marrow, or foie gras pâté may sound as everyday as a turkey sandwich.

In The Palazzo, 3327 Las Vegas Blvd. S. www.publichouselv.com. ✆ **702/407-5310.** Reservations recommended for dinner. Main courses $14–$44. AE, DISC, MC, V. Sun–Thurs 11am–11pm; Fri–Sat 11am–midnight.

Sensi ★★ ECLECTIC   It's usually a truism, as far as restaurants go, "jack of all trades, master of none." Sensi seems to be an exception, given that its menu is made up of Italian (fancy pizzas and pastas), wood-grilled American options (burgers, fish, chicken), and Asian-influenced dishes (and they mean "Pan-Asian," thus tandoori and sushi both). And yet, it does it all very well indeed. A fun menu in a fun-looking space, laid out to surround one very busy and versatile kitchen.

In Bellagio, 3600 Las Vegas Blvd. S. www.bellagio.com. ✆ **702/693-7223.** Main courses $18–$60. AE, DC, DISC, MC, V. Mon–Thurs 5–9:45pm; Fri–Sat 5–10:15pm.

Table 10 ★★ AMERICAN   Emeril Lagasse's imprint is easy to spot on the menu here, from the subtle Louisiana influences on some dishes to the more obvious inclusions of things like his signature banana cream pie. That may a good or bad thing, depending on your feelings about the celebrity chef, but you really should forget about that entirely because this delightful restaurant stands on its own as a creation that, if you didn't know better, was completely outside of Lagasse's world. Start with the candied bacon served with maple syrup or the fried Great Lakes smelt with lemon mayo, and work your way up to Colorado filet or, better yet, the Hawaiian snapper, simply dressed and steamed to perfection. The menu is seasonal so details may change, but it is also wide-ranging and eclectic from things like suckling pig to lobster spaghetti to sea scallops, so there should be something for just about every taste. And if you want to finish off with the banana cream pie, we certainly won't blame you, but do consider the malassadas, which are like cinnamon powdered donut holes stuffed with white chocolate. Bam, indeed.

In The Palazzo, 3327 Las Vegas Blvd. S. www.emerils.com. ✆ **702/607-6363.** Reservations recommended for dinner. Main courses $15–$38 lunch, $26–$48 dinner. AE, DISC, MC, V. Sun–Thurs 11am–10pm; Fri–Sat 11am–11pm.

Moderate

Cabo Wabo Cantina ★ MEXICAN   Should you really be taking culinary recommendations from Sammy Hagar? If it's at a place like his Cabo Wabo Cantina, then the answer is a resounding "why not?" Part restaurant and part party pit, this Vegas version of his famous (or is it infamous?) Cabo San Lucas joint definitely tries to bring a spring-break-in-Mexico vibe to the Strip with loud music, bright colors, and a waitstaff that may burst into the Cha Cha Slide at any

FAMILY-FRIENDLY restaurants

Buffets   Cheap meals for the whole family. The kids can choose what they like, and there are sometimes make-your-own sundae machines. See "Buffets & Brunches" (p. 146) for buffet reviews. Those with reduced prices for kids are noted.

Cypress Street Marketplace (p. 124) Caesars Palace's food court (stylish enough to offer real plates and cloth napkins) offers a range of food (from very good hot dogs to wrap sandwiches to Vietnamese noodles) wide enough to ensure that bottomless-pit teenagers, picky grade schoolers, and health-conscious parents will all find something that appeals, at affordable prices.

Fellini's (p. 129)   With a menu that admittedly veers toward Italian-American rather than authentic food from the motherland, this is all the more appropriate for families, who probably want a good red-sauce pasta dish and some solid pizza rather than anything more elaborate.

Theme Restaurants   Although the cuisine usually won't win any awards, theme restaurants are often great places to take kids for their wide-ranging menus and plenty of distractions to keep them entertained. See "You Gotta Have a Theme" p. 106.

moment. The drink menu (featuring margaritas made with Hagar's Cabo Wabo Tequila, of course) is bigger than the food menu but if you need something to soak up all that alcohol, the Mexican dishes are certainly up to the task. All the basics are covered—tacos, burritos, nachos (including a Cadillac variety where every chip is loaded separately), fajitas, and so forth—and it's all good, though not fantastic . . . although if you have enough of the tequila, you'll probably be too busy doing the Cha Cha Slide with the waitresses to care.

In Planet Hollywood Resort & Casino, 3663 Las Vegas Blvd. S. www.cabowabocantinalv.com. **℘ 702/385-2226.** Main courses $10–$24. AE, DISC, MC, V. Sun–Thurs 8am–midnight; Fri–Sat 8am–1am.

Central Michel Richard ★ ECLECTIC   Washington, D.C., Chef Richard is aiming to reinvent the 24-hour Las Vegas cafe with upscale bistro. The trappings are certainly more luxe; instead of vinyl booths and keno boards, you get sleekly modern design, a full bar, and big windows overlooking the plaza in front of Caesars Palace. The menu is eclectic, with hints of Chef's French cuisine background in the mussels and cheese plate, but options run the gamut from American classics like burgers and steaks to comfort food like spaghetti and meatloaf. Although there are occasional bum notes in the main courses (the meatloaf was a little overdone), delightful "lighter" options like the bacon-and-onion tart or the signature Faux Gras made with chicken liver, butter, and cream keep things moving briskly. Breakfasts include simple fare to full-on feasts (steak and eggs, anyone?), while the late-night dining offers a little bit of everything so you can nosh after a night of clubbing.

In Caesars Palace, 3570 Las Vegas Blvd. S. www.centrallv.com. **℘ 702/650-5921.** Main courses lunch $17–$39, dinner $17–$59. AE, DISC, MC, V. Daily 24 hr.

FIRST Food and Bar ★★ AMERICAN   You kind of have to hunt to find this place, tucked away as it is in an almost forgotten corner of The Shoppes at The Palazzo, but make the effort because this is one unique and interesting restaurant. Chef Sammy DeMarco brings an offbeat New York energy to both the decor, which features tattoo-inspired artwork and a working photo booth among other contemporary touches, and the menu, offering twisted takes on classic diner food. The Philly cheesesteak potstickers are a silly success and the pastrami sandwich, served inside a bag of potato chips, is worthy of its NYC roots. There's a little something for everyone, including sandwiches, pizza, salads, pasta, chicken and waffles, fish and chips, steaks, chops, breakfast, and much, much more. The place lives up to its motto: "Hard to find, easy to love."

In The Palazzo, 3325 Las Vegas Blvd. S. www.firstfoodandbar.com. ℂ **702/607-3478.** Main courses lunch $12–$30, dinner $15–$35. AE, DISC, MC, V. Daily 11am–2am.

Gilley's ★★ BARBECUE   You don't have to be a cowboy to love this place. Located along the sidewalk with great people-watching and pirate-battle views, this bright and airy space is done like a roadhouse saloon, all rustic wood and metal, with two big bars. And, yes, they have a mechanical bull. His name is TItem (TI—Treasure Island—see what they did there?) and if you want to work off your lunch, you can ride him for $5 a pop. And you may just need to do that with the massive portions of down-home country cooking served here. Do not miss the award-winning pork-green chili, which is not green at all but filled with succulent, melt-in-your-mouth hunks of pork and not-too-spicy hatch and poblano chiles. The burgers are roughly the size of your head, made of deliciously smoky certified Black Angus beef and just waiting for one of the custom barbecue sauces (the roasted onion is our personal favorite). The pulled pork is as barbecue perfect as you're going to find west of the Mississippi, and the rest of the menu is waistline expanding with hot links, fried chicken, chicken-fried steak, ribs, and more—most of it served with two sides, including such favorites as molasses baked beans, white cheddar–and–green chili grits, and corn on the cob. It's all moderately priced, which is not to say exactly cheap ($15 for a burger), but the combination of tasty food, friendly service, and a great location make it worth putting on your ten-gallon and moseying on down.

At Treasure Island, 3300 Las Vegas Blvd. S. www.gilleyslasvegas.com. ℂ **702/894-7111.** Main courses $9–$35. AE, DISC, MC, V. Daily 11am–midnight.

Hash House a Go Go ★★★ AMERICAN   Back when this place was located on the west side of town, we told you to go but we understood if it was too far to drive or cab. Now that there are multiple locations, including one at the Imperial Palace on the Strip, you only have yourself to blame if you miss it. Yes, you could go to a breakfast buffet and pay $15 for scrambled eggs warmed under a heat lamp, but why not experience the "twisted farm food" here instead? The brainchild of a couple of Midwest natives, breakfast (and dinner) go beyond the typical into realms of the almost unimaginable. Pancakes (traditional buttermilk to coconut mango) are the size of large pizzas, and waffles the size of checkerboards (and some come with bacon baked right inside). The signature hashes come in varieties from corned beef to meatloaf, and "scrambles" throw everything but the kitchen sink into a frying pan and serve it hot to your table that way. Been out partying too late? Try the O'Hare of the Dog special, a 24-ounce Budweiser served in a paper bag with a side of bacon.

Lunch and dinner add salads, sandwiches, burgers, fried chicken, potpie, and more, all with the same fun sensibility and a farm-fresh flavor that you can practically taste before you put it in your mouth. But it's breakfast that we dream about as we write this. **Note:** There are outlets at the Plaza Hotel in Downtown Las Vegas; the M Resort in south Las Vegas; and another at 6800 W. Sahara Ave. Check the website for contact info and directions.

In Imperial Palace, 3535 Las Vegas Blvd. S. www.hashhouseagogo.com. (© **702/731-3311.** Main courses $10–$24. AE, DC, DISC, MC, V. Sun–Thurs 7am–11pm; Fri–Sat 7am–2am.

Holstein's Shakes and Buns ★★ AMERICAN   We have to admit that we are getting a little tired of the gourmet burger trend. Don't get us wrong—we like burgers as much as the next guy, but we're usually just as happy with the ones that are ordered through a clown's mouth as we are with ones that are topped with foie gras and cost more than most fine meals. Sometimes, even more happy. But Holstein's has reaffirmed our faith in the concept by tempering the fancy with fun. They've got everything from classic burgers (love the sirloin with smoked bacon and garlic-chive aioli) to Kobe beef with tempura avocado, beef topped with brisket (beef on beef!), tandoori chicken with apricot-date chutney, and duck stuffed with, yes, foie gras. But burgers aren't their only option. There is a big selection of sausages, including a kicky bratwurst on a soft sandwich-type bun loaded with sauerkraut and bacon; some salads; sliders; and a big selection of appetizers, of which we highly recommend the chicken and waffles. Not as good as those served at the famed L.A. restaurant Roscoe's, but still darned tasty. And, of course, don't forget the shake part of their name— gourmet-worthy ice-cream concoctions that can be ordered straight or spiked with various booze options. Note that the bar out front and its proximity to the Marquee nightclub mean that late-night dining can be a loud experience, so lunch might be a better option.

In The Cosmopolitan of Las Vegas, 3708 Las Vegas Blvd. S. www.holsteinslv.com. (© **877/551-7772.** Reservations recommended. Main courses $12–$30. AE, DC, DISC, MC, V. Daily 11am–midnight.

KGB: Kerry's Gourmet Burgers ★★★ BURGERS   Finding the best burger in a particular city is like a vision quest; a culinary rite of passage for gastronomes. That quest should start and end right here at rock-'n'-roll chef Kerry Simon's entry into the crowded gourmet burger market. You can build your own from dozens of meat (beef, chicken, turkey, lamb, and so on), bun, cheese, and topping choices, or you can put your faith in their signature concoctions like the barbecue burger (topped with smoky applewood bacon, Gouda, and crispy onion straws) or sloppy Joe burger (topped with tangy short-rib meat—meat on meat!). The appetizers, like deep-fried macaroni and cheese with white-cheddar sauce or the insanely delicious waffle fry nachos (topped with that killer sloppy Joe), are tempting, but the burgers are huge, so don't get filled up on the starters. A casually fun atmosphere and relatively moderate prices are great but will seem like icing on the cake once you take a bite of the best burgers in Vegas.

In Harrah's, 3475 Las Vegas Blvd. S. www.kerrysimon.com. (© **702/369-5065.** Main courses $10–$18. AE, DC, DISC, MC, V. Daily 11am–6am.

Lagasse's Stadium ★ AMERICAN   This is what you get when you mix Emeril Lagasse's cooking with sports of every conceivable variety. Whether it's a good thing probably depends on which of those ingredients you care more about. Emeril fans will find a mix of some of his trademark New Orleans–style dishes (crab cakes, muffaletta pasta, Creole boiled shrimp) but mostly it's fairly standard pub grub: soups, salads, pizza, burgers, sandwiches, barbecue, and the like. While everything we sampled was certainly good, it may be disappointing to those looking for a true Lagasse experience. Sports fans will find more than 100 HDTVs showing everything from the NFL to girls' high school basketball, and just about all of it can be bet on at the sports book conveniently located in the main dining room. They'll probably love it and not care a whit about the chef that designed the menu. Prices are affordable until you get to the table minimums ($25–$50 per person, depending on if you choose a table on the main floor, the upper mezzanine, or the big comfy couches in a stadium-like setting), and it's worth noting that sports fans and the games they watch are not terribly conducive to a quiet dining experience.

In The Palazzo, 3325 Las Vegas Blvd. S. www.emerils.com. (C) **702/607-2665.** Reservations recommended. Main courses $13–$35. AE, DC, DISC, MC, V. Mon–Fri 11am–10pm; Sat 7:30am–10pm; Sun 8:30am–10pm.

Max Brenner Chocolate Restaurant ★★ AMERICAN   We're convinced that restaurants like this exist solely to torture us. After all, what else would you call a place that offers so many different chocolate meal and dessert items that it would be impossible to eat them all in one sitting without risking some sort of diabetic coma? You don't have to sit through a real meal to justify going directly to the chocolate if you don't want to, but not doing so will make you miss some compelling arguments for nonchocolate-based food items. Appetizers like chicken, bacon, and cheddar rolls (exactly what they should taste like) are not to be missed, and their flatbread pizzas are meaty wonders. Burgers, salads, and entrees from steak to pasta round out the offerings, and they tease you with hints of chocolate here and there throughout. The fries are dusted with chile and cocoa powder and the onion rings are served with a chocolate ranch dipping sauce (the former was yummy, the latter just kind of weird). But then comes the 10-page-long dessert menu and heaven kicks in. The chocolate pizza, hot chocolate, cookies, milkshakes, fondue, and more and more and more will leave you breathless and wishing you really could eat nothing else. Not that we're encouraging that kind of behavior.

In The Forum Shops at Caesars Palace, 3500 Las Vegas Blvd. S. www.maxbrenner.com. (C) **702/462-8790.** Reservations recommended. Main courses $13–$27. AE, DC, DISC, MC, V. Mon–Thurs 10am–11pm; Fri 10am–midnight; Sat 9am–midnight; Sun 9am–11pm.

Mon Ami Gabi ★★★ BISTRO   Although dinner is certainly a good option, lunch is the primary reason we want to send you to this charming French bistro, especially if you can get a seat on the Strip-facing patio or in the sunny garden atrium. You may be tempted to just people-watch for an hour or so, interspersed with viewings of the Bellagio Fountains across the street. But pay attention to the plates coming to your table, filled with safely Americanized versions of Parisian cafe cuisine, including sandwiches (croque-monsieur is really just a deliciously gooey ham sandwich), crepes, salads, quiche, hamburgers, steaks with french fries (sorry, *pommes frites*), and more. The baked cheese appetizer, served with a zesty tomato purée and garlic bread, is a must, and the ham-and-cheese crepe is a delightfully light lunch option. Dinner adds more substantial entrees (and higher prices), while breakfast serves up everything from omelets to Belgian waffles.

In Paris Las Vegas, 3655 Las Vegas Blvd. S. www.monamigabi.com. © **702/944-4224.** Reservations recommended. Main courses $10–$25 lunch, $18–$45 dinner. AE, DC, DISC, MC, V. Sun–Fri 7am–11pm; Sat 7am–midnight.

munchbar ★★★ AMERICAN   This small eatery tucked into a corner near Caesars' race and sports book appears to be nothing more than a glorified snack bar. But don't judge a cafe by its cover. This casual diner serves up some of the most deliriously enjoyable food in town at prices that will leave you with plenty left over for other pursuits—or you could just order more food. With a nod to the name, it's mostly munchie-type stuff such as wings, sliders, and the like, with some additional "Big Munch" items including salads, burgers, and tacos. Start with the mini–grilled cheese sandwiches served with a creamy tomato dipping sauce (comfort food heaven) or the Pizzadilla, which is basically a quesadilla stuffed with pizza fixings, then move on to one of their juicy hamburgers, so loaded with fixings atop sweet, soft buns that you will never want to eat at McDonald's again. Don't forget about dessert—huge soft-serve ice-cream cones and sundaes that are too big for normal human beings to consume, but so good you'll want to try. It's not exactly cheap but it's certainly more affordable than most Strip restaurants, and the food is better than places that will charge you three times as much.

In Caesars Palace, 3570 Las Vegas Blvd. S. www.munchgroup.com. © **702/731-7778.** Reservations not accepted. Main courses $9–$17. AE, DC, DISC, MC, V. Sun–Mon and Wed–Thurs 11am–2am; Tues and Fri–Sat 11am–4am.

Payard Patisserie & Bistro ★★★ BISTRO   Breakfast here offers one of the few real remaining bargains in Vegas, given quality-to-price ratio. Surely it can't last, considering the state of things in modern-day Vegas, but for now you can look forward to a continental breakfast like no other. Just $22 gets you cereals, fruits, yogurts, lox and bagels, and, most significantly, all the breakfast pastries you can eat. Because the chef has his roots in Paris, these buttery bits of brioche and croissant are as good as any you could consume by the Seine. One can easily spend that much on a breakfast buffet or a lunch entree elsewhere in town, but there is no comparison for quality. Lunch is light and of the French variety, while evening brings dessert tastings of inspired flights of sugary whimsy. Both are of particularly high quality and worth investigating, but it's the breakfast that has already earned the strong reputation.

In Caesars Palace, 3570 Las Vegas Blvd. S. www.caesarspalace.com. © **702/731-7110.** Breakfast $15–$18; lunch $16–$28; dinner $18–$42. Daily 6:30–11:30am breakfast, 11:30am–2pm lunch; Wed–Sun 5–10pm dinner. Pastry counter daily 6:30am–11pm.

PJ Clarke's ★★ AMERICAN   Any business that has been operating for more than 125 years has to be doing something right, and at PJ Clarke's, the "right" involves good food, affordable prices, and a total absence of the kind of haughty attitude that Las Vegas seems to embrace. Based on the famous New York City watering hole (it's the place where Johnny Mercer wrote "One for My Baby"), the Vegas version is a casual saloon-style oasis located amid the high-priced retail outlets of The Forum Shops. It feels almost out of place here, but once you get inside it's as if you are embraced by the warm woods, cool tile work, and historic

Las Vegas photos that seem to say, "Hey, relax! It's just food." But what good food! It's mostly classic American, from pub grub like sandwiches and salads to more grown-up fare like steak and lobster. Lunch is most highly recommended for the signature burgers of lean Montana Angus beef or the classic Reuben piled high with sauerkraut and Swiss. An extensive raw bar is a good way to get things moving, and the desserts—especially the traditional New York cheesecake or the warm apple cobbler—are a fantastic way to bring things to a close.

In The Forum Shops at Caesars Palace, 3500 Las Vegas Blvd. S. www.pjclarkes.com. ✆ **702/434-7900.** Reservations recommended. Main courses $10–$32. AE, DC, DISC, MC, V. Daily 11am–midnight.

Serendipity 3 ★ AMERICAN   Yes, it has the famous foot-long hot dogs from the New York City original, along with a full menu of quite good cafe food (including some very well-made hamburgers on freshly baked spiral buns), but it's really the frozen hot chocolate and other signature desserts that are bringing you here, right? That frozen hot chocolate, so beloved by generations of New Yorkers and tourists alike, is served in a giant overflowing glass with two straws. If that's not decadent enough for your sensibilities, perhaps you want to go for the Treasure Chest, made of chocolate and filled with cookies, cakes, ice cream, and more. It's $88, but it serves four! Still not hitting the over-the-top mark for you? How about the Golden Opulence dessert, recognized as the most expensive in the country? A cool $1,000 will get you a sundae made from rare ice creams and chocolate and topped with edible gold leaf. What else are you going to do with that slot-machine jackpot?

In Caesars Palace, 3570 Las Vegas Blvd. S. www.caesarspalace.com. ✆ **702/731-7373.** Reservations not accepted. Main courses $10–$20; desserts $10–$1,000. AE, DISC, MC, V. Sun–Thurs 8am–11pm; Fri–Sat 8am–midnight.

Sugar Factory ★★ AMERICAN   Perhaps most famous for their celebrity-endorsed, over-the-top lollipops (Britney Spears has a whole line of them), Sugar Factory has moved up in the world with this multifunction, full-service restaurant, bar, lounge, gift shop, and, yes, candy store. A fantastic location right on the Strip allows for great people-watching and Bellagio Fountain views while you nosh on a wide selection of menu choices, including signature crepes (try the ham and brie topped with apples as a brunch option) and other breakfast items, soups, salads, sandwiches, burgers, pizza, pastas, and even entrees like steak or pork chops. Start with the fried macaroni and cheese, served with a delicate tomato-herb sauce, and end with one of their deliriously iced cupcakes (because in Vegas there are no calories). Despite the gimmicky nature, the food is surprisingly good; it's one of the best theme joints in town. Afterward, visit the chocolate lounge, where the bar has built-in fondue heaters, and then blow all your casino winnings in the candy shop; Britney reportedly dropped three grand on one visit. To put it briefly, this place is sweet! (Sorry, it had to be done.)

In Paris Las Vegas, 3655 Las Vegas Blvd. S. www.sugarfactory.com. ✆ **702/776-7770.** Reservations not required. Main courses $10–$25. AE, DC, DISC, MC, V. Daily 24 hr.

Inexpensive

Cypress Street Marketplace ★★ ☺ FOOD COURT   Often when we go to a Vegas buffet (and we are not alone in this), we sigh over all the choices, all

Deli Delights

It's East Coast versus West Coast in the battle of the famous delis, here in sister properties The Mirage and Treasure Island. The former has brought in New York's beloved **Carnegie Deli ★★** (www.mirage.com; ℂ 702/791-7310; daily 24 hr.), home of the towering sandwich, so large that no mere mortal can clamp his or her jaws around it. It's hardly the same joint New Yorkers are used to, given that this sleek and modern interpretation is crammed into a small corner of a casino. Bad puns still run amok on the menu (Tongues for the Memory, Nova on a Sunday, and The Egg and Oy!). We aren't happy that the famously huge sandwiches come with huge prices to match, along with a miserly $3 sharing fee. Treasure Island is home to the first offshoot of Los Angeles's **Canter's Deli ★★** (www.treasureisland.com; ℂ 702/894-7111; daily 11am–midnight), where many a musician has whiled away many an hour. As much as we admit that NYC is right to claim it has superior bagels, and this Carnegie definitely has better hours, the Canter's smells just like the one we spent much pleasurable time in during our formative years. Ah, just go do some pastrami taste testing yourselves, youse.

those different kinds of pretty good, if not better, cuisines there for the taking, but of course we can't possibly try everything. And yet, in some of the higher-priced venues, we are charged as if we can. Here, in this modern version of the classic food court, it's sort of like being at a well-stocked buffet: There's darn fine barbecue (including North Carolina–influenced pulled pork), wrap sandwiches (grilled shrimp, for one example), Asian (including pot stickers and Vietnamese noodles), decent New York pizza, plump Chicago hot dogs, peel-and-eat shrimp and lobster chowder, a bargain-priced salad bar, plus pastries and even wine. And with the range of food, an entire family with very different tastes will all find something satisfactory.

In Caesars Palace, 3570 Las Vegas Blvd. S. www.caesarspalace.com. ℂ **702/731-7110.** Most items under $15. AE, MC, V. Daily 11am–11pm.

Earl of Sandwich ★★★ SANDWICHES It seems credulity straining, but the sandwich was something that had to be invented, and thus someone got their simple yet ingenious idea named after them. At least, so the story goes, so sufficiently accepted as historical lore that it carries enough weight for the intrepid inventor's descendant, the 11th earl of Sandwich, to lend his name to a chain of sandwich shops. It's a gimmick, but a good one, and so is the food. The eponymous, and largely excellent, sandwiches are served warm (wraps are cold) on bread made for the shop and include varieties such as grilled Swiss, blue and brie with applewood-smoked bacon, and roast beef with horseradish cream and cheddar cheese. There are also complex if unoriginal salads, smoothies, and breakfast sandwiches. Portions aren't huge, but it's not a problem if you are devoted to Vegas-size meals; the low prices make it possible to order two of everything if appetites demand.

In Planet Hollywood Resort & Casino, 3667 Las Vegas Blvd. S. www.earlofsandwichusa.com. ℂ **702/463-0259.** Most items under $6. AE, MC, V. Daily 24 hr.

Pink's ★★★ DELI   The hot dogs served by Pink's are legendary in Los Angeles—almost mythic, in fact. In business at the same location for more than 70 years, the little shack draws hordes, with lines down the block turning peak dining times into waits of more than an hour. Why? Well, the all-beef dogs, cooked to "snapping" perfection, are certainly good, but it's the toppings that make it different: chili, bacon, guacamole, mushroom and Swiss, sauerkraut, pastrami, nacho cheese—you name it and they probably put it on the bun. This Vegas location at Planet Hollywood is Pink's second full outlet, and while the lines aren't as crazy, the dogs are just as good. All the traditional versions are on the menu—the bacon chili cheese, piled high with tomatoes and onions, is virtually impossible to pick up and a favorite of ours—but they also throw in some Vegas-only options like the Showgirl (relish, onions, bacon, tomato, sauerkraut, and sour cream), the Vegas Strip (two dogs in one bun with guacamole and jalapeños), and the Planet Hollywood (a Polish with grilled onions and mushrooms, bacon, and cheese). There are also burgers, burritos, and some nonbeef varieties, but that's just background noise as far as we are concerned. Nothing on the menu is over $10, which only adds to the allure.

At Planet Hollywood Resort & Casino, 3663 Las Vegas Blvd. S. www.planethollywoodresort.com. ℂ **702/405-4711.** Main courses $5–$10. AE, MC, V. Sun–Thurs 10:30am–midnight; Fri–Sat 10:30am–3am.

NORTH STRIP
Very Expensive

Bartolotta Ristorante di Mare ★★★ ITALIAN/SEAFOOD   James Beard Foundation Award–winning chef Paul Bartolotta trained in Italy under master chefs before opening his highly acclaimed Spiaggia in Chicago. Now he's here, in this gorgeously designed, multilevel, indoor/outdoor space, yet more proof that celebrity chefs are all very well and good, but it's not the same as having them on the premises. In this case, the result is as authentic Italian food as one can find outside Italy. Determined to produce just that, Bartolotta went to his boss, Steve Wynn, and insisted that his fish not just be ultrafresh but also be flown daily straight from the Mediterranean to his Vegas kitchen. Choices may vary seasonally, but expect a wide array from the familiar to the virtually unknown; the server will walk you through the choices, all lovingly displayed in a tableside case. Most are prepared in light butter and/or olive oil and filleted at your table, allowing the rich, decidedly nonfishy taste to burst through. A Mediterranean sea bass seemed like a safe choice, but we were rewarded with a robust flavor that would convert all but the most vehement of anti-seafood campaigners. Langoustines are grilled to charred smoky rightness, and seared scallops with porcini mushrooms in browned butter are what scallops should be. Pastas are perfect, especially the *maccheroni,* a hand-rolled spaghetti in Tuscan meat sauce. And don't miss desert (like we need to tell you that), especially the selection of house-made ice cream, gelato, and sorbet. Prices are palpitation inducing, but this is one of the rare instances where it is totally worth it.

In Wynn Las Vegas, 3131 Las Vegas Blvd. S. www.wynnlasvegas.com. ℂ **888/352-3463** or 702/248-3463. Reservations recommended. Main courses $23–$110. AE, DC, DISC, MC, V. Daily 5:30–10pm.

North Strip Restaurants

New York Av	
Chicago Av	Oakey Blvd
Philadelphia Av	
St. Louis Av	
	Stratosphere ❶
Baltimore Av	St. Louis Av
Cleveland Av	
Cincinnati Av	
Sahara Av	

Highland Av, Western Av, Industrial Rd, Tam Dr, Fairfield Av, Main St, Paradise Rd, Santa Rita Dr, Rexford Dr, Rancho Dr

Palace Station

Rancho Dr, Westwood Dr, Highland Dr, Industrial Rd

Circus Circus Dr
Circus Circus ❷

(THE STRIP)

Sahara
Karen Av

Riviera Blvd
Riviera

Post Office

LVH
LVH: Las Vegas Hotel

Las Vegas Country Club

Convention Center Dr

Desert Inn Rd

Channel 8 Dr

Paradise Rd

Encore Las Vegas ❸

Wynn Golf and Country Club

Fashion Show Dr

Fashion Show Mall

Wynn Las Vegas ❹

Spring Mountain Rd
Treasure Island
The Palazzo
Sands Av

••• Las Vegas Monorail
••• Free monorail
━━ Pedestrian bridge

RESTAURANTS
Bartolotta Ristorante di Mare **4**
Fellini's **1**
Red 8 **4**
Rock & Rita's **2**
Sinatra **3**
The Steakhouse **2**
Top of the World **1**
BUFFETS
Circus Circus Buffet **2**
Wynn Las Vegas Buffet **4**

Sinatra ★★★ ITALIAN   Old Blue Eyes is the theme here, with memorabilia (including an Oscar and a Grammy), giant pictures of Frank, and even a few of his favorite menu items (*Ossobuco Milanese*, clams *Possilipo*) to choose from. But this swank restaurant is so much more than its gimmick. The dining room is one of the most gorgeous in town, with giant windows facing a garden patio and plush, eclectic, vaguely retro furnishings encouraging the kind of laid-back dining experience that is rare in this rush-to-get-the-check town. Chef Theo Schoenegger was born and raised in Italy, gaining fame in the U.S. during his stint as the executive chef at Los Angeles–based Patina, and his short but satisfying selection of northern Italian dishes is bursting with fresh flavors. Start with the prosciutto appetizer, almost sweet with a fire-roasted pepper accompaniment, then move on to the *agnolotti*, a handmade ravioli pasta stuffed with ricotta cheese and drenched in a buttery asparagus sauce. Or go crazy with the lasagna made with beef, veal, and pork. Seafood and meat options include Maine lobster and a delicious, herb-crusted rack of lamb served with a pepper stuffed with ratatouille. Desserts are equally satisfying, as is the exceptional cocktail and wine list. Allow the expert sommelier to pair the perfect glass of *vino* with whatever you are having.

In Encore Las Vegas, 3121 Las Vegas Blvd. S. www.encorelasvegas.com. © **702/248-3463.** Reservations required. Main courses $27–$55. AE, DISC, MC, V. Daily 5:30–10pm.

Top of the World ★★ CONTINENTAL   It really is impossible to beat the views from this revolving restaurant more than 800 feet up atop the Stratosphere Tower, but for a long time the food didn't live up to the surroundings. Good news: A revised menu is much more interesting, the prices are much more affordable, and the food is much better. Although there are shades of a steakhouse in the offerings, they go way beyond those borders with eye-catching options throughout the menu. Check out the roasted pork belly appetizer served with an Argentinian chimichurri sauce, or maybe the grilled portobello mushroom with roasted red pepper and buffalo mozzarella. The steaks are tempting—the filet with a red wine–mushroom sauce is especially noteworthy—but don't miss the more unique offerings such as the pork tenderloin wrapped in bacon and served with apple-and-cranberry chutney or the rack of lamb with Moroccan couscous. Even though the menu is seasonal and offerings may be different when you visit, the originality and inventiveness remains throughout the year. And did we mention that view?! It takes about an hour and 20 minutes to make the full rotation, and the best part is when you're under the SkyJump (p. 68) platform so you see people dropping off the top of the building as you dine (and perhaps laugh at the level of their insanity).

In Stratosphere Casino Hotel, 2000 Las Vegas Blvd. S. www.topoftheworldlv.com. © **702/380-7777.** Reservations required. Main courses lunch $14–$31, dinner $40–$64. AE, DISC, MC, V. Daily 11am–3:30pm; Sun–Thurs 4:30–10pm; Fri–Sat 4:30–10:30pm.

Expensive

The Steakhouse ★ STEAK   Most of the steakhouses in Las Vegas have fallen prey to modernization, adding faux-elegant lounge-worthy design schemes, fancy extraneous dishes, cocktail menus, and prices that push into the stratosphere. What happened to the traditional meat–and-potatoes steakhouse? It's right here, my friends. In business for more than 2 decades, The Steakhouse at Circus Circus does things the old-fashioned way, with a dark cigar club–style design (think high-backed booths and faux animal heads on the wall), familial but professional service, classic cuts cooked over a wood flame, and prices that won't make you dip into your gambling budget. Regarding the latter, it may seem like $50 is not exactly cheap, but unlike most Strip steakhouses, the price is inclusive of soup or salad and a side dish, things that will cost you extra just about everywhere else. It's a retro delight in a town that currently seems ruthless about weeding out such things.

In Circus Circus, 2880 Las Vegas Blvd. S. www.circuscircus.com. © **702/794-3767.** Reservations recommended. Main courses $40–$50. AE, DC, DISC, MC, V. Daily 5–10pm.

Moderate

Fellini's ★ ☺ ITALIAN   A Vegas institution in its original but now-closed West Las Vegas location, much beloved by in-the-know locals, Fellini's is a classic Italian restaurant—you know, gloopy red sauce, garlicky cheesy bread—which isn't meant to be an insult at all. It might not be ambitious, but it is reliable and more than satisfying. Fellini's does a strong version of pasta (rigatoni, in this case) *amatriciana*, and they are generous with the pancetta. And while some Italian food purists would shudder at the gnocchi with tenderloin tips, topped with Gorgonzola and shallot cream sauce, they are just missing out, that's all. The well-proportioned menu offers a variety of options from osso buco to basic pizza, and, given the prices, that makes it a good option for families with a similar range of tastes and needs.

In Stratosphere Casino Hotel, 2000 Las Vegas Blvd S. www.fellinislv.com. ✆ **702/383-4859.** Main courses $13–$29. AE, DISC, MC, V. Daily 5–11pm.

Red 8 ★★ ASIAN   Such a relief, in the otherwise pricey Wynn, to find a dining spot that is both good and affordable. This visual standout is a small cafe—as you wander by, you think "Cool! Some of the tables overlook the casino!" Then you realize those are *all* of the tables—with a decor that screams the place's colorful name. It's popular, given the location, size, and pricing—not to mention the quality of the food. Covering a sort of Pan-Asiatic (Southeast Asia, anyway) terrain, look for noodle dishes both wet (soup) and dry (pan-fried), rice (including porridge), dim sum, Korean barbecue, Mongolian beef, vegetarian options, and more. There are some "market price" specials that can quadruple a bill pretty fast, but otherwise, this is a pretty budget-friendly option.

In Wynn Las Vegas, 3131 Las Vegas Blvd. S. www.wynnlasvegas.com. ✆ **702/770-3380.** No reservations required. Main courses $12–$30. AE, DISC, MC, V. Sun–Thurs 11:30am–11pm; Fri–Sat 11:30am–1am.

Inexpensive

Rock & Rita's ★ AMERICAN   They serve drinks in souvenir cups shaped like toilet bowls. We mention this at the outset to give you a very quick glimpse into the kind of place this is. If the idea of drinks served in toilet bowls horrifies you, don't come here. We think it's kind of funny (in an admittedly 12-year-old boy kind of way), so we have a warm spot in our party-down hearts for this raucous restaurant and bar. The food is all big portions of high-calorie American cuisine. Don't believe us? One of their few salad options is a creamy bacon fried-chicken salad topped with barbecue potato chips. Again, horrified? Stay away. It's probably best for appetizer-type munchies—we loved the warm, gooey quesadilla and tender, breaded chicken fingers—but they have breakfast, lunch, full dinners, and late-night bites, so no matter the time of day you can find something to bump up your cholesterol by a few points. The music, TVs, frequent live entertainment, flair bartenders, and general merriment mean this is not a place for a quiet meal.

In Circus Circus, 2880 Las Vegas Blvd. S. www.rockandritas.com. ✆ **702/691-5991.** Reservations not accepted. Main courses $8–$17. AE, DISC, MC, V. Daily 24 hr.

DOWNTOWN

Very Expensive

Hugo's Cellar ★ CONTINENTAL   Hugo's Cellar is indeed in a cellar, or at least below street level in the Four Queens hotel. No, they aren't ashamed of it—quite the opposite. This is their pride and joy, and it is highly regarded by the locals. This is Old School Vegas Classy Dining. Each female guest is given a red rose when she enters the restaurant—the first of a series of nice touches.

The meal is full of ceremony, perfectly delivered by a well-trained and cordial waitstaff. Salads, included in the price, are prepared at your table, from a cart full of choices. In Vegas style, though, most choices are on the calorie-intensive side, ranging from chopped egg and blue cheese to pine nuts and bay shrimp. Unfortunately, the main courses are not all that novel (various cuts of meat, seafood, and chicken prepared in different ways), but satisfying in an old-school Vegas dining experience kind of way. The fact that salad and a small dessert are included makes an initially hefty-seeming price tag appear a bit more reasonable, especially compared to Strip establishments that aren't much better and can cost the same for just the entree. While it's not worth going out of your way for the food, perhaps it is worth it for the entire package.

In the Four Queens, 202 Fremont St. www.hugoscellar.com. 𝄢 **702/385-4011.** Reservations required. Main courses $38–$56. AE, DC, DISC, MC, V. Daily 5:30–11pm.

Expensive

Chart House ★ SEAFOOD   Downtown Las Vegas is a bit of a wasteland when it comes to fine-dining experiences, so it was exciting when the Landry's restaurant chain took over the Golden Nugget. Among their additions is a branch of the Chart House, which is usually found overlooking some body of water to go along with a predominantly seafood menu. Because there are no bodies of water in Downtown Vegas, they built a 75,000-gallon aquarium as the focal point. It's beautiful, but may be a little unsettling if you choose a table right next to it and have a variety of colorful fish watching as you chow down on their brethren. If you can't decide between the lobster bisque, New England clam chowder, and gazpacho for your soup course, get all three in the Ménage sampler. The flounder stuffed with jumbo lump crab on a bed of Yukon gold potatoes was as close to perfect as you're going to get with fish in the Nevada desert. Although the menu is obviously seafood intensive, there are a few steak and chicken options available.

In Golden Nugget, 129 E. Fremont St. www.chart-house.com. 𝄢 **702/386-8364.** Reservations recommended. Main courses $18–$39. AE, DC, DISC, MC, V. Mon–Thurs 11:30am–11pm; Fri–Sat 11:30am–11:30pm; Sun 11:30am–10:30pm.

Oscar's Steakhouse ★★ STEAK   Located in the iconic dome at The Plaza Hotel in Downtown Las Vegas, this traditional steakhouse is the brainchild of flamboyant former Las Vegas Mayor Oscar Goodman. An unrepentant imbiber, the Mayor's quote on the menu reads, in part, "eat, talk, have fun, and get drunk!" All of that is easy to do here even though the "eat" part of the offerings here don't necessarily break any new ground. Steak and seafood rules the menu but you can find some interesting options here and there like a bone-in veal chop billed as "Wiener" schnitzel and house made latkes as a side. Prices are downright reasonable compared to most Strip steakhouses and the service is fantastic but it's really

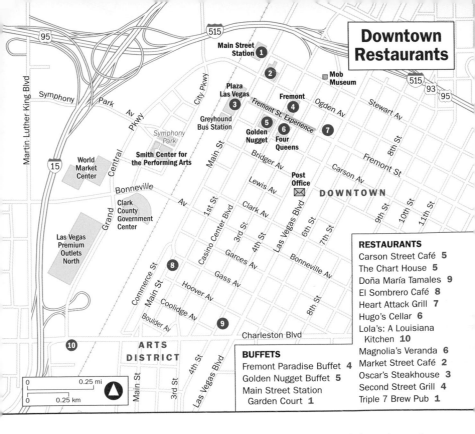

Downtown Restaurants

RESTAURANTS
Carson Street Café **5**
The Chart House **5**
Doña María Tamales **9**
El Sombrero Café **8**
Heart Attack Grill **7**
Hugo's Cellar **6**
Lola's: A Louisiana Kitchen **10**
Magnolia's Veranda **6**
Market Street Café **2**
Oscar's Steakhouse **3**
Second Street Grill **4**
Triple 7 Brew Pub **1**

BUFFETS
Fremont Paradise Buffet **4**
Golden Nugget Buffet **5**
Main Street Station Garden Court **1**

the ambience—with an unparalleled view of the Glitter Gulch light and sound show across the street—that make this a one-of-a-kind Vegas experience.

In The Plaza, 1 Main St. www.plazahotelcasino.com. ☏ **702/386-7227.** Reservations recommended. Main courses $23–$46. AE, DC, DISC, MC, V. Daily 5pm–close.

Second Street Grill ★ 🏢 CONTINENTAL/PACIFIC RIM   Our categorization notwithstanding, Second Street Grill calls itself "Continental American with Euro and Asian influences." And, yes, that translates to a bit of a muddle, but the portions are extremely generous, and it's hard to resist a place that plants two long potato chips in a pile of mashed potatoes, thereby creating a bunny rabbit. You are probably best off with grill dishes (various steaks and other cuts of meat), though here might be your best ratio of quality to price for lobster tail. Play around with the Hunan pork–and-beef lettuce-wrap appetizers, and the Peking duck and shrimp tacos. The waist-conscious will be very pleased with the bamboo-steamed snapper in a nice broth, while others may want to try the grilled salmon with goat cheese–Parmesan crust. Desserts are disappointing, unfortunately. Overall, a nice place for a family event dinner Downtown, and certainly more affordable than fancy places on the Strip.

In Fremont Hotel & Casino, 200 E. Fremont St. www.fremontcasino.com. ☏ **702/385-3232.** Reservations recommended. Main courses $17–$30. AE, DC, DISC, MC, V. Sun–Mon and Thurs 5–10pm; Fri–Sat 5–11pm.

Moderate

Lola's: A Louisiana Kitchen ★★★ 🎁 CAJUN/CREOLE

Regional cuisine often inspires passionate arguments about authenticity, but you'll rarely find anyone more deeply protective of their food than those who love Cajun and Creole cooking. They will say, often with a fervor reserved for tent revivals, that you simply cannot get authentic Louisiana cooking outside of Louisiana. They have probably never been to Lola's. Run by a New Orleans native, this charming bistro would be right at home in the Garden District or French Quarter, with Big Easy favorites like jambalaya, po' boys, gumbo, red beans and rice, gulf shrimp, and blackened catfish among others. Forget how genuine the food is for a moment (the po' boys are served on the revered Liedenheimer bread, flown in from NOLA) and just relish how flavorful and masterfully prepared the dishes are. The roast beef debris po' boy is a work of sweet-and-sour genius, while the traditional bread pudding will have you asking for seconds. *Laissez les bons temps rouler*, indeed!

201 W. Charleston Ave, no. 101 (at Grand Central Pkwy). www.lolaslasvegas.com. ℂ **702/227-5652.** Main courses $8–$25. AE, DC, DISC, MC, V. Mon–Thurs 11am–9pm; Fri 11am–10pm; Sat noon–9pm.

Inexpensive

Carson Street Cafe AMERICAN

Here's a slightly better-than-adequate hotel coffee shop, though it's a mixed bag in terms of quality of food. Sandwiches are better than ribs, burgers, and fries, all of which are merely just filling. On the other hand, the linguine with shrimp is surprisingly good, while desserts, especially pecan pie a la mode, more than earn their rep.

In Golden Nugget, 129 E. Fremont St. www.goldennugget.com. ℂ **702/385-7111.** Reservations not accepted. Main courses $6–$18. AE, DC, DISC, MC, V. Daily 24 hr.

Doña María Tamales ★★ MEXICAN

Decorated with Tijuana-style quilt work and calendars, this quintessential Mexican diner is convenient to both the north end of the Strip and Downtown. The cooks use lots of lard, lots of cheese, and lots of sauce. As a result, the food is really good—and really fattening. Yep, the folks who did those health reports showing how bad Mexican food can be for your heart probably did some research here. The fat just makes it all the better, in our opinion. Locals apparently agree; even at lunchtime, the place is crowded.

You will start off with homemade chips and a spicy salsa served in a mortar. Meals are so large that it shouldn't be a problem getting full just ordering off the sides, which can make this even more of a budget option. Naturally, the specialty is the fantastic tamales, which come in red, green, cheese, or sweet. There are also excellent enchiladas, *chiles rellenos*, burritos, and fajitas. All dinners include rice, beans, tortillas, and soup or salad. Sauces are heavy but oh so good. For dessert, there is flan, fried ice cream, and Mexican-style pumpkin pie.

910 Las Vegas Blvd. S. (at Charleston Blvd.). www.donamariatamales.com. ℂ **702/382-6538.** Main courses $8–$12 breakfast and lunch, $12–$15 dinner. AE, MC, V. Daily 8am–10pm.

El Sombrero Cafe ★★ MEXICAN

This kind of hole-in-the-wall Mexican joint can be found all over California, but not always so readily elsewhere. It's also the kind of family-run place (since 1950) increasingly forced out of Vegas by giant hotel conglomerates, making it even more worth your time. Mexican-food fans in particular should seek out this friendly place, though it's not in an attractive part of town. Portions are generous and unexpectedly spicy. The staff also caters to special requests—changing the beef burrito to a chicken one (an option that comes highly recommended), for example, without batting an eyelash. The enchilada-and-taco combo also won raves.

807 S. Main St. (at Gass Ave.). (✆ **702/382-9234.** Main courses $8–$10 lunch, $13–$18 dinner. MC, V. Mon–Thurs 11am–4pm; Fri–Sat 11am–8:30pm.

Heart Attack Grill ★ BURGERS

There's something pure, and purely ridiculous, about the concept here, which can be boiled down to this: Their food is hazardous to your health. The medical theme is kooky fun with waitresses dressed as (naughty) nurses, bartenders in scrubs, and diners in hospital johnnies, but it's their artery-hardening burgers, fries, and shakes that will make you want to set up an appointment with your cardiologist afterward. Their signature Quadruple Bypass Burger is 8,000 calories of meat, bacon, and cheese, and if you finish it you get a wheelchair ride back to your car (or a waiting ambulance, perhaps). Shakes are billed as having the highest butterfat content in the world, and that's before you they add a pat of butter on top. Fries cooked in pure lard, nonfilter cigarettes, and a full bar serving blended margaritas that are 50% alcohol round out the limited choices here. The burgers are merely okay but it's really the experience, and surviving it, that makes this place worth knowing about, especially if you weigh over 350 pounds. If you do and are willing to prove it by stepping on the scale in the center of the restaurant, you eat for free.

450 E. Fremont St. www.heartattackgrill.com. (✆ **702/254-0171.** Main courses $8–$15. Cash only. Daily 11am–2am.

Magnolia's Veranda DINER

So there you are . . . you can't possibly eat at another buffet, and yet you don't want to spend $50 for a meal at a typical Vegas restaurant. Magnolia's Veranda seems to have been invented for folks just like you. This 24-hour cafe isn't going to win an epicurean award, but the food is better than coffee-shop average and is, without exception, affordable. With a menu that is more wide ranging than most buffets (soups, salads, sandwiches, burgers, pizza, pasta, breakfasts, steak, seafood), you'll be sure to find something here to please just about any taste. And meal-deal hunters should definitely pay attention to such things as the $8.95 prime rib dinners served nightly.

In the Four Queens, 202 E. Fremont St. www.fourqueens.com. (✆ **702/385-4011.** Main courses $6–$19. MC, V. Daily 24 hr.

Market Street Café DINER

Twenty-four-hour diners are ubiquitous in Las Vegas. After all, you need something to eat at 4am after a night of gambling, drinking, and general Sin City debauchery. The Market Street Café is exactly the kind of place you want to stumble into in the wee hours. Bargain-priced regula~ items (hamburgers for $5) and meal-deal type specials abound (a steak an~ shrimp combo for $8), all served in generous portions and with a minimum c frippery.

In the California Hotel, 12 Ogden Ave. www.thecal.com. (✆ **702/385-1222.** Reservations nc accepted. Main courses $5–$12. AE, DC, DISC, MC, V. Daily 24 hr.

Triple 7 Brew Pub ★ PUB FARE

The wide-ranging menu of pub gru includes everything from salads to sushi, but it is the almost shockingly affordabl~

pizza and sandwiches that you should focus most of your attention on. The crispy-crust, simple pepperoni pie is "Mamma Mia!" worthy and the cheesesteak, loaded with onions and peppers, is a victory by just about any measure. A huge selection of beers includes their own micro-brews, which you can sample while you watch sports on one of the omnipresent TV screens or enjoy the frequent evening enter-tainment. Note the operating hours—perfect for a place to stop in at 4am after you've hit all the Fremont Street bars.

In Main Street Station, 200 N. Main St. www.mainstreetcasino.com. © **702/387-1896.** Main courses $6–$18. AE, DC, DISC, MC, V. Daily 11am–7am.

JUST OFF THE STRIP
Very Expensive

Alizé ★★★ FRENCH   Just a perfect restaurant, thanks to a combination of the most divine dining room and view in Vegas, not to mention one of the best chefs in Vegas. Situated at the top of the Palms hotel, three sides of full-length windows allow a panoramic view of the night lights of Vegas; obviously, window-side tables are best, but even seats in the center of the room have a good view. Many great chefs have restaurants locally but are rarely in their kitchens (we love Emeril and Wolfgang, but they can't be in 25 different places at once). This operation is carefully overseen by André Rochat, he of the eponymous (and excellent) restaurant in the Monte Carlo. The menu changes seasonally, but this is a close-your-eyes-and-point kind of place; anything you order will be heavenly. If you can swing it, do the tasting menus; if not, go a la carte and go home happy. A recent visit included a divine pork belly appetizer, served in a sweet apple–and-cream sauce; an insanely rich Maine lobster and tomato bisque; and two cuts of beef—a filet in a green-peppercorn crust and cognac cream sauce and a rib-eye with a smoky pinot noir glaze—that would shame the best of steak-houses in Vegas. Desserts are similarly outstanding and often of great frivolity, such as an inside-out raspberry cheesecake (cubes with graham cracker crust on the outside, raspberry compote inside) and mint chocolate mousse. Like we said: perfect!

In Palms Resort & Casino, 4321 W. Flamingo Rd. www.alizelv.com. © **702/951-7000.** Fax 702/951-7002. Reservations strongly recommended. Main courses $40–$75; 5-course tasting menu $105, 7-course tasting menu $125. AE, DC, DISC, MC, V. Daily 5:30–10:30pm.

Lawry's The Prime Rib ★★★ STEAK   Eating at Lawry's—a branch of the famed Los Angeles eatery in business since 1938—is a ceremony, with all the parts played the same way for the past 60 years. Waitresses in brown-and-white English-maid uniforms, complete with starched white cap, take your order; giant metal carving carts come to the table so you can select your cut; and salad bowls are literally spun in a bed of ice while their famous dressing is applied. The prime rib is, of course, the main attraction (and deservedly so; this is the gold standard) but they also have fresh fish (halibut, salmon, or swordfish, depending on the evening), steaks, and even a vegetarian option or two. But back to the prime rib—it comes with terrific Yorkshire pudding, nicely browned and not soggy, and some creamed horseradish that is combined with fluffy whipped cream, simultane-ously sweet and tart. Flavorful, tender, perfectly cooked, and lightly seasoned, this will be the best prime rib you will ever have.

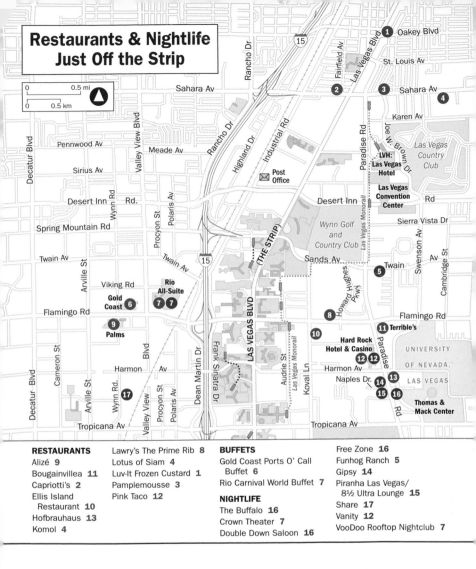

Restaurants & Nightlife Just Off the Strip

RESTAURANTS
Alizé **9**
Bougainvillea **11**
Capriotti's **2**
Ellis Island Restaurant **10**
Hofbrauhaus **13**
Komol **4**

Lawry's The Prime Rib **8**
Lotus of Siam **4**
Luv-It Frozen Custard **1**
Pamplemousse **3**
Pink Taco **12**

BUFFETS
Gold Coast Ports O' Call Buffet **6**
Rio Carnival World Buffet **7**

NIGHTLIFE
The Buffalo **16**
Crown Theater **7**
Double Down Saloon **16**

Free Zone **16**
Funhog Ranch **5**
Gipsy **14**
Piranha Las Vegas/ 8½ Ultra Lounge **15**
Share **17**
Vanity **12**
VooDoo Rooftop Nightclub **7**

4043 Howard Hughes Pkwy. (at Flamingo Rd., btw. Paradise Rd. and Koval Lane). www.lawrysonline.com. *(C)* **702/893-2223.** Reservations recommended. Main courses $28–$54. AE, DC, DISC, MC, V. Mon–Fri 11:30am–2pm; Sun–Thurs 5–10pm; Fri–Sat 5–11pm.

Pamplemousse ★ FRENCH   A little bit off the beaten path, Pamplemousse is a long-established Vegas restaurant that shouldn't be overlooked in the crush of high-profile eateries. Evoking a cozy French-countryside inn (at least, on the interior), it's a catacomb of low-ceilinged rooms and intimate dining nooks with rough-hewn beams. It's all very charming and un-Vegasy. The restaurant's name, which means "grapefruit" in French, was suggested by the late singer Bobby Darin, one of the many celebrity pals of owner Georges La Forge.

CHEF ANDRÉ ROCHAT'S TOP 10 THINGS ONE SHOULD NEVER ASK A french chef

French born Chef André Rochat has been delighting Las Vegas audiences with his fine cuisine since 1973. His restaurants Alizé at the Palms and André's at Monte Carlo are among the most popular and best-reviewed French restaurants in the city, so who better to ask what you *shouldn't* ask him?

1. May I have my duck breast well done?

2. May I have A-1 sauce with steak au poivre?

3. I brought this from my garden; can you cook it for me?

4. I want the lobster Thermidor; but can you hold the cream?

5. Can I have the crème brûlée as an appetizer?

6. May I order a soufflé to go?

7. Can we do the seven-course chef's tasting menu in 45 minutes?

8. Can I have mint jelly with the rack of lamb?

9. Will you keep the food under the heat lamps in the kitchen while we go smoke?

10. May I have ketchup with the lobster Thermidor?

And yes . . . Chef André says he's actually been asked these questions. Welcome to Las Vegas!

Your waiter recites the menu, which changes nightly. The meal always begins with a large complimentary basket of crudités (about 10 different crisp, fresh vegetables), a big bowl of olives, and, in a nice country touch, a basket of hard-boiled eggs. Recent menu offerings have included out-of-this-world soups (French onion and cream of asparagus, to name a couple) and appetizers such as shrimp in cognac cream sauce, and Maryland crab cakes with macadamia-nut crust. Recommended entrees include a sterling veal with mushrooms and Dijon sauce, and an even better rack of lamb with pistachio-nut crust and rosemary cream sauce (all sauces, by the way, are made with whatever the chef has on hand that evening in the kitchen). Leave room for the fabulous desserts, such as homemade ice cream in a hard chocolate shell.

400 E. Sahara Ave. (btw. Santa Paula and Santa Rita drives, just east of Paradise Rd.). www. pamplemousserestaurant.com. ℂ **702/733-2066.** Reservations required. Main courses $28–$40. AE, DC, DISC, MC, V. Tues–Sun 5:30–10pm.

Moderate

Hofbrauhaus ★ GERMAN   Leave it to Las Vegas to bring an exact replica of a 400-year-old beer garden to the Nevada desert. Based on the Munich landmark in business since 1589, the beer brewed for the establishment was, according to legend, so good that Swedes called off their planned plundering of the city in 1614 in exchange for 344 buckets of the stuff. They fly it in to the Vegas location and re-create the schnitzel, strudel, and bratwurst specialties to give you something to wash down. Portions are huge and often drenched in butter or cream; if you're looking for a light lunch, you probably aren't going to find here, but it's a good place to go to put a little oomp in your pah-pah. **Note:** Polka fans should check the website to see when they have their frequent live entertainment.

4150 Paradise Rd. (at Harmon Ave). www.hofbrauhauslasvegas.com. ✆ **702/853-2337.** Reservations accepted. Main courses $10–$25. AE, DC, DISC, MC, V. Sun–Thurs 11am–11pm; Fri–Sat 11am–midnight.

Inexpensive

Bougainvillea ★★ ✦ DINER   Oh, how we love a Vegas coffee shop. You've got your all-day breakfasts, your graveyard-shift specials, your prime rib, and, of course, your full Chinese menu. And it's all hearty and well priced; we're talkin' build your own three-egg, three-ingredient omelet for around $5. You can get a full dinner entree or a nice light lunch of a large half sandwich and soup, also for around $5. And 24-hour specials—a slab of meat, potato or rice, veggies, soup or salad, and a 12-ounce draft beer—are an astounding $10. Yep. That's the ticket.

In Terrible's, 4100 Paradise Rd. www.terriblescasinos.com. ✆ **702/733-7000.** Main courses $5–$13. AE, MC, V. Daily 24 hr.

Capriotti's ★★★ 💼 SANDWICHES   It looks like a dump, but Capriotti's is one of the great deals in town, for quality and price. It roasts its own beef and turkey on the premises and stuffs them (or Italian cold cuts, or whatever) into sandwiches mislabeled "small," "medium," and "large"—the last clocks in at 20 inches, easily feeding two for under $10 total. And deliciously so. The Bobby (turkey, dressing, and cranberry sauce, like Thanksgiving dinner in sandwich form) would be our favorite sandwich in the world had we not tried the Slaw B Joe: roast beef, coleslaw, and Russian dressing. But other combos, such as the aforementioned Italian cold cuts, have their fans, too, and Capriotti's even has veggie varieties. There are outlets throughout the city, but this one is not only right off the Strip but also right by the freeway. We never leave town without a stop here, and you shouldn't either.

322 W. Sahara Ave. (at Las Vegas Blvd. S.). www.capriottis.com. ✆ 702/474-0229. Most sandwiches under $10. AE, MC, V. Mon–Sat 10am–8pm; Sun 11am–7pm.

Ellis Island Restaurant ★ ✦ DINER   Believe it or not, this simple little 24-hour coffee shop–style restaurant is pretty famous in Las Vegas. Why? The most expensive thing on the menu is around $13 and that's a king cut of prime rib that comes with soup or salad, a baked potato, and a glass of beer. Yes, this is the epicenter of the much beloved meal deal, with most items under $10. The surprising thing is that the food is pretty good, the portions are huge, and the selections (burgers, sandwiches, salads, pasta, pizza, and so on) are epic. You can even get selections from a separate barbecue joint in this restaurant later in the afternoon. If budget is a concern, take a detour from the pricey Strip and find yourself a bargain here.

In Ellis Island Casino, 4178 Koval Lane (at Flamingo Rd.). www.ellisislandcasino.com. ✆ **702/733-8901.** Main courses $5–$14. AE, MC, V. Daily 24 hr.

Komol THAI   This is a hole-in-the-wall dive, like most good ethnic places, with a large menu of poultry, beef, pork, vegetarian, rice, and noodle selections.

1

They'll spice the food to your specifications, but unless you're a Thai expert, it might be best to play it on the safe side. Although we don't want things bland, too much heat can overwhelm all other flavors. The mild to medium packs enough of a kick for most people.

Among the items tried during a recent visit were a vegetarian green curry and the *pad-kee-mao* (flat rice noodles stir-fried with ground chicken, mint, garlic, and hot peppers). *Nam sod* is ground pork with a hot-and-sour sauce, ginger, and peanuts, all of which you wrap up in lettuce leaves—sort of an Asian burrito. The Thai iced tea was particularly good—just the right amount of sweetness and tea taste for a drink that is often served overly sweet.

Note: The Commercial Center also has a number of other ethnic (mostly Asian) restaurants, including Korean barbecue.

In the Commercial Center, 953 E. Sahara Ave. www.komolrestaurant.com. (✆ **702/731-6542.** Main courses $8–$15. AE, DISC, MC, V. Mon–Sat 11am–10pm; Sun noon–10pm.

Lotus of Siam ★★★ 🍴 THAI   Much has been written about this out-of-the-way Thai joint (Jonathan Gold of *Gourmet* magazine called it the best Thai restaurant in North America), but what makes this place so darn special? First of all, in addition to all the usual beloved Thai favorites, there is a separate menu featuring lesser known dishes from northern Thailand—the staff doesn't routinely hand this one out (because most of the customers are there for the more pedestrian, if still excellent, $10 lunch buffet). Second, the owner drives at least twice a week back to Los Angeles to pick up the freshest herbs and other ingredients needed for his dishes' authenticity. That's dedication that should be rewarded with superlatives.

You might be best off letting them know you are interested in northern food (with dried chilies and more pork; it's not un-Cajunlike, says the owner) and letting them guide you through, though you must assure them that you aren't of faint heart or palate (some customers complain the heat isn't enough, even with "well-spiced" dishes, though others find even medium spice sufficient). Standouts include the Issan sausage (a grilled sour pork number), the *nam kao tod* (that same sausage, ground up with lime, green onion, fresh chile, and ginger, served with crispy rice), *nam sod* (ground pork mixed with ginger, green onion, and lime juice, served with sticky rice), jackfruit *larb* (spicy ground meat), and *sua rong hai* ("weeping tiger"), a dish of soft, sliced, and grilled marinated beef. If you insist on more conventional Thai, that's okay, in that it's unlikely you are going to have better *mee krob* noodles or *tom kah kai*.

In the Commercial Center, 953 E. Sahara Ave. www.saipinchutima.com. (✆ **702/735-3033.** Reservations strongly recommended for dinner, call at least a day in advance. Main courses $10–$29; lunch buffet $10. AE, MC, V. Mon–Fri 11:30am–2pm and 5:30–9:30pm; Sat–Sun 5:30–10pm.

Pink Taco ★ MEXICAN   A megahip Mexican cantina, this folk art–bedecked spot is a scene just waiting to happen. There are no surprises in terms of the food; you know the drill—tacos, burritos, quesadillas—but it's all tasty and filling, and some of it comes with some surprising accompaniments, such as tapenade, along with the usual guacamole and sour cream. Despite it attempting to appear like a hole-in-the-wall, mom-and-pop joint, it's really a slick, hip operation and so the food and overall experience feels much more processed than Mexican restaurants that look like this usually are.

In the Hard Rock Hotel & Casino, 4455 Paradise Rd. www.hardrockhotel.com. ☏ **702/693-5525.** Reservations accepted only for groups of 10 or more. Main courses $7.50–$15. AE, DC, DISC, MC, V. Sun–Thurs 7am–10pm; Fri–Sat 7am–2am. Bar stays open later.

SOUTH & EAST OF THE STRIP

Expensive

Todd's Unique Dining ★★★ CONTINENTAL   Las Vegas is filled with some great dining options, most of which are located within steps of wherever you are staying. But true foodies know that to find the best culinary experiences you need to get away from the tourist areas, and that's most definitely true of Todd's Unique Dining. Located in a boring strip mall in Henderson, about 20 minutes from the Strip, this small bistro is the brainchild of Chef Todd Clore, former chef de cuisine for the Sterling Brunch at Bally's. It's intimate and friendly—a family restaurant where you'll often find the chef's wife waiting tables. The menu changes almost daily, focusing on the freshest ingredients Clore can get his hands on, which is most obvious in the seafood selections that rival, and in many cases beat, the fish you'll find at much more expensive restaurants on the Strip. Genius items like the lobster-wrapped sole, dressed in a simple yet flavorful butter sauce, prove that you don't need the backing of a big hotel to get the best catches. Signature items include grilled skirt steak "on fire," so spicy delicious it'll make your eyes water (in a good way) and served with fun chili-cheese fries; and a boneless braised short rib, slow-cooked for days and served in a red-wine gravy atop a bed of jalapeño mashed potatoes. The latter is like the best, most tender, most mouth-watering pot roast you'll ever have and is the reason you should put down this book, get in a cab, and head here for dinner right this second.

4350 E. Sunset Rd., Henderson (just east of Green Valley Pkwy.). www.toddsunique.com. ☏ **702/ 259-8633.** Reservations recommended. Main courses $25–$35. AE, DC, DISC, MC, V. Mon–Sat 4:30–10pm.

Moderate

Memphis Championship Barbecue ★★ BARBECUE   We simply refuse to get into the debate about Texas vs. Kansas City vs. Mississippi barbecue (and if you've got another place with the best dang barbecue, we really don't want to hear about it). But we can say that if you aren't physically in those places, you gotta take what you can get—and luckily for Vegas visitors, eating at Memphis Championship Barbecue is hardly settling. Its vinegar-based sauce is sweet but has a kick. Food is cooked over mesquite applewood, and the meat falls off the bone just the way you want it to. It offers hot links, baked beans, everything you would want and hope for. Standouts include a pulled-barbecue-chicken sandwich, onion straws, and delicious mac and cheese. ***Note this special:*** A $70 feast includes a rack of St. Louis or baby back ribs, a half-pound of pork, a half-pound of beef brisket, a half-pound of hot links, a whole chicken, baked beans, coleslaw, rolls, cream corn, and fries. It feeds four; we think even if two of those four are teenage boys, you might have leftovers.

2250 E. Warm Springs Rd. (near I-215). www.memphis-bbq.com. ☏ **702/260-6909.** Main courses $8–$23; special barbecue dinner for 4 $70. AE, MC, V. Mon–Fri 11am–10pm; Sat–Sun 8am–10pm.

PT's Gold ★ PUB GRUB   There are dozens of these locals' favorite diners around Las Vegas under the monikers PT's Gold, PT's Pubs, and PT's Place and all of them are pretty much the same as the others. That's not necessarily a bad thing when you get lots of beers on tap, a little gambling in the form of video poker and sports wagers, lots of TVs on which to watch your favorite game, and plenty of hearty, American pub grub–style food at prices that only veer into the moderate price territory when you are going for full entrees like steaks. Most of the time, though, you'll be more than satisfied with their burgers, pizzas, sandwiches (everything from Cuban to French Dip), breakfasts, and more, the bulk of which are under $10. The reason we are pointing out this particular location is because of it's unique views—the main runway of McCarran International Airport is directly across the street. You'll be surprised to find that watching planes land and take off can be so hypnotic.

1661 E. Sunset Rd. (at Spencer St.). www.ptstaverns.com. ℭ **702/616-0723.** Reservations not accepted. Main courses mainly under $15. AE, DC, MC, V. Daily 24 hours.

Inexpensive

Jason's Deli ★ DELI   A chain popular with locals, there are four Jason's in the area, but this one is convenient to those staying east of the Strip. It's a busy, bustling deli where all items are advertised as free of artificial trans fat and offering a selection of "slimwiches," so as multipurpose diner/delis go, this may be a fairly healthy option. Jason's also does a brisk take-out business, again useful for those staying in nearby chain hotels without much in the way of room service. There is the usual deli fare—at least a dozen soups, sandwiches, wraps, and junior meals. The wraps tip you off that this is not a Brooklyn-style pastrami deli, but fancy California-influenced versions of sandwiches. A wild card is the New Orleans–inspired muffalettas. The sandwiches are piled with meat, and the chicken potpie is huge. Naturally, the salad bar contains pudding and vanilla wafers—wouldn't want to carry "healthy" too far.

3910 S. Maryland Pkwy. www.jasonsdeli.com. ℭ **702/893-9799.** All items under $10. AE, DISC, MC, V. Daily 10am–9pm.

Paymon's Mediterranean Café & Lounge ★ MEDITERRANEAN   If you can get past the overwrought Mediterranean and Middle Eastern decor, you'll discover yet another interesting and authentic ethnic cuisine experience in a strip mall in Vegas. The menu skips around the region with stops in Greece (gyros, pitas, moussaka), Italy (lasagna, spaghetti, chicken parm'), and the Middle East (kabobs, kibbe, *fesenjan*), plus a detour to India (tandoori and chicken curry), which is geographically questionable but with food this good we'll let it slide. As the menu warns, kabobs take 20 minutes, so order an appetizer plate with various dips to while away the time. The hummus here is too reminiscent of its chickpea origins, but the *baba ghanouj* is properly smoky and the falafel has the right crunch. Gyros may not be the most adventurous thing to order, but who cares about that when you've got a well-stuffed pocket pita, gloopy with yogurt sauce. *Fesenjan* is a dish of falling-apart chicken swimming in a tangy pomegranate sauce; ask them to ensure that the ratio of sauce to chicken is greater than 10:1. Bonus points for the honest-to-goodness hookah lounge!

4147 S. Maryland Pkwy. (at Flamingo Rd., in the Tiffany Sq. strip mall). www.paymons.com. ℭ **702/731-6030.** Reservations not accepted. Main courses $9–$21; most sandwiches under $10. AE, DISC, MC, V. Daily 11am–1am.

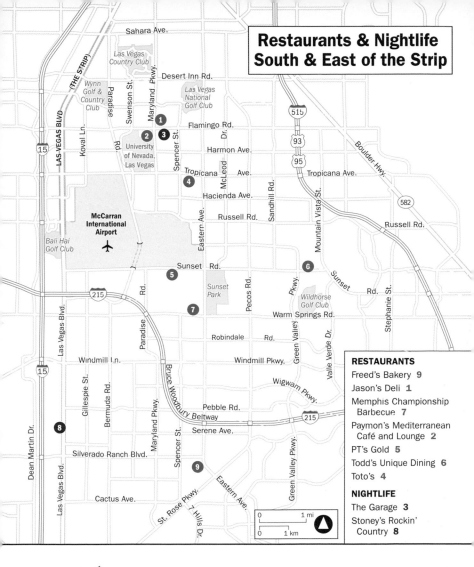

Restaurants & Nightlife
South & East of the Strip

Toto's ★ 🏷 MEXICAN A family-style Mexican restaurant favored by locals, with enormous portions and quick service, this is good value for your money. With all that food, you could probably split portions and still be satisfied. There are no surprises on the menu, though there are quite a few seafood dishes. Everything is quite tasty, and they don't skimp on the cheese. The nongreasy chips come with fresh salsa, and the nachos are terrific. Chicken tamales got a thumbs up, while the veggie burrito was happily received by non–meat eaters (although it's not especially healthy, all the ingredients were fresh, with huge slices of zucchini and roasted bell peppers). The operative word here is *huge*; the burritos are almost the size of your arm. The generous portions continue with dessert—a piece of flan was practically pie size. The Sunday margarita brunch is quite fun, and the drinks are large (naturally) and yummy.

2055 E. Tropicana Ave. ⓒ **702/895-7923.** Main courses $9–$18. AE, DISC, MC, V. Mon–Thurs 11am–10pm; Fri–Sat 11am–11pm; Sun 9:30am–10pm.

NORTH & WEST OF THE STRIP
Expensive

Austins Steakhouse ★ ★ 📖 STEAK/SEAFOOD   Now, understand that we don't send you out to nether regions such as Texas Station lightly. We do so here because, improbably, Austins Steakhouse has gained a reputation for serving what many consider to be the best steaks in town. Really. Even the snooty critics at the *Las Vegas Review-Journal* agree with the hubbub about this place. The filet is not only so tender and juicy that you can literally cut it with a fork, but it is one of the few filets in town that doesn't require some sort of accompaniment to make it interesting—it does that on its own in a smoky, woodhouse kind of way. The bone-in rib-eye is Texas epic and the prime rib (which you can often get on special) competes with the gold standard Lawry's for best in class. Note that a comparable meal on the Strip would cost $10 to $20 more per person—yet another reason to head out to the hinterlands.

In Texas Station, 2101 Texas Star Lane. www.texasstation.com. ⓒ **702/631-1033.** Reservations recommended. Main courses $19–$54. AE, DC, DISC, MC, V. Sun–Thurs 5–10pm; Fri–Sat 5–11pm.

Moderate

Cathay House CHINESE   Ordering dim sum, for those of you who haven't experienced it, is sort of like being at a Chinese sushi bar, in that you order many individual, tasty little dishes. Of course, dim sum itself is nothing like sushi. Rather, it's a range of pot stickers, pan-fried dumplings, *baos* (soft, doughy buns filled with such meat as barbecued pork), translucent rice noodles wrapped around shrimp, sticky rice in lotus leaves, chicken feet, and so forth. Some of it is steamed; some is fried—for that extra-good grease! You can make your own dipping sauce by combining soy sauce, vinegar, and hot-pepper oil. The waitstaff pushes steam carts filled with little dishes; point, and they'll attempt to tell you what each one is. Better, just blindly order a bunch and dig in. Each dish ranges from approximately $1 to $3; each server makes a note of what you just received, and the total is tallied at the end. (For some reason, it almost always works out to about $9 per person.) Dim sum is usually available only until midafternoon.

   Note: The 24/7 Café at the Palms, 4321 W. Flamingo Rd. (www.palms. com; ⓒ **702/980-8888**), serves Cathay House specialties and dim sum.

5300 W. Spring Mountain Rd. ⓒ **702/876-3838.** Reservations recommended. Main courses $6.75–$19. AE, DC, DISC, MC, V. Daily 10:30am–10pm.

M&M Soul Food ★ ★ 📖 SOUL FOOD   Though we've listed this in the North/West area, it's really not too far from the Strip. At first glance, the neighborhood seems intimidating, but it's not actually threatening. Why come here? Because locals have voted this their favorite soul-food place, and while the competition may not be all that high, the quality stands out regardless. Appropriately, it's a hole in the wall, with somewhat higher prices than one might expect, but the generous portions make up for it. Mini cornbread pancakes are served to every table. Smothered fried chicken is moist, slightly spicy, and topped with a robust gravy. The menu includes hot links, collard greens, and other typical options.

Restaurants North & West of the Strip

Smoke Ranch Rd.

Lake Mead Blvd.

Vegas Dr.

1

Simmons St.

Martin Luther King Blvd.

Vegas Dr.

Owens Ave.

95

Summerlin Pkwy.

Jones Blvd.

Decatur Blvd.

Las Vegas
Golf Course

Lorenzi
Park

Washington Ave.

93

15

Rancho Dr.

Rampart Blvd.

Alta Dr.

95

Springs
Preserve

DOWNTOWN

Charleston Blvd.

2

Oakey Blvd.

Rancho Dr.

Cimarron Rd.

Buffalo Dr.

Rainbow Blvd.

Sahara Ave.

Fort Apache Rd.

Durango Dr.

Tenaya Way

Torrey Pines Dr.

Jones Blvd.

Lindell Rd.

Decatur Blvd.

Arville St.

Valley View Blvd.

15

Las Vegas
Country Club

Desert Inn Rd.

Spring Mountain Rd.

5

3 **4**

Twain Ave.

Spring Mtn. Rd.

Wynn Golf
and
Country Club

Flamingo Rd.

LAS VEGAS BLVD. (THE STRIP)

UNLV

Austins Steakhouse **1**
Cathay House **4**
M&M Soul Food **2**
Raku Grill **3**
Viva Mercados **5**

0 ____ 1 mi
0 ____ 1 km

Tropicana Ave.

Hacienda Ave.

McCarran
Int'l Airport

3923 W. Charleston. www.mmsoulfoodcafe.com. ☎ **702/453-7685.** Main courses $6–$18. AE, DISC, MC, V. Daily 7am–8pm.

Raku Grill ★★★ JAPANESE   At first glance, it's not the kind of place you'd expect to get rave notices in *GQ* and *New York*. It's also not the kind of place you'd expect master chefs like Paul Bartolotta to frequent. But get past the run-down Strip mall location on the west side of town and you'll find one of the most interesting, unique, and purely divine restaurants in all of Las Vegas. It's tiny, with seats for fewer than three dozen, and what with all the deserved attention it has gotten, those seats are hard to come by (make reservations at least a week if not more in advance). But if you get one, you'll be treated to a litany of taste bud–popping flavors from the *robata* grill.

Everything is small plates, most served on skewers. It's the esoteric items that have gotten most of the press—pork ear, pork cheek, Kobe beef liver—but the long list includes perfectly moist chicken breast, Kobe with milder-than-expected wasabi, a miniature lamb chop, seared foie gras, grilled duck, asparagus or tomato wrapped in bacon (both joy inducing in their freshness), ground chicken, and much more. Daily specials include seafood flown in from Japan, and there is also an *odin* (broth pot) section and rice, noodle, and soup dishes. But it is that *robata* grill that should dominate your choices—the smoky charcoal-grill flavor brings everything to life but allows each dish to have its own distinct flavors. Even the somewhat less than mainstream options are heavenly, with the

sweet SENSATIONS

Plenty of opportunities exist in Vegas for satisfying your sweet tooth, but for the discriminating, here are five spots that you may have to make a detour for.

Jean-Philippe Patisserie ★★★ (pictured), in Bellagio, 3600 Las Vegas Blvd. S. (www.jpchocolates.com; ✆ **702/693-8788**), makes us swoon, not just because it has the world's largest chocolate fountain (20 ft. high! Though only 11 ft. are on view, and they won't let us drink from it. Darn.), but perhaps, more to the point, it's the home of World Pastry champion Jean-Philippe Maury. (Yes, you can win gold medals for pastries.) Each visit causes us to spin around distractedly, trying to take in all the choices, both visually and gastronomically. From perfect gourmet chocolates to ice cream to diet-conscious sorbets to the eponymous pastries, each of which are little works of art, we hit greed overload. For us, this is true Vegas decadence—if only "what happens in Vegas, stays in Vegas" applied to calories. The patisserie also serves some solidly good sandwiches, and some adequate savory crepes. It is open Sunday through Thursday from 7am to 11pm and Friday and Saturday from 7am until midnight.

A local favorite is **Freed's Bakery,** 9815 S. Eastern Ave., at Silverado Ranch Blvd. (www.freedsbakery.com; ✆ **702/456-7762**), open Monday through Saturday from 8am to 8pm and Sunday from 8am to 6pm. If you've got a serious sugar craving, this is worth the 20-minute drive from the Strip. It's like walking into Grandma's kitchen, provided you had an old-fashioned granny who felt pastries should be gooey, chocolaty, and buttery. Their signature wedding cakes will make you want to rush down the aisle, but you'll want to bring a basket for the fresh bread, Napoleons, strawberry cheesecake, cream puffs, sweet rolls, Danishes, and doughnuts, many of which are made with surprisingly fresh ingredients. Some may find the goodies too heavy and rich, but for those of us with a powerful sweet tooth, this place hits the spot. There is no dining area so everything is to go; do try to at least make it to your car before you start digging in.

We used to try to send you to Henderson to experience the delights of **The Cupcakery ★★★**, but now there's a branch open at Monte Carlo, 3770 Las Vegas Blvd. S. (✆ **702/207-2253**; www.thecupcakery.com). The delectable cakes here aren't large, but they pack a wallop of moist cake and creamy frosting. Clever combinations include the Boston cream pie (filled with

pork cheek tasting basically like a hunk of bacon lard, and we mean that in a good way. Although most of the selections are only a few bucks (most under $5), it is easy to rack up a big bill here because after the first bite you'll be tempted to just have them bring you everything on the menu. And we would not blame you for doing so.

5030 W. Spring Mountain Rd., no. 2 (at Decatur). www.raku-grill.com. ✆ **702/367-3511.** Reservations required. *Robata* grill items $3–$16. AE, MC, V. Mon–Sat 6pm–3am.

Viva Mercado's ★★ MEXICAN   Ask any local about Mexican food in Vegas, and almost certainly they will point to Viva Mercado's as the best in town. That recommendation, plus the restaurant's health-conscious attitude, makes this worth the roughly 10-minute drive from the Strip.

custardy cream), but even the basic chocolate-on-chocolate is a buttercream pleasure. There are even sugarfree cupcakes for those with such dietary needs. The Cupcakery is open Monday to Friday 8am to 6pm, Saturday 10am to 8pm, and Sunday noon to 6pm.

As long as we're on the topic, national chain **Gigi's Cupcakes** has opened a branch at the Plaza Hotel in Downtown Las Vegas at 1 Main St. (www.gigiscupcakesusa.com; ✆ **702/386-2110**). The frosting is piled high just the way we like it, and many of the cakes have chocolate chunks baked right so you get a double-dose of sweetness. Check out the minicupcakes, which are just as good but may make you feel as though you are practicing restraint—even if you get a dozen of them. The store is open Sunday through Monday from 10am until 10pm and Friday and Saturday from 10am until 11pm.

Hot Vegas days call for cool desserts, and frozen custard (softer than regular ice cream, but harder than soft serve) is a fine way to go. Head for **Luv-It Frozen Custard,** 505 E. Oakey (www.luvitfrozencustard.com; ✆ **702/384-6452**), open Sunday through Thursday from 1 to 10pm and Friday and Saturday from 1 to 11pm. Because custard has less fat and sugar than premium ice cream, you can even fool yourself into thinking this is somewhat healthful (ha!). Made every few hours using fresh cream and eggs, the custard is available in basic flavors for cup or cone, but more exotic flavors (maple walnut, apple spice, and more) come in tubs.

Given all those warnings about Mexican food and its heart-attack-inducing properties, the approach at Viva Mercado's is nothing to be sniffed at. No dish is prepared with or cooked in any kind of animal fat. Nope, the lard so dear to Mexican cooking is not found here. The oil used is an artery-friendly canola. This makes the place particularly appealing to vegetarians, who will also be pleased by the regular veggie specials. Everything is quite fresh, and particularly amazing things are done with seafood. Try the Mariscos Vallarta, which is fillet of *basa,* scallops, langostino, and shrimp cooked in a tomato sauce, with capers and olives. There are all sorts of noteworthy shrimp dishes and a dozen different salsas, ranked 1 to 10 for degree of spice. The staff is friendly (try to chat with owner Bobby Mercado) and the portions hearty.

3553 S. Rainbow Rd. (near Spring Mountain Rd.). www.vivamercadoslv.com. ☎ **702/871-8826.** Reservations only accepted for large parties. Main courses $14–$25. AE, DISC, MC, V. Sun–Thurs 11am–9:30pm; Fri–Sat 11am–10pm.

BUFFETS & BRUNCHES

Like so much else that was Vegas tradition, the buffets have evolved. Gone, mostly, are the days of trays and cafeteria-style lines serving heaping mounds of warmed-over blandness at bargain-basement prices. The modern buffet uses come-and-go serving areas, live-action cooking stations, multiple ethnic and regional cuisines, and a general rise in quality that puts many on par with traditional restaurants. Of course, as the quality has gone up so, too, have the prices, which now make them less of a bargain. But consider it this way: You would pay much more, per person, at one of the fancier restaurants in town, where you would order just one, potentially disappointing, item. At a buffet there's more variety and more chance to find something you love. More variety per person means less likelihood for disappointment, so if you hate what you picked you can simply dump your plate and start all over. They are, generally speaking, not nearly as atmospheric as a proper restaurant, but how else can you combine good barbecue with excellent Chinese and a cupcake or 10?

There is a lot of variety within the buffet genre. Some are still buffet basic with the perfunctory steam-table displays and salad bars that are heavy on the iceberg lettuce, while others are unbelievably opulent spreads with caviar and free-flowing champagne. Some are quite beautifully presented as well. Some of the food is awful, some of it is decent, and some of it is memorable.

Buffets are extremely popular, and reservations are not taken so be prepared for a long line at peak times. Eating at offbeat hours (lunch at 2pm for example) will mean a shorter wait to get in, as will some hotel/casino players' club cards, which can get you line cuts.

Note: At press time, several hotels were offering all-you-can-eat all-day-long packages where you could pay one flat fee and come back to the buffets as many times as you like in a given day. Caesars Entertainment (Harrah's, Flamingo, Rio, and so on) is even offering a full-day pass to all of their buffets for $45 so you can mix and match. Details and pricing on these change often, so visit the hotel's website or call ahead to see if they are offering any special deals when you're in town.

South Strip
EXPENSIVE

The Buffet at Aria ★ BUFFET   While the food here may not be the pinnacle of all-you-can-eat delights, it is certainly a cut above standard buffet fare. Various regional and ethnic food stations (love the tandoori oven!) serve up enough variety to keep your stomach confused for days (pizza, pot stickers, and hummus on one plate?) and the quality is evident with every bite, although very little of it is so good that it makes you want to go back for seconds. Well, maybe the full rack of bacon at the carving station during the weekend brunches is worth another helping. The room is bright, airy, modern, and totally forgettable, except for the very nice outdoor dining patio.

At Aria Las Vegas, 3730 Las Vegas Blvd. S. www.arialasvegas.com. ☎ **702/590-7111.** Breakfast $17; lunch $21; dinner $31–$39; Sat–Sun champagne brunch $31. AE, DC, DISC, MC, V. Daily 7am–10pm.

Mandalay Bay's Bayside Buffet ★ BUFFET   This is a particularly pretty, not overly large buffet. Floor-to-ceiling windows overlooking the beach part of the elaborate pool area make it less stuffy and eliminate the closed-in feeling that so many of the other buffets in town have. The buffet itself is adequately arranged but features nothing particularly special, though there are some nice salads, hearty meats, and a larger and better-than-average dessert bar—they make their own desserts, and it shows.

In Mandalay Bay, 3950 Las Vegas Blvd. S. www.mandalaybay.com. ℰ **702/632-7402.** Breakfast $16; lunch $20; dinner $28; Sun brunch $25. Reduced prices for children 5–11; free for children 4 and under. AE, DC, DISC, MC, V. Daily 7am–2:30pm and 4:45–9:45pm.

MGM Grand Buffet BUFFET   On paper, this cavernous buffet certainly sounds interesting. Consider the made-to-order Belgian waffle station at breakfast, the Argentinean grill station at brunch, and the endless crab legs and prime rib at dinner. Still, the high prices and lackluster preparation put this on the second tier of our preferred buffet list.

In MGM Grand, 3799 Las Vegas Blvd. S. www.mgmgrand.com. ℰ **702/891-7777.** Breakfast $17; weekday brunch $23; dinner $30–$36; Sat–Sun brunch $25. Reduced prices for children 4–11; free for children 3 and under. AE, DC, DISC, MC, V. Daily 7am–2:30pm and 4:30–10pm.

MODERATE

Excalibur's Roundtable Buffet ★ BUFFET   This one strikes the perfect balance of moderate prices, forgettable decor, and adequate food. It's what you want in a cheap Vegas buffet—except it's just not that cheap anymore. Then again, none are anymore, so this still qualifies and, thus, usually has long lines.

In Excalibur, 3850 Las Vegas Blvd. S. www.excalibur.com ℰ **702/597-7777.** Breakfast $15; lunch $16; dinner $20. AE, DC, DISC, MC, V. Daily 7am–10pm.

Monte Carlo Buffet ★ BUFFET   A "courtyard" under a painted sky, the Monte Carlo's buffet room has a Moroccan market theme, with murals of Arab scenes, Moorish archways, Oriental carpets, and walls hung with photographs of and artifacts from Morocco. Dinner includes a rotisserie (for chicken and pork loin, or London broil), a Chinese food station, a taco/fajita bar, a baked potato bar, numerous salads, and more than a dozen desserts, plus frozen yogurt and ice-cream machines. Lunches are similar. At breakfast, the expected fare is supplemented by an omelet station, and choices include crepes, blintzes, and corned-beef hash. Fresh-baked bagels are a plus.

In Monte Carlo Resort & Casino, 3770 Las Vegas Blvd. S. www.montecarlo.com. ℰ **702/730-7777.** Brunch $17–$20; dinner $20–$25. Reduced prices for children 5–11; free for children 4 and under. AE, DC, DISC, MC, V. Daily 7am–3pm and 4–10pm.

MORE, The Buffet at Luxor ★ BUFFET   Once one of our favorite buffets not just for the excellent price-to-quality ratio, but also because of its Indiana Jones–invoking decor, the Luxor buffet has been redesigned and renamed as part of the ongoing de-Egypt-ing of the hotel. Dang. We are sick of neato modern classy already and want our mummies back. That said, the food is the best in its price range, and it is one of the top buffets in town. There's a Mexican station with some genuinely spicy food, a Chinese stir-fry station, and different Italian pastas. Desserts were disappointing, though they do offer a pretty large selection of diabetic-friendly options. The quality-to-price ratio is no secret, and, as a result, the lines are always enormous.

In Luxor, 3900 Las Vegas Blvd. S. www.luxor.com. ☎ **702/262-4000.** Breakfast $15; lunch $16; dinner $20. Reduced prices for children 4–10; free for children 3 and under. AE, DC, DISC, MC, V. Daily 7am–10pm.

Mid-Strip
EXPENSIVE

Bellagio Buffet ★★ BUFFET   Though one of the priciest of the buffets, the Bellagio still gets high marks from visitors. The array of food is fabulous, with one ethnic cuisine after another (Japanese, Chinese that includes dim sum, build-it-yourself Mexican items, and so on). There are elaborate pastas and semitraditional Italian-style pizza from a wood-fired oven. The cold fish appetizers at each end of the line are not to be missed—scallops, smoked salmon, crab claws, shrimp, oysters, and assorted condiments. Other specialties include breast of duck and game hens. There is no carving station, but you can get the meat precarved. The salad bar is more ordinary, though prepared salads have some fine surprises, such as the eggplant-tofu salad and an exceptional Chinese chicken salad. Desserts, unfortunately, look better than they actually are.

In Bellagio, 3600 Las Vegas Blvd. S. www.bellagio.com. ☎ **877/234-6358.** Mon–Thurs breakfast $16, lunch $20, dinner $30; Fri breakfast $16, lunch $20, dinner $37; Sat brunch $24–$29, dinner $36; Sun brunch $24–$29, dinner $30. Free for children 2 and under. AE, DC, DISC, MC, V. Daily 7am–10pm.

Le Village Buffet ★★★ BUFFET   One of the more ambitious buffets, with a price to match—still, you do get a fine assortment of food and more value for the dollar than you are likely to find anywhere else. The Paris buffet is housed in a Disneyland-esque replica of a French village that is either a charming respite from Vegas lights or sickening, depending on your perspective. Buffet stations are grouped according to French regions, and though in theory entrees change daily, there do seem to be some constants like their famous made-to-order crepes and bananas Foster. Although there are some French spins on dishes, most of it is good old-fashioned American grub, so don't let the Parisian flair scare you away.

In Paris Las Vegas, 3655 Las Vegas Blvd. S. www.parislasvegas.com. ☎ **888/266-5687.** Mon–Fri breakfast $16, lunch $20, dinner $30–$37; Sat–Sun brunch $30. Reduced prices for children 4–10; free for children 3 and under. AE, DC, DISC, MC, V. Daily 7am–10pm.

Mirage Cravings Buffet ★ BUFFET   This buffet features a gleaming, streamlined look, all shining steel and up-to-the-minute high-design concept. Gone are the heaping mounds of shrimp and other symbols of Vegas excess and bargain. In its place are plenty of live-action stations, with noteworthy items such as an excellent pizza, pot stickers and Chinese barbecue pork, quite good barbecue, tangy Japanese cucumber salad, and slightly dry but flavorful Mexican slow-roasted pork. A trip to the made-to-order salad station is so pokey, you'll need to find the other salads that are hidden with the open-faced sandwiches (where you can also find the gefilte fish). The hand-scooped gelato is yummy but the rest of the desserts are generally disappointing. Despite the drawbacks, this remains popular with buffet connoisseurs.

In The Mirage, 3400 Las Vegas Blvd. S. www.mirage.com. ☎ **702/791-7111.** Breakfast $16; lunch $20; dinner $27; Sat–Sun brunch $25. Reduced prices for children 5–10; free for children 4 and under. AE, DC, DISC, MC, V. Daily 8am–10pm.

Wicked Spoon Buffet ★ BUFFET   Although the bulk of this buffet is pretty standard (food in trays that you spoon onto a plate), they twist things up a bit by doing lots of "small plate" offerings—eggs Benedict served in a miniature copper pan, for instance. It's interesting although it does make carting your food back to your table a little more challenging. They have the full range of cuisines (American to Chinese, Mexican to seafood, and beyond) plus some live-action cooking stations that you'd expect of a modern buffet. That said, there's really nothing here that makes it stand out as a must-visit all-you-can-eat experience.

In The Cosmopolitan of Las Vegas, 3708 Las Vegas Blvd. S. www.cosmopolitanlasvegas.com. ☏ **877/551-7772.** Weekday brunch $22; weekend brunch $29; dinner $35. AE, DC, DISC, MC, V. Brunch Mon–Fri 8am–2pm, Sat–Sun 8am–3pm; dinner Sun–Thurs 5–9pm, Fri–Sat 5–10pm.

MODERATE

The Buffet at TI ★ BUFFET   This handsome buffet space is done as sort of contemporary diner, all dark gleaming wood, mirrors, and geometric lines. We feel mixed on the food choices; this is a smaller buffet than one might expect for such a big hotel, and while there is a reasonable range of cuisines (Italian; Japanese, with sushi chefs who will make up fresh plates for you; Southern, including unexpected spoon bread; deli), there isn't the overwhelming bounty we've come to consider our right when it comes to Vegas buffets. However, there are some well-considered and fine-tasting deli sandwiches (brie and honey, roast beef with goat cheese), plus better-than-decent barbecue ribs and Chinese options. Some of the most charming dessert choices focus on such childhood tastes as cupcakes, fresh cotton candy, and quite good crème brûlée (yes, not exactly real kiddie fare, but, let's face it, it's just exceptionally good vanilla custard!). Best of all are the adorable minidoughnuts, fresh out of the fryer; we ate two dozen and we are not ashamed.

In Treasure Island, 3300 Las Vegas Blvd. S. www.treasureisland.com. ☏ **702/894-7111.** Breakfast $17; lunch $19; dinner Mon–Thurs $23, Fri–Sun $27; Sat–Sun champagne brunch $24. Reduced prices for children 4–10; free for children 3 and under. AE, DC, DISC, MC, V. Daily 7am–10pm.

Flamingo Paradise Garden Buffet ★ BUFFET   This buffet occupies a vast room, with floor-to-ceiling windows overlooking a verdant tropical landscape of cascading waterfalls and koi ponds. At dinner, there is an extensive international food station (which changes monthly), presenting French, Chinese, Mexican, German, or Italian specialties. A large salad bar, fresh fruits, pastas, vegetables, potato dishes, and a vast dessert display round out the offerings. Lunch is similar, featuring international cuisines as well as a stir-fry station and a soup/salad/pasta bar. At breakfast, you'll find all the expected fare, including a made-to-order omelet station and fresh-baked breads. The seafood is dry and tough, and desserts are uninspired.

In Flamingo Las Vegas, 3555 Las Vegas Blvd. S. www.flamingolv.com. ☏ **702/733-3111.** Breakfast $16; lunch $17; dinner $20–$22; Sat–Sun champagne brunch $20. Reduced prices for children 4–10; free for children 3 and under. AE, DC, DISC, MC, V. Daily 7am–10pm.

Flavors at Harrah's ★ BUFFET   A casually comfortable room may not be all that special, but the food at least approaches it. Oddly, here it's the carving station that stands out, with simultaneous servings of turkey, ham, prime rib, chicken, game hen, sausage, roast vegetables, and lamb. The other stations are typical—Mexican, Italian, seafood, Chinese. A particularly good dessert area is

5

WHERE TO EAT

Buffets & Brunches

heavy on the cookies, cakes, and little pastries, such as Oreo mousse tarts and mini crème brûlées.

In Harrah's, 3475 Las Vegas Blvd. S. www.harrahslv.com. ℭ **702/369-5000.** Breakfast $18; lunch $19; dinner $22–$24; brunch Sat–Sun $21. Reduced prices for children 4–10; free for children 3 and under. AE, MC, V. Daily 7am–10pm.

Spice Market Buffet ★★ BUFFET   This is one of the better choices in the city, thanks to unexpected (and pretty good) Middle Eastern specialties, including the occasional Moroccan entrees. Look for tandoori chicken, hummus, couscous, stuffed tomatoes with ground lamb, and, at dinner, lamb skewers. The Mexican station is particularly good as well, even if it confuses the palate to go from guacamole to hummus. The dim sum also gets a vote of confidence. There is cotton candy at lunch and a crepe-making station at dinner. We still wish it were a bit cheaper; at these prices, it's edging toward the high end.

3667 Las Vegas Blvd. S. www.planethollywoodresort.com. ℭ **702/785-5555.** Breakfast $18–$21; lunch $21; dinner $30; Sat–Sun champagne brunch $27. AE, DC, DISC, MC, V. Daily 7am–10pm.

North Strip
VERY EXPENSIVE
Wynn Las Vegas Buffet ★★★ BUFFET   Goodness, we do love a nice buffet, and this one is particularly nice (if notably superexpensive). It's thoughtful and artful, starting with the *Alice in Wonderland*–evoking atrium styled with towers of fruit flowers and foliage and even some natural light. Don't worry if you don't score one of the few tables set there; it's a bit far from the food lines, and you want to be close to the action, after all. Look for such items as jerk chicken, wood-fired pizza, honey-glazed pork, nice little salmon rolls, five kinds of *ceviche*, sweet Kansas City–style barbecue, and tandoori chicken among the stations, which include Mexican, Southern, seafood, and Italian. Desserts are superior to those at probably all the other buffets, in construction and in taste, giving the impression that a pastry chef is active on the premises. Don't miss the mini floating islands, the unusual tiramisu, the excellent chocolate mousse and ice creams, and even a plate full of madeleines.

In Wynn Las Vegas, 3131 Las Vegas Blvd. S. www.wynnlasvegas.com. ℭ **702/248-3463.** Breakfast $20; lunch $24; dinner $37–$40; Sat–Sun brunch $32–$44. AE, DC, DISC, MC, V. Sun–Thurs 8am–10pm; Fri–Sat 8am–10:30pm.

INEXPENSIVE
Circus Circus Buffet BUFFET   Here's a trade-off: It's just about the cheapest buffet on the Strip but also what some consider the worst in town. Here you'll find 50 items of typical cafeteria fare, and none of them is all that good. If food is strictly fuel for you, you can't go wrong here. Otherwise, find another buffet.

In Circus Circus, 2880 Las Vegas Blvd. S. www.circuscircus.com. ℭ **702/734-0410.** Breakfast $12; lunch $14; dinner $15. AE, DC, DISC, MC, V. Daily 7am–2pm and 4:30–10pm.

Downtown
MODERATE
Golden Nugget Buffet ★★ BUFFET   This buffet has often been voted number one in Las Vegas, and while we wouldn't go that far, it certainly is top

quality. Most of the seating is in plush booths. The buffet tables are laden with an extensive salad bar (about 50 items), fresh fruit, and marvelous desserts. Fresh seafood is featured every night. Most lavish is the all-day Sunday champagne brunch, which adds such dishes as eggs Benedict, blintzes, pancakes, creamed herring, and smoked fish with bagels and cream cheese.

In Golden Nugget, 129 E. Fremont St. www.goldennugget.com. ☎ **702/385-7111.** Breakfast $11; lunch $12; dinner Mon–Thurs $19, Fri–Sun $22; Sat–Sun brunch $20. Discounts for children 3–12; free for children 2 and under. AE, DC, DISC, MC, V. Mon–Fri 7am–10pm; Sat–Sun 8am–10pm.

INEXPENSIVE

Fremont Paradise Buffet ★ BUFFET   A combination buffet and coffee shop offers you the choice to do the all-you-can-eat strategy or order off a menu of diner favorites. Nothing is terribly surprising here except, perhaps, for the larger-than-average selection of Asian specialties (the hotel caters to Pacific Rim tourists), but everything is hearty, satisfying, and warm when it should be. Plus it's hard to beat these kinds of prices.

At the Fremont Hotel, 200 Fremont St. www.fremontcasino.com. ☎ **702/385-3232.** Breakfast $8; lunch $9; dinner $15–$19; Sat–Sun champagne brunch $12. AE, DC, DISC, MC, V. Mon–Fri 7–10:30am, 11am–3pm, and 4–10pm; Sat–Sun 7am–3pm and 4–10pm.

Main Street Station Garden Court ★★★ 🍴 BUFFET   Set in what is truly one of the prettiest buffet spaces in town (and certainly in Downtown), with very high ceilings and tall windows bringing in much-needed natural light, the Main Street Station Garden Court buffet is one of the best in town, let alone Downtown. It features nine live-action stations where you can watch your food being prepared, including a wood-fired brick-oven pizza (delicious); many fresh salsas at the Mexican station; a barbecue rotisserie; fresh sausage at the carving station; Chinese, Hawaiian, and Southern specialties (soul food and the like); and so many more we lost count. On Friday night, it has all this and nearly infinite varieties of seafood, all the way up to lobster. We ate ourselves into a stupor and didn't regret it.

At Main Street Station, 200 N. Main St. www.mainstreetcasino.com. ☎ **702/387-1896.** Breakfast $8; lunch $9; dinner $12–$23; Sat–Sun champagne brunch $12. Free for children 3 and under. AE, DC, DISC, MC, V. Daily 7–10:30am, 11am–3pm, and 4–10pm.

Just Off the Strip

EXPENSIVE

Rio's Carnival World Buffet ★★ BUFFET   This buffet has long been voted by locals as the best in Vegas, and for good reason. It's laid out as a food court of sorts with "South American" cooked-to-order stir-fries, Mexican taco fixings and accompaniments, Chinese fare, a Japanese sushi bar and *teppanyaki* grill, a Brazilian mixed grill, Italian pasta and antipasto, and fish and chips. There's even a diner setup for hot dogs, burgers, fries, and milkshakes. All this is in addition to the usual offerings of most Las Vegas buffets. Best of all, a dessert station features at least 70 kinds of pies, cakes, and pastries from an award-winning pastry chef, plus a large selection of gelatos and sorbets.

In Rio All-Suite Hotel & Casino, 3700 W. Flamingo Rd. www.riolasvegas.com. ☎ **702/252-7777.** Breakfast $19; lunch $22; dinner $30; Sat–Sun champagne brunch $30. Reduced prices for children 4–8; free for children 3 and under. AE, DC, MC, V. Daily 8am–10pm.

INEXPENSIVE

Gold Coast Ports O' Call ★ BUFFET   As formerly bargain buffet prices skyrocket—and we aren't helping matters by highly recommending $30-and-up places such as the Wynn buffet—it's getting harder and harder to find anything budget-minded on the Strip. Well, anywhere worth eating, certainly. This isn't on the Strip, but it is nearby, and the prices are cheaper than at any buffet on the Strip. Plus, you are less likely to find tremendous lines here. Having said that, don't expect anything miraculous, though they get points for keeping the food at the correct temperature (many a buffet's hot food suffers from a cooling effect as it sits out). Options run the usual gamut: Asian (decent pot stickers), Mexican (fine beef fajitas), and a carving station (with full rotisserie chickens).

In Gold Coast, 4000 W. Flamingo Rd. www.goldcoastcasino.com. ☎ **702/367-7111.** Breakfast $7; lunch $9; dinner $13–$18; Sun brunch $12. Reduced prices for children 4–9; free for children 3 and under. Mon–Sat 7–10am, 11am–3pm, and 4–9pm; Sun 8am–3pm and 4–9pm.

PRACTICAL MATTERS: THE DINING SCENE

GETTING IN   There are tricks to surviving dining in Vegas. If you can, make reservations in advance, particularly for the better restaurants. You might get to town, planning to check out some of the better spots, only to find that they are totally booked throughout your stay. Eat during off hours when you can. Know that noon to, say, 1:30 or 2pm is prime time for lunch, and 5:30 to 8:30pm (and just after the early shows get out) is prime time for dinner. Speaking of time, give yourself plenty of it, particularly if you have to catch a show. Even casual restaurants can take up longer-than-expected chunks of your time that could make you late for the curtain.

SAVING MONEY   So you want to sample the creations of a celebrity chef, but you took a beating at the craps table? Check our listings to see which of the high-profile restaurants are open for lunch. Sure, sometimes the more interesting and exotic items are found at dinner, but the midday meal is usually no slouch and can be as much as two-thirds cheaper.

Or skip that highfalutin' stuff altogether. The late-night specials—a complete steak meal for just a few dollars—are also an important part of a good, decadent Vegas experience. And having complained about how prices have gone up, we'll also tell you that you can still eat cheaply and decently all over town. The locals repeatedly say that they almost never cook, because in Vegas it is always cheaper to eat out. To locate budget fare, check local newspapers (especially Friday editions) and free magazines (such as *What's On in Las Vegas*), which are given away at hotel reception desks. Sometimes these sources also yield money-saving coupons.

Be on the lookout for weekday night specials as well. Many high-end restaurants offer prix-fixe menus on their off nights or for pretheater audiences for significantly less money. You may not be able to sample the truly extravagant dishes, but it'll get you a taste of the good life.

BEING ADVENTUROUS   Virtually every major national chain restaurant has an outlet in Las Vegas, from Applebee's to Yoshinoya (sorry, we couldn't think of a Z). We understand the inclination to want to stick with something safe and known, but the city is packed with one-of-a-kind (or at least one-of-a-very-few) eateries of all different cuisines and price points that will make your vacation more memorable for having dined there. You can go to Olive Garden when you get home.

A FINAL WORD   As welcome as the influx of designer chefs is, you can't help but notice that the majority are simply re-creating their best work (and sometimes not even that) from elsewhere rather than producing something new. So the Vegas food scene remains, like its architecture, a copy of something from somewhere else. And as happy as we are to encourage you to throw money at these guys, please don't forget the mom-and-pop places, which struggle not to disappear into the maw of the big hotel machines and which produce what comes the closest to true local quality. If you can, get in a car and check out some of the options listed below that are a bit off the beaten track. Show Vegas you aren't content—you want a meal you can brag about and afford, now!

RESTAURANTS BY CUISINE

AMERICAN
Carson Street Cafe ($, p. 132)
Dick's Last Resort ★★ ($$, p. 105)
FIRST Food and Bar ★★ ($$, p. 120)
Hard Rock Cafe ★ ($$, p. 106)
Hash House a Go Go ★★★ ($$, p. 120)
Holstein's Shakes and Buns ★★ ($$, p. 121)
Lagasse's Stadium ★ ($$, p. 121)
Margaritaville ★ ($$, p. 106)
Max Brenner Chocolate Restaurant ★★ ($$, p. 122)
munchbar ★★★ ($$, p. 123)
PBR Rock Bar & Grill ★ ($$, p. 107)
Planet Hollywood ($$, p. 107)
PJ Clarke's ★★ ($$, p. 123)
Rainforest Café ($$, p. 107)
Rock & Rita's ★ ($, p. 129)
Serendipity 3 ★ ($$, p. 124)
The Sporting House ($$, p. 107)
Sugar Factory ★★ ($$, p. 107)
Table 10 ★★ ($$$, p. 118)

ASIAN
Grand Wok ★★ ($$, p. 105)
Red 8 ★★ ($$, p. 129)

BARBECUE
BB King's Blues Club ★ ($$, p. 106)
Gilley's ★★ ($$, p. 120)
Lynyrd Skynyrd Beer & BBQ ★ ($, p. 109)
Memphis Championship Barbecue ★★ ($$, p. 139)

BISTRO
Bouchon ★★★ ($$$, p. 115)
Mon Ami Gabi ★★★ ($$, p. 122)
Payard Patisserie & Bistro ★★★ ($$, p. 123)
Pinot Brasserie ★★ ($$$, p. 117)

BUFFETS/BRUNCHES
Bellagio Buffet ★★ ($$$, p. 148)
The Buffet at Aria ★ ($$$, p. 146)
The Buffet at TI ★ ($$, p. 149)
Circus Circus Buffet ($, p. 150)
Excalibur's Roundtable Buffet ★ ($$, p. 147)
Flamingo Paradise Garden Buffet ★ ($$, p. 149)
Flavors at Harrah's ★ ($$, p. 149)
Fremont Paradise Buffet ★ ($, p. 151)
Gold Coast Ports O' Call ★ ($, p. 152)

KEY TO ABBREVIATIONS:
$$$$** = Very Expensive   **$$$** = Expensive   **$$** = Moderate   **$ = Inexpensive

Golden Nugget Buffet ★★ ($$, p. 150)

Le Village Buffet ★★★ ($$$, p. 148)

Main Street Station Garden Court ★★★ ($, p. 151)

Mandalay Bay's Bayside Buffet ★ ($$$, p. 147)

MGM Grand Buffet ($$$, p. 147)

Mirage Cravings Buffet ★ ($$$, p. 148)

Monte Carlo Buffet ★ ($$, p. 147)

MORE, The Buffet at Luxor ★ ($$, p. 147)

Rio's Carnival World Buffet ★★ ($$$, p. 151)

Spice Market Buffet ★★ ($$, p. 150)

Wicked Spoon Buffet ★ ($$$, p. 149)

Wynn Las Vegas Buffet ★★★ ($$$$, p. 150)

BURGERS

Heart Attack Grill ★ ($, p. 133)

KGB: Kerry's Gourmet Burgers ★★★ ($$, p. 121)

CAJUN/CREOLE

Delmonico Steakhouse ★★ ($$$$, p. 110)

Emeril's New Orleans Fish House ★ ($$$, p. 103)

Lola's: A Louisiana Kitchen ★★★ ($$, p. 132)

CALIFORNIA

Spago ($$$$, p. 113)

CHINESE

Blossom ★★ ($$, p. 104)

Cathay House ($$, p. 142)

China Poblano ★ ($$$, p. 115)

CONTINENTAL

Fleur by Hubert Keller ★★★ ($$$, p. 103)

Hugo's Cellar ★ ($$$$, p. 130)

Red Square ★★ ($$$$, p. 101)

Second Street Grill ★ ($$$, p. 131)

Todd's Unique Dining ★★★ ($$$, p. 139)

Top of the World ★★ ($$$$, p. 128)

DELI

Canter's Deli ★★ ($, p. 125)

Carnegie Deli ★★ ($, p. 125)

Jason's Deli ★ ($, p. 140)

Pink's ★★★ ($, p. 126)

DINER

Bougainvillea ★★ ($, p. 137)

Burger Bar ★ ($$, p. 104)

Ellis Island Restaurant ★ ($, p. 137)

Magnolia's Veranda ($, p. 133)

Market Street Café ($, p. 133)

ECLECTIC

Central Michel Richard ★ ($$, p. 119)

Sensi ★★ ($$$, p. 118)

FOOD COURT

Cypress Street Marketplace ★★ ($, p. 124)

FRENCH

Alizé ★★★ ($$$$, p. 134)

Andre's ★★ ($$$$, p. 99)

Comme Ça ★★ ($$$, p. 116)

Joël Robuchon Restaurant ★★★ ($$$$, p. 100)

L'Atelier de Joël Robuchon ★★★ ($$$$, p. 100)

Le Cirque ($$$$, p. 112)

Pamplemousse ★ ($$$$, p. 135)

Picasso ★★★ ($$$$, p. 114)

GASTROPUB

Public House ★ ($$$, p. 117)

GERMAN

Hofbrauhaus ★ ($$, p. 136)

GREEK

Estiatorio Milos ★★★ ($$$$, p. 112)

IRISH

Rí Rá Irish Pub ★★ ($$, p. 107)

ITALIAN

B&B Ristorante ★★ ($$$$, p. 110)

Bartolotta Ristorante di Mare ★★★ ($$$$, p. 126)

Circo ★★ ($$$$, p. 110)

Fellini's ★ ($$, p. 129)

Olives ★★ ($$$, p. 117)
Rao's ($$$, p. 113)
Sinatra ★★★ ($$$$, p. 127)
Sirio Ristorante ★★ ($$$, p. 104)

JAPANESE

Raku Grill ★★★ ($$, p. 143)

MEDITERRANEAN

Olives ★★ ($$$, p. 117)
Paymon's Mediterranean Café &
   Lounge ★ ($, p. 140)

MEXICAN

Border Grill ★★ ($$$, p. 102)
Cabo Wabo Cantina ★ ($$, p. 118)
China Poblano ★ ($$$, p. 115)
Diablo's Cantina ★★ ($$, p. 105)
Doña María Tamales ★★ ($, p. 132)
El Sombrero Cafe ★★ ($, p. 132)
Hussong's Cantina ★ ($$, p. 105)
Pink Taco ★ ($, p. 138)
Tacos & Tequila ★★ ($$, p. 108)
Toto's ★★ ($, p. 141)
Viva Mercado's ★★ ($$, p. 144)

NEW AMERICAN

Aureole ★★★ ($$$$, p. 99)
Mix ★ ($$$$, p. 101)

PACIFIC RIM

Second Street Grill ★ ($$$, p. 131)

PUB FARE

PT's Gold ★ ($$, p. 140)
The Pub at Monte Carlo ★ ($$,
   p. 107)
Todd English P.U.B. ★★★ ($$,
   p. 109)
Triple 7 Brew Pub ★ ($, p. 133)

RUSSIAN

Red Square ★★ ($$$$, p. 101)

SANDWICHES

Capriotti's ★★★ ($, p. 137)
Earl of Sandwich ★★★ ($, p. 125)

SEAFOOD

Austins Steakhouse ★★ ($$$, p. 142)
Bartolotta Ristorante di Mare ★★★
   ($$$$, p. 126)
Chart House ★ ($$$, p. 130)
Emeril's New Orleans Fish House ★
   ($$$, p. 103)
Estiatorio Milos ★★★ ($$$$, p. 112)
Michael Mina ($$$$, p. 112)

SOUL FOOD

M&M Soul Food ★★ ($, p. 142)

SOUTHERN

Harley-Davidson Café ★ ($$, p. 106)
House of Blues ★★ ($$, p. 106)

SOUTHWESTERN

Mesa Grill ★★ ($$$$, p. 113)

SPANISH

Beso ($$$, p. 112)
Julian Serrano ★★ ($$$, p. 103)

STEAK

Austins Steakhouse ★★ ($$$, p. 142)
Charlie Palmer Steak ★★ ($$$$,
   p. 99)
Delmonico Steakhouse ★★ ($$$$,
   p. 110)
Lawry's The Prime Rib ★★★ ($$$$,
   p. 134)
Old Homestead Steakhouse ★★★
   ($$$$, p. 114)
Oscar's Steakhouse ★★ ($$$, p. 130)
The Palm ($$$$, p. 113)
The Steakhouse ★ ($$$, p. 128)
Strip House ★★ ($$$$, p. 115)

THAI

Komol ($, p. 137)
Lotus of Siam ★★★ ($, p. 138)

6

SHOPPING

L as Vegas is one of the top shopping destinations in the world and many visitors list the malls, stores, outlets, and boutiques as one of their primary reasons for coming to the city. Several top-grossing retail outlets are in Las Vegas, including The Forum Shops at Caesars Palace, which makes more money per square foot than any other mall in the United States. But in between the big malls and high-end luxury stores are lots of fun and offbeat boutiques that help to make Vegas a shopper's paradise, no matter your taste or budget.

SOUTH STRIP

Your retail options on the southern end of the Strip are mostly limited to the stores, arcades, and malls associated with the big hotels. Excalibur, Luxor, New York–New York, and MGM Grand all have a few stores each but nothing to go out of your way for. They are more for finding clothes, accessories, and sundries you forgot to pack and for that last-minute, overpriced souvenir for the person in your life for whom you forgot to get something actually interesting.

The noteworthy destinations include **Mandalay Place** (p. 166), a collection of stores, restaurants, and boutiques on a bridge in between Mandalay Bay and Luxor, and **Crystals** (p. 160), the insanely high-end mall at CityCenter. The former is fairly small but has a few interesting outlets like a Nike Golf store, and the latter is big and modern and features items from luxury retailers like **Tiffany's** (p. 172) and **Tom Ford** (p. 172) that most normal people can't afford.

Also worth at least a visit is the **Showcase Mall** (p. 166), if for no other reason than to visit **M&M's World** (p. 173), where you can stock up on lots and lots and lots of chocolate.

MID-STRIP

Shopping aficionados should focus on this part of the Strip for their retail bliss. This is where you'll find the most noteworthy and fun malls, lots of high-end retailers, and a few shopping arcades worth knowing about.

Buying things becomes more of an experience at the highly themed malls in this neighborhood. **The Forum Shops at Caesars Palace** (p. 162) is done like an ancient Roman street scene—if ancient Rome had talking statues and really expensive stores from designers like Gucci and Armani; high-end cosmetics from **Kiehl's** (p. 169), **Sephora** (p. 170), and **MAC** (p. 170); and fun specialty retailers like **Agent Provocateur** (p. 170) selling sexy lingerie and **Auto Veloce** (p. 175) with its lifelike model cars. **The Grand Canal Shoppes** at The Venetian (p. 163) features an actual Venice-style canal with singing gondoliers running up the center of it and a host of more affordable stores, while its sister **The Shoppes at The Palazzo** (p. 166) may not have a canal but it does have a

PREVIOUS PAGE: **Tiffany's, in Crystals, is a great place to blow your winnings.**

Barney's New York (p. 171). The **Miracle Mile Shops** at Planet Hollywood Resort (p. 165) is partly Rodeo Drive blandness and partly ancient road to Morocco silliness, the latter left over from the days when this was the *Arabian Nights*–themed Desert Passage. Many of the stores here are more offbeat, including the one-of-a-kind accessories at **Ollin Arm Candy** (p. 172) and the peek-a-boo fashions of the **Bettie Page Boutique** (p. 171).

In between these big malls are smaller shopping arcades that range from the very high-end **Via Bellagio** (p. 167) to the flea-market sensibilities of the outdoor **Carnaval Court** (p. 159) at Harrah's Las Vegas.

NORTH STRIP

The northern end of the Strip is a study in shopping contrasts. At one end you have the luxury retailers at the **Fashion Show** mall (p. 162)—including Nordstrom's, Saks Fifth Avenue, and Bloomingdales, to name a few—and the **Esplanade at Wynn Las Vegas** (p. 161) that has boutiques from famous names like Chanel, Cartier, and Dior. At the other end, both geographically and economically, you have the **Stratosphere Tower Shops** (p. 166), a mostly forgettable collection of somehow cheap but still overpriced, off-brand retailers.

In between is the sweet spot with the **Bonanza Gift and Souvenir Shop** (p. 173), which claims to be the biggest gift shop in the world and has every possible Las Vegas knickknack that you could think of.

DOWNTOWN

Downtown Las Vegas used to be a wasteland when it came to shopping opportunities, but these days it is probably the most interesting and original place to go for some retail therapy.

Start in the 18b Arts District, where you'll find funky art galleries like those at **The Arts Factory** (p. 168); specialty boutiques including **Gamblers General Store** (p. 174) serving up all things casino; and antique and collectible stores, such as the divine **Retro Vegas** (p. 167) and treasure hunter heaven **Not Just Antiques Mart** (p. 167).

Over in the Union Park area, just to the west of the Arts District, bargain hunters will love to scour the discounts at the high-end retailers in the **Las Vegas Premium Outlets North** (p. 164) and home-decor junkies will go crazy at the **Las Vegas Design Center** (p. 174).

Fremont Street in the heart of Downtown is mostly made up of a bunch of unimaginative, tourist trap–style souvenir stores, but in between the tacky you can find some real treasures, like the blast-from-the-past **Toy Shack** (p. 176) and the arts collective at **Emergency Arts** (p. 168).

JUST OFF THE STRIP

As soon as you start getting away from the Strip, the glitz starts to fade, and so do the prices. The **Las Vegas Premium Outlets South** (p. 164) is a large, indoor discount mall where you can find even better values than its sister to the north. Meanwhile, **Town Square** (p. 166) is a handsomely designed outdoor shopping district that has more affordable shopping, cheaper restaurants, movie theaters, and even its own park. Tech junkies will want to make a beeline to **Fry's Electronics** (p. 175) and history buffs should go directly to the gift shop at the

National Atomic Testing Museum (p. 74) for some morbidly fun atomic-age souvenirs.

SOUTH & EAST OF THE STRIP

Once you have left the bright lights of the Strip in your rear-view mirror, you enter territory that is mostly shopped by the people who live in Las Vegas. The Boulevard (see below) on Maryland Parkway and the Galleria at Sunset (p. 163) are suburban malls that are pretty much like the one in your hometown, which means that you won't find anything terrible special but you also won't pay an arm and a leg for the things you want and need.

In fact, Maryland Parkway, which runs parallel to the Strip on the east, has just about one of everything: Target, Toys "R" Us, several major department stores, major drugstores (in case you forgot your shampoo and don't want to spend $10 on a new bottle in your hotel's sundry shop), some alternative-culture stores and hip clothing stores including the Buffalo Exchange (p. 171), and so forth.

Specialty stores worth knowing about include the Gambler's Book Club (p. 170), selling everything you need to learn how to at least think you will do better in the casinos, and Bass Pro Shops (p. 175) for outdoors enthusiasts.

Finally, if you head south—*really* south—to Primm, Nevada, at the border of California, you'll discover the Fashion Outlets (p. 161), which is probably the best of the area's discount outlet malls.

NORTH & WEST OF THE STRIP

Continuing the suburban shopping theme, heading north and west of the Strip will get you to malls like the Meadows (p. 165) and offbeat finds like the end-of-the-world supplies at the Zombie Apocalypse Store (p. 174); the heavenly used-book emporium Dead Poet Bookstore (p. 170); and a slap to the face of the downloadable music revolution in Zia Record Exchange (p. 175).

MALLS & SHOPPING ARCADES

The Boulevard ★ The Boulevard is the second-largest mall in Las Vegas—Fashion Show on the Strip has it beat. Its 140-plus stores and restaurants are arranged in arcade fashion on a single floor occupying 1.2 million square feet. Geared to the average consumer, it has anchors such as Sears, JCPenney, Macy's, and Marshalls. There's a wide variety of shops offering all sorts of items—moderately priced shoes and clothing for the entire family, books and gifts, jewelry, and home furnishings. There are also more than a dozen fast-food eateries. In short, you can find just about anything you need here. The mall is open Monday through Saturday from 10am to 9pm and Sunday from 11am to 6pm. 3528 S. Maryland Pkwy. (btw. Twain Ave. and Desert Inn Rd.). www.boulevardmall.com. ✆ **702/735-7430.**

Carnaval Court This small outdoor shopping promenade, a concept unique to the Strip, consists mostly of little stalls selling bits and bobs, such as hippie-inspired floaty dresses and tops, saucy underwear with catchy phrases on it, jewelry, and knock-off purses. A store highlight is a Ghirardelli chocolate shop, a branch of the famous San Francisco–based chocolate company. It's a smaller version of the one in San Francisco (alas, without the vats of liquid chocolate being mixed up), and in addition to candy, you can get a variety of delicious sundaes and other ice-cream treats. Hours vary by store. At Harrah's Las Vegas, 3475 Las Vegas Blvd. S. www.harrahslv.com. ✆ **800/214-9110.**

The Cosmopolitan of Las Vegas Shops ★   Roughly a dozen stores surround the giant chandelier on the second floor, mostly offering clothing, jewelry, and other stylish accessories. None of the places have names that are familiar to most Americans, but Allsaints, Beckley, Droog, and Skins 6/2 may be known to international visitors. One fun store is EatDrink, a bodega of sorts where you can create your own minipicnic with wine, cheese, meats, and other savories. Hours vary by store. In The Cosmopolitan of Las Vegas, 3708 Las Vegas Blvd. S. www.cosmopolitan lasvegas.com. ✆ **702/698-7000.**

Crystals ★   Architecturally speaking, Crystals is as evocative a building as you'll find in Vegas. All sharp angles jutting into the sky, the shape is meant to evoke a pile of crystals (get it?), and it is nothing if not dramatic. Inside, the soaring ceilings and plenty of windows give an airy feeling, but too much white space makes it a little bland once you get past the way the place was built. We're willing to forgive it since it is part of an extended environmental building plan that includes radiant heating in the floors and recycled construction materials. Stores are all almost exclusively the highest of high end, including a 10,000-square-foot **Tiffany & Co.** (p. 172), **Tom Ford** (p. 172), **Harry Winston** jewelers (p. 172), Louis Vuitton, Prada, and Porsche Design (in case you can't actually afford to own the vehicle but want to look like you do). Restaurants include actress Eva Longoria Parker's **Beso** (p. 112), the fantastic **Todd English P.U.B.** (p. 109), a couple of Wolfgang Puck eateries, Mastro's Ocean Club, and the return of the much-beloved sushi restaurant/nightclub Social House. Don't miss the two water features by the same folks who did the Bellagio Fountains. These are smaller and not as "wow," but still cool. The mall is open daily 10am to midnight, but individual store and restaurant hours may vary. 3720 Las Vegas Blvd. S. (at City-Center). www.crystalsatcitycenter.com. ✆ **702/590-9299.**

Carnaval Court is small and unassuming by Vegas standards, but you may well find something that catches your eye in its many stalls.

One of several cool art installations inside Crystals.

The Esplanade at Wynn Las Vegas ★★   The Esplanade is along the same rarified lines of the Bellagio shopping area, in that it's a Euro-style-esque (love those Vegas qualifiers!) shopping street lined with pricey places with famous names—Oscar de la Renta, Manolo Blahnik, Chanel, Cartier, Dior, Alexander McQueen, and Louis Vuitton. We prefer it to the one at Bellagio because it seems like it has just enough shops that nearly reach an average person's budget. There are additional stores along the walkway between Wynn Las Vegas and neighboring Encore. Hours vary by store. In Wynn Las Vegas, 3131 Las Vegas Blvd. S. www.wynnlasvegas.com. © **702/770-8000.**

Fashion Outlets Las Vegas ★★★
Dedicated bargain hunters (we stop here every time we drive by) may want to make the roughly 40-minute drive along I-15 to this big outlet complex in Primm, Nevada, right on the border of California. There's also a shuttle from the MGM Grand, Fashion Show mall, Miracle Mile Shops at Planet Hollywood, and LVH: The Las Vegas Hotel. Round-trip fare is $15 and includes a savings book for discounts at the outlets. Also, check the website for a shuttle discount coupon. This large factory outlet has some designer names prominent enough to make the trip worthwhile—Kenneth Cole, Juicy Couture, Coach, Gap, Banana Republic, Old Navy, even a rare Williams-Sonoma, among several others. Fashion Outlets is open daily from 10am to 8pm. 32100 Las Vegas Blvd. S. www.fashion outletlasvegas.com. © **888/424-6898** or 702/ 874-1400.

Esplanade at Wynn Las Vegas.

Fashion Show ★★ What was once a nondescript, if large, mall now has a *yowsa!* exterior much more fitting of Las Vegas. It's capped by a giant . . . well . . . they call it a "cloud," but we call it "that weird thingy that looks like a spaceport for UFOs." Inside, it's still, more or less, a basic mall, including Nevada's only Nordstrom, a Bloomingdale's Home store, Saks Fifth Avenue, a Neiman Marcus, and other high-end retailers. The mall hosts more than 250 shops, restaurants, and services. And the cloud/alien spaceport thingy has giant LED screens, music, and other distractions—again, much more fitting for Vegas, where even the malls have to light up. Valet parking is available, and you can even arrange to have your car hand washed while you shop. Fashion Show is open Monday through Saturday from 10am to 9pm and Sunday from 11am to 7pm. 3200 Las Vegas Blvd. S. (at the corner of Spring Mountain Rd.). www.thefashionshow.com. *©* **702/396-8382.**

Fashion Show is an architectural wonder . . . and a good place to shop.

The Forum Shops at Caesars Palace ★★★ This Rodeo-Drive-meets-the-Roman-Empire affair comes complete with a 48-foot triumphal arch entranceway, a painted Mediterranean sky, acres of marble, lofty Corinthian columns with gold capitals, and a welcoming goddess of fortune under a central dome. Then there is the Festival Fountain, where some seemingly immovable "marble" animatronic statues of Bacchus (slightly in his cups), a lyre-playing Apollo, Plutus, and Venus come to life for a 7-minute revel with dancing waters and high-tech laser-light effects. The shows take place every hour on the hour. Other nonretail highlights include a 50,000-gallon aquarium with another fountain show involving fire (don't stand too close, it gets really hot) and a circular escalator, said to be one of only two in the world. The entire thing is pretty incredible, but also very Vegas—particularly the Bacchus show, which is truly frightening and bizarre. Even if you don't like shopping, it's worth the stroll just to giggle.

Oh, right, the stores. With all the gawking opportunities, it may be easy to forget that you can shop and buy things here (so much so that Caesars claims this is the most profitable mall in America). Tenants are mostly of the exclusive variety, although there are a few more Average Joe kind of stores (yes, of course there's a Gap). Some examples: Louis Vuitton, bebe, Christians Dior, *and* Louboutin, **Agent Provocateur** (p. 170), A/X Armani Exchange, Gucci, Versace, Brooks Brothers, Juicy Couture, cosmetics giants **Kiehl's** (p. 169), **MAC** (p. 170), **Sephora** (p. 170), and Vosges Haut Chocolate—makeup and sweets, that sounds like shopping heaven to us! If that's not enough, they now have the largest H&M in the United States, with three stories of affordable fashion bliss.

The majority of The Forum Shops are open Sunday through Thursday from 10am to 11pm and Friday and Saturday from 10am to midnight. In Caesars Palace, 3570 Las Vegas Blvd. S. www.forumshops.com. $©$ **702/893-4800.**

The Galleria at Sunset ★   This is the farthest-away mall of the bunch (9 miles southeast of Downtown Las Vegas, in Henderson) but the most aesthetically pleasing, a 1-million-square-foot Southwestern-themed shopping center, with topiary animals adding a sweet touch to the food court. Anchored by Dillard's, Kohl's, JCPenney, Dick's Sporting Goods, and Macy's, the Galleria's 140 emporia include branches of American Eagle Outfitters, Vans, Abercrombie & Fitch, bebe, Caché, Lane Bryant, Victoria's Secret, and Hot Topic. In addition to shoes and clothing for the entire family, you'll find electronics, eyewear, gifts, books, home furnishings, jewelry, and luggage here. Dining facilities include an extensive food court and several restaurants. It's open Monday through Saturday from 10am to 9pm and Sunday from 11am to 6pm. 1300 W. Sunset Rd. (at Stephanie St., just off I-15), Henderson. www.galleriaatsunset.com. $©$ **702/434-0202.**

The Grand Canal Shoppes ★★   After you've shopped Ancient Rome at Caesars, come here to amble through Venice. This is a re-created Italian village, complete with a painted, cloud-studded blue sky overhead, and a canal right down the center on which gondoliers float and sing. Pay them ($16), and you can take a lazy float down and back, serenaded by your boatman (actors hired especially for this purpose and with accents perfect enough to fool Roberto Benigni). The stroll (or float) ends at a miniature version of St. Mark's Square, the central landmark of Venice. Here, you'll find opera singers, strolling musicians, glass blowers, and other bustling marketplace activity. It's all most ambitious and beats the heck out of animatronic statues.

The Shoppes are accessible directly from outside (so you don't have to navigate miles of casino and other clutter) via a grand staircase whose ceiling features more of those impressive hand-painted art re-creations. It's quite smashing.

Caesars Forum Shops.

The stores feature fewer luxury nameplates and more that at least approach affordability including: Cache, Davidoff, Kenneth Cole, Ann Taylor, BCBG, bebe, Banana Republic, Rockport, and more, plus Venetian glass and paper shops. **Madame Tussauds Las Vegas** (p. 62) is also located here, and so is the **Canyon Ranch SpaClub** (p. 93). The Shoppes are open Sunday through Thursday from 10am to 11pm and Friday and Saturday from 10am to midnight. In The Venetian, 3355 Las Vegas Blvd. S. www.thegrandcanalshoppes.com. ℂ **702/414-4500.**

Las Vegas Premium Outlets North   We had such high hopes for this, the most conveniently located and largest outlet mall in Las Vegas. We can say that it looks nice, in that pretty outdoor mall kind of way. But the key here is "outdoor." It's fine on a regular day, but on a hot Vegas day—and there are plenty of those—this is an open oven of misery. They should put a roof over the thing or at least install a lot more misters. You'll roast away while shopping among disappointingly dull stores, some of which are "outlets" only because they aren't in regular malls. Maybe we are just feeling bitter about that pair of Bass shoes that were half a size too small. Or that we can't quite fit into the Dolce & Gabbana sample sizes. Still, bring a lot of water if you go during the summer. Stores include Brooks Brothers, Armani, Dolce & Gabbana, Lacoste, Bose, Kenneth Cole, Wilson's Leather, Calvin Klein (including an entire store devoted to their underwear), Coach, Nike, Perry Ellis, Crabtree & Evelyn, Samsonite, Timberland, Tommy Hilfiger, TAG Heuer, and Zales. The mall is open Monday through Saturday from 10am to 9pm and Sunday from 10am to 8pm. 875 S. Grand Central Pkwy. (at I-15). www.premiumoutlets.com. ℂ **702/474-7500.**

Las Vegas Premium Outlets South ★   A 2010 makeover of both the look and lineup of this outlet center is both a good and a bad thing. It's bigger—there are now more than 140 stores—and it is prettier if that matters to you. But several of the more affordable stores that offered the real bargains have been forced out in favor of high-end shops like DKNY and Sean John. The good news is that

Las Vegas Premium Outlets North.

it is enclosed and air-conditioned unlike its North sibling, so if you aren't finding the kind of deals you were hoping for you can at least do it while staying cool. Among other stores you'll find Perry Ellis, Converse, Levi's, Nike, Lane Bryant, Reebok, Jockey, Van Heusen, Hot Topic, True Religion jeans, Tommy Hilfiger, Burlington, Corningware/Corelle/Revere, and Calvin Klein. There is also a carousel and a food court. The mall is open Monday through Saturday from 10am to 9pm and Sunday from 10am to 8pm. 7400 Las Vegas Blvd. S. (at Warm Springs Rd.). www.premiumoutlets.com. ✆ **702/896-5599.**

Meadows Mall ★   Another immense mall, this one has more than 140 shops, services, and eateries, anchored by four department stores: Macy's, Dillard's, Sears, and JCPenney. In addition, there are more than a dozen shoe stores, a full array of apparel for the entire family (including maternity wear, petites, and large sizes), an extensive food court, and shops purveying toys, books, music, luggage, gifts, jewelry, home furnishings, accessories, and so on. Fountains and trees enhance Meadows Mall's ultramodern, high-ceilinged interior, and there are a few comfortable seating areas for resting your feet a moment. The Meadows Mall is open Monday through Saturday from 10am to 9pm and Sunday from 10am to 6pm. 4300 Meadows Lane (at the intersection of Valley View and U.S. 95). www.meadows mall.com. ✆ **702/878-3331.**

Miracle Mile Shops at Planet Hollywood ★★   Though not without some eye-catching details, these shops aren't all that glamorous: It's pretty much a new-Vegas, whiz-bang version of every nice upper-end mall in America, a letdown all the worse because the original version was so charming. Although some of the original *Arabian Nights* details from when this mall was known as the Desert Passage still exist, most of the mall is pretty generic. At least the shops somewhat stand out, including several listed separately below, plus Frederick's of Hollywood, Crocs, Two Lips Shoes (affordable, stylish, and comfortable shoes), a giant Urban Outfitters, Steve Madden, American Apparel, Urban Outfitters, bebe, BCBG, Sephora, and a branch of the insanely popular H&M clothing store. The shops are open Sunday through Thursday from 10am to 11pm and Friday and Saturday from 10am to midnight. In Planet Hollywood Resort & Casino, 3663 Las Vegas Blvd. S. www.miraclemileshopslv.com. ✆ **702/866-0703.**

Miracle Mile Shops at Planet Hollywood.

Neonopolis   When this $100 million shopping complex opened on Fremont Street in 2002 it had movie theaters, stores, and restaurants but a series of ownership missteps led to the place becoming mostly abandoned. There is new life here these days with the addition of terrific stores like

The Toy Shack (p. 176) and restaurants like **Heart Attack Grill** (p. 133), plus more on the way. If nothing else, the restored neon signs throughout the complex are worth a gander. Hours vary by store. 450 E. Fremont St. www.neonopolislv.com. ℭ **702/232-5539.**

The Shoppes at Mandalay Place ★ In appearance, more like an actual indoor mall than a hotel shopping arcade, but in content it has neither the rarified atmosphere of Via Bellagio or the Wynn Promenade, nor does it have the collection of The Forum Shops. But there is a men's shop called the Art of Shaving, a couple of art galleries, an Urban Outfitters and Ron John Surf Shop for the younger set, a NIKE Golf store for your husband, and a Frederick's of Hollywood if you're feeling the need to make your husband happy with something other than golf. Hours vary by store. In Mandalay Bay, 3930 Las Vegas Blvd. S. www.mandalaybay. com. ℭ **702/632-9333.**

The Shoppes at The Palazzo ★★ The sister hotel to The Venetian couldn't hold its resort head up without its own luxury shopping area. As with the super high-end experience at Bellagio and Wynn, this brings all kinds of names to town, names sure to thrill the souls—and diminish the wallets—of dedicated fashionistas. A branch of **Barneys New York** (p. 171) is the star of the retail show, but Christian Louboutin, Bottega Veneta, Chloe, Diane von Furstenberg, Michael Kors, and Van Cleef & Arpels are hardly second string. It's like the pages of *Vogue* come to life! Hours vary by store but generally are open Sunday through Thursday from 10am until 11pm and Friday and Saturday from 10am until midnight. In The Palazzo, 3327 Las Vegas Blvd. S. www.theshoppesatthepalazzo.com. ℭ **702/414-4525.**

Showcase Mall ★ Less a traditional mall than an entertainment center, this place has plenty of shopping and fun—we rarely miss a chance to drop by **M&M's World** (p. 173). Other occupants include the World of Coca-Cola store, Grand Canyon Experience, United Artists theaters—the only regular movie theater complex on the Strip—a few fast-food eateries, and the Strip's first **Hard Rock Cafe** (p. 106). Hours vary by store. 3785 Las Vegas Blvd. S. (right next to the MGM Grand). ℭ **702/597-3122.**

Stratosphere Tower Shops The internationally themed (though in a high-school-production kind of way, compared to what's over at Planet Hollywood and The Venetian) second-floor promenade, housing more than 40 stores, is entered via an escalator from the casino. Some shops are in Paris, along the Rue Lafayette and Avenue de l'Opéra (there are replicas of the Eiffel Tower and the Arc de Triomphe in this section). Others occupy Hong Kong and New York City streetscapes. It's mostly useless, non-brand-name stuff that isn't worth a special trip for. Hours vary by store. In the Stratosphere Hotel, 2000 Las Vegas Blvd. S. www. stratospherehotel.com. ℭ **702/380-7777.**

Town Square ★ Instead of an enclosed mall or boring box store shopping center, Town Square is designed to look like, well, a town. Tree-lined streets bisect the 117-acre property, and if you're lucky, you can grab a parking space right in front of whatever store you're visiting (or park in one of the huge lots or garages nearby). The facades of the buildings resemble small-town America, only cleaner and more crowded than most. It's a great place to stroll and window-shop, at least on the roughly 27 days a year when it isn't either insanely hot or blustery and chilly. More than 150 shops and boutiques include plenty of typical mall favorites, such as Gap, American Eagle, Old Navy, J. Crew, Abercrombie

When the weather's good, it's a pleasure to stroll the shops that line Town Square.

and Fitch, and Banana Republic—plus some unique outlets, such as H&M, an Apple store, Sephora, and even a Whole Foods market. More than a dozen restaurants (among them Claim Jumper, California Pizza Kitchen, and Texas de Brazil) provide sustenance, and bars, movie theaters, parks, and playgrounds offer entertainment. Hours vary by store. 6605 Las Vegas Blvd. S. (at I-215). www.mytownsquarelasvegas.com. ☎ **702/269-5000.**

Via Bellagio ★★   This collection of stores isn't as big as some of the other megahotel shopping arcades, but here it's definitely quality over quantity. It's a veritable roll call of glossy magazine ads: Armani, Prada, Chanel, Tiffany & Co., Fred Leighton, Gucci, Dior, Fendi, and Hermés. That's about it. You need anything else? Well, yes—money. If you can afford this stuff, good for you, you lucky dog. Hours vary by store. In Bellagio, 3600 Las Vegas Blvd. S. www.bellagio.com. ☎ **702/693-7111.**

SHOPPING A TO Z
Antiques & Collectibles

Not Just Antiques Mart ★   More than 12,000 square feet of antiques ranging from trash to treasure fills this building, giving it a vibe that bargain hunters will die for. Although the name implies something more, the merchandise consists only of antiques, collectibles, and consignment items. If you get exhausted from all the scavenging, you can stop at their tea room for a respite. It's open Monday through Saturday from 10:30am to 5:30pm. 1422 Western Ave. (just south of Charleston Ave.). www.notjustantiquesmart.com. ☎ **702/384-4922.**

Retro Vegas ★★   This fun and funky antiques and collectible boutique is not entirely about Sin City—the large selection of midcentury and Danish modern furnishings is definitely worth drooling over—but it is the Vegas history on display that will probably offer the biggest thrill. Go small with a '60s era ashtray from the Sands or go big with a '70s era smoked-glass chandelier from the Desert Inn, with lots of bric-a-brac from across the eras in between. It's open Monday through Saturday from 11am to 6pm. 1131 S. Main St. (at Charleston Ave.). www.retrovegas.com. ☎ **702/384-2700.**

Visit Retro Vegas and you may wind up going home with a piece of Vegas history.

Arts, Crafts & Museum Stores

The Arts Factory ★   Sitting at the geographic and spiritual center of the 18b Arts District is this multifunction gallery, boutique, bistro, and bar that houses local artists and their wares. Some of it is only for looking, but enough of it is for buying that you can find some really interesting artistic keepsakes. And yes, you can get wine at the bar, but don't drink and shop! Gallery and boutique hours vary but are generally 9am until 6pm daily. 107 E. Charleston Ave. (at Main St.). www.the artsfactory.com. ℂ **702/383-3133.**

Emergency Arts ★★   Located in a former medical clinic, this gallery and boutique collective is similar in concept to the above Arts Factory, only with funkier finds. They have everything from clothes to jewelry to classic vinyl, all created or curated by local talent. There's also a fun coffee shop on the first floor that feels like the perfect place to sit and discuss Nietzsche. Gallery and boutique hours vary, but are generally 10am until 6pm. 520 E. Fremont St. www. emergencyartslv.com. ℂ **702/409-5663.**

Martin Lawrence Gallery ★★   A word of advice: If you decide to purchase a multimillion-dollar Picasso or Dali from this high-end gallery, they will ship it for you so you don't have to try to cram it into the overhead compartment on the plane ride home. Serious art lovers need to visit even if they can't afford to actually buy anything. It's open Sunday through Thursday from 10am until 11pm and Friday, Saturday 10am until midnight. In the Forum Shops at Caesars Palace, 3500 Las Vegas Blvd. S. www.martin lawrence.com. ℂ **702/991-5990.**

National Atomic Testing Museum ★★   For mixed emotions, little can beat items emblazoned with vintage images of bomb tests and other glories to the good old days of atomic blasts. Plus they often have Albert Einstein action figures, which makes it worth visiting alone. Hours are Monday

Gift shop at the Atomic Testing Museum.

through Saturday 10am until 5pm and Sunday noon until 5pm. 755 E. Flamingo Rd. (just east of Paradise Ave.). www.nationalatomictestingmuseum.org. ℂ **702/794-5161.**

Oh My Godard Gallery ★★ Artist Michael Godard attended the University of Nevada Las Vegas, and his work has a decidedly Sin City spin to it. Dubbed the "Rock Star of the Art World," Godard's inspirations include tattoos and alcohol, with his "Martini Olive" series perfectly capturing his whimsical aesthetic as they do everything from play golf to gamble. The gallery is open daily at 10am until 11pm weekdays and until midnight weekends. In the Miracle Mile Shops at Planet Hollywood Resort, 3667 Las Vegas Blvd. S. www.michaelgodard.com. ℂ **702/699-9099.**

Beauty & Cosmetics

Kiehl's ★ In business since 1851, this purveyor of high-end cosmetics can be found in boutiques and department stores across the country, but that doesn't mean you shouldn't make a special pilgrimage to the Vegas store, which features an epic array of skin- and hair-care products for women and men. Yes, it's a thing of beauty. It's open Sunday through Friday 10am until 11am and Saturday 10am until midnight. In The Forum Shops at Caesars Palace, 3500 Las Vegas Blvd. S. www.kiehls. com. ℂ **702/784-0025.**

SHOPPING gets real

The proliferation of reality TV shows has turned an island's worth of Average Joes, from ice road truck drivers to overly tanned Jersey boys, into pop-culture stars. Although you can't go trawling on a fishing boat (for instance) with your favorite demi-celebrities, In Las Vegas you can visit a couple of the places that made them famous by way of two of the History Channel's most popular series.

Pawn Stars is sort of like the more desperate version of PBS' *Antiques Roadshow,* where people bring in their treasures and trash to the **Gold & Silver Pawn Shop,** 713 Las Vegas Blvd. S. (www.gspawn.com; ℂ **702/385-7912**), hoping to make a mint (or at least enough to keep them gambling in the casinos). Operated by the colorful Harrison family, the store is heavy on the hocked jewelry but there are lots of other odds and ends worth a quick browse. The bad news is that the Harrisons themselves are rarely on-site anymore, which can be a disappointment to the hordes of people waiting in line (seriously!) at all times of the day to get inside. The store is open daily from 9am until 9pm.

You'll have a much better chance of seeing people you've seen on TV at

Rick's Restorations, 1112 S. Commerce St. (www.ricksrestorations.com; ℂ **702/ 366-7030**), where *American Restoration* is filmed. Owner Rick Dale, his wife Kelly, and a crew of lovable oddballs restore classic Americana (soda machines, gas pumps, bicycles, slot machines, and more) in a rambling facility that offers tours, a showroom, a gift shop, and more. Big windows in the public areas give you a glimpse into the working facility and people from the show, including Rick, will often pop out to say hi and sign autographs. The restorations themselves are stunning accomplishments, but you're going to need a high credit limit to afford any of it. The store is open Monday through Friday from 9am until 5pm.

MAC ★ Originally founded with an eye (or eyeliner, perhaps) toward professional makeup artists, the brand has grown into one of the most coveted in North America, even name-checked in song ("Unpretty" by TLC). The pro-grade quality makes the wide selection of lipsticks, blushes, mascara, and more worth the above-average prices. It's open Sunday through Thursday 10am until 11am and Saturday 10am until midnight. In The Forum Shops at Caesars Palace, 3500 Las Vegas Blvd S. www.maccosmetics.com. ✆ 702/369-8770.

Sephora ★★ With more than 750 stores worldwide, you'd think a trip to cosmetics giant Sephora would be a fairly pedestrian event. Not so. It is often viewed by the cosmetically inclined to be a practically holy experience—one best completed by carrying out giant shopping bags full of makeup. Hours are Sunday through Thursday 10am until 11am and Saturday 10am until midnight. In The Forum Shops at Caesars Palace, 3500 Las Vegas Blvd S. www.sephora.com. ✆ 702/228-3535.

Books

Alternate Reality Comics ★ This is the best place in Vegas for all your comic-book needs. It has a nearly comprehensive selection, with a heavy emphasis on underground comics. But don't worry—the superheroes are here, too. It's open Sunday through Tuesday from 11am to 6pm and Wednesday through Saturday from 10am to 7pm. 4110 S. Maryland Pkwy., no. 8. www.alternaterealitycomics.net. ✆ 702/736-3673.

Bauman Rare Books ★ The books you'll find at this high-end purveyor of classic and rare literary works are probably not the kinds of things you'll be reading on the plane home. First editions from Joyce, Hemingway, and Twain are among the treasures, some of which are signed by their authors. They also have documents signed by Abraham Lincoln and Napoleon, which are cool to look at if nothing else. The store is open daily from 10am until 11pm. In The Shoppes at The Palazzo, 3327 Las Vegas Blvd. S. www.baumanrarebooks.com. ✆ 702/948-1617.

Dead Poet Bookstore ★★ 🎁 The dead poet in question was the man from whose estate the owners bought their start-up stock. He had such good taste in books that they "fell in love with him" and wanted to name the store in his memory. Just one problem—they never did get his name. So they just called him "the dead poet." His legacy continues at this book-lover's haven. It's open Monday through Saturday from 10am to 6pm. 937 S. Rainbow Blvd. ✆ 702/227-4070.

Gambler's Book Club ★ Here you can buy a book on any system ever devised to beat casino odds. The store carries more than 4,000 gambling-related titles, including many out-of-print books, computer software, and videotapes. On request, knowledgeable clerks provide on-the-spot expert advice on handicapping the ponies and other aspects of sports betting. The store's motto is "knowledge is protection." The shop is open Monday through Friday from 9am to 7pm and Saturday 10am to 6pm. 5473 S. Eastern Ave. www.gamblersbookclub.com. ✆ 800/522-1777 or 702/382-7555.

Clothing & Accessories

Agent Provocateur ★★★ Vegas doesn't lack for lingerie stores (including Frederick's of Hollywood), but if you can only make time for one, it has to be this British import. The designs are clever and witty, in addition to being drop-dead sexy and ultracool. Kate Moss has long been the face and body of the line and even starred in a short movie ad for the line directed by Mike Figgis. Seduction should start someplace special. Agent Provocateur is open Sunday through Thursday from 10am to 11pm and Friday and Saturday from 10am to midnight. In The Forum Shops at Caesars Palace, 3500 Las Vegas Blvd. S. www.agent provocateur.com. ✆ **702/696-7174.**

Barney's New York ★ Founded in 1923, Barney's has long reigned as the standard for luxury department stores, and this Vegas version lives up to the reputation. The designer women's and men's fashions are certainly not cheap, but if you're in the mood to dress to impress you'll have a hard time finding a bigger selection anywhere in the city. It's open Sunday through Thursday from 10am until 11pm and Friday and Saturday from 10am until midnight. In The Shoppes at The Palazzo, 3327 Las Vegas Blvd. S. www.barneys.com. ✆ **702/629-4200.**

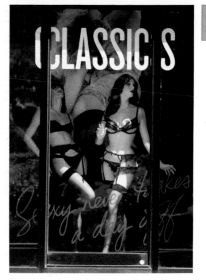

If you're in the market for lingerie, make ultracool Agent Provocateur your first stop.

Bettie Page Boutique ★★ It's the old story. Needing a job, curvaceous gal poses for naughty photos, and her cheery good humor in all kinds of bondage photos, not to mention a gleaming black pageboy hairdo, makes her an icon. The next thing you know, there's a store dedicated to all things Bettie. Dress like a pin-up thanks to a line of Page-inspired '50s-style dresses, corsets, hosiery, and more. You can't have a venture like this without a wink, and so the shop, all done up in leopard, is a hoot. There is also plenty of Bettie artwork by renowned pin-up artist Olivia de Berardinis for sale. The boutique is open Sunday through Thursday from 10am to 11pm and Friday and Saturday from 10am to midnight. There's also another branch of the boutique in the Fashion Show mall. In the Miracle Mile Shops at Planet Hollywood Resort, 3663 Las Vegas Blvd. S. www.bettiepageclothing.com. ✆ **702/636-1100.**

Buffalo Exchange ★ This is actually a branch of a chain of stores spread out across the United States. If the chain part worries you, don't let it—this merchandise doesn't feel processed. Staffed by plenty of incredibly hip alt-culture kids (ask them what's happening in town during your visit), it is stuffed with dresses, shirts, pants, and so forth. You can easily go in and come out with 12 fabulous new outfits, but you can just as easily go in and come up dry. But it's still probably the most reliable of the local vintage shops. The store is open Monday through Saturday from 10am to 8pm and Sunday from 11am to 7pm. 4110 S. Maryland Pkwy. (at Flamingo Rd.). www.buffaloexchange.com. ✆ **702/791-3960.**

Club Tattoo ★ If you're not brave (or perhaps drunk) enough to get inked or pierced here, you can look like you are with tattoo-inspired fashions, jewelry, and accessories they sell. Just remember that this is a working tattoo parlor, so if you faint at the sight of blood, you may want to focus on the T-shirts and not the people getting their body art. It's open Sunday through Thursday from 10am until 11pm and Friday and Saturday from 10am until 11pm. In the Miracle Mile Shops at Planet Hollywood Resort, 3667 Las Vegas Blvd. S. www.clubtattoo.com. ✆ **702/363-2582.**

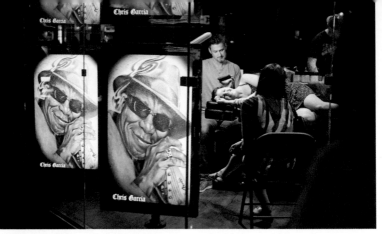

Whether you're looking for new ink or just tattoo-inspired fashions, jewelry, and accessories, Club Tattoo has you covered.

Harry Winston ★   When you see a celebrity at some awards show or on a random red carpet dripping with millions of dollars in fine jewelry, there's a good chance that it came from Harry Winston. Although he passed away in 1978, Winston was famed for his extensive collection of diamonds—he was the one who donated the Hope Diamond to the Smithsonian—and his legacy lives on in this salon full of baubles designed for the rich and famous. The store is open daily 10am until 11pm weekdays and until midnight weekends. In Crystals at CityCenter, 3720 Las Vegas Blvd. S. www.harrywinston.com. ✆ **702/262-0001.**

Ollin Arm Candy ★★   Sure, you could pay thousands for a designer handbag from the likes of Fendi or Hermes, but why not get something more original, and more ecologically friendly, like the delightful purses at this boutique made out of candy wrappers, license plates, seat belts, and other found objects. These are not just recycled bits turned into something disposable, they are funky works of art that make accessorizing fun again. It's open Sunday through Thursday from 10am until 11pm, Friday and Saturday from 10am until midnight. In the Miracle Mile Shops at Planet Hollywood Resort, 3667 Las Vegas Blvd. S. www.ollinarmcandy.com. ✆ **702/260-3223.**

Tom Ford ★   Designer Tom Ford's career has taken him from the house of Gucci to his own successful label and even to Hollywood, where he directed the Oscar-nominated *A Single Man*. This dramatic flagship store, with big windows looking out on the Strip, features his men's and women's lines of stylishly mod clothing plus eyewear, shoes, fragrances, and more. Hours are Sunday through Thursday from 10am until 11pm and Friday and Saturday from 10am until midnight. In Crystals at CityCenter, 3720 Las Vegas Blvd S. www.tomford.com. ✆ **702/740-2940.**

Tiffany & Co. ★   You may be tempted to walk down the big staircase in this 10,000-square-foot, two-story store awash in their jewels, pretending you are no less than Audrey Hepburn, but they will probably frown on that. The biggest Tiffany's in Vegas is a veritable superstore of bracelets, necklaces, rings, and more, and while much of it is only for those with very high credit limits, there are a few smaller trinkets that will allow the rest of us to walk out with a signature blue Tiffany & Co. bag. It's open daily from 10am until 11pm weekdays and until midnight weekends. In Crystals at CityCenter, 3720 Las Vegas Blvd. S. www.tiffany.com. ✆ **702/545-9090.**

Food & Drink

Ethel's Chocolate Lounge ★   A creation of local confectioner Ethel M that is part cafe, part lounge. "You love chocolate. We are here to help." is the shop's motto. This location isn't as large or as immediately fun as others around the country, but it's still a fun blood-sugar pick-me-up. Choose fancy chocolates from the carefully designed ones on display, such as pomegranate, champagne cocktail, and even Margarita flavor, or savor a fondue or other appropriate nosh. Because it keeps mall hours—Monday through Saturday from 10am to 9pm and Sunday from 11am to 7pm—Ethel's is more of a midafternoon snack spot than a postdinner wind-down option. In Fashion Show mall, 3200 Las Vegas Blvd. S. www.ethelm.com. ✆ **702/796-6662.**

M&M's World ★★ ☺   What can one do when faced with a wall of M&Ms in colors never before seen by man or woman (purple! teal! lime green!)? Overpriced? Yeah! Who cares? There are doodads galore, replete with the M&M's logo, and a surprisingly enjoyable short film and comedy routine, ostensibly about the "history" of the candy but really just a cute little adventure with a decent budget behind it. It's open Sunday through Thursday from 9am until 11pm and Friday and Saturday from 9am until midnight. In the Showcase Mall, 3785 Las Vegas Blvd. S. (just north of the MGM Grand Hotel). www.mymms.com. ✆ **702/736-7611.**

Gifts & Souvenirs

Bonanza Gift and Souvenir Shop ★★   If you prefer your souvenirs to be a little less class and a little more kitsch, head here to the self-proclaimed "World's Largest Gift Shop." It certainly is big. T-shirts; Native American "handicrafts;" all kinds of playing cards, both new and used (casinos have to change decks frequently, so this is where used packs go); dice; things covered in rhinestones; snow globes—in short, something for everyone, provided "everyone" has a certain sensibility. We looked, and we felt the tackiest item available was the pair of earrings made out of poker chips. The coolest? Some inexpensive, old-fashioned-style dice. It's open daily from 8am until midnight. 2470 Las Vegas Blvd. S. (at Sahara Ave.). www.worldslargest giftshop.com. ✆ **702/384-0005.**

M&M's World.

Gamblers General Store ★ This is a gambler's paradise stocked with a massive book collection, antique and modern slot machines, gaming tables (blackjack, craps, and so on), roulette wheels, collectible chips, casino dice, classic Vegas photos, and a ton of gaming-related souvenirs. The store is open daily from 9am to 5pm. 800 S. Main St. (Downtown). www.gamblersgeneralstore. com. ⓒ **800/322-2447** or 702/382-9903.

Zombie Apocalypse Store ★★ Although you can stock your bunker with enough supplies to survive any type of apocalypse from the selections at this store, we're putting it under "Gifts &

Bonanza Gift and Souvenir Shop.

Souvenirs" for the delightfully silly zombie paraphernalia in which they wrap their end-of-the-world fear feeding. In addition to the survivalist store staples like knives, stun guns, and food rations, they have bumper stickers with sayings like "Fast Zombies suck," T-shirts that read "Zombies should get a life," helpful posters with zombie killing and survival tips, zombie-shaped target practice sheets, books, DVDs, and even a bunker-style den where you can sit and watch zombie movies. The store is open Monday through Saturday from 9am to 7pm. 3420 Spring Mountain Rd. (at Polaris Ave.). www.zombieapocalypsestore.com. ⓒ **866/784-7882.**

Home Design, Furnishings & Housewares

Las Vegas Design Center ★ More than 40 showrooms packed with designer furnishings and accessories are open to the public at the World Market

Mural on the exterior of the Gamblers General Store.

Center, one of the biggest home-design expo facilities in the world. You'll find everything from living room sets to objets d'art, most of which is insanely expensive but still fun to look at. If nothing else you can get some ideas for how you want to redo your own home, but ladies, take heed: Don't let your guy see the home-theater-seating showroom. He'll want it all for his man cave. The center is open Tuesday through Saturday from 10am until 6pm. In the World Market Center, 495 S. Grand Central Parkway. www.lvdesigncenter.com. ℂ **702/599-3093.**

Music

Zia Record Exchange ★★   A sign that individual Vegas culture might not be dead after all, these fairly large shops mix new and used records. The emphasis is on CDs, but there is a big vinyl section, and both show a varied selection of music styles (rock, punk, jazz, soundtracks, and so on). Cleverly, the stores spotlight bands coming to Vegas, both large and small, with special displays, plus there are always bins of music from local acts. They also feature occasional in-store CD signings, events, and concerts. Please note the signs cautioning against slam dancing! Both locations are open daily from 10am to midnight. 4503 W. Sahara Ave. www.ziarecords.com. ℂ 702/233-4942. 4225 S. Eastern Ave., no. 17. ℂ **702/735-4942.**

Sporting & Camping Goods

Bass Pro Shops ★   So you're in Vegas and you think, "Man, I really could use a fishing boat right about now." Luckily, Bass Pro Shops is there to help with that and pretty much any other outdoor sporting good need you may have. The store is almost as big as the great outdoors and offers numerous workshops and classes to help you become the nature lover you've always wanted to be. It's open Monday through Saturday from 9am until 9pm and Sunday from 9am until 7pm. In the Silverton Resort and Casino, 8200 Dean Martin Dr. (at Blue Diamond Rd.). www.basspro.com. ℂ **702/730-5200.**

Technology & Cameras

Fry's Electronics ★   There are a couple of dozen of these shrines to the techno-geek gods in the U.S., but each has a different, wacky theme so no two are exactly alike. Here the theme is, appropriately enough, Las Vegas; there's a giant slot machine on the outside and what seems like acres of all things electronic inside, from computers and TVs to home theater systems and those little random plugs and cables that you inevitably forget to pack. It's open Monday through Friday from 8am until 9pm, Saturday from 9am until 9pm, and Sunday from 9am until 7pm. 6845 Las Vegas Blvd. S. www.frys.com. ℂ **702/932-1400.**

Toys & Games

Auto Veloce ★   You probably won't be racing these immaculately designed, 1/18th-scale reproductions of everything from Aston Martins to Volkswagens around your living room floor, but it sure will be tempting. The detail of the models is stunning, with working doors, hoods, trunks, and more allowing you to live out your Ferrari fantasies without having to pay the hundreds of thousands of dollars a full-size one would cost. The shop is open Sunday through Thursday from 10am until 11pm and Friday and Saturday from 10am until midnight. In The Forum Shops at Caesars Palace, 3500 Las Vegas Blvd. S. www.autovelocemodels.com. ℂ **702/650-2440.**

The Toy Shack ★★★   Fans of the History Channel's *Pawn Stars* may recognize the name Jimmy Jiminez, who acts as the toy expert on the show. He's the brains behind this blast-from-the-past (and present) store that celebrates all things play with new and collectible toys of all stripes, from action figures and dolls to model cars and trucks (and one of the biggest selections of Hot Wheels in the country). If you had a favorite from your childhood, you'll probably find three of them here, and if you don't, they can probably get it for you. The Toy Shack is open Sunday through Thursday from 10am until 10pm and Friday and Saturday from 10am until midnight. In Neonopolis, 450 E. Fremont St. www.lasvegas toyshack.com. ✆ **702/538-8600.**

PRACTICAL MATTERS: THE SHOPPING SCENE

HOURS OF OPERATION   Because they are as much tourist attractions as shopping destinations, the malls, stores, and boutiques on the Strip are open longer than you may expect, generally from 10am until 11pm on weekdays and until midnight on weekends. Once you get off the Strip, things become more normal, with typical operating hours between 9am and 6 or 7pm. Some of the smaller independent stores are closed on Sundays.

SALES TAX   The effective sales tax rate in Clark County, where Las Vegas is located, is 8.1% as of 2012. This applies to most purchases of goods and products.

FINDING BARGAINS   Generally speaking, the farther you get away from the Strip, the cheaper things get. This applies to just about all categories of merchandise, even at name-brand chain stores where they will bump up prices by a few bucks just because they can. So if you're planning on getting a pair of shoes or jeans, for instance, at a familiar chain store, check to see if they have an outlet elsewhere in the city and you can often save yourself some dough.

This also holds true for sundry items like toothpaste, shampoo, and deodorant. If you buy these at the hotel gift shops, expect to pay significantly more than you would if you go off the Strip to a regular retailer like Target or Wal-Mart.

GETTING THINGS HOME   It's usually best to only buy what you can fit in your suitcase or carry-on for the plane ride home, but if you see that lamp or giant framed painting or Ferrari that you just have to have, most stores will arrange for shipping. But before you blindly accept the store's sometimes inflated charges, check with your hotel's concierge desk, which usually offer FedEx, UPS, USPS, and other shipping services that can save you a few bucks. Also check the "Mail" heading under "Fast Facts" in chapter 11 for more information on where local branches of shipping and mailing services are located in Las Vegas.

ENTERTAINMENT & NIGHTLIFE

A

ccording to an advertising slogan, Hollywood is the "Entertainment Capital of the World." But consider for a moment the sheer number of shows, headliners, bars, nightclubs, lounges, and other forms of entertainment and nightlife in Las Vegas. Your options are almost limitless: Cirque du Soleil has a half-dozen permanent shows here; virtually every hotel has at least one showroom, if not four; Celine Dion, Elton John, and Garth Brooks are among the big names who perform only in Vegas; most bars are open 24 hours a day; the number of nightclubs pounding out the beats until dawn seems to grow every week; and yes, there are even a few showgirls left. Hollywood may have the slogan, but Las Vegas is the real capital.

You certainly won't be lacking in things to do; in fact, the opposite may be true in that there are simply not enough hours in your vacation to do all the things you may want to do. The key is to cover the basics—a Cirque show if you've never seen one; a headliner if they are in town; a fun bar; a high-energy nightclub—and then start layering in the off-the-beaten-track, the one-of-a-kind, and the less-high-profile shows, clubs, and entertainment offerings that will make your trip more memorable.

What follows are the things you should not miss—and some that are not worth your time no matter what you may have heard—in the categories of performing arts, which includes shows both big, small, and in between; the bar scene, including lounges, piano bars, and pubs; the club and music scene, which covers the big dance clubs, ultralounges, comedy clubs, and more; and, of course, the strip clubs, which are big business in Vegas. There's also a section for gay and lesbian visitors showcasing the best and brightest bars and clubs around town.

Sprinkled throughout are some handy tips, tricks, and advice on how to maximize your entertainment offerings, including some "Practical Matters" at the end of the chapter on things like showroom policies, dress codes, and more.

THE PERFORMING ARTS

This category covers all the major Las Vegas production shows, and a few of the minor ones as well. Note that shows can close without warning, even ones that have been running just shy of forever, so please call first. You might also want to double-check on days and times of performances; schedules can change without notice. **Note:** Most ticket prices do not include taxes, fees, or drinks, so you might also check for those potential hidden costs.

PREVIOUS PAGE: **Cirque du Soleil's** *Mystère*.

Hot Tip!

Tix4Tonight (© **877/849-4868;** www. tix4tonight.com) is a service that puts unsold seats for that evening on sale for as little as half the normal ticket price. There is no way to know in advance what shows will have tickets available for that evening, so the very nature of the service means you can't plan; you have to stand in line and take your chances. Sales start at 10am but lines start forming well ahead of that. Also, although some of the bigger shows, like those from Cirque du Soleil, will sometimes have discounted tickets, they may not be half price and they may not be the best seats. And if you're hoping to find Céline or Garth tickets here, don't hold your breath. So if you have your heart set on a specific show or a specific seat, don't rely on Tix4Tonight, but if, like a good gambler, you like taking chances, head for any of their nine Las Vegas locations, including the one at 3785 Las Vegas Blvd. S. (in the giant Coke bottle, at the Showcase Mall).

Absinthe ★★★ Like the supposedly hallucinatory drink it is named after, this Cirque du Soleil–style revue may leave you reeling, but, boy, will that hangover be worth it. The show is performed in the round in a small tentlike structure in front of Caesars Palace, with a tiny circular stage and only a few rows of seating. This gives new meaning to the phrase "death-defying stunts," with acrobats, trapeze artists, high-wire walkers, and even high-speed roller skaters literally feet– and in some cases inches—from your face. Adding to the thrills are the raunchy host, The Gazillionaire, and his faithfully dimwitted sidekick Penny, who introduce the acts with a dirty glee and X-rated humor than will leave you laughing so hard you'll forget to be offended or shocked. Penny's sock-puppet

segment is so deliriously over the top that it transcends its inherent vulgarity to become virtually awe-inspiring—it's worth the price of admission alone. Definitely not for kids or prudes! Shows are Tuesday and Thursday through Saturday at 8 and 10pm, Wednesday and Sunday at 8pm only. In Caesars Palace, 3570 Las Vegas Blvd. S. www.absinthevegas.com. © **877/423-5463.** Tickets $69–$99.

Blue Man Group ★★ Are they blue? Indeed they are—three hairless, nonspeaking men dipped in azure paint, doing decidedly odd stunts with marshmallows, art supplies, audience members, tons of paper, and an amazing array of percussion instruments fashioned fancifully from PVC piping. If that doesn't sound very Vegas, well, it's not—at least not originally. Although they have become as synonymous with Vegas entertainment as

Penny, one of the delightful hosts at _Absinthe_.

Cirque du Soleil, now currently in their third hotel showroom (after Luxor and The Venetian), they are actually a franchise of a New York–born performance-art troupe that seems to have slipped into town through a side door opened by Cirque's groundbreaking successes. Don't get the wrong idea: This is no Cirque clone. There are no acrobatics or flowing choreography, no attempt to create an alternate universe—just a series of surreal, unconnected bits. It's funny in the weirdest and most unexpected ways, and the crowd is usually roaring by the end. Fans of typical Vegas shows may leave scratching their heads, but we are glad there is another color in the Vegas entertainment spectrum. Shows are nightly at 7 and 10pm. At Monte Carlo Resort & Casino, 3770 Las Vegas Blvd. S. www.blueman.com. ✆ 866/641-7469. Tickets $75–$160.

Céline Dion ★ The French-Canadian songstress's return to Vegas after a 3-year absence is backed by a 31-piece orchestra, making this a more dignified affair than her dance-heavy 2003-2008 show. As usual, her voice is pure and clear; she is probably one of the most naturally gifted singers in the world. And when she sings stirring signature ballads like "Because You Loved Me" and the inevitable "My Heart Will Go On," it's easy to understand how she can sell out a 4,000-seat theater on a regular basis. But despite a wide-ranging catalogue, she only sings a handful of her own songs, mostly ballads, and spends the rest of the evening doing others' music, including languid tributes to Michael Jackson, Ella Fitzgerald, and the music of James Bond movies, all of which are, at best, mid-tempo. Even her virtual duets with Andrea Bocelli and, oddly, herself (doing "How Do You Keep the Music Playing"—look up the lyrics, you'll see why it's odd) are sleepy. There are some up-tempo moments, but not enough to sustain the energy of a Vegas audience, buffet stuffed and ready to get back to the slot machines. Note that the show is not performed every week and nights vary, but shows are usually Tuesday and Wednesday, and Friday through Sunday at 7:30pm. In Caesars Palace, 3570 Las Vegas Blvd. S. www.celinedion.com. ✆ 877/423-5463. Tickets $55–$250.

Blue Man Group.

Cirque du Soleil's KÀ ★★★ ☺
KÀ subverts expectations by largely
eschewing the usual Cirque format—
wide-eyed innocent is taken on surreal
adventure, beautiful but aimless, complete with acrobats and clowns and lots
of weird floaty things—in favor of an
actual plot, as a brother and sister from
some mythical Asian kingdom are separated by enemy raiders and have to
endure various trials and tribulations
before being reunited. Gleefully bor-
rowing imagery from magical realist
martial-arts movies such as *Crouching
Tiger, Hidden Dragon,* the production
makes use of a technically extraordinary set that shifts the stage not just
horizontally but vertically, as the action
moves from under the sea to the side of
a steep cliff and beyond. The circus
elements—acrobats and clowns—are
for once incorporated into the show in
a way that makes some loose narrative

Céline Dion.

sense, though this does mean that the physical stunts are mostly pretty much in
service to the story rather than random feats of derring-do.

The story is by turns funny, tragic, and whimsical, with moments that are
nothing less than exquisitely perfect bits of theater. It might be too long and
intense for younger children, but older ones will be enthralled—and so will you.
Performances are held Tuesday through Saturday at 7 and 9:30pm. In the MGM
Grand, 3799 Las Vegas Blvd. S. www.cirquedusoleil.com/ka. ✆ **866/740-7711.** Tickets $69–
$180, discounts for children 5–12.

Cirque du Soleil's LOVE ★ ☺   A collaboration between the Beatles (by way
of Sir George Martin's son, who remixed and reconfigured the music with a free
hand that may distress purists) and Cirque du Soleil, this is the usual Cirque
triumph of imaginative design, but it also feels surprisingly hollow. In one sense,
it's an inspired pairing, in that the Beatles' music provides an apt vehicle for
Cirque's joyous spectacle. But while Cirque shows have never been big on plot,
the particular aimlessness of this production means that the show too quickly
dissolves into simply the introduction of one novel staging element after another.
In other words, its visual fabulousness ends up repetitious rather than thrilling.
Beatles fans will still have a good time, but others may wish to spend their Cirque
money on one of the other options. Shows are held Thursday through Monday at
7 and 9:30pm. At The Mirage, 3400 Las Vegas Blvd. S. www.cirquedusoleil.com/love.
✆ **800/963-9634** or 702/792-7777. Tickets $79–$180.

Cirque du Soleil's Mystère ★★★ ☺   2013 marks the 20th anniversary of
the first (and many would still say the best) of the multiple Las Vegas Cirque du
Soleil productions. Although there have been some tweaks here and there and a
few new acts were added in 2012, the show is pretty much the same as it always
has been, which, in a word, is *stunning*. It is the closest to the original ethos of
the Montréal-based company's unique circus experience, which not only shuns

CIRQUE DU thriller

For years there had been rumors of a possible collaboration between Cirque du Soleil and Michael Jackson, but it took the singer's untimely death in 2009 to make the dream a reality. A new Cirque production featuring Jackson's music will debut at Mandalay Bay in early 2013 after a touring version of the production moonwalks around the world throughout 2012. The creators say the permanent and touring versions will be substantially different, but that is yet to be seen. The show will accompanied by additional Cirque and Michael Jackson–themed attractions at the hotel, including a Jackson memorabilia exhibit, a night-club, and a retail outlet. For updates, visit www.cirquedusoleil.com/mj.

traditional animal acts in favor of gorgeous feats of human strength and agility, but also adds elements of the surreal and the absurd. The show features one simply unbelievable act after another (seemingly boneless contortionists and acrobats, breathtakingly beautiful aerial maneuvers), interspersed with Dadaist/ *Commedia dell'arte* clowns. All this and a giant snail! The thesaurus runs dry trying to describe it: dreamlike, suspenseful, funny, erotic, mesmerizing, and just lovely. At times, you might even find yourself moved to tears. Catch it Saturday through Wednesday at 7 and 9:30pm. In Treasure Island, 3300 Las Vegas Blvd. S. www. cirquedusoleil.com/mystere. ✆ **800/392-1999** or 702/894-7722. Tickets $69–$109, discounts for children under 12.

Cirque du Soleil's O ★★★ How to describe the seemingly indescribable wonder and artistry of Cirque du Soleil's still utterly dazzling display? An Esther Williams–Busby Berkeley spectacular on peyote? A Salvador Dalí painting come to life? A stage show by Fellini? The French-Canadian troupe has topped itself with this production—and not simply because it's situated its breathtaking acrobatics in, on, around, and above a 1.5-million-gallon pool (*eau*—pronounced O— is French for "water"). Even without those impossible feats, this might be worth the price just to see the presentation, a constantly shifting dreamscape that's a marvel of imagination and staging. If you've seen *Mystère* at Treasure Island, or other Cirque productions, you'll be amazed that they've once again raised the bar to new heights without losing any of the humor or stylistic trademarks, including the sensuous music. Performances are held Wednesday through Sunday at 7:30 and 10pm. In Bellagio, 3600 Las Vegas Blvd. S. www.cirquedusoleil.com/o. ✆ **888/488-7111** or 702/796-9999. Tickets $109–$180.

Cirque du Soleil's Zumanity ✋ This adult show, dedicated to celebrating human sexuality, features a bevy of acts are all meant to be lewd or alluring or both, if you pay attention. They are mostly just basic Cirque acts (and worse, just basic striptease acts, which you can see anywhere in town for a great deal less money), though instead of giving the illusion of near nakedness, they give the illusion of total nakedness (an illusion that works better the farther you sit from the stage). As they contort and writhe and feign pleasure or apathy, we feel sympathy for all the parents who spent money on gymnastics and ballet lessons over the years, only to have their poor kids end up in this. See, Cirque is naturally sexy and erotic, so all this is gilding the lily until it chokes from lack of oxygen and dies. There are some visually stunning moments (two women splashing about in a large glass, a woman performing with a dozen hula hoops), but there are better ways to get your thrills in this town. Shows are held Friday through Tuesday at 7:30 and 10pm. In New York–New York, 3790 Las Vegas Blvd. S. www.zumanity.com. ✆ **866/606-7111** or 702/740-6815. Tickets $69–$135. Only ages 18 and over admitted.

Chippendales ★ Of the several beefcake revues in town, this one gets the most attention simply because of its well-known brand name. The show ticks all of the boxes: inhumanly handsome and fit men; fantasy fulfillment sketches featuring the guys as cowboys and fireman and the like; and an audience of (mostly) women who go quite, quite crazy. The latter is almost as fun to watch as the guys themselves. But something feels overprocessed here and our man-candy money goes to rival **Thunder From Down Under** (p. 192). Shows are held Sunday through Wednesday and Thursday at 8pm and Friday and Saturday at 8 and 10:30pm. In the Rio Hotel, 3700 W. Flamingo. www.chippendales.com. ✆ **702/777-7776.** Tickets $40–$60. Ages 18 and over.

Crazy Girls *Crazy Girls* is probably the raciest revue on the Strip. It features sexy showgirls with perfect bodies in erotic song-and-dance numbers enhanced by innovative lighting effects. Think of *Penthouse* poses coming to life. Perhaps it was best summed up by one older man from Kentucky: "It's okay if you like boobs and butt. But most of the girls can't even dance." The show is held nightly except Tuesday at 9:30pm. In the Riviera Hotel & Casino, 2901 Las Vegas Blvd. S. www.rivierahotel. com. ✆ **800/634-3420.** Tickets $45–$60. Only ages 18 and over admitted.

Criss Angel: Believe ★★ Forget what you may have heard about early versions of illusionist Criss Angel's show and hear this: *Believe* is probably the best traditional (and in many ways untraditional) magic shows in Vegas. Angel has always been a compelling showman, astounding audiences with his bigger-than-life stunts that are mixed with a kind of rock-'n'-roll aesthetic. Although he can't do stuff in this showroom like float above the Luxor pyramid or walk on water as he has on his popular *Mindfreak* TV show, he still manages to bring out the "wow" factor with tricks both big (a gruesomely awesome sawing-the-woman-in-half bit) and small (is he really swallowing those razor blades?). There are more illusions packed into this 90-minute show than any other in Vegas, and since he is constantly adding and changing pieces, the show will continue to evolve.

Interestingly, the changes seem to have extended to Angel himself, who now comes across as less of a Hollywood bad boy and more of a thoughtful artist, complete with home video of him as a kid and honorifics to his favorite

---

😊 family-friendly **SHOWS**

Appropriate shows for kids, all described in this chapter, include the following:

- **Cirque du Soleil's KÀ,** at the MGM Grand (p. 181)
- **Cirque du Soleil's LOVE,** at The Mirage (p. 181)
- **Cirque du Soleil's Mystère,** at Treasure Island (p. 181)
- **Mac King,** at Harrah's (p. 189)
- **Tournament of Kings,** at Excalibur (p. 192)

For a long time, Vegas headliners were something of a joke; only those on the downhill side of fame were thought to play here. But with all the new performance spaces—and high fees—offered by the new hotels, Vegas suddenly has respect again, especially, on (of all things) the rock scene. Both the Hard Rock Hotel's The Joint and the House of Blues attract very current and very popular acts who find it hip, rather than humiliating, to play Sin City, and there are several bigger venues that draw in the arena-size concerts and events. Major headliner showrooms in Vegas include the following:

o **The Boulevard Pool** is an outdoor concert venue overlooking the Las Vegas Strip that sees concerts from smaller music acts (in The Cosmopolitan of Las Vegas, 3708 Las Vegas Blvd S.; www.cosmopolitanlasvegas. com; ✆ **877/551-7778**).

o **The Colosseum** is home to no fewer than four big headliner names. In addition to **Céline Dion**'s and **Elton John**'s regular shows (reviewed separately in this chapter), the 4,000-seat theater also hosts extended runs by **Rod Stewart** and **Shania Twain** in addition to shorter stands by big-name singing and comedy acts (in Caesars Palace, 3570 Las Vegas Blvd S.; www.caesarspalace.com; ✆ **866/ 227-5938**).

o Hard Rock Hotel's **The Joint** was rebuilt in 2009 and now holds 4,000

people for rock concerts and special events (in the Hard Rock Hotel, 4455 Paradise Rd.; www.hardrockhotel. com; ✆ **800/693-7625** or 702/ 693-5000).

o The **House of Blues** can hold several hundred people for smaller rock and blues concerts and their weekly gospel brunch (in Mandalay Bay, 3950 Las Vegas Blvd. S.; www.hob. com; ✆ **877/632-7400** or 702/ 632-7600).

o **Mandalay Bay Events Center** seats 12,000 people for arena-style concert tours and indoor sporting events (in Mandalay Bay, 3950 Las Vegas Blvd. S.; www.mandalaybay.com; ✆ **877/ 632-7400** or 702/632-7580).

o **MGM Grand Garden Events Arena** can hold over 17,000 people and is

magicians. Shows are held Tuesday through Saturday at 7pm, with an additional show at 9:30pm on Tuesday, Friday, and Saturday. In the Luxor, 3900 Las Vegas Blvd. S. ✆ **800/557-7428**. www.crissangel.com. Tickets $59–$160.

Divas Las Vegas ★ Star impersonator Frank Marino hosted the similar *La Cage* for more than 2 decades up the street at the Riviera. His new show at the Imperial Palace isn't really all that new, in that it still features Marino as Joan Rivers in a series of Bob Mackie–esque gowns telling groan-worthy jokes and introducing a lineup of female impersonators. The "ladies" vary in quality and illusion: "Beyoncé" is done more for laughs and "Madonna" and "Dolly" are good, but "Céline Dion" is dead-on and "Lady Gaga" is frighteningly accurate (but hey, she kind of looks like a drag queen anyway). They lip-synch their way through hits, often accompanied by scantily clad male dancers, which gives you something to look at if the impersonator isn't up to snuff. Shows are held Saturday through home to big-name concert tours and events (in the MGM Grand, 3799 Las Vegas Blvd. S.; www.mgmgrand.com; (C) 800/929-1111 or 702/891-7777).

o **MGM Grand Hollywood Theatre** is an intimate 740-seat venue that is home to dozens of shows per year by illusionist David Copperfield, plus shorter runs from comedians and singers (in the MGM Grand, 3799 Las Vegas Blvd. S.; www.mgmgrand.com; (C) 800/929-1111 or 702/891-7777).

o **The Orleans Showroom** seats 9,500 people and often has concerts, ice hockey, traveling circuses, and other events (in The Orleans, 4500 W. Tropicana Ave.; www.orleanscasino. com; (C) 800/675-3267).

o **The Pearl Theater** is a three-level venue that seats up to 2,500 people for pop, rock, R&B, and comedy concerts (in the Palms, 4321 W. Flamingo Rd.; www.palms.com; (C) 866/942-7770).

o **Sam Boyd Stadium** is a 36,800-seat stadium that features big concerts

and sporting events (7000 E. Russell Rd.; www.ticketmaster.com; (C) 800/745-3000).

o **The Smith Center for the Performing Arts** has a 2,000 seat concert hall for big stage shows (including a Broadways series), a 300-seat Cabaret Jazz theater, and a 200-seat theater for smaller productions. See p. 71 for more details (361 Symphony Park Ave.; www.thesmithcenter.com; (C) 702/614-0109).

o The **Theatre for the Performing Arts** is a 7,000-seat concert hall dating back to 1972 (but modernized) that hosts touring Broadway shows and other events (in Planet Hollywood Hotel & Casino, 3667 Las Vegas Blvd. S.; www.planethollywood resort.com; (C) 877/333-9474 or 702/785-5555).

o **The Thomas and Mack Center** is a 19,522-seat arena that hosts concerts and sporting events (UNLV Campus; www.ticketmaster.com; (C) 800/745-3000).

Thursday at 10pm. In Imperial Palace, 3535 Las Vegas Blvd. S. www.imperialpalace.com. (C) 888/777-7664. Tickets $39–$79.

Donny and Marie ★ Yes, proving that a good fainting spell on *Dancing with the Stars* is worth a lot more than you'd expect, the wholesome brother-sister duo of Donny and Marie has made a comeback on the stages of Las Vegas, performing their personal blend of music, comedy, and variety at the Flamingo. The show is a lot more fun than it has any right to be as long as you go in with your tongue placed firmly in cheek. But really, $260? Really? Shows are held Tuesday through Saturday at 7:30pm. In the Flamingo, 3555 Las Vegas Blvd. S. www.flamingolv.com. (C) 702/733-3333. Tickets $95–$260.

Elton John: The Million Dollar Piano ★★ Sir Elton's canon of work is irreproachable: "Benny and the Jets," "Rocket Man," "Don't Let the Sun Go Down on Me." We could be here all day just listing his 5 decades worth of hits. He's also a master showman; king of the bling and the tricked-out pianos like the one used in this production complete with LED video panels built into it. Great songs and a great performer. So why does it feel like something is missing here? The staging is part of the problem. John spends the bulk of his time onstage sitting at the piano, naturally, so the computer-generated graphics on the massive background LED panels provide the bulk of the "movement" on stage, and, sadly, they are little more than glorified screensavers. The set list could use some energizing as well, as it is heavy on the ballads and deep album cuts that only the most rabid of fans will recognize. Musically speaking, Elton John is a genius and this production highlights that well, but those looking for a little more "show" for their $250 show tickets may be disappointed. Note that the show is not performed every week and nights vary, but shows are usually Tuesday, Wednesday, and/or Thursday and Friday through Sunday at 7:30pm. In Caesars Palace, 3570 Las Vegas Blvd. S. www.caesarspalace.com. ℂ **888/435-8665.** Tickets $55–$250.

Garth Brooks ★★★   Back before Garth Brooks retired, his concerts regularly broke box office records with tens of thousands lured to the stadium-size spectacles he put on around the world. Now, Brooks has been lured out of retirement for a series of weekend shows at Encore Las Vegas, and his return to the stage is both triumphant and completely unexpected. The spectacle is gone; instead, what you get is a guy and a guitar. No sets, no band, no special effects, just a laser focus on what made this man and his music. Brooks comes across as Everyman—your very funny best friend who wants to tell stories and play a few songs on his guitar. Although it is acoustic, what he does is electrifying, taking the audience on a journey through his life and the music that formed him. He doesn't actually play that many of his own songs, instead covering classics by everyone from Merle Haggard to Elton John, then uses those tunes to showcase the influences in his music. For instance, an exploration of a dark Bob Seger song ("the chords paint a picture") leads to his own "Thunder Rolls." He even responds to shouted-out requests, in one instance pulling an entire catalog of Jim Croce songs out of his trucker cap without breaking a sweat. You don't need to like country music—heck, you don't even need to like Garth Brooks's music—you just need to like music, period. The show is performed on select Fridays and Sundays at 8pm and Saturdays at 8 and 10:30pm. In the Encore Las Vegas, 3121 Las Vegas Blvd. S. www.encorelasvegas.com. ℂ **877/654-2784.** Tickets $253.

Jersey Boys Vegas ★★   Between 1962 and 1975, Frankie Valli and the Four Seasons racked up an astonishingly long string of catchy, well-crafted pop hits that are as beloved as any in pop music. These time-tested songs are the central draw of the massively popular, Tony Award–winning (for Best Musical) *Jersey Boys.* But this is far more than a rote musical revue, or just another re-creation of a popular oldies act. It's a real musical play, with a compelling street-to-suite storyline, a fair share of drama, and enough humor and uplift to satisfy both the theater veteran and the vacationing family (with a mild warning for some salty, Jersey-esque language). A dazzlingly visual production that crackles with energy and shines with precision stagecraft, *Jersey Boys* has already had an enthusiastic post-Broadway life. With its visual wow factor and an excitingly faithful re-creation of the Four Seasons' music, it is successful enough that it is now in a new home at Paris Las Vegas. Performances are Wednesday through Friday and Sunday at 7pm, Tuesday and Saturday at 6:30 and 9:30pm. In Paris Las Vegas, 3655 Las Vegas Blvd. S. www.jerseyboysinfo.com/vegas. ℂ **702/777-7776.** Tickets $100–$227.

Jubilee! ★ This, the last of the classic Vegas showgirl spectaculars, is crammed with singing, dancing, magic, acrobats, elaborate costumes and sets, and, of course, bare breasts. While interesting from a historic perspective—pretty much *all* Vegas entertainment used to be like this—the show itself is a musty, dusty relic; sad to say, but there's a reason that this type of show is mostly extinct. To be sure, the costumes by the legendary Bob Mackie are fantastic and the set pieces are impressive, including a *Temple of Doom*–style Samson-and-

Delilah bit and a water-filled sinking of the Titanic segment, but even those come with less-than-impressive dancing, singing, and music that often veers uncomfortably into misogynistic territory. Much more entertaining and historically enlightening is the backstage walking tour Monday, Wednesday, and Saturday at 11am (tickets are $17, with $5 off if you buy a ticket to see the show). Shows are held Saturday through Thursday at 7:30 and 10:30pm. In Bally's Las Vegas, 3645 Las Vegas Blvd. S. www.ballyslv.com. **℗ 800/237-7469**. Tickets $58–$118. Ages 18 and over.

Legends in Concert ★ The parade of faux celebrities who do their best to make you believe they are the real thing (with varying results) has been running in Vegas for more than 25 years, noteworthy on its own in a

TOP: **An Elton John impersonator performs in** *Legends in Concert.* BOTTOM: *Jubilee!*

Hot Tip!

Options are a good thing, and Caesars Entertainment is offering more than 20 of them for one price. Their All Stage Pass allows Vegas visitors to pay $99 (with free membership to their Total Rewards players' club) for the opportunity to see as many of their shows and attractions as possible in 48 hours. This includes productions like Chippendales, *Absinthe, Jubilee!, Divas Las Vegas, Legends in Concert*, Mac King, and more plus attractions such as the Eiffel Tower Ride and Auto Collections at Imperial Palace. If you're really committed, you could see a couple of afternoon shows and both an early- and late-evening show during your 2 days and save hundreds of dollars, but even if you only see two or three you're probably still coming out ahead. Note that you don't get the best seats, and high-end shows at Caesars Entertainment hotels like Céline Dion, Elton John, and Donny and Marie are not included. You must purchase the passes in person at the Show Tickets Direct box office at Bally's, Caesars Palace, or Planet Hollywood (no phone orders, sorry). For more information, visit www.caesars.com/allstagepass.

town like this. Performers will vary depending on when you see the show; you may catch "Janet Jackson" and "Diana Ross," or you could get "Dolly Parton" and "Cher," but you will almost always get "Elvis." Unlike other impersonator shows, the singing is live (no lip-syncing, even when "Britney" is performing), which can enhance the illusion or destroy it. Some performers succeed more in appearance and others do better with vocal mimicry, and while most are at least passable, there are a few that will leave you wondering if he or she is the real thing playing a joke on the audience. Don't scoff; Ellen Degeneres did that very thing during at 2008 show and captured the audience reactions ("didn't look anything like her") for her daytime talkfest. Shows are Sunday through Friday at 7 and 9:30pm. In Harrah's Las Vegas, 3475 Las Vegas Blvd. www.harrahslv.com. ✆ **702/396-5111.** Tickets $50–$60.

Le Rêve ★★   Challenged from the get-go, thanks to a decision to base this Cirque-like show around a stage of water, thus prompting inevitable comparisons with *O* down the street, this production has received major revamps, both in staging and choreography. By and large, the choices—particularly to get revered avant-garde choreographer and MOMIX-genius Moses Pendleton to take over the choreography (thus increasing the presence of dance)—have been good ones, and this production now stands on its own as a visual spectacle and emotionally satisfying entertainment.

Le Rêve, named for the most significant of the paintings owned by Steve Wynn, is an extravaganza featuring all the usual elements: gorgeously sculpted athletic performers who twist, contort, and mostly pose in filmy tattered outfits before and after diving in and splashing out of a giant pool. Intermittently funny clowns do their thing. Magritte figures float by. Fountains rise out of the stage. The result is pure spectacle, with a slight narrative suggesting the proceedings are the dreams of a woman dealing with a turbulent romantic issue. It's like the biggest, most impressive Esther Williams production you can imagine. Speaking of which, you may wish to avoid sitting in the front rows, unless you don't mind spending 90 minutes huddling under the provided towels—there is splashing involved. Shows are held Friday through Tuesday at 7 and 9:30pm. In Wynn Las

PENN & TELLER'S TOP 10 THINGS ONE SHOULD NEVER DO IN A VEGAS magic show

Penn & Teller have been exercising their acerbic wit and magical talents in numerous forums together for more than 25 years, and their show at the Rio is one of Vegas's best and most intelligent. We must confess that we couldn't get the quieter half of the duo, Teller, to cough up a few words, but the more verbose Penn Jillette was happy to share.

1. Costume yourself in gray business suits totally lacking in rhinestones, animal patterns, Mylar, capes, bell-bottoms, shoulder pads, and top hats.

2. Wear your hair in any style that could not be described as "feathered" or "spiked."

3. Use really good live jazz music instead of canned sound-alike cheesy rip-off fake pop "music."

4. Cruelly (but truthfully) make fun of your siblings in the magic brotherhood.

5. Do the dangerous tricks on each other instead of anonymous show women with aftermarket breasts and/or endangered species.

6. Toss a cute little magic bunny into a cute little chipper-shredder.

7. Open your show by explaining and demonstrating how other magicians on the Strip do their most amazing tricks, and then do that venerable classic of magic "The Cups and Balls," with transparent plastic cups.

8. Treat the audience as if they had a brain in their collective head.

9. Allow audience members to sign real bullets, load them into real guns, and fire those bullets into your face.

10. Bleed.

(You will find many of these "don'ts" in the Penn & Teller show at the Rio All-Suite Hotel & Casino.)

Vegas, 3131 Las Vegas Blvd. S. www.wynnlasvegas.com. ℭ **888/320-7110.** Tickets $105–$195. Only ages 13 and over admitted.

Mac King ★★★ ☺ 🎫 One of the best entertainment values in Vegas, this is an afternoon comedy-magic show—and note the order of precedence in that introduction. King does magic, thankfully, emphasizing the only kind that's really mind-blowing these days—those close-up tricks that defy your eyes and mind. But he surrounds his tricks with whimsy and wit, and sometimes gut-busting guf-faws, which all serve to make you wonder how someone else can still perform stunts with a straight face. Check out how he takes a $100 bill and—wait, we don't want to give it away, but suffice it to say it involves an old shoe, a Fig New-ton, and several other unexpected props. Perfect for the kids, perfect for the budget, perfect timing if you need something in the afternoon before an evening of gambling, dining, and cavorting. Simply perfect. Shows are held Tuesday through Saturday at 1 and 3pm. In Harrah's, 3475 Las Vegas Blvd. S. www.harrahslv.com. ℭ **800/427-7247** or 702/369-5222. Tickets $33.

Nathan Burton ★ After competing in NBC's *America's Got Talent* show, Burton doubled-down on his popularity by bringing his light-hearted magic show to Vegas. There's nothing particularly ground-breaking about the production, but illusions are done with style and a healthy dose of good-natured humor. With a relatively low

Penn & Teller.

ticket price, it's a good way to spend an afternoon—provided you've already seen Mac King. Shows are Tuesday through Sunday at 4pm. In the Flamingo, 3555 Las Vegas Blvd. S. www.nathanburton.com. ℭ **702/733-3333.** Tickets $34–$44.

Peepshow ★★ The concept is utterly ridiculous: a retelling of classic fairy tales like Little Bo Peep and the Three Little Pigs as a topless musical revue. Yet somehow it works. The songs, both original and covers, are as titillating as the cast singing them, and the staging is inventive with candy-colored set pieces and evocative lighting. Throw in a headlining B- or C-level star like Holly Madison or Mel B. of the Spice Girls (who have each done stints in the show) and you have an enjoyably silly and surprisingly sexy show. Shows are nightly at 7 and 9:30pm. At Planet Hollywood Resort & Casino, 3667 Las Vegas Blvd. S. www.lasvegaspeepshow.com. ℭ **800/745-3000.** Tickets $66–$126. Ages 18 and over.

Penn & Teller ★★★ 📷 The most intelligent show in Vegas, as these two— magicians? illusionists? truth-tellers? BS artists? geniuses?—put on 90 minutes of, yes, magic and juggling, but also acerbic comedy, mean stunts, and quiet beauty. Looking like two characters out of Dr. Seuss, big, loud Penn and smaller, silent Teller (to reduce them to their basic characteristics) perform magic, reveal the secrets behind a few major magic tricks, discuss why magic is nothing but a bunch of lies, and then turn around and show why magic is as lovely an art form as any other. We won't tell you much about the various tricks and acts for fear of ruining punch lines, but watching Teller fish money out of an empty glass aquarium or play with shadows is to belie Penn's earlier caveats about learning how tricks are done—it doesn't ruin the wonder of it, not at all, nor the serenity that settles in your Vegas-sensory-overloaded brain. Shows are held Saturday through Wednesday at 9pm. In the Rio All-Suite Hotel & Casino, 3700 W. Flamingo Rd. www.riolas vegas.com. ℭ **888/746-7784.** Tickets $75–$95. Only ages 5 and over admitted.

The Price Is Right Live ★ If the casinos aren't paying off for you, maybe you should try your luck as a contestant on a live stage version of a classic game show instead. Here, select audience members get to play classic TPIR games like Plinko and Mountain Climber for a chance to win prizes that range from free-play in the casino to washing machines to cars. The chances of getting on stage are about as slim as those in the real televised show, but even audience members get a chance to win gift certificates and other small prizes with a series of interactive pricing challenges. Check the schedules for the frequent C- and D-list celebrity guest hosts, which have ranged from Jerry Springer to Joey Fatone. Shows are Tuesday through Thursday and Saturday at 2:30pm and Friday at

JUST FOR laughs

Depressed over all the money you lost in the casino? A surefire way to get cheered up is to check out one of the shows from stand-up comics currently paying in Las Vegas.

Louie Anderson has his own theater at Palace Station, 2411 W. Sahara Ave. (www.palacestation.com; ✆ **800/634-3101;** Tues–Sat 8:30pm; tickets $50), where he does his laid-back riffs on whatever happens to be amusing him that day. Frequent opening acts and improv guest stars make this a comedy bonanza.

George Wallace, at the Flamingo, 3555 Las Vegas Blvd. S. (www.flamingolv.com; ✆ **702/733-3333;** Tues–Sat 10pm; tickets $50), specializes in rants about

things that bug him, which in many cases will be things that bug you also.

Or, if you're feeling absurdist, you can try the outrageous, stream-of-consciousness prop comedy of **Carrot Top,** at Luxor Las Vegas, 3900 Las Vegas Blvd. S. (www.luxor.com; ✆ **800/557-7428;** Mon and Wed–Sun 8:30pm; tickets $50).

Also be sure to see who is playing at the comedy clubs in Vegas; a couple of which are listed later in this chapter.

7:30pm. At Bally's Las Vegas, 3645 Las Vegas Blvd. S. www.ballyslv.com. ✆ **800/237-7469.** Tickets $56.

Terry Fator ★ *America's Got Talent* winner Fator is no Susan Boyle, that's for sure, but his shtick—ventriloquism meets impersonation—is downright entertaining. The format of the 80-minute show is fairly standard: A series of puppets joins Fator on stage, and they proceed to do a song or three impersonating a famous voice. Winston the Turtle does a serviceable Roy Orbison and an eerily familiar James Blunt, while Walter the Cowboy kills on a Brooks and Dunn song—or rather Fator does, of course. Even the less than perfect impressions are

The Price is Right Live.

still impressive considering the fact that he's doing it all with his mouth closed. Fator's overall demeanor is a little too laconic, especially when he doesn't have a piece of felt on his hand, but the show mostly hits its middle-of-the-road target on the bull's eye, offering up some decent chuckles and a nice night of music. Try to get a seat in the center section, otherwise you'll spend most of your time watching the giant TV screens instead of the guy (and his friends) on stage. Shows are Tuesday through Saturday at 7:30pm. At The Mirage, 3400 Las Vegas Blvd. S. www.mirage.com. © **800/963-9634** or 702/792-7777. Tickets $60–$150.

Thunder from Down Under ★★   If you only have the time, money, and energy to see one male strip show, it should be this one. It's not that the guys are any hotter or the dancing any better than what you'll find in the better-known Chippendales at the Rio, but this production has an edgier, anything-could-happen vibe that amps up the energy and the fun. Plus, the guys here are all Australian. Oh, those accents! Shows are daily at 9pm with an additional 11pm show on Friday and Saturday. In Excalibur, 3850 Las Vegas Blvd. S. © **702/597-7600**. www.thunderfromdownunder.com. Tickets $41–$61. No one under 18 allowed; guests 18–20 must be accompanied by an adult.

Tournament of Kings ★ ☺   "Lords and Ladies, Wizards and Wenches, hasten thee to thy throne, for the battle is about to commence." Yes, that's how they talk at this dinner show—like a Renaissance fair, only with better production values. If you're familiar with the Medieval Times chain, this will look familiar. For a fixed price, you get a dinner that's better than you might expect (Cornish game hen, very fine baked potato, and the like), which you eat with your hands (in keeping with the theme), while Merlin (or someone like him) spends too much time trying to work the crowd up with a singalong. This gives way to a competition among the kings of various medieval countries, competing for titles in knightly contests (jousting, horse races, and such) that are every bit as unrehearsed and spontaneous as a professional wrestling match. Eventually, good triumphs over evil and all that. Younger kids will like it, teenagers will be too jaded, and adults will probably be bored. Shows are Monday and Wednesday at 6pm and Thursday through Sunday at 6 and 8:30pm. In Excalibur, 3850 Las Vegas Blvd. S. www.excalibur.com. © **800/933-1334** or 702/597-7600. Tickets $44–$59.

Thunder from Down Under.

You never know what you'll see at *V: The Ultimate Variety Show.*

V: The Ultimate Variety Show ★★   Although not as big budget as the Cirque productions, V can still offer some big thrills if you happen to see it on the right night. It's a collection of variety acts that could include acrobats, magicians, musicians, dancers, and more, but since the acts vary, so does the quality. Check to see if the thrilling roller-skating couple, Vittorio and Jenny Aratas, are on the roster. If so, their daredevil stunts are worth the ticket price alone. Shows are nightly at 7 and 9:30pm. In the Miracle Mile Shops at Planet Hollywood Resort, 3667 Las Vegas Blvd. S. www.vtheshow.com. ⓒ **866/932-1818** or 702/932-1818. Tickets $70–$90.

Vegas! The Show ★★★   What would happen if you took the best bits of classic Las Vegas entertainment from the last 70 years or so and put it in one package? That's the basic question behind this loving look back at the ghosts of the Sin City stages and the answer is this: it would be a heck of a lot of fun. It's all here—beautiful showgirls with skimpy costumes and big head dresses; headliners like The Rat Pack and Elvis; variety acts (tap dancing! magic!); dancing; singing; even Elton John and implosions. The show plays like a history channel special done by Busby Berkeley as the talented troupe leads the audience from the tuxedo and showgirl 1940s, the rock and roll '50s, the Frank and Dino '60s, the disco '70s, and beyond with performances that are more homages than impersonations. The singing and dancing are among the best you'll find in Vegas, which may very well make you long for the days before those French acrobats took over the showrooms. Shows are nightly at 7 and 9pm. In the Miracle

Take a trip back through time at *Vegas! The Show.*

WAYNE NEWTON'S TOP 10 FAVORITE lounge SONGS

Wayne Newton is the consummate entertainer. He has performed more than 25,000 concerts in Las Vegas alone, and in front of more than 25 million people worldwide. Wayne has received more standing ovations than any other entertainer in history. Along with his singing credits, his acting credits are soaring—one of his most fun credits is *Vegas Vacation*.

1. "You're Nobody, 'Til Somebody Loves You" (You don't have a body unless somebody loves you!)

2. "Up a Lazy River" (or "Up Your Lazy River!")

3. "Don't Go Changing (Just the Way You Are)" (The clothes will last another week!)

4. "Having My Baby" (Oh, God!)

5. "The Windmills of My Mind" (A mind is a terrible thing to waste!)

6. "The Wind Beneath My Wings" (Soft and Dry usually helps!)

7. "Copacabana"

8. "When the Saints Go Marching In"

9. "I Am, I Said" (Huh?!)

10. "The Theme from *The Love Boat*" (or "Would a Dinghy Do?")

Mile Shops at Planet Hollywood Resort, 3667 Las Vegas Blvd. S. www.vegastheshow.com. ✆ **800/933-1334** or 702/597-7600. Tickets $80–$100.

THE BAR SCENE

In addition to the venues listed below, you might also check out the incredible nighttime view at the bars and lounges atop the **Stratosphere Casino Hotel & Tower** (p. 288)—nothing beats it. Except for maybe the more up-close view of the bar adjacent to the 23rd-floor lobby at the **Mandarin Oriental** (p. 254). The floor-to-ceiling windows make you feel like you're floating in the middle of the Strip, especially at night.

There's also the **Viva Las Vegas Lounge** at the Hard Rock Hotel (p. 299), which every rock-connected person in Vegas will eventually pass through.

Bars & Cocktail Lounges

Beauty Bar ★ Popular with the young hipster set in Los Angeles and New York, the Vegas outpost of this bar done as a retro beauty salon draws a more diverse crowd owing to its location near the businesses and tourists of Downtown Las Vegas. Having said that, you'll probably do a lot better here if you know who Stephen Colbert is. It's open nightly from 9pm until 2am. 517 E. Fremont St. www. thebeautybar.com. ✆ **702/598-1965.** No cover except for special events.

Double Down Saloon ★★★ 🎁 "House rule: You puke, you clean." Okay, that about sums up the Double Down. Well, no, it doesn't really do the place justice. This is a big local hangout, with management quoting an old *Scope* magazine description of its clientele: "Hipsters, blue collars, the well-heeled lunatic fringe." Rumored to have been spotted here: director Tim Burton and the late Dr. Timothy

Leary. Trippy hallucinogenic graffiti covers the walls, the ceiling, and the tables, while decor includes thrift-store battered armchairs and sofas, a couple of pool tables, and a jukebox that holds everything from the Germs to Link Wray, Dick Dale, and Reverend Horton Heat. Oddly, the Double Down swears it invented the bacon martini here. Live bands perform on many nights (from punk to alt to blues). There's no cover unless an out-of-town band is playing that actually has a label. The Double Down is open daily 24 hours. 4640 Paradise Rd. (at Naples Dr.). www.doubledownsaloon.com. ☏ **702/791-5775.** No cover except for special events.

Griffin ★★ Part of the delightful revitalization of the Fremont East District (just a couple of blocks from the Fremont Street Experience), the fun starts with the old stone facade and eponymous sign and continues inside with the stone pillars, arched cave ceiling, and two fire pits. Just what you want in a stylish bar that revels in its history but at the same time doesn't try too hard. Given its proximity to other top-notch downtown hangouts, such as Downtown Cocktail Lounge, this is a must-stop on the anti–Strip and hotel bar tour. There are DJs on the weekends. It's open Monday through Friday from 5pm until close and Saturday and Sunday 8pm until close. 511 E. Fremont St ☏ **702/382-0577.** No cover except for special events.

Hogs & Heifers Saloon ★ While there is a chain of Coyote Ugly nightclubs (including one here in Vegas), the movie of the same name was based on the hijinks that happened at the New York version of this rowdy roadhouse saloon. In Sin City since 2005, the hogs here are of the motorcycle variety, and the place definitely draws a crowd that can look intimidating but is usually a friendly (and boisterous) bunch. Saucy bar maidens and outdoor barbecues on select weekends make this a fun spot for a beer. It's open daily, usually 1pm to 6am (call to check, as hours vary by month). 201 N. 3rd St. (btw. Ogden and Stewart aves., 1 block from the Fremont Street Experience). www.hogsandheifers.com. ☏ **702/676-1457.** No cover.

Insert Coin(s) ★★★ The pinnacle of Fremont East entertainment district has to be this wildly original bar and nightclub that features dozens of restored classic video games right alongside the drinking and dancing. Grab a moderately priced beer and start chewing your way through Ms. Pac Man, or sidle up to the main bar where you can play Nintendo and X-Box games (among others) on the giant overhead monitors. Or you can even get a private booth with bottle service and your own gaming station. The crowd skews young but gamers of all ages will feel at home here. It's open Monday through Thursday from 4pm to 4am, Friday from 4pm to 6am, Saturday from noon to 6am, and Sunday from noon until 4am. 512 E. Fremont St. www.insertcoinslv.com. ☏ **702/477-2525.** No cover.

Hogs & Heifers Saloon.

Insert Coin(s).

Mob Bar ★   Capitalizing on the nearby Mob Museum, this little slip of a place isn't quite the roaring '20s speakeasy that you would like it to be with a name like it has, but it's still worth a stop by if for no other reason than alcohol infused cupcakes they sell in conjunction with a local boozy bakery. Sugar and alcohol in one bite? Sounds like a roaring good time to us. Open Monday through Thursday from 11am until midnight, Friday and Saturday from 11am until 2am, and Sunday from 1pm until 8pm. 201 N. 3rd St. (at Ogden Ave). www.mobbarlv.com. 𝄐 **702/ 259-9700.** No cover.

Peppermill's Fireside Lounge ★ 📷   Walk through the classic Peppermill's coffee shop (not a bad place to eat, by the way) on the Strip, and you land in this fabulously dated bar. It has low, circular banquette seats, fake floral foliage, a whole bunch of pink neon, and electric candles. But best of all is the water and fire pit as the room's centerpiece—a piece of kitsch thought to be long vanished from earth and attracting nostalgia buffs like moths to a flame. Recently added neon detracts somewhat from the fire-pit centerpiece, but it's still wonderfully retro for unwinding a bit after some time spent on the hectic Strip. You might well be joined by entertainers and others winding down after a late night. The enormous, froufrou tropical drinks (including the signature bathtub-size margaritas) will ensure that you sink into a comfortable stupor. Peppermill's is open daily 24 hours. 2985 Las Vegas Blvd. S. www.peppermilllasvegas.com. 𝄐 **702/735-4177.** No cover.

Rock & Rita's ★   Circus Circus may not be the first place that comes to mind when you're thinking about a place to go party, but Rock & Rita's is actually a pretty fun bar even if you don't need something to do while your kids are playing in the circus midway upstairs. The surprisingly huge space has multiple bars, including one shaped like a bus, and they are staffed by competition-winning flair bartenders, meaning you get a show with your cocktails. There's a small dance floor and a stage for frequent live entertainment, and they serve cheap eats 24 hours a day. Oh, and you can get a drink served in a container shaped like a toilet bowl, so there's that. The bar and restaurant are open 24 hours. In Circus Circus, 2880 Las Vegas Blvd. S. www.rockandritas.com. 𝄐 **702/691-5991.** No cover.

Vanguard Lounge ★★   The space itself is not much to look at—a small, narrow room of polished concrete, a long bar, and a couple of couches—but that allows the cocktails to create all the noise and fury necessary to keep you entertained. A staff of professional mixologists create avant garde concoctions using a lot of house-made, seasonal ingredients (jams, bitters, and the like) that are bursting with flavor and freshness. That they are better than, and half the price of, drinks like this on the Strip is a miracle. Vanguard is open Monday through Saturday from 4pm until late. 516 E. Fremont St. www.vanguardlv.com ✆ **702/868-7800.** No cover.

Hotel Bars

Bond ★★   In any other building this would probably just be another hotel bar, but because it's at the boldly visual Cosmopolitan they had to amp it up a few thousand notches. The relatively small space is covered with LED and LCD screens that broadcast eye-popping visuals alongside the window boxes looking out toward the Strip, where you'll find everything from street performers to artists. Get your groove on, have a drink, and enjoy the spectacle. Bond is open daily from 3pm until 4am. In The Cosmopolitan of Las Vegas, 3708 Las Vegas Blvd. S. www.cosmopolitanlasvegas.com. ✆ **702/698-7979.** Cover varies.

The Chandelier ★★★   One of the most dramatic elements of the very dramatic Cosmopolitan of Las Vegas hotel is the massive, three-stories-tall chandelier, but it is not just for decoration. Inside are three separate bars, including a casual casino lounge on the main floor, a mixology-focused space on the second level serving high-end cocktails, and an ultralounge space on the top floor that acts as an adjunct, of sorts, to the nearby Marquee nightclub. It's all sleek and modern and cool looking, yet somehow manages to be a lot less intimidating than most of the other nightlife spaces in the hotel. The Chandelier is open 24 hours. In The Cosmopolitan of Las Vegas, 3708 Las Vegas Blvd. S. www.cosmopolitanlasvegas.com. ✆ **702/698-7979.** No cover.

Eiffel Tower Bar ★   From this chic and elegant room, in the restaurant on the 11th floor of the Eiffel Tower, you can look down on everyone, just like a real

Peppermill's Fireside Lounge.

Parisian! (Just kidding, Francophiles.) But really, this is a date-impressing bar, and, because there's no cover or minimum, it's a cost-effective alternative to the overly inflated food prices at the restaurant. Drop by for a drink, but try to look sophisticated. And then you can cop an attitude and dismiss everything as gauche—or droit, depending on which way you are seated. A business-attire dress code is enforced after 4:30pm. It's open daily 11:30am to 11pm. In Paris Las Vegas, 3655 Las Vegas Blvd. S. www.parislasvegas.com. ✆ **702/948-6937.** No cover.

Petrossian ★★★   Those despairing of a grown-up place to drink, a place for people who want a real cocktail made by people who know that martinis really do require vermouth (none of this "just wave the bottle in the general direction of the glass" nonsense and that "shaken not stirred" is a silly debate), rejoice and come here. Located just off the Bellagio lobby, this is one of the prettiest places to imbibe in the city as the glorious Dale Chihuly glass flowers "bloom" near your head. The bartenders are required to attend ongoing cocktail education, so they really know their stuff. Said stuff is made with the finest ingredients, which means none of the drinks come cheap. But the extra is worth it if you want it done right. They also have a good selection of high-end snacks. A little beluga with your booze? It's open daily 24 hours. In Bellagio, 3600 Las Vegas Blvd. S. www.bellagio.com. ✆ **702/693-7111.** No cover.

Piano Bars

The Bar at Times Square ★   If you're looking for a quiet piano bar, this is not the place for you. Two pianos are going strong every night, and the cigar-smoking crowd overflows out the doors. It always seems to be packed with a singing, swaying throng full of camaraderie and good cheer—or at least, full of booze. Hugely fun, provided you can get a foot in the door. Shows are daily from 8pm to 2am. In New York–New York, 3790 Las Vegas Blvd. S. www.newyorknewyork.com. ✆ **702/740-6969.** Cover $10 after 7pm.

Don't Tell Mama ★   The famed original Mama in NYC is a favorite of singers from Broadway to karaoke and everything in between. While the Vegas version

Dueling pianos at The Bar at Times Square.

Triple 7 Brew Pub.

may not have the same celebrities-might-show-up-to-sing energy that the Gotham version does, it is still a fun place to either listen to some good singers or belt out a tune or two yourself. The crowd is very hit and miss—packed with boisterous partiers one night and pretty much you and the staff on others—but there is no better place in town in which to live out your cabaret dreams. Hours are Tuesday through Sunday from 8pm until late. 517 E. Fremont St. www.donttell mama.com. (②) **702/207-0788.** No cover.

Pubs

The Pub at Monte Carlo ★   More than 300 beers are on tap here, which may be reason enough to visit for some people, but the appeal of this middle-of-the-road pub goes beyond just what they serve at the bar. Nightly entertainment like dueling pianos, DJs, or live bands keep you moving while the full menu of pub-grub-style fare keeps you fat and happy. Come during happy hour for their $1 snacks and two-for-one drink specials. It's open Sunday through Thursday from 11am to 11pm and Friday and Saturday from 11am until 3am. In Monte Carlo Resort, 3770 Las Vegas Blvd S. www.montecarlo.com. (②) **702/730-7777.** No cover.

Todd English P.U.B. ★★   This is a drinker's paradise with a list of beers, wines, and specialty cocktails that is longer than the food menu (p. 109) and a variety of games designed to get you smashed. Can you finish a pint in 7 seconds? If you can, it's free! Nickel beer nights, beer pong, darts, and sports on the omnipresent flat screen TVs make this a lively place to party. It's open daily from 11am until 2am. In Crystals at CityCenter, 3720 Las Vegas Blvd. S. www.toddenglishpub.com. (②) **702/489-8080.** No cover.

Triple 7 Brew Pub ★ 📷   Yet another of the many things the Main Street Station hotel has done right. Stepping into its microbrew pub feels like stepping out of Vegas. The place has a partially modern warehouse look (exposed pipes, microbrew fixtures visible through exposed glass at the back, and a very high ceiling), but a hammered-tin ceiling continues the hotel's Victorian decor; the overall effect seems straight out of San Francisco's North Beach. It's a bit yuppified but escapes being pretentious. This place has its own brew master and a number of microbrews ready to try, and if you want a quick bite, there's also an oyster-and-sushi bar, plus fancy burgers and pizzas. Triple 7 is open daily 11am to 7am. In Main Street Station, 200 N. Main St. (②) **702/387-1896.** No cover.

THE CLUB & MUSIC SCENE

Most of the clubs in town have DJs, and on those rare occasions when you do have live entertainment, it's usually a pop or cover band. If you prefer alternative or real rock music, your choices used to be limited, but that's all changed. Most touring rock bands make at least one stop in the city. But otherwise, the alternative club scene in town is no great shakes. If you want to know what's playing during your stay, consult the local free alternative papers: the *Las Vegas Weekly* (biweekly, with great club and bar descriptions in its listings; www.lasvegas weekly.com), and *City Life* (weekly, with no descriptions but comprehensive listings of what's playing where all over town; www.lasvegascitylife.com). Both can be picked up at restaurants, bars, record and music stores, and hip retail stores. If you're looking for good alt-culture tips, try asking the cool staff at **Zia Records (© 702/735-4942)**; not only does it have bins dedicated to local artists, but local acts also play live in stores on the weekend.

Dance Clubs

The nightclub scene in Vegas rivals Ibiza, New York, and Los Angeles for its scope and popularity. Almost every hotel has at least one club and almost all of them are packed whenever their doors are open.

Many of the following have absurdly high cover charges, prices that go up—way, way, way up—if you either encounter one of those doormen who will accept discrete (and significant) tips to let you bypass the inevitable line, or if you reserve one of the obnoxious "bottle-service tables." Many of the clubs reserve all tables (and thus, chairs) for "bottle service," which requires the purchase of a bottle or two of booze, usually running triple digits and way up. By the time you factor in the inflated cost of the bottle (which is often smaller than usual), taxes, and other fees, your evening out has hit mid–three figures or more. Unless your wallets are heavy, skip this racket and resign yourself to maneuvering for a place to stand on the floor.

Fergie celebrating her birthday at celebrity fave 1 OAK.

The Bank.

One bright note—women are often charged less for admission than men (sometimes even allowed in free), and any guest can get a comped ticket to even the hottest clubs, if you play it right. If you are gambling for any length of time, ask the pit boss for comps.

1 OAK ★　This Big Apple transplant is a favorite for celebrities and the impossibly hip alike. Fergie, Pitbull, and Katy Perry are among the big names who have made appearances, and the VIP booths are often filled with other famous folk drawn to the multiroom club with a beat-pounding dance floor, lots of dramatic black-and-white visuals, a dark and moody vibe, and an undeniable energy. All of this is great fun *if* you can get inside. It's a snap if you're rich, famous, or connected, but everyone else will be stuck with the uncontrolled hordes that are often clamoring for access outside the velvet ropes. BTW and FYI, 1 OAK = One of a Kind. It's open Friday and Saturday from 10:30pm until dawn. In The Mirage, 3400 Las Vegas Blvd. S. www.1oaklasvegas.com. ☎ **702/588-5656.**

The Bank ★★　The entrance lined with 500 bottles of Cristal champagne, with crystal hanging from the ceiling, and the bar lined with gold crocodile skin put a guest on notice: This is high-end clubbing. Look for hefty cover charges (though ladies are often free), and as a result, it attracts the deep-pocket crowd. Top-of-the-line everything nearly justifies prices; the lights respond to the music, 10 machines pump snow effects over the hot crowd, and the staff is in couture suits. They may or may not let you in if you aren't dressed to the nines. The Bank is open Thursday through Sunday from 10:30pm to 4am. In Bellagio, 3600 Las Vegas Blvd. S. www.bellagio.com. ☎ **702/693-8300.** Cover $30 and up.

Chateau ★　This hot-spot entry from Paris Las Vegas holds a unique position—literally. It is the only major nightclub in town that offers direct access to the Strip; you don't have to walk through the casino to get there. That kind of cool, but really it's the high-energy, high-gloss, high-price digs that you care about, and Chateau has them in spades. It's a long, narrow room, but the high ceiling provides some much needed vertical relief, especially with the throngs packed in so tightly on the horizontal. If you need air, head outside to the beer garden overlooking the Strip and the Bellagio Fountains. Crowds are young and a bit on the aggressive side in both demeanor and dress, but that's par for the course at most Vegas nightclubs. Chateau is open Tuesday, Friday, and Saturday

crowd **CONTROL**

Huge lines outside are a point of pride for Vegas clubs. So if you're into dancing, you may spend a good chunk of the night single file, double file, or in an enormous, unwieldy cluster out in front of a club—particularly on Friday or Saturday. We're not kidding: Lines can be hours long (see below), and once you get to the front, you'll find that there's no actual order. You're at the mercy of a power-wielding, eye-contact-avoiding "executive doorman"—bouncer—who gives attractive women priority. To minimize your time in line, try the following strategies:

Arrive before 11pm. You'll have a harder time getting in if you show up between 12:30 and 1am, the busiest period at clubs.

Group yourself smartly. The larger the group, the longer the wait—especially a large group of mostly (or all) guys. Split up if you have to, but always keep some women with each part of your group (it's much harder for unaccompanied men to get into the clubs).

If you're trying to tip your way in, don't make it obvious. It's a negotiation. Don't wave cash above your head (the IRS has recently been clamping down on unreported tip income, so that tactic will make you very unpopular). Discreetly and respectfully hand the doorman $20 and ask if he can take care of you.

Don't buy a VIP Pass. Can you say "scam"? Many passes require you get there before midnight (a time when there'd normally be no line), and with others you're paying big bucks just to have someone make the call ahead that you could have made yourself. Again: Don't fall for this scam.

Do check the websites. Many clubs will offer front-of-line passes, cover discounts, and drink specials via text alerts and/or if you check-in via a social networking site like Facebook or Twitter. Details change often, so check the club's website for the latest offer.

Dress to impress. For women: Antediluvian but true—showing more cleavage is a line-skipping tactic. If that's not an option, stick with a little black dress or nice jeans and a sexy or club-wear-style top. For men: Look good. Avoid baggy jeans, shorts, tennis shoes, or work boots. Nice jeans or pants and a collared shirt work well.

Look confident. While cockiness never helps, assertiveness never hurts.

from 10pm until dawn. In Paris Las Vegas, 3655 Las Vegas Blvd. S. www.chateaunightclub lv.com. ℂ 702/776-7770. Cover varies, usually $30 and up.

Coyote Ugly ★   You've seen the movie, now go have some of that prepackaged fun for yourself. Oh, come on—you don't think those bartender girls really dance on the bar and hose down the crowd just because they are so full of spontaneous rowdy high spirits, now do you? Not when the original locale built a reputation (and inspired a bad movie) on just such behavior, creating a success strong enough to start an entire chain of such frat-boy fun places? By the way, sarcastic and cynical as we are, can we say it's a totally fun place? It's open daily from 6pm until "late." In New York–New York, 3790 Las Vegas Blvd. S. (at Tropicana Ave.). www.coyoteuglysaloon.com. ℂ 702/740-6969. Cover varies, usually $10 and up after 9pm.

Crown Theater ★   Several nightclubs have tried and, to one degree or another, failed in this space at the Rio, but the pedigree of the operators, who once ran the famed Viper Room on the Sunset Strip, probably give it the best chance it has ever had to succeed. It is a great space. The circular layout puts the dance floor at the center of the action and there are plenty of bottle-service booths and tables for the moneyed set. Concerts and special events take advantage of the big stage (where Prince used to perform when this was his place) and the drink and cover prices, while not cheap, are not as outrageous as those at clubs on the Strip. The Crown is open Wednesday, Friday, and Saturday from 10pm until dawn. In Rio All-Suite Hotel & Casino, 3700 W. Flamingo Rd. www.thecrown vegas.com. ℂ 888/727-6966. Cover varies, usually $20 and up.

Gallery ★   The nightclub that used to be in this space, Prive, got a reputation for being an anything-goes kind of place. That made it wildly fun, but also got the hotel in trouble when it was socked with a $750,000 fine for the less-than-legal goings-on. They remodeled it with a boudoir-meets–art gallery theme and cracked down on the shenanigans, which is good, but unfortunately makes Gallery feel routine and a bit pedestrian. On the upside, the cover charge also gets you into the adjacent Pussycat Dolls Saloon so you get two clubs in one. Gallery is open Wednesday through Saturday from 10pm until 4am. In Planet Hollywood Resort, 3667 Las Vegas Blvd. S. www.gallerylv.com. ℂ 702/818-3700.

Haze ★   From the same people who brought you Bank at Bellagio comes this place that has all the ingredients that seem to make Las Vegas nightclubs popular these days. It is crowded, dark, insanely expensive, loud, attitudinal, at times downright obnoxious, and yet somehow it all works. If you manage to make it past the crazy long lines, the dimly lit interior of the club features multiple levels, several bars, a big dance floor, lots of VIP bottle-service booths and tables, and a killer light-and-sound system, plus strange little exhibition rooms where costumed models pose in various states of repose. Are those wood nymphs? Okay. It's like a fever dream with a bass beat. Haze! Got it. It's open Thursday through Saturday from 10:30pm until 4am. In Aria Las Vegas, 3730 Las Vegas Blvd. S. www. hazelv.com. ℂ 702/693-8300. Cover varies, usually $30 and up.

LAX ★   Dimly lit to the point of needing a flashlight at times, the decor (when you can see it) is swank supper club gone mad; deep-red padded vinyl walls, richly textured curtains in red and purple, and plenty of high-gloss black marble lend an air of sophistication that the aggressively young and trendy clientele probably don't appreciate as much as the multiple bars and ultra-high-tech dance floor. LAX is open Wednesday through Saturday 10pm until dawn. In Luxor Las Vegas, 3900 Las Vegas Blvd. S. www.laxthenightclub.com. ℂ 702/242-4529. Cover varies, usually $30 and up.

future **BEATS**

The nightlife scene in Vegas is almost constantly changing, balancing atop the shifting tastes and moods of the club crowd as carefully as some women navigate their way to the bar in 5-inch heels. Although the details of coming attractions are often a closely guarded secret, we have some info on what the future has in store for the dance floor.

Mandalay Bay's Rumjungle was part restaurant/part nightclub and a heck of a lot of fun. It closed after disputes and lawsuits between the club owners and the hotel. So what will replace it? A **Cirque du Soleil**–produced and –themed club that will feature some of its performers as atmospheric entertainment. The club should be open around the same time as a **Michael Jackson**–themed lounge, which will accompany the King of Pop–themed Cirque show debuting in early 2013. Visit www.mandalaybay.com for updates.

As a part of its major makeover, MGM Grand is redoing several of its nightlife offerings. The long-running Studio 54 is gone and will be replaced by **Hakkasan Las Vegas,** a co-venture between the Hakkasan restaurant group (with outlets from Miami to Mumbai) and Angel Management, the same Las Vegas company that does PURE at Caesars Palace. The new venue will have both a restaurant and a nightclub and will feature a large

outdoor patio overlooking the Strip. It should be open by the end of 2012. Also on the docket for MGM Grand is the **Pink Elephant Club,** a version of the popular New York City dance club and a revision of their ultralounge **Tabu.** Visit www. mgmgrand.com for updates.

Speaking of popular New York clubs, **The Box** will bring its nightclub-meets–performance art space antics to The Venetian. It should be open by the time you read this. Visit www.venetian.com for information.

The Palms is also redoing many of its nightlife venues, including revamps to the long-running ghostbar and replacements for the shuttered Rain and Playboy Club. There were no details at press time on what would replace them, but the hotel has long made a name for itself for creating exciting, must-visit hot spots so be sure to check www.palms.com for the latest information.

Marquee ★★★ The hottest club in town is usually the newest, but even though others have come after it, Marquee still reigns as one of *the* places to see and be seen. The multilevel space is a stunner, with no fewer than four separate clubs. Marquee is the main space with a huge dance floor, lots of table-service booths (some tucked into more private spaces), multiple bars, and a high-energy vibe. It also has a giant outdoor space with a pool, cabanas, another bar, and gaming tables if you prefer to party alfresco. Boombox is more of an ultralounge space with a DJ spinning different music (hip-hop, for example, if the main club is dance). Most appealing, at least to our sensibilities, is The Library, a cozy den of a space with a fireplace, pool table, and actual books on shelves (although the chances of anyone spending a lot of time reading here are minimal). Prices are high and lines are long, but would you expect anything different? Marquee is open Monday and Thursday through Saturday from 10pm until dawn. The pool club is open seasonally on weekend afternoons. In The Cosmopolitan of Las Vegas, 3708 Las Vegas Blvd. S. www.marqueelasvegas.com. ℭ **702/333-9000.** Cover varies, usually $30 and up.

PURE ★★ PURE is everything a big, loud nightclub ought to be. People line up hours before opening for the chance to share in the mayhem. (This is the place where Britney passed out on New Year's instead of completing her hostess duties, while Christina Aguilera held an after-show party here.) The theme is reflected in the decor—or lack of it, because just about everything is as white as Ivory Soap (get the name?). The noise and lack of cushy corners means this is a definite get-your-booty-in-motion kind of place, though there is ample space (seriously, there are airline hangars that are smaller) for just standing around watching other booties in motion. There is also a rooftop club, itself bigger than most regular Vegas clubs, with views of the Strip. PURE is open Thursday through Sunday and Tuesday 10pm to dawn. In Caesars Palace, 3570 Las Vegas Blvd. S. www.purelv.com. ✆ **702/731-7873.** Cover varies, usually $30 and up.

Tao Nightclub ★ Although newer competition has stolen some of its must-see status, this is still one of the hottest of the Vegas hot spots. Done as a Buddhist temple run amok, this multilevel club is drawing the party faithful and the celebrity entourages in droves, so expect long lines and high cover charges. Some may find the wall-to-wall crowds, flashing lights, pounding music, and general chaos overwhelming, but Tao is obviously doing something right. It's open Thursday through Saturday from 10pm until dawn. In The Venetian, 3355 Las Vegas Blvd. S. www.taolasvegas.com. ✆ **702/388-8588.** Cover varies.

Tryst ★ The clubs at Wynn Las Vegas and Encore are, generally speaking, more grown up and refined than the competition, not necessarily in age but in attitude. This is good because there are fewer instances of unruly 22-year-old drunken behavior, although if you are an unruly 22-year-old maybe you should go somewhere else. The bad news is that grown-up and refined attitudes bring grown-up and refined prices, meaning higher-than-average covers and drinks. If you can afford it, you'll be rewarded with a gorgeous, semicircular club complete with a dance floor that opens up onto a 90-foot waterfall. Then again, this was

Tao Nightclub.

briefly Paris Hilton's Vegas nightspot of choice (before that unpleasantness with a "pack of gum" and the police), so "refined" is definitely open to interpretation. Tryst is open Thursday through Saturday 10pm to 4am. In Wynn Las Vegas, 3131 Las Vegas Blvd. S. www.trystlasvegas.com. ✆ **702/770-3375.** Cover varies, usually $30 and up.

Vanity ★★   The Hard Rock knows how to do nightclubs, with the near-legendary Baby's and Body English once ruling the party scene in Vegas. Those clubs are gone now, replaced by this multilevel indoor/outdoor space, which includes lots of cozy banquettes (a few of which are even open to the general public, not just bottle-service buyers), fireplaces, cabanas, and a slamming dance floor. Hanging above the latter is the club's centerpiece, a "chandelier" made up of more than 20,000 crystal LED lights, allowing shapes, patterns, and images to be broadcast above the booty-shaking crowd. It should come as no surprise that lines are long and attitude is high, so bring your A game. Vanity is open Thursday through Saturday 10pm to 4am. In the Hard Rock Hotel, 4455 Paradise Rd. www.vanitylv.com. ✆ **702/693-5555.** Cover varies, usually $20 and up.

XS ★★   If you've been to the other Wynn club, Tryst, you'll definitely recognize the relationship when you walk into sister property Encore's version. The aptly named XS has the same basic floor plan as Tryst, only bigger and, well, more of just about everything. Done in an eye-catching gold, pink, and purple color scheme, the semicircular rings of booths and tables cascade down to a center dance floor that opens up onto a giant outdoor patio complete with its own pool, fireplaces, and lounge spaces. More grown up than most Vegas nightclubs, XS offers the same kind of high-energy vibe with a bit more sophistication and lighting—you can actually see who you're bumping into as you try to navigate the crowds. XS is open Friday through Monday 10pm to 4am. In Encore Las Vegas, 3121 Las Vegas Blvd. S. www.xslasvegas.com. ✆ **702/770-0097.** Cover varies, usually $30 and up.

Tryst.

Vanity.

XS.

Ultralounges

What, you may be asking, is an ultralounge? That's an excellent question since the definition is loosely defined at best. Generally speaking, ultralounges are smaller than traditional nightclubs, offering a more intimate vibe. Some have dance floors and some don't, although even the ones that don't usually have DJs and people will dance wherever they can find the room to do so. You'll also usually find a lot more seating at an ultralounge, but most of it will probably be reserved for people willing to pay for bottle service. Drink and cover prices may be a bit less than the big nightclubs as well. The type of crowd they draw depends on the location and theme, with the most popular bringing in the same young and pretty crowd that goes to the hot dance clubs (they'll often come to an ultralounge first, and then head to the dance floor elsewhere).

Downtown Cocktail Room ★★   One of several friendly and individualistic bars just a couple blocks from the Fremont Street Experience, this is the place to go for true modern Vegas cool, as opposed to the prefab (not to mention costly) Strip-side hotel bars. Once you find the door (it's hidden behind an industrial metal sheet on the left), you enter an Asian *moderne* space, complete with lounges that invite posing. It feels a little more young-executive-friendly than its neighbor, the gothic Griffin (p. 195). The cocktail menu is as substantial as it ought to be. It's open Monday through Friday from 4pm until 2am and Saturday from 7pm until 2am. 111 Las Vegas Blvd. www.thedowntownlv.com. © **702/880-3696.**

Hyde Bellagio ★★   It's hard to figure out how to categorize this place. Early evenings it's a cocktail lounge focusing on mixology and small-plate appetizers from nearby Circo; some late nights it's more of an ultralounge, all sleek and sexy with DJs keeping the makeshift dance floor moving; and late on weekends it becomes a full-fledged nightclub with the requisite pretty people and long lines to get in. Regardless of which version you experience, the multilevel, multiroom club done as an Italian villa has the best views of the Bellagio Fountains you'll find anywhere. It's open nightly 5pm until close. In Bellagio, 3600 Las Vegas Blvd. S. www.hydebellagio.com. © **702/693-8700.**

Mix ★   If you took away the stunning view from the top floor of THEhotel's tower, this would be little more than an overpriced cocktail lounge. But those views elevate (pun intended) the club into a cool, sexy, laid-back place to have a drink. It's open daily from 5pm until close. In Mandalay Bay, 3950 Las Vegas Blvd S. www.mandalaybay.com. ✆ **702/632-9500.**

Pussycat Dolls Saloon ★   No, Nicole Scherzinger will not be riding the carousel horse or lounging in the on-stage bathtub when you visit. Of course, the comely lasses that are strutting their stuff in this burlesque bar are still worthy of your attention. The vibe is heavy on the testosterone and there's a bit of a frat house feel to the place, but what else would you expect from a place where women in pasties ride a carousel horse and frolic in an on-stage bathtub? Note that one cover charge gets you into here and the adjacent Gallery nightclub. The saloon is open Tuesday through Saturday from 9pm until 4am. In Planet Hollywood Resort, 3667 Las Vegas Blvd. S. www.planethollywoodresort.com. ✆ **702/818-3700.**

Revolution ★   This place is tied to the Beatles-themed Cirque *LOVE* show, so think *White Album,* not Chairman Mao. While we dig the Union Jack–mini-skirt-clad greeters, we wish the somewhat sterile interior was more shagadelic. Apart from some random Beatles-esque elements, the furnishings are pretty much beanbag chairs, silver mirrors, and a whiff of Austin Powers. Plus, the music relates not at all to the '60s. Note that an *Abbey Road*–themed bar at the front is open daily starting at noon, while the nightclub portion is open Thursday through Sunday 10pm to 4am. In The Mirage, 3400 Las Vegas Blvd. S. www.mirage.com. ✆ **702/791-1111.**

Surrender ★★   Although it's a sexy space all by itself, with low-slung couches, a decent-size dance floor, and the requisite stripper poles for the go-go dancers to hold onto, the coolest thing about this ultralounge space is the big wall of windows that opens up onto the Encore Beach Club (p. 210). It acts as an extension of that space when the main party is outside, and things reverse themselves late at night when things move indoors. Surrender is open Wednesday through Saturday from 10:30pm until dawn. In Encore Las Vegas, 3121 Las Vegas Blvd. S. www.surrender nightclub.com. ✆ **702/770-7300.** Cover varies, usually $30 and up.

VooDoo Rooftop Nightclub ★   Occupying, along with a restaurant, two floors atop the Rio, the VooDoo almost successfully combines Haitian voodoo and New Orleans Creole in its decor and theme. There are two main rooms: one with a large dance floor and stage for live music, and a disco room, which is filled with large video screens and serious light action. Big club chairs in groups form conversation pits, where you might actually be able to have a conversation. And if you don't suffer from paralyzing vertigo, be sure to check out the dramatic outdoor, multilevel patio, which offers some amazing views of the Strip. The mid- to late-20s crowd is more heavily local than you might expect. The lounge portion is open nightly 5pm to 3am and the nightclub operates nightly from 9pm until dawn. In the Rio All-Suite Hotel & Casino, 3700 Las Vegas Blvd. S. www.riolasvegas.com. ✆ **702/252-7777.** Cover varies, usually $20 and up.

Hotel Lounges

Most of the nightclubs in town are ruled by the young and pretty type—you know who we mean: the 23-year-olds with impossibly short dresses, tiny waists, and an attitude that can be seen from space. Not that there's anything wrong with that. If we were thin and pretty, we'd want to hang out at these nightclubs, too.

Gilley's.

But what about the rest of us? What about older people who may not have a tiny waist anymore but still want to go out, dance, and have a good time?

For them we offer what some consider to be a dinosaur of a bygone age: the hotel lounge. Don't roll your eyes, because many of the hotel lounges offer entertainment, dance floors, low or no cover charge, cheaper drink prices, and an almost total absence of the kind of "hey look at me" posing that comes along with the trendy nightclubs. These are great places to go to simply have a night out of fun that doesn't involve a slot machine or blackjack table. All of the major hotels have at least one, so you can just wander by to see if it strikes your fancy, but here are a few that might be worth the extra effort to visit.

Carnaval Court ★   Flair bartenders work the crowd into a frenzy almost as well as the frequent live entertainment that plays here. Although certainly not cheap, it's a relatively affordable place to party the night away, provided the weather cooperates. The bar is located outside, so you may want to find somewhere else to play on extremely warm or cool evenings. It's open daily at noon until 2am Sunday through Thursday and 3am Friday and Saturday. At Harrah's Las Vegas, 3475 Las Vegas Blvd. S. www.harrahslv.com. (©) **702/731-7778.**

eyecandy sound lounge ★   Located in the center of the casino, eyecandy has a younger look and feel (bold colors, interactive screens built into the tables), but still draws a more grown-up crowd than most of the nightclubs. DJs spin all types of music nightly from 6pm until late and there is no cover charge. In Mandalay Bay, 3950 Las Vegas Blvd. S. www.mandalaybay.com. (©) **702/632-7777.**

Mizuya Lounge ★★   In addition to some darned good sushi, Mizuya's nightly entertainment makes it noteworthy in this category. It usually features no-name cover bands, but they are usually really good no-name cover bands who do a great job of whipping the crowd into a party-all-the-time lather. The lack of a cover, lower-than-nightclub drink prices, and more casual atmosphere make this one a must. It's open nightly until 2am or later, depending on the crowds. In Mandalay Bay, 3950 Las Vegas Blvd. S. www.mandalaybay.com. (©) **702/632-7777.**

Country/Western Clubs

Gilley's ★★   Yeehaw! When Gilley's former location at the Frontier closed, it was a sad day for the boot-scootin' boogie crowd in Las Vegas, but this institution, made famous in the movie *Urban Cowboy*, is back at Treasure Island and significantly upgraded. The dance floor is small, but there is still room for line dancing

cool BY THE POOL

A critical part of the nightclub scene is that it takes place at night. Maybe that's why they call them "night" clubs. But you don't have to wait until the sun goes down to start partying, especially in Vegas, where a host of daytime pool clubs gives you an opportunity to boogie down while working on your tan.

Most of the major hotels have some form of a poolside day club that usually operates on weekends and only in season (Mar–Oct mostly). They all feature DJs or live music, bars, private cabanas, and lots of opportunity to splash around in pools that are separated from the main recreational facilities for people over 21 years of age only. All charge a cover (although they vary as much as nightclub covers do) and some offer table games (like blackjack) and topless sunbathing. All are open to the general public (you don't have to be staying at the host hotel).

It should go without saying that these usually draw a younger, fit crowd who aren't embarrassed about how they look in a bikini or board shorts. If that isn't you, you may want to consider alternate afternoon entertainment.

Here are the most noteworthy of the current pool clubs:

- **Bare** At The Mirage, 3400 Las Vegas Blvd. S. (www.barepool.com; ✆ **702/588-5656**). Small pool, cabanas, DJ, and bar. Topless sunbathing allowed. Open daily 8am–6pm. Cover $10 and up.

- **Encore Beach Club** At Encore Las Vegas, 3121 Las Vegas Blvd. S. (www. encorebeachclub.com; ✆ **702/770-7300**). 60,000-square-foot facility, three pools, cabanas, DJ, gaming, bar, grill. No topless sunbathing. Open Thurs–Mon from noon until 7pm. Cover $25 and up.

(with lessons on select nights) and the mechanical bull is ready to embarrass all of you tenderfoots. DJs or live bands provide the country-music accompaniment, and there is even Cowboy Karaoke if you feel like emulating Garth or Gretchen. Gilley's is open nightly from 8pm until 2am, later on weekends. In Treasure Island, 3300 Las Vegas Blvd. S. www.gilleyslasvegas.com. ✆ **702/894-7111.**

Stoney's Rockin' Country ★ After the original Gilley's at the Frontier closed back in 2007, Stoney's threw its ten-gallon hat into the (mechanical) bull-ring as the only major country-western nightclub in town. Gilley's is back and better than ever in a more convenient location, but there's still a lot of fun to be had here for cowpokes of all stripes. There's a big dance floor, a mechanical bull, arcade and carnival-style games, and frequent drink specials that keep it affordable. It's open Thursday through Sunday from 7pm until late. 9151 Las Vegas Blvd S., no. 300. www.stoneysrockincountry.com. ✆ **702/435-2855.**

Comedy Clubs

Brad Garrett's Comedy Club Although it has his name on it, the comic (best known as the long-suffering brother Robert on *Everybody Loves Raymond*) only appears here periodically. The rest of the time you'll find both moderately known and "who?" level comics, but the caliber seems to be a bit better here than the no-name clubs elsewhere in Vegas. Shows are Sunday through Thursday at

DJ, gaming, bar, food service. No topless sunbathing. Open Fri–Sun noon–6pm. Cover $25 and up.

o **Rehab** At the Hard Rock Hotel, 4455 Paradise Rd. (www.rehablv.com; © **800/473-7625**). Several pools, sandy beaches, cabanas, DJ, gaming, bar, food service. No topless sunbathing. Open Sun 11am–6pm. Cover $25 and up.

o **Tao Beach** At The Venetian, 3355 Las Vegas Blvd. S. (www.taobeach. com; © **702/388-8588**). One pool, cabanas, DJ, bar, food service. Topless sunbathing allowed. Open daily 10am–sunset. Cover $20 and up.

o **Wet Republic** At MGM Grand, 3799 Las Vegas Blvd. S. (www.wetrepublic. com; © **800/851-1703**). Two pools, cabanas, DJ, bar, food service. No topless sunbathing. Open Fri–Sun 11am–6pm. Cover $20 and up.

o **Liquid** At Aria Las Vegas, 3730 Las Vegas Blvd. S. (www.arialasvegas. com; © **702/693-8300**). Three pools, cabanas, DJ, bar, restaurant. No topless sunbathing. Open Thurs–Sun 11am–6pm. Cover $20 and up.

o **Marquee Dayclub** At The Cosmopolitan of Las Vegas, 3801 Las Vegas Blvd. S. (www.marqueelas vegas.com; © **702/333-9000**). Two pools, cabanas with private pools,

8pm and Friday and Saturday at 8 and 10pm. In MGM Grand, 3799 Las Vegas Blvd. S. www.bradgarrettcomedy.com. © **866/740-7711**. Tickets $43–$87.

The Improv ★★ This offshoot of Budd Friedman's famed comedy club (the first one opened in 1963 in New York City) presents about four comedians per show in a 400-seat showroom. Only stand-up junkies will have heard of most of the people who perform here, and whether or not it's worth the ticket price totally depends on the comics of the evening, but in general there are more hits than misses. Shows are Tuesday through Sunday at 8:30 and 10:30pm. In Harrah's Las Vegas, 3475 Las Vegas Blvd. S. www.harrahslv.com. © **800/392-9002** or 702/369-5000. Tickets $30–$45.

THE GAY & LESBIAN SCENE

Hip and happening Vegas locals know that some of the best scenes and dance action can be found in the city's gay bars. And no, they don't ask for sexuality ID at the door. All are welcome at any of the following establishments—as long as you don't have a problem with the people inside, they aren't going to have a problem with you. For women, this can be a fun way to dance and not get hassled by overeager Lotharios.

In addition to the dedicated clubs and bars listed below, a growing number of the straight clubs are having nights dedicated to the gay and lesbian crowds, like "Closet Sundays" at the **Revolution Lounge** in The Mirage (p. 208).

If you want to know what's going on in gay Las Vegas during your visit, pick up a copy of **Q Vegas,** which is also available at any of the places described below. You can also call ✆ **702/650-0636** or check out the online edition at www.qvegas.com.

The Buffalo ★   Close to Gipsy and several other gay establishments, this is a leather/Levi's bar popular with Average Joe tourists and locals alike. It features beer busts (all the beer you can drink for a small cover) and other drink specials throughout the week. There are pool tables and darts, and music videos play in this austere environment, where concrete floors are not of the fancy polished variety. It's very cheap, with longnecks going for a few bucks, and it gets very, very busy, very late (3 or 4am). The Buffalo is open daily 24 hours. 4640 Paradise Rd. (at Naples Dr.). ✆ **702/733-8355.**

Free Zone ★   One of several bars within a few steps of each other on the corner of Paradise Road and Naples Drive, Free Zone plays the role of friendly neighborhood club (as opposed to the nearby swank lounges or leather bars) with a variety of theme nights (everything from country to karaoke), lots of comfortable sitting areas, chatty bartenders, video poker, and inexpensive drinks. A moderately sized dance floor gets busy on weekend nights, but for the most part this is a place to sit and drink with friends. Free Zone is open 24 hours. 610 E. Naples Dr. (at Paradise Rd.). www.freezonelv.com. ✆ **702/794-2300.** Cover varies.

Funhog Ranch   You know those trendy nightclubs where you stand in line for hours, pay outrageously high cover charges and drink prices, and are surrounded by opulence and beauty everywhere you turn once you finally get inside? This isn't one of them. As down-home as it gets, Funhog Ranch is just a bar, a few booths, some video poker, a jukebox, and an electronic dartboard. Drinks are rock-bottom cheap and the clientele, which skews a bit older and is more of the leather/Levi's crowd, is enormously friendly. There is no standing and posing allowed and nobody is going to care what you are wearing unless you go out of your way to try to make them. Funhog is open daily 24 hours. 495 E. Twain Ave. (just east of Paradise Rd.). www.funhogranchlv.com. ✆ **702/791-7001.**

The Garage ★★   If you're looking for a more authentic and friendly Vegas experience than you'll find at gay bars near the Strip, this is the type of place you should visit. The garage theme with gas-station signs, corrugated metal on the walls, and employees in mechanic's uniforms is a bit overdone, but the vibe is decidedly down to earth and much less intimidating than the tourist-driven bars. Women are welcome, but it's predominantly a men's bar and its proximity to UNLV means a younger-than-average median age, which may or may not be a good thing depending on your point of view. The Garage is open daily 24 hours. 1487 E. Flamingo Rd. www.thegaragelv.com. ✆ **702/440-6333.**

Gipsy ★   For years, Gipsy reigned supreme as the best gay dance place in the city due to its great location (Paradise Rd., near the Hard Rock) and excellent layout (sunken dance floor and two bars). Competition has rendered this a second-tier choice, but drink specials, along with theme nights, shows, and male dancers, still make this a good party bar. These days it is only open Friday and Saturday from 10pm to dawn, but the party goes all week at sister club Piranha right next door. 4605 Paradise Rd. (at Naples Dr.). ✆ **702/731-1919.** Cover varies but is usually $5 and up.

Krave ★★   After breaking new ground as the only gay nightclub on the Strip, Krave is poised to blaze trails once more as it moves to Neonopolis in Downtown Vegas by early 2013. The new Krave will be the world's largest gay nightclub,

Krave.

with 80,000 square-feet of themed dance clubs, bars, a theater, a swimming pool, and more. Visit the club's website to learn when Downtown Vegas will become a lot more fabulous. In the meantime, the existing club is open daily from 8pm until late. At Planet Hollywood Resort & Casino, 3667 Las Vegas Blvd. S. (entrance on Harmon). www.kravelasvegas.com. © **702/836-0830.** Cover varies.

Piranha Las Vegas/8½ Ultra Lounge ★★ Although they are connected, these two gay hot spots operate as distinct bars. Piranha is the dance club, a high-energy space done in lush colors and fabrics complete with a VIP area (that has reportedly drawn everyone from Janet to Britney) and several skyboxes that overlook the always-packed dance floor. Of note here is the outdoor patio, complete with fireplaces and comfortable seating. The aquariums that used to hold the signature piranhas are empty, a victim of city regulations that apparently govern things like killer fish in a gay bar. The 8½ is cool and groovy, with lots of space to relax, video screens to keep you entertained, and lots of comfy seating. This is one of the most popular gay clubs in town; as a consequence, lines are often long, and cover and drink prices are both high. Dress to impress. Both are open nightly 9pm to dawn. 4633 Paradise Rd. (at Naples Dr.). www.piranhavegas.com. © **702/791-0100.** Cover varies, usually $20.

Share Las Vegas ★★ A high-energy nightclub downstairs, a laid-back ultralounge upstairs, and a cavalcade of Chippendales worthy go-go dancers make this one of the most interesting and sexy gay clubs in town. The location west of the Strip near The Orleans is a bit of a bummer—there are no other clubs (or anything else for that matter) nearby—but with a vibe as intriguing as this one you won't mind making the trek. Be sure to check their website for specials and discounts on drinks and cover charges. Open daily at 6pm until 2am Sunday through Wednesday and 4am Thursday through Saturday. 4636 Wynn Rd. www.share nightclub.com. © **702/258-2681.**

STRIP CLUBS

No, we don't mean entertainment establishments on Las Vegas Boulevard South. We mean the other kind of "strip." Yes, people come to town for the gambling and the wedding chapels, but the lure of Vegas doesn't stop there. Though prostitution is not legal within the city, the sex industry is an active and obvious force in town. Every other cab carries a placard for a strip club, and a walk down the Strip at night will have dozens of men thrusting fliers at you for clubs, escort services, phone-sex lines, and more. And some of you are going to want to check it out.

And why not? An essential part of the Vegas allure is decadence, and naked flesh would certainly qualify, as does the thrill of trying something new and daring. Of course, by and large, the nicer bars aren't particularly daring, and if you go to more than one in an evening, the thrill wears off, and the breasts don't look quite so bare.

For Men Only?

Many of the strip clubs will not allow women in unless they're escorted by a man—presumably to protect ogling husbands from suspicious wives. If you're looking for a ladies' night out and want to check out the topless action, be sure and call ahead to find out what each individual club allows.

In the finest of Vegas traditions, the "something for everyone" mentality extends to strip clubs. Here is a guide to the most prominent and heavily advertised; there are plenty more, of increasing seediness, out there. You don't have to look too hard. The most crowded and zoolike times are after midnight, especially on Friday and Saturday nights. Should you want a "meaningful" experience, you might wish to avoid the rush and choose an off hour for a visit.

Cheetah's ★ This is the strip club used as the set in the movie *Showgirls,* but thanks to renovations by the club, only the main stage will look vaguely familiar to those looking for Nomi Malone. There's also a smaller stage, plus three tiny "tip stages" so that you can really get close to (and give much money to) the woman of your choice. The management believes "if you treat people right, they will keep coming back," so the atmosphere is friendlier than at other clubs. They encourage couples to come here, though on a crowded Saturday night, some unescorted women were turned away, despite policy. Lap dances are $20. Cheetah's is open daily 24 hours. 2112 Western Ave. www.cheetahslasvegas.com. ✆ **702/384-0074.** Topless. Cover $20.

Club Paradise ★ Until the new behemoths moved into town, this was the nicest of the strip clubs. Which isn't to say it isn't still nice; it's just got competition. The outside looks a lot like the Golden Nugget; the interior and atmosphere are rather like that of a hot nightclub where most of the women happen to be topless. The glitzy stage looks like something from a miniature showroom. The lights flash and the dance music pounds. There are two big video screens (one featuring soft porn, the other showing sports), and the chairs are plush and comfortable. The place is relatively bright by strip-club standards, and it offers champagne and cigars. Not too surprisingly, the crowd is very white collar here. Lap dances are $20. Club Paradise is open daily from 5pm to 8am. 4416 Paradise Rd. ✆ **702/734-7990.** Topless. Cover $30. Unescorted women allowed.

Girls of Glitter Gulch ★ Right there in the middle of the Fremont Street Experience, Glitter Gulch is either an eyesore or the last bastion of Old Las Vegas, depending on your point of view. One of the most venerable strip clubs in town, updates over the years have kept the place current with an interior that rivals some of the midlevel Strip ultralounges. It's still a little cramped and naturally dark. The location is the most convenient of all of the strip clubs but it's also the most conspicuous, given that you have to exit right on Fremont Street. Not so good for the bashful or discrete. Still, it means customers include groups of women and even a 90-year-old couple. Given its convenient location, this is the perfect place for the merely curious—you can easily pop in, check things out, goggle and ogle, and then hit the road. Lap dances are $20 and up. Glitter Gulch is open daily 1pm to 4am. 20 Fremont St. ℭ **702/385-4774.** Topless. No cover; 2-drink minimum.

Larry Flynt's Hustler Club ★ Leave it to the founder of *Hustler* magazine to take the concept of a strip club and turn it into something tacky. We aren't talking about the dancers or what they are doing, we're talking about the building itself, a 70,000-square-foot facility that is lit up on the outside like a piece of space junk on re-entry and filled on the inside with signs pointing you to things like the Beaver Stage and Honey Rooms. Sigh. Having said that, it's hard to argue with the completeness of three levels of stripper paradise, including a rooftop "oasis," multiple stages and bars, VIP booths, and a gift shop where you can pick up something special on your way home. Lap dances are $30. The Hustler Club is open daily 4pm until 9am. 6007 Dean Martin Dr. www.hustlerclubs.com. ℭ **702/795-3131.** Topless. Cover $30 (includes first lap dance).

OG Gentlemen's Club ★ Once known as Olympic Gardens, the name is about the only thing that has changed here. There are two rooms: one with large padded tables for the women (and men on select nights) to dance on, the other featuring a more classic strip runway. The crowd is a mix of 20s to 30s geeks and blue-collar guys. As the place fills up and the chairs are crammed in next to each other, it's hard to see how enjoyable, or intimate, a lap dance can be when the guy next to you is getting one as well. That didn't seem to stop all the guys there, who seemed appropriately blissed out. Lap dances are $20, more in the VIP room. The club is open daily 24 hours. 1531 Las Vegas Blvd. S. ℭ **702/385-9361.** www.og vegas.com. Topless. Cover $30 after 6pm. Unescorted women allowed.

The Palomino ★ This one-time classically elegant nudie bar—you know, red flocked wallpaper and the like—became pretty run down over the years, as places like that generally do. Even the offer of total nudity was not quite enough to lure visitors to this seedy part of town. The owners then came up with an ingenious makeover. In addition to updating the downstairs (gone, sadly, is the aforementioned vintage look in favor of a flashy runway, neon, flatscreen TVs, and other modern gizmos; it's new, but it's also generic), they had the inspiration to introduce male stripping—yes, still totally nude—upstairs on the weekends. This something-for-

> ## Question Your Cabbie
>
> If there's a particular strip club that you want to visit, don't let your cabdriver talk you out of it. Clubs give cabdrivers kickbacks for delivering customers. So be leery of drivers who suggest one club over another. They may be making $20 for delivering you there. And don't accept a higher cover charge than we've listed here; the clubs are trying to get you to cover the kickback they just gave the cabbie.

everyone equality approach results in a bustling crowd packed with women, with an atmosphere that can be a little intense rather than bachelorette ribald. Expect a largely urban crowd and a lot of couples. And in case you were wondering, the guys do lap dances, too. Topless lap dances are $20; totally nude dances are $40. The Palomino is open daily 4pm to 5am. 1848 Las Vegas Blvd. N. www.palominolv.com. ℭ **702/642-2984.** Totally nude. Cover $20.

Sapphire Gentleman's Club ★★★ Ladies and gentlemen (particularly the latter), Las Vegas, home of the largest everything else, now brings you—drum roll—the largest strip club *in the world!* That's right, 71,000 square feet of naked-ity. Expect three stages in a bridge shape (including one where gawkers who paid for the privilege can watch the action from below, thanks to a glass floor), and a fourth in a separate—and still large—room, with several poles and strippers all working it at the same time. Giant video screens occasionally act as a JumboTron for the action on the other side of the cavernous room. Upstairs are incredibly posh and incredibly expensive rooms for wealthy sports and movie figures to utilize. And as if that all weren't enough, now they have a pool you can lounge by in between lap dances, which start at $20. Sapphire is open daily 24 hours. 3025 S. Industrial. (✆ **702/796-6000.** Topless. Cover $30 6pm–6am. Unescorted women allowed.

Spearmint Rhino ★ Did you know that even strip bars come in chains? They do, and this is a familiar brand to those in the know, or to those who read bill-boards close to airports. The runway (where some of the dancers get a little per-sonal with each other) is actually in a separate back area, so it is possible to have a drink at the front (where there are many TVs) and never see a naked girl (save for the smaller stage and pole nearby). On a busy night, it's crammed with grown-up frat boys enjoying a clubby space. There can be a veritable assembly line of lap dances during these busy periods, which frankly seems the opposite of a turn-on to us. Unescorted women should also note that while normally they are permit-ted, lately it seems that they might be taken for hookers and turned away from the door (lest they come inside and lure customers away). Lap dances are $20. Spearmint Rhino is open daily 24 hours. 3344 S. Highland Dr. www.spearmintrhinolv. com. (✆ **702/796-3600.** Topless. Cover $30. Unescorted women allowed.

Treasures ★★★ Right now, along with Sapphire, this is our favorite of the strip clubs, for several reasons. From the outside, this looks like one of the new fancy casino-hotels (if considerably smaller), but inside it's straight out of a Victorian sporting house (that's a brothel, by the way), down to replicas of 19th-century girlie pictures on the walls. On stage, the performers actually perform; anyone who has witnessed the desultory swaying of the hips and vacant stare of a bored stripper will appreciate not just the bump-and-grind (some of which gets on the raunchy side) dance routines but also the spe-cial effects, from hair-blowing fans to smoke machines to a neon pole. We are suckers for this combination of period-inspired style and contemporary approach to the business at hand. This is an excellent and comfortable venue for couples and first-timers. Lap dances are $30 and up. Treasures is open daily 4pm to 6am. 2801 Westwood Dr. www. treasureslasvegas.com. (✆ **702/257-3030.** Topless. Cover $30. No unescorted women.

Treasures.

SPECTATOR SPORTS

Las Vegas isn't known for its sports teams. Except for minor-league baseball and hockey, the only consistent spectator sports are those at UNLV. For the pros, if watching Triple-A baseball (in this case, a Toronto Blue Jays farm team) in potentially triple-degree heat sounds like fun, the charmingly named and even-better merchandized **Las Vegas 51s** (as in Area 51, as in alien-themed gear) is a hot ticket. The team's schedule and ticket info are available at www.lv51.com, or call ℂ **702/386-7200.** Ice hockey might be a better climate choice; get info for the **Las Vegas Wranglers** at www.lasvegaswranglers.com or call ℂ **702/471-7825.**

Cosmo, the official mascot of the Las Vegas 51s.

The **Las Vegas Motor Speedway** (p. 77) is a main venue for car racing that draws major events to Las Vegas.

Because the city has several top-notch sporting arenas, important annual events take place in Las Vegas, details for which can be found in the "Las Vegas Calendar of Events" in chapter 2. The **Justin Timberlake Shriners Hospitals for Children Open** (www.jtshrinersopen.com) takes place in Las Vegas every October. The **National Finals Rodeo** (www.nfrexperience.com) is held in UNLV's Thomas & Mack Center in December. From time to time, you'll find

The MGM Grand's Garden Events Arena hosts some of the biggest events in boxing, like 2012's Mayweather vs. Cotto match.

NBA exhibition games, professional ice-skating competitions, or gymnastics exhibitions. Finally, Las Vegas is well known as a major location for **boxing matches.** These are held in several Strip hotels, most often at MGM Grand or Mandalay Bay. Tickets are hard to come by and quite expensive.

Tickets to sporting events at hotels are available either through **Ticketmaster** (© **702/893-3000;** www.ticketmaster.com) or through the hotels themselves. (Why pay Ticketmaster's exorbitant service charges if you don't have to?)

Major Sports Venues in Hotels

The **MGM Grand's Garden Events Arena** (© **800/929-1111** or 702/891-7777) is a major venue for professional boxing matches, rodeos, tennis, ice-skating shows, World Figure Skating Championships, and more.

Mandalay Bay (© **877/632-7400**) has hosted a number of boxing matches in its 12,000-seat Events Center.

PRACTICAL MATTERS: THE ENTERTAINMENT & NIGHTLIFE SCENE

WHO'S PLAYING? To find out who's performing during your stay and for up-to-date listings of shows (prices change, shows close), you can call the various hotels, using their toll-free numbers. Or call the **Las Vegas Convention and Visitors Authority** (© **877/847-4858** or 702/892-0711), and ask them to send you a free copy of *Showguide* or *What's On in Las Vegas* (one or both of which will probably be in your hotel room). You can also check out what's playing at www.visitlasvegas.com. It's best to plan well ahead if you have your heart set on seeing one of the most popular shows or catching a major headliner.

SHOWROOM POLICIES Unless otherwise noted, all of the shows in this chapter have preassigned seating. There are a few showrooms that still have a tuxedo-clad maître d' ushering you to your seat, but the days where they got to decide where you sit based on how much you tip them are gone. Having said that, in those rare maître d' situations, a tip could get you a *better* seat providing there isn't already someone sitting in it. A tip of $10 to $20 per couple should suffice, but only if you are dying to sit closer to the stage.

If you buy tickets for an assigned-seat show in person, you can look over a seating chart. Avoid sitting right up by the stage, if possible, especially for big-production shows. Dance numbers are better viewed from the middle of the theater. With headliners, you might like to sit up close. All these caveats and instructions aside, most casino-hotel showrooms offer good visibility from just about every seat in the house.

There are no official dress codes at the Las Vegas showrooms other than the typical "no shirt, no shoes, no service." Some people like to dress up for their evening at the theater, while others take a come-as-you-are approach. This will often mean a theater with a couple in a suit and cocktail dress next to a couple in shorts and T-shirts. We advise going somewhere in between and to remember that many showrooms go heavy on the air-conditioning, so bringing a light layer to add to your ensemble may be a good idea.

All showrooms are nonsmoking.

NIGHTCLUB & BAR TIPS   The nightlife scene doesn't really get started in Vegas until very late—often after midnight—but it also goes late, with many of the clubs staying open until the last person leaves or the sun comes up, whichever happens first.

Dress codes are much more stringent at the big dance clubs than they are at most bars. Policies vary from place to place and change often, so check their website or call ahead, but in general try to stay away from shorts, flip-flops, sleeveless shirts, and baseball caps.

Safety is a big issue when you're checking out the nightlife scene. Regardless of your gender, don't ever accept a drink from a stranger (unless you watch the bartender make it), and once you have your own drink don't let it out of your sight. Although it certainly is not common, there have been instances of people getting something slipped into their drinks without their knowledge and it usually doesn't end well.

ADULTS ONLY   Be aware that there is a curfew law in Vegas: Anyone under 18 is forbidden from being on the Strip without a parent after 9pm on weekends and holidays. In the rest of the county, minors cannot be out without parents after 10pm on school nights and midnight on weekends.

ENTERTAINMENT & NIGHTLIFE

Practical Matters: The Entertainment & Nightlife Scene

8

ABOUT CASINO GAMBLING

Las Vegas is no longer the gambling capital of the world. That title belongs to Macau, China, where casinos with familiar names like MGM Grand, The Venetian, and Wynn pull in more money in 2 months than the casinos on the Strip generate all year. Even in the United States, the proliferation of legal gambling in other areas is eclipsing Las Vegas in terms of revenue and scope. As of this writing there are more than two dozen states that have Indian or riverboat casinos and nearly that many that have commercial casinos, with more on the way. And in Las Vegas, gambling is no longer the biggest revenue generator, earning an average of about 46% in 2011 of a resort's income. The remaining 54% comes from rooms, dining, entertainment, shopping, nightclubs, and other sources.

But strip away all the facts and figures and what you are left with is the undeniable lure of Las Vegas as a gambling mecca. It is, in no small part, what built this city and what continues to drive it, as evidenced by the fact that you can find gaming almost everywhere. There are slot machines in the airport, waiting for you to get off the plane or giving you something to do while you wait for your baggage. Convenience stores and gas stations have video poker so you can play a few hands while filling up. And the average Strip casino has literally dozens of blackjack, craps, roulette, and other gaming tables.

People come here to play, and although they may lose more often than they win, it doesn't stop anyone from trying to win the Big One. You know, like that woman in 2010 that won $2.9 million on a "Wizard of Oz" penny slot (whose name was Dorothy, by the way). That only a few ever do win big doesn't stop them from trying again and again and again. That's how the casinos make their money.

It's not that the odds are stacked so incredibly high in their favor—though the odds *are* in their favor, and don't ever think otherwise. Rather, it's that if there is one constant in this world, it's human greed. Look around in any casino, and you'll see countless souls who, having doubled their winnings, are now trying to quadruple them and are losing it all and then trying to recoup their initial bankroll and losing still more in the process.

The first part of this chapter tells you the basics of betting. Knowing how to play the games not only improves your odds but also makes playing more enjoyable. In addition to the instructions here, you'll find dozens of books on how to gamble at all casino hotel gift shops, and many casinos offer free gaming lessons.

The second part describes most of the major casinos in town. Remember that gambling is supposed to be entertainment. Picking a gaming table where the other players are laughing, slapping each other on the back, and generally enjoying

PREVIOUS PAGE: **Casino chips.**

themselves tends to make for considerably more fun than a table where everyone is sitting around in stony silence, morosely staring at their cards. Unless you really need to concentrate, pick a table where all seem to be enjoying themselves, and you probably will, too, even if you don't win.

THE GAMES

As you walk through the labyrinthine twists and turns of a casino floor, your attention will likely be drawn to the various games and, your interest piqued, your fingers may begin to twitch in anticipation of hitting it big. Before you put your money on the line, it's imperative to know the rules of the game you want to play. Most casinos offer free gambling lessons at scheduled times on weekdays and occasionally on weekends. This provides a risk-free environment for you to learn the games that tickle your fancy. Some casinos follow their lessons with low-stakes game play, enabling you to put your newfound knowledge to the test at small risk. During those instructional sessions, and even when playing on your own, dealers in most casinos will be more than happy to answer any questions you might have. Remember, the casino doesn't need to trick you into losing your money . . . the odds are already in their favor across the board; that's why it's called *gambling.* Another rule of thumb: Take a few minutes to watch a game being played in order to familiarize yourself with the motions and lingo. Then go back and reread this section—things will make a lot more sense at that point. Good luck!

Baccarat

The ancient game of baccarat, or *chemin de fer,* is played with eight decks of cards. Firm rules apply, and there is no skill involved other than deciding whether to bet on the bank or the player. No, really—that's all you have to do. The dealer does all the other work. You can essentially stop reading here. Oh, all right, carry on.

Any beginner can play, but check the betting minimum before you sit down, as baccarat tends to be a high-stakes game. The cards are shuffled by the croupier and then placed in a box called the "shoe." Players may wager on "bank" or "player" at any time. Two cards are dealt from the shoe and given

A roulette wheel.

to the player who has the largest wager against the bank, and two cards are dealt to the croupier, acting as banker. If the rules call for a third card, the player or banker, or both, must take the third card. In the event of a tie, the hand is dealt over. **Note:** The guidelines that determine whether a third card must be drawn (by the player or banker) are provided at the baccarat table upon request.

The object of the game is to come as close as possible to the number 9. To score the hands, the cards of each hand are totaled and the *last digit* is used. All cards have face value. For example: 10 plus 5 equals 15 (score is 5); 10 plus 4 plus 9 equals 23 (score is 3); 4 plus 3 plus 3 equals 10 (score is 0); and 4 plus 2 plus 2 equals 9 (score is 9). The closest hand to 9 wins.

Each player has a chance to deal the cards. The shoe passes to the player on the right each time the bank loses. If the player wishes, he may pass the shoe at any time.

Note: When you bet on the bank and the bank wins, you are charged a 5% commission. This must be paid at the start of a new game or when you leave the table.

Big Six

Big Six provides pleasant recreation and involves no study or effort. The wheel has 56 positions on it, 54 of them marked by bills from $1 to $20. The other two spots are jokers, and each pays 40 to 1 if the wheel stops in that position. All other stops pay at face value. Those marked with $20 bills pay 20 to 1, the $5 bills pay 5 to 1, and so forth. The idea behind the game is to predict (or just blindly guess) what spot the wheel will stop at and place a bet accordingly.

Blackjack

In this popular game, the dealer starts by dealing each player two cards. In some casinos, they're dealt to the player face up, in others face down, but the dealer always gets one card up and one card down. Everybody plays against the dealer. The object is to get a total that is higher than that of the dealer without exceeding 21. All face cards count as 10; all other number cards, except aces, are counted at their face value. An ace may be counted as 1 or 11, whichever you choose it to be.

Starting at her left, the dealer gives additional cards to the players who wish to draw (be "hit") or none to a player who wishes to "stand" or "hold." If your count is nearer to 21 than the dealer's, you win. If it's under the dealer's, you lose. Ties are a "push" (standoff) and nobody wins. After all the players are satisfied with their counts, the dealer exposes her face-down card. If her two cards total 16 or less, the dealer must hit until reaching 17 or over. If the dealer's total exceeds 21, she must pay all the players whose hands have not gone "bust." It is important to note here that the blackjack dealer has no choice as to whether she should stay or draw. A dealer's decisions are predetermined and known to all the players at the table.

If you're a novice or just rusty, do yourself a favor and buy one of the small laminated cards available in shops all over town that illustrate proper play for every possible hand in blackjack. Even longtime players have been known to pull them out every now and then, and they can save you from making costly errors.

HOW TO PLAY

Here are eight "rules" for blackjack:

1. Place the number of chips that you want to bet on the betting space on your table.

223

1. *Never* touch your cards (or anyone else's), unless it's specifically stated at the table that you may. While you'll receive only a verbal slap on the wrist if you violate this rule, you *really* don't want to get one.

2. Players must use hand signals to indicate their wishes to the dealer. All verbal directions by players will be politely ignored by the dealer, who will remind players to use hand signals. The reason for this is the "eye in the sky," the casino's security system, which focuses an "eye" on every table and must record players' decisions to avoid accusations of misconduct or collusion.

---

2. Look at the first two cards the dealer gives you. If you wish to stand, then wave your hand over your cards, palm down (watch your fellow players), indicating that you don't wish any additional cards. If you elect to draw an additional card, you tell the dealer to hit you by tapping the table with a finger (again, watch your fellow players).

3. If your count goes over 21, you are bust and therefore lose, even if the dealer also goes bust afterward.

4. If you make 21 in your first two cards (any picture card or 10 with an ace), you've got blackjack. The payout for this used to be 3:2, meaning if you bet $5 you'd win an additional $7.50. In some casinos and at some tables it still is, but more and more have switched to a 6:5 payout for blackjacks, meaning they are only going to pay you $6 on your $5 bet. This has caused no small amount of outrage among the blackjack faithful, and if you're one of them, you can still find 3:2 tables—you just have to look a little harder for them.

5. If you find a "pair" in your first two cards (say, two 8s or two aces), you may "split" the pair into two hands and treat each card as the first card dealt in two separate hands. You will need to place an additional bet, equal to your original bet, on the table. The dealer will then deal you a new *second* card to the first split card, and play commences as described above. This will be done for the second split card as well. **Note:** When you split aces, you will receive only one additional card per ace and must stand.

6. After seeing your two starting cards, you have the option to "double down." You place an amount equal to your original bet on the table and you receive only one more card. Doubling down is a strategy to capitalize on a potentially strong hand against the dealer's weaker hand. **Tip:** You may double down for less than your original bet, but never for more.

7. Anytime the dealer deals herself an ace for the "up" card, you may insure your hand against the possibility that the hole card is a 10 or face card, which would give him or her an automatic blackjack. To insure, you place an amount up to one-half of your bet on the "insurance" line. If the dealer does have a blackjack, you get paid 2 to 1 on the insurance money while losing your original bet: You break even. If the dealer does not have a blackjack, she takes your insurance money and play continues in the normal fashion.

8. The dealer must stand on 17 or more and must hit a hand of 16 or less.

PROFESSIONAL TIPS

Advice of the experts in playing blackjack is as follows:

1. *Do not* ask for an extra card if you have a count of 17 or higher, *ever.*

2. *Do not* ask for an extra card when you have a total of 12 or more if the dealer has a 2 through 6 showing in his or her "up" card.

3. *Ask* for an extra card or more when you have a count of 12 through 16 in your hand if the dealer's "up" card is a 7, 8, 9, 10, or ace.

There's a lot more to blackjack strategy than the above, of course. So consider this merely as the bare bones of the game. Blackjack is played with a single deck or with multiple decks; if you're looking for a single-deck game, your best bet is to head to a Downtown casino.

A final tip: Avoid insurance bets; they're sucker bait!

Craps

The most exciting casino action is usually found at the craps tables. Betting is frenetic, play fast paced, and groups quickly bond while yelling and screaming in response to the action.

THE POSSIBLE BETS

The craps table is divided into marked areas (Pass, Come, Field, Big Six, Big Eight, and so on), where you place your chips to bet. The following are a few simple directions.

PASS LINE   A "Pass Line" bet pays even money. If the first roll of the dice adds up to 7 or 11, you win your bet; if the first roll adds up to 2, 3, or 12, you lose your bet. If any other number comes up, it becomes your "point." If you roll your point again, you win, but if a 7 comes up again before your point is rolled, you lose.

DON'T PASS LINE   Betting on the "Don't Pass Line" is the opposite of betting on the Pass Line. This time, you lose if a 7 or an 11 is thrown on the first roll, and you win if a 2 or a 3 is thrown on the first roll.

If the first roll is 12, however, it's a "push" (standoff), and nobody wins. If none of these numbers is thrown and you have a point instead, in order to win, a 7 will have to be thrown before the point comes up again. A Don't Pass bet also pays even money.

COME   Betting on "Come" is the same as betting on the Pass Line, but you must bet after the first roll or on any following roll. Again, you'll win on 7 or 11 and lose on 2, 3, or 12. Any other number is your point, and you win if your point comes up again before a 7.

DON'T COME   This is the opposite of a Come bet. Again, you wait until after the first roll to bet. A 7 or an 11 means you lose; a 2 or a 3 means you win; 12 is a push, and nobody wins. You win if 7 comes up before the point. (The point, you'll recall, was the first number rolled if it was none of the above.)

FIELD   This is a bet for one roll only. The "Field" consists of seven numbers: 2, 3, 4, 9, 10, 11, and 12. If any of these numbers is thrown on the next roll, you win even money, except on 2 and 12, which pay 2 to 1 (at some casinos 3 to 1).

BIG SIX AND EIGHT   A "Big Six and Eight" bet pays even money. You win if either a 6 or an 8 is rolled before a 7. Mathematically, this is a sucker's bet.

ANY 7   An "Any 7" bet pays the winner 5 to 1. If a 7 is thrown on the first roll after you bet, you win.

"HARD WAY" BETS   In the middle of a craps table are pictures of several possible dice combinations together with the odds the casino will pay you if you bet and win on any of those combinations being thrown. For example, if double 3s or 4s are rolled and you had bet on them, you will be paid 7 to 1. If double 2s or 5s are rolled and you had bet on them, you will be paid 9 to 1. If either a 7 is rolled or the number you bet on was rolled any way other than the "Hard Way," then the bet is lost. In-the-know gamblers tend to avoid "Hard Way" bets as it is an easy way to lose money.

ANY CRAPS   Here you're lucky if the dice "crap out"—if they show 2, 3, or 12 on the first roll after you bet. If this happens, the bank pays 7 to 1. Any other number is a loser.

PLACE BETS   You can make a "Place Bet" on any of the following numbers: 4, 5, 6, 8, 9, or 10. You're betting that the number you choose will be thrown before a 7 is thrown. If you win, the payoff is as follows: 4 or 10 pays at the rate of 9 to 5, 5 or 9 pays at the rate of 7 to 5, and 6 or 8 pays at the rate of 7 to 6. "Place Bets" can be removed at any time before a roll.

SOME PROBABILITIES

The probability of a certain number being rolled at the craps table is not a mystery. Because there are only 36 possible outcomes when the dice are rolled, the probability for each number being rolled is easily ascertained. See the "Dice Probabilities" chart below to help you, in case you decided it was fun to pass notes or sleep during math classes.

Dice Probabilities

NUMBER	POSSIBLE COMBINATIONS	ACTUAL ODDS	PERCENTAGE PROBABILITY
2	1	35:1	2.8%
3	2	17:1	5.6%
4	3	11:1	8.3%
5	4	8:1	11.1%
6	5	6.2:1	13.9%
7	6	5:1	16.7%
8	5	6.2:1	13.9%
9	4	8:1	11.1%
10	3	11:1	8.3%
11	2	17:1	5.6%
12	1	35:1	2.8%

So 7 has an advantage over all other combinations, which, over the long run, is in favor of the casino. You can't beat the law of averages, but if you can't beat 'em, join 'em (that is, play the "Don't Pass" bet).

Keno

Originating in China, this is one of the oldest games of chance. Legend has it that funds acquired from the game were used to finance construction of the Great Wall of China.

Although fading in popularity—maybe because *the house percentage is greater than that of any other casino game*—you can still find the game in dedicated keno lounges and in some casino restaurants, most often at older Strip casinos, Downtown, and in the off-Strip casinos.

For those of you with state lotteries, this game will appear very familiar. You can select from 1 to 15 numbers (out of a total of 80), and if all of your numbers come up, you win. Depending on how many numbers you've selected, you can win smaller amounts if less than all of your numbers have come up. For example, if you bet a "3-spot" (selecting a total of three numbers) and two come up, you'll win something but not as much as if all three had shown up. A one-number mark is known as a 1-spot, a two-number selection is a 2-spot, and so on. After you have selected the number of spots you wish to play, write the amount you want to wager on the ticket, in the right-hand corner where indicated. The more you bet, the more you can win if your numbers come up. Before the game starts, you have to give the completed form to a keno runner, or hand it in at the keno lounge desk, and pay for your bet. You'll get back a duplicate form with the number of the game you're playing on it. Then the game begins. As numbers appear on the keno board, compare them to the numbers you've marked on your ticket. After 20 numbers have appeared on the board, the game is over; if you've won, turn in your ticket to collect your winnings.

The more numbers on the board matching the numbers on your ticket, the more you win (in some cases, you get paid if *none* of your numbers come up). If you want to keep playing the same numbers over and over, you can replay a ticket by handing in your duplicate to the keno runner; you don't have to keep rewriting it.

In addition to the straight bets described above, you can split your ticket, betting various amounts on two or more groups of numbers. It does get a little complex, as combination-betting options are almost infinite. Helpful casino personnel in the keno lounge can assist you with combination betting.

Poker

Poker is the game of the Old West (there seems to be at least one sequence in every Western where the hero faces off against the villain over a poker hand). In Las Vegas, poker is just about the biggest thing going, thanks to the popularity of celebrity poker TV shows, poker tours, books, and magazines. Just about every casino now has a poker room, and it's just a matter of time before the others catch up.

There are lots of variations on the basic game, but one of the most popular is **Texas Hold 'Em.** Two cards are dealt, face down, to the players. After a betting round, five community cards (everyone can use them) are dealt face up on the table. Players make the best five-card hand, using their own cards and the "board" (the community cards), and the best hand wins. The house dealer takes care of the shuffling and the dealing, and moves a marker around the table to alternate the start of the deal. The house usually rakes around 10% (it depends on the casino) from each pot. Most casinos also provide tables for playing Seven-Card Stud, Omaha High, and Omaha Hi-Lo. A few even have Seven-Card Stud Hi-Lo split. To learn how these variations are played, either read a book or take lessons.

Warning: If you don't know how to play poker, don't attempt to learn at a table. Card sharks are not a rare species in Vegas; they will gladly feast on fresh meat. Find a casino that provides free gaming lessons and learn, to quote Kenny Rogers, when to hold 'em and when to fold 'em.

PAI GOW

Pai Gow is a variation on poker that has become popular. The game is played with a traditional deck plus one joker. The joker is a wild card that can be used as an ace or to complete a straight, a flush, a straight flush, or a royal flush. Each player is dealt seven cards to arrange into two hands: a two-card hand and a five-card hand. As in standard poker, the highest two-card hand is two aces, and the highest five-card hand is a royal flush. The five-card hand *must* be higher than the two-card hand (if the two-card hand is a pair of 6s, for example, the five-card hand must be a pair of 7s or better). Any player's hand that is set incorrectly is an automatic loser. The object of the game is for both of the players' hands to rank higher than both of the banker's hands. Should one hand rank exactly the same as the banker's hand, this is a tie (called a "copy"), *and the banker wins all tie hands.* If the player wins one hand but loses the other, this is a "push," and no money changes hands. The house dealer or any player may be the banker. The bank is offered to each player, and each player may accept or pass. Winning hands are paid even money, less a 5% commission.

CARIBBEAN STUD

Caribbean Stud is yet another variation of poker that is gaining in popularity. Players put in a single ante bet and are dealt five cards, face down, from a single deck; they play solely against the dealer, who receives five cards, one of them face up. Players are then given the option of folding or calling, by making an additional bet that is double their original ante. After all player bets have been made, the dealer's cards are revealed. If the dealer doesn't qualify with *at least an ace/king combination,* players are paid even money on their ante, and their call bets are returned. If the dealer does qualify, each player's hand is compared to the dealer's. On winning hands, players receive even money on their ante bets, and call bets are paid out on a scale according to the value of their hands. The scale ranges from even money for a pair, to 100 to 1 on a royal flush, although there is usually a cap on the maximum payoff, which varies from casino to casino.

An additional feature of Caribbean Stud is the inclusion of a progressive jackpot. For an additional side bet of $1, a player may qualify for a payoff from a progressive jackpot. The jackpot bet pays off only on a flush or better, but you can win on this bet even if the dealer ends up with a better hand than you do. Dream all you want of getting that royal flush and taking home the jackpot, but the odds of it happening are astronomical, so don't be so quick to turn in your resignation letter. Most veteran gamblers will tell you this is a bad bet (from a strict mathematical standpoint, it is), but considering that Caribbean Stud already has a house advantage that is even larger than the one in roulette, if you're going to play, you might as well toss in the buck and pray.

LET IT RIDE

Let It Ride is another popular game that involves poker hands. You place three bets at the outset and are dealt three cards. The dealer is dealt two cards that act as community cards (you're not playing against the dealer). Once you've seen your cards, you can choose to pull the first of your three bets back or "let it ride." The object of this game is to get a pair of 10s or better by combining your cards with the community cards. If you're holding a pair of 10s or better in your first three cards (called a "no-brainer"), you want to let your bets ride the entire way through. Once you've decided whether or not to let your first bet ride, the dealer exposes one of his two cards. Once again, you must make a decision to take back your middle bet or keep on going. Then the dealer exposes the last of his cards; your third bet must stay. The dealer then turns over the hands of the players and determines whether you've won. Winning bets are paid on a scale, ranging from even money for a single pair up to 1,000 to 1 for a royal flush. These payouts are for each bet you have in play. Similar to Caribbean Stud, Let It Ride has a bonus that you can win for high hands if you cough up an additional $1 per hand, but be advised that the house advantage on that $1 is obscene. But hey, that's why it's called gambling.

THREE-CARD POKER

Three-Card Poker has become one of the most popular table games in Las Vegas, with gamblers appreciating the relatively low mental input requirements and relatively high payout possibilities. It's actually more difficult to explain than to play. For this reason, we recommend watching a table for a while. You should grasp it pretty quickly.

Basically, players are dealt three cards with no draw and have to make the best poker hand out of those three cards. Possible combinations include a straight flush (three sequential cards of the same suit), three of a kind (three queens, for example), a straight (three sequential cards of any suit), a flush (three cards of the same suit), and a pair (two queens, for example). Even if you don't have one of the favored combinations, you can still win if you have cards higher than the dealer's.

On the table are three betting areas—Ante, Play, and Pair Plus. There are actually two games in one on a Three-Card Poker table—"Pair Plus" and "Ante and Play." You can play only Pair Plus or only Ante, or both. You place your chips in the areas in which you want to bet.

In Pair Plus, you are betting only on your hand, not competing against anyone else at the table or the dealer. If you get a pair or better, depending on your hand, the payoff can be pretty fab –straight flush: 40 to 1; three of a kind: 30 to 1; straight: 6 to 1; flush: 3 to 1; and pair: 1 to 1.

In Ante and Play, you are betting that your hand will be better than the dealer's but you're not competing against anyone else at the table. You place an Ante bet, view your cards, and then, if you decide you like your hand, you place a bet in the Play area equal to your Ante bet. If you get lousy cards and don't want to go forward, you can fold, losing only your Ante bet and your Pair Plus bet, if you made one. Once all bets are made, the dealer's hand is revealed—he must have at least a single queen for the bet to count; if not, your Ante and Play bets are returned. If you beat the dealer's hand, you get a 1 to 1 payoff, but there is a bonus for a particularly good winning hand: straight flush, 5 to 1; three of a kind, 4 to 1; straight, 1 to 1.

Your three cards are dealt. If you play only Pair Plus, it doesn't matter what the dealer has—you get paid if you have a pair or better. If you don't, you lose your bet. If you play the Ante bet, you must then either fold and lose the Ante bet or match the Ante bet by placing the same amount on the Play area. The dealer's hand is revealed, and payouts happen accordingly. Each hand consists of one fresh 52-card deck.

There are several variants to this game, including a bonus bet that can win a progressive jackpot (usually $1) and a six-card version where your cards are combined with the dealer's cards to come up with the best five- or six-card hand. Caesars Entertainment casinos are even offering a million-dollar top prize in their six-card games if, between you and the dealer, you come up with the 9-10-J-Q-K-A of diamonds. Don't scoff—several people have actually won it already!

OTHER POKER VARIANTS

Meanwhile, as if all this weren't enough, new variations on poker games keep popping up. There's Crazy 4 Poker, similar to Three-Card Poker, only with five cards dealt, no draw, and make your best four-card poker hand out of it; a version of Texas Hold 'em where you are not competing against other players; several riffs on Three-Card poker that include secondary bonus bets, progressive jackpots, and multiple betting strategies; and more. All of them follow the basic tenets of poker (highest hand wins), but each has its own set of rules, betting strategies, and payouts; if you see one of these games, look for an instructional pamphlet at the table or ask the dealer for a quick lesson before you sit down.

Roulette

Roulette is an extremely easy game to play, and it's really quite colorful and exciting to watch. The wheel spins and the little ball bounces around, finally dropping into one of the slots, numbered 1 to 36, plus 0 and 00. You can place bets "Inside" the table and "Outside" the table. Inside bets are bets placed on a particular number or a set of numbers. Outside bets are those placed in the boxes surrounding the number table. If you bet on a specific number and it comes up, you are paid 35 to 1 on your bet. Bear in mind, however, that the odds of a particular number coming up are actually 38 to 1 (don't forget the 0 and 00!), so the house has an advantage the moment you place an inside bet. The methods of placing single-number bets, column bets, and others are fairly obvious. The dealer will be happy to show you how to make many interesting betting combinations, such as betting on six numbers at once. Each player is given different-colored chips so that it's easy to follow the numbers you've bet on.

Slots

You put the coin in the slot and pull the handle. What, you thought there was a trick to this?

Actually, there is a bit more to it. But first, some background. Old-timers will tell you slots were invented to give wives something to do while their husbands gambled. Slots used to be stuck at the edges of the casino and could be counted on one hand, maybe two. But now they *are* the casino. The casinos make more from slots than from craps, blackjack, and roulette combined. There are more than 150,000 slot machines (not including video poker) in the county. Some of these are at the airport, steps from you as you deplane. It's just a matter of time before the planes flying into Vegas feature slots that pop up as soon as you cross the state line.

But to keep up with the increasing competition, the plain old machine, where reels just spin, has become nearly obsolete. Now they are all computerized and have buttons to push so you can avoid getting carpal tunnel syndrome from yanking the handle all night (though the handles are still there on some of them). Many don't even have reels anymore but are entirely video screens, which offer a number of little bonus extras that have nothing to do with actual play. The idea is still simple: Get three (or four or ten) cherries (clowns, sevens, dinosaurs, whatever) in a row, and you win something. Each machine has its own combination.

Slot machine in the MGM Grand's casino.

ABOUT CASINO GAMBLING | The Games

Some will pay you something with just one symbol showing; on most, the more combinations there are, the more opportunities for loot. Some will even pay if you get three blanks. Study each machine to learn what it does. **Note:** The **payback** goes up considerably if you bet the limit (from 2 to hundreds of coins on penny slots, for instance).

Progressive slots are groups of linked machines (sometimes spread over several casinos) where the jackpot gets bigger every few moments (just as lottery jackpots build up). Some machines have their own progressive jackpot, which can be slightly less stressful because you're not competing with other players to win the top prize.

Themes and interactivity are the watchwords these days. Pick a pop culture reference and there's probably a slot machine dedicated to it. **Wizard of Oz, The Amazing Race, Airplane!** (don't call me Shirley!), **Jaws, Sex and the City,** and **American Idol** (with Simon!) are just a few of the familiar titles you'll see on casino floors. Each of them features bonus rounds and side games that have animations, video clips, music, competitions between other players, and, in some cases, even motion-activated seats.

Penny and nickel slots, which for a long time had been overlooked, relegated to a lonely spot somewhere by a back wall because they were not as profitable for the casinos as quarter and dollar slots, have made a comeback. You can bet just a penny or nickel, but maximum bets for the bigger jackpots are usually in the $2 to $3 range, sometimes even more. As a result, more cash is pocketed by the casino (which keeps a higher percentage of cash off of lower denomination slots than it does off of higher ones), which is happy to accommodate this trend by offering up more and more cheaper slots. See how this all works? Are you paying attention?

Cashless machines are the standard in Vegas these days. Now when gambling, players insert their money, they play, and when they cash out, they get—instead of the clanging sound of coins cascading out into the tray—a little paper ticket with their total winnings on it. Hand in your ticket at a cashier's window (or use the omnipresent ATM-style redemption machines), and you get your winnings. Purists howl, bemoaning the loss of the auditory and tactile thrill of dealing with coins, but most of them are the type of people who would put $5 in a machine, lose it, and then be done with gambling for the rest of the trip. Those

PLAYERS' clubs

If you play slots or video poker, or, indeed, just gamble quite a bit, or even just gamble, it definitely pays to join a players' club. These so-called clubs are designed to attract and keep customers in a given casino by providing incentives: meals, shows, discounts on rooms, gifts, tournament invitations, discounts at hotel shops, VIP treatment, and (more and more) cash rebates. Join a players' club (it doesn't cost a cent to sign up), and soon you, too, will be getting those great hotel-rate offers—$20-a-night rooms, affordable rooms at the luxury resorts, even free rooms. This is one way to beat the high hotel rates. Of course, your rewards are often greater if you play just in one casino, but your mobility is limited.

When you join a players' club (inquire at the casino desk), you're given a card that looks like a credit card, which you must insert into an ATM-like device whenever you play. Yes, many casinos even have them for the tables as well as the machines. The device tracks your play and computes bonus points. Don't forget, as we sometimes do, to retrieve your card when you leave the machine—though that may work in your favor if someone comes along and plays the machine without removing it. Hand over your card when you join a gaming table (blackjack, for example) and they will monitor your play as well.

These days, players' clubs go beyond the casino as well. Many of them track your overall spending at participating casinos, including what you pay for meals, shopping, rooms, spa treatments, and more. This means you can earn points toward rewards pretty much anytime you pull out your wallet.

Which players' club should you join? Actually, you should join one at any casino where you play because even the act of joining usually entitles you to some benefits. It's convenient to concentrate play where you're staying; if you play a great deal, a casino-hotel's players' club benefits may be a factor in your accommodations choice. Consider, though, particularly if you aren't a high roller, the players' clubs Downtown. You get more bang for your buck, because you don't have to spend as much to start raking in the goodies.

Another advantage is to join a players' club that covers many hotels under the same corporate umbrella. Caesars Entertainment operates the Total Rewards club, which is good at any of their casinos in Vegas (Harrah's, Rio, Caesars Palace, the Flamingo, Paris Las Vegas, Bally's, and Planet Hollywood; www.harrahs.com/total_rewards) or elsewhere around the world. The same goes for the M life program for casinos in the MGM Resorts International stable (Aria Las Vegas, The Mirage, Bellagio, MGM Grand, Mandalay Bay, Luxor, New York–New York, and Excalibur; www.mlife.com), the locals' favorite Station Casinos Boarding Pass (Palace, Sunset, Texas, and more; www.stationcasinos.com/gaming/boarding-pass), and their main competition at Boyd/Coast, B Connected (Orleans, Suncoast, Fremont, and more; www.bconnectedonline.com).

Choosing the best club(s) for you can be a complex business. To get into it in-depth, see www.lasvegasadvisor.com. Also visit the sites for the individual casinos, many of which allow you to join their clubs online. Try it, and you might find yourself receiving discounts and freebies before you even set foot in Vegas.

who are more than just casual players love the convenience and simplicity of the tickets and wouldn't go back to the days of having to lug big buckets of change around if you promised them better payoff odds.

The biggest revolution in gaming is the advent of server-based slots and video poker. This allows you or the casino to switch out themes and denominations on a single machine. Tired of playing the Double Diamond quarter machine? No problem! Hit a button and it can become a Lucky 7 dollar machine in an instant. These high-tech gadgets are also often integrated to a virtual version of the hosting hotel's concierge, allowing you to find out restaurant and show information without ever getting up. You will have to get up to actually go see the show or eat at the restaurant, but we're sure they're working on a way around that, too.

Are there surefire ways to win on a slot machine? No. But you can lose more slowly. The slot machines use minicomputers known as random number generators (RNGs) to determine the winning combinations on a machine, and though each spin may indeed be random, individual machines are programmed to pay back different percentages over the long haul. As a result, a machine programmed to return a higher percentage might be "looser" than others. A bank of empty slots probably (but not certainly) means the machines are tight. Go find a line where lots of people are sitting around with lots of credits on their meters. A good rule of thumb is that if your slot doesn't hit something in four or five pulls, leave it and go find another. Also, each casino has a bank of slots that they advertise as more loose or with a bigger payback. Try these. It's what they want you to do, but what the heck.

Video Poker

Video poker works the same way as regular poker, except you play against the machine. You are dealt a hand, you pick which cards to keep and which to discard, and then you get your new hand. And, it is hoped, you collect your winnings. This is somewhat more of a challenge and more active than slots because you have some control (or at least the illusion of control) over your fate, and it's easier than playing actual poker with a table full of serious poker players.

There are a number of varieties of video poker machines, including **Jacks or Better, Deuces Wild,** and so forth. Be sure to study your machine before you play. (The best returns are offered on the **Bonus Poker** machines; the payback for a pair of jacks or better is two times your bet, and three times for three of a kind.) The Holy Grail of video-poker machines is the 9/6 (it pays nine coins for a full house, six coins for a flush), but you'll need to pray a lot before you find one in town. Some machines offer **dou-**

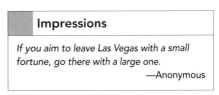

Impressions

If you aim to leave Las Vegas with a small fortune, go there with a large one.

—Anonymous

ble down: After you have won, you get a chance to draw cards against the machine, with the higher card the winner. If you win, your money is doubled, and you are offered a chance to go again. Your money can increase nicely during this time, and you can also lose it all very quickly, which is most annoying.

Other options include multihand video poker, where you play anywhere from 3 to 100 hands at the same time; bonus spin poker, allowing you to spin a wheel for extra credits when you get certain hands; and progressive jackpots for things like royal flushes or four aces.

Technology is catching up with video poker, too. Now they have touch screens, which offer a variety of different poker games, blackjack, and video slots—just touch your screen and choose your poison.

Sports Books

Most of the larger hotels in Las Vegas have sports-book operations, which look a lot like commodities-futures trading boards. In some, almost as large as theaters, you can sit comfortably, occasionally in recliners, and sometimes with your own video screen, and watch ball games, fights, and, at some casinos, horse races on huge TV screens. To add to your enjoyment, there's usually a deli/bar nearby that serves sandwiches, hot dogs, soft drinks, and beer. As a matter of fact, some of the best sandwiches in Las Vegas are served next to the sports books. Sports books take bets on virtually every sport (and not just who'll win, but what the final score will be, who'll be first to hit a home run, who'll be MVP, who'll wear red shoes, you name it). They are best during important playoff games or big horse races, when everyone in the place is watching the same event—shrieking, shouting, and moaning, sometimes in unison. Joining in with a cheap bet (so you feel like you, too, have a personal stake in the matter) makes for bargain entertainment.

Some sports books have started doing in-line betting. Popular in Europe, this allows you to bet on events within the game in addition to the actual game itself. Yes, you can still wager on which team will win the baseball game, but you can also wager on, say, if the next person up at bat is going to get a hit or strike out. As of this writing only a few are doing this (**M Resort, Venetian,** and **Palazzo,** to name a few), but it seems to be the wave of the future.

Speaking of the future, in early 2010, the Nevada Gaming Commission approved rules that would allow casino sports books to take wagers on the outcomes of nonsporting events such as the Academy Awards, *American Idol,* and even presidential elections. In the past, you couldn't bet on these types of events because in many of them the outcome is known by someone before the results are announced (those Oscar accountants get all the luck!) or there was too high a risk that the outcomes could be influenced. At press time, no major casino in Vegas was offering these types of wagers because of all of the restrictions the commission put on them to guard against the concerns that made them illegal before, but it is only a matter of time—the casinos smell big money here and they'll figure out a way to make it work. So who do you think is going to win *Dancing With the Stars?* Wanna bet?

Mobile Gaming

So you're lying there by the pool and you're thinking, "Golly, I really wish I didn't have to get up to make a wager at the sports book or play a hand of blackjack." Well, lazybones, you are in luck. Mobile gaming has arrived in Las Vegas, and it is already changing the way some people play.

The mobile devices vary in size and scope at the relatively few places that offer this type of gambling (again at **Venetian** and **Palazzo,** for instance). Some are about the size of an iPad, while others are more like an iPhone on steroids. Sports betting is the most popular application, but most of them have other games as well, including slots, video poker, blackjack, and more.

You sign out a device with a driver's license, credit card, and your room information if you are guest of the hotel where it is offered; buy in for however much money you want to load on it; and then you can go roam and gamble at the same time.

Although popular with sports bettors, the devices are not catching on as rapidly as the makers had envisioned. This may seem odd, especially considering our iEverything lives these days, but there's something undeniably "missing" about the experience. No matter how much technology runs our lives or how addicted you may be to Angry Birds, there's just something about sitting at an actual blackjack table or in front of a real, live slot machine that can't be replicated with a handheld gadget.

THE CASINOS

Casino choice is a personal thing. Some like to find their lucky place and stick with it, while others love to take advantage of the nearly endless choices that Las Vegas offers. Everyone should casino hop at least once to marvel (or get dizzy) at the decor/spectacle and the sheer excess of it all.

Virtually all casinos make sure they have no clocks—they do not want you to interrupt your losing streak by realizing how much time has passed. Of course, we've all heard the legend that Las Vegas casinos pump in fresh oxygen to keep the players from getting tired and wanting to pack it in. The veracity of this is hard to confirm, but we can only hope it's true, especially when we think of that time we looked up after a long stretch of gambling and discovered it was Thursday.

You can expect to find in every casino the usual and expected assortment of games—slot machines, of course, video poker, blackjack, table poker (making a big comeback after years of decline), a race and sports book, a keno lounge, a poker room, baccarat, minibaccarat, Caribbean Stud, Let It Ride, craps, roulette, Pai Gow, and more, more, more. If you want a particular game, and it's not one of the most obvious, you might want to call before heading over to a particular casino, just to make sure it's available there.

What follows is a description of most of the major casinos in Vegas, including their level of claustrophobia, and a completely arbitrary assessment based on whether we won there.

South Strip

Aria Las Vegas   This is, without a doubt, one of the most dramatic casinos in town. Heavy use of wood, steel, glass, fabric, and stone, accompanied by moody lighting, give the expansive 150,000-square-foot room a look and feel that is dazzling and distinctly modern, although admittedly not to everyone's taste, especially the casino purists among us. "Why is there sunlight?!" The good news is that those architectural details break up the space to provide a more intimate feeling without increasing the claustrophobia quotient. Offerings include thousands of slots (traditional reel, video, and server based) of all denominations, dozens of table games, two high-limit lounges, a race and sports book, and a poker room. As a member of MGM

> ### Impressions
>
> *Tip Number 3: Win a bunch of money. I can't recommend this too highly. If it hasn't occurred to you, win $1,200 and see for yourself. It's very energizing and really adds to your Vegas fun.*
>
> —Merrill Markoe, *Viva Las Wine Goddesses!*

Resorts International, Aria takes part in their M life rewards program, which is also used at Bellagio, Mandalay Bay, New York–New York, and others. 3730 Las Vegas Blvd. S. www.arialasvegas.com. ✆ **702/590-7111.**

The Cosmopolitan of Las Vegas If Aria is dramatic, then The Cosmo is *bold,* both from a visual and aural standpoint. There is eye-candy everywhere from blown glass to LED panels to the three-story chandelier housing a multi-level bar. Multiple soundtracks pump up the sonic energy depending on where you are standing. ***Warning:*** It can sometimes tip over into overwhelming, especially if you prefer a more sedate gambling experience. My ears were ringing after a few hours spent there one evening. Despite its size (around 100,000 sq. ft.), it's also one of the most easily accessible and navigable casinos in town. The underground parking garage and Strip entrances mean you can pop right up into the heart of the action, and the long, narrow layout means you should never get lost. There are lots of the latest slots in all denominations, plenty of table games, a small race and sports book bar, a high-limit area, and even casino cabanas—areas that can be cordoned off around slots or tables to provide a semiprivate gaming session. There is no poker room, keno, or bingo. The casino features its own Identity club program that tracks play and other money spent around the hotel for rewards. 3708 Las Vegas Blvd. S. www.cosmopolitanlasvegas.com. ✆ **702/698-7000.**

Excalibur As you might expect, the Excalibur casino is replete with suits of armor, stained-glass panels, knights, dragons, and velvet-and-satin heraldic banners, with gaming action taking place beneath vast iron-and-gold chandeliers fit for a medieval castle fortress. This all makes it fine for kitsch seekers, but anyone who hates crowds or is sensitive to noise will hate it. The overall effect is less like a castle than like a dungeon. One of us won a lot of money here and refused to share it with the other, so our final judgment about the casino is, well, mixed. Excalibur is part of the MGM Resorts International M life program, which is also used at MGM Grand, The Mirage, Bellagio, Luxor, Mandalay Bay, and others. 3850 Las Vegas Blvd. S. www.excalibur.com. ✆ **702/597-7777.**

Luxor Las Vegas The good news: It is more accessible than you might think, thanks to the air-conditioned people-mover from Excalibur and the monorail from Mandalay Bay. The bad news: Luxor has systematically stripped away most of its Egyptian wackiness. The result—a casino that looks like all the other casinos in town, with lots of sleek lines, cool blue tones, and boring blandness. Bring back the talking camels and King Tut! Having said that, the casino does have a much airier feel without all the fake hieroglyphic stonework, which produces a low claustrophobia level—in parts of the place, you can see all the way up the inside of the pyramid. There is also a casino lounge called Aurora that is very nice. The MGM Resorts International M life program offers rewards of cash, merchandise, meals, and other rewards. Sports action unfolds on both large screen and individual monitors in Luxor's race and sports book. We felt inclined to like this casino, thanks to a good run at blackjack, but we are most cranky about the de-Egypt-ification. 3900 Las Vegas Blvd. S. www.luxor.com. ✆ **702/262-4444.**

Mandalay Bay You'll find "elegant" gaming in a prefab, deliberate way, with a very high ceiling that produces a very low claustrophobia factor. This is definitely the right place to gamble if you're looking for less hectic, less gimmick-filled play. The layout makes it look airy, and it's marginally less confusing and certainly less overwhelming than many other casinos. Because it is so far down the Strip, there are fewer walk-in players, but the presence of the House of Blues and a couple of popular casino lounges can mean a late-night influx of customers. There's a big, ultracomfortable sports-book area (complete with armchairs that could well encourage a relaxed gambler to fall asleep). Players can sign up for the M life reward program. 3950 Las Vegas Blvd. S. www.mandalaybay.com. ☎ **702/632-7777.**

MGM Grand   At more than 171,000 square feet, this is the largest casino in Las Vegas, and it feels like it in both good and bad ways. Getting from one end to the other requires comfortable shoes and intimate spaces are in short supply, but the sheer number of options available means that if one machine, table, or area isn't giving you any luck, you have a seemingly endless amount of other options for your gaming dollars. There are a couple of nice high-limit lounges, a poker room, and a superluxe sports book (complete with VIP skyboxes) make this the most complete casino on the Strip. This hotel takes part in the M life rewards program. 3799 Las Vegas Blvd. S. www.mgmgrand.com. ☎ **702/891-7777.**

Monte Carlo Resort & Casino   A 2009 remodel turned this bland white room into a slightly less bland beige room. You wouldn't think beige would decrease the blandness, but anytime you throw in new carpets, wall coverings, furnishings, and gaming tables, it's a definite improvement. Unfortunately, they didn't do anything to change the fact that it is still essentially one big room, so it leaves gamblers often feeling a bit exposed. There are plenty of slots and table games to distract you from that, of course, and the sports book and poker rooms offer some sanctuary. This casino takes part in the M life rewards program. 3770 Las Vegas Blvd. S. www.montecarlo.com. ☎ **702/730-7777.**

New York–New York   Just like sister casino Luxor, the theme-gone-mad here has been scaled way back, removing a lot of the wacky details that made this place fun. The Central Park effect has been replaced by smooth, modern lines (blech), generic styling, and an overall sense of "classy" that, while admittedly pretty, is certainly not as entertaining. Having said that, you can still get your game on here with a full array of slots, tables, sports betting, and more; and, if you feel the need to immerse yourself in the faux-Gotham glory, you can wander into the adjacent Greenwich Village shops and restaurant areas for a breather. New York–New York participates in the M life rewards program. 3790 Las Vegas Blvd. S. www.nynyhotelcasino.com. ☎ **702/740-6969.**

Tropicana   After nearly a decade of promises (or was it threats?) to remodel this aging and somewhat dingy casino, the latest owners have finally come through and completely transformed the Trop into a modern, South Beach–themed showplace. White is the predominate color here in the marble floors, plantation-shutter-clad columns, and gaming table borders and chairs, all set off by vibrant splashes of orange, gold, and red. It's modern and fun, but still maintains a nod to the casino's history with a famous vintage Tiffany glass ceiling over the main gaming pit. It's impossible to deny that the place looks a billion times better than it did. It's a relatively small space, at least in comparison to the behemoths nearby, but there are still plenty of slot, video poker, and table game options. 3801 Las Vegas Blvd. S. www.troplv.com. ☎ **702/739-2222.**

Mid-Strip

Bally's Las Vegas   Bally's casino is large (the size of a football field), with lots of colorful signage. The big ceiling makes for a low claustrophobia level, although the open floor plan can leave gamblers who want a sense of privacy scuttling to the more secluded corners. There's a keno room as well as a poker area, plus a

Casino floor at New York–New York.

big, modern sport book. Note that the latter is located in the shopping promenade at the back of the hotel, away from the main casino. As a part of the Caesars Entertainment family, this casino takes part in their Total Rewards players' club. 3645 Las Vegas Blvd. S. www.ballyslv.com. (℃ **702/739-4111.**

Bellagio   The slot machines here are mostly encased in marble and fine woods. How's that for upping the ante on classy? Bellagio comes the closest to re-creating the feel of gambling in Monte Carlo (the country, not the nearby casino), but its relentless good taste means that this is one pretty forgettable casino. After all, we are suckers for a wacky theme that screams "Vegas," and European class just doesn't cut it. Sure, there are good touches—we always like a high ceiling to reduce the claustrophobia index, and the place is laid out in an easy-to-navigate grid with ultrawide aisles, so walking through doesn't seem like such a crowded collision-course maze. And we won big here, so there's that. Anyway, the cozy sports book has individual TVs and entirely denlike leather chairs—quite, quite comfortable. Bellagio is part of the M life rewards program. 3600 Las Vegas Blvd. S. www.bellagio. com. (℃ **888/987-6667.**

Bill's Gamblin' Hall & Saloon   Bill's Gamblin' Hall & Saloon is an 1890s-style casino ornately decorated with $2 million worth of gorgeous stained-glass skylights and signs, as well as immense crystal-dangling globe chandeliers over the gaming tables. It's kind of small, dark, and cluttered, but it's also Old Las Vegas (and we mean "old" loosely, certainly not true "old" like Downtown Vegas), and small is rare on the Strip. Although the property is owned by Caesars Entertainment, it does not participate in their Total Rewards players' club. 3595 Las Vegas Blvd. S. www.billslasvegas.com. (℃ **702/737-7111.**

Caesars Palace   The Caesars casino is simultaneously the ultimate in gambling luxury and the ultimate in Vegas kitsch. Where else can you gamble under the watchful gaze of faux-marble Roman statues? The very high ceiling in certain newer areas of the casino makes for a very low claustrophobia level, but older areas still feel cramped. Although we love it, the casino has become somewhat confusing and unmanageable because of its size and meandering layout, like Caesars itself.

A notable facility is the state-of-the-art race and sports book, with huge electronic display boards and giant video screens. Caesars pioneered computer-generated wagering data that can be communicated in less than half a second, and it has sophisticated satellite equipment that can pick up the broadcast of virtually any sporting event in the world. It's quite comfortable, but is located right by the line of foot traffic. The domed arena of The Forum Casino is a plush, crystal-chandeliered precinct with table games and slots adjacent. Gamblers can accumulate bonus points toward cash back, gifts, gratis show tickets, meals, and rooms by joining the Total Rewards players' club. It's a gorgeous and elegant place to gamble, and we've actually won some money here so we love it. 3570 Las Vegas Blvd. S. www.caesarspalace.com. ℭ **702/731-7110.**

Flamingo Las Vegas   If you've seen the movie *Bugsy*, you won't recognize this as Mr. Siegel's baby. The updated main area right off the Strip is a bit crowded, but improved lighting and a general softening of the glaring colors have made it more tolerable than it used to be. Back toward the lobby is a darker den of a space that is most notable for its reputedly loose Blazing 7 slot machines. A Margaritaville-themed minicasino (think parrots) opened in 2011 and is fun in a beachy kind of way. We never win here but that doesn't change our respect for the place, if for no other reason than its history. The Flamingo takes part in the Total Rewards players' club. 3555 Las Vegas Blvd. S. www.flamingolasvegas.com. ℭ **702/733-3111.**

Harrah's   This is a mixed bag of a casino, one that is both dated (low ceilings, old lighting, stuffy) and fun (parts have high-enough ceilings and there are special attractions). It's also supercrowded, noisy, flashy, and claustrophobic. At night, the popular party pit (allegedly fun dealers, rowdy music) packs them in, but the entire place gets crowded by the end of the day. The good news is that we have won here more often than not and the staff is among the most efficient and friendly on the Strip. Win a hand-pay jackpot and you'll get paid in a fraction of the time that most casinos take. Harrah's participates in Caesars Entertainment's Total Rewards players' club. 3475 Las Vegas Blvd. S. www.harrahs.com. ℭ **702/369-5000.**

The Mirage   The Mirage is more inviting now than in its chaotic past, thanks to a design switch from heavy tropics to more soothing Asian wood accents. But it's still twisting and meandering, and the relatively low ceiling and black walls are still a medium claustrophobia issue. Facilities include a plush European-style *salon privé* for high rollers at baccarat, blackjack, and roulette; an elegant dining room serves catered meals to gamblers there. Players can join the M life program and work toward bonus points for cash rebates, special room rates, complimentary meals and/or show tickets, and other benefits. The elaborate race and sports book offers theater stereo sound and a movie-theater-size screen. It's one of the most pleasant and popular casinos in town, so it's crowded more often than not. 3400 Las Vegas Blvd. S. www.mirage.com. ℭ **702/791-7111.**

The Palazzo   This casino is so lacking in distinguishing features that when it came time to write it up, we couldn't remember if The Palazzo even *had* a casino. See the review below for the one at the adjoining Venetian and just lather, rinse, and repeat. Sure it's big and grand, but it's also beige and bland. Signage is just as confusing as over at The Venetian. Slots are almost all multipayline video screen rather than the traditional single-payline model, which is disappointing. The sports book is located on a different level, incorporated into an Emeril Lagasse restaurant, but it does offer in-line betting (wagers placed during the game instead of just on the game as a whole) and mobile gaming with handheld devices that can be used in many areas of the hotel. Their Grazie players' reward program (clubgrazie.venetian.com) offers comps, cash back, and more. 3325 Las Vegas Blvd St. www.palazzo.com. ℭ **866/263-3001.**

Paris Las Vegas Casino   Surrounded by a rather Disney-esque one-third-scale replica of the streets of Paris, this 83,000-square-foot casino is a very pleasant place to gamble, in that Vegas gimmick kind of way. It's one of those kitschy places that "real" gamblers are appalled by. To heck with them, we say. A tall ceiling gives the illusion that you are trying to bust the bank while strolling outside and results in an airy effect. The place doesn't feel all that large, thanks to its layout. It has more than 2,000 slot machines and more than 100 table games. A state-of-the-art race and sports book features live satellite feeds of sporting events from around the world. The Paris casino participates in the Total Rewards players' club. 3655 Las Vegas Blvd. S. www.parislasvegas.com. ☏ **702/946-7000.**

Planet Hollywood Resort & Casino   Although the outside of the casino is a jumbled mess of lights, signs, and video screens, the interior is impressive, classic Hollywood glamour, with plenty of curving lines and dramatic folderol on columns and the like. All the usual casino suspects are still around, including thousands of slots, video-poker machines, plenty of table games, a high-limit salon, a poker room, and more. Guys and their tolerant female significant others will probably enjoy the Passion Pit, a group of tables where buxom lasses deal the cards and/or dance on stripper poles. The hotel is owned by Caesars Entertainment, so gambling here gets you points in the corporate Total Rewards club. 3667 Las Vegas Blvd. S. www.planet hollywoodresort.com. ☏ **702/785-5555.**

Treasure Island   We really loved it when this place was a casino set in Disneyland's Pirates of the Caribbean—or so it seemed. It doesn't seem like a big deal, the loss of those pirate chests dripping gold, jewels, and skulls with eye patches, but with the removal of the theme, this is now just a very nice casino. But it is that, so you should come here. There are nonsmoking gaming tables in each pit. A race and sports book boasts state-of-the-art electronic information boards and TV monitors at every seat, as well as numerous large-screen monitors. 3300 Las Vegas Blvd. S. www.treasureisland.com. ☏ **702/894-7111.**

The Venetian   Once a fairly bland but at least manageable casino, recent revisions have turned this into a chaotic, overwhelming mess, especially for slot players. The densely packed floor means little or no personal space and the proliferation of whiz-bang, graphics intensive machines creates a visual overload that left us turning in circles, desperately looking for the exit to the Strip, which seems almost tame in comparison. Sports wagers should note that this is one of the few casinos in town that offers in-line betting and mobile gambling devices. Their Grazie players' reward program (clubgrazie.venetian.com) offers comps, cash back, and more. 3355 Las Vegas Blvd. S. www.venetian.com. ☏ **702/414-1000.**

North Strip

Circus Circus   Even more important than the actual gambling is the circus midway above the main casino, with trapeze stunts and other feats of derring-do going on over your head. If that isn't Vegas gimmickry, we don't know what is. Unfortunately, the casino is crowded and noisy, and there are lots of children passing through (making it more crowded and noisy). That, plus some low ceilings (not in the Big Top, obviously), makes for a very high claustrophobia rating. 2880 Las Vegas Blvd. S. www.circuscircus.com. ☏ **702/734-0410.**

Encore Las Vegas   If you are looking for a unique casino experience, this should definitely be on your list. First, the room is smaller than most Strip casinos at only about 50,000 square feet, so it's much easier to navigate and you don't have to drop bread crumbs. The space is further broken up by lovely plantation shutters and heavy drapes that give the effect of a series of intimate gaming

Planet Hollywood casino.

Circus acts above the crowds at the Circus Circus casino.

salons instead of one big room. Most notable, though, is the use of natural light, which floods the entire space from the skylights in front to the wall of windows facing the pool in the back. It's unlike any other casino in town—in a good way. Having said that, the smaller square footage means less choice of machines and tables, the majority of which have higher denominations and limits (although there are a few penny, nickel, and quarter machines lurking around). Encore takes part in parent company Wynn Resorts Red Card players' reward program. 3121 Las Vegas Blvd. S. www.encorelasvegas.com. © **800/320-7125.**

Riviera   The word "classic" in Las Vegas usually means "old and out of date." The Riviera's casino is definitely "classic," but they have managed to spruce up the old gal (dating back to 1955) with some modern slots, plenty of low-limit tables (including 3-to-2 single-deck blackjack payouts), and the Strip's only bingo parlor, which is located at the back of the hotel near the front desk. The sports book flies under the Lucky's banner and is linked to their other outlets across Nevada. If you're in a hurry, you can place your bets on the ponies at a walk-up window facing the Strip. 2901 Las Vegas Blvd. S. www.rivierahotel.com. © **702/734-5110.**

Stratosphere Casino Hotel & Tower   Although fairly basic in terms of offerings and decor, this is still a comfortably upscale place to play, with a soft design scheme, good machine spacing, and modern touches. It is geared toward the budget gambler with only a handful of $1 and above slots, and lower limits available on the table games. A poker room and a race and sports book offer lively options; their ACE rewards club sponsors frequent tournaments, and its members can earn points toward gifts, VIP perks, discounted room rates, meals, and cash rebates. 2000 Las Vegas Blvd. S. www.stratospherehotel.com. © **702/380-7777.**

Wynn Las Vegas   Sprawling off the registration and conservatory/atrium/garden walkway, this simply laid-out but almost gaudily designed casino offers more than initially meets the eye. There are plenty of slots of all denominations (pennies to hundreds of dollars), more video poker than you'd expect in a major Strip casino, and dozens of table games with some surprisingly friendly dealers. It may not be the most memorable casino in town, but it's a place where you can gamble in a tastefully grown-up kind of way, although whether you actually want that is a question only you can answer. All the games you could want, plus a poker room and the rest, are here, though good luck trying to find a blackjack table under $15 a hand. The casino is tied to sister property Encore both physically and via the Wynn Red Card players' club. 3131 Las Vegas Blvd. S. www.wynnlasvegas.com. ✆ **702/770-7700**.

Downtown

Binion's 🎁 Despite the soap opera of the last few years (multiple owners, loss of the World Series of Poker, a brief closure), Binion's is still a must-visit for the serious gambler, especially those who like their casinos dark, smoky, and full of a classic "Vegas, Baby!" vibe. A remodel a few years back took out a bunch of slot machines in an effort to improve flow, and some parts got painted so it looks less dingy, but otherwise it remains essentially the same. That includes the relatively high claustrophobia level. It offers single-deck blackjack and low minimums, 10-times odds on craps, and high progressive jackpots. Real gamblers still won't consider going anywhere else. 128 E. Fremont St. (btw. Casino Center Blvd. and 1st St.). www.binions.com. ✆ **702/382-1600**.

California Hotel & Casino Despite its name, this friendly facility actually has a Hawaii theme, complete with dealers in Hawaiian shirts and lots of tropical floral patterns in the fabrics and carpet. It draws a healthy number of tourists from the Aloha state and other Pacific Rim areas, although which came first is probably best left up to the chicken and egg. There are over 1,000 slot and video poker machines (most with lower-than-average limits), all the usual table games, a keno room, a sport book, and more. Players can join the B Connected players' club (which is also good at Main Street Station and the Fremont Hotel & Casino). 12 Ogden Ave. (at 1st St.). www.thecal.com. ✆ **702/385-1222**.

The D Las Vegas Casino Hotel New owners acquired the former Fitzgerald's in 2011 and did a major makeover that not only changed the name but revamped the casino as well. The lower-than-Strip limits on table games and slots help keep it in line with Downtown standards, while the sleeker look and feel give it a modern edge that most of its competitors in the area don't have. There's a little something for everyone here; downstairs are modern machines and sexy, dancing dealers, while upstairs has a more vintage feel with "classic" slots that take and dispense coins. 301 Fremont St. (at 3rd St.). www.thed.com. ✆ **702/388-2400**.

El Cortez One of the last shreds of pre-1980s Las Vegas, this old gal got a fantastic face-lift a couple of years ago, with a natural appeal based less on kitsch. By removing half the slot machines, the casino has been opened up and aired out. Plus, it has a more contemporary decor. Former owner and local legend Jackie Gaughin (who lives in the penthouse) still wanders through and dines in the restaurants from time to time. It features frequent big-prize drawings and special events designed to bring the locals in. It's also popular for low limits and high odds (25¢ roulette and 10-times odds on craps). 600 Fremont St. (btw. 6th and 7th sts.). www.elcortezhotelcasino.com. ✆ **702/385-5200**.

Four Queens The Four Queens is New Orleans themed, with late-19th-century-style globe chandeliers, which make for good lighting and a low claustrophobia level. It's small, but the dealers are helpful, which is one of the pluses of

ABOUT CASINO GAMBLING

The Casinos

8

THE world series, LAS VEGAS-STYLE

Binion's was internationally known as the home of the **World Series of Poker.** "Nick the Greek" Dondolos first approached Benny Binion in 1949 with the idea for a high-stakes poker marathon between top players. Binion agreed, with the stipulation that the game be open to public viewing. The competition, between Dondolos and the legendary Johnny Moss, lasted 5 months, with breaks only for sleep. Moss ultimately won about $2 million. As Dondolos lost his last pot, he rose from his chair, bowed politely, and said, "Mr. Moss, I have to let you go."

In 1970, Binion decided to re-create the battle of poker giants, which evolved into the annual World Series of Poker. Johnny Moss won the first year and went on to snag the championship again in 1971 and 1974. Thomas "Amarillo Slim" Preston won the event in 1972 and pop-ularized it on the talk-show circuit.

The lure of big winnings has drawn everyone from casual poker players to celebrities. During one memorable year, the participants included actors Matt Damon and Edward Norton, fresh from *Rounders,* a movie in which they played a couple of card sharks. They decided to try out their newly acquired moves against the pros, who were unhappy that these kids were barging in on their action and so, rumor has it, offered a separate, large bounty to whichever player took them out. Both actors got knocked out on the first day but took it with good grace and apparently had a blast. Matt's buddy Ben Affleck, an experienced player, tried in 2003—the line on him to win (he didn't) was 400:1.

In 2005, the World Series of Poker moved to the Rio, under the auspices of Caesars Entertainment, which bought the rights to the event the year before. The following year set a record when 42-year-old Jamie Gold won the main event at pocketed a cool $12 million.

Today the event draws thousands of competitors—almost 7,000 of them in 2011, each of whom ponied up the $10,000 entrance fee in an effort to win the top prize, which eventually went to a 22-year-old German, Pius Heinz. He walked away with $8.72 million.

The qualifying rounds are held in June and July with the final table held in November. The action is broadcast on ESPN and online at www.wsop.com.

gambling in the more manageably sized casinos. Slots tournaments are frequent events, and there are major poker tournaments throughout the year. 202 Fremont St. (at Casino Center Blvd.). www.fourqueens.com. ☏ **702/385-4011.**

Fremont Hotel & Casino   This 32,000-square-foot casino—it's much bigger than it initially looks—offers a relaxed atmosphere. In some ways, it's more com-fortable gambling here than on the Strip, possibly in part because the beautiful people don't bother with places like this. But lots of other people do, and so it can be more crowded than other Downtown casinos, even during the day. Low gam-bling limits ($5 blackjack, 25¢ roulette, though not as many tables with these as we would like) help. It's also surprisingly open and bright for a Downtown casino. Casino guests can accumulate bonus points redeemable for cash by joining the B Connected club (which is also good at Main Street Station and the California Hotel & Casino). 200 E. Fremont St. (btw. Casino Center Blvd. and 3rd St.). www.fremont casino.com. ☏ **702/385-3232.**

The Golden Gate   This is the oldest casino in Downtown, and though it's certainly not glitzy, it's still fun to go there due to recent upgrades and remodeling that have kept it classic yet current. Despite the name, historic Vegas is the theme, with old slot machines, photos from bygone days, and even hotel and gambling ledgers from the early 1900s. Big windows to Fremont Street help to reduce the claustrophobia level. Oh, and don't forget about their famous $1.99 shrimp cocktail! 1 Fremont St. www.goldengatecasino.com. ✆ **702/382-3510.**

Golden Nugget   While this is not the standout among casino properties originally developed by Steve Wynn (now owned by Landry's Restaurants), it's still one of the nicest places to gamble, looks-wise, in Downtown. We prefer Main Street Station, but you might prefer the more obvious attempts at class that this place exudes. The looks are all warm, golden hues, giving it a lovely aura, but we do wish they didn't try to cram so much into such a small space; it can be overwhelming at peak times. Some tables are only $5 minimum, at least during the day. And compared to most other Downtown properties, this is the most like the Strip. Of course, it has a players' club. 129 E. Fremont St. (at Casino Center Blvd.). www.goldennugget.com. ✆ **702/385-7111.**

The Gold Spike   What a difference a few million dollars makes. Once a haven for '70s-era wood paneling, shag carpeting, and homeless people, the Gold Spike has gotten a complete makeover, turning the small, 10,000-square-foot space into a delightfully modern casino. Generous use of stone, fabrics, and wood give it a warm vibe, and the new machines definitely bring it up-to-date. Note that they only have a couple of blackjack tables and a roulette wheel, and they are not open 24 hours a day. Check with the hotel for operating hours. They also have keno and offer sports betting at the bar. This isn't a destination casino. While nice, it's just too small to give people enough options to keep them entertained for long periods of time. But if you're doing some casino hopping in the Downtown area, you should definitely check this one out. 217 Las Vegas Blvd. N. (at Ogden Ave.). www.goldspike.com. ✆ **702/384-8444.**

Main Street Station ♟   This is the best of the Downtown casinos, at least in terms of comfort and a pleasant environment. The decor here is, again, classic Vegas/old-timey (Victorian-era) San Francisco, but with extra touches (check out the old-fashioned fans above the truly beautiful bar) that make it work much better than other attempts at the same decor. Strangely, it seems just about smoke-free, perhaps thanks in part to a very high ceiling. The claustrophobia level is zero. Players can join the B Connected club, which is also good at Fremont Hotel & Casino and the California Hotel & Casino. 200 N. Main St. (btw. Fremont St. and U.S. 95). www.mainstreetcasino.com. ✆ **702/387-1896.**

The Plaza   After falling on tough times, this stalwart casino-hotel at the head of Fremont Street got new owners, who shut it down for a year while they completely remodeled it. The decor and furnishings came from a never-completed, $4-billion Strip hotel, and the quality is obvious. No longer a smoky, dingy pit, the Plaza is now a lively, up-to-date casino offering over a thousand slots, table games, a race sports book, and a bingo room. 1 Main St. www.plazahotelcasino.com. ✆ **702/386-2110.**

Just Off the Strip

Gold Coast   Geared to a locals' audience, this simple casino has a higher ratio of video-poker machines to slot machines than you'll find at most casinos on the Strip. It's a light and bright affair, with plenty of windows giving it an airy feeling and a high ceiling reducing the claustrophobia affect. In addition to the usual table games and machines, they have a race and sports book and a bingo room, plus they participate in the B Connected players' club, which is also good at other Boyd/Coast Gaming properties, such as The Orleans and Sam's Town. 4000 W. Flamingo Rd. www.goldcoastcasino.com. **☎ 702/367-7111.**

Main Street Station is the best place to gamble Downtown.

Hard Rock Hotel & Casino The Hard Rock certainly took casino decor to an entirely new level. The attention to detail and the resulting playfulness is admirable, if not incredible. Gaming tables have piano keyboards at one end, some slots have Fender guitar fret boards as arms, gaming chips have band names and/or pictures on them, slot machines are similarly rock themed (check out the Jimi Hendrix machine), and so it goes. Rock blares over the sound system, allowing boomers to boogie while they gamble—the noise level is above even that of a normal casino, and we just hated it. We are in the minority, though; most people love it, so assume you will be one of them. A 2009 expansion added more gaming space in a much more luxe room (black walls, lots of crystal). The race and sports book here provides comfortable seating in leather-upholstered reclining armchairs. 4455 Paradise Rd. www.hardrockhotel.com. **☎ 702/693-5000.**

LVH: Las Vegas Hotel The name has changed—it used to be the Las Vegas Hilton—but other than the signs and gaming chips, pretty much everything else is the same and that's actually a good thing. The trademark Austrian-crystal chandeliers are still over the main casino area, adding a touch of class, and the enormous sports book (30,500 sq. ft. and 300 seats) is still one of the world's largest and one of Las Vegas' most popular and technologically advanced. In fact, its video wall is second in size only to NASA's. 3000 Paradise Rd. www.thelvh.com. **☎ 702/732-5111.**

The Orleans This is not a particularly special gambling space, though it does have a low claustrophobia level. Another plus is that it sometimes plays Cajun and zydeco music over the sound system, so you can two-step while you gamble, which can make losing somewhat less painful. It has all the needed tables—blackjack, craps, and so forth—plus plenty of slots and video poker. And because it's not on the Strip, you'll find better odds for craps and cheaper table minimums. The B Connected players' club card gains you points at all Boyd/Coast Gaming casinos, such as the Suncoast and Sam's Town. 4500 W. Tropicana Ave. www.orleanscasino.com. **☎ 702/365-7111.**

Palms Resort & Casino This desperately seeking-the-hip hotel has a bit of an identity crisis: It also wants to be a place where locals feel comfortable gambling. You know, like Palace and Texas Station. Huh? That's right, the Palms wants to mirror those hotels off the Strip that offer loose slots and other incentives to

The Casinos

Gold Coast casino.

make the locals feel at home. This rarely makes for a chic playing area (because locals don't want to have to get glammed up to go out and play some slots). On the other hand, the area—especially on weekend nights—is ringed with the beautiful and aloof, desperate to get into the hip nightclubs that abound. If they aren't inside, they are surly about it. It's actually a pretty fun place to play, so something works. The gaming area covers most of the ground floor and is replete with Miami tropical–inspired details. 4321 W. Flamingo Rd. www.palms.com. (✆ **702/942-7777.**

Rio All-Suite Hotel & Casino   This Brazilian-themed resort's 85,000-square-foot casino is, despite the presence of plenty of glitter and neon, very dark. It has about the highest claustrophobia rating of the major casinos and seems very dated these days. Drink slingers will randomly jump onto small stages and burst into song and/or dance in between beer deliveries. Why? Why not. The part of the casino in the Masquerade Village is considerably more pleasant (the very high ceilings help), though still crowded, and the loud live show (performed evenings Thurs–Sun) adds even more noise. If you're looking for a casino in which to get your Zen on, look elsewhere. The Rio participates in the Total Rewards players' club. 3700 W. Flamingo Rd. www.riolasvegas.com. (✆ **702/252-7777.**

North & West of the Strip

Cannery   Located in North Las Vegas about 8 miles north of the Stratosphere, Cannery has a charming World War II theme. True, very little was charming about World War II, but what there is, they found it with big Rosie the Riveter–style artwork amidst a factory theme. It's mainly a draw for locals, but it can be worth the drive for visitors for its low limits and famously generous slot machines and video poker. They have all the modern games plus some throwbacks, including a few that actually still accept and dispense coins! The Cannery's Can Club players' reward program earns points here and at sister casinos Eastside Cannery and the Rampart Casino at the JW Marriott. 2121 E. Craig Rd. (just west of I-15), North Las Vegas. www.cannerycasino.com. (✆ **702/507-5700.**

Rampart Casino   Although in the same building as the JW Marriott resort on the northwest side of town, the Rampart Casino is operated as a wholly separate facility and a sister to The Cannery and Eastside Cannery casinos. It primarily draws a local crowd for its lower limits gaming and lots of video poker, so those looking for a more affordable gambling experience should add it to their list. In addition to table games like blackjack and craps, they have a race and sports book and lots of the latest and classic slots, including some that take and dispense coins. Their Rampart Rewards players' club is connected to the Cannery casino's Can Club, so you can earn and use points at any of their properties. 221 N. Rampart (at Summerlin Pkwy.). www.rampartcasino.com. ✆ **702/507-5900.**

Red Rock Resort   It's a bit of a distance to travel just for gambling, but perhaps worth it because this is one of the best-looking casinos in town. It utilizes natural woods, glass ornaments, and stone to provide a sense of texture to the space, and as with the rest of the resort, it's a stunner. It's also a convivial place to play, but our good wins at blackjack probably had very little to do with that. Not only does Red Rock have traditional gaming tables, slots (from penny slots to high-roller $100 pulls), a race and sports book, and a 24-hour Poker Room, it also has bingo. Part of Station Casinos Boarding Pass players' club, Red Rock offers points toward cash back and other rewards that can be redeemed here and at other casinos in the family, such as Palace Station and Boulder Station. 10973 W. Charleston Blvd. www.redrocklasvegas.com. ✆ **702/767-7773.**

Santa Fe Station   The rambling north side casino is done in the same style as the lovely Green Valley Ranch with lots of warm lighting, stone, and greenery, giving it a comfortable, laid-back vibe. There are more than 2,700 slot and video poker machines of all denominations (although the bulk are lower-limit penny, nickel, and quarter varieties), 40 table games from blackjack to craps and various poker variations, a bingo hall, a race and sports book, and a keno lounge. As a part of the Station Casinos chain, this casino participates in the Boarding Pass players' reward program, along with other casinos in their portfolio like Sunset Station and Red Rock Resort. 4949 N. Rancho Dr. (at I-95). www.santafestationlasvegas.com. ✆ **702/658-4900.**

Sports book at LVH.

Silverton It's only a few miles away from the Strip, but the casino here is a million miles away in terms of attitude and experience. Done with a gorgeous, amber-hued ski-lodge theme, the room is warm, inviting, and comfortable—the kind of place you could feel good just hanging out in for long periods of time. The 90,000-square-foot facility has more than 2,000 slot and video poker machines, more than two-dozen table games like roulette and blackjack, a poker room, a keno lounge, a high-limit salon, and a race and sports book. Their Silverton Rewards program earns players points while playing any of the games. 3333 Blue Diamond Rd. (at I-15). www.silvertoncasino.com. ✆ **702/263-7777.**

South & East of the Strip

Eastside Cannery Just like sister casino Cannery, this locals joint also has a retro theme, only this one is the '60s Flower Power era. Don't worry; the theme is pretty subtle, allowing the focus to be on the games—and there are lots of them. Ultramodern slot machines with 3-D graphics share floor space with classic devices that take and dispense real coins instead of tickets. Now that's what we call retro! They have more than 20 gaming tables (blackjack, craps, roulette, and so forth), a poker room, a race and sports book, and a bingo parlor. Because it is mainly geared to a neighborhood crowd, limits throughout are lower than you'll find on the Strip so you can stretch your gambling dollar here. The Can Club players' reward program earns points here and at sister casinos Cannery and Rampart Casino at the JW Marriott. 5255 Boulder Hwy. (at Sunset Dr.). www.eastside cannery.com. ✆ **702/856-5300.**

Green Valley Ranch Resort It's probably too far for the average traveler to drive—after all, when there is a casino just steps (or floors) away from your hotel room (and between you and anywhere in the world apart from your hotel room), to say nothing of several dozen more within a few blocks, you may be disinclined to drive out to one that is isolated from many other decent casinos. But given that this is a swank resort, that it's smallish and elegant, and that despite all this the limits are low and the dealers are friendly, we think it's worth your time and effort. The casino participates in the Station Casinos players' club. 2300 Paseo Verde Dr. (at I-215), Henderson. www.greenvalleyranchresort.com. ✆ **702/617-7777.**

M Resort Although it has a Henderson address, M Resort is a straight shot down Las Vegas Boulevard about 10 miles from Mandalay Bay, the first casino people traveling in from Los Angeles see as they get to town. Done in similar tones to competitor Red Rock Resort, the heavy use of natural wood and stone mix well with lots of natural light to provide a lovely gaming space. Its 92,000 square feet of gaming space offers up slots of all denominations, more than 60 table games, a poker room, and a sports book that is tied to The Venetian and The Palazzo and offers in-line betting (wagers on plays during the game). 12300 Las Vegas Blvd. S. (at St. Rose Pkwy.), Henderson. www.themresort.com. ✆ **702/797-1000.**

Sam's Town On its two immense floors of gaming action, Sam's Town maintains the friendly, just-folks ambience that characterizes the entire property. The casino is adorned with Old West paraphernalia (horseshoes, Winchester rifles, holsters, and saddlebags) and is looking a bit less dated, thanks to some recent sprucing up (it's subtle, but believe us, it's better). Sam's Town claims its friendliness extends to looser slots. The B Connected players' club card gains you points at all Boyd/Coast Gaming casinos. 5111 Boulder Hwy. (at Nellis Blvd.). www.samstownlv. com. ✆ **702/456-7777.**

ABOUT CASINO GAMBLING | The Casinos

PRACTICAL MATTERS: THE CASINO SCENE

THE BASICS   Most Las Vegas casinos are open 24 hours a day, 365 days a year. You must be 21 years of age to even be inside the casino, much less play the games, so be sure to have a government-issued ID (passport, driver's license, or the like) on you, especially if you look young.

GAMBLING AS ENTERTAINMENT   Everyone dreams of hitting it big in Las Vegas, but the reality is that very, very few people actually do. Gambling should not be viewed as way of making money. Instead, look at it the same way you would look at going to see a show—entertainment, a fun distraction. Although it may not help you lose less money, it may help you have more fun while you're doing it.

Remember also that there is no system that's sure to help you win. Reading books and listening to others at the tables will help you pick up some tips, but if there were a surefire way to win, the casinos would have taken care of it (and we will leave you to imagine just what that might entail). Try to have the courage to walk away when your bankroll is up, not down. Remember, your children's college fund is just that, and not a gambling-budget supplement.

TAKING ADVANTAGE OF THE FREEBIES   Most casinos offer free or heavily discounted drinks to keep you well lubricated and happy. Just don't forget to tip your cocktail server a buck or two per drink and more if you are winning.

Many casinos have free gambling lessons on several popular table games, including blackjack, craps, and roulette. These lessons also often come with coupon books or other perks that the casinos hope will get you to stay and play. Check with the casino players' club desk for details and schedules.

Speaking of players' clubs, be sure to join the one at whatever casino you choose to play in. You'll earn points that can get you all sorts of free stuff, from meals to hotel rooms and even free money to gamble with. See p. 232 for more information about players' clubs.

EXPLORE YOUR OPTIONS   Don't be a snob and don't be overly dazzled by the fancy casinos. Sometimes you can have a better time at one of the older places Downtown, where stakes are lower, pretensions are nonexistent, and the clientele is often friendlier. Frankly, real gamblers—and by that we don't necessarily mean high rollers, but those who play to win, regardless of the amount of said win—head straight for Downtown for these precise reasons, caring not a whit about glitz and glamour. Even if you don't take your gambling as seriously as that, you may well want to follow their example. After all, it's getting harder and harder to find cheap tables (where you can play a hand of blackjack, for example, for less than $10) on the Strip—so take your hard-earned money to where you can lose it more slowly.

We would also call your attention to less glamorous, less readily accessible casinos, such as local favorites Sunset Station, Texas Station, Cannery, Fiesta Rancho, Fiesta Henderson, and Fiesta Santa Fe, where payoffs are often higher than on the Strip, and the limits are lower.

WHERE TO STAY

9

T here are about 150,000 hotel rooms in Las Vegas. If you stayed in a different room every night it would take you 411 years to get through them all. You could give one to every single resident of Topeka, Kansas, and still have enough left over for you and about 25,000 of your closest friends. The point is, finding a hotel room in Las Vegas is not hard; it's finding the right one for *you* that can be more challenging. Do you want a luxurious suite where you can lounge in bed and order room service, or basic accommodations where you'll dump your luggage and then not see it again until you stumble back to it as the sun is coming up the next morning? Do you want classic Glitter Gulch glitz or contemporary Sin City glamour? Do you want high tech or low cost? Las Vegas has all of the above and just about everything in between.

BEST LAS VEGAS HOTEL BETS

- o **Best Classic Vegas Hotel:** Most of historic Las Vegas has been imploded (often spectacularly), but at **Caesars Palace** you can still get a taste of it as themed Roman decadence meets classic Sin City opulence. See p. 269.

- o **Best Modern Vegas Hotel: The Cosmopolitan of Las Vegas** offers a blueprint for what the next generation of Las Vegas hotels will be like: as over-the-top visually as any theme hotel, but with a sexy, contemporary edge. See p. 271.

- o **Best for a Romantic Getaway:** No, it's not the real Eiffel Tower, but the one at **Paris Las Vegas** is almost as charming as the rest of this ooo-la-la themed resort, providing you ample opportunity to re-create a romantic French retreat. See p. 273.

- o **Best for Families:** Las Vegas is not a family destination, but if you can't leave the little ones with Grandma, your only choice for a major Vegas hotel is **Circus Circus,** where there are almost as many things for the wee ones to do as there are for adults. See p. 289.

- o **Best for Business Travelers: LVH: Las Vegas Hotel's** location next to the Convention Center makes this a no-brainer from a geographical perspective, but the swank rooms, casino, and restaurants give it a decidedly Vegas spin. See p. 303.

- o **Best Rooms on the Strip:** The condolike units at **The Cosmopolitan of Las Vegas** are not only sizeable but they have cool design touches (art! real books!) and terraces offering amazing views of the Strip. See p. 271.

PREVIOUS PAGE: **A Renaissance Suite at The Venetian.**

Guest room at The Cosmpolitan of Las Vegas.

- **Best Rooms Downtown:** The Plaza got a massive makeover using furnishing and fixtures once destined for a $4 billion hotel, turning once-dingy rooms into rare Downtown showplaces. See p. 298.

- **Best Rooms Off the Strip:** Red Rock Resort lives up to the resort part of its name as a true desert retreat, complete with gorgeous, modern rooms that you'll never want to leave. See p. 316.

- **Best Bathrooms:** This one is a toss-up for us, with the bigger-than-many-apartment-size retreats at **The Venetian** (p. 275) and the sumptuous luxury fixtures at **Wynn Las Vegas** (p. 286) both winning our hearts.

- **Best Bang for Your Buck:** Almost everything you can find at a Strip hotel (nice rooms, full casino, multiple restaurants, sharks!) can be gotten at the **Golden Nugget** in Downtown Las Vegas for a fraction of the cost. See p. 291.

- **Best Non-Casino Hotel:** They can't get your money gambling, so they get it through high room rates, but to stay at the **Mandarin Oriental** is to immerse yourself in luxury. See p. 254.

- **Best Splurge:** Rooms at **Encore Las Vegas** will almost always be among the most expensive in town, but you'll totally feel like you are getting your money's worth, especially with the gorgeous spa, pools, casino, and other amenities at your disposal. See p. 284.

PRICE CATEGORIES

Very Expensive	$250 and up
Expensive	$175–$250
Moderate	$100–$175
Inexpensive	Under $100

The rack rate is the maximum rate that a hotel charges for a room. It's the rate you'd get if you walked in off the street and asked for a room for the night. Hardly anybody pays these prices, however, especially in Vegas, where prices fluctuate wildly with demand.

Low seasons like the insanely hot summer months and parts of December and January offer the lowest rates, where a room at a hotel like Aria Las Vegas that would go for north of $250 during a busy time can be had for as low as $129. Of course, the law of supply and demand cuts both ways—during peak periods that same room could go for over $400 a night.

The best prices can usually be found online at each individual hotel website or through their social media pages on Facebook and Twitter. All usually offer cheaper rates, special discounts, and sometimes even give low-price guarantees. A recent check of hotels like Mandalay Bay, where they'll quote $200 a night as their base rate, showed rooms for as low as $79 midweek.

As far as room prices go, keep in mind that our price categories are rough guidelines, at best. If you see a hotel that appeals to you, even if it seems out of your price range, give them a call anyway. They might be having a special, a slow week, or some kind of promotion, or they may just like the sound of your voice (we have no other explanation for it). You could end up with a hotel in the Expensive category offering you a room for $60 a night. It's a toll-free call or a few clicks on a website, so it's worth a try.

Note: Quoted discount rates almost never include breakfast, hotel tax, or any applicable resort fees, the latter of which can send up the price by $20 or more per night.

SOUTH STRIP

The southern third of the Strip, from roughly Russell Road to Harmon Avenue, is home to some of the biggest and most extravagant hotels in the world.

Best for: First-time visitors who want to experience all of the Vegas insanity they have read about and seen on TV.

Drawbacks: Prices are higher here than in non-Strip locations; the sheer number of people can cause major traffic jams (and we're not just talking about on the street).

Very Expensive

Four Seasons Hotel Las Vegas ★★★ ☺   Various mammoth Vegas hotels attempt to position themselves as luxury resorts, insisting that service and fine cotton sheets can be done on a mass scale. But this is one of the few that can truly lay claim to that title. It's located on the top five floors of Mandalay Bay, though in many ways, the Four Seasons is light-years away from the vibe of the host hotel. A separate driveway and portico entrance, plus an entire registration area, set you up immediately with hushed elegance. This is one fancy hotel in town where you are not greeted, even at a distance, with the clash and clang and general hubbub that is the soundtrack of Vegas.

Inside the hotel, all is calm and quiet. But it's really the best of both worlds—all you have to do is walk through a door, and instantly you are in Mandalay Bay, with access to a casino, nightlife, and, yes, general hubbub. The difference is quite shocking, and frankly, once you've experienced Vegas this way, it's kind of hard to go back to the constant sensory overload.

The rooms don't look like much at first—slightly bland but in good taste—but when you sink down into the furniture, you appreciate the fine quality. Here at last is a Vegas hotel where they really don't care if you ever leave your room, so the beds are never-get-up cozy, robes are plush, and amenities are really, really nice. Because Four Seasons has the southernmost location on the Strip, its Strip-view rooms (the most expensive units) give you the whole incredible panorama.

In addition to all of the dining available at Mandalay Bay, there are two on-site restaurants, including the exercise in gluttony that is **Charlie Palmer Steak** (p. 99).

Service is superb—if they say 20 minutes for room service, you can expect your food in 19½ minutes. Children are encouraged and welcomed with gifts of toys and goodies, rooms are childproofed in advance, and the list of comforts available for the asking is a yard long. Once you factor in all the freebies (gym/spa access and various other amenities), not to mention the service and the blessed peace, the difference in price between Four Seasons and Bellagio (with all its hidden charges) is nothing.

3960 Las Vegas Blvd. S., Las Vegas, NV 89119. www.fourseasons.com. ✆ **877/632-5000** or 702/632-5000. Fax 702/632-5195. 424 units. $199 and up double; $399 and up suite. Resort fee $20 per night. Extra person $35. Children 17 and under stay free in parent's room. AE, DC, DISC, MC, V. Valet parking $22; no self-parking. Pets under 25 lb. accepted. **Amenities:** 2 restaurants; concierge; executive-level rooms; fitness center (free to guests); heated outdoor pool; room service; spa. *In room:* A/C, TV/DVD w/pay movies, fridge (on request), hair dryer, high-speed Internet, minibar.

Mandarin Oriental ★★★ With the much-lamented closure of the Ritz-Carlton at Lake Las Vegas in 2010, a window has opened up for another hotel to

Pool at the Four Seasons Hotel Las Vegas.

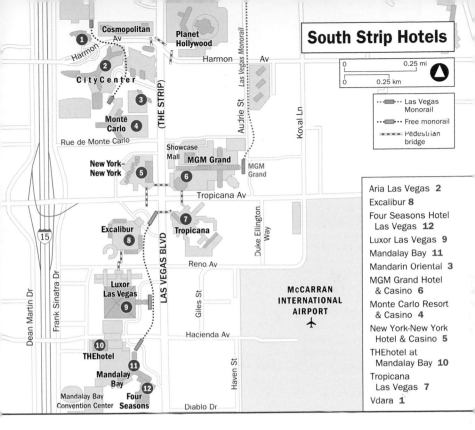

South Strip Hotels

	0	0.25 mi
	0	0.25 km

··■···· Las Vegas Monorail
··■···· Free monorail
×××× Pedestrian bridge

Aria Las Vegas **2**
Excalibur **8**
Four Seasons Hotel Las Vegas **12**
Luxor Las Vegas **9**
Mandalay Bay **11**
Mandarin Oriental **3**
MGM Grand Hotel & Casino **6**
Monte Carlo Resort & Casino **4**
New York-New York Hotel & Casino **5**
THEhotel at Mandalay Bay **10**
Tropicana Las Vegas **7**
Vdara **1**

slip in and battle for the crown of Most Luxurious in Vegas. The Mandarin Oriental seems more than up for the fight. The Asian hotelier chain is better known in Europe and the Far East, but they have come to Vegas with a bold statement of true boutique luxury in a city that likes to pretend that a 3,000-room hotel can be either of those things.

This property has just under 400 hotel rooms and another 200 residential units—small by Vegas standards—allowing for a level of service and amenities that simply can't be replicated at a larger hotel. The accommodations are not huge, but are still comfortable and roomy; all with a subtle Asian decor scheme, decadently comfortable beds, plush robes and towels, and even a valet closet so the "help" doesn't need to come into the room to pick up your laundry or drop off a newspaper. Classy.

But you don't need to wait to get to your room—the playground of the rich vibe greets you as soon as you walk in the door. The top hat–wearing doorman will greet you and attendants will guide you to an elevator that whisks you to the 23rd-floor Sky Lobby. With floor-to-ceiling windows facing the Strip, it is without a doubt the most dramatic lobby in town. A tearoom, bar, and a French restaurant from world-renowned chef Pierre Gagnaire complete this floor, all with similar stunning views.

The pool and spa area are on the seventh and eighth floors with still more windows, including in the treatment rooms and whirlpool areas. Have a soak while sipping vitamin-infused water and gazing out at the city lights? Why, yes, thank you.

Spa Orchid Room at the Mandarin Oriental.

Although there is little else in the building (no casino, no showroom, no roller coaster), the very deep catalog of restaurants, nightclubs, bars, shopping, gambling, and entertainment options at the other properties within CityCenter are just a short walk away.

3752 Las Vegas Blvd. S., Las Vegas, NV 89109. www.mandarinoriental.com. ✆ **888/881-9578** or 702/590-8888. Fax 702/590-8880. 392 units. $199 and up double; $399 and up suite. Resort fee $24 per night. Extra person $50. Children 11 and under stay free in parent's room. AE, DC, DISC, MC, V. Free self- and valet parking. **Amenities:** 3 restaurants; concierge; executive-level rooms; health club; heated pool; room service; spa. *In room:* A/C, TV w/pay movies, fridge (on request), hair dryer, high-speed Internet, minibar.

Expensive

Aria Las Vegas ★★★ Sitting at the virtual center of the massive CityCenter complex, Aria Las Vegas seems to elicit the classic "love it or hate it" reaction from visitors. To be sure, it is unlike any Vegas megaresort that has come before it—all gleaming, glass skyscraper and contemporary interior design instead of the themed

Resort Fees

As room rates have plummeted due to the sagging economic fortunes of Las Vegas, hotels have found new ways to increase their bottom line, mainly through the addition of what we consider to be nefarious and often outrageous "resort fees." These extra charges are tacked on top of the nightly room rate and variously include things like Internet access, entry to the fitness center, printing of boarding passes, local and toll-free phone calls, and the like. Some hotels throw in extra goodies like bottles of water, discounted cocktails or meals, and credits for future stays. It can be a good deal if you take advantage of what the fee covers, but even if you don't, you still have to pay the fee. We indicate which hotels charge resort fees in the listings in this chapter and include their current prices, but do note that the amount and what they include changes often; be sure to ask when booking your room or take some time to read the fine print if making arrangements online.

A deluxe queen room at Aria Las Vegas.

wackiness or faux old-school luxury of its predecessors. It feels almost out of place here, like someone picked up a big chunk of some ultracosmopolitan city (which Vegas most certainly is not, no matter how much it wants to be) and dropped it down in the middle of the Strip. It is dramatic and unexpected, modern without being cold or sterile, and for the record we are firmly in the "love it" camp.

The sinuous glass-and-steel exterior of the building gives way to a gorgeously appointed series of public spaces, each filled with the kind of attention to design detail that evokes reactions from "cool!" to "wow!" There is no such thing as a blank wall here—everything has a texture or pattern, using wood, stone, glass, fabric, metal, and other natural elements to create a richness that is lacking in other Vegas hotels. Throw in a lot of natural light and some exciting artworks (yes, that is a sculpture by Maya Lin hanging behind the check-in desk) and you have a unique and endlessly gawkable space.

More than 4,000 rooms come in all shapes and sizes, with standard rooms continuing the warm modern theme. Deep hues in the woods and fabrics would lend a cavelike air in other places, but the full wall of floor-to-ceiling windows fixes that nicely here. Standard amenities are plentiful and virtually everything (drapes, temperature, entertainment systems, lights) is controlled by an integrated touch-screen device that will even warn you if you've left the door unlocked. Bathrooms are generously sized, with abundant frosted glass and marble, as well as one seriously odd design element: Although the shower and tub are separate, they are in one enclosure so you have to pass through the former to get to the latter—space saving but strange.

Back downstairs you'll find a lively casino (p. 235), more than a dozen restaurants, including tapas from **Julian Serrano** (p. 103), fine Chinese at **Blossom** (p. 104), and upscale Italian at **Sirio** (p. 104). And if that's not enough, there are nearly a dozen more restaurants at the neighboring mall and hotels in CityCenter. There is also the requisite high-energy dance club **Haze** (p. 203), several other bars and lounges, a gorgeous spa, salon, workout facility, and lushly landscaped pool area. A showroom will feature a new Cirque du Soleil production in 2013.

Downsides are the size (which is leviathan and feels it), parking (both self-parking and the valet pickup are a long trek from where you want to be), and the outrageous resort fee.

3730 Las Vegas Blvd. S., Las Vegas, NV 89109. www.arialasvegas.com. ⓒ **866/359-7757** or 702/590-7757. 4,004 units. $159 and up double; $359 and up suite. Resort fee $25. Extra person $35. No discount for children. AE, DC, DISC, MC, V. Free self- and valet parking. **Amenities:** 17 restaurants; casino; concierge; executive-level rooms; health club; heated outdoor pools; room service; spa; showroom. In room: A/C, TV w/pay movies, hair dryer, high-speed Internet, minibar.

Mandalay Bay ★★ ☺ Its relative isolation on the far southern end of the Strip and its comparatively serene atmosphere make this seem more like an actual resort hotel than just a Vegas version of one. You don't have to walk through the casino to get to any of these public areas or the guest-room elevators, the pool

9

WHERE TO STAY

South Strip

area is spiffy, and the entire complex is marginally less confusing and certainly less overwhelming than some of the neighboring behemoths.

The spacious rooms in the main tower may not seem as luxe when compared to newer options at places like Aria or The Cosmopolitan, but they are still lovely. They are all sleek modernity, like everyone else in town, but the furnishings are cozy (love the window seats) and the fixtures fine. The bathrooms are downright large with impressive, slightly sunken tubs, glassed-in showers, double sinks, and separate water closets, plus lots of fab amenities. Rooms on higher floors have some of the best Strip views in town, but usually cost an additional fee.

Much more covetable are the gorgeous suites in a second tower known as THEhotel. Once billed as a completely separate hotel, the rooms here are now considered to be just another configuration available to Mandalay

The lobby of Mandalay Bay.

Bay guests. It still has its own check-in, valet parking, spa, and other amenities that make it feel like a plush nongaming space away from the main madness.

The multiroom suites here are posh, with gleaming woods and plasma-screen TVs in every room, including the enormous marble bathroom, where the tub is so deep the water comes up to your chin when you sit down. Bathroom amenities are high end, the comforters are down, and the sheets have a soft heft that makes you want to sink into them and never leave. For once, a hotel room in Vegas is designed to make you want to stay put. You'll usually pay a premium for them, but it's totally worth it.

Reservations at many of the nearly two dozen restaurants in Mandalay Bay are among the most sought after in town. **Aureole, Border Grill, Fleur by Hubert Keller, Red Square,** the **House of Blues,** and the **Bayside Buffet** are reviewed in chapter 5. A showroom will be the home of the new Michael Jackson–themed Cirque du Soleil production scheduled to open in 2013, and there is a separate arena for bigger concerts and events. There's also a big, comfortable casino (p. 236); several lounges, including the fun **Mizuya** (p. 209); the 1.5-million gallon **Shark Reef** aquarium (p. 60); and a massive outdoor beach area including a wave pool (more of a ripple pool, really), a lazy river ride, a sandy-bottomed pool, a cafe and bar, a dedicated casino, and more. The pools are a great place for families but they are extremely popular, so a quiet respite by the water is probably not on the agenda. A well-equipped workout facility, full-service spa, and a salon complete the recreation package.

A monorail system connects the hotel with Luxor and Excalibur, which are located in the heart of the Strip action, and this should more than help you get over any feelings of isolation.

Much has been written about CityCenter, the $9-billion (yes, you read that right) development in the heart of the Las Vegas Strip that opened in late 2009. What is confusing, however, is that CityCenter is not a hotel, specifically, but rather a collection of them, along with other facilities. Aria Las Vegas (the only one with a casino), Mandarin Oriental, and Vdara are the hotels, each listed separately in this chapter; the Crystals mall is reviewed in chapter 6. Another hotel, The Harmon, was due to open in 2011, but will probably be torn down due to construction irregularities.

The complex features its own monorail, connecting Monte Carlo to the south and Bellagio to the north, and has multiple parking garages and valets. Although it is considered to be the largest privately funded construction project in history, the developers went out of their way to remain as green as possible, with heavy reuse of material (93% of the construction waste was recycled), energy-saving devices (radiant cooling, sunshades over the windows), and even the world's first fleet of natural gas–powered limousines.

3950 Las Vegas Blvd. S. (at Hacienda Ave.), Las Vegas, NV 89119. www.mandalaybay.com. (*) **877/632-7800** or 702/632-7108. Fax 702/632-7228. 3,309 units (excluding THEhotel). $99 and up double; $149 and up suite; $149 and up House of Blues Signature rooms. Resort fee $25. Extra person $30. Children 14 and under free in parent's room. AE, DC, DISC, MC, V. Free self- and valet parking. **Amenities:** 22 restaurants; aquarium; casino; concierge; 12,000-seat events center; executive-level rooms; health club; Jacuzzi; 1,700-seat performing-arts theater; 4 outdoor pools w/lazy river and wave pool; room service; sauna; spa; watersports equipment/rentals. *In room:* A/C, TV w/pay movies, hair dryer, high-speed Internet, minibar.

MGM Grand Hotel & Casino ★★   The biggest hotel in Vegas, with more than 5,000 rooms, has always felt like it was in search of a personality. It started as a family-friendly destination complete with a Wizard of Oz theme and an amusement park out back, then tried for a more upscale approach with fancy restaurants and high-end nightclubs. For a time it even attempted to be a solid middle-market offering with a little something for all tastes.

A 2012 makeover attempted to put more of a focus on the proceedings by revamping huge swaths of the hotel, including all of the rooms in the main towers. Once-bland accommodations are now sexy stunners with bold accents of green or magenta making the visuals pop, floor-to-ceiling padded headboards and mirrors making them seem bigger than they are, and lots of new technology such as 40-inch flatscreen televisions and a connectivity center, making them feel cutting edge.

Although this style makes up the bulk of the offerings, there are other layouts, including the smaller but equally modern West Wing rooms; the condominium-style units in the Signature towers out back; and the dramatic, multilevel Skylofts, which come with their own 24-hour butler.

Other changes affect the casino, lobby, shopping areas, and many of the hotel's nightlife and entertainment offerings, including the removal of the beloved Lion Habitat (don't worry, the lions are fine and living in comfort just outside Las Vegas). While most of these changes are mainly cosmetic, they have certainly have bumped up the look and feel of the now 20-year-old hotel. Sure, it may not be as visually arresting as The Cosmopolitan or Aria, but it is definitely an improvement over what had become a fairly pedestrian experience.

MGM houses a prestigious assemblage of dining rooms, among them **Joël Robuchon**'s two sterling entries and **Emeril's New Orleans Fish House.** These, and other on-site restaurants, are reviewed in chapter 5.

As befits a behemoth of this size, there's an appropriately gigantic casino (p. 237). The show is **KÀ,** a dazzling offering from Cirque du Soleil. Plus, there are other entertainment, bar, and club offerings; a headliner showroom; and a larger events arena that hosts sporting events and bigger concerts. See chapter 7 for details on all the nightlife options.

A mammoth bronze lion guards the entrance to the MGM Grand Hotel & Casino.

The MGM Grand's **Grand Spa** is a Zen-Asian minimalist wonder, all natural stone and aged wood (a full litany of services is offered); the fitness center is state of the art, in case you need to work off a few buffet pounds. The swimming pool area is a rousing success. The 6½ acres of landscaped grounds feature five pools, including the longest lazy river in town (though we wish portions of it weren't closed off for nonsummer months). The "pool club"—sort of like a nightclub, but during the day—called Wet Republic only further pushes kids out of the picture.

3799 Las Vegas Blvd. S. (at Tropicana Ave.), Las Vegas, NV 89109. www.mgmgrand.com. © **800/ 929-1111** or 702/891-7777. Fax 702/891-1030. 5,034 units. $99 and up double; $159 and up suite. Resort free $25. Extra person $35. Children 13 and under stay free in parent's room. AE, DC, DISC, MC, V. Free self- and valet parking. **Amenities:** 21 restaurants; nightclub; cabaret theater; casino; concierge; events arena; executive-level rooms; large health club; Jacuzzi; 5 outdoor pools w/lazy river; room service; salon; shopping arcade; spa; 2 wedding chapels. In room: A/C, TV w/pay movies, hair dryer, high-speed Internet.

Monte Carlo Resort & Casino ★

Overshadowed by its high-profile, more luxe-intensive neighbors, Monte Carlo has staked a claim as a middle-of-the-road alternative for Vegas lodging. Once you get past the Corinthian colonnades, triumphal arches, and big and busy statuary outside, the inside is a fairly sedate affair, with little in the way of wow-worthy moments. Everything is fairly beige, both in terms of color scheme and ambience. We love that the guest rooms are accessible without going through the casino, but we don't really love the rooms themselves, as they are smaller than what we've grown accustomed to, especially in terms of bathroom square footage. The pool area, once the very last word in local pool fun, is now put to shame by better versions (including superior lazy rivers) at Mandalay Bay and the MGM Grand. It does have a number of child-/family-/budget-friendly restaurants.

The top level operates as a mini–boutique hotel called Hotel 32. A free limo ride whisks you to a greeter, who puts you in your private elevator straight to the top and checks you into your handsome and masculine room or suite, which comes with some pretty swish details. Don't miss the club room with the free snacks. You're going to pay much more for these perks, but it might work out to be a better deal for luxury than the Four Seasons, so comparison shop.

Among the many restaurant options, **Diablo's Cantina, The Pub, Monte Carlo Buffet,** and **Andre's** are described in chapter 5; the casino is covered in chapter 8; and the show starring the wild and wacky **Blue Man Group** is reviewed in chapter 7.

3770 Las Vegas Blvd. S. (btw. Flamingo Rd. and Tropicana Ave.), Las Vegas, NV 89109. www. montecarlo.com. *C* **800/311-8999** or 702/730-7777. 3,002 units. $99 and up double; $145 and up suite. Daily resort fee $20. Extra person $30. No discount for children. AE, DC, DISC, MC, V. Free self- and valet parking. **Amenities:** 8 restaurants; food court; casino; concierge; executive-level rooms; fitness center; Jacuzzi; outdoor pool w/wave pool and lazy river; room service; showroom; spa; watersports equipment/rentals; wedding chapel. *In room:* A/C, TV w/pay movies, hair dryer, high-speed Internet.

New York–New York Hotel & Casino ★★   Isn't this exactly the kind of hotel you think about—or dream about or fear—when you think "Las Vegas?" There it is; a jumbled pile mock-up of the venerable Manhattan skyline—the Empire State Building, the Chrysler Building, the Public Library—all crammed together, along with the 150-foot Statue of Liberty and Ellis Island, all built to approximately one-third scale. And as if that weren't enough, they threw in a roller coaster running around the outside and into the hotel and casino itself.

Inside is a different story these days. Once as highly themed as the outside, the main casino space has gotten a makeover that has removed much of the New York detail. Gone are the Big Apple Bar and Central Park–themed gaming areas, replaced by a sleekly modern decor that, while pretty, is nowhere near as entertaining. The replica of Greenwich Village, down to the cobblestones, the man-hole covers, the tenement-style buildings, and the graffiti, remains, and you'll still find enough of the Gotham silliness elsewhere to probably evoke a smile or three, but dizzy laughter over the sheer spectacle is a thing of the past.

A suite in the Monte Carlo's top-level Hotel 32.

Rooms are housed in different towers, each with a New York–inspired name. The place is so massive and mazelike that finding your way to your room can take a while. There are 64 different layouts for the rooms, which have moved them ever farther from the original Deco-inspired decor to something bland, albeit comfortable, and though the bathrooms are small, they are pleasantly decorated. There can be a loooonnnggg walk from the elevators, so if you have ambulatory issues, you had best mention this while booking. Light sleepers should request a room away from the roller coaster. The health club and spa are nice but nothing to write home about, and the mediocre pool is right next to the parking structure.

In addition to a particularly good food court and several restaurants, there are some festive bars, clubs, and activities offered, including **The Bar at Times Square** (p. 198); the aforementioned **Roller Coaster** (p. 60); and the topless and adults-only Cirque du Soleil production *Zumanity,* which we think is improving but not the best that Cirque has to offer. Chapter 7 offers more on the hotel's nightlife.

3790 Las Vegas Blvd. S. (at Tropicana Ave.), Las Vegas, NV 89109. www.nynyhotelcasino.com. © **800/693-6763** or 702/740-6969. 2,024 units. $79 and up double. Daily resort fee $18. Extra person $30. No discount for children. AE, DC, DISC, MC, V. Free self- and valet parking. **Amenities:** 7 restaurants; food court; casino; executive-level rooms; fitness center; Jacuzzi; outdoor pool; room service; showroom; spa. *In room:* A/C, TV w/pay movies, hair dryer, high-speed Internet.

Vdara ★   This nongaming property is a condominium-hotel, designed to be a residential facility first and tourist accommodations second. Many of the units are owned by someone who then puts them into a rental pool when they are not in residence, allowing Average Joes like us the opportunity to see how folks who can afford places like this live. This is important because it may help to explain why Vdara feels so sedate and restrained when compared to the rest of the outrageously audacious CityCenter complex.

New York–New York replicates the Manhattan skyline.

Lobby bar at Vdara.

Most of the units are studios with a very small kitchenette and dining table and a combo living room/bedroom. The design scheme is sleekly modern, muted brown and gray with a few splashes of color, and all distinctly grown-up. Bathrooms are big, bright white affairs with all the comforts of home. One- and two-bedroom units are also available with full kitchens and separate living spaces if you need more room to stretch out.

On-site there is a small shop for groceries (make your own picnic!) and a lobby bar plus a pool and spa, but there is nary a restaurant, slot machine, showroom, or white tiger in sight. Luckily the hotel is connected via a very long walkway to Bellagio next door, and the CityCenter monorail will take you to the heart of the development if you get bored. And quite frankly, you just might. Don't get us wrong, it's all very nice and some people may appreciate the anti-Vegas feeling (and it's certainly a good place for families), but if you're looking for Vegas-style excitement you may want to look elsewhere.

One fun fact: This is the hotel that got a lot of press for its **"Death Ray,"** a strange phenomenon wherein the sunlight would bounce off the glass facade of the building and fry things on the pool deck (there were reports of melted plastic and singed hair). It was all completely overblown and steps were taken to fix whatever issues did exist. But it's still fun to say "Death Ray!"

2600 W. Harmon Ave., Las Vegas, NV 89109. www.vdara.com. © **866/745-7767** or 702/590-2767. 1,500 units. $159 and up double; $299 and up suite. Resort fee $25. Extra person $35. No discount for children. AE, DC, DISC, MC, V. Free valet parking; no self-parking. **Amenities:** Restaurant; concierge; executive-level rooms; health club; heated outdoor pool; room service; spa. *In room:* A/C, TV w/pay movies, hair dryer, high-speed Internet, kitchen or kitchenette, minibar.

Moderate

Excalibur ★ ☺ One of the largest resort hotels in the world, Excalibur is a gleaming white, turreted castle complete with moat, drawbridge, battlements, and lofty towers. And it's huger than huge. To heck with quiet good taste; kitsch is cool. And it's becoming harder and harder to find in a town that once wore tacky proudly. If your soul is secretly thrilled by overblown fantasy locations—or if you just want a pretty good budget option on the Strip—the Excalibur is still here for you.

FAMILY-FRIENDLY hotels

We've said it before, and we'll say it again: Vegas is simply not a good place to bring your kids. Most of the major hotels have backed away from being perceived as places for families, no longer offering babysitting, much less exciting children's activities. Further, fewer hotels offer discounts for children staying in a parent's room, and many others have lowered the age for children who can stay for free.

In addition to the suggestions below, you might consider choosing a non-casino hotel, particularly a reliable chain, and a place with kitchenettes.

○ **Circus Circus Hotel & Casino** (p. 289) Centrally located on the Strip, this is our first choice if you're traveling with the kids. The hotel's mezzanine level offers ongoing circus acts daily from 11am to midnight, dozens of carnival games, and an arcade. And behind the hotel is a full amusement park.

○ **Excalibur** (p. 263) Though the sword-and-sorcery theme has been considerably toned down, Excalibur features an entire floor of midway games and a large video-game arcade. It also has some child-oriented eateries and shows, but there's a heavily promoted male-stripper show, too, so it's not perfect.

○ **Four Seasons** (p. 253) For free goodies, service, and general child pampering, the costly Four Seasons is probably worth the dough. Your kids will be spoiled!

○ **Mandalay Bay** (p. 257) Mandalay Bay certainly looks grown up, but it has a number of factors that make it family-friendly: good-size rooms, to start, which you do not have to cross a casino to access; a variety of restaurants; a big ol' shark attraction; and, best of all, the swimming area—wave pool, sandy beach, lazy river, lots of other pools—fun in the Vegas sun!

○ **The Orleans** (p. 305) Considered a "local" hotel, its proximity to the Strip makes it a viable alternative, especially for families seeking to take advantage of its plus-size pool area, kid's activity area, bowling, and movie theaters.

○ **Stratosphere Casino Hotel** (p. 288) For families looking for reasonably priced, if not particularly exciting, digs, this is a good choice. Plus, it's not in the middle of the Strip action, so you and your kids can avoid that. Thus far, it's not moving in the "adult entertainment" direction, and it has thrill rides at the top.

WHERE TO STAY | **South Strip**

9

Some of the original "family-friendly" elements have been stripped out—gone is the animatronic dragon and wizard show out front, although the carnival-style midway and the SpongeBob SquarePants–themed virtual reality ride remain. It's really too bad because, without the excess, this is just another hotel—a mighty big and chaotic hotel, thanks to a sprawling casino full of families and small-time gamblers which is located smack-dab in the middle of everything, including, naturally, the path between you and the elevators to your room. Parents should be warned that on the way to the SpongeBob ride you may see posters for the male-stripper act *Thunder from Down Under,* also in residence at the hotel.

Newer "widescreen" rooms only slightly reflect the Olde English theme and feature the brown suede headboards that are all the rage, flatscreen TVs, spiffed-up bathrooms with new marble fixtures, and nice wallpaper. Older "standard" rooms are about as motel basic as they come. Guests who have stayed in Tower 2 have complained about the noise from the roller coaster across the street at New York–New York (it runs till 11pm, so early birds should probably ask to be put in a different part of the hotel). Frankly, we prefer stopping in for a visit rather than actually settling here, but if budget is a major concern we'd understand if you felt differently.

The second floor holds the Medieval Village, where several of Excalibur's restaurants and shops are peppered along winding streets and alleyways, a sort of permanent Renaissance Faire, which could be reason enough to stay away (or to come). Up here you can access the enclosed, air-conditioned, moving sidewalk that connects with the Luxor. The pool area has some nice landscaping, fancy cabanas,

Medieval architecture rules the realm at Excalibur.

and the like. There are plenty of restaurants, including a branch of the popular Buca di Beppo, plus the **Roundtable Buffet, Lynyrd Skynyrd Beer & BBQ,** and **Dick's Last Resort,** all reviewed in chapter 5. The **Tournament of Kings** and *Thunder From Down Under* are covered in chapter 7, and there's a very loud, claustrophobic casino discussed in chapter 8.

3850 Las Vegas Blvd. S. (at Tropicana Ave.), Las Vegas, NV 89109 www.excalibur.com. ✆ **800/937-7777** or 702/597-7700. 4,008 units. $59 and up double. Daily resort fee $15. Extra person $20. No discount for children. AE, DC, DISC, MC, V. Free self- and valet parking. **Amenities:** 5 restaurants; buffet; food court; casino; concierge; outdoor pools; room service; showrooms; wedding chapel. *In room:* A/C, TV w/pay movies, hair dryer, high-speed Internet.

Pet-Friendly Hotels

Up until recently, if you wanted to bring Fido or Fluffy to Vegas with you, your options on lodging were fairly limited, with only one major hotel on the Strip allowing pets (the Four Seasons). Now, more hotels are jumping on the pet-friendly bandwagon, including all of the Caesars Entertainment properties. Their popular PetStay program allows dogs up to 50 pounds to get a taste of Sin City. There are fees associated, of course ($25–$40), and there are plenty of restrictions, but you get things like food and water dishes, recommended dog walking routes, and more. The program is good at Caesars Palace, Paris Las Vegas, Planet Hollywood, Harrah's, the Flamingo, Bally's, Rio Suites, and Imperial Palace. For more information on *PetStay,* check out www.caesars.com/petstay. You can also contact the Las Vegas Convention and Visitors Authority (✆ **877/ 847-4858;** www.visitlasvegas.com) for information on other pet-friendly accommodations in town.

Luxor Las Vegas ★★   Kitsch worshipers were dealt a blow when the people behind this hotel came to the inexplicable decision to eliminate most of the Egypt theme from the inside of it, casting aside identity in favor of generic luxury. Obviously, they can't get rid of certain elements—the main hotel is, after all, a 30-story onyx-hued pyramid, complete with a really tall 315,000-watt light beam at the top. (Luxor says that's because the Egyptians believed their souls would travel up to heaven in a beam of light. We think it's really because it gives them something to brag about: "The most powerful beam on earth!") Replicas of Cleopatra's Needle and the Sphinx still dominate the exterior, and touches of Egypt remain in the lobby and main entrance (you figure out what to do with those three-story-high statues of Ramses). But other than that, virtually every other trace of the land of the Pharaohs is gone. And some magic is now gone from Vegas. Now guests will be attracted only by the generally good prices, not by the giddy fun the theme produced.

But they can't take away fundamentals, and so staying in the pyramid part means you get to ride the 39-degree high-speed inclinators—that's what an elevator is when it works inside a pyramid. Really, they are part conveyance, part thrill ride—check out that jolt when they come to a halt. Rooms are pretty basic in the pyramid, although there were rumors of a remodeling at press time, so by the time you visit they could be a bit nicer. Marvelous views are offered through the slanted windows (the higher up, the better, of course), but the bathrooms are shower only, no tubs. Furnishing and bathrooms are better in the Tower rooms, including deep tubs.

Among the many restaurants are the margarita heaven of **Tacos & Tequila** and the archaeological dig–themed **MORE, The Buffet at Luxor,** both covered in chapter 5. **Criss Angel:** *Believe* pairs the popular exotic magician with the spectacle of Cirque du Soleil (p. 183). Comedian Carrot Top is also in residency. Enormous nightclub **LAX** (p. 203) is state of the art, and attracting a fashionable crowd. Two notable attractions here are **Titanic: The Exhibition** (p. 61) and **Bodies . . . The Exhibition** (p. 58).

The Luxor atrium is the largest of its kind in the world.

Suite, Tropicana Las Vegas.

3900 Las Vegas Blvd. S. (btw. Reno and Hacienda aves.), Las Vegas, NV 81119. www.luxor.com.
© **888/777-0188** or 702/262-4000. 4,400 units. $69 and up double; $150 and up whirlpool suite;
$249–$800 other suites. Resort fee $18. Extra person $30. No discount for kids. AE, DC, DISC,
MC, V. Free self- and valet parking. **Amenities:** 5 restaurants; buffet; food court; nightclub;
casino; concierge; executive-level rooms; health club; 5 outdoor pools; room service; showrooms; spa. *In room:* A/C, TV w/pay movies, hair dryer, high-speed Internet.

Tropicana Las Vegas ★★ For years we've been telling you about major
potential changes at the Tropicana, and for years we have been made to look the
fools when absolutely nothing changed. But now everything has changed—and
we mean that almost literally. New owners took the place out of bankruptcy and
immediately dumped more than $100 million into the property, revamping rooms,
the casino, restaurants, the exterior, the pool area, the convention center, and
more. Just about the only thing not getting a makeover is the parking structure.

Gone is the faded and dusty Caribbean/tropical theme, replaced with a bright,
white-and-orange South Beach/tropical theme. New carpets, marble, gaming tables,
and slots liven up the casino by about a million percent with a sunny vibe (think
white marble and plantation shutter–clad support columns). And that continues
upstairs, where all the rooms were basically stripped to the cement and redone with
sandy rattan and bamboo furnishings, crisp white linens, bright orange chaise
longues or sofas, white plantation shutters on the windows, and even a white-framed
42-inch TV. Bathrooms were similarly updated, and although they couldn't make
them any bigger, they certainly are more modern and comfortable.

There are a few restaurants, bars, and a nightclub. The revised Tiffany
Showroom no longer has the classic *Folies Bergere* (sad!), but does still serve up
variety-style entertainment. As mentioned, the already stunning pool area also
got a face-lift, changing it from a tropical paradise into a Miami party spot, but
it's still one of the nicest in town. The casino is covered in chapter

We made fools of ourselves for a long time waiting for the changes at this
hotel. It was totally worth it.

3801 Las Vegas Blvd. S. (at Tropicana Ave.), Las Vegas, NV 89109. www.troplv.com. © **888/826-
8767** or 702/739-2222. 1,375 units. $99 and up double. Resort fee $15. Extra person $25. No
discount for kids. AE, DC, DISC, MC, V. Free self- and valet parking. **Amenities:** 3 restaurants;
food court; casino; executive-level rooms; health club; 3 outdoor pools; showroom; wedding
chapel. *In room:* A/C, TV w/pay movies, hair dryer, high-speed Internet, minibar.

MID-STRIP

The middle of the Strip is from Harmon Avenue to Spring Mountain/Sands Road and features many of the grand Vegas gambling destinations you have seen in the movies.

Best for: People without transportation who want to be able to walk to everything they want to see.

Drawbacks: Peak times bring out massive crowds and higher prices.

Very Expensive

Bellagio ★★★   Over the last few years, Bellagio has been walking a bit of a tightrope, attempting to retain the elegant features and ambience that established it as the most luxurious hotel in Las Vegas, while trying to update and modernize it to compete with the more contemporary resorts that have come along to challenge its dominance in the high-end market. That they have navigated the tightrope with ease is worthy of applause.

Most of the changes have been subtle—a new nightclub here; a new restaurant there—but the biggest update has been to the rooms in the main tower, which were completely revamped in 2011. These previously staid accommodations are now gorgeously rendered, modern masterpieces with funky retro-mod furnishings; bold purple, green, and golden design schemes; high-tech touches including a connectivity station for computers and devices of all kinds; and marble lined bathrooms that are big enough to share and luxurious enough that you'll never want to leave.

Rooms in the Spa Tower are not quite as eye-catching but are still insanely comfortable in all the ways you would expect them to be.

The things that drew crowds and appreciative goggling are still there: the 8-acre lake in front with a dazzling choreographed water-ballet extravaganza (p. 66); an eye-popping Dale Chihuly blown-glass flower sculpture on the lobby ceiling (the largest of its kind in the world); an art gallery (p. 61); and a downright lovely conservatory (p. 66), complete with brightly colored flowers and plants, changed every few months to go with the season (the holiday and Chinese New Year exhibits are favorites).

Dale Chihuly's *Fioro di Como* glass sculpture adorns the ceiling of Bellagio's lobby.

There are also still a host of fine restaurants including **Picasso, Le Cirque, Circo, Michael Mina, Sensi,** and **Olives,** plus the **Bellagio Buffet,** all of which are reviewed in chapter 5; upscale bars and clubs like **Petrossian, The Bank,** and **Hyde Bellagio** (reviewed in chapter 7); the stunning Cirque du Soleil show **O** (p. 181); a classically designed casino with plenty of fine fabrics, wood, and marble (p. 238); and **Via Bellagio,** a high-end shopping gallery (p. 167).

On the downside, you still can't avoid a walk through the casino to get

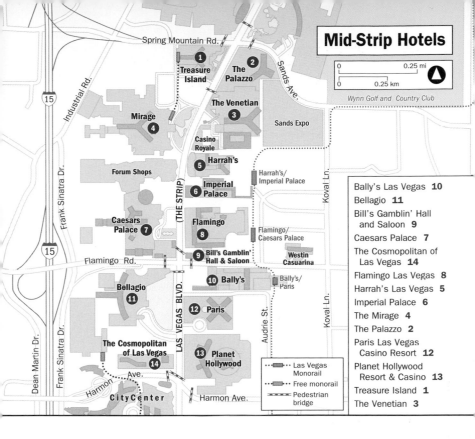

just about anywhere and there are extra charges galore, such as a pricey resort fee and another one for poolside cabanas. If you wish to splurge for the latter, you'll find them next to no fewer than six swimming pools set in a neoclassical Roman garden with flowered, trellised archways, and a fitness center and 40,000-square-foot spa (p. 93), all designed to pamper you into submission.

3600 Las Vegas Blvd. S. (at the corner of Flamingo Rd.), Las Vegas, NV 89109. www.bellagio.com. ℂ **888/987-6667** or 702/693-7111. 3,933 units. Resort fee $25. $169 and up double; $450 and up suite. Extra person $35. No discount for children. AE, DC, DISC, MC, V. Free self- and valet parking. **Amenities:** 20 restaurants; nightclub; casino; concierge; executive-level rooms; large health club; 6 outdoor pools; room service; showrooms; spa; wedding chapel. *In room:* A/C, TV w/pay movies, hair dryer, high-speed Internet.

Caesars Palace ★★ Since 1966, Caesars has stood simultaneously as the ultimate in Vegas luxury and the nadir (or pinnacle, depending on your values) of Las Vegas cheese. It's the most Vegas-style hotel you'll find, covering all the bases, from the tacky fabulous schmaltz of the recent past (Roman colonnades, pillars, and statues) to the current trend in high-end luxury (sleekly designed, high-tech rooms). It's what Vegas ought to be.

Accommodations occupy five towers. The older Roman and Forum Tower rooms are comparatively basic, although some still have the Roman-style baths in the room (as opposed to in the bathroom). Decor is simple but plush, and they

The neoclassical pool area at Bellagio was inspired by the one at Hearst Castle in San Simeon, California.

have a raft of amenities including flat-panel TVs, minibars (in some rooms), motorized drapes, and the like. The Palace Tower ups the ante with more floor space, a small sitting area, bigger bathrooms, spa tubs, and more. The newest Augustus and Octavius towers have the biggest rooms with ultraluxe furnishings and design—all sleek lines and muted colors with big floor-to-ceiling windows offering some cool views if you get the right room. They have their own check-in and valet entrance off of Flamingo, plus some newfangled gimmickry in an online application that allows you to do things like order room service or have your car pulled up at the valet through your computer or mobile device.

A sixth tower has been converted into a boutique hotel within the hotel under the Nobu brand name, after the Japanese restaurant group. It has a subtle Asian theme, its own check-in, and amenities including room service from a new branch of Nobu in the casino.

Caesars has a well-deserved reputation for superior in-house restaurants. The meat-lover's paradise **Old Homestead Steakhouse,** the Bobby Flay brainchild **Mesa Grill,** the casual **munchbar,** and more are described in chapter 5.

Other on-site amenities include the Roman-themed shopping experience of **The Forum Shops** (p. 162); the huge and hugely popular nightclub **PURE** (p. 205) and several other bars and lounges; the diving respite of the **Qua Baths** (p. 93); a fully stocked fitness center; an opulent, rambling casino (p. 238); and a 4,000-seat showroom, home to **Céline Dion, Elton John, Shania Twain,** and others (see chapter 7).

Notable is the **Garden of the Gods** pool area, a tasteful, undeniably Caesaresque masterpiece. With eight pools on three levels, there is plenty of space for frolicking in the hot sun. Each has the classic granite columns and intricately carved sculptures that you'd expect from an area that names each of its pools after Roman deities or words that lend context to its unique mission (Fortuna has swim-up blackjack, Bacchus is for VIP guests only, and Apollo gets the most sun of any of them).

3570 Las Vegas Blvd. S. (just north of Flamingo Rd.), Las Vegas, NV 89109. www.caesarspalace. com. © **877/427-7243** or 702/731-7110. 3,960 units. $129 and up double; $299 and up suite. No resort fee. Extra person $30. No discount for children. AE, DC, DISC, MC, V. Free self- and valet parking. **Amenities:** 26 restaurants; nightclub; casino; concierge; executive-level rooms; health club; 8 outdoor pools; room service; spa; 3 wedding chapels. *In room:* A/C, TV w/pay movies, hair dryer, minibar (in some rooms), high-speed Internet (for a fee).

The Cosmopolitan of Las Vegas ★★★ Due to economic turbulence, it's likely that this is the last major megaresort to open on the Las Vegas Strip for quite some time. If that's the case, they really went out on a high note. The Cosmo is audacious, bold, stunningly visual, and one of the most interesting hotels in Vegas, or anywhere else for that matter.

The interior design was envisioned as an art project—a series of curated experiences creating a dramatic whole. The big spectacles will get your attention first: the three-story chandelier with a multilevel bar inside; the video panels on the lobby columns; the six-foot-tall sculptures of women's pumps in random places. But take time to notice the smaller details: the restored cigarette machines that dispense packs of art instead of smokes; the banquettes in the lobby of tufted velvet with a working, rotary-style phone; the wall of record album covers leading to the "hidden" pizza place. It's like staying in a contemporary art museum with slot machines.

The hotel's small footprint required a vertical design that is much more easily navigable than most Strip behemoths. Parking is under the hotel, with the casino and multiple bars on the first floor, shopping and some casual restaurants on the second, fine dining on the third, and one of the pools and a nightclub on the fourth and fifth floors respectively.

Rooms are in two towers and all are big, with at least 600 square feet of upscale amenities including flatscreen televisions; a small kitchenette with a minibar, sink, and microwave (at the very least); huge bathrooms, some with Japanese soaking tubs; and all of the nice touches you would expect. There are even some touches you wouldn't expect, like actual books scattered about the room. You can pick them up and read them and everything! About two-thirds of the rooms also come with terraces—gorgeous outdoor patios with comfy furnishings that offer some stunning views of the city from the higher floors.

Reproductions of classical Roman statues are situated throughout Caesars Palace.

The Atlantis Fountain Show in The Forum Shops at Caesars Palace.

The hotel has over a dozen restaurants, many of which are reviewed in chapter 5; a major nightclub, **Marquee** (p. 204); three pools, a spa, and a gym; a 100,000-square-foot **casino** (p. 238); and an outdoor performance venue for concerts.

It is worth noting that the bold design, big crowds, and loud music at every turn can be a bit overwhelming. People who are looking for a sedate Vegas getaway should avoid this place at all costs. But those who want to see what the future of Las Vegas looks like should head here. It may be the last hotel for a while, but it may very well also be the best.

By the way, that "hidden" pizza place? It's down an unmarked hallway on the third floor between the Jaleo and Blue Ribbon Sushi restaurants. Don't tell them we told you.

3708 Las Vegas Blvd. S., Las Vegas, NV 89109. www.cosmopolitanlasvegas.com. ℂ **877/551-7778** or 702/698-7000. Fax 702/698-7007. 2,995 units. $159 and up double. No resort fee. Extra person $30. Children under 17 stay free in parent's room. AE, DC, DISC, MC, V. Free self- and valet parking. **Amenities:** 12 restaurants; buffet; casino; concierge; executive-level rooms; health club; heated outdoor pools; room service; spa. *In room:* A/C, TV w/pay movies, hair dryer, high-speed Internet (for a fee), kitchenette, minibar.

The Palazzo ★★   The Palazzo is an expansion of the impressive Venetian, but one that functions as a separate hotel, with its own massive grand lobby, own restaurants, and own casino. The rooms are virtually identical to its sister hotel but that's a good thing, really—they are some of the nicest in town. Each is a "suite"—a bedroom plus a sunken living room, with a sectional couch perfect for crashing and channel surfing. Three flatscreen TVs (two quite big, one smaller one badly positioned in the bathroom), a particularly squishy white bed with superior linens and pillows, remote-control curtain and shades, and a deep bathtub in a generously sized, gleaming bathroom add up to the kind of accommodations that are hard to leave. Stay here only if what you mostly wanted to see in the city is your fabulous hotel room.

The Chandelier at the Cosmopolitan.

Guest room at The Palazzo.

Should you leave, there are 14 restaurants, including **Table 10** and **Lagasse's Stadium,** both from celebrity chef Emeril, and **FIRST Food & Bar** and **Public House,** all of which are covered in chapter 5. The high-end shopping area (covered in chapter 6) is anchored by Barneys New York (p. 171). The excellent Canyon Ranch spa and health club (p. 93) will set you back an additional $35 a day.

3325 Las Vegas Blvd. S., Las Vegas, NV 89109. www.palazzo.com. (C) **877/883-6423** or 702/414-4100. 4,027 units. $199 and up double; $229 and up suite. Resort fee $20. Extra person $35. Children 12 and under stay free in parent's room. AE, DC, DISC, MC, V. Free self- and valet parking. **Amenities:** 16 restaurants; casino; concierge; executive-level rooms; health club and spa shared w/Venetian; nightclubs; 7 outdoor pools shared w/Venetian; room service; showroom. *In room:* A/C, TV w/pay movies, fax, fridge (on request), hair dryer, high-speed Internet.

Paris Las Vegas Casino Resort ★ *Sacre bleu!* The City of Light comes to Sin City in this, one of the few theme-run-amok hotels left to its giddy devices. Stay here if you came to Vegas for the silly fantasy. The outside reproduces various Parisian landmarks (amusing anyone familiar with Paris, as the Hotel de Ville is crammed on top of the Louvre), complete with a half-scale perfect replica of the Eiffel Tower. The interior puts you in the middle of a dollhouse version of the city. You can stroll down a mini Rue de la Paix, ride an elevator to the top of the Eiffel Tower, stop at an overpriced bakery for a baguette, and have your photo taken near several very nice fountains.

Quel dommage, this attention to detail does not extend to the rooms, which are nice enough but uninteresting, with furniture that only hints at mock French Regency. Bathrooms are small but pretty, with deep tubs. If you don't mind the upgraded price, go for the newer Red rooms on the upper floors, done in a modern French-bordello theme complete with suede sofas that look like puckered lips. Try to get a Strip-facing room so that you can see Bellagio's fountains across the street; note also that north-facing rooms give you nice Peeping Tom views right into neighboring Bally's. The monorail has a stop out back, which adds to the convenience factor. Overall, not a bad place to stay, but a great place to visit—*quel hoot!*

boutique **HOTELS**

In most cities, a "boutique" hotel is one that offers some sort of unique experience in a smaller package than the bigger chain properties. That's true in Vegas as well, but on a significantly larger scale. Whereas most true boutique hotels have only a few dozen rooms at most, in Vegas having a few hundred still puts you on the smaller end of the size scale. And because most of the major hotels are unique experiences in and of themselves (Paris! Venice!), the boutique properties have to try a little harder to stand out.

Here a few of the more notable entries in the genre, each offering a one-of-a-kind feeling in a much smaller package.

Rumor Las Vegas, 455 E. Harmon Ave. (✆ **877/997-8667** or 702/369-5400; www.rumorvegas.com), is a 150-room property directly across the street from the Hard Rock. It's done in a Hollywood-hip style, with lots of modern and artistic flourishes (witness the big pewter pig in the lobby) and bold splashes of color against sleek white backgrounds. The overall effect is, perhaps, trying a bit too hard to be as cool as their next-door neighbor, but it's still fun if you don't take it too seriously. Rooms are big and well equipped, there's a fun pool and courtyard complete with hammocks for lazing about, and one on-site restaurant. Beware the noise levels though—the hotel is located directly under the approach for one of McCarran International Airport's main runways.

Sister property **The Artisan Hotel,** 1501 W. Sahara Ave. (✆ **800/554-4092** or 702/214-4000; www.artisanhotel.com), is much more in line with the boutique concept in terms of size, offering 64 rooms all done in a deliriously over-the-top art collection theme. Paintings and sculptures cover every square inch of the joint and each room features its own reproductions of masterworks from artists like Cezanne, Da Vinci, van Gogh, and others. It's gaudy and ostentatious, but we don't mean that in a bad way (really!). A small but gorgeous pool has regular parties and the on-site restaurant and lounge are popular among the hipster

set. Noise can also be an issue here because of its stone's throw proximity to I-15.

Ravella, 1610 Lake Las Vegas Pkwy., Henderson (✆ **888/810-0440** or 702/567-4700; www.ravellavegas.com), is the new name for the hotel that used to be one of our favorites, the Ritz-Carlton. Located about 17 miles east of the Strip at the scenic Lake Las Vegas complex, the hotel is still just as beautiful as it was when it had a more famous name. Many of the 370 rooms are on a replica of the Ponte Vecchio Bridge in Italy, jutting out over the lake, and the rest of the property is peaceful and luxurious. There is an on-site restaurant and more just steps away in the adjacent MonteLago Village area, plus you have tons of recreation opportunities from swimming to hiking and beyond. It's more of a luxury resort than a true boutique hotel, but the smaller size and unique setting make it worth knowing about, regardless of what category you want to put it in.

Paris Las Vegas features re-creations of various Parisian landmarks.

The hotel has eight more-or-less French-themed restaurants, including the highly lauded **Le Village Buffet,** the **Eiffel Tower Restaurant** (located guess where), the **Sugar Factory,** and bistro **Mon Ami Gabi,** all of which are covered in chapter 5. Celebrity chef and professional yeller Gordon Ramsay will have a steakhouse here by the time you read this. The bread for all these restaurants is made fresh on-site at the bakery. You can buy delicious, if pricey, loaves of it at the bakery, and we have to admit, that's kinda fun. For entertainment (as if it wasn't entertaining enough already) there are lounges and a nightclub **Chateau** (p. 201), the **Eiffel Tower** attraction (p. 62), and the Broadway hit *Jersey Boys* in the Parisian opera house–themed showroom (p. 186).

3655 Las Vegas Blvd. S., Las Vegas, NV 89109. www.parislv.com. © **888/266-5687** or 702/946-7000. 2,916 units. $119 and up double; $350 and up suite. No resort fee. Extra person $30. No discount for children. AE, DC, DISC, MC. V. Free self- and valet parking. **Amenities:** 12 restaurants; buffet; casino; concierge; executive-level rooms; health club; outdoor pool; room service; showrooms; spa; 2 wedding chapels. *In room:* A/C, TV w/pay movies, hair dryer, high-speed Internet (for a fee).

The Venetian ★★   One of the most elaborate hotel spectacles in town, The Venetian falls squarely between an outright adult Disneyland experience and the luxury resort experience currently dominating the Vegas landscape. The hotel's exterior, which re-creates most of the top landmarks of Venice (the Campanile, a portion of St. Mark's Square, part of the Doge's Palace, a canal or two), ranks right up there with New York–New York as a must-see. As stern as we get about re-creations *not* being a substitute for the real thing, we have to admit that the attention to detail here is impressive indeed. Stone is aged for that weathered look, statues and tiles are exact copies of their Italian counterparts, security guards wear Venetian police uniforms—all that's missing is the smell from the canals, but we are happy to let that one slide.

Inside, it's more of the same, particularly in the lobby area and the entrance to the extraordinary shops, as ceilings are covered with hand-painted re-creations of Venetian art. With plenty of marble, soaring ceilings, and impressive pillars and archways, it's less kitschy than Caesars but more theme park than Bellagio.

Rooms in the main and Venezia towers are virtually identical to those in the sister hotel Palazzo, with a sleeping area and living room separated by a couple of steps and rich fabrics and woods adorning the surfaces. The marbled bathrooms are enormous wonders that will tempt you to spend your entire vacation just luxuriating in the tub.

Many celebrity chefs and high-profile restaurants are in residence at The Venetian. Reviews of **Bouchon** (by Thomas Keller, perhaps America's top chef), **Delmonico Steakhouse,** Mario Batali's **B&B Ristorante,** and **Pinot Brasserie** can be found in chapter 5. As of this writing the hotel's two showrooms are empty, but there will most likely be new productions in place by the time you read this; check the website for details. Other amusements include an elegant but confusingly laid-out casino (p. 240); the largest spa facility in town at the **Canyon Ranch SpaClub** (p. 93); and **The Grand Canal Shoppes** (p. 163), a mall complete with its own canal and singing gondoliers.

The Venetian has five pools and whirlpools, but its pool area is disappointingly sterile and bland. Pools are neoclassical (think rectangles with the corners lopped off), and the fourth-floor location probably means that more dense foliage is not going to be forthcoming. The Venezia Tower has a courtyard pool area that is amusing, but the water space is tiny.

3355 Las Vegas Blvd. S., Las Vegas, NV 89109. www.venetian.com. ✆ **888/283-6423** or 702/414-1000. 4,027 units. $169 and up double. Resort fee $20. Extra person $35. Children 12 and under stay free in parent's room. AE, DC, DISC, MC, V. Free self- and valet parking. **Amenities:** 18 restaurants; casino; concierge; executive-level rooms; health club; 6 outdoor pools; 24-hr. room service; extensive shopping arcade; showrooms; spa; wedding chapels. *In room:* A/C, TV w/pay movies, fax, hair dryer, high-speed Internet, minibar.

Elaborate frescoes decorate the soaring ceilings of The Venetian.

The lovely Wildlife Habitat at the Flamingo is home to a number of the resort's namesake birds.

Expensive

Flamingo Las Vegas ★   The Flamingo is the Strip's senior citizen, boasting a colorful history. It's changed a great deal since Bugsy Siegel opened his 105-room oasis "in the middle of nowhere" in 1946. It was so luxurious for its time that even the janitors wore tuxedos. (Hey, new Vegas? That's class.)

By Vegas standards, the old girl is Paleozoic, but not only is it hanging in there, some of the changes over the last few years have made us reconsider it entirely. Rushing headlong into the Dean Martin/Rat Pack retro vibe, the GO rooms are kicky candy modern, with hot pink (the signature Flamingo color) accent walls, hot pink lights in the bathroom where you can also find TV screens embedded in the mirror, candy-striped wallpaper, black-and-white photos of the Flamingo from its early days, squishy white beds with chocolate accents and vinyl padded headboards, huge flatscreens with HDTV, iPod docking stations, and more. They are ring-a-ding fun, and Dino would surely have approved.

The standard FAB rooms are not quite as fun but still very nice with comfy furnishings, some retro touches in the artwork, and a unique-for-Vegas touch with wood laminate floors. The latter make the rooms feel more spacious than they really are, but if you are visiting in the chillier months you may want to consider bringing your slippers.

The **Paradise Garden Buffet** (p. 149) is a decent choice. There are also several bars, a huge casino reviewed in chapter 8, and a showroom featuring **Donny and Marie** and **Nathan Burton,** both of which are reviewed in chapter 7. The monorail has a stop out back.

For those planning some leisure time outside the casino, the Flamingo's exceptional pool area, spa, and tennis courts are big draws. Five gorgeous swimming pools, two whirlpools, and water slides are located in a 15-acre Caribbean landscape amid lagoons, meandering streams, fountains, waterfalls, a rose garden, and islands of live flamingos. Ponds have ducks, swans, and koi, and a grove of 2,000 palms graces an expanse of lawn. Although the water can be a little chilly, kids should be able to spend hours in the pool area.

3555 Las Vegas Blvd. S. (btw. Sands Ave. and Flamingo Rd.), Las Vegas, NV 89109. © **800/732-2111** or 702/733 3111. www.flamingolv.com. 3,517 units. $85 and up double; $199 and up suite. No resort fee. Extra person $30. No discount for children. Timeshare suites available. AE, DC, DISC, MC, V. Free self- and valet parking. **Amenities:** 8 restaurants; buffet; food court; casino; executive-level rooms; health club; 5 outdoor pools; room service; showrooms; spa; wedding chapels. *In room:* A/C, TV w/pay movies, hair dryer, high-speed Internet (for a fee).

Harrah's Las Vegas ★   Here's another property that is doing its best to keep up with the pace in Vegas, to mixed success. Though parts of Harrah's benefited from a reworking of the place a few years ago, the rest of it evokes Old Las Vegas in the way the Riviera does—as in dark, dated, and claustrophobic. Still, there is much to like here, and occasional quite good rates might make the so-so bits worth overlooking. Certainly, it wants to be the fun and convivial place we wish more of Vegas were (instead of pretty much catering to high rollers and simply tolerating the rest of us with normal budgets).

The rooms are simple, with comfy mattresses and those white bed covers that are now more or less standard in most local hotels. No flash here, but they are reliable for what is ultimately a gamblers' hotel and provide guests with most of the necessary amenities.

A variety of restaurants include a steakhouse (with great views of the Strip), a fine Italian bistro, a Toby Keith–themed joint, featuring down-home cooking and nightly entertainment, a buffet (p. 149), the fantastic burgers at **KGB** (p. 121), and a food court for quick bites to eat. The casino (p. 239) has a fun, festive atmosphere. There's a showroom that used to be home to Sammy Davis, Jr., back in the day and is now showcasing **Mac King**'s wonderful comedy/magic act (p. 189) in the daytime and the long-running impersonator show *Legends in Concert* (p. 187) at night. **Carnaval Court** (p. 209) is a festive, palm-fringed shopping plaza where strolling entertainers perform.

It isn't flashy, but Harrah's has a friendly and fun vibe.

Harrah's has an Olympic-size swimming pool and sundeck area with a waterfall, trellised gardens, and a whirlpool. It's a pretty underwhelming pool by Vegas standards, but the adjacent health club and spa are nice enough.

3475 Las Vegas Blvd. S. (btw. Flamingo and Spring Mountain roads), Las Vegas, NV 89109. www. harrahslasvegas.com. (✆ **800/427-7247** or 702/369-5000. 2,526 units. $79 and up double; $199 and up suite. No resort fee. Extra person $30. No discount for children. AE, DC, DISC, MC, V. Free self- and valet parking. **Amenities:** 9 restaurants; buffet; casino; concierge; executive-level rooms; health club; outdoor pool; room service; showrooms; spa. *In room:* A/C, TV w/pay movies, hair dryer, high-speed Internet (for a fee).

The Mirage ★★ In many ways, The Mirage invented the concept of the modern Las Vegas resort. When it opened in 1989 there was nothing like it—a spectacle of excess that, though often repeated since, set a new standard for the outrageous fortune of Las Vegas. It has changed since then, of course—much more dark wood, Asian minimalist decor (at least in the casino)—but the wonder still exists and so does our love for the place.

Occupying 102 acres, The Mirage is fronted by more than a city block of cascading waterfalls and tropical foliage centering on a "volcano," which, after dark, erupts every hour, spewing fire 100 feet above the lagoons below. (That volcano cost $30 million, which is equal to the entire original construction cost for Caesars next door.) The lobby is dominated by a 53-foot, 20,000-gallon simulated coral-reef aquarium stocked with more than 1,000 colorful tropical fish. This gives you something to look at while waiting for check-in.

Next, you'll walk through the rainforest, which occupies a 90-foot domed atrium—a path meanders through palms, banana trees, waterfalls, and serene pools. If we must find a complaint with The Mirage, it's with the next bit, because you have to negotiate 8 miles (or so it seems) of casino mayhem to get to your room, the pool, food, or the outside world. It gets old fast.

Fresh room renovations have turned the lodgings into that white bed/bold, solid colors/70s-inspired look that everyone is sporting a variation of these days. Admittedly, it does fit the current mod look of the hotel. Plus, a pillow-top mattress and 42-inch LCD TVs do wonders for overcoming any decor concerns. The bathrooms remain small—though they have been given a solid makeover as

SO YOUR TRIP GOES swimmingly . . .

Part of the delight of the Vegas resort complexes is the gorgeous pools—what could be better for beating the summer heat? But there are pools and there are *pools*, so you'll need to keep several things in mind when searching for the right one for you.

During the winter, it's often too cold or windy to do much lounging, and even if the weather is amenable, the hotels often close part of their pool areas during winter and early spring. The pools also are not heated for the most part, but in fairness, they largely don't need to be.

Most hotel pools are shallow, chest-high at best, only about 3 feet deep in many spots (the hotels want you gambling, not swimming). Diving is impossible—not that a single pool allows it anyway.

And finally, during those hot days, be warned that sitting by pools next to heavily windowed buildings such as The Mirage and Treasure Island allows you to experience the same thing a bug does under a magnifying glass with a sun ray directed on it (see the Vdara "Death Ray" on p. 263). Regardless of time of year, be sure to slather on the sunscreen; there's a reason you see so many unhappy lobster-red people roaming the streets. Many pool areas don't offer much in the way of shade. On the other hand, if your tan line is important to you, head for Caesars, Mandalay Bay, Wynn Las Vegas, or Stratosphere (to name a few), all of which have topless sunbathing areas where you can toast even more flesh than at the other hotels.

At any of the pools, you can rent a cabana (which often includes a TV, special lounge chairs, and—even better—poolside service), but these should be reserved as far in advance as possible, and, with the exception of the Four Seasons' complimentary shaded lounging area, most cost a hefty fee. If you are staying at a chain hotel, you will most likely find an average pool, but if you want to spend some time at a better one, be aware that most of the casino-hotel pool attendants will ask to see your room key. If they are busy, you might be able to sneak in, or at least blend in with a group ahead of you.

When it comes to our favorites, we tend to throw our support to those that offer luxurious landscaping, plenty of places to lounge, multiple dipping options, and some shade for those times when the desert sun gets to be too much. This is a good description of the pools at both **The Mirage** and the **Flamingo,** which offer acres of veritable tropical paradises for you to enjoy. Ditto the renovated pool area at the **Tropicana,** serving up a sunny Miami Beach feeling among lush grounds.

If you're looking for something a little more adventurous, try the epic facility at **Mandalay Bay,** complete with a wave pool, a lazy-river ride, and good old-fashioned swimming holes along with a sandy beach. **MGM Grand** has a similar facility, although not as big and without the waves.

Partying is not confined to the night-clubs these days. Many of the hotels offer pool-club experiences (p. 88), but even when they aren't in full-on party mode, the pools at **Hard Rock** (sandy beaches, swim-up blackjack), the **Palms** (multilevel, high-end cabanas), **Aria Las Vegas** (acres of sexy modernity), and **The Cosmopolitan of Las Vegas** (not one but two party pools overlooking the Strip) serve up high-energy frolicking.

well—which won't bother you unless you have space issues and/or have seen the bigger ones elsewhere on the Strip. The **Mirage Cravings Buffet** is detailed in chapter 5. The Cirque production *LOVE* is reviewed in chapter 7, as is a show starring Terry Fator, winner of *America's Got Talent.* The Mirage has one of our favorite casinos (p. 208) and some excellent nightclubs and bars (see chapter 7).

Out back is the pool, one of the nicest in Vegas, with a quarter-mile shoreline, a tropical paradise of waterfalls and trees, water slides, and so forth. It looks inviting, but truth be told, it's sometimes on the chilly side and isn't very deep. But it's so pretty you'll hardly care. There is also Bare, a "European-style pool" offering a more adult aquatic experience. Behind the pool are the **Dolphin Habitat** and Siegfried & Roy's **Secret Garden** (p. 63).

A sculpture of Siegfried, Roy, and one of the duo's famous white tigers in front of The Mirage.

3400 Las Vegas Blvd. S. (btw. Flamingo and Spring Mountain roads), Las Vegas, NV 89109. www. mirage.com. ℂ **800/627-6667** or 702/791-7111. 3,044 units. $109 and up double; $275 and up suite. Resort fee $25. Extra person $35. No discount for children. AE, DC, DISC, MC, V. Free self- and valet parking. **Amenities:** 12 restaurants; buffet; casino; concierge; executive-level rooms; health club; beautiful outdoor pool; room service; showrooms; spa. *In room:* A/C, TV w/ pay movies, hair dryer, high-speed Internet.

Planet Hollywood Resort & Casino ★★   Fronted by a jumble of LED screens and bright signs, you may think you're in for the same kind of sensory overload that the pop-culture restaurants of the same name provide. But once you get inside you may be pleasantly surprised by classy, modern design that manages to evoke Hollywood glamour without resorting to overuse of glitter.

From a size and amenities perspective, the rooms are pretty average until you get to the memorabilia displays. Each has a movie or entertainment theme, such as *Pulp Fiction,* which might have John Travolta's suit in a glass case and a glass coffee table filled with more original memorabilia from the film. Although more than one room may share the same movie theme, no two rooms will have the same objects. The vibe of the room can vary radically depending on whether the theme is Judy Garland in some charming musical or Wesley Snipes in *Blade,* so ask when booking. As gimmicks go, it's a catchy one, and a good use for all that junk the company's accumulated over the years.

There are also a couple of thousand additional rooms in the connected but separately managed Elara, a Hilton Grand Vacations timeshare/hotel. They offer the typical sleek design and decor of modern Vegas hotels but throw in a Hollywood twist through art and amenities. Studios through four-bedroom suites each have kitchens (from wee to wow), projector televisions that use the blackout shades for truly gigantic screen viewing, and whirlpool tubs. You have to book rooms here separately through Hilton, but they are definitely nicer than those in the main tower, albeit with a little less personality.

Note: The parking lot is all the way on the other side of the Miracle Mile shopping area, thus requiring guests to drag their suitcases all the way through the mall and a good chunk of the hotel before getting to registration. Do not self-park here if you have mobility issues of any kind. Instead, follow the signs for casino (as opposed to mall) valet parking (free, except for the tip), which is right outside the front desk.

A long list of restaurants includes Sammy Hagar's **Cabo Wabo Cantina; Strip House,** a New York steakhouse with a bordello theme; **PBR Rock Bar & Grill;** and the **Earl of Sandwich**—all covered in chapter 5. For entertainment there are a host of bars and clubs including **Gallery** and **Pussycat Dolls Saloon** (see chapter 7); a showroom with the silly but sexy *Peepshow* (p. 190), plus more in the various theaters in the **Miracle Mile** shopping area (p. 165); and the **Theater for the Performing Arts** for touring shows and concerts.

3667 Las Vegas Blvd. S., Las Vegas, NV 89109. www.planethollywoodresort.com. (℃ **877/333-9474** or 702/785-5555. 2,400 units. $99 and up double. No resort fee. Extra person $30. No discount for children. AE, DC, DISC, MC, V. Free self- and valet parking. **Amenities:** 20 restaurants; buffet; bars/lounges; casino; concierge; executive-level rooms; health club; 2 Jacuzzis; performing-arts center; 2 outdoor pools; room service; showroom; spa; wedding chapel. *In room:* A/C, TV w/pay movies, hair dryer, high-speed Internet (for a fee).

Treasure Island ★★ Huh? What happened to Treasure Island? What happened to the pirates? Why, Vegas grew up, that's what. Or, rather, it wants the kids it once actively tried to court to grow up, or at least not come around until they are able to drink and gamble properly.

Originally the most modern family-friendly hotel, Treasure Island (commonly referred to as "TI" by most folks) was a blown-up version of Disneyland's

Hollywood Hip room, Planet Hollywood Resort & Casino.

Pirates of the Caribbean. But that's all behind them now, and the slight name change is there to make sure you understand that this is a grown-up, sophisticated resort. One victim is the pirate stunt show out front; it was revamped so that the pirates (and you have no idea how much we wish we were making this up) now "battle" scantily clad strippers . . . er, "sirens."

And now, a new captain has taken over the ship. Former Frontier owner Phil Ruffin threw several hundred million dollars at MGM Resorts International in 2009, and TI is no longer part of that family of hotels. Ruffin has already made changes, mostly designed to make the hotel more palatable to the mid-market with less expensive restaurants and more in-room amenities.

The good-size rooms are pleasant but not postcard-worthy, although additions of niceties like in-room refrigerators make them more comfy than they already were. Good bathrooms feature large soaking tubs—a bather's delight. Best of all, Strip-side rooms have a view of the pirate battle—views are best from the sixth floor on up. You know, so you can see right down the sirens' dresses.

The hotel offers half a dozen restaurants, including **Dishes, The Buffet at TI** (p. 149); a branch of Los Angeles's **Canter's Deli** (p. 125); and a return of the country-western favorite **Gilley's** (p. 120). Treasure Island is home to Cirque du Soleil's *Mystère* (p. 181), one of the best shows in town.

Neither the spa nor pool is all that memorable, so if those things are important to you, stay elsewhere, like at the neighboring Mirage, which is connected to the TI by a free tram.

Note: As with most hotels in Vegas, this one charges a resort fee, but here the list of what is included is much longer. Details change frequently but expect things like Internet access, admission to the fitness center and spa, two-for-one drinks and buffet coupons, and credits for future stays.

3300 Las Vegas Blvd. S. (at Spring Mountain Rd.), Las Vegas, NV 89109. www.treasureisland.com. © **800/944-7444** or 702/894-7111. 2,885 units. $89 and up double; $140 and up suite. Resort

Treasure Island stages a free pirate "battle" outside its doors every night.

fee $20. Extra person $30. Free for children 14 and under in parent's room. Inquire about packages. AE, DC, DISC, MC, V. Free self- and valet parking. **Amenities:** 9 restaurants; buffet; casino; concierge; executive-level rooms; health club; outdoor pool; room service; showrooms; spa; wedding chapels. *In room:* A/C, TV w/pay movies, fax, hair dryer, high-speed Internet.

Moderate

Bally's Las Vegas ★
With all the fancy-pants new hotels in town, it's hard to keep up with the Joneses—or the Wynns, as the case may be. And here's poor Bally's, with a perfect location, and it's got no big fountain or Eiffel Tower or anything to make a passerby think "Gotta go gamble there," much less a tourist booking long distance to think "Gotta stay there." And we aren't really going to make you change your mind, though we might give you a reason to consider it. After all, you can get a room for a ridiculously low rate these days, and those rooms, which are larger than average, have some swell touches, including modern curvy couches, big TVs, and marble this and that. The public areas still feel a little dated, but the hotel is connected to its sister property, Paris Las Vegas, which is swanky and modern enough. Also, it's a stop on the monorail system, so you'll be able to go just about everywhere by foot or by swift train, and, thanks to those nice rooms, you've got someplace pleasant to return to.

Bally's has the usual range of dining choices, with many more next door at Paris Las Vegas. The casino is large, well lit, and colorful, and there's also a headliner showroom and the splashy *Jubilee!* revue (p. 187).

3645 Las Vegas Blvd. S. (at Flamingo Rd.), Las Vegas, NV 89109. www.ballyslv.com. ℂ **800/634-3434** or 702/739-4111. 2,814 units. $99 and up double; $199 and up suite. No resort fee. Extra person $30. No discount for children. AE, DC, MC, V. Free self- and valet parking. **Amenities:** 6 restaurants; casino; concierge; health club; outdoor pool; room service; showrooms; spa; 8 night-lit tennis courts. *In room:* A/C, TV w/pay movies, hair dryer, high-speed Internet (for a fee).

Bill's Gamblin' Hall and Saloon
You can't fault the location of this hotel. It's right on the busiest corner of the Strip, smack in the middle of the action. With all the hotel business (the itty-bitty reception desk and tiny sundries/gift-shop counter) set on the fringes of the small, dark, cluttered casino, this is very Old Vegas, which is sort of a good thing; but unfortunately, it's becoming harder to wrap one's mind around it in these days of megacasino complexes.

Each room has an extra corner of space for a couple of chairs or a couch alongside the very cramped bathroom. *Beware:* The very loud intersection outside can make rooms noisy.

3595 Las Vegas Blvd. S. (at Flamingo Rd.), Las Vegas, NV 89109. www.billslasvegas.com. ℂ **866/245-5745** or 702/737-2100. 200 units. $60 and up double. No resort fee. Extra person $30. No discount for children. AE, DC, DISC, MC, V. Free self- and valet parking. **Amenities:** 2 restaurants; casino; room service. *In room:* A/C, TV w/pay movies, hair dryer, high-speed Internet (for a fee).

Inexpensive

Imperial Palace
Big changes are in store for this long-running budget-minded hotel, not the least of which is the name, which won't be Imperial Palace by the end of 2013. The entire hotel is getting a revamp, remodel, and rebranding as part of the half-billion dollar entertainment complex going in next door that will include shopping, nightclubs, and the world's tallest observation wheel. Details are sketchy at press time, but they will most likely bump up the amenities and

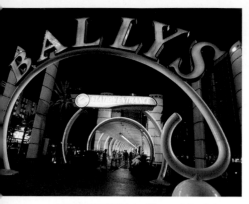

FROM LEFT: **Bally's Las Vegas; stained glass inside Bill's Gamblin' Hall and Saloon.**

the price so this may no longer be a truly "inexpensive" hotel. Then again, this is not the first time that the owners have said they were going to make changes here, so we're taking a believe-it-when-we-see-it approach.

For now, what you get are basic accommodations and not much more. It's the kind of hotel where you dump your bags and then go have fun elsewhere.

If you feel like staying on-site for entertainment, there is a casino with relatively low limits; a few shows, bars, and restaurants, including the delightful **Hash House a Go Go** (p. 120); and a pretty basic pool. Of course, all that could change, too, so be sure to check the website for updates.

3535 Las Vegas Blvd. S., Las Vegas, NV 89109. www.imperialpalace.com. © **800/351-7400** or 702/731-3311. 2,550 units. $59 and up double; $159 and up suite. No resort fee. Extra person $30. No discount for children. AE, DC, DISC, MC, V. Free self- and valet parking. **Amenities:** 8 restaurants; buffet; casino; concierge; executive-level rooms; health club; heated outdoor pool; room service; spa; showrooms; salon; auto museum; wedding chapel. *In room:* A/C, TV, high-speed Internet (for a fee).

NORTH STRIP

The northern end of the Strip, from Spring Mountain/Sands Road to Charleston Avenue, is not quite as densely populated with major casinos, but still has enough Vegas flair to make it worth your while.

Best for: Visitors who want to be on the Strip but want a slightly more manageable experience from a crowd and congestion perspective.

Drawbacks: It's a longer walk to most of what you'll want to see; some of the hotels here are past their prime.

Very Expensive

Encore Las Vegas ★★   What do you do after you have built a casino empire, sold it all, and then reentered the fray by creating an all-new paradigm for modern Vegas luxury? Well, you have an encore, of course.

The thusly named Encore is the second act for Vegas impresario Steve Wynn and his eponymous Wynn Las Vegas. Located just north of that hotel and sharing its gracefully curved bronze exterior look, the baby sister of the family is

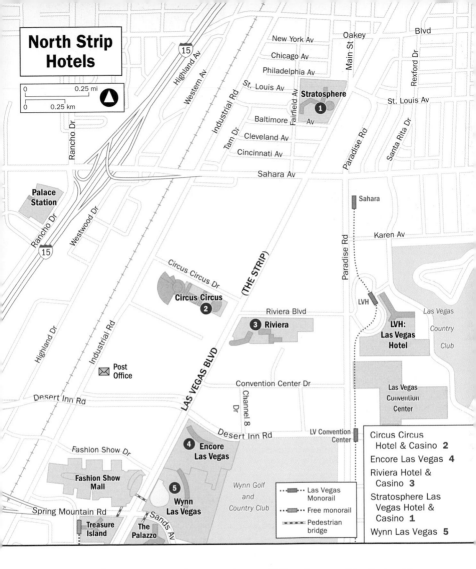

New York Av

Oakey

Blvd

Chicago Av

Philadelphia Av

St. Louis Av

Highland Av

Western Av

Industrial Rd

Tam Dr

Fairfield Av

Stratosphere
1

Main St

St. Louis Av

Rexford Dr

Santa Rita Dr

Baltimore Av

Cleveland Av

Cincinnati Av

Paradise Rd

Rancho Dr

Sahara Av

Sahara

Palace
Station

Rancho Dr

Westwood Dr

Karen Av

Paradise Rd

Circus Circus Dr

(THE STRIP)

Circus Circus
2

Riviera Blvd

3 Riviera

LVH

LVH:
Las Vegas
Hotel

Las Vegas

Country

Club

Highland Dr

Industrial Rd

LAS VEGAS BLVD

Post
Office

Convention Center Dr

Channel 8 Dr

Las Vegas
Convention
Center

Desert Inn Rd

Desert Inn Rd

LV Convention
Center

Fashion Show Dr

4 Encore
Las Vegas

Fashion Show
Mall

Wynn Golf
and
Country Club

Spring Mountain Rd

5

Wynn
Las Vegas

Treasure
Island

Sands Av

The
Palazzo

···■··· Las Vegas
Monorail

···■··· Free monorail

⬤⬤⬤⬤ Pedestrian
bridge

Circus Circus
Hotel & Casino **2**

Encore Las Vegas **4**

Riviera Hotel &
Casino **3**

Stratosphere Las
Vegas Hotel &
Casino **1**

Wynn Las Vegas **5**

intended to be at once more luxurious (no, really!) and more whimsical, with a design scheme that is heavy on the springtime cues (think butterflies) with Greek and Moroccan touches liberally applied everywhere you look. Oh, and red. Lots of red. It shouldn't work, really, and yet it does, somehow.

While they follow a similar aesthetic, the rooms at Encore are grander than those at Wynn both in terms of size and amenities. Most are "suites" with a sleeping area separated from a living room space by a partial wall (and a giant flatscreen TV). Furnishings are modern but with an elegant panache, and high-tech, thus allowing you to operate everything from the lights to the TVs to the drapes to the air-conditioning from a single remote that remembers your preferences. Bathrooms are massive and packed with plush towels and robes, high-quality bath amenities, and enough marble to build your own Colosseum.

The main pool area in the center of the property is yet another winner, done as a European garden with more of the springtime touches and Greek statuary. A second pool, the Encore Beach Club, is a 60,000-square-foot pool/nightclub/restaurant concept with luxury cabanas, an indoor/outdoor dance club, and restaurant. The 70,000-square-foot **Spa at Encore** is gorgeous (p. 94).

You'll find butterfly motifs throughout Encore Las Vegas.

Five restaurants serve up high-end cuisine, including a shrine to the Chairman of the Board at **Sinatra** (p. 127) and the 24-hour **Society Café** among others. And, of course, the restaurants at Wynn are just a short walk away. A small casino inspired by European gaming salons is covered in chapter 8, and the showroom featuring **Garth Brooks** is reviewed in chapter 7.

As with its big sister, prices here are not for the faint of heart. While the recession may have knocked down the overall bill during its inaugural run, room rates will almost always be more expensive here than just about anywhere else on the Strip. Ditto restaurant prices, table game limits, and the cost of a bottle of water in the sundry store.

3121 Las Vegas Blvd. S. (near Spring Mountain Rd.), Las Vegas, NV 89109. www.encorelasvegas.com. ✆ **888/320-7125** or 702/770-7171. 2,034 units. $159 and up double. Resort fee $25. Extra person $50. No discount for children. AE, DC, DISC, MC, V. Free self- and valet parking. **Amenities:** 5 restaurants; casino; concierge; executive-level rooms; health club; 2 outdoor pools; room service; spa. *In room:* A/C, TVs w/pay movies, CD/DVD player, fax, hair dryer, high-speed Internet.

Wynn Las Vegas ★★ Steve Wynn, a modern-day Vegas legend (he built The Mirage and Bellagio, among others) spent nearly $3 billion to create this eponymous shrine to luxury. While that's a drop in the bucket compared to some of the hotels that came after it, one can still see evidence of the investment at every turn.

The hotel feels a little bit cramped when you first enter—we are used to swooping Vegas lobby displays—and the reception area is impractically proportioned, resulting in some check-in waits. The suspicion is that all this makes the place seem less behemoth and more resort size. The hotel has no discernible theme (apart from that tendency to prompt constant comparisons to Bellagio), which may be disappointing for those looking for theme-aganza. The interior has some superior moments, including considerable use of natural light via various skylights and atriums, unusual in this town and most welcome; a floral motif reflected in eye-catching, brightly hued floor mosaics; artistic fresh-flower arrangements throughout; and, best of all, the atrium that runs down the center and, like its predecessor at Bellagio, features frequently changed displays. As with all other Wynn hotels, there is an installation in front of the building, a 150-foot-tall man-made mountain covered in trees (many mature trees taken from the old Desert Inn golf course) and waterfalls, and, like the others, this comes with a free show (p. 205).

The rooms are gorgeous: large with much-appreciated floor-to-ceiling views (west side shows off the mountain and waterfalls, east side the golf course; both are choice); deeply comfortable beds, with high-thread-count sheets and feather beds atop good-quality mattresses; flatscreen TVs; and excellent up-to-the-minute bathrooms, complete with quite long and deep tubs, their own flatscreen TVs, and lemony amenities. Take note of the silky-satiny robes (the best we've ever had in a hotel) and plush velour slippers. It's all done in creamy tones that make it modern without being garish.

The gym is excellent, stuffed with up-to-the-minute equipment, most with individual TV screens, though we could do without the windows looking onto an interior hallway that make our workout visible to all passersby. The spa area is serene and particularly pretty, with an atrium emitting natural light into the bathing areas. The pool area has four oval-shaped numbers connected by some stretches long enough for laps, plus a "European sunbathing" (read: topless) area that includes outdoor blackjack tables.

Dining options are superb (though generally exceptionally pricey), including **Bartolotta, Red 8,** and the **Wynn Las Vegas Buffet,** all reviewed in chapter 5. A shopping street (p. 161) features high-end choices—Chanel, Cartier, Manolo Blahnik, Gaultier—but if that's not enough for you there's also a Ferrari dealership—no, really. A showroom features the Cirque-like production *Le Rêve* (p. 188).

3131 Las Vegas Blvd. S. (corner of Spring Mountain Rd.), Las Vegas, NV 89109. www.wynnlasvegas.com. (C) **888/320-9966** or 702/770-7100. Fax 702/770-1571. 2,716 units. $199 and up double. Resort fee $25. Extra person $50. No discount for children. AE, DC, DISC, MC, V. Free self- and valet parking. **Amenities:** 13 restaurants; buffet; casino; concierge; executive-level rooms; health club; 4 outdoor pools; room service; showrooms; spa; 3 wedding chapels. *In room:* A/C, TVs w/pay movies, CD/DVD player, fax, hair dryer, high-speed Internet.

Whimsical lanterns overlook the viewing area for the Lake of Dreams at Wynn Las Vegas.

Moderate

Riviera Hotel & Casino  Its best days long past, this former Strip star is taking minor steps toward a comeback with changes to its casino offerings and a focus on being a bargain for both gamblers and guests. That being said, it still has a long way to go before you should consider this seriously for any other reason than the bargain basement pricing you can often get here.

Opened in 1955 (Liberace cut the ribbon, and Joan Crawford was the official hostess of opening ceremo-

Old-school signage marks the exterior of the Riviera Hotel & Casino.

nies), the Riviera was the first "high-rise" on the Strip, at nine stories. Today it tries to evoke the Vegas of the good old days—"come drink, gamble, and see a show"—and while it is appropriately dark and glitzy, it's also very crowded and has a confusing layout. Don't miss your chance to have your photo taken with the bronze memorial to the *Crazy Girls* (their premier, largely nekkid, show), and their butts, outside on the Strip. There is a pool here, but it's very dull.

Some rooms received makeovers, bringing in modern furnishings, the ubiquitous white comforters, flatscreen TVs, and the like. Be sure to ask for one of these but understand that no matter which room you get it'll be bland, basic, and totally forgettable. There is the predictable assortment of dining options, from steakhouse to food court. The Riviera's enormous casino is a rambling, affair (see chapter 8), and there are several low-rent shows including the aforementioned *Crazy Girls,* a topless Las Vegas–style revue (p. 183).

2901 Las Vegas Blvd. S. (at Riviera Blvd.), Las Vegas, NV 89109. www.rivierahotel.com. © **800/ 634-6753** or 702/734-5110. Fax 702/794-9451. 2,074 units. $59 and up double; $155 and up suite. Resort fee $11. Extra person $20. No discount for children. AE, DC, MC, V. Free self- and valet parking. **Amenities:** 5 restaurants; buffet; food court; casino; executive-level rooms; health club; outdoor pool; room service; showrooms; spa; wedding chapel. *In room:* A/C, TV w/pay movies, high-speed Internet.

Stratosphere Las Vegas Hotel & Casino ★ ☺ At 1,149 feet, the Stratosphere Tower looms large above the Vegas skyline, but over the years the hotel has struggled to find its place in the city's pantheon of megaresorts. It started as a family-friendly destination, morphed into a low-frills budget option, and now, with some recent renovations, is trying to aim somewhere in the middle.

About half of the rooms have gotten a grown-up makeover, turning what were Motel 6 basic accommodations into something more akin to maybe a Holiday Inn Express. That's actually a good thing—we like Holiday Inn Express and we like the new lodgings here as well. Modern furnishings, comfortable beds, tastefully decor, upgraded (although still smallish) bathrooms, and plenty of amenities make them much more interesting. They'll cost you a few bucks more than the standard rooms (which are still Motel 6), but are totally worth it.

Note: Contrary to popular belief, there are no hotel rooms in the observation tower itself. Sorry.

Downstairs, the casino (p. 241), lobby, many of the restaurants (including **Fellini's** and the **Courtyard Buffet**), and front entrance have all been upgraded with more subtle fabrics and fixtures that give the entire place a more upscale feel. Luckily they didn't upscale the prices, which can still be downright cheap.

Upstairs, you'll find a rather pedestrian shopping mall with few brand names, a pool with some great views, a health club, spa, and a showroom.

Way upstairs—that it to say up more than 100 stories—is the observation tower with restaurants, lounges, bars, and some extreme thrill rides covered in more detail on p. 68. Guests of the hotel get free access to the tower as part of the daily resort fee.

For the price, this might be the right place for you. Just remember that its location on the far northern end of the Strip means you need a rental car or a lot of cash for cabs to get to the true thrills down the street.

2000 Las Vegas Blvd. S. (btw. St. Louis and Baltimore aves.), Las Vegas, NV 89104. www.stratospherehotel.com. © **800/998-6937** or 702/380-7777. 2,444 units. $49 and up double; $109 and up suite. Resort fee $7.50. Extra person $15. Children 12 and under stay free in parent's room. AE, DC, DISC, MC, V. Free self- and valet parking. **Amenities:** 4 restaurants; buffet; several fast-food outlets; arcade; casino; concierge; executive-level rooms; large pool area w/great views of the Strip; room service; showrooms; wedding chapel. *In room:* A/C, TV w/pay movies, hair dryer, high-speed Internet (for a fee).

Inexpensive

Circus Circus Hotel & Casino ★ ☺
This is the last bastion of family-friendly Las Vegas—indeed, for years, the only

FROM TOP: **The Stratosphere Las Vegas Hotel & Casino Tower is a Strip landmark and marks its northern boundary;** Midway arcade at Circus Circus Hotel & Casino.

coming ATTRACTIONS

For years, the list of what was being built, what was about to be built, and what was a possibility of being built was almost as long as the list of things that actually had been built in Vegas. But the global economic smackdown that started in 2008 has put the kibosh on almost every major construction project in Las Vegas, and now the coming attractions list is almost empty.

The two biggest Strip megaresort projects are "on hold" officially and it will probably be years before they ever get started back up again, if they do at all. These are **Echelon,** a multibillion-dollar development that was to replace the Stardust, and **Fontainebleau,** a $4-billion high-rise hotel north of Riviera. Progress ranged from little built (Echelon) to a lot built (Fontainebleau), but both are now mothballed for the foreseeable future.

So instead of building new hotels, revisions to existing hotels seem to be the direction most gaming companies are going. The **MGM Grand, Imperial Palace,** and the **Palms** are all undergoing some level of transformation that include everything from new rooms to new names. You can read more detail in the reviews of each of those properties.

Downtown Las Vegas will see the return of the long dormant Lady Luck, only it won't have that name. **The Downtown Grand** is the new moniker for the property that will come along with a top-to-bottom renovation and expansion, due in 2013.

As with everything about the recession, it's hard to predict Vegas's future; but it is possible that when you read this, the cranes could be back in action at the construction sites. It's also possible that they will still be collecting dust. Just put a very large asterisk next to anything that isn't open yet and, in fact, next to some things that already are.

hotel with such an open mind, which is also not to say that you should confuse this with a theme-park hotel. All the circus fun is still built around a busy casino. The midway level features dozens of carnival games, a large arcade (more than 300 video and pinball games), trick mirrors, and ongoing circus acts under the big top from 11am to midnight daily. The world's largest permanent circus, it features renowned trapeze artists, stunt cyclists, jugglers, magicians, acrobats, and high-wire daredevils. Spectators can view the action from much of the midway, or get up close and comfy on benches in the performance arena.

The thousands of rooms here occupy sufficient acreage to warrant a free Disney World–style aerial shuttle (another kid pleaser) connecting its many components. Tower rooms have newish, just slightly better-than-average furnishings. The Manor section comprises five white, three-story buildings out back, fronted by rows of cypresses. These rooms are usually among the least expensive in town, but we've said it before and we'll say it again: You get what you pay for. All sections of this vast property have their own swimming pools, and additional casino space serves the main tower and sky-rise buildings.

The fact that all of this feels kind of dated and a bit worn in spots is really more of a function of changing times than any particular slam against the hotel. Compare it to places like The Cosmopolitan or Aria and it looks like a joke, but on its own it's a perfectly acceptable option and, as mentioned, one of the few places on the Strip for families.

Adjacent to the hotel is **Circusland RV Park,** which is KOA run, with 399 full-utility spaces and up to 50-amp hookups. It has its own 24-hour convenience store, swimming pools, saunas, whirlpools, kiddie playground, fenced pet runs, video game arcade, community room, and Wi-Fi. The rate is $55 and up, with peak rates around $100. For gorging, there's always the **Circus Circus Buffet** (p. 150), party bar/restaurant **Rock & Rita's** (p. 129), and, for a classic steakhouse experience, try the appropriately, if unimaginatively, named **The Steakhouse** (p. 128).

In addition to the ongoing circus acts, there's also the upgraded **Adventuredome** (p. 64) indoor theme park out back.

2880 Las Vegas Blvd. S. (btw. Circus Circus and Convention Center drives), Las Vegas, NV 89109. www.circuscircus.com. © **877/434-9175** or 702/734-0410. Fax 702/734-5897. 3,774 units. $59 and up double. Resort fee $8.95. Extra person $15. Children 17 and under stay free in parent's room. AE, DC, DISC, MC, V. Free self- and valet parking. **Amenities:** 7 restaurants; buffet; several fast-food outlets; casino; circus acts and midway-style carnival games; executive-level rooms; 2 outdoor pools; room service; wedding chapel. *In room:* A/C, TV w/pay movies, hair dryer, high-speed Internet.

DOWNTOWN

The original Las Vegas, with classic and historic hotels, is Downtown; the glare of Glitter Gulch has become the must-see tourist destination of the Fremont Street Experience.

Best for: Budget-minded tourists; those looking for a friendlier atmosphere than the snooty Strip.

Drawbacks: Harder-to-find upscale experiences; the surrounding neighborhoods can be a bit rough.

Expensive

Golden Nugget ★★ Always the standout hotel in the Downtown area, a recent face-lift and expansion has made it more appealing than ever. Everything feels brighter, lighter, and more spacious. The redo is a good complement of the best of old and new Vegas; new enough not to be dated, but still user-friendly.

The Golden Nugget opened in 1946 as the first building in Las Vegas constructed specifically for casino gambling. Steve Wynn, who is basically responsible for the "new" Vegas hotel look, took over the Golden Nugget as his first major project in Vegas in 1973. He gradually transformed the Old West/Victorian interiors (typical for Downtown) into something more high rent and genuinely luxurious. The sunny interior spaces are a welcome change from the Las Vegas tradition of dim artificial lighting. Don't forget their mascot (well, it ought to be): the world's largest gold nugget. The *Hand of Faith* nugget weighs in at 61 pounds, 11 ounces and is on display for all to see. Want your own gold? They have an "ATM" that dispenses bars of the stuff.

Standard rooms are attractive and comfortable, but do splurge a bit (maybe an extra $25 per night) for the newer Rush Tower rooms. Opened in 2009, the rooms here are stunning—rough-hewn wood accents, leather furnishings, and an enormous wall of built-ins that features everything from a minibar to a DVD player for the flatscreen TV. You don't have to walk through the casino to get to your room, but you do have to walk a distance to get to the newly redone pool, a chic and snazzy highlight, complete with a water slide that goes right through a glass tunnel in the shark tank. The Rush Tower has its own adults-only (not topless, just no kids) heated infinity pool with cabanas and a bar. The presence of the pool, and general overall quality, makes this the best hotel Downtown for families; the other Downtowners seem geared toward the much older set and/or the single-minded-gambler set.

The **Golden Nugget Buffet,** which is home to a fine Sunday brunch, is described in chapter 5. Oh, and yes, there is a casino. Don't think they'd forget that!

129 E. Fremont St. (at Casino Center Blvd.), Las Vegas, NV 89101. www.goldennugget. com. **②** **800/846-5336** or 702/385-7111. Fax 702/386-8362. 2,425 units. $69 and up double; $275 and up suite. No resort fee. Extra person $20. No discount for children. AE, DC, DISC, MC, V. Free self- and valet parking. **Amenities:** 7 restaurants; buffet; bars, lounges, and nightclub; casino; executive-level rooms; health club; outdoor pool; room service; showroom; spa. *In room:* A/C, TV w/pay movies, hair dryer, high-speed Internet (for a fee).

Hand of Faith, **Golden Nugget.**

Moderate

The D Las Vegas Casino Hotel   The same company that has done such a great job revitalizing The Golden Gate (see below) took on the Luck of the Irish–themed Fitzgerald's and gave it a sleek makeover that includes its somewhat too-hip-for-its-own-good new name. What does the D stand for? Well, it's a combination of sorts, paying homage to its Downtown Las Vegas location, the Detroit area from which the owners hail, and the nickname for CEO Derek Stevens. We're willing to overlook it if only so we can dream about the D, the M Resort, and LVH (formerly the Las Vegas Hilton) all getting into some sort of alphabetical street fight.

Silly name aside, the Fitz was getting long in the tooth and needed an update. Whether you like the sleek, modern look of the place is a matter of taste, but it is impossible not to see it as an improvement over what had become a tired, worn-around-the-edges blarney stone. An outdoor bar fronts Fremont Street under a new facade of light-emitting diode screens; inside, the two-level casino has contemporary trappings downstairs with vintage throwbacks upstairs (the slots dispense coins!). New restaurants and lounges have been added to the list of amenities that also includes a pool, which not all Downtown hotels have.

The rooms mainly got a cosmetic freshening, but they did thrown in niceties like pillow-top mattresses, flatscreen TVs, iPod docking stations, high-speed wired and wireless Internet access, and more. They can't really compete with the luxurious rooms on the Strip, but they aren't trying to, especially when you consider the significantly lower bill you will get upon checkout.

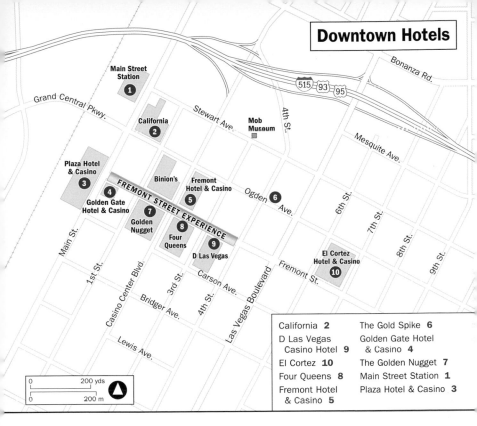

Main Street
Station
1

Grand Central Pkwy.

California
2

Stewart Ave.

Mob
Museum

4th St.

Bonanza Rd.

515 93 95

Mesquite Ave.

Plaza Hotel
& Casino
3

Binion's

Fremont
Hotel & Casino

Ogden **6** Ave.

6th St.

7th St.

8th St.

9th St.

FREMONT STREET EXPERIENCE

4

Golden Gate
Hotel & Casino

Fremont
Hotel & Casino
5

7

Golden
Nugget

8

Four
Queens

9

D Las Vegas

El Cortez
Hotel & Casino
10

Main St.

1st St.

Casino Center Blvd.

Bridger Ave.

3rd St.

Carson Ave.

4th St.

Las Vegas Boulevard

Fremont St.

Lewis Ave.

0 ___ 200 yds
0 ___ 200 m

California **2**	The Gold Spike **6**
D Las Vegas Casino Hotel **9**	Golden Gate Hotel & Casino **4**
El Cortez **10**	The Golden Nugget **7**
Four Queens **8**	Main Street Station **1**
Fremont Hotel & Casino **5**	Plaza Hotel & Casino **3**

301 Fremont St. (at 3rd St.), Las Vegas, NV 89101. www.thed.com. ℂ **800/274-5825** or 702/388-2400. 638 units. $59 and up double. No resort fee. Extra person $20. Children 11 and under stay free in parent's room. AE, DC, DISC, MC, V. Free self- and valet parking. **Amenities:** 4 restaurants; lounge; casino; concierge; unheated outdoor pool; room service. *In room:* A/C, TV w/pay movies, hair dryer, high-speed Internet (for a fee).

Four Queens ★   Opened in 1966 with a mere 120 rooms, the Four Queens (named for the owner's four daughters) has evolved over the decades into a major Downtown property, occupying an entire city block. One of the last bastions of original Vegas glamour that still exists, if this isn't the luxurious place it once was, there is still plenty to like here, including sometimes very low rates. As the staff says, this is the place to stay if you just want to gamble—or if you want a genuine retro experience. Rooms come in a bright color palette, which is jarring given the monochromes that otherwise rule local decor. They can be rather wee, but the ones in the South Tower are a shade larger than the others, though we wouldn't hold any multiperson slumber parties in there, either. In most cases, rooms in the North Tower offer views of the Fremont Street Experience. The restaurant, **Hugo's Cellar** (p. 130), has a cozy lounge with a working fireplace; the inexpensive yet satisfying **Magnolia's Veranda** (p. 133) is open 24 hours a day; two bars serve the casino.

202 Fremont St. (at Casino Center Blvd.), Las Vegas, NV 89101. www.fourqueens.com. ℂ **800/634-6045** or 702/385-4011. 690 units. $49 and up double; $119 and up suite. No resort fee. Extra person $15. Children 11 and under stay free in parent's room. AE, DC, DISC, MC, V.

Free self- and valet parking. **Amenities:** 3 restaurants; food court; 2 bars; casino; room service. *In room:* A/C, TV w/pay movies, hair dryer, high-speed Internet (for a fee).

Inexpensive

California Hotel & Casino   This is a hotel with a unique personality. California themed, it markets itself mostly in Hawaii, and because 85% of its guests are from the Aloha State, it offers Hawaiian entrees in several of its restaurants and even has an on-premises store specializing in Hawaiian foodstuffs. You'll also notice that dealers are wearing colorful Hawaiian shirts. The rooms, however, reflect neither California nor Hawaii; they have solid furnishings and attractive marble bathrooms.

If it sounds like we are giving this place short shrift, it's only because there isn't a lot that makes it stand out (other than that Hawaii thing). What you will find is decent, middle-of-the-road accommodations (at very reasonable prices) that you will probably spend little time in because excitement is found elsewhere.

12 Ogden Ave. (at 1st St.), Las Vegas, NV 89101. www.thecal.com. 📞 **800/634-6255** or 702/385-1222. Fax 702/388-2660. 781 units. $40 and up double. No resort fee. Extra person $10. Children 12 and under stay free in parent's room. AE, DC, DISC, MC, V. Free self- and valet parking. **Amenities:** 5 restaurants; casino; small rooftop pool. *In room:* A/C, TV w/pay movies, hair dryer, high-speed Internet (for a fee).

El Cortez Hotel & Casino ★★   Finally, a much-needed (as opposed to just done because everyone else is doing it) and well-conceived renovation has given an old-timer an unexpected new shot of life. The public areas are totally refreshed: Check out those cherrywood and oxidized metal panel sheets on the walls—you just don't see something that contemporary and design-intensive all that often in Downtown. By daringly removing half the slot machines, the casino floor has been opened up and aired out. The entrance exterior, with its stonework, planters, hitching posts, and stone driveway, makes this feel like an entirely new hotel. Even more exciting, a proper plaza, with trees, fountains, and the like, which seems totally alien to the concept of Vegas, welcomes visitors from Las Vegas Boulevard. Rooms in the main hotel (some quite large) have traditional furnishings; admittedly, nothing stands out, but with such amenities as flatscreen TVs, nice new (if small) bathrooms, armoires with actual minifridges, and Wi-Fi (for a fee), they are right behind Main Street Station for recommendable, affordable Downtown lodgings.

Most notable here are the Cabana Suites. Formerly the rattrap Ogden House across the street, the building

A palm tree–studded courtyard leads into the surprisingly modern interiors of the El Cortez Hotel & Casino.

was remodeled into a modern/retro wonder complete with mod decor, Swarovski crystal chandeliers, custom furnishings, a small gym, and a funky lobby with a fireplace and concierge service. They took 102 tiny rooms and turned them into 64 bigger rooms, all with updated appointments, modern bathrooms, and a full host of amenities.

There are a couple of dependable restaurants, including a steakhouse on-site, plus bars and lounges. Many of the employees have been here well over a dozen years, which says a lot. Local legend Jackie Gaughan still lives in the penthouse and wanders through the property. Forget the manufactured versions—this is the real thing, updated but without losing its identity, and for at least half the price.

Second Street Grill, Fremont Hotel & Casino.

600 Fremont St. (btw. 6th and 7th sts.), Las Vegas, NV 89101. www.elcortezhotelcasino. com. (C) **800/634-6703** or 702/385-5200. Fax 702/474-3626. 428 units. $35 and up double; $55 and up suite. No resort fee. Extra person $10. No discount for children. AE, DISC, MC, V. Free self- and valet parking. **Amenities:** 2 restaurants; small food court; casino. In room: A/C, TV, high-speed Internet (for a fee).

Fremont Hotel & Casino   When it opened in 1956, the Fremont was the first high-rise in Downtown Las Vegas. Wayne Newton got his start here, singing in the now-defunct Carousel Showroom. Step just outside the front door, and there you are, in the **Fremont Street Experience** (p. 69). Rooms are larger (the bathrooms, however, are the opposite of large) and more comfortable than you might expect. (Though, up until midnight, you can hear, sometimes all too well, music and noise from the Fremont Street Experience show. But then again, if you are in bed before midnight in Vegas, it's your own fault.) The staff is shockingly friendly, partly because you actually can have personal service with hotels this size (another advantage of staying Downtown), partly because they just are. The hotel encourages environmental awareness by changing linens only every other day; upon request, it can be more often, but why not help out the planet a bit? For that matter, why not help out your wallet a bit and stay here?

The Fremont boasts an Art Deco restaurant called the **Second Street Grill** (p. 131), along with the **Paradise Buffet** (p. 149). Guests can use the swimming pool at the nearby California Hotel, another Sam Boyd enterprise.

200 E. Fremont St. (btw. Casino Center Blvd. and 3rd St.), Las Vegas, NV 89101. www.fremont casino.com. (C) **800/634-6182** or 702/385-3232. 447 units. $40 and up double. No resort fee. Extra person $10. No discount for children. AE, DC, DISC, MC, V. Free valet parking; no self-parking. **Amenities:** 5 restaurants; casino; access to outdoor pool at nearby California Hotel. In room: A/C, TV w/pay movies, hair dryer.

Gold Spike ♪   Once a figurative (if not literal) rattrap, a major renovation has turned this into a charming boutique hotel, perfect for people who want character, but don't want to pay an arm and a leg for it. Guest rooms are housed in two buildings that have a retro-'50s feeling (sleek lines, old Vegas photos, white-and-teal color schemes), but with modern touches like flatscreen TVs, iPod radios, and Wi-Fi. They are small and simple but tastefully done. There's a surprisingly swank pool with cabanas and nice lounge chairs, a couple of fitness machines passing as a gym, a 24-hour restaurant serving diner grub at bargain-basement prices, a snack shop, and a bar—but that's about it for on-site facilities. There is a casino, but it is microscopic in comparison to the big boys on the Strip—only 200 slot and video poker machines and a handful of gaming tables, the latter of which are not open 24 hours (call ahead for exact hours). Luckily there are about a dozen other casinos on Fremont Street about a block away, so you're actually closer to more gaming options than you would be at a Strip hotel. It's worth noting that Downtown in general is not as shiny or as safe as the Strip. You should stick to the well-lit tourist areas and not wander far afield. The prices they charge here rival what you'd pay at an econobox motel, so people looking for a budget alternative that doesn't skimp on personality should give this place a look-see.

217 Las Vegas Blvd. N., Las Vegas, NV 89101. www.goldspike.com. ☎ **866/600-8600** or 702/384-8444. Fax 702/382-6428. 164 units. $25 and up for up to 4 people in a room. Resort fee $7.95. AE, DC, DISC, MC, V. Free self-parking. **Amenities:** 2 restaurants; casino; fitness room; heated outdoor pool. *In room:* A/C, TV w/pay movies, high-speed Internet.

The Golden Gate ⚑   The Hotel Nevada, as it was known when it opened in 1906, was the state's first hotel, and despite its San Francisco–referencing moniker, it is firmly embracing its history. It's up-to-date in terms of modernity but everywhere you turn there are blasts from past, including antique slot machines and some of the original furnishings, plus hotel and gambling ledgers from its earliest days. It's all charming and especially noteworthy in a town that seems to delight in blowing up its bygone eras.

In 1906 the 100-square-foot guest rooms were stately accommodations, but today they are tiny by just about any standard. Thankfully the gorgeous, retro furnishings almost make up for a lack of floor space with dark woods, warm leather, and bold touches of red livening the space. All have a flatscreen TV, iPod radios, and Wi-Fi; one or two double beds; and a comfy chair; some also have writing desks.

Bathrooms are also small, so don't expect to be sharing the mirror with anyone. A 2012 expansion added 16 larger, modern suites including two massive, 1,600 square-foot high-roller palaces.

Downstairs there's a cozy casino (p. 244) and both a restaurant and deli managed by the Du-Par's coffee shop chain. Note that the deli still serves the shrimp cocktail that has been featured in more than a few Travel Channel specials, though the price is up to $1.99 these days. There are only a couple of bars for on-site entertainment, but the hotel's location on Fremont Street means that you are just steps away from most of the Glitter Gulch casinos and fun.

Old-school slot machines are just some of the charming features of The Golden Gate.

When the hotel first opened they charged $1 per day. Unsurprisingly, it's a bit more expensive than that now, but not by a lot. You can usually get a room here for less than $40 a night, making it a great alternative for the budget-minded.

1 Fremont St., Las Vegas, NV 89101. www. goldengatecasino.com. (C) **800/426-1906** or 702/385-1906. Fax 702/382-5349. 122 units. $25 and up for up to 4 people. No resort fee. AE, DC, DISC, MC, V. Free self- and valet parking. **Amenities:** 2 restaurants; casino; bars. *In room:* A/C, TV w/pay movies, high-speed Internet (for a fee).

Main Street Station ★★

Though not actually on Fremont Street, Main Street Station is just 2 short blocks away, barely a 3-minute walk. Considering how terrific it is, this is hardly an inconvenience. Having taken over an abandoned hotel space,

Period details help create a warm atmosphere at the Main Street.

Main Street Station, in our opinion, remains one of the nicest hotels in Downtown and one of the best bargains in the city.

The overall look here, typical of Downtown, is early-20th-century San Francisco. However, unlike everywhere else, the details here are outstanding, resulting in a beautiful hotel by any measure. Outside, gas lamps flicker on wrought-iron railings and stained-glass windows. Inside, you'll find hammered-tin ceilings, ornate antique-style chandeliers, and lazy ceiling fans. The small lobby is filled with wood panels, long wooden benches, and a front desk straight out of the Old West, with an old-time key cabinet with beveled-glass windows. Check out the painting of a Victorian gambling scene to the left of the front desk. Even the cashier cages look like antique brass bank tellers' cages. They are proud of their special antiques, such as stained glass from the Lillian Russell mansion and doors from the Pullman mansion. It's all very appealing and just plain pretty. An enclosed bridge connects the hotel with the California Hotel across the street, where you will find shopping and a kids' arcade.

The long and narrow rooms are comfortably sized, and although the ornate decorating downstairs does not extend up here, the rooms are plenty nice enough. The bathrooms are small but well appointed. Rooms on the north side overlook the freeway, and the railroad track is nearby. The soundproofing seems quite strong—we couldn't hear anything when inside, but then again, we're from L.A. A few people have complained about noise in these rooms, but the majority of guests haven't had any problems. If you're concerned, request a room on the south side.

The stylish **Triple 7 Brew Pub** is described in detail in chapter 7. The excellent buffet, **Main Street Station Garden Court,** is described in chapter 5. And the casino, thanks to some high ceilings, is one of the most smoke-free around.

200 N. Main St. (btw. Fremont St. and I-95), Las Vegas, NV 89101. www.mainstreetcasino.com. ℂ **800/465-0711** or 702/387-1896. Fax 702/386-4466. 406 units. $59 and up double. No resort fee. Extra person $10. No discount for children. AE, DC, DISC, MC, V. Free self- and valet parking. **Amenities:** 3 restaurants; casino; access to outdoor pool at nearby California Hotel; free shuttle to Strip and sister properties; free Wi-Fi in lobby. *In room:* A/C, TV w/pay movies and games, high-speed Internet (for a fee).

The Plaza Hotel & Casino ⚑ The Fontainebleau was supposed to be a flashy $4-billion megaresort on the Strip, with amenities and decor elements designed to be competitive with other nearby luxury hotels. That project went bankrupt during construction and was picked up for a fraction of the money that had been spent on it by billionaire investor Carl Icahn (former owner of the Stratosphere), who mothballed the half-completed hotel and started selling off all the stuff that was supposed to go into it. Furniture, carpet, drapes, artwork, light fixtures, bathroom fixtures, marble floors, and more all went to the highest bidder.

Enter The Plaza. After years of neglect left this Downtown stalwart a dingy dump, the hotel has gotten a new lease on life by taking advantage of the Fontainebleau's misfortunes. The entire property has been remodeled and upgraded with all the stuff that was supposed to go into a multibillion hotel on the Strip, meaning that the place feels richer and more luxurious than it ever has and, for the rock-bottom prices it charges, has any right to be.

Rooms are gorgeous, earth-toned delights with sleek modern lines, comfy beds and chairs, and up-to-date technology (flatscreens, Wi-Fi, and so forth) plus fun, retro touches in the black-and-white photography of Old Vegas on the walls. Bathrooms are small but fancy due to the Font's sinks and tile work. As a package, they are the nicest standard rooms in Downtown Vegas, bar none.

The rest of the hotel got the full makeover as well, with new restaurants including **Oscar's** (p. 130) from former Mayor Oscar Goodman and branch of the fantastic **Hash House a Go Go** (p. 120); an upgraded salon; a small theater home to the Insurgo acting company; upgrades to the pool and tennis courts; and a top-to-bottom remodeling of the casino, which is light, bright, and airy.

The fact that they have done all this and still keep the prices as low as they are (we've seen them at $29 during the week) is nothing short of a miracle. Welcome back Plaza! We've missed you.

217 Las Vegas Blvd. N., Las Vegas, NV 89101. www.goldspike.com. ℂ **866/600-8600** or 702/384-8444. Fax 702/382-6428. 164 units. $25 and up for up to 4 people in a room. No resort fee. AE, DC, DISC, MC, V. Free self-parking. **Amenities:** 2 restaurants; casino; fitness room; heated outdoor pool. *In room:* A/C, TV w/pay movies, high-speed Internet.

JUST OFF THE STRIP

Within about a mile east, west, and south of the Strip are dozens of hotels, many of which offer the same kind of casino-resort experience but usually at significantly cheaper rates.

Best for: People with a car at their disposal; those who want to be near the action but not in the thick of it.

Drawbacks: Traffic to and from the Strip can be a nightmare, even if you are only driving a mile.

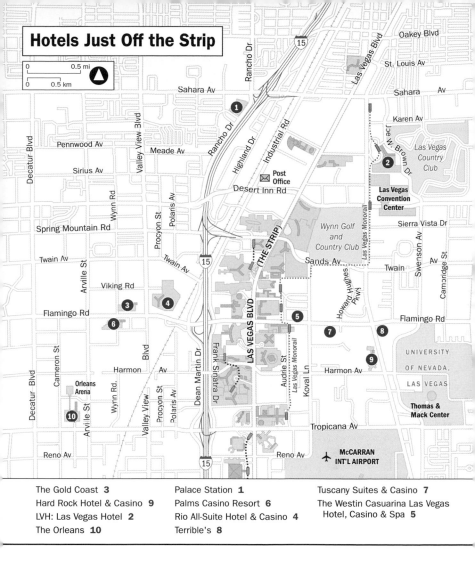

Hotels Just Off the Strip

The Gold Coast **3**
Hard Rock Hotel & Casino **9**
LVH: Las Vegas Hotel **2**
The Orleans **10**

Palace Station **1**
Palms Casino Resort **6**
Rio All-Suite Hotel & Casino **4**
Terrible's **8**

Tuscany Suites & Casino **7**
The Westin Casuarina Las Vegas
Hotel, Casino & Spa **5**

Expensive

Hard Rock Hotel & Casino ★★   As soon as you check out the Hard Rock clientele, you'll know you are in a Vegas hotel that's like no other. The body-fat percentage (and median age) plummets; the percentage of black clothing skyrockets. Yep, the hip—including Hollywood and the music industry, among others—still flock to the Hard Rock, drawn by the cool 'n' rockin' ambience and the goodies offered here. Our problem is that we are not famous pop stars and we do not look enough like any of the Kardashians to warrant the kind of attention that the staff seems to reserve for those types.

It's that Boomer-meets–Gen X sensibility that finds tacky chic so very hip. Original rooms are spacious and almost painfully self-aware in how cool they are trying to be, with mod furnishings and funky amenities. Balconies are a nice touch here. The newer Paradise Tower has a touch more sophistication with a black-and-gray design scheme, contemporary furnishings, and bathrooms that are sleek enough to be in a nightclub (note they only have showers, no tubs). The HRH Tower is the pinnacle in terms of amenities—and cost. The gleaming white suites are plush and feature multiple TVs and an entertainment system that allows you to plug your MP3 player into the wall and create your own playlist or listen to one of theirs.

Rock music memorabilia at the Hard Rock Hotel & Casino.

The casino is loud and boisterous (p. 245) and there are several fine restaurants, including **Pink Taco** (p. 139) serving up funky Mexican food in fun, folk art–inspired surroundings; and **Mr. Lucky's 24/7** (p. 109), a round-the-clock coffee shop displaying rock memorabilia and old Las Vegas hotel signs. The **Hard Rock Cafe** (p. 106) is adjacent to the hotel. **The Joint** (p. 184) is a major showroom that often hosts big-name rock musicians, and there are multiple nightclubs covered in chapter 9.

On the perimeter of the casino is a collection of rock memorabilia, ranging from sad (a Kurt Cobain tribute) to cool (various guitars and outfits) to useless (various other guitars and outfits).

If you've ever dreamed of being in a beach-party movie, or on the set of one of those MTV summer beach-house shows, the pool at the Hard Rock is for you. Multiple pools are joined by a lazy river and fringed in spots by actual sand beaches. You won't get much swimming done—the water is largely so shallow that it won't hit your knees—but there is swim-up blackjack (they give you little plastic pouches to hold your money), and a stage that features live music in the summer and is fronted by a sandy area, so you can make like Frankie, Annette, and Erik Von Zipper and do the Watusi. Or just pose in a thong bikini and new breasts. Whichever. On warm days and nights, this is *the* hangout scene.

A spa facility mixes Moroccan details with stripper poles. Oh but that we were making that up. There is actually a room in the spa where you can practice your, um, technique under the disguise of exercise. Whatever makes you happy.

Plus there's a tattoo shop, so yeah, it's that kind of place (or trying to be).

4455 Paradise Rd. (at Harmon Ave.), Las Vegas, NV 89109. www.hardrockhotel.com. © **800/473-7625** or 702/693-5000. 1,500 units. $109 and up double; $250 and up suite. Resort fee $20. Extra person $35. Children 12 and under stay free in parent's room. AE, DC, MC, V. Free self- and valet parking. **Amenities:** 7 restaurants; casino; concert venue; concierge; fitness center; executive-level rooms; 2 outdoor pools w/lazy river and sandy-beach bottom; room service; spa. *In room:* A/C, TV w/pay movies, hair dryer, high-speed Internet.

Palms Casino Resort ★★   The Palms was Britney Spears's base for her (first) wedding debacle, and is still the retreat of choice for tabloid staples. In keeping with the tropical-foliage name, it's more or less Miami themed (but without the pastels), with a strange aversion to straight lines (really, check out all those curves). Inside a bland building is a pretty nice complex with some down-right family-friendly touches—which we say only because it's a puzzle that the place is such a hot spot. That's mostly due to the nightlife options, which usually sport lines of people every night the facilities are open, offering to sell their first-born sons for a chance to go inside. Why did the clubs catch on so? Quite possibly MTV's *The Real World: Las Vegas,* which featured seven strangers picked to live in the Palms and have their lives taped . . . oh, never mind . . . what you need to know is that the entrances to the clubs stand right by the elevators to your hotel room, which means on a busy weekend night, there can be upwards of 4,000 gorgeous and antsy (if not angry) people standing between you and access to your bed. If you are a Hilton sister, or wish to see whether one will date you, this could be heaven, but if encountering the beautifully dressed and coifed, with 0% body fat and sullen expressions of entitlement, and the 19-year-olds who seek to become all that (and usually affect a thuggish demeanor) makes you, like us, itch, this might not be the most comfortable place to stay. And yet there is an excellent child-care facility, Kid's Quest, plus movie theaters, and a family-ready food court (with a McDonald's, Panda Express, pizza, and subs). So it's both totally wrong for kids and rather right at the same time.

The Palms has perhaps some of the most comfortable beds in Vegas, thanks to fluffy pillows and duvets that make one reluctant to rise, plus big TVs and huge bathrooms. The workout room is decent size, but the spa is underwhelming, though it does offer yoga and Pilates classes. The pool areas are party-spot havens; the kind of trendy must-visit beach areas this kind of crowd loves. Also on the property is the gorgeous and romantic **Alizé** (p. 134), one of the best restaurants in town.

4321 W. Flamingo Rd. (just west of I-15), Las Vegas, NV 89103. www.palms.com. © **866/942-7777** or 702/942-7777. Fax 702/942-6859. 703 units. $99 and up double. Resort fee $15. Extra person $30. No discount for children. AE, DC, DISC, MC, V. Free self- and valet parking. **Amenities:** 9 restaurants; buffet; food court; casino; concierge; executive-level rooms; health club; movie theater; nightclub/showroom; outdoor pool; room service; spa. *In room:* A/C, TV w/ pay movies, hair dryer, high-speed Internet.

Rio All-Suite Hotel & Casino ★

Rio bills itself as a "carnival" atmosphere hotel, which means hectic, crowded, and noisy in most of the public spaces. This is fine for party seekers, but families and those seeking a quiet respite may want to look elsewhere.

The hotel touts its room size. Every one is a "suite," which does not mean two separate rooms, but rather one large room with a sectional, corner sofa, and coffee table at one end. The dressing areas are certainly larger than average and feature a number of extra amenities, such as fridges. Windows, running the entire length of the room,

Rio All-Suite Hotel & Casino.

are floor to ceiling, with a pretty impressive view of the Strip, suburban Vegas, or the mountains (depending on which way you're facing). The furniture doesn't feel like hotel-room standard, but otherwise the decor is fairly bland.

The hotel's first-rate **Carnival World Buffet** is described on p. 151. You might consider checking out the **Wine Cellar Tasting Room,** which bills itself as "the world's largest and most extensive collection of fine wines," and, hyperbole aside, it's certainly impressive and a must-do for any wine aficionado.

Penn & Teller, the smartest show in town, is reviewed in chapter 7, as are the **Chippendales** male stripper show and **VooDoo Rooftop Nightclub.** The casino, alas, is dark and claustrophobic. The party/carnival theme gets a distinct R rating, most notably from the late-night editions of the **Show in the Sky** (p. 66), which features scantily clad dancers and lots of pelvic thrusting.

Out back is a pool with a sandy beach, and two others in imaginative fish and shell shapes that seem inviting until you get up close and see how small they are. It could be especially disappointing after you have braved the long, cluttered walk to get there. Three whirlpool spas nestle amid rocks and foliage, there are two sand-volleyball courts, and blue-and-white-striped cabanas (equipped with rafts and misting coolers) can be rented for $250 to $500 per day. The 18-hole championship **Rio Secco golf course,** located on the south side of town (transportation included), was designed by Rees Jones (p. 91).

3700 W. Flamingo Rd. (just west of I-15), Las Vegas, NV 89103. www.riolasvegas.com. ☏ **888/752-9746** or 702/777-7777. Fax 702/777-7611. 2,582 units. $99 and up suite. No resort fee. Extra person $30. No discount for children. AE, DC, MC, V. Free self- and valet parking. **Amenities:** 8 restaurants; 2 buffets; sports book dining; casino; concierge; executive-level rooms; golf course; health club; 4 outdoor pools; room service; showrooms; spa. *In room:* A/C, TV w/pay movies, fridge, hair dryer, high-speed Internet (for a fee).

The Westin Casuarina Las Vegas Hotel, Casino & Spa ★

When the ever-more-seedy Maxim was more or less stripped to its bones and turned into a Westin, we were thrilled. What Vegas needs, we kept saying, was a true kicky boutique hotel, one that puts real service and real style ahead of slot machines. This Westin won't fill that bill, but business travelers who want a little style, and don't mind if said style is just a tad generic and sterile, will be pleased with this hotel.

There is nothing wrong with the rooms. Although small, they are in excellent taste, done in eye-pleasing sages and wheats, complete with The Westin's self-congratulatory trademarked Heavenly Beds, which are quite heavenly in a plushy pillow-top kind of way. The bathrooms are gleaming—but they pale compared to some of the (admittedly occasionally lurid) fantasies around town in both size and amenities. For the price, especially if you were looking for something Vegas-riffic, you might be disappointed. It doesn't help that the cool exec-style lobby/check-in area melds into a similarly bland casino area and some subtly tasteful lounge and restaurant spaces. Even the gym, spa, and pool are forgettable. Ultimately, it's too good a property not to give a relatively high rating, but you need to understand that, by Vegas standards—which means different things to different people—it's boring.

Note: Like many other Vegas hotels, this one is going through significant financial turbulence at press time, including foreclosure and a probable ownership change. It will most likely remain open but there may be changes in its future.

160 E. Flamingo Rd., Las Vegas, NV 89109. www.westin.com/lasvegas. ☏ **866/837-4215** or 702/836-5900. Fax 702/836-5996. 825 units. $129 and up double. Resort fee $12. Extra person $30. Children 17 and under stay free in parent's room. AE, DC, DISC, MC, V. Free self- and valet

parking. Pets accepted, $35 fee and a deposit. **Amenities:** Restaurant; bar; coffee shop; casino; concierge; health club; outdoor heated pool; room service. *In room:* A/C, TV, hair dryer, high-speed Internet (for a fee), minibar.

Moderate

LVH: Las Vegas Hotel & Casino ★

For the better part of 40 years this place was known as the Las Vegas Hilton, a favorite for business travelers owing to its location next door to the Las Vegas Convention Center. The licensing deal for the Hilton name expired at the end of 2011, hence the new moniker; while uninventive, at least means they don't have to change their initials. Other than the signs and the stationery, everything else is pretty much the same.

Rooms are a bit boring in comparison to the wilder, newer digs on the Strip, but they are larger than you'll find at most hotels of this age and well stocked with comfy furnishings. You may want to fork over the extra few bucks for a Superior room, which comes with views of the Strip, a minifridge, and a few other extras. Nicer still are the Grand rooms, measuring out at a spacious 600 square feet; plenty of room for a sitting area.

Downstairs is an old-fashioned glitzy casino that is small enough to navigate without a GPS device; several restaurants, including a branch of the popular **Benihana** Japanese grill; bars and lounges, including the **Shimmer Cabaret,** which often has fun local cover bands; a showroom; a small shopping arcade with no-name stores; and lots of businessmen and women here for whatever convention is going on next door. A sunny recreation deck features a big pool, tennis courts, and a Jacuzzi with a well-stocked fitness center and spa adjacent.

There's good news/bad news in terms of prices. You can often find rooms here for much cheaper rates that you'll find at comparable hotels on the Strip unless (and here's the bad part) there is a convention of any size happening, and then rates are often sky high.

One bit of history: Before it was LVH and even before it was the Hilton, back when it was known as the International, Elvis Presley played 837 sold-out shows here. One of Elvis's sequined jumpsuits is enshrined in a glass case in the front, near the entrance to the lobby/casino. Feel free to say "thank you very much" when you pass it. No one will judge you.

3000 Paradise Rd. (at Riviera Blvd.), Las Vegas, NV 89109. www.thelvh.com. ⓒ **888/ 732-7117** or 702/732-5111. Fax 702/732-5805. 3,174 units. $49 and up double. No resort fee. Extra person $35. Children 17 and under stay free in parent's room. AE, DC, DISC, MC, V. Free self- and valet parking. **Amenities:** 13 restaurants; food courts; casino; executive-level rooms; health club; outdoor pool; room service; showrooms; spa; 6 night-lit tennis courts. *In room:* A/C, TV w/ pay movies, fridge (in some), hair dryer, high-speed Internet (for a fee).

Shimmer Cabaret, Las Vegas Hilton.

Tuscany Suites & Casino ★

This may be the right kind of hybrid between chain hotel and fancy resort—not as lush as the latter but not anywhere near as expensive,

RELIABLE CHAIN alternatives

Most people who come to Las Vegas want to stay in one of the big megaresorts on the Strip. But sometimes budget, timing, or just your own personal taste may necessitate a more traditional approach to lodging. Just about every hotel chain has at least one outlet in the city and all offer the kind of reliable, comfortable, and often affordable accommodations that they are known for. Here are some examples, all of which are located within a mile or two of the Strip so you can have the best of both worlds.

Best Western Mardi Gras, 3500 Paradise Rd.; ✆ **800/634-6501**

Best Western McCarran, 4970 Paradise Rd.; ✆ **800/780-7234**

Candlewood Suites, 4034 Paradise Rd.; ✆ **877/834-3613**

Clarion Hotel, 305 Convention Center Dr.; ✆ **800/633-1777**

Courtyard by Marriott, 3275 Paradise Rd.; ✆ **888/236-2427**

Courtyard by Marriott, 5845 Dean Martin Dr.; ✆ **888/236-2427**

Embassy Suites, 3600 Paradise Rd.; ✆ **800/560-7782**

Embassy Suites, 4315 Swenson St.; ✆ **800/560-7782**

Fairfield Inn by Marriott, 3850 S. Paradise Rd.; ✆ **888/236-2427**

Fairfield Inn Suites, 5775 Dean Martin Dr.; ✆ **888/236-2427**

Hampton Inn, 4975 S. Dean Martin Dr.; ✆ **800/426-7866**

Holiday Inn Express, 5760 Polaris Ave.; ✆ **888/890-0224**

Hyatt Place, 4520 Paradise Rd.; ✆ **888/492-8847**

La Quinta Inn and Suites, 3970 Paradise Rd.; ✆ **800/753-3757**

Las Vegas Marriott, 325 Convention Center Dr.; ✆ **888/236-2427**

Ramada Las Vegas, 325 E. Flamingo Rd.; ✆ **888/288-4982**

Renaissance Las Vegas, 3400 Paradise Rd.; ✆ **800/750-0980**

Residence Inn, 3225 Paradise Rd.; ✆ **888/236-2427**

Residence Inn, 370 Hughes Center Dr.; ✆ **888/236-2427**

Staybridge Suites, 5735 Dean Martin Dr.; ✆ **800/238-8000**

Super 8, 4250 Koval Lane; ✆ **888/288-5081**

Travelodge, 3735 Las Vegas Blvd. S.; ✆ **800/578-7878**

either, with far more personal detail and indulgent touches than you can find at chains. It's another all-suite hotel, and another where "suite" really means "very big room." The rooms aren't memorable, just like the chain rooms, but they are smart enough that you won't get depressed like you might when you see some of the rooms in similarly priced hotels. The large complex (27 acres, complete with a winding pool) isn't so much Italian as it is vaguely evocative of the idea of Italian architecture, but it, too, is more stylish than most of the chains in town. And, unlike those other chains, this one comes with a small casino, roped off in such a way that this is still an appropriate place for families who want the best of all worlds (price, looks, family-friendly atmosphere, and gambling), especially as each room has a separate dining area, a kitchenette, and large TVs, plus convertible couches, on request. While the kids play, there is a large soaking tub for their folks to relax in. There are three on-site restaurants (Italian, Mexican, and diner), plus a lounge.

255 E. Flamingo Rd., Las Vegas, NV 89169. www.tuscanylasvegas.com. ✆ **877/887-2261** or 702/893-8933. Fax 702/947-5994. 700 units. $79 and up suite. No resort fee. Extra person $20.

Children 12 and under stay free in parent's room. AE, DISC, MC, V. **Amenities:** 3 restaurants; lounge; casino; concierge; fitness center; outdoor pool; room service. *In room:* A/C, TV w/ Nintendo, fridge, hair dryer, high-speed Internet (for a fee).

Inexpensive

The Gold Coast 🍴 Although its less than half a mile from the Strip, this budget-minded hotel couldn't be more different than the glittery palaces in whose shadow it sits. Geared mostly to locals, everything here is noticeably cheaper—from the room rates to the gambling limits to the cost of a beer at the casino bar. People who want to be close to the Strip but don't want to pay Strip prices should absolutely pay attention here.

Rooms are small and simple, but unexpectedly stylish with modern furnishings (think IKEA), flatscreen TVs, a writing desk, a coffeemaker, hair dryer, iron and board, and other niceties. The bathrooms won't win any awards for size or style, but they are more than adequate for all but the snootiest of visitors.

On-site facilities include a big, brightly lit casino (p. 244); a 70 lane bowling alley; a basic pool and fitness center; a barber shop and beauty salon; a showroom and lounge for regular entertainment; and six affordable restaurants, including the **Ports O' Call buffet** (p. 152) and a T.G.I. Friday's. A free shuttle ferries people from the hotel to the Strip and sister property The Orleans.

4000 W. Flamingo Rd. Las Vegas, NV 89103. www.goldcoastcasino.com. 🎧 **800/331-5334** or 702/367-7111. 711 units. $39 and up double. Resort fee $3. Extra person $15. Children under 15 stay free in parents' room. AE, DC, DISC, MC, V. Free self- and valet parking. **Amenities:** 6 restaurants; buffet; bowling alley; casino; executive-level rooms; fitness center; heated outdoor pool; room service; salon. *In room:* A/C, TV w/pay movies, hair dryer, high-speed Internet (for a fee).

The Orleans ★ ☺ 🍴 The Orleans is a little out of the way, and there is virtually nothing around it (at least nothing interesting to tourists), but with an 18-screen movie complex, a food court, a day-care center, a 24-hour bowling alley, and a 9,000-seat arena for a minor-league hockey team (but also available for concerts and the like), this is a reasonable alternative to staying on the hectic Strip. Plus, there is a shuttle that runs continuously to the Gold Coast, Sam's Town, and Suncoast. The facade is aggressively fake New Orleans, more reminiscent of Disneyland than the actual Big Easy. Inside, it's much the same.

As long as prices hold true (as always, they can vary), this hotel is one of the best bargains in town, despite the location. "Standard" rooms live up (or down as the case may be) to their name with lots of beige and fairly utilitarian furnishings. Pay the premium for the also aptly named "Premium" rooms, which have much more stylish furnishings, modern decor, built-in desks, and other niceties. Don't expect to want to spend any time in the microscopic bathrooms.

The hotel has your basic Vegas-type places to eat. Worth noting are **Big Al's Oyster Bar,** a not-unauthentic Creole/Cajun-themed restaurant; and **Don Miguel's,** a basic but satisfying Mexican restaurant that makes its own tortillas while you watch. There are several bars, including one with live music at night. **The Orleans Showroom** is an 827-seat theater, featuring live entertainment; **The Orleans Arena** is a large facility for concerts and sporting events; and, of course, there's a casino (p. 245).

4500 W. Tropicana Ave. (west of the Strip and I-15), Las Vegas, NV 89103. www.orleanscasino. com. 🎧 **800/675-3267** or 702/365-7111. 1,886 units. $59 and up double; $185 and up suite. Extra person $15. Children 15 and under stay free in parent's room. Resort fee $3. AE, DC, DISC,

The Orleans.

MC, V. Free parking. **Amenities:** 10 restaurants; buffet; food court; 9,000-seat arena; 70-lane bowling center; casino; children's center offering amusements and day care for kids 3–12; concierge; executive-level rooms; health club; 18-screen movie theater; 2 outdoor pools; room service; showroom; spa. *In room:* A/C, TV w/pay movies, hair dryer, high-speed Internet (for a fee).

Palace Station ★ ⚔ Anybody who wants a Vegas experience but doesn't want to pay typical Vegas prices should take a look at Palace Station. It's close to the north end of the Strip—just on the other side of I-15, about a mile from the Stratosphere—but it is definitely not a Strip hotel in ways both good and not so good. Rooms in the hotel tower are modern and functional with crisp white linens, flatscreen TVs, and solid (if basic) furnishings. They are not particularly large and certainly not showy—these are not the kind of rooms that you'll want to take pictures of to make your friends back home jealous—but they do offer dependably comfortable lodging at bargain rates. Rooms in the low-rise motel-style buildings are even more basic and really should only be considered by those for whom money is the primary concern when picking where they stay. There's nothing expressly wrong with them, but if you can afford to pay a few more bucks per night there are better places to stay. All have the usual conveniences for rates as low as $29 a night, and that's a lot of bang for your Vegas buck.

The rest of the hotel offers plenty of low-cost entertainment and dining options, including a big, rambling low-limit casino, a showroom featuring comedian Louie Anderson (p. 191), bars and lounges, two pools, a fitness room, seven restaurants (from a buffet to a steakhouse), and free shuttle service for guests to both the Strip and the airport. Unless you want to depend on that shuttle, you will need a car to get to most of the places you'll want to visit in Las Vegas, but with all the money you'll save it could very well be worth it.

2411 W. Sahara Ave., Las Vegas, NV 89102. www.palacestation.com. ✆ **800/678-2846** or 702/367-2411. 1,011 units. $29 and up for up to 4 people. $15 resort fee. AE, DC, DISC, MC, V. Free self- and valet parking. **Amenities:** 7 restaurants; airport and Strip shuttle; arcade; casino;

locals' HOTELS

Most residents of Las Vegas—the locals—never go anywhere near the Strip. They prefer to play, eat, be entertained, and occasionally stay at casino-hotels in their own neighborhoods, partly because of convenience but mostly because it will usually cost a lot less money. All of the following hotels are admittedly located away from the main tourist areas, but if you have a car at your disposal, you can save yourself some dough by being flexible with your location. Several offer free shuttles to other sister properties.

Just south of the Strip along I-15 is **Silverton,** 3333 Blue Diamond Rd. (www. silvertoncasino.com; ☏ 866/946-4373 or 702/263-7777), a delightful ski lodge–themed hotel and casino with a warm casino, surprisingly stylish rooms (considering how cheap they usually are; figure in the $40–$75 range), and several affordable restaurants. The sports-minded may want to stop here just for the massive Bass Pro Shops (p. 175) attached to the complex offering everything from skis to the boats with which to pull people wearing them.

About 5 miles west of the Strip along Boulder Highway are a couple of locals' hotel options. **Boulder Station** ★, 4111 Boulder Hwy. (www.boulderstation.com; ☏ **800/683-7777** or 702/432-7777), has more than 300 guest rooms, a 75,000-square-foot casino, movie theaters, restaurants, bars, and a concert venue. Rates usually run from $75 to $125 a night, but rooms can be had for as little as $49 per night. **Arizona Charlie's East** ★, 4575 Boulder Hwy. (www. arizonacharlies.com; ☏ **888/236-9066** or 702/951-5900) features 300 minisuites, a 37,000-square-foot casino, several restaurants, and a casino lounge. It's only a step or two above budget accommodations but still very well maintained and usually priced like the former.

Just down the street, you'll find locals' favorite **Fiesta Henderson** ★, 777 W. Lake Mead Dr., Henderson (www.fiestahendersonlasvegas.com; ☏ 888/899-7770 or 702/558-7000). The Southwestern-themed hotel has basic yet comfortable lodgings, plus plenty of gaming options, restaurants, bars, movie theaters, and more. Things are cheap here, with rooms going for as low as $30 a night during the week.

On the north and west sides of town are several smaller properties popular with locals. **Fiesta Rancho** ★, 2400 N. Rancho Rd. (http://fiestarancholasvegas. com; ☏ **888/899-7770** or 702/631-7000) is similar in concept and execution to its sister property mentioned above. In addition to the 100 rooms, there is a big casino and a regulation-size ice-skating rink, complete with equipment rentals and lessons (p. 87). Prices go as low as $40 a night. If you continue north—about as far north as you can go without running into a mountain—you'll find **Aliante Station** ★★, 7300 Aliante Pkwy., North Las Vegas (www.aliantecasinohotel.com; ☏ **877/477-7627** or 702/692-7777), a beautifully done resort with smallish rooms that are gorgeously decorated with all of the latest amenities. The facility boasts several restaurants, bars and lounges, a Strip-worthy pool, and a big casino, all wrapped up in warm design elements. It's a solid 25-minute drive from the Strip without traffic, but with prices as low as $29 a night for rooms this nice, it might just be worth it.

executive-level rooms; fitness center; outdoor pools; room service. *In room:* A/C, TV w/pay movies, hair dryer, high-speed Internet.

Terrible's ★ 🎁   First of all, this place isn't terrible at all. (The hotel was created by Ed "Terrible" Herbst, who operated a chain of convenience stores and gas stations.) Second, it isn't a bit like the hotel it took over, the rattrap known as the Continental. The Continental is gone, and good riddance. In its place is an unexpected bargain, a hotel frequently offering ridiculously low prices. Try this on for size: as low $24 a night! Near the Strip! Near a bunch of really good restaurants! Hot diggity! So what do you get?

Well, don't expect much in the way of memorable rooms; they are as basic as can be (despite some sweet attempts with artwork depicting European idylls), and some have views of a wall (though even those get plenty of natural light). Some, however, are considerably larger than others, so ask. A newer tower has both suites and standard rooms, with slightly nicer furnishings and flatscreen TVs, plus high-speed Internet. The pool area is a surprise; it looks like what you might find in a nice apartment complex (which, actually, is what Terrible's resembles on the outside), with plenty of palms and other foliage. There's a small but thoroughly stocked casino (with lots of penny slots, continuing the budget theme), plus a convenience store. How could you want for anything more? Did we mention the price and location? Plus a free airport shuttle? Okay, so we wish they had used a bit more imagination with the rooms.

A buffet and the affordable **Bougainvillea** (p. 137) take care of the dining options.

4100 Paradise Rd. (at Flamingo Rd.), Las Vegas, NV 89109. www.terriblescasinos.com. **☎ 800/640-9777** or 702/733-7000. 330 units. $39 and up double. No resort fee. Extra person $12. Children 17 and under stay free in parent's room. AE, DC, DISC, MC, V. Free self-parking. **Amenities:** 2 restaurants; outdoor pool; room service. *In room:* A/C, TV w/pay movies and Nintendo (for a fee), hair dryer, high-speed Internet (for a fee).

SOUTH & EAST OF THE STRIP

The main areas worth knowing about are the Boulder Highway strip on the far east side of town, the bedroom community of Henderson, and Lake Las Vegas—all of which offer a range of casino and non-casino hotels that can save you money and/or provide a unique Vegas experience.

Best for: Repeat visitors who want to try something new; value hunters.

Drawbacks: You'll have to drive to get to most of the major tourist attractions; upper-end restaurants and shows are harder to find.

Expensive

Green Valley Ranch Resort, Spa and Casino ★★   This flat-out fabulous resort makes up for its somewhat far-flung local with earnest efforts and slightly lower prices than comparable accommodations on the Strip. It seems that Green Valley's designers took careful notes on places like the now-closed Ritz-Carlton when coming up with their design—the interiors, rooms, and public spaces feel completely influenced by the same, while the exterior pool area borrowed much from hip hotel concepts such as the Standard and the W. This sounds like a potentially risky combination, but it works smashingly. You can stay here with your parents or your kids, and every age group should be happy.

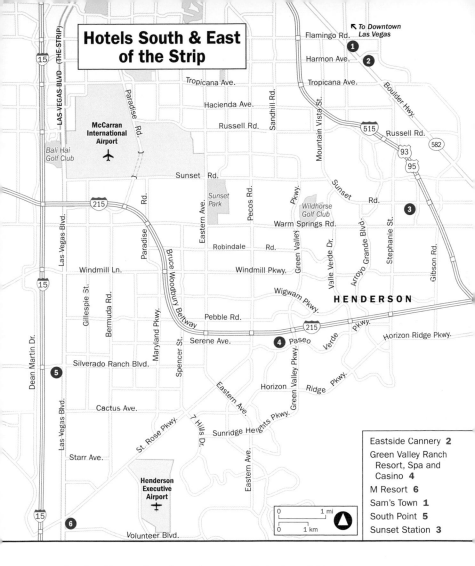

Hotels South & East of the Strip

LAS VEGAS BLVD. (THE STRIP)

To Downtown Las Vegas

Flamingo Rd. **1**

Harmon Ave. **2**

Tropicana Ave.

Tropicana Ave.

Hacienda Ave.

Russell Rd.

Sandhill Rd.

Mountain Vista St.

Boulder Hwy.

McCarran International Airport

Paradise Rd.

Russell Rd.

Bali Hai Golf Club

Sunset Rd.

Rd.

Sunset Park

Pecos Rd.

Eastern Ave.

Pkwy.

Sunset

Rd.

Wildhorse Golf Club

3

Warm Springs Rd.

Green Valley

Stephanie St.

Valle Verde Dr.

Arroyo Grande Blvd.

Gibson Rd.

Robindale

Rd.

Windmill Pkwy.

Windmill Ln.

Paradise

Rd.

Bruce Woodbury Beltway

Wigwam Pkwy.

H E N D E R S O N

Gillespie St.

Bermuda Rd.

Maryland Pkwy.

Spencer St.

Pebble Rd.

Serene Ave.

Paseo

4

Verde

Pkwy.

Horizon Ridge Pkwy.

Silverado Ranch Blvd.

5

Dean Martin Dr.

Las Vegas Blvd.

Horizon

Green Valley Pkwy.

Ridge

Pkwy.

Cactus Ave.

Eastern Ave.

St. Rose Pkwy.

7 Hills Dr.

Sunridge Heights Pkwy.

Eastern Ave.

Starr Ave.

Henderson Executive Airport

6

Volunteer Blvd.

Eastside Cannery	**2**
Green Valley Ranch Resort, Spa and Casino	**4**
M Resort	**6**
Sam's Town	**1**
South Point	**5**
Sunset Station	**3**

0   1 mi

0   1 km

Inside, all is posh and stately—a dignified, classy lobby; large rooms with the most comfortable beds in town (high-thread-count linens, feather beds, plump down comforters); and luxe marble bathrooms.

Outside is the hippest pool area this side of the Hard Rock: part lagoon, part geometric, with shallow places for reading and canoodling, and your choice of poolside lounging equipment, ranging from teak lounge chairs to thick mattresses strewn with pillows. The tiny health club is free, and the spa is also modern and hip.

At night, you can hang out at **Drop Bar,** a swank casino lounge in the middle of the satisfying and budget-conscious casino (p. 248), or have a bite to eat at any of the cheaper-than-the-Strip restaurants and then catch a flick at the

Drop Bar in Green Valley Ranch Resort, Spa & Casino.

multiscreen movie theater. A shopping area, the District, conveniently located next door, features a simulated street scene, where you'll find your usual mall and catalog favorites (Williams-Sonoma, Pottery Barn), plus still more restaurants.

2300 Paseo Verde Pkwy. (at I-215), Henderson, NV 89052. www.greenvalleyranchresort.com. *C* **866/782-9487** or 702/617-7777. 490 units. $129 and up double. Resort fee $25. Extra person $35. Children 17 and under stay free in parent's room. AE, DC, DISC, MC, V. Free self- and valet parking. **Amenities:** 7 restaurants; buffet; food court; casino; concierge; executive-level rooms; health club; lounge; movie theater; outdoor pool; room service; free shuttle service to the airport and the Strip; spa. *In room:* A/C, TV w/pay movies, hair dryer, high-speed Internet.

Moderate

M Resort ★★   Red Rock Resort is one of our favorite hotels in the entire city. We bring this up here because in many ways, M Resort is a lot like Red Rock: beautifully designed, lots to do, great value (in comparison to the Strip), and roughly 9 bazillion miles from anything you're going to want to do in Las Vegas. Okay, that's an exaggeration, but when you're sitting in the inevitable traffic on the roughly 10-mile slog north on I-15 to the southern end of the Strip, it will seem like 9 bazillion miles. But that's really the only downside here. The hotel is stunning, with an abundant use of natural elements (wood, stone, crystal, mother-of-pearl ceilings) and huge windows that flood the entire property with light. The designers wanted to bring the outside in and they succeeded, creating one of the most airy and light spaces in town.

Rooms are large at about 550 square feet, many with great views of the city off in the distance (9 bazillion miles, remember), which you can even see while soaking in the tubs—there are windows from the bathroom into the bedroom. Glossy streamlined furnishings give them a mod feeling and everything is the highest of high tech. To power up the room you have to insert your key into a holder next to the door. Remove it and everything shuts off, maintaining your settings for when you return.

On-site you'll find a 95,000-square-foot casino with all the latest bells and whistles, several restaurants include a branch of the fantastic **Hash House a Go Go** (p. 120) and the interactive Studio B Buffet (complete with its own television studio), multiple bars and lounges, a spa/salon/gym facility, a very nicely landscaped pool area, and the hotel's very own wine cellar.

With prices, on average, about half of what you would pay for similar digs on the Strip, it almost makes that 9-bazillion-mile tick worth considering.

12300 Las Vegas Blvd. S. (at St. Rose Pkwy.), Henderson, NV 89044. www.themresort.com. ℭ **877/673-7678** or 702/797-1000. 390 units. $129 and up double. No resort fee. Extra person $30. Children 17 and under stay free in parent's room. AE, DC, DISC, MC, V. Free self- and valet parking. **Amenities:** 5 restaurants; buffet; casino; concierge; executive-level rooms; health club; heated outdoor pool; room service; shuttle service to the Strip; spa and salon. *In room:* A/C, TV w/pay movies, hair dryer, high-speed Internet (for a fee), minibar.

Inexpensive

Eastside Cannery ★★ 🏊 Most of the hotels on the Boulder Highway ministrip (Sam's Town, Boulder Station, and the like) are older and nowhere near as fancy as the big hotels on the actual Strip, but they aren't trying to be, either. What they are trying to be is budget alternatives to the Strip and places where the locals in the neighborhood can gamble, eat, be entertained, and occasionally stay without spending an arm and a leg. The Eastside Cannery is unique in this area because it tries to be fancier than its neighbors, but still maintains a low-cost ethos that keeps it from being ignored by the budget-conscious—it's the best of both worlds.

The hotel has a subtle '60s flower-power theme, but that's not really important. What is are the gorgeous rooms that, while perhaps not as stylish or big as those in Strip hotels, certainly stand out in this neighborhood. Contemporary furnishings mix with a generous use of textures (wood, leather, marble) to create a modern yet warm look, and the list of standard amenities is long, including

Pool area of the M Resort.

Standard guest room, Eastside Cannery.

floor-to-ceiling windows and flatscreen TVs. The fact that you can often get rooms for as low as $40 a night is like some sort of Vegas miracle.

The hotel's casino (p. 248) is fun, especially for those who appreciate lower limits; the pool is small but satisfactory; the restaurants are all cheaper than similar places on the Strip; and their ballroom-style events center hosts some pretty big names (Gretchen Wilson and Dwight Yoakam put in appearances recently).

The only things you'd really need to change to make this a Strip hotel are the size, the location, and the prices. Thank goodness they aren't considering doing any of that.

5225 Boulder Hwy, Las Vegas, NV 89122. www.eastsidecannery.com. ✆ **866/999-4899** or 702/856-5300. Fax 702/856-5588. 307 units. $40 and up double. $15 extra person. Children 17 and under stay free in parent's room. AE, DC, DISC, MC, V. Free self- and valet parking. **Amenities:** 4 restaurants; buffet; casino; executive-level rooms; outdoor pool; room service. *In room:* A/C, TV w/pay movies, fridge, hair dryer, high-speed Internet (for a fee).

Sam's Town ★ ✦ Just 5 miles from the Strip, the Western-themed Sam's Town is immensely popular with locals and tourists alike. This unexpectedly pleasing resort is well worth considering for the price. Off the beaten track though it may be, regular, free shuttles to the Strip and Downtown may help you with any feelings of isolation.

Rooms are basic but well tended, with comfortable, modern furnishings that, thankfully, no longer follow the yee-haw look and feel of the public areas. At roughly 375 square feet, they aren't the biggest in town but they are plenty big for most casual visitors and feature the usual niceties.

Sam's Town's main draw is its centerpiece atrium, a high-rising edifice that is part park, part Western vista. With living trees and splashing fountains, plus silly animatronic animals, it's a nice, albeit artificial (not unusual for Vegas) place to wander through and sit (definitely unusual for Vegas). And if it's a bit noisy, well, we'll take the splashing sounds of the water over the ka-chinging of slots any day.

There are about a dozen restaurants, including a food court with a McDonald's and Subway among others; several bars; an 18-screen movie theater complex; a 56-lane bowling alley; a pool; a salon; and, unsurprisingly, a casino. The latter is one of the biggest in town, covered in more detail on p. 248.

Value is the watchword here—you can get perfectly decent lodging for a fraction of the cost you'd pay 5 miles to the west. That fraction could well make it worth the drive.

5111 Boulder Hwy., Las Vegas, NV 89122. www.samstownlv.com. © **866/897-8696** or 702/456-7777. 646 units. $39 and up double. Resort fee $4.50. Extra person $20. Children under 15 stay free in parent's room. AE, DC, DISC, MC, V. Free self- and valet parking. **Amenities:** 4 restaurants; buffet; food court; casino; executive-level rooms; fitness room; heated outdoor pool; room service; salon. *In room:* A/C, TV w/pay movies, fridge (for a fee), hair dryer, high-speed Internet (for a fee).

South Point ★★ 🏊 Located about 6 miles south of Mandalay Bay, South Point is still on Las Vegas Boulevard but certainly not within walking distance of anything else of interest except for maybe a convenience store. Still, this hotel is a worthwhile addition both to the city and to this category, offering an expensive level of accommodations at a moderate price.

South Point follows the same formula established by its ancestors: nice rooms at reasonable prices; plenty of low-priced food outlets; tons of entertainment options, including movie theaters, a bowling alley, and more; and a massive casino with lower-than-average limits on everything from slots to craps tables. There's also a giant Equestrian Center out back, large enough for just about any rodeo, complete with air-conditioned horse stalls and a pen for thousands of head of cattle. It's a unique offering to be sure, but we'd recommend you choose a nonevent time to stay here, if possible, because no matter how many odor-absorbing wood chips you throw at them, 2,000 head of cattle emit a less-than-pleasant scent that may make an afternoon by the pool rather unenjoyable.

Atrium, Sam's Town.

The overall scheme is Southern California modern, with plenty of sunny paint schemes and airy architectural details. Think Santa Barbara instead of Hollywood, and you're probably in the ballpark. Rooms are large and aesthetically pleasing, each over 500 square feet and crammed full with expensive and luxurious furnishings, 42-inch plasma televisions, and all the other pampering amenities one would expect in a room three times the price. Seriously, a weekend rate check had rooms here at less than $100 per night, while Bellagio and Wynn were well over $250. Although we wouldn't put these rooms on quite the same level as the ones at those two ultraluxe establishments, we have a hard time coming up with a $150 amount of difference. Venerable local restaurant Michael's relocated here, and you'll also find a number of other restaurants.

9777 Las Vegas Blvd. S., Las Vegas, NV 89183. www.southpointcasino.com. ☎ **866/796-7111** or 702/796-7111. 2,100 units. $79 and up double. No resort fee. Extra person $20. Children 16 and under stay free in parent's room. AE, DC, DISC, MC, V. Free self- and valet parking. **Amenities:** 8 restaurants; buffet; several fast-food outlets; 70-lane bowling center; casino; concierge; 4,400-seat equestrian and events center; 16-screen movie theater; outdoor pool; room service; spa. *In room:* A/C, TV w/pay movies, hair dryer, high-speed Internet (for a fee).

Sunset Station ★ ✦ One of the things that made the Station Casinos chain so successful for so long was its ability to create high-value, low-cost hotels like Sunset Station. Okay, yes, the parent company sunk into bankruptcy and reorganization, but that was more a function of their debt load than whether or not they offered good hotel experiences, which they did and continue to do. Need proof? Take a look at the list of things they offer at Sunset Station: a 110,000-square-foot casino with a sunny, Spanish missionary theme; a 72-lane bowling alley; a 13-screen movie theater with IMAX; a 5,000-seat outdoor concert amphitheater; a pool with cabanas; a fitness room; a Kids Quest play center; a free airport shuttle; and more than a dozen places to eat. What else could you possibly want for rates that are as low as $35 a night? Well, you could want it to be closer to the Strip. Its Henderson location means you will absolutely need a car to get to most of the places you'll want to visit. And the rooms, while comfortable and packed with amenities like Wi-Fi, are pretty basic and not exactly what you might call large. But if you do want it to be closer and the rooms to be nicer, you're going to have to accept the fact that you'll probably be paying a lot more than you would here.

1301 W. Sunset Rd., Henderson, NV 89014. www.sunsetstation.com. ☎ **800/678-2846** or 702/547-7777. Fax 702/547-7744. 448 units. $40 and up for up to 4 people. Resort fee $15. AE, DC, DISC, MC, V. Free self- and valet parking. **Amenities:** 7 restaurants; buffet; food court; airport shuttle; casino; child-care facility; executive-level rooms; fitness center; outdoor pool; room service. *In room:* A/C, TV w/pay movies, hair dryer, high-speed Internet.

NORTH & WEST OF THE STRIP

Summerlin, on the far west side of town, and North Las Vegas (north of the city, appropriately enough) are suburbs that have pockets of casino-hotel options ranging from budget to luxury, and lots of outdoor opportunities from golf to hiking and beyond.

Best for: The recreation-minded; people who want a more relaxing Vegas vacation.

Drawbacks: Long drives to the Strip and fewer entertainment options.

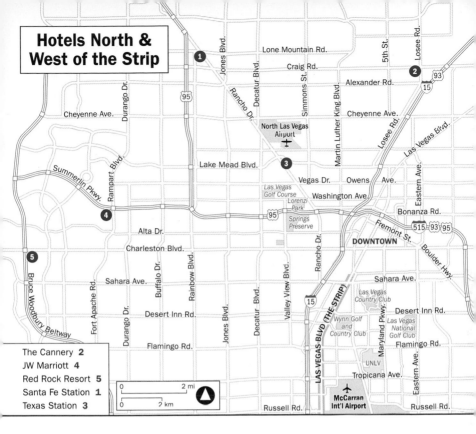

Hotels North &
West of the Strip

Lone Mountain Rd.
Craig Rd.
Alexander Rd.
Cheyenne Ave.
Cheyenne Ave.
North Las Vegas Airport
Lake Mead Blvd.
Vegas Dr. Owens Ave.
Las Vegas Golf Course
Washington Ave.
Lorenzi Park
Springs Preserve
Bonanza Rd.
Alta Dr.
DOWNTOWN
Charleston Blvd.
Sahara Ave.
Sahara Ave.
Las Vegas Country Club
Desert Inn Rd.
Desert Inn Rd.
Wynn Golf and Country Club
Las Vegas National Golf Club
Flamingo Rd.
Flamingo Rd.
UNLV
Tropicana Ave.
McCarran Int'l Airport
Russell Rd.
Russell Rd.

The Cannery 2
JW Marriott 4
Red Rock Resort 5
Santa Fe Station 1
Texas Station 3

0   2 mi
0   2 km

Expensive

JW Marriott ★★ 🎁 Many hotels in Vegas throw the "resort" word around a lot but few of them feel as true to the spirit of the word as the JW Marriott. Located in the northwest part of town, seemingly a million miles from the crazy that is Sin City, the entire place feels like an oasis in the middle of a neon desert. Nestled on 54 acres of lushly landscaped grounds, the Spanish missionary–style buildings are gorgeous reminders that you don't need exposed steel, acres of glass, or dancing water fountains to create a luxury feeling.

There are more than 500 rooms in two wings that sweep out around the grounds in low-rise buildings. All are done in muted gold and earth tones and are finely appointed with plush, classical furnishings, ceiling fans, big TVs, minibars, coffee service, Wi-Fi, and more. The lush bathrooms feature Jacuzzi tubs with separate "rainfall" showers and plenty of marble to make things feel upscale. If you can, try to get a unit on the ground floor so you can take advantage of the patios they offer—sitting outside on a warm night enjoying the scenery is a must.

Spread across the 54 acres are walking paths, babbling brooks, footbridges, secluded benches, and a beautiful pool area. These are the kinds of grounds that you simply can't find on the Strip, where they pack every square inch with a building or a parking structure or a slot machine. They have the latter here, too. The **Rampart Casino** (p. 247) is separated from the main hotel by a long

315

Guest room with a view of the mountains at Red Rock Resort.

hallway, but it is there if you want it as are several restaurants, a buffet, bars and lounges, and the extreme pampering available at the **Aquae Sulis spa** (p. 93).

Although certainly not cheap, prices here are no more expensive than the pricier places on the Strip—you know, the ones that call themselves resorts.

221 N. Rampart Blvd., Las Vegas, NV 89128. www.jwlasvegasresort.com. ⓒ **877/869-8777** or 702/869-7777. Fax 702/869-7339. 200 units. $129 and up for up to 4 people. No resort fee. AE, DC, DISC, MC, V. Free self- and valet parking. **Amenities:** 8 restaurants; casino; concierge; fitness center; outdoor pool; room service; spa. *In room:* A/C, TV w/pay movies, hair dryer, high-speed Internet (for a fee).

Red Rock Resort ★★★ The same people who brought you the fantastic Green Valley Ranch Resort trumped themselves by opening the swank Red Rock Resort in 2006, a hotel and casino complex that pretty much outdoes every other non-Strip hotel and most of the Strip hotels, also.

Built at a cost of nearly a billion dollars (an outrageous sum for an 800-room hotel not located on Las Vegas Blvd.), the hotel is named for its perch right on the edge of the **Red Rock Canyon National Conservation Area** (see chapter 10), a stunning natural wonderland of red-hued rock formations and desert landscape. It's a toss-up, really, which view you should choose—to the west, you get the beautiful natural vistas, and to the east, you get an unimpeded view of the Strip and Downtown Las Vegas, about 11 miles away.

Yes, it is a bit of a trek out here, but people seeking a luxury resort experience with the added bonus of a casino, restaurants, and more will find it worth the drive. Start with that casino, an 80,000-square-foot monster that is one of the most appealing in town, meandering through the building wrapped in natural woods, stonework, glass sculptures, and stunning amber-hued chandeliers. Nine restaurants serve up a wide variety of food selections, among them a buffet and a food court that knocks it up a notch with a **Capriotti's** outlet, offering some of the best submarine sandwiches we've ever tasted. Throw in a 16-screen movie theater; a day-care center; nightclubs and bars; a bowling alley; a sumptuous spa and health club; and a 3-acre circular "backyard" area with a sandy beach, swimming and wading pools, Jacuzzis, private cabanas, and a stage where big-name entertainers perform, and you've got a terrific recipe for success.

The rooms are impressive, modern wonders with high-end furnishings and linens, 42-inch high-def plasma TVs, iPod sound systems, giant bathrooms, and more, all wrapped up in clean, sleek lines and vibrant earth tones. Once ensconced in one, we were hard-pressed to leave.

11011 W. Charleston Rd., Las Vegas, NV 89135. www.redrocklasvegas.com. © **866/767-7773** or 702/797-7777. 816 units. $160 and up (up to 4 people). Resort fee $25. Extra person $35. Children 15 and under stay free in parent's room. AE, DC, DISC, MC, V. **Amenities:** 8 restaurants; buffet; food court; bars and lounges; casino; concierge; day-care center; health club; 16-screen movie theater; outdoor pools and beach area; room service; spa. *In room:* A/C, TV w/pay movies, hair dryer, high-speed Internet, minibar.

Inexpensive

The Cannery ★ ✦ It's kind of odd to suggest that World War II was in any way charming, but that's the theme at this North Las Vegas casino hotel and, darn it, they somehow made it work. Large posters of big band–era pin-up girls and Rosie the Riveter–style Americana dominate the public spaces, decorated to resemble a 1940s factory complete with a 120-foot-tall smokestack outside to use as a navigation guide. There are 200 guest rooms in motel-style buildings, all done in a simple and modern style with flatscreen TVs, dark-wood furnishings, and colorful orange-and-red throws and fabrics. They have a few conveniences like Wi-Fi, but these are not luxury digs so you'll forego such niceties as bathrooms the size of airplane hangars. For entertainment, there's a big casino (p. 246), a 16-screen movie theater, several bars and lounges, a handful of restaurants, and a venue that can be an indoor/outdoor space for everything from concerts to food festivals. Cost is the main reason you would consider staying here; rates as low as $50 a night prove that there are still opportunities for value in Las Vegas.

2121 E. Craig Rd., North Las Vegas, NV 89030. www.cannerycasino.com. © **866/999-4899** or 702/507-5700. 200 units. No resort fee. $50 and up double. $15 extra person. Children 17 and under stay free in parent's room. AE, DC, DISC, MC, V. Free self- and valet parking. **Amenities:** 4 restaurants; buffet; casino; fitness center; outdoor pool; room service. *In room:* A/C, TV w/pay movies, hair dryer, high-speed Internet (for a fee).

Santa Fe Station ✦ There are few casino-hotels in Las Vegas that are farther afield from the main tourist areas than Santa Fe Station. Its far north location means at least a 20-minute drive to get to most of what you'll want to do, and even more when traffic is bad (which it often is). So why are we bothering to tell you about it? Well, Santa Fe Station is one of those rare hotels that offers so many positives that it balances out whatever negatives you may be able to find. True, it's a long drive, but with all the money you'll save on hotel rooms that go as low as $39 a night, you can afford to rent a car. Yes, the rooms themselves may be motel basic, but you can spend most of your time in the massive casino (p. 247), eat at one of their half-dozen restaurants or at the food court (they have a Fatburger!), go to a movie in their 16-screen complex, knock down a few pins at their bowling alley, check out the entertainment in one of their lounges or bars, and/or just lounge in the pool. Although it is primarily geared toward locals, you don't need to be a Las Vegas resident to take advantage of all they offer here—you just need to be smart. And have a car.

4949 N. Rancho Rd., Las Vegas, NV 89130. www.santafestationlasvegas.com. (C) **800/678-2846** or 702/658-4900. Fax 702/658-4919. 200 units. $39 and up double. Resort fee $13. Extra person $20. Children 12 and under stay free in parent's room. AE, DC, DISC, MC, V. Free self- and valet parking. **Amenities:** 5 restaurants; buffet; food court; bowling alley; casino; child-care facility; movie theaters; outdoor pool; room service. *In room:* A/C, TV w/pay movies, hair dryer, high-speed Internet.

Texas Station ✦ Take everything we said about sister hotel Santa Fe Station above, throw some country-western accoutrements at it (think longhorns and lots of plank wood), and move it a few miles closer to the Strip, and you pretty much have Texas Station covered. They have the movie theaters and the bowling alley; the big casino with all of the gaming action you could want; a pool; a fitness center; and lots of restaurants, including one of the best steakhouses in town, **Austins** (p. 142). The rooms here are motel basic, but they are clean, comfortable, and full of the expected amenities. And, more importantly, they are rock-bottom cheap with rates sometimes falling as low as $25 a night. You will give up a lot of the luxury appointments that you will find at Strip hotels, but when you get the bill at the end of your stay you probably won't care. The location on the north side of town does mean you'll need transportation to go see all the cool tourist things Vegas has to offer, but, again, take a look at your bill! Are you caring yet?

2101 Texas Star Lane, Las Vegas, NV 89032. www.texasstation.com. (C) **800/678-2846** or 702/631-1000. Fax 702/288-7985. 200 units. $29 and up double. Resort fee $13. Extra person $20. Children 12 and under stay free in parent's room. AE, DC, DISC, MC, V. Free self- and valet parking. **Amenities:** 4 restaurants; buffet; food court; bowling alley; casino; child-care facility; fitness center; outdoor pool; room service. *In room:* A/C, TV w/pay movies, hair dryer, high-speed Internet.

PRACTICAL INFORMATION
The Big Picture

With a few exceptions in the very expensive category, most hotel rooms in Las Vegas are pretty much the same. After you factor in location and price, there isn't that much difference between rooms, except for perhaps size and the quality of their surprisingly similar furnishings.

Hotel prices in Vegas are anything but fixed, so you will notice wild price ranges. The same room can routinely go for anywhere from $60 to $250, depending on demand. So use our price categories with a grain of salt, and don't rule out a hotel just because it's listed as Very Expensive—on any given day, you might get a great deal on a room in a pricey hotel. On the negative side, some hotels start with their most typical lowest rate, adding "and up." Don't be surprised if "up" turns out to be way up. Just look online or call and ask.

Yes, if you pay more, you'll probably (but not certainly) get a "nicer" establishment and clientele to match (perhaps not so many loud drunks in the elevators). On the other hand, if a convention is in town, the drunks will be there no matter how upscale the hotel—they'll just be wearing business suits and/or funny hats. And frankly, the big hotels, no matter how fine, have mass-produced rooms; at

3,000 rooms or more, they are the equivalent of '60s tract housing. Consequently, even in the nicest hotels, you can (and probably will) encounter plumbing noises, notice scratch marks on the walls or furniture, overhear conversations from other rooms, or be woken by the maids as they knock on the doors next to yours that don't have the do not disturb sign up.

Getting the Best Deal

Here are some tips for landing a low rate.

○ **Book online.** Most Las Vegas hotels are offering their best rates via their Internet sites, with discounts and specials that you won't get if you call.

○ **Be social.** Almost every major resort in town has some presence in the social media world, including Facebook pages, Twitter feeds, and smartphone apps. Connect with them and you may find yourself getting exclusive offers that the luddites out there won't be hearing about.

○ **Dial direct.** When booking a room in a chain hotel (Courtyard by Marriott, for example), call the hotel's local line, as well as the toll-free number, and see where you get the best deal. A hotel makes nothing on a room that stays empty. The clerk who runs the place is more likely to know about vacancies and will often grant deep discounts in order to fill up. *Beware:* Many Vegas hotels are now charging a fee if you book via phone, preferring you use the Internet instead.

○ **Don't be afraid to bargain.** Get in the habit of asking for a lower price than the first one quoted. Always ask politely whether a less expensive room is available than the first one mentioned, or whether any special rates apply to you. If you belong to the players' club at the hotel casino, you may be able to secure a better deal on a hotel room there. Of course, you will also be expected to spend a certain amount of time, and money, gambling there.

○ **Rely on a qualified professional.** Certain hotels give travel agents discounts in exchange for steering business their way, so if you're shy about bargaining, an agent may be better equipped to negotiate discounts for you.

○ **Remember the law of supply and demand.** Las Vegas hotels are most crowded and therefore most expensive on weekends. So the best deals are offered midweek, when prices can drop dramatically. If possible, go then. You can also call the **Las Vegas Convention and Visitors Authority** (www.visitlasvegas. com; ℂ **877/847-4858**) to find out whether an important convention is scheduled at the time of your planned visit; if so, you might want to change your date. Some of the most popular conventions are listed under "When to Go," on p. 29. Remember also that planning to take your vacation just a week before or after official peak season can mean big savings.

○ **Beware of hidden extras.** Almost all the major hotels charge extra for things that are always free in other destinations, such as health-club privileges. Expect to pay anywhere from $15 to $35 to use almost any hotel spa/health club. Wi-Fi also doesn't come free; usually there is a $12-to-$15 charge per 24-hour period. (We've noted when there is a fee in the listings so that you won't be taken by surprise.)

○ **Beware of not-so-hidden extras.** Room rates have dropped dramatically in the last couple of years, but many Vegas hotels have found ways to add to their bottom line through the addition of the infamous "resort fee." These fees range anywhere from $5 to $25 per night, and although the specifics vary from property to property, they often cover amenities like Internet service, health club access, newspapers, printing of boarding passes, maybe a bottle of water or two, and the like. So what if you're not going to use any of that? Too bad—you still have to pay it. Many hotels include this in their totals when you book your room, but a few wait and sock it to you at check-out, so be sure to ask ahead. (We have noted those hotels with resort fees in the listings, but do note that they change often.)

o Watch for coupons and advertised discounts. Scan ads in your local Sunday travel section, an excellent source for up-to-the-minute hotel deals.

o Consider a suite. If you are traveling with your family or another couple, you can pack more people into a suite (which usually comes with a sofa bed) and thereby reduce your per-person rate. Remember that some places charge for extra guests and some don't.

Reservation Services

All of the major Las Vegas hotels require a major credit card to reserve a room, although most do not charge anything until you arrive. Cancellation policies vary, but generally speaking you can usually back out of your booking anywhere from 24 to 48 hours ahead of your check-in date without penalty. Exceptions to both of these general rules are often found on major holidays like New Year's Eve or during big event weekends like the Super Bowl.

BOOKING AGENCIES

The Las Vegas Convention and Visitors Authority runs a **room-reservations hot line** (www.visitlasvegas.com; © **877/847-4858** or 702/892-0711) that can be helpful. The operators can apprise you of room availability, quote rates, contact a hotel for you, and tell you when major conventions will be in town.

A couple words of warning: Make sure they don't try to book you into a hotel you've never heard of. Try to stick with the hotels listed in this book. Always get your information in writing, and then make some phone calls just to confirm that you really have the reservations that they say they've made for you.

What Am I Looking for in a Hotel?

If gambling is not your priority, what are you doing in Vegas? Just kidding. But not 100% kidding. Vegas's current identity as a luxury, and very adult, resort destination means there are several hotels that promise to offer you all sorts of alternatives to gambling—lush pool areas, fabulous spas, incredible restaurants, lavish shopping. But if you look closely, much of this is Vegas bait-and-switch; the pools are often chilly (and often partially closed during nonsummer months), and it will be years before there is more foliage than concrete in these newly land-scaped environments. The spas cost extra (sometimes a whole lot extra), the best restaurants can require a small bank loan, and the stores are often the kinds of places where average mortals can't even afford the oxygen. So what does that leave you with? Why, that's right—gambling.

The other problem with these self-proclaimed luxury hotels is their size. True luxury hotels do not have 3,000 rooms—they have a couple of hundred, at best, because you simply can't provide first-class service and Egyptian-cotton sheets in mass quantity. But while hotels on the upper end of the price spectrum (Wynn, Encore, Bellagio, The Venetian, and so on) have done their best to offer sterling service and to make their rooms more attractive and luxurious than those at other Vegas hotels, there's only so much that any place that big can do. Don't get us wrong—these places are absolutely several steps up in quality from other large hotels, and compared to them, even the better older hotels really look shabby. But they are still sprawling, frequently noisy complexes.

If the hubbub of a casino makes you itch, there are a few nongaming hotels and even nongaming towers within casino-hotels that could help reduce your stress level. Check out Vdara or Mandarin Oriental at CityCenter or the Venezia and THEhotel towers at The Venetian and Mandalay Bay respectively. Just make certain the hotel has a pool, however, especially if you need some recreation. There is nothing as boring as a non-casino, nonpool Vegas hotel—particularly if you have kids.

Sadly, it's relatively easy for both you and us to make a mistake about a hotel; either of us may experience a particular room or two in a 1,000-plus-room hotel and, from there, conclude that a place is nicer than it is or more of a dump than it is. Maintenance, even in the best of hotels, can sometimes be running a bit behind, so if there is something wrong with your room, don't hesitate to ask for another. Of course, if it's one of those busy weekends, there may not be another room to be had, but at least this way you've registered a complaint, perhaps let-ting a busy hotel know that a certain room needs attention. And who knows? If you are gracious and persistent enough, you may be rewarded with a deal for some future stay.

If you want a true luxury-resort hotel, there are only two options: the Four Seasons and the Mandarin Oriental. In addition to that same service and level of comfort only found at a smaller hotel, both offer those extra goodies that pile on the hidden charges at other hotels—health club, poolside cabanas, and so on—as part of the total package, meaning that their slightly higher prices may be more of a bargain than you'd think. Actually, there is a third option: The Red Rock Resort is attracting well-heeled and high-profile tabloid types, who, presumably, know luxury. However, Red Rock charges for all the extras you get as a regular part of your stay at the Four Seasons and the Mandarin.

Casino hotels, by the way, are not always a nice place for children. It used to be that the casino was a separate section in the hotel, and children were not allowed inside. (We have fond memories of standing just outside the casino line, watching Dad put quarters in a slot machine "for us.") But in almost all the new hotels, you have to walk through the casino to get anywhere—the lobby, the res-taurants, the outside world. This makes sense from the hotel's point of view; it gives you many opportunities to stop and drop $1 or $10 into a slot. But this often long, crowded trek gets wearying for adults—and it's far worse for kids. The rule is that kids can walk through the casinos, but they can't stop, even to gawk for a second at someone hitting a jackpot nearby. The casino officials who will immediately hustle the child away are just doing their job, but, boy, it's annoying.

So, take this (and what a hotel offers that kids might like) into consideration when booking a room. Again, please note that those gorgeous hotel pools are often cold (and again, sometimes closed altogether) and not very deep. They look like places you would want to linger, but often (from a kid's point of view) they are not. Plus, the pools close early. Hotels want you inside gambling, not outside swimming.

Finally, the thing that bothers us the most about this latest Vegas phase: It used to be that we could differentiate between rooms, but that's becoming harder and harder. Nearly every major hotel has changed to more or less the same effect; gone is any thematic detailing and in its place is a series of disappointingly similar (if handsome and appealing) looks. Expect clean-lined wood furniture, plump white beds, and monochromes everywhere you go. All that may distinguish one from another would be size of the room or quality of furnishings.

Ultimately, though, if it's a busy time, you'll have to nab any room you can, especially if you get a price you like. How much time are you going to spend in the room anyway?

10

SIDE TRIPS FROM LAS VEGAS

Though Vegas is designed to make you forget that there is an outside world, it might do you and your pocketbook some good to reacquaint yourself with the non-Vegas realm. Actually, if you're spending more than 3 days in Vegas, this may become a necessity; 2 days with kids, and it absolutely will.

Plus, there is such a startling contrast between the artificial wonders of Sin City and the natural wonders that, in some cases, lie just a few miles away. Few places are as developed and modern as Vegas; few places are as untouched as some of the canyons, desert, and mountains that surround it. The electrical and design marvel that is the Strip couldn't exist without the extraordinary structural feat that is Hoover Dam. Need some fresh air? There are plenty of opportunities for outdoor recreation, all in a landscape all the more jarring for the contrast it has with the city.

With the exception of the Grand Canyon, the excursions covered in this chapter will take you from 20 to 60 miles out of town. Every one of them offers a memorable travel experience.

10

HOOVER DAM, LAKE MEAD & LAKE LAS VEGAS

30 miles SE of Las Vegas

This is one of the most popular excursions from Las Vegas. Hoover Dam is visited by as many as 3,000 people daily. Why should you join them? Because Hoover Dam is an engineering and architectural marvel, and it changed the Southwest forever. Without it, you wouldn't even be going to Vegas. Kids may be bored, unless they like machinery or just plain big things, but expose them to it anyway, for their own good. Buy them ice cream and a Hoover Dam snow globe as a bribe. If you are visiting Lake Mead, it's a must.

Getting There

Drive east on Flamingo Road or Tropicana Avenue to U.S. 515 S, which automatically turns into I-93 S and takes you right to the dam. This involves a dramatic drive as you go through Boulder City and come over a rise, and Lake Mead suddenly appears spread out before you. It's a beautiful sight. At about this point, the road narrows to two lanes, and traffic can slow considerably. After the 2010 opening of a bypass bridge (dramatic on its own for its soaring height over the canyon), vehicles no longer pass directly over the bridge to get from Nevada to Arizona, but despite hopes that the bypass would make the commute better, it hasn't helped much. On a normal day, getting to the dam will take about an hour.

Go past the turnoff to Lake Mead to Nevada State Route 172, the well-marked Hoover Dam Access Road. As you near the dam, you'll see a five-story

PREVIOUS PAGE: **Hoover Dam.**

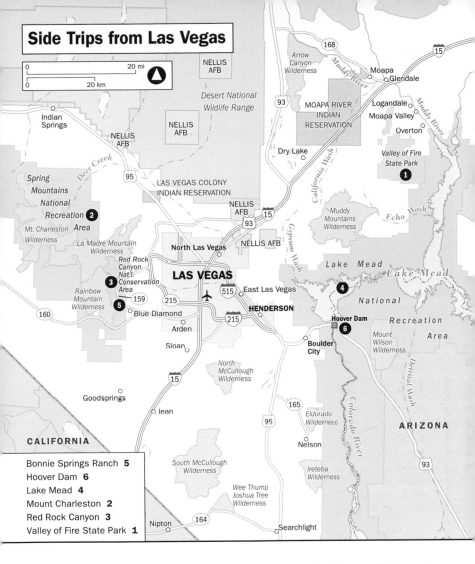

Side Trips from Las Vegas

parking structure tucked into the canyon wall on your left. Park here ($7 charge) and take the elevators or stairs to the walkway leading to the visitor center.

If you would rather go on an **organized tour,** check out **Gray Line** (www.grayline.com; ℭ **800/634-6579**), which offers a half-day tour of the dam from $60 or a daylong tour that includes a paddleboat cruise of Lake Mead and a tour of the Ethel M Chocolate factory from $99.

Hoover Dam ★★★

There would be no Las Vegas as we know it without Hoover Dam. Certainly, the neon and glitz that we know and love would not exist. In fact, the growth of the entire Southwest can be tied directly to the electricity created by the dam.

Winged Figures of the Republic, **Hoover Dam.**

Until Hoover Dam was built, much of the southwestern United States was plagued by two natural problems: parched, sandy terrain that lacked irrigation for most of the year and extensive flooding in spring and early summer, when the mighty Colorado River, fed by melting snow from its source in the Rocky Mountains, overflowed its banks and destroyed crops, lives, and property. On the positive side, raging unchecked over eons, the river's turbulent, rushing waters carved the Grand Canyon.

In 1928, prodded by the seven states through which the river runs during the course of its 1,400-mile journey to the Gulf of California, Congress authorized construction of a dam at Boulder Canyon (later moved to Black Canyon). The Senate's declaration of intention states, "A mighty river, now a source of destruction, is to be curbed and put to work in the interests of society." Construction began in 1931. Because of its vast scope and the unprecedented problems posed in its realization, the project generated significant advances in many areas of machinery production, engineering, and construction. An army of more than 5,200 laborers was assembled, and work proceeded 24 hours a day. Completed in 1936, 2 years ahead of schedule and $15 million under budget (it is, no doubt, a Wonder of the Modern Fiscal World), the dam stopped the annual floods and conserved water for irrigation, industry, and domestic uses. Equally important, it became one of the world's major electrical-generating plants, providing low-cost, pollution-free hydroelectric power to a score of surrounding communities. Hoover Dam's $165-million cost has been repaid with interest by the sale of inexpensive power to a number of California cities and the states of Arizona and Nevada. The dam is a government project that paid for itself—a feat almost as awe inspiring as its engineering.

The dam itself is a massive curved wall, 660 feet thick at the bottom, tapering to 45 feet where a road crosses it at the top. It towers 726 feet above bedrock (about the height of a 60-story skyscraper) and acts as a plug between the canyon walls to hold back up to 9.2 trillion gallons of water in Lake Mead, the reservoir created by its construction. Four concrete intake towers on the lake side drop the water down about 600 feet to drive turbines and create power, after which the water spills out into the river and continues south.

All the architecture is on a grand scale, and the design has beautiful Art Deco elements, unusual in an engineering project. Note, for instance, the monumental 30-foot bronze sculpture, *Winged Figures of the Republic,* flanking a 142-foot flagpole at the Nevada entrance. According to its creator, Oskar Hansen, the sculpture symbolizes "the immutable calm of intellectual resolution, and the enormous power of trained physical strength, equally enthroned in placid triumph of scientific achievement."

Seven miles northwest of the dam on U.S. 93, you'll pass through **Boulder City,** which was built to house managerial and construction workers. Sweltering summer heat (many days it is 125°F/52°C) ruled out a campsite by the dam. The higher elevation of Boulder City offered lower temperatures. The city emerged within a single year, turning a desert wasteland into a community of 6,000. By 1934, it was Nevada's third-largest town.

TOURING THE DAM

The very nice **Hoover Dam Visitor Center,** a vast three-level circular concrete structure with a rooftop overlook, opened in 1995. Once you pass through security (small bags and purses are allowed if scanned) you'll enter the main lobby, where you can buy tour tickets; peruse informational exhibits, photographs, and memorabilia; and view video presentations about the importance of water to life, the events leading up to the construction of Hoover Dam, and the construction itself. Exhibits on the Plaza Level include interactive displays on the environment, habitation, the development of the Southwest, the people who built the dam, and related topics.

Yet another floor up, galleries on the Overlook Level demonstrate, via sculpted bronze panels, the benefits of Hoover Dam and Lake Mead to the states of Arizona, Nevada, and California. The Overlook Level additionally provides an unobstructed view of Lake Mead, the dam, the power plant, the Colorado River, and Black Canyon. There are multiple photo opportunities throughout this trip.

You can visit an exhibit center across the street, where a 10-minute presentation in a small theater focuses on a topographical map of the 1,400-mile Colorado River. It also has a cafeteria. It costs $8 to visit just this portion, but for an extra $3 you can get the Powerplant Tour as well (see below). The center closes at 6pm (5:15pm is the last admission time), though hours vary seasonally.

There are two tours available, the Powerplant Tour and the Hoover Dam Tour. The cost of the former is $11 for adults; $9 for seniors, children 4 to 16, and

Hoover Dam installations at Lake Mead.

military personnel and their dependents; and free for children 3 and under and military in uniform. It is self-guided and takes about 2 hours if you really stop to look at and read everything (less if you're a skimmer). The more extensive Hoover Dam Tour includes the self-guided portion but adds an hour-long guided tour into the deeper recesses of the facility. It is $30 per person; no children age 7 and under are allowed. Tickets for the Hoover Dam Tour must be purchased at the Visitor Center, while admission to the Visitor Center and tickets for the Power-plant Tour are available online. Parking is $7 no matter which tour you take, and the lot takes cash only. There is no need to call ahead to reserve a place, but for more information, call ⓒ **866/730-9097** or 702/494-2517.

On the Powerplant Tour, visitors go to the center, see a movie, and walk on top of the dam. While both tours include a 530-foot descent via elevator into the dam to view the massive generators, the Powerplant Tour is a self-guided tour aided by the occasional information kiosk or guide/docent stationed at intervals along the way; the pricier Hoover Dam Tour offers the same attractions and view-ing opportunities, but it is guided, lasts an hour, and is limited to 20 people. If you plan on taking that tour, be aware that it covers over a mile and a half of walk-ing on concrete and gravel, with no handicapped access. The Hoover Dam Tour is offered every half-hour, with the last tour at 3:30pm, while the final Powerplant Tour admission is at 5:15pm.

Some fun facts you might hear on the tour: It took 6½ years to fill the lake. Though 96 workers were killed during construction, contrary to popular myth, none were accidentally buried as the concrete was poured (it was poured at a level of 8 in. at a time). Look for a monument outside dedicated to the workers who were killed—"they died to make the desert bloom"—along with a tombstone for their doggy mascot who was also killed, albeit after the dam was completed. Compare their wages of 50¢ an hour to those of their Depression-era peers, who made 5¢ to 30¢. For more information on the dam, and sometimes discount cou-pons, visit www.usbr.gov/lc/hooverdam.

Lake Mead National Recreation Area ★★

Under the auspices of the National Park Service, 1.5-million-acre Lake Mead National Recreation Area was created in 1936 around Lake Mead (the reservoir lake that is the result of the construction of Hoover Dam) and later Lake Mohave to the south (formed by the construction of Davis Dam). Before the lakes emerged, this desert region was brutally hot, dry, and rugged—unfit for human habitation. Today, it's one of the nation's most popular playgrounds, attracting millions of visitors annually. The two lakes comprise 247 square miles. At an elevation of just over 1,000 feet, Lake Mead itself extends some 110 miles upstream toward the Grand Canyon. Its 700-mile shoreline, backed by spectacu-lar cliff and canyon scenery, forms a perfect setting for a wide variety of waters-ports and desert hiking.

Having said all that, Lake Mead is in the beginning stages of a crisis so large that if unchecked, it would spell the end for Vegas entirely. The nation's largest res-ervoir has experienced a severe drop-off in levels since 2000, a combination of drought, global warming, and increased use. Whole portions of the lake's edges are now dry, in the process exposing the remains of some of the small towns that were flooded to build the thing in the first place. These have become tourist spots them-selves. In 2010, the lake was at 39% of its capacity and hit a record low height of 1,083 feet above sea level. Things got a little better in 2011 and 2012 with increased water flow into the lake, but it is still a fraction of its former self and the long-term risk is still present. According to a research study published in 2008, there is a 50% chance the lake will go dry by 2021 and because it supplies water to Las Vegas (not to mention hydroelectric power), that has grave implications for that city. Let's encourage those fancy new hotels to put in drought-tolerant plants instead of more grass. And don't ask for your towels to be changed every day.

Keep in mind that if the lake water shortage continues, many of the following outdoor activities will probably be affected in one way or another, if they aren't already.

The **Alan Bible Visitor Center,** also known as the Lake Mead Visitor Center, 4 miles northeast of Boulder City on U.S. 93, at NV 166 (© **702/293-8990**), can provide information on all area activities and services. You can pick up trail maps and brochures here, view informative films, and find out about scenic drives, accommodations, ranger-guided hikes, naturalist programs and lectures, bird-watching, canoeing, camping, lakeside RV parks, and picnic facilities. The center has some sweet exhibits about the area and is staffed by friendly folks full of local pride. It's open daily from 8:30am to 4:30pm except Thanksgiving, Christmas, and New Year's Day.

For information on camping, boat rentals, fishing, tours, and more, visit the National Parks Service website at www.nps.gov/lame.

The **entry fee** for the area is $10 per vehicle, which covers all passengers, or $5 per person if you're walking, motorcycling, or biking in. Entry fees cover 1 to 7 days and yearly passes are available for $30 per vehicle or individual.

Outdoor Activities

This is a lovely area for scenic drives amid the dramatic desert landscape. One popular route follows the Lakeshore and Northshore scenic drives along the edge of Lake Mead. From these roads, there are panoramic views of the blue lake, set against a backdrop of the browns, blacks, reds, and grays that make up the desert mountains. Northshore Scenic Drive also leads through areas of brilliant red boulders and rock formations, and you'll find a picnic area along the way.

Boating on Lake Mead.

BOATING & FISHING The **Las Vegas Boat Harbor** (www.boatinglakemead. com; ✆ **702/293-1191**) rents powerboats, pontoon boats, personal watercraft, and watersports equipment. It also carries groceries, clothing, marine supplies, sporting goods, water-skiing gear, fishing equipment, and bait and tackle. Similar services are offered at the **Callville Bay Resort & Marina** (www.callvillebay.com; ✆ **800/255-5561** or 702/565-8958), which is usually less crowded. Nonresidents can get a fishing license here ($69 for a year or $18 for 1 day plus $7 for each additional day; discounts for children 14 and under are available; additional fees apply for special fishing classifications, including trout, which require a $10 stamp for taking or possessing that fish). Largemouth bass, striped bass, channel catfish, crappie, and bluegill are found in Lake Mead; rainbow trout, largemouth bass, and striped bass are in Lake Mohave. You can also arrange here to rent a fully equipped houseboat at **Echo Bay,** 40 miles north.

CAMPING Lake Mead's shoreline is dotted with campsites, all of them equipped with running water, picnic tables, and grills. Available on a first-come, first-served basis, they are administered by the **National Park Service** (www.nps.gov/ lame; ✆ **702/293-8990**). There's a charge of $10 per night at each campsite.

CANOEING The **Alan Bible Visitor Center** (see above) can provide a list of outfitters that rent canoes for trips on the Colorado River. A canoeing permit ($12 per person) is required in advance and is available from livery services licensed by the Bureau of Reclamation. Questions about launch permits should be directed to Black Canyon River Adventures (www.black canyonadventures.com; ✆ **702/494-2204**). You can apply for and receive the permit on the same day that you plan to canoe.

HIKING The best season for hiking is November through March (it's too hot the rest of the year). Some ranger-guided hikes are offered via the **Alan Bible Visitor Center** (see above), which also stocks detailed trail maps. Three trails, ranging in length from .75 mile to 6 miles, originate at the visitor center. The 6-mile trail goes past remains of the railroad built for the dam project. Be sure to take all necessary desert-hiking precautions. (See "Desert Hiking Advice," below.)

LAKE CRUISES A delightful way to enjoy Lake Mead is on a cruise aboard the **Lake Mead Cruises** boat *Desert Princess* ★ (www.lakemeadcruises. com; ✆ **702/293-6180**), a Mississippi-style paddle-wheeler. It's a relaxing, scenic trip (enjoyed from an open promenade deck or one of two fully enclosed, climate-controlled decks) through Black Canyon and past colorful rock formations known as the Arizona Paint Pots en route to Hoover Dam, which is lit at night. Options include narrated midday cruises ($25 adults, $13 children), brunch cruises ($45 adults, $20 children), and dinner cruises ($58 adults, $25 children). Dinner is served in a pleasant, windowed, air-conditioned dining room. There's a full onboard bar. Brunch and dinner cruises run April through October, and the midday cruises run February through November. Call for departure times.

SCUBA DIVING October through April, there's good visibility, lessened in summer months when algae flourishes. A list of good dive locations, authorized instructors, and nearby dive shops is available at the **Alan Bible Visitor Center** (see above). There's a designated underwater-diving area near Lake Mead Marina.

DESERT hiking **ADVICE**

Except in summer, when temperatures can reach 120°F (49°C) in the shade, the Las Vegas area is great for hiking. The best hiking season is November through March. Great locales include the incredibly scenic Red Rock Canyon (p. 336) and Valley of Fire State Park (p. 333).

Hiking in the desert is exceptionally rewarding, but it can be dangerous. Here are some safety tips:

1. Don't hike alone.

2. Carry plenty of water and drink it often. Don't assume that spring water is safe to drink. A gallon of water per person per day is recommended for hikers.

3. Be alert for signs of heat exhaustion (headache, nausea, dizziness, fatigue, and cool, damp, pale, or red skin).

4. Gauge your fitness accurately. Desert hiking may involve rough or steep terrain. Don't take on more than you can handle.

5. Check weather forecasts before starting out. Thunderstorms can turn into raging flash floods, which are extremely hazardous to hikers.

6. Dress properly. Wear sturdy walking shoes for rock scrambling, long pants (to protect yourself from rocks and cacti), a hat, and sunglasses.

7. Wear sunscreen and carry a small first-aid kit.

8. Be careful when climbing on sandstone, which can be surprisingly soft and crumbly.

9. Don't feed or play with animals, such as the wild burros in Red Rock Canyon. (It's actually illegal to approach them.)

10. Be alert for snakes and insects. Though they're rarely encountered, you'll want to look into a crevice before putting your hand into it.

11. Visit park or other information offices before you start out and acquaint yourself with rules and regulations and any possible hazards. It's also a good idea to tell the staff where you're going, when you'll return, how many are in your party, and so on. Some park offices offer hiker-registration programs.

12. Follow the hiker's creed: Take only photographs and leave only footprints.

Boulder City

You might want to consider poking around Boulder City on your way back to Vegas. Literally the company town for those building Hoover Dam, it was created by the wives who came with their husbands and turned a temporary site into a real community, since aided by the recreational attractions and attendant businesses of Lake Mead. It doesn't look like much as you first approach it, but once you are in the heart, you'll discover that it's quite charming, an old-fashioned town all the more preserved and quiet due to its status as the only city in Nevada where gambling is illegal. It's worth getting out and taking a little stroll. There are some antiques and curio shops, and a number of burger and Mexican-food joints and family-style restaurants, including the **Coffee Cup Diner,** 512 Nevada Hwy. (www.worldfamouscoffeecup.com; © **702/294-0517**), which is right on the road to and from the dam. A '50s diner in looks and menu, it has the usual

LEADING (lake) LAS VEGAS

Originally created as a playground for the rich and famous (Céline Dion had a house here), Lake Las Vegas is a man-made reservoir created in a formerly dry, dusty valley about 20 miles east of the city on the way to Lake Mead. Surrounded by multimillion-dollar houses and rambling upscale condominium complexes, the bulk of the area is privately owned; but curving gracefully around the western lip of the lake is Monte-Lago Village, an homage to an Italian seaside community that features accommodations, dining, shopping, entertainment, and recreation options for those with a taste (and a budget) for the finer things in life.

But the area has been hit hard by the global economic recession, and many of the reasons to visit have vanished. The fantastic Ritz-Carlton hotel, the casino, and two of the three golf courses closed. Many of the stores and restaurants went out of business, and most of sank into bankruptcy.

Things are improving, with new life in the hotel and a return of the casino, but it's still a far cry from what its developers hoped it would be.

There are still several shops and restaurants at **MonteLago Village,** Lake Las Vegas Parkway at Strada di Villagio, Henderson (www.montelagovillage.com; ℭ **877/997-6667**). Done as an Italianate village with cobblestone streets and candy-colored buildings, it's a nice place to stroll on spring days. On hotter days you can go inside to the **Casino Monte-Lago,** 8 Strada di Villagio, Henderson (www.casinomontelago.com; ℭ **702/898-7777**), which has a couple of hundred slot machines and a few electronic table games like blackjack and roulette, but no live tables.

On the other side of the lake, the **Westin Lake Las Vegas,** 101 MonteLago Blvd. (www.westinlakelasvegas.com; ℭ **702/567-6000**), is new but in name only, having formerly been a Loews and before that a Hyatt. Not much has changed with the new ownership except the addition of their trademark "Heavenly" beds and some toning down of the Moroccan-themed decor. It is a true resort facility that may look familiar if you remember the Julia Roberts/John Cusack movie *America's Sweethearts,* which was largely filmed here. There are more than 500 rooms, a spa, several pools, restaurants, recreation programs, kids programs, and more, so you won't be lacking in things to do here or in ways to be pampered.

The former Ritz-Carlton was purchased by the luxury hotelier Dolce Group and reopened in 2011 as Ravella. Though not much has changed in the room and amenities department, a focus on the business traveler has diminished some of the personal touches that made it special.

burgers, shakes, and fries, plus complete breakfasts, and is inexpensive, friendly, and a good place to take the kids. *Note:* The restaurant is only open for breakfast and lunch, from 6am until 2pm.

WHERE TO STAY

There are no hotels on Lake Mead proper anymore, so if you want to do an overnight visit that doesn't involve a tent, your closest options include the resorts at Lake Las Vegas (covered separately in this chapter) or nearby Boulder City. The latter offers several small no-frills motels, RV parks, and a couple of noteworthy accommodations, including the historic **Boulder Dam Hotel,** 1305 Arizona St. (www.boulderdamhotel.com; ℂ **702/293-3510**), which was built in 1933 as a place for high-level government supervisors to stay during construction of the dam; and the **Quality Inn,** 110 Ville Dr. (ℂ **702/293-6444**), part of the reliable chain that offers a host of up-to-date amenities and some pretty good views of the lake.

For more information on Boulder City accommodations, call the **Las Vegas Convention and Visitors Authority** at ℂ **877/847-4858.**

VALLEY OF FIRE STATE PARK ★★

60 miles NE of Las Vegas

Most people visualize the desert as a vast expanse of undulating sands punctuated by the occasional cactus or palm-fringed oasis. But the desert of America's Southwest bears little relation to this Lawrence of Arabia image. Stretching for hundreds of miles around Las Vegas in every direction is a seemingly lifeless tundra of vivid reddish earth, shaped by time, climate, and subterranean upheavals into majestic canyons, cliffs, and ridges.

The 36,000-acre Valley of Fire State Park typifies the mountainous, red Mojave Desert. It derives its name from the brilliant sandstone formations that were created 150 million years ago by a great shifting of sand, and that continue to be shaped by the geologic processes of wind and water erosion. These are rock formations like

you'll never see anywhere else. There is nothing green, just fiery red rocks swirling unrelieved as far as the eye can see. No wonder various sci-fi movies have used this place as a stand-in for another planet—it has a most otherworldly look. The entire place is very mysterious, loaded with petroglyphs, and totally inhospitable. It's not hard to believe that for the Indians it was a sacred place, where men came as a test of their manhood. It is a natural wonder that must be seen to be appreciated.

Although it's hard to imagine in the sweltering Nevada heat, for billions of years, these rocks were under hundreds of feet of ocean. This ocean floor began to rise some 200 million years ago, and the waters became more and more shallow. Eventually, the sea made a complete retreat, leaving a muddy terrain traversed by ever-diminishing streams. A great sandy desert covered much of the southwestern part of the American continent until about 140 million years ago. Over eons, winds, massive fault action, and water erosion sculpted fantastic formations of sand and limestone. Oxidation of iron in the

One of the Seven Sisters rock formations at Valley of Fire State Park.

Lost City Museum.

sands and mud—and the effect of groundwater leaching the oxidized iron—turned the rocks the many hues of red, pink, russet, lavender, and white that can be seen today. Logs of ancient forests washed down from faraway highlands and became petrified fossils, which can be seen along two interpretive trails.

Getting There

From Las Vegas, take I-15 north to exit 75 (Valley of Fire turnoff). However, the more scenic route is I-15 north to Lake Mead Boulevard east to Northshore Road (NV 167) and then proceed north to the Valley of Fire exit. The first route takes about an hour, the second 1½ hours.

There is a $10-per-vehicle admission charge to the park ($8 for Nevada residents), regardless of how many people you cram inside.

Plan on spending a minimum of an hour in the park, though you can spend a great deal more time. It can get very hot in there (there is nothing to relieve the sun beating down on and reflecting off of all that red), and there is no water, so be certain to bring a liter, maybe two, per person in the summer. Without a guide, you must stay on paved roads, but don't worry if they end; you can always turn around and go back to the main road. You can see a great deal from the car, and there are also hiking trails.

Numerous **sightseeing tours** go to the Valley of Fire; inquire at your hotel tour desk.

The Valley of Fire can also be visited in conjunction with Lake Mead. Take NV 166 (Lakeshore Rd.) north, make a right turn on NV 167 (Northshore Rd.), turn left on NV 169 (Moapa Valley Blvd.) W—a spectacularly scenic drive—and follow the signs. Valley of Fire is about 65 miles from Hoover Dam.

What to See & Do

There are no food concessions or gas stations in the park; however, you can obtain meals or gas on NV 167 or in nearby **Overton** (15 miles northwest on NV 169). Overton is a fertile valley town replete with trees, agricultural crops, horses, and herds of cattle—quite a change in scenery. On your way in or out of the teeming metropolis, do stop off at **Inside Scoop** ★, 395 S. Moapa Valley Blvd. (⌀ **702/397-2055**), open Monday through Saturday from 11am to 8pm and Sunday from 11am to 7pm. It's a sweet, old-fashioned ice-cream parlor run by extremely friendly people, with a proper menu that, in addition to sandwiches and the like, features full dinners several evenings a week. Everything is quite tasty and fresh. Inside Scoop also does box lunches, perfect for picnicking inside the park.

At the southern edge of town is the **Lost City Museum ★**, 721 S. Moapa Valley Blvd. (© **702/397-2193**), a sweet little museum, very nicely done, commemorating an ancient ancestral Puebloan village that was discovered in the region in 1924. Artifacts dating back 12,000 years are on display, as are clay jars, dried corn and beans, arrowheads, seashell necklaces, and willow baskets from the ancient Pueblo culture that inhabited this region between a.d. 300 and 1150. Other exhibits document the Mormon farmers who settled the valley in the 1860s. A large collection of local rocks—petrified wood, fern fossils, iron pyrite, green copper, and red iron oxide, along with manganese blown bottles turned purple by the ultraviolet rays of the sun—are also displayed here. The museum is surrounded by reconstructed wattle-and-daub pueblos. Admission is $5 for adults, free for children 17 and under. It's open Thursday through Sunday 8:30am to 4:30pm, but closed Thanksgiving, December 25, and January 1.

Information headquarters for Valley of Fire is the **Visitor Center** on NV 169, 6 miles west of Northshore Road (© **702/397-2088**). It's open daily 8:30am to 4:30pm and is worth a quick stop for information and a bit of history before entering the park. Exhibits on the premises explain the origin and geologic history of the park's colorful sandstone formations, describe the ancient peoples who carved their rock art on canyon walls, and identify the plants and wildlife you're likely to see. Postcards, books, slides, and films are for sale here, and you can pick up hiking maps and brochures. Rangers can answer your park-related questions. For online information about the park, which is open sunrise to sunset, go to www.parks.nv.gov/vf.htm.

There are **hiking trails, shaded picnic sites,** and **two campgrounds** in the park. Most sites are equipped with tables, grills, water, and restrooms. A $20-per-vehicle, per-night camping fee is charged for use of the campground (plus $10 for utility hook-ups); if you're not camping, it costs $10 per vehicle to enter the park.

A hiker in Valley of Fire State Park.

Some of the notable formations in the park have been named for the shapes they vaguely resemble—a duck, an elephant, seven sisters, domes, beehives, and so on. Mouse's Tank is a natural basin that collects rainwater, so named for a fugitive Paiute called Mouse, who hid there in the late 1890s. **Native American petroglyphs** etched into the rock walls and boulders—some dating from 3,000 years ago—can be observed on self-guided trails. Petroglyphs at Atlatl Rock and Petroglyph Canyon are both easily accessible. In summer, when temperatures are usually over 100°F (38°C), you may have to settle for driving through the park in an air-conditioned car.

RED ROCK CANYON ★★★

19 miles W of Las Vegas

If you need a break from the casinos of Vegas, Red Rock Canyon is balm for your overstimulated soul. Less than 20 miles away—but a world apart—this is a magnificent unspoiled vista that should cleanse and refresh you (and if you must, a morning visit should leave you enough time for an afternoon's gambling). You can drive the panoramic 13-mile **Scenic Drive** (daily 6am–dusk) or explore more in-depth on foot, making it perfect for athletes and armchair types alike. There are many interesting sights and trail heads along the drive itself. The **National Conservation Area** (www.nv.blm.gov/redrockcanyon) offers hiking trails and internationally acclaimed rock-climbing opportunities. Especially notable is 7,068-foot Mount Wilson, the highest sandstone peak among the bluffs; for information on climbing, contact the **Red Rock Canyon Visitor Center** at ☏ 702/515-5350. There are picnic areas along the drive and in nearby **Spring Mountain Ranch State Park** (www.parks.nv.gov/smr.htm), 5 miles south, which also offers plays in an outdoor theater during the summer. Because Bonnie Springs Ranch (see later in this chapter) is just a few miles away, it makes a great base for exploring Red Rock Canyon. The entrance fee is $7 per vehicle.

Getting There

Just drive west on Charleston Boulevard, which becomes NV 159. As soon as you leave the city, the red rocks will begin to loom around you. The visitor center will appear on your right, though the sign is not the best, so keep a sharp eye out.

You can also go on an **organized tour. Gray Line** (www.grayline.com; ☏ 800/634-6579), among other companies, runs bus tours to Red Rock Canyon. Inquire at your hotel tour desk.

Finally, you can go **by bike.** Not very far out of town (at Rainbow Blvd.), Charleston Boulevard is flanked by a bike path that continues for about 11 miles to the visitor center/scenic drive. The path is hilly but not difficult, if you're in reasonable shape. However, exploring Red Rock Canyon by bike should be attempted only by exceptionally fit and experienced bikers.

Just off NV 159, you'll see the turnoff for the **Red Rock Canyon Visitor Center** (www.nv.blm.gov/redrockcanyon; ☏ 702/515-5350), which marks the actual entrance to the park. Redesigned and revamped in 2010, the center now features outdoor exhibits on the flora and fauna found in the canyon. There, you can also pick up information on trails and the driving route. The center is open daily from 8am to 4:30pm.

About Red Rock Canyon

The geological history of these ancient stones goes back some 600 million years. Over eons, the forces of nature have formed Red Rock's sandstone monoliths into arches, natural bridges, and massive sculptures painted in a stunning palette of gray-white limestone and dolomite, black mineral deposits, and oxidized minerals in earth-toned sienna hues ranging from pink to crimson and burgundy. Orange and green lichens add further contrast, as do spring-fed areas of lush foliage. And formations, such as **Calico Hill,** are brilliantly white where groundwater has leached out oxidized iron. Cliffs cut by deep canyons tower 2,000 feet above the valley floor.

During most of its history, Red Rock Canyon was below a warm, shallow sea. Massive fault action and volcanic eruptions caused this seabed to begin rising some 225 million years ago. As the waters receded, sea creatures died, and the calcium in their bodies combined with sea minerals to form limestone cliffs studded with ancient fossils. Some 45 million years later, the region was buried beneath thousands of feet of windblown sand. As time progressed, iron oxide and calcium carbonate infiltrated the sand, consolidating it into cross-bedded rock.

About 100 million years ago, massive fault action began dramatically shifting the rock landscape here, forming spectacular limestone and sandstone cliffs and rugged canyons punctuated by waterfalls, shallow streams, and serene oasis pools.

Red Rock's valley is home to more than 45 species of mammals, about 100 species of birds, 30 different reptiles and amphibians, and an abundance of plant life. Ascending the slopes from the valley, you'll see cactus and creosote bushes, aromatic purple sage, yellow-flowering blackbrush, yucca and Joshua trees, and, at higher elevations, clusters of forest-green pinyon, juniper, and ponderosa pines. In spring, the desert blooms with extraordinary wildflowers.

In the latter part of the 19th century, Red Rock was a mining site and later a sandstone quarry that provided materials for many buildings in Los Angeles, San Francisco, and early Las Vegas. By the end of World War II, as Las Vegas developed, many people became aware of the importance of preserving the canyon. In 1967, the secretary of the interior designated 62,000 acres as Red Rock Canyon Recreation Lands, under the auspices of the Bureau of Land Management, and later legislation banned all development except hiking trails and limited recreational facilities. In 1990, Red Rock Canyon became a National Conservation Area, further elevating its protected status. Its current acreage is 197,000.

Calico Basin, Red Rock Canyon.

What to See & Do

Begin with a stop at the **Visitor Center;** while there is a $7-per-vehicle fee for entering the park, you also can pick up a variety of helpful literature: history, guides, hiking trail maps, and lists of local flora and fauna. You can also view exhibits that tell the history of the canyon and depict its plant and animal life. You'll see a fascinating video here about Nevada's thousands of wild horses and burros, protected by an act of Congress since 1971. Call ahead to find out about ranger-guided tours as well as informative guided hikes offered by such groups as the Sierra Club and the Audubon Society. And if you're traveling with children, ask about the free *Junior Ranger Discovery Book,* filled with fun family activities. Books and videotapes are for sale here, including a guidebook that identifies more than 100 top-rated climbing sites.

The easiest thing to do is to **drive the 13-mile scenic loop ★★★** (or you can bike it, if you wish). It really is a loop, and it only goes one way, so once you start, you are committed to driving the entire thing. You can stop the car to admire a number of fabulous views and sights along the way, or have a picnic, or take a walk or hike. As you drive, observe how dramatically the milky-white limestone alternates with iron-rich red rocks. Farther along, the mountains become solid limestone, with canyons running between them, which lead to an evergreen forest—a surprising sight in the desert.

If you're up to it, however, we can't stress enough that the way to really see the canyon is by **hiking.** Every trail is incredible—glance over your options and decide what you might be looking for. You can begin from the Visitor Center or drive into the loop, park your car, and start from points therein. Hiking trails range from a .7-mile-loop stroll to a waterfall (its flow varying seasonally) at Lost Creek to much longer and more strenuous treks. Actually, all the hikes involve a certain amount of effort, as you have to scramble over rocks on even the shortest hikes. Unfit or undexterous people should beware. Be sure to wear good shoes, as the rocks can be slippery. You must have a map; you won't get lost forever (there usually are other hikers around to help you out, eventually), but you can still get lost. Once deep into the rocks, everything looks the same, even with the map, so give yourself extra time for each hike (at least an additional hour), regardless of its billed length.

A popular 2-mile round-trip hike leads to **Pine Creek Canyon** and the creekside ruins of a historic home site surrounded by ponderosa pine trees. Our hiking trail of choice is the **Calico Basin,** which is accessed along the loop. After an hour walk up the rocks (which is not that well marked), you end up at an oasis surrounded by sheer walls of limestone (which makes the oasis itself inaccessible, alas). In the summer, flowers and deciduous trees grow out of the walls.

Biking the scenic loop at Red Rock Canyon.

As you hike, keep your eyes peeled for lizards, the occasional desert tortoise, herds of bighorn sheep, birds, and other critters. But the rocks themselves are the most fun, with small caves to explore and rock formations to climb on. On trails along Calico Hills and the escarpment, look for "Indian marbles," a local name for small, rounded sandstone rocks that have eroded off larger sandstone formations. Petroglyphs are also tucked away in various locales.

Biking is a tremendous way to travel the loop. There are also terrific off-road mountain-biking trails, with levels from amateur to expert.

The gleaming luxurious **Red Rock Resort** (p. 316) gives day-trippers a new, highly desirable refueling point on a trip to the canyon. Be sure to stop by the food court Capriotti's, the economical submarine sandwich shop. The subs are ideal for takeout for picnics in the park (buy a cheap Styrofoam ice chest at a convenience store) or for in-room dining as you rest up in your hotel post-hike.

MOUNT CHARLESTON ★★

About 35 miles NW of Las Vegas

Although officially known as the Springs Mountains National Recreation Area, this region is more popularly referred to by the name of its most prominent landmark, the 11,918-foot-high Mount Charleston. Visible from Las Vegas proper, the mountain and its surrounding recreation areas have been a popular getaway for locals and vacationers alike for decades.

Comprising more than 316,000 acres of the Humboldt-Toiyabe National Forest (the largest in the lower 48), the area is practically an earth science class covering geography of such variety that it almost causes whiplash. As you start up the road toward the peak, you are surrounded by the kind of desert sagebrush and Joshua trees that are most predominant at the lower levels. Suddenly the road takes a curve and a dip, and the desert gives way to a pinyon-juniper based eco-system, full of craggy canyons and trees. Finally you dive into the full-on forests of ponderosa and bristlecone pines, which create a lush oasis powered by more than 100 natural springs formed by water and snow runoff that soaks through the porous limestone rock and eventually bubbles to the surface.

Outdoor activities are the predominant lure and include hiking, camping, rock climbing, horseback riding, and, during the winter months, skiing and snowboarding.

Getting There

Head north on I-15 away from the Strip and then transition to U.S. 95 N. About 18 miles of freeway-style driving will bring you to the first of two roads up to the Mount Charleston area. Kyle Canyon Road/NV 157 will take you about 17 miles up toward the summit and is where you'll find the **Spring Mountain Visitor Center** (✆ **702/229-3111**), many of the campgrounds and hiking trails, the Mount Charleston Resort, and the Mount Charleston Lodge. A few miles farther is Lee Canyon Road/NV 156, which runs about 18 miles up to the Las Vegas Ski and Snowboard Resort (see "Snow Sports," below). It's only about 35 miles or so from Downtown Las Vegas, but traffic on the freeways in town is often difficult (to say the least) so give yourself an hour to be safe. **Note:** Chains are often required during or after snowfalls, which can be epic in the area. A December 2010 storm dumped a record 90 inches here over the course of several days.

Also note that there are no gas stations, convenience stores, or other services (and that often includes cellphone service) in the area, so be sure to fill up the tank and bring whatever supplies you may need with you.

Outdoor Activities

You might well be satisfied with a drive up to the region and, if it's wintertime, gazing at the snow from the warmth of your vehicle. We know that many of you come to Las Vegas in the winter to get away from the snow, but for those who don't get to see it very often, snow-covered Mount Charleston could very well be an entertaining sight. But if you want to actually get out of the car, there are a number of recreation activities available.

CAMPING   There are seven campgrounds available in the Mount Charleston area, although only the McWilliams, Fletcher View, and Kyle Canyon sites are open year-round. Some have hookups if you are bringing your camper with you, while others are good for just tents and your sleeping bag; most have toilets, fire pits, and other outdoorsy conveniences. Fees range from $8 to $47, depending on the number of people and vehicles. A full listing of the campgrounds is available at the USDA Forest Service website at www.fs.usda.gov (then search for the Spring Mountains National Recreation Area). To make reservations for any of the sites, use the National Recreation Reservation Service at ✆ **877/ 444-6777** or head online to www.recreation.gov.

HIKING   Whether you are an expert hiker or a casual walker, there is probably a trail here for you—more than two dozen total. The Echo/Little Falls trail is a relatively easy mile or so through forests that lead to a small waterfall. On the other end of the scale is the South Loop, an 8-mile trek that will lead you almost all the way to the summit of Mount Charleston more than 11,000 feet up. You can pick up a trail guide at the Spring Mountain Visitor Center. There is no fee to use the trails, but be sure to stick to the marked routes and follow all of the admonitions about bringing plenty of water and not drinking from the natural springs (they are pretty but contain parasites that can make you sick).

HORSEBACK RIDING   Almost all of the hiking trails are open to horses, and there are several companies that offer riding services and supplies in the area. Chief among them is **Mount Charleston Trail Rides** (www. mountcharlestontrailrides.com; ✆ **702/596-6715**), a family-owned and -operated establishment that has been offering trail, carriage, and sleigh rides for more than 30 years. Hourly rates start at $40 and they have special breakfast and lunch rides, plus pony rides for kids 7 and over. During the winter you can take a sleigh ride (bring along your own warm apple cider).

ROCK CLIMBING   There are several rock-climbing opportunities available in the Mount Charleston area, but all of them are do-it-yourself—no cushy controlled environments here. The most popular sites are the Hood along the unfortunately named Trail Canyon Trail, or Robber's Roost, accessed from the trail head along Highway 158. For more information, pick up a guide at the Spring Mountain Visitor Center.

SNOW SPORTS   The **Las Vegas Ski and Snowboard Resort,** Highway 156, Mount Charleston (www.skilasvegas.com; ✆ **702/385-2754**), offers 11 trails ranging from beginner to advanced, including a half-pipe and the Darkside Park with tabletop jumps and assorted rails. Lift tickets are $40 to $60

SIDE TRIPS | Mount Charleston

for adults, and $30 to $45 for children 12 and under and seniors 60 and over. The facility offers a full array of equipment and clothing rentals; there's also a small snack bar and sundry shop if you forgot to bring a camera with which to record yourself in full downhill glory (or falling repeatedly, if you are like us). It is usually open late November through early April from 9am until 4pm, but that may vary based on conditions. **Note:** A major expansion and renovations of the facilities here is underway, due to be complete by winter 2013 season. As a result, some features may be unavailable periodically.

Where to Stay & Dine

In addition to the aforementioned snack shop at the Las Vegas Ski and Snowboard Resort, there is only one other dining option outside of the Mount Charleston Resort (see below). The **Mount Charleston Lodge,** 5375 Kyle Canyon Rd., (www.mtcharlestonlodge.com; ✆ **702/872-5708**), has a rustic dining room with 20-foot ceilings in an A-frame, ski-lodge type building; a big bar; an open fireplace in the center of the room; and big windows and an outdoor patio from which you can enjoy the scenic views from its 7,717-foot elevation. They serve a wide range of American comfort food, from burgers to ribs, and are open for breakfast, lunch, and dinner from 8am until 9pm Sunday through Thursday; and from 8am until 10pm on Friday and Saturday. The lounge is open daily until midnight.

Mount Charleston Resort ★   Purchased in 2010 by the Siegel Group—the same company that rescued the Gold Spike in Downtown Las Vegas—the Mount Charleston Resort has undergone some serious improvements that have kept the charm of the place, but modernized it and moved it upscale a notch or two. The ski-chalet style buildings (log and stone exteriors) are tucked into a canyon providing a gorgeous backdrop for a peaceful retreat. The lobby has a big fireplace perfect for warming up after a winter hike, along with a small menagerie of stuffed animals that seem *de rigueur* in a place like this.

The rooms range from standard motel size to presidential suites, all with comfortably modern furnishings, flatscreen TVs, faux fireplaces, iPod radios, DVD players, and more.

On-site there is a small spa and fitness center; a full-service restaurant serving breakfast, lunch, and dinner (classic American fare); a sundry store/bistro with quick bites; and a bar and lounge complete with a few video poker machines if you're going into gambling withdrawal.

2 Kyle Canyon Rd., Las Vegas, NV 89124. www.mtcharlestonresort.com. ✆ 888/559-1888 or 702/872-5500. Fax 702/872-5374. 61 units. $40 and up double. Resort fee $9.95. Extra person $15. Children 17 and under stay free in parent's room. AE, MC, V, DISC. Free self-parking. Amenities: 2 restaurants; bar/lounge; spa. In room: A/C, TV, hair dryer, Wi-Fi.

BONNIE SPRINGS RANCH/OLD NEVADA ★★

About 24 miles W of Las Vegas, 5 miles past Red Rock Canyon

Bonnie Springs Ranch/Old Nevada is a kind of Wild West theme park with accommodations and a restaurant. If you're traveling with kids, a day trip to Bonnie Springs is recommended, but it is appealing for adults, too. It could even be a romantic getaway, as it offers horseback riding, gorgeous mountain vistas, proximity to Red Rock Canyon, and temperatures 5° to 10° cooler than on the Strip.

If you're **driving,** a trip to Bonnie Springs Ranch can be combined easily with a day trip to Red Rock Canyon; it is about 5 miles farther. But you can also stay overnight.

Jeep tours to and from Las Vegas are available through **Action Tours.** Call ✆ **888/288-5200** or 702/566-7400 or visit www.actiontours.com for details.

What to See & Do

Old Nevada is a re-creation of an 1880s frontier town, built on the site of a very old ranch. As tourist sights go, this is a classic one, if a bit worn around the edges; it's a bit cheesy, but knowingly, perhaps even deliberately, so. It's terrific for kids up to about the age of 12 or so (before teenage cynicism kicks in), but not all that bad for adults fondly remembering similar places from their own childhoods. Many go expecting a tourist trap, only to come away saying that it really was rather cute and charming. Still others find it old in the bad way.

Old Nevada looks authentic, with rustic buildings made entirely of weathered wood. And the setting, right in front of beautiful mountains with layered red rock, couldn't be more perfect for a Western. They offer shoot-'em-up stunt shows, stage melodramas (complete with moustache-twirling villains for you to hiss and boo at), and an Old West town that you can wander through for souvenir shopping and tourist attraction–type activities (dress up in a period costume and get your picture taken!).

The Bonnie Springs Zoo is a petting zoo with the usual suspects (deer, sheep, goats, and rabbits) and some unusual animals (potbelly pigs and snooty llamas) to caress and feed, and there is also a mazelike enclosure with wire-mesh pens that contain a variety of livestock, some of which should not be penned up (though they are well taken care of), including wolves and bobcats. Still, it's more than diverting for kids.

Less politically and ecologically distressing is the aviary, which houses peacocks, Polish chickens, peachface and blackmask lovebirds, finches, parakeets, ravens, ducks, pheasants, and geese. Keep your eyes peeled for the peacocks roaming free; with luck, they will spread their tails for a photo op. With greater

Old Nevada.

Bonnie Springs is full of hokey but fun tourist options.

Trail ride at Bonnie Springs ranch.

luck, some of the angelic, rare white peacocks will do the same. It may be worth dropping by just in the hopes of spotting one in full fan-tailed glory.

Riding stables offer guided hour-long trail rides into the mountain area on a continuous basis throughout the day (spring–fall 10:30am–5pm, summer until 6pm). Children must be at least 6 years old to participate. Cost is $55 per person. There are also breakfast, lunch, and dinner rides, which cost from $118 to $140 per person. For more information, call ✆ **702/875-4191.**

There is a small on-site restaurant and bar serving good old-fashioned grub (barbecue, steaks, and the like) and even a motel if you love the place so much that you must spend the night here. Chance are you won't—this is better for an afternoon distraction before you head back to the bright lights of Vegas—but more information on the cowboy-themed, basic motel accommodations are available on their website (listed below).

On Monday and Tuesday, only the petting zoo is open and admission is $5 per person. Wednesday through Friday the petting zoo and Old Nevada are up and running but admission is still $5 per person. Saturday and Sunday admission bumps up to $7 per person. From November through April, Old Nevada is open weekdays from 11am until 5pm and Saturday and Sunday from 10:30am until 5pm. The rest of the year it is open until 6pm daily.

For additional information, you can call **Bonnie Springs Ranch/Old Nevada** at ✆ **702/875-4191,** or visit them on the Web at www.bonniesprings.com.

THE GRAND CANYON

About 270 miles E of Las Vegas

The geographically challenged among us believe that the Grand Canyon is just a hop, skip, and a jump from Las Vegas and therefore a great idea for a side trip while visiting Sin City. While this may be true from a strictly comparative basis— the canyon is closer to Vegas than it is to, say, London—it is not exactly what you might call "close." The South Rim is about 270 miles from Las Vegas via two- and four-lane highways. This equates to a solid 5-hour drive on a good day and an hour or two more than that during peak traffic times. In other words, if you want to take a quick day trip to the Grand Canyon from Las Vegas, you better accept the fact that it's going to be a very long day and you won't have much time at the park. An overnight visit or taking advantage of an air tour is probably a better bet.

But if you have the time and the energy, visiting the Grand Canyon is a breathtaking experience. There's a reason why it is considered one of the seven natural wonders of the world.

Open year-round, the South Rim is the most popular area of the park and the one that you should visit if you have never been, as it offers the most options in terms of lodging, tours, activities, restaurants, and more. Keep in mind, however, that there are other areas of the park worth visiting. For more information on the North Rim and other Grand Canyon National Park destinations, visit www.frommers.com.

Getting There

If you're taking your own car, head east on Flamingo Road or Tropicana Boulevard to I-515 S. This becomes NV 93, which crosses over Hoover Dam into Arizona and will lead to I-40 at Kingman. Take the interstate east to NV 64 at Williams, Arizona, and follow the signs north. Drivers should be advised that much of the route to the Grand Canyon from Las Vegas is along narrow, twisty roads that can be a challenge and are often jammed with traffic.

Lipan Point, the Grand Canyon's South Rim.

PLANNING YOUR TRIP TO LAS VEGAS

Whether you are visiting Las Vegas for the first time or the 50th, planning a trip here can be an overwhelming experience—as overwhelming as the city itself. With about 150,000 hotel rooms, nearly as many slot machines, thousands of restaurants, and dozens of shows and attractions, there are seemingly endless ways to lose or waste your money. This chapter is designed to help you navigate the practical details of designing a Vegas experience that is tailored to your needs, from getting to and around the city to advice on the best times to visit and more.

Lots of people, both from the U.S. and abroad, believe that Las Vegas is the way it is portrayed in movies and television. For the most part, it isn't. Well, okay, you are more likely to run into a random showgirl or Elvis impersonator here than you are in say, Wichita, but they aren't in the background of every photo opportunity. International visitors, especially, should pay close attention to the material that follows in order to prepare for the most common nonshowgirl issues you may encounter in Las Vegas or on your way here. We also suggest that you check out chapter 7, "Entertainment & Nightlife," before you leave home. If you want to see the most popular shows, it's a good idea to call ahead and order tickets well in advance to avoid disappointment. Ditto if you want to dine in one of the city's top restaurants: see chapter 5, "Where to Eat," for reviews and contact information.

GETTING THERE

By Plane

Las Vegas is served by **McCarran International Airport,** 5757 Wayne Newton Blvd. (℃ **702/261-5211,** TDD 702/261-3111; www.mccarran.com), just a few minutes' drive from the southern end of the Strip, where the bulk of casinos and hotels are concentrated. The airport is known online by the code **LAS.**

Most major domestic and many international airlines fly into Las Vegas, and the city acts as a major routing point for low-cost Southwest Airlines.

The airport has two terminals. Terminal 1 serves mostly domestic carries with four sets of gates. A and B gates are accessible to the main ticketing area and baggage claim by (very long) hallways, while most of the C and all of the D gates are reached by taking a tram. The ultramodern Terminal 3 opened in 2012 and primarily services international and long-haul flights with its 14 gates.

In case you're wondering what happened to Terminal 2, it closed when Terminal 3 opened.

Each terminal has its own baggage-claim facility and services such as dining, shopping, and traveler assistance, along with ground transportation areas for taxis, buses, and shuttles to the rental-car facility.

PREVIOUS PAGE: **The city's iconic neon sign greets visitors at the southern end of the Strip.**

And yes, all of the terminals and baggage claims have slot machines just in case you want to lose a few bucks while you're waiting for your luggage.

By Car

The main highway connecting Las Vegas with the rest of the country is **I-15**; it links Montana, Idaho, and Utah with Southern California. The drive from Los Angeles is quite popular and can get very crowded on Friday and Sunday afternoons as hopeful weekend gamblers make their way to and from Las Vegas.

From the east, take **I-70** or **I-80** west to Kingman, Arizona, and then **U.S. 93** north to Downtown Las Vegas (Fremont St.). From the south, take **I-10** west to Phoenix, and then U.S. 93 north to Las Vegas. From San Francisco, take I-80 east to Reno, and then **U.S. 95** south to Las Vegas.

Vegas is 286 miles from Phoenix, 759 miles from Denver, 421 miles from Salt Lake City, 269 miles from Los Angeles, and 586 miles from San Francisco.

International visitors should note that insurance and taxes are almost never included in quoted rental-car rates in the U.S. Be sure to ask your rental agency about these. They can add a significant cost to your car rental.

For information on car rentals and gasoline (petrol) in Las Vegas, see "Getting Around: By Car," below.

By Bus

Bus travel is often the most economical form of public transit for short hops between U.S. cities, but it's certainly not an option for everyone. Though getting to Vegas this way is cheaper, especially if you book in advance, it's also time consuming (a 1-hr. flight from L.A. becomes a 5- to 8-hr. trek by bus) and usually not as comfortable. So you need to figure out how much time and comfort mean to you. **Greyhound** (www.greyhound.com; ✆ **800/231-2222** in the U.S.; ✆ **001/ 214/849-8100** outside the U.S. with toll-free access) is the sole nationwide bus line. International visitors can obtain information about the **Greyhound North American Discovery Pass.** The pass, which offers unlimited travel and stopovers in the U.S. and Canada, can be obtained outside the United States from travel agents or through www.discoverypass.com.

The main Greyhound terminal in Las Vegas is located Downtown next to The Plaza hotel, 200 S. Main St. (✆ **702/383-9792**), and is open 24 hours. Although it's just a block from the Fremont Street Experience, it's several miles from the Strip in both location and atmosphere (why can't they put bus stations in nice neighborhoods?). Cabs are usually available right out front to whisk you to more scenic areas, but guard your valuables on arrival.

By Train

Amtrak (✆ **800/872-7245;** www.amtrak.com) does not currently offer direct rail service, although plans have been in the works to restore the rails between Los Angeles and Las Vegas for years. We've been hearing these reports for so long now, they just make us roll our eyes.

In the meantime, you can take the train to Los Angeles or Barstow, and Amtrak will get you to Las Vegas by bus, which takes 5 to 6 hours depending on traffic.

GETTING AROUND

It isn't too hard to navigate your way around Vegas. But do remember: Thanks to huge hotel acreage, increased and very slow traffic, and lots and lots of people—like you—trying to explore, getting around takes a lot longer than you might think. Heck, it can take 15 to 20 minutes to get from your room to another part of your hotel! Always allow for plenty of time to get from point A to point B.

Getting into Town from the Airport

Getting to your hotel from the airport is a cinch. You can grab one of the roughly nine gajillion cabs that are lined up waiting for you (see "By Taxi," p. 352) or you can grab a shuttle bus. **Bell Transportation** (www.bell-trans.com; ✆ **800/274-7433** or 702/739-7990) runs 20-passenger minibuses daily (3:30am–1am) between the airport and all major Las Vegas hotels and motels. The cost is $7 per person each way to hotels on the Strip or around the Convention Center, $8.50 to Downtown, and $8 to other off-Strip properties (north of Sahara Ave. and west of I-15). Several other companies run similar ventures—just look for the signs for the shuttle bus queues, located just outside of the baggage-claim area. Buses from the airport leave every few minutes. When you want to check out of your hotel and head back to the airport, call at least 2 hours in advance to be safe (though often you can just flag down one of the buses outside any major hotel).

Even less expensive are **Citizens Area Transit (CAT)** buses (www.rtcsnv.com/transit; ✆ **702/228-7433**). The no. 109 bus goes from the airport to the South Strip Transfer Terminal at Gilespie Street and Sunset Road, where you can transfer to the Strip and Downtown Express (SDX) or Deuce lines that runs along the Strip into Downtown. Alternately, the no. 108 bus departs from the airport and takes you to the Stratosphere, where you can transfer to the SDX or Deuce lines. The fares for buses on Strip routes are $5 for adults for 2 hours or $7 for 24 hours. *Note:* You might have a long walk from the bus stop to the hotel entrance, even if the bus stop is right in front of your hotel. Vans are able to get right up to the entrance, so choose a van if you're lugging lots of baggage.

If you have a large group with you, you might also try one of the limos that wait curbside at the airport, and charge $45 to $65 for a trip to the Strip. The price may go up with additional passengers, so ask about the fee very carefully. The aforementioned Bell Transportation is one reputable company that operates limousines in addition to their fleet of shuttle buses (call in advance).

By Car

If you plan to confine yourself to one part of the Strip (or one cruise down to it) or to Downtown, your feet will suffice. Otherwise, we highly recommend that visitors rent a car. The Strip is too spread out for walking (and Las Vegas is often too hot or too cold to make strolls pleasant); Downtown is too far away for a cheap cab ride, and public transportation is often ineffective in getting you where you want to go. Plus, return visits call for exploration in more remote parts of the city, and a car brings freedom, especially if you want to do any side trips at your own pace.

You should note that places with addresses some 60 blocks east or west of the Strip are actually less than a 10-minute drive—provided there is no traffic.

Having advocated renting a car, we should warn you that traffic is getting worse, and it's harder and harder to get around town with any certain swiftness. A general rule of thumb is to avoid driving on the Strip whenever you can, and avoid driving at all during peak hours (8–9:30am and 4:30–6pm), especially if you have to make a show curtain.

Parking is usually a pleasure because all casino hotels offer free valet service. That means that for a mere $2 to $3 tip, you can park right at the door, though the valet usually fills up on busy nights. In those cases, you can use the gigantic self-parking lots (free on the Strip, nominal fees Downtown) that all hotels have.

If you're visiting from abroad and plan to rent a car in the United States, keep in mind that foreign driver's licenses are usually recognized in the U.S., but you may want to consider obtaining an international driver's license. Also, international visitors should note that insurance and taxes are almost never included in quoted rental-car rates in the U.S. Be sure to ask your rental agency about these. They can add a significant cost to your car rental.

At press time, in the U.S., the cost of gasoline (also known as gas, but never petrol), is around $3.40 per gallon and tends to vary unpredictably. Taxes are already included in the printed price. One U.S. gallon equals 3.8 liters or .85 imperial gallons. Fill-up locations are known as gas or service stations. Las Vegas prices typically fall near the nationwide average. You can also check **www.vegas gasprices.com** for recent costs.

Renting a Car

If there is one bit of advice we can give you about visiting Las Vegas that we stress above most others, it is this: Rent a car! Not only will it allow you greater freedom and flexibility in what you can see and do, but it can also save you money in the long run. If you are planning on getting off the Strip at all, cabs will cost you more than a small rental, and if you are truly budget-minded, you can get a cheaper hotel elsewhere in town that will more than make up for the money you spend on a vehicle. Parking is abundant and usually free, so the only real downside is the traffic, which can be a nightmare at peak times (see p. 353 for some helpful tips on how to get around the worst of it).

Major companies with outlets in Las Vegas include **Advantage** (✆ 800/777-5500; www.advantagerentacar.com), **Alamo** (✆ 877/227-8367; www.alamo.com), **Avis** (✆ 800/230-4898; www.avis.com), **Budget** (✆ 800/527-0700; www.budget.com), **Dollar** (✆ 800/800-3665; www.dollar.com), **Enterprise** (✆ 800/261-7331; www.enterprise.com), **Hertz** (✆ 800/654-3131; www.hertz.com), **National** (✆ 800/227-7368; www.nationalcar.com), **Payless** (✆ 800/729-5377; www.paylesscarrental.com), and **Thrifty** (✆ 800/847-4389; www.thrifty.com).

Rental policies vary from company to company, but generally speaking you must be at least 25 years of age with a major credit or debit card to rent a vehicle in Las Vegas. Some companies will rent to those between 21 and 24, but will usually charge extra ($20–$30 per day) and will require proof of insurance and a major credit card; also, they may restrict the type of vehicle you are allowed to rent (forget those zippy convertibles).

All of the major car-rental companies are located at a consolidated facility at 7135 Gilespie St., just a block off Las Vegas Boulevard near Warm Springs Road and about 2½ miles from the airport. When you arrive, look for the signs for buses and shuttles in the baggage-claim area and follow them outside, where you'll find blue-and-white buses marked mccarran rent-a-car center. It takes about 10 minutes to make the trip, although it's worth noting that the lines for buses and at the car-rental counters can be long—budget some extra time if you have somewhere to be right after you get to town.

The rental-car facility is modern and easily navigable, and just in case you resisted while at the airport, there are slot machines next to the rental counters as well. Welcome to Vegas!

When exiting the facility, take three right turns and you are on the Strip, about 2 miles south of Mandalay Bay.

Car-rental rates vary even more than airline fares. The price you pay depends on the size of the car, where and when you pick it up and drop it off, the length of the rental period, where and how far you drive it, whether you purchase insurance, and a host of other factors. A few key questions could save you hundreds of dollars.

- Are weekend rates lower than weekday rates? In Vegas this is usually true, although holiday or special events weekends can be more costly. Ask if the rate is the same for pickup Friday morning, for instance, as it is for Thursday night.

- Is a weekly rate cheaper than the daily rate? Even if you need the car for only 4 days, it may be cheaper to keep it for 5.

- Does the agency assess a drop-off charge if you don't return the car to the same location where you picked it up? Is it cheaper to pick up the car at the airport than at a Downtown location?

- Are special promotional rates available? If you see an advertised price in your local newspaper, be sure to ask for that specific rate; otherwise, you may be charged the standard cost. Terms change constantly, and reservations agents are notorious for not mentioning available discounts unless you ask.

- Are discounts available for members of AARP, AAA, frequent-flier programs, or trade unions? If you belong to any of these organizations, you may be eligible for discounts of up to 30%.

- In Las Vegas, expect to add about 35% to 40% on top of the rental fee, including a $2.35-per-day vehicle license fee, a $3.75-per-day facility fee, a 10% airport concession fee, and about 20% in taxes and state government surcharges. Ouch.

- What is the cost of adding an additional driver's name to the contract?

- How many free miles are included in the price? Free mileage is often negotiable, depending on the length of the rental.

Some companies offer "refueling packages," in which you pay for an entire tank of gas up front. The price is usually fairly competitive with local gas prices, but you don't get credit for any gas remaining in the tank and because it is virtually impossible to use up every last bit of fuel before you return it, you will usually wind up paying more overall than you would if you just filled it up yourself. There are several gas stations within a few blocks radius of the car-rental center, including three at the intersection of Las Vegas Boulevard and Warm Springs Road. You may pay a few extra pennies at them than you would at stations elsewhere in town, but in the long run it's still a better deal.

Many available packages include airfare, accommodations, and a rental car with unlimited mileage. Compare these prices with the cost of booking airline tickets and renting a car separately to see if such offers are good deals. Internet resources can make comparison shopping easier.

Surfing for Rental Cars

For booking rental cars online, the best deals are usually found at rental-car company websites, although all the major online travel agencies also offer rental-car

DRIVE IN style

If the idea of tooling around Las Vegas in a pedestrian rent-a-box just doesn't sound appealing, you can always indulge your fantasies by going with something more exotic.

Las Vegas Exotic Car Rentals (© 866/871-1893 or 702/736-2592; www.vegasexoticrentals.com) has a fleet from makers such as Lamborghini, Bentley, Ferrari, Lotus, and Porsche, plus a stable of classic American muscle like the Chevrolet Corvette. They even feature an Aston Martin, if you want to work out your inner James Bond while buzzing between casinos. Rates start at about $300 per day and go up from there—sometimes, way up. The Ferrari F40 $1,284 per day, or roughly what you'll pay for a week in a standard room at a nice Vegas hotel.

reservations services. **Priceline** (www.priceline.com) and **Hotwire** (www.hot wire.com) work well for rental cars; the only "mystery" is which major rental company you get, and for most travelers, the difference between Hertz, Avis, and Budget is negligible. Also check out **Breezenet.com,** which offers domestic rental-car discounts with some of the most competitive rates around.

Demystifying Rental-Car Insurance

Before you drive off in a rental car, be sure you're insured. Hasty assumptions about your personal auto insurance or a rental agency's additional coverage could end up costing you tens of thousands of dollars—even if you are involved in an accident that was clearly the fault of another driver.

If you already hold a **private auto insurance** policy in the United States, you are most likely covered for loss of or damage to a rental car, and liability in case of injury to any other party involved in an accident. Be sure to find out whether you are covered in Vegas, whether your policy extends to all persons who will be driving the rental car, how much liability is covered in case an outside party is injured in an accident, and whether the type of vehicle you are renting is included under your contract. (Rental trucks, sport utility vehicles, and luxury vehicles may not be covered.)

Most **major credit cards** provide some degree of coverage as well—provided they were used to pay for the rental. Terms vary widely, however, so be sure to call your credit card company directly before you rent. If you don't have a private auto insurance policy, the credit card you use to rent a car may provide primary coverage if you decline the rental agency's insurance. This means that the credit card company will cover damage or theft of a rental car for the full cost of the vehicle. If you do have a private auto insurance policy, your credit card may provide secondary coverage—which basically covers your deductible. *Credit cards do not cover liability* or the cost of injury to an outside party and/or damage to an outside party's vehicle. If you do not hold an insurance policy, you may want to seriously consider purchasing additional liability insurance from your rental company. Be sure to check the terms, however: Some rental agencies cover liability only if the renter is not at fault; even then, the rental company's obligation varies from state to state. Bear in mind that each credit card company has its own peculiarities; call your own credit card company for details before relying on a card for coverage. Speaking of cards, members of AAA should be sure to carry their membership ID card with them, which provides some of the benefits touted by the rental-car agencies at no additional cost.

The basic insurance coverage offered by most rental-car companies, known as the **Loss/Damage Waiver (LDW)** or **Collision Damage Waiver (CDW),** can cost $20 per day or more. The former should cover everything, including the loss of income to the rental agency, should you get in an accident (normally not covered by your own insurance policy). It usually covers the full value of the vehicle, with no deductible, if an outside party causes an accident or other damage to the rental car. You will probably be covered in case of theft as well. Liability coverage varies, but the minimum is usually at least $15,000. If you are at fault in an accident, you will be covered for the full replacement value of the car—but not for liability. In Nevada, you can buy additional liability coverage for such cases. Most rental companies require a police report in order to process any claims you file, but your private insurer will not be notified of the accident. Check your own policies and credit cards before you shell out money on this extra insurance because you may already be covered.

It's worth noting that rental-car companies seem to be pushing the extra coverage especially hard these days. Doing your research on what types of coverage you do and do not need will allow you to smile politely and decline if it is appropriate. Don't let them pressure or scare you into spending extra money for items you don't need.

By Taxi

Because cabs line up in front of all major hotels, an easy way to get around town is by taxi. Cabs charge $3.30 at the meter drop and $2.60 per mile after that, plus an additional $1.80 fee for being picked up at the airport and time-based penalties if you get stuck in a traffic jam. A taxi from the airport to the Strip will run you $15 to $23, from the airport to Downtown $18 to $25, and between the Strip and Downtown about $12 to $18. You can often save money by sharing a cab with someone going to the same destination (up to five people can ride for the same fare). All this implies that you have gotten a driver who is honest; many cabbies take you the long way around, which sometimes means the shortest physical distance between two points—right down the Strip—but longest time on the clock and, thus, on the meter. Either way, you could end up paying a fare that . . . let's just say a new pair of shoes would have been a much more fun way to spend that jackpot. Your only recourse is to write down the cab number and call the company and complain. They may not respond, but you can try.

If you just can't find a taxi to hail and want to call one, try the following companies: **Desert Cab Company** (✆ **702/386-9102**), **Whittlesea Blue Cab** (✆ **702/384-6111**), or **Yellow/Checker Cab/Star Company** (✆ **702/ 873-2000**).

By Monorail

The monorail opened in 2004, offering riders their first and best shot of getting from one end of the Strip to the other with a minimum of frustration and expense. The 4-mile route runs from the MGM Grand, at the southern end of the Strip, to the then-open Sahara, at the northern end, with stops at Paris/Bally's, the Flamingo, Harrah's, the Las Vegas Convention Center, and LVH: Las Vegas Hotel along the way. Despite the Sahara's closure in 2011, there is still a stop there that

Traffic in Las Vegas can be frustrating at times, especially near the Strip on evenings and weekends. Here are a few tips to help you get around the worst of it.

o **Spaghetti Bowl:** The "Spaghetti Bowl" is what locals call the mess where I-15 intersects U.S. 95. The entire thing was reconstructed in 2000, but some studies indicate that it's carrying more traffic than it was designed for, so don't expect a congestion-free ride. Avoid it if you can.

o **U.S. 95:** A 7-year project to widen the west leg of U.S. 95 (connecting to the busy northwest valley) is now complete. Though still busy in weekday rush hours, this freeway hasn't moved better in 20 years.

o **Keep Your Feet off the Streets:** Local engineers have been trying to improve traffic on the Strip by separating the cars from the pedestrians. The first overhead pedestrian walkways opened at Tropicana Avenue, in 1995; similar bridges were completed at Flamingo Avenue in 2000, Spring Mountain in 2003, and Harmon Avenue in 2009.

o **Do D.I. Direct:** Most visitors seem to get a lot of mileage out of the Strip and I-15. But if you're checking out the local scene, you can bypass both of those, using Desert Inn Road, which is now one of the longest streets running from one side of the valley to the other. Plus, the 2-mile "Superarterial" section between Valley View and Paradise zips you nonstop over the interstate and under the Strip.

o **Grin and Bear It:** Yes, there are ways to avoid traffic jams on the Strip. But

at least these traffic jams are entertaining! If you have the time and patience, go ahead and take a ride along the Strip from Mandalay Bay to the Stratosphere. The 4-mile drive might take an hour, but while you're grinding along, you'll see a sphinx, an active volcano, a water ballet, and some uniquely Vegas architecture.

o **Rat Pack Back Doors:** Frank Sinatra Drive is a bypass road that runs parallel to the Strip from Russell Road north to Industrial. It's a great way to avoid the traffic jams and sneak in the back of hotels such as Mandalay Bay, Luxor, and Monte Carlo. On the other side of I-15, a bunch of high-end condo developers talked the city into rechristening a big portion of Industrial Road as Dean Martin Drive. It's still called Industrial from near Downtown to Twain, and it lets you in the back entrances to Circus Circus, Treasure Island, and others. It's a terrific bypass to the Strip and I-15 congestion.

o **Beltway Bypass:** The 53-mile 215 Beltway was completed in 2003, wrapping three-quarters of the way around the valley, allowing easy access to the outskirts while bypassing the Resort Corridor. While the initial beltway is done, some portions still need to be built out from half-beltway and frontage road systems to a full freeway—a process that will take until 2014 at least.

dumps you off about a block from the Strip. Note that some of the actual physical stops are not particularly close to their namesakes, so there can be an unexpected—and sometimes time-consuming—additional walk from the monorail stop to wherever you intended to go. Factor in this time accordingly.

These trains can accommodate more than 200 passengers (standing and sitting) and make the end-to-end run in about 15 minutes. They operate Monday through Thursday from 7am until 2am and Friday through Sunday from 7am until 3am. Fares are $5 for a one-way ride (whether you ride from one end to the other or just to the next station); discounts are available for round-trips and multiride/multiday passes.

A variety of behind-the-scenes issues, mostly having to do with money and bankruptcy, may change the way it's run, extend the route, or even shut it down altogether. Be sure to check the website to make sure it's still operating normally before you take the long walk to the station.

For more information visit the Las Vegas Monorail website at **www.lvmonorail.com**.

By Bus

The Deuce and SDX (Strip to Downtown Express) buses operated by the **Regional Transportation Commission** (**RTC;** www.rtcsouthernnevada.com; ☎ **702/228-7433**) are the primary public transportation on the Strip. The double-decker Deuce and double-carriage SDX run a route between the Downtown Transportation Center (at Casino Center Blvd. and Stewart Ave.) and a few miles beyond the southern end of the Strip. The fare is $5 for adults for 2 hours; an all-day pass is $7 and a 3-day pass is $20. There are no discounts for children or seniors. CAT buses run 24 hours a day and are wheelchair accessible. Exact change is required.

Although they are certainly economical transportation choices, they are not the most efficient as it relates to time or convenience. They run often but are usually very crowded and are not immune to the mind-numbing traffic that clogs the Strip at peak times. Patience is required.

There are also a number of **free transportation services,** courtesy of the casinos. A free monorail connects Mandalay Bay with Luxor and Excalibur; another connects Monte Carlo, Bellagio, and CityCenter; and a free tram shuttles between The Mirage and Treasure Island. Given how far apart even neighboring hotels can be, thanks to their size, and how they seem even farther apart on really hot (and cold and windy) days, these are blessed additions.

[Fast FACTS]

Area Codes   The local area code is 702.

Business Hours   Casinos and most bars are open 24 hours a day; nightclubs are usually open only late at night into the early morning hours, and restaurant and attraction hours vary.

Car Rental   See "Getting Around: By Car," earlier in this chapter.

Cellphones   See "Mobile Phones," below.

Crime   See "Safety," later in this section.

Customs   Every visitor 21 years of age or older may bring in, free of duty, the following: (1) 1 liter of alcohol as a gift or for personal use; (2) 200 cigarettes, 100 cigars (but not from Cuba), or 3 pounds of smoking tobacco; and (3) $100 worth of gifts. These exemptions are offered to travelers who spend at least 72 hours in the United States and who have not claimed them within the preceding 6 months. It is forbidden to bring into the country almost any meat products (including canned, fresh, and dried-meat products such as bouillon, soup mixes, and so forth). Generally, condiments, including vinegars, oils, pickled goods, spices, coffee, tea, and some cheeses and baked goods, are permitted. Avoid rice products, as rice can often harbor insects. Bringing fruits and vegetables is prohibited since they may harbor pests or disease. International visitors may carry in or out up to $10,000 in U.S. or foreign currency with no formalities; larger sums must be declared to U.S. Customs on entering or leaving, which includes filing form CM 4790. For details regarding U.S. Customs and Border Protection, consult your nearest U.S. embassy or consulate, or **U.S. Customs** (www.cbp.gov).

For information on what you're allowed to take home, contact your home country's Customs agency.

Disabled Travelers On the one hand, Las Vegas is fairly well equipped for travelers with disabilities, with virtually every hotel having wheelchair-accessible rooms and ramps and other requirements. On the other hand, the distance between hotels (particularly on the Strip) makes a vehicle of some sort virtually mandatory for most people with disabilities, and it may be extremely strenuous and time consuming to get from place to place (even within a single hotel, because of the crowds). Even if you don't intend to gamble, you still may have to go through the casino, and casinos can be quite difficult to maneuver in, particularly for a guest in a wheelchair. Casinos are usually crowded, and the machines and tables are often arranged close together, with chairs, people, and such blocking easy access. You should also consider that it is often a long trek through larger hotels between the entrance and the room elevators (or, for that matter, anywhere in the hotel), and then add a crowded casino to the equation.

For more on organizations that offer resources to travelers with limited mobility, go to **www.frommers.com**.

Doctors Hotels usually have lists of doctors, should you need one. In addition, doctors are listed in the Yellow Pages. For physician referrals, call the **Desert Springs Hospital** (www.desertspringshospital.com; ✆ **702/388-4888**). Hours are Monday to Friday from 8am to 8pm and Saturday from 9am to 3pm except holidays. Also see "Hospitals," later in this section.

Drinking Laws The legal age for purchase and consumption of alcoholic beverages is 21; proof of age is required and often requested at bars, nightclubs, and restaurants, so it's always a good idea to bring ID when you go out.

Beer, wine, and liquor are sold in all kinds of stores pretty much around the clock in Vegas; trust us, you won't have a hard time finding a drink in this town.

Do not carry open containers of alcohol in your car or any public area that isn't zoned for alcohol consumption, which includes the Strip and the Fremont Street Experience downtown. The police can fine you on the spot. And nothing will ruin your trip faster than getting a citation for DUI (driving under the influence), so don't even think about driving while intoxicated.

Driving Rules See "Getting Around," earlier in this chapter.

Electricity Like Canada, the United States uses 110–120 volts AC (60 cycles), compared to 220–240 volts AC (50 cycles) in most of Europe, Australia, and New Zealand. Downward converters that change 220–240 volts to 110–120 volts are difficult to find in the United States, so bring one with you.

Embassies & Consulates

All embassies are in the nation's capital, Washington, D.C. Some consulates are in major U.S. cities, and most nations have a mission to the United Nations in New York City. If your country isn't listed below, call for directory information in Washington, D.C. (📞 **202/555-1212**), or check **www.embassy.org/embassies**.

The embassy of **Australia** is at 1601 Massachusetts Ave. NW, Washington, DC 20036 (www.usa.embassy.gov.au; 📞 **202/797-3000**). Consulates are in New York, Honolulu, Houston, Los Angeles, and San Francisco.

The embassy of **Canada** is at 501 Pennsylvania Ave. NW, Washington, DC 20001 (www.canadianembassy.org; 📞 **202/682-1740**). Other Canadian consulates are in Chicago, Detroit, Los Angeles, New York, Seattle, and many other major U.S. cities.

The embassy of **Ireland** is at 2234 Massachusetts Ave. NW, Washington, DC 20008 (www.embassyofireland.org; 📞 **202/462-3939**). Irish consulates are in Boston, Chicago, New York, San Francisco, and other cities. See website for complete listing.

The embassy of **New Zealand** is at 37 Observatory Circle NW, Washington, DC 20008 (www.nzembassy.com; 📞 **202/328-4800**). New Zealand consulates are in Los Angeles, Salt Lake City, San Francisco, and Seattle.

The embassy of the **United Kingdom** is at 3100 Massachusetts Ave. NW, Washington, DC 20008 (www.britainusa.com; 📞 **202/588-6500**). Other British consulates are in Atlanta, Boston, Chicago, Cleveland, Houston, Los Angeles, New York, San Francisco, and Seattle.

Emergencies

Dial 📞 **911** to contact the police or fire department, or to call an ambulance.

Family Travel

Family travel can be immensely rewarding, giving you new ways of seeing the world through smaller pairs of eyes. That said, Vegas is hardly an ideal place to bring the kids. For one thing, they're not allowed in casinos at all. Because most hotels are laid out so that you frequently have to walk through their casinos to get to where you are going, you can see how this becomes a headache.

Note also that the Strip is often peppered with people distributing fliers and other information about decidedly adult entertainment options in the city. Sex is everywhere. Just walking down the Strip might give your kids an eyeful of items that you might prefer they avoid. (They don't call it "Sin City" for nothing!)

On top of everything else, there is a curfew law in Vegas: Kids younger than 18 are not permitted on the Strip without a parent after 9pm on weekends and holidays. In the rest of the county, minors can't be out without parents after 10pm on school nights and midnight on the weekends.

Although still an option at most smaller chain hotels and motels, the major casino-hotels on the Strip offer no discount for children staying in your room, so you may have to pay an additional fee ($10–$40 per person per night) to have them bunk with you. You'll definitely want to book a place with a pool. Some hotels also have enormous video arcades and other diversions.

To locate accommodations, restaurants, and attractions that are particularly kid friendly, look for the "Kids" icon throughout this guide.

Gasoline

Please see "Getting Around: By Car," earlier in this chapter.

Health

By and large, Las Vegas is like most other major American cities in that the water is relatively clean, the air is relatively clear, and illness-bearing insects and animals are rare. However, in a city with this many people coming and going from all over the world, there are a couple of specific concerns worth noting.

o **Food Poisoning**   Food preparation guidelines in Las Vegas are among the strictest in the world, but when you're dealing with the sheer volume that this city is, you're bound to run into trouble every now and then. All restaurants are required by law to display a health certificate and letter grade (A, B, or C) that indicate how well they did on their last Health Department inspection. An A grade doesn't mean you won't get food poisoning, but it does mean the staff does a better-than-average job in the kitchen.

o **Norovirus**   Over the past few years, there have been a few outbreaks of norovirus at Las Vegas hotels. This virus, most commonly associated with cruise ships, is rarely serious but can turn your vacation into a very unpleasant experience of intestinal illness. Because it is spread by contact, you can protect yourself by washing your hands often, especially after touching all of those slot machines.

o **Sun Exposure**   In case you weren't paying attention in geography, Las Vegas is located in the middle of a desert and so it should come as no surprise that the sun shines particularly bright here. Heat and sunstroke are dangers that all visitors should be concerned about, especially if you are considering spending any amount of time outdoors. Sunscreen (stick to a minimum SPF 30) is a must even if you are just traveling from one hotel to another, and you should always carry a bottle of water with you to stay hydrated even when temperatures are moderate. The low desert humidity means that your body has to work harder to replenish moisture, so help it along with something other than a free cocktail in the casino. The good news: Low humidity means it's hard to have a bad hair day.

Hospitals   The closest full-service hospital to the Strip is **Sunrise Hospital,** 3186 Maryland Pkwy. (www.sunrisehospital.com; (C) **702/731-8000**), but for lesser emergencies, the **Harmon Medical Urgent Care,** 150 E. Harmon (www.harmonmedicalcenter.com; (C) **702/796-1116**), offers treatment from 8am until 5pm Monday through Friday. Additionally, most major hotels in Las Vegas can provide assistance in finding physicians and/or pharmacies that are well suited to your needs.

Insurance   Traveler's insurance is not required for visiting Las Vegas, and whether or not it's right for you depends on your circumstances. For example, most Las Vegas travel arrangements that include hotels are refundable or cancelable up to the last moment, so insurance is probably not necessary. If, however, you have prepaid a nonrefundable package, then it could be worth considering insurance.

For information on traveler's insurance, trip cancellation insurance, and medical insurance while traveling, please visit www.frommers.com/planning.

Internet & Wi-Fi   Most resort hotels in Vegas offer wireless access, but for a hefty daily fee (usually starting around $14). Some chain hotels offer free Wi-Fi in public areas, while others still offer high-speed access. In Las Vegas, you can find free Wi-Fi at most stand-alone McDonald's, Starbucks, and in the Fashion Show mall. To find additional public Wi-Fi hot spots, go to www.jiwire.com; its Wi-Fi Finder holds the world's largest directory of public wireless hot spots.

For dial-up access, most business-class hotels in the U.S. offer dataports for laptop modems.

Wherever you go, bring a connection kit of the right power and phone adapters, a spare phone cord, and a spare Ethernet network cable—or find out whether your hotel supplies them to guests.

Most major airports have Internet kiosks that provide basic Web access for a per-minute fee that's usually higher than hotel prices. Check out copy shops, such as FedEx Office, which offer computer stations with fully loaded software (as well as Wi-Fi).

Legal Aid   While driving, if you are pulled over for a minor infraction (such as speeding), never attempt to pay the fine directly to a police officer; this could be construed as attempted bribery, a much more serious crime. Pay fines by mail, or directly into the hands of the clerk of the court. If accused of a more serious offense, say and do nothing before consulting a lawyer. In the U.S., the burden is on the state to prove a person's guilt beyond a reasonable doubt, and everyone has the right to remain silent, whether he or she is suspected of a crime or actually arrested. Once arrested, a person can make one telephone call to a party of his or her choice. The international visitor should call his or her embassy or consulate.

LGBT Travelers   For such a licentious, permissive town, Las Vegas has its conservative side, and it is not the most gay-friendly city. This does not manifest itself in any signs of outrage toward open displays of gay affection, but it does mean that the local gay community is largely confined to the bar scene. This may be changing, with local gay-pride parades and other activities gathering steam each year. See listings for gay bars, in chapter 7. For gay and lesbian travel resources, visit **www.frommers.com**.

Mail   At press time, domestic postage rates were 32¢ for a postcard and 45¢ for a letter. For international mail, a first-class letter of up to 1 ounce costs $1.05 (85¢ to Canada and Mexico); a first-class postcard costs the same as a letter. For more information go to **www.usps.com**.

If you aren't sure what your address will be in the United States, mail can be sent to you, in your name, c/o General Delivery at the main post office in Las Vegas, which is located Downtown at 200 S. Main St., near the Fremont Street casinos and hotels. (Call ☎ **800/275-8777** for information on the nearest post office for other locations.) The addressee must pick up mail in person and must produce proof of identity (such as a driver's license or passport). The main Las Vegas post office is open Monday through Friday from 8:30am until 5pm.

Always include a zip code when mailing items in the U.S. If you don't know a zip code, visit www.usps.com/zip4.

The most convenient post office to the Strip is immediately behind Circus Circus at 3100 S. Industrial Rd., between Sahara Avenue and Spring Mountain Road (☎ **800/275-8777**). It's open Monday through Friday from 8:30am to 5pm. You can also mail letters and packages at your hotel, and there's a drop-off box in The Forum Shops at Caesars Palace.

Medical Requirements   Unless you're arriving from an area known to be suffering from an epidemic (particularly cholera or yellow fever), inoculations or vaccinations are not required for entry into the United States. Also see "Health," above.

Mobile Phones   Just because your mobile phone works at home doesn't mean it'll work everywhere in the U.S. (thanks to our nation's fragmented mobile phone system). Whether or not you'll get a signal depends on your carrier and where you happen to be standing when you are trying to make a call. Hotel rooms and casinos are notoriously bad places to be if you want to chat with someone back home on your cellphone, but step outside and things will usually improve dramatically. Note that if you can get a signal in a casino, don't try to use your phone while sitting at a gaming table—that's a big no-no.

Once you leave Las Vegas proper, you are in the wilds of the Nevada desert, and so unless you are near a major byway (like I-15) expect to get very few, if any, bars on your phone.

If you're not from the U.S., you'll be appalled at the poor reach of the GSM (Global System for Mobile Communications) wireless network, which is used by much of the rest of the world. Your phone will probably work in Las Vegas but it probably won't once you get into more rural areas. To see where GSM phones work in the U.S., check out www.t-mobile.com/coverage. And you may or may not be able to send SMS (text messaging) home.

US$	Aus$	Can$	Euro (€)	NZ$	UK£
1	.93	1	.76	1.20	.63

Money & Costs   Frommer's lists exact prices in the local currency. The currency conversions quoted above were correct at press time. However, rates fluctuate, so before departing consult a currency exchange website such as **www.xe.com** to check up-to-the-minute rates.

Because Las Vegas is a town built on the concept of separating you from your money, it should come as no surprise that gaining access to money is very easy—sometimes too easy. There are ATMs (also known as "cash machines" or "cashpoints") conveniently located about every 4 feet (okay, an exaggeration, but not by a lot); and check cashing, credit card–advance systems, and traveler's check services are omnipresent.

And while Vegas visitors used to require a great deal of change in order to play the slots and other gaming machines, few, if any, still accept coins. Gone are the once-prevalent change carts. All machines now take bills in most denominations, and you get "change" in the form of a credit slip that appears when you cash out. You then take this slip to the nearest cashier's cage to exchange for actual money.

So getting to your money isn't a problem. Keeping it may be.

WHAT THINGS COST IN LAS VEGAS	US$
Taxi from the airport to the Strip	15.00 25.00
Taxi from the airport to Downtown Las Vegas	18.00–27.00
One-way Las Vegas monorail ticket	5.00
All-day Deuce or SDX bus pass	7.00
Standard room at Bellagio, Fri–Sat	175.00–400.00
Standard room at MGM Grand, Fri–Sat	150.00–300.00
Standard room at Bally's, Fri–Sat	100.00–200.00
Dinner for two at Picasso, prix fixe	226.00
Dinner for two at Austins Steakhouse	75.00
Wynn Las Vegas buffet, weekend champagne brunch	44.00
Main Street Station Garden Court buffet champagne brunch	12.00
Ticket to Cirque du Soleil's O	109.00–180.00
Ticket to Mac King (comedy magic show)	33.00
Domestic beer at Haze	8.00
Domestic beer at the Double Down Saloon	4.00

Las Vegas has grown progressively more expensive, with the concept of a cheap Sin City vacation a distant memory. The average room rate on the Strip on weekends is over $200 a night, those formerly cheap buffets have been replaced by $30-a-person lavish spreads, and top-show tickets easily surpass $100 a head. And then, of course, there are the casinos, a money-losing proposition for the traveler if there ever was one.

But there are Las Vegas vacations available for just about any budget, so pay (no pun intended) close attention to chapter 9, "Where to Stay," and chapter 5, "Where to Eat," which break down your choices by cost.

Beware of hidden credit card fees while traveling. International visitors should check with their credit or debit card issuer to see what fees, if any, will be charged for transactions in the U.S.

For help with currency conversions, tip calculations, and more, download Frommer's convenient Travel Tools app for your mobile device. Go to **www.frommers.com/go/ mobile** and click on the "Travel Tools" icon.

Newspapers & Magazines The *Las Vegas Review-Journal* is the major daily periodical in the city, which is now partnered with the *Las Vegas Sun,* its former newspaper rival. Both offer the latest news, weather, and information and can be valuable resources for coupons and up-to-the-minute show listings.

What's On Las Vegas is a local magazine listing shows, restaurants, happenings, and more, and it often features discount offers to attractions that could save you some dough.

Packing Most Las Vegas hotel rooms are fully stocked with basics—shampoo, conditioner, hand lotion, mouthwash, and in some cases things like sewing kits and cotton swabs. If you don't have allergy or skin sensitivity issues to contend with, you may want to consider leaving those types of sundry items at home to free up some room in your suitcase. The same goes for your travel iron, as most rooms have a full-size iron and ironing board or they are available by request through housekeeping.

Comfortable walking shoes are a must for Las Vegas as you'll be doing a lot of it. Yes, your Jimmy Choo's will look fabulous for your night out at the party spots, but do you really want to navigate the crowds across a 100,000-square-foot casino in them?

Checking the weather forecast before your trip can provide you with guidance on what types of clothes to bring, but packing a light sweater or jacket even during the summer months is not a bad idea. It gets windy in Las Vegas and there can be a chill in the evenings, plus many of the casinos and showrooms set the air-conditioning on "Siberia," so light layers that you can peel off when you go back outside into the heat are recommended.

If you are bringing your computer or other mobile devices, don't forget to bring your power cords, chargers, and other imperatives like an Ethernet cord. Most hotels offer Wi-Fi service, but if you can't connect and need to use their cords, you could get charged extra for it.

Lastly, consider safety when packing by tossing in a small flashlight. During an emergency, this could become invaluable in helping you navigate your way out of a 4,000-room hotel.

For more helpful information on packing for your trip, download our convenient Travel Tools app for your mobile device. Go to www.frommers.com/go/mobile and click on the "Travel Tools" icon.

Passports Virtually every air traveler entering the U.S. is required to show a passport. All persons, including U.S. citizens, traveling by air between the United States and Canada, Mexico, Central and South America, the Caribbean, and Bermuda are required to present a valid passport. **Note:** U.S. and Canadian citizens entering the U.S. at land and sea ports of entry from within the Western Hemisphere must now also present a passport or other documents compliant with the Western Hemisphere Travel Initiative (WHTI; www.getyou home.gov). Children 15 and under may continue entering with only a U.S. birth certificate, or other proof of U.S. citizenship.

Passport Offices

- **Australia   Australian Passport Information Service** (www.passports.gov.au; *℃* **131-232**).

- **Canada   Passport Office,** Department of Foreign Affairs and International Trade, Ottawa, ON K1A 0G3 (www.ppt.gc.ca; *℃* **800/567-6868**).

- **Ireland   Passport Office,** Setanta Centre, Molesworth Street, Dublin 2 (www. foreignaffairs.gov.ie; *℃* **01/671-1633**).

- **New Zealand   Passports Office,** Department of Internal Affairs, 47 Boulcott St., Wellington, 6011 (www.passports.govt.nz; *℃* **0800/225-050** in New Zealand or 04/463-9360).

- **United Kingdom**   Visit your nearest passport office, major post office, or travel agency or contact the **Identity and Passport Service (IPS),** 89 Eccleston Sq., London, SW1V 1PN (www.ips.gov.uk; *℃* **0300/222-0000**).

- **United States**   To find your regional passport office, check the U.S. State Department website (http://travel.state.gov/passport) or call the **National Passport Information Center** (*℃* **877/487-2778**) for automated information.

Petrol   Please see "Getting Around: By Car," earlier in this chapter.

Police   For nonemergencies, call *℃* **702/795-3111.** For emergencies, call *℃* **911.**

Safety   *CSI: Crime Scene Investigation,* a popular U.S. TV show, may turn up new corpses in Vegas each week, but the crime rate in real-life Vegas isn't higher than in any other major metropolis of its size.

With all that cash floating around town, pickpockets and thieves are predictably active. At gaming tables and slot machines, men should keep wallets well concealed and out of the reach of pickpockets, and women should keep handbags in plain sight (on laps). If you win a big jackpot, ask the pit boss or slot attendant to cut you a check rather than give you cash—the cash may look nice, but flashing it can attract the wrong kind of attention. Outside casinos, popular spots for pickpockets and thieves are restaurants and outdoor shows, such as the volcano at The Mirage or the fountains at Bellagio. Stay alert. Unless your hotel room has an in-room safe, check your valuables into a safe-deposit box at the front desk.

When in your room, be sure to lock and bolt the door at all times and only open it to hotel employees that you are expecting (such as room service).

A special safety concern for women (and even men occasionally) centers on behavior at nightclubs. Do not ever accept a drink from a stranger no matter how handsome he is and keep your cocktail in your hand at all times, even on the dance floor. Instances of people getting something slipped into their drink are rare but they have happened, so it's best to take precautions.

Senior Travel   One of the benefits of age is that travel to most destinations often costs less—but that's rarely true in Las Vegas. Discounts at hotels, shows, restaurants, recreation, and just about anything else you want to do are rare. About the only discounts offered to seniors are at some of the local attractions, which will give a few bucks off to those over 62 or 65 (see chapter 4).

Members of **AARP,** 601 E St. NW, Washington, DC 20049 (www.aarp.org; ☎ **888/687-2277**), get discounts on hotels, airfares, and car rentals. AARP offers members a wide range of benefits, including *AARP The Magazine* and a monthly newsletter. Anyone over 50 can join.

The U.S. National Park Service (NPS) offers an **America the Beautiful—National Park and Federal Recreational Lands Pass—Senior Pass** (formerly the **Golden Age Passport**). You'll find it useful for some of the side trips covered in chapter 10. The pass gives seniors 62 years or older lifetime entrance to all properties administered by the National Park Service—national parks, monuments, historic sites, recreation areas, and national wildlife refuges—for a one-time processing fee of $10. The pass must be purchased in person at any NPS facility that charges an entrance fee. Besides free entry, the America the Beautiful Senior Pass also offers a 50% discount on some federal-use fees charged for such facilities as camping, swimming, parking, boat launching, and tours. For more information, go to **www.nps.gov/findapark/passes.htm** or call the **United States Geological Survey (USGS),** which issues the passes, at ☎ **888/275-8747.**

Smoking Vegas is decidedly no longer a smoker's haven. Increasingly strict smoking laws prohibit puffing virtually everywhere indoors except in designated hotel rooms, nightclubs and bars, and on the casino floor itself. Because it's frequently hard to tell where a casino ends and basic public area begins, don't fret too much about stepping across some invisible line. Hotels still have dedicated floors for smokers and nonsmokers. There is a significant charge, approximately $300, for smoking anything in a nonsmoking room.

Taxes The United States has no value-added tax (VAT) or other indirect tax at the national level. Every state, county, and city may levy its own local tax on all purchases, including hotel and restaurant checks and airline tickets. These taxes will not appear on price tags.

The sales tax in Las Vegas is 8.1% and is added to food and drink bills. Hotel rooms on the Strip come with a 12% tax, while those in the Downtown area carry 13%. Taxes are also added to show tickets.

Telephones Generally, Vegas hotel surcharges on long-distance and local calls are astronomical. You are often charged even for making a toll-free or phone-card call. You're better off using your **cellphone** or a **public pay telephone.** Some hotels are now adding on an additional "resort fee" to the cost of the room, which is supposed to cover local calls (as well as using the pool and other elements that ought to be givens). The fee can range from $1 (Motel 6) to $25 per day.

Many convenience groceries and packaging services sell **prepaid calling cards** in denominations up to $50. Many public pay phones at airports now accept American Express, MasterCard, and Visa. **Local calls** made from most pay phones cost either 25¢ or 35¢. Most long-distance and international calls can be dialed directly from any phone. **To make calls within the United States and to Canada,** dial 1 followed by the area code and the seven-digit number. **For other international calls,** dial 011 followed by the country code, city code, and the number you are calling.

Calls to area codes **800, 888, 877,** and **866** are toll-free. However, calls to area codes **700** and **900** (chat lines, bulletin boards, "dating" services, and so on) can be expensive—charges of 95¢ to $3 or more per minute. Some numbers have minimum charges that can run $15 or more.

For **reversed-charge or collect calls,** and for person-to-person calls, dial the number 0 then the area code and number; an operator will come on the line, and you should specify whether you are calling collect, person-to-person, or both. If your operator-assisted call is international, ask for the overseas operator.

For **directory assistance** ("Information"), dial 411 for local numbers and national numbers in the U.S. and Canada. For dedicated long-distance information, dial 1, then the appropriate area code plus 555-1212.

Time   The continental United States is divided into **four time zones:** Eastern Standard Time (EST), Central Standard Time (CST), Mountain Standard Time (MST), and Pacific Standard Time (PST). Alaska and Hawaii have their own zones. Las Vegas is in the Pacific Time zone, 8 hours behind Greenwich Mean Time (GMT), 3 hours behind the East Coast and 2 behind the Midwest. For example, when it's 9am in Las Vegas (PST), it's 7am in Honolulu (Hawaii Standard Time), 10am in Denver (MST), 11am in Chicago (CST), noon in New York City (EST), 5pm in London (GMT), and 2am the next day in Sydney.

Daylight saving time (summer time) is in effect from 1am on the second Sunday in March to 1am on the first Sunday in November, except in Arizona, Hawaii, the U.S. Virgin Islands, and Puerto Rico. Daylight saving time moves the clock 1 hour ahead of standard time.

For help with time translations, and more, download our convenient Travel Tools app for your mobile device. Go to **www.frommers.com/go/mobile** and click on the "Travel Tools" icon.

Tipping   Las Vegas is a hospitality-driven economy, meaning many of the people you encounter depend on tips for their livelihood. This doesn't necessarily mean you *need* to tip more than you would anywhere else, but average tips in other cities can be viewed as somewhat stingy here.

In the casinos, it's common to tip **cocktail waitresses** $1 to $2 per drink and to tip **dealers** 5% of any big wins.

In hotels, tip **bellhops** at least $1 per bag ($2–$3 if you have a lot of luggage) and tip the **chamber staff** $1 to $2 per day (more if you've left a big mess for him or her to clean up). Tip the **doorman** or **concierge** only if he or she has provided you with some specific service (for example, calling a cab for you or obtaining difficult-to-get theater tickets). Tip the **valet-parking attendant** $2 to $3 every time you get your car.

In restaurants, bars, and nightclubs, tip **service staff** and **bartenders** 15% to 20% of the check, and tip **checkroom attendants** $1 per garment.

As for other service personnel, tip **cabdrivers** 15% of the fare; tip **skycaps** at airports at least $1 per bag ($2–$3 if you have a lot of luggage); and tip **hairdressers** and **barbers** 15% to 20%.

For help with tip calculations, currency conversions, and more, download our convenient Travel Tools app for your mobile device. Go to **www.frommers.com/go/mobile** and click on the "Travel Tools" icon.

Toilets   In Las Vegas, you are almost always near a bathroom as long as you are in one of the tourist areas, with the casinos being the most obvious example. All have multiple facilities and they are usually among the cleanest you'll find in any public location. One small annoyance is that many hotel restaurants do not have their own restrooms, meaning you may need to go into the casino to find the nearest one.

You won't find public toilets or "restrooms" on the streets in most U.S. cities, but they can be found in hotel lobbies, bars, restaurants, museums, department stores, railway and bus stations, and service stations. Large hotels and fast-food restaurants are often the best bet for clean facilities. Restaurants and bars in resorts or heavily visited areas may reserve their restrooms for patrons.

VAT   See "Taxes," above.

Visas   The U.S. State Department has a **Visa Waiver Program (VWP)** allowing citizens of the following countries to enter the United States without a visa for stays of up to 90 days: Andorra, Australia, Austria, Belgium, Brunei, Czech Republic, Denmark, Estonia, Finland, France, Germany, Greece, Hungary, Iceland, Ireland, Italy, Japan, Latvia, Liechtenstein, Lithuania, Luxembourg, Malta, Monaco, the Netherlands, New Zealand, Norway, Portugal, San Marino, Singapore, Slovakia, Slovenia, South Korea, Spain, Sweden, Switzerland, and the United Kingdom. (**Note:** This list was accurate at press time; for the most up-to-date list of countries in the VWP, consult http://travel.state. gov/visa.) Even though a visa isn't necessary, in an effort to help U.S. officials check travelers against terror watch lists before they arrive at U.S. borders, visitors from VWP countries must register online through the Electronic System for Travel Authorization (ESTA) before boarding a plane or a boat to the U.S. Travelers must complete an electronic application providing basic personal and travel eligibility information. The Department of Homeland Security recommends filling out the form at least 3 days before traveling. Authorizations will be valid for up to 2 years or until the traveler's passport expires, whichever comes first. Currently, there is a US$14 fee for the online application. Existing ESTA registrations remain valid through their expiration dates. **Note:** Any passport issued on or after October 26, 2006, by a VWP country must be an **e-Passport** for VWP travelers to be eligible to enter the U.S. without a visa. Citizens of these nations also need to present a round-trip air or cruise ticket upon arrival. E-Passports contain computer chips capable of storing biometric information, such as the required digital photograph of the holder. If your passport doesn't have this feature, you can still travel without a visa if the valid passport was issued before October 26, 2005, and includes a machine-readable zone; or if the valid passport was issued between October 26, 2005, and October 25, 2006, and includes a digital photograph. For more information, go to **http://travel.state.gov/visa**. Canadian citizens may enter the United States without visas, but will need to show passports and proof of residence.

Citizens of all other countries must have (1) a valid passport that expires at least 6 months later than the scheduled end of their visit to the U.S.; and (2) a tourist visa.

For information about U.S. visas go to **http://travel.state.gov** and click on "Visas." Or go to one of the following websites:

Australian citizens can obtain up-to-date visa information from the **U.S. Embassy Canberra,** Moonah Place, Yarralumla, ACT 2600 (② **02/6214-5600**) or by checking the U.S. Diplomatic Mission's website at **http://canberra.usembassy.gov/visas.html**.

British subjects can obtain up-to-date visa information by calling the **U.S. Embassy Visa Information Line** (② **09042-450-100** from within the U.K. at £1.20 per minute; or ② **866/382-3589** from within the U.S. at a flat rate of $16 and is payable by credit card only) or by visiting the "Visas to the U.S." section of the American Embassy London's website at **http://london.usembassy.gov/visas.html**.

Irish citizens can obtain up-to-date visa information through the **U.S. Embassy Dublin,** 42 Elgin Rd., Ballsbridge, Dublin 4 (**http://dublin.usembassy.gov**; ② **1580-47-8472** from within the Republic of Ireland at €2.40 per minute**)**.

Citizens of **New Zealand** can obtain up-to-date visa information by contacting the **U.S. Embassy New Zealand,** 29 Fitzherbert Terrace, Thorndon, Wellington (**http://newzealand.usembassy.gov**; ✆ **644/462-6000**).

Visitor Information   The Las Vegas Convention and Visitors Authority (www.visitlasvegas.com; ✆ **877/847-4858** or 702/892-7575) provides information, hotel reservation assistance, show guides, convention calendars, and more.

Other popular Las Vegas travel websites include www.vegas.com, www.vegas4visitors.com, and www.cheapovegas.com.

Many hotels have their own mobile apps that you can download for special information and offers and you can also download the Frommer's Las Vegas app with tons of great information about the city at **www.frommers.com/go/mobile**.

Water   Ongoing drought conditions mean water is a concern in terms of its long-term availability, but for now it is plentiful from faucets, drinking fountains, and endless bottles of the stuff. As in most of the United States, the drinking water is considered safe and there have been no reported instances of sickness from it. Still, bottles of water are often free in the casinos, so you might as well pick one up.

Wi-Fi   See "Internet & Wi-Fi," earlier in this section.

Women Travelers   Thanks to the crowds, Las Vegas is as safe as any other big city for a woman traveling alone. A woman on her own should, of course, take the usual precautions and should be wary of hustlers and drunken businessmen who may mistake her for a "working girl." (Alas, million-dollar proposals à la Robert Redford are a rarity.) Many of the big hotels have security guards stationed at the elevators at night to prevent anyone other than guests from going up to the room floors. If you're anxious, ask a security guard to escort you to your room. *Always* double-lock your door *and* deadbolt it to prevent intruders from entering.

For general travel resources for women, go to **www.frommers.com/planning**.

Index

Accommodations

Restaurants